THIS DAY IN MUSIC

Copyright ©2010 Neil Cossar
This edition ©2010 Omnibus Press
(A Division of Music Sales Limited)

Cover and book designed by Paul Tippett and Adrian Andrews at Vitamin P
Cover and Memorabilia Photography by Jacqui Black
Cover layout by Liz Sanchez, Jacqui Black and Paul Tippett
Picture research by Jacqui Black, Neil Cossar and Paul Tippett

ISBN: 978.1.84938.543.5
Order No: OP53625

Exclusive Distributors,
Music Sales Limited,
14/15 Berners Street,
London, W1T 3LJ.

Music Sales Corporation
257 Park Avenue South,
New York, NY 10010, USA.

Macmillan Distribution Services,
56 Parkwest Drive,
Derrimut, Vic 3030,
Australia.

Every effort has been made to trace the copyright holders of the photographs in
this book but one or two were unreachable. We would be grateful if the
photographers concerned would contact us.

Printed in China.

A catalogue record for this book is available from the British Library.

Visit Omnibus Press on the web at www.omnibuspress.com

For more musical facts and feats visit www.thisdayinmusic.com

THIS DAY IN MUSIC

An Every Day Record of Musical Feats and Facts

By Neil Cossar

OMNIBUS PRESS

London/New York/Paris/Sydney/Copenhagen/Berlin/Madrid/Tokyo

Dedication

For Liz for making it all happen and much more and Matthew, Danny, Simon, Ace, Lyle and Chloe and Mum and Dad for all being part of one big family.

Acknowledgements

Very special thanks to: Pete Hawkins, Chris Charlesworth, Andy Neill, John Wadlow, Paul at Vitamin P, Jacqui Black, Andy Murray, Pete and Davin at 39 Ventures, Olly Walsh at Rhino Records, Rupert Vereker at Sonic, David Barraclough, Steve Davis, Mark Goodier and all at Wise Buddah.

About the author

Neil Cossar played guitar in the late 70s-80s group The Cheaters, who were signed to Parlophone Records, but never troubled the charts. Continually gigging until 1982, the band was awarded "Hardest Working Band Of The Year" by BBC Radio 1 after playing 321 gigs as well as recording an album.

During the 90s Neil worked as a radio DJ in Manchester, England, presenting a late night show which featured countless 'new acts' in session, including Radiohead, Blur, The Charlatans, Lenny Kravitz, PJ Harvey, The Cranberries and Tori Amos. He also runs a PR company with his partner Liz Sanchez – their clients have included Def Leppard, INXS, Joan Baez, Glen Campbell, Jean Michel Jarre, The Proclaimers, Natalie Imbruglia, The Hollies, Feist, The Stranglers, Atomic Kitten, Barenaked Ladies and UB40.

Neil first started to collect music facts and trivia while working in radio in the early 90s. Over the years this became an obsession and evolved into his website thisdayinmusic.com, which was launched in 1999.

The Author is thrilled at seeing The Rolling Stones on *Top Of The Pops* on Jan 1, 1964.

Introduction

This Day In Music brings together all the significant events in the history of rock and pop music in one giant volume. Here are the facts, the figures, the dates, the times and the places, and most of all the stars that made rock and pop the most vibrant art form of the 20th and 21st centuries.

From Elvis to Lady Ga Ga, from rock 'n' roll to rap, from *6.5 Special* to *X Factor*, from Abba to ZZ Top and from New Year's Day to New Year's Eve, here is all the information you need to know, set out chronologically so you can look up those dates that interest you or simply pore through the year month by month, day by day.

For example in 2001 Kiss added another product to their merchandising universe: the 'Kiss Kasket', a coffin featuring the faces of the four founding members of the band. Pantera guitarist Dimebag Darrell was buried in one after he was shot and killed on-stage in December 2004.

When The Beatles made their US live concert debut on February 11, 1964 at the Washington Coliseum, they had to stop three times to turn Ringo's drum kit around and re-position their microphones so that they faced a different section of the audience.

Fast forward 40 odd years to May 2, 2009 when Bob Dylan mingled unnoticed with other Beatles tourists during a minibus tour to John Lennon's childhood home. Dylan, who was on a day off on a European tour, paid £16 for the public trip to the 1940s house in Woolton, Liverpool.

In 2008 a 1976 Rolling Stones album bought for £2 at a car boot sale sold for £4,000 at an auction. The *Black And Blue* LP was signed by John Lennon, Yoko Ono, Paul and Linda McCartney and George Harrison as well as members of The Rolling Stones.

Fancy a night out? On May 29, 1967 you could've seen The Move, Cream, The Jimi Hendrix Experience and Pink Floyd all on the same bill for £1.

And if you were filling up with petrol in Dublin in the mid 70s, you could've been served by a young man named Paul Hewson, as he once worked as a petrol pump attendant. You might have seen his band U2 on December 15, 1979 when they appeared for free at the Windsor Castle Pub, Harrow Road, London.

What's the worst job you ever had? Mark Stoermer bass guitarist with The Killers once worked as an organ/blood/body part delivery boy. Jamie Cook, guitarist with Arctic Monkeys, worked as a bathroom tiler.

Or how about when The Inspiral Carpets headlined Reading Festival in 1990 and they brought on a pantomime cow. The band's guitar roadie Noel Gallagher was half of that cow, making his first headline appearance.

Did you see T. Rex at Sheffield City Hall in 1971? You might have sat next to Def Leppard singer Joe Elliott, since he was there.

Do you own any records (are they called that?) by Florian Cloud De Bounevialle Armstrong (that's Dido to you) or Alecia Moore (Pink)? You'll find more of them inside.

And in the new digital world Freddie Mercury's 1974 Rolls Royce was offered for auction on eBay by his family. The Silver Shadow luxury car attracted bids of up to £8,400. It came with an unused box of tissues the singer always stored in the car.

But if you missed that one you could've bid on buybritneyshair.com during February 2007, when the hair salon where Britney Spears shaved her own head set up a website to auction her hair for more than $1m. As well as the hair, the winning bidder also got a blue lighter she left at the salon and the can of Red Bull she was drinking at the time.

It might dismay Beatles fans to learn that Ringo is 70 in 2010, Doors fans to learn that Jim Morrison would have been 67 and Jimi Hendrix fans to learn that the man many still regard as the greatest electric guitarist who ever lived would have been 68. It's now 45 years since Dylan 'went electric' at the Newport Folk Festival and over 50 years since Buddy Holly and others died in a plane crash in Iowa, the first great rock tragedy.

From drug busts, historic recordings, gigs, festivals, birthdays, deaths and arrests, *This Day in Music* continues to search and document key moments in music history. I hope you enjoy this updated second edition, which includes even more musical facts, figures and features. And if you're a musician, keep breaking, making and bending the rules so we can continue to write about you.

Neil Cossar, February 2010.

January 1

1953
Country singer Hank Williams, best known for 'Your Cheatin' Heart', dies aged 29 of a heart attack brought on by drugs and alcohol. Over 20,000 mourners attend his funeral.

1955
Elvis Presley appears at The Eagles Hall in Houston, Texas. He went on to play over 250 shows in 1955.

1960
Johnny Cash plays at San Quentin Prison, San Francisco.

1962
The Beatles audition for Decca Records in London but A&R boss Dick Rowe turns them down.

1964
BBC TV transmits the first *Top Of The Pops* from an old church hall in Manchester, England. Introduced by DJ Jimmy Savile, acts miming to their latest releases include The Rolling Stones ('I Wanna Be Your Man'), The Dave Clark Five ('Glad All Over'), The Hollies ('Stay') and The Swinging Blue Jeans ('Hippy Hippy Shake'). The opening song is Dusty Springfield's 'I Only Want To Be With You'. Also featured, on disc and film, are The Beatles ('I Want To Hold Your Hand'), Freddie & The Dreamers, Cliff Richard & The Shadows and Gene Pitney.

1969
Marmalade are at No. 1 on the UK singles chart with their version of The Beatles song 'Ob-La-Di Ob-La-Da'.

1977
Genesis play the first of three nights at the newly renovated Rainbow Theatre in London, where tickets cost £2.50.

The Clash play the opening night at punk's first real venue, The Roxy Club, in Covent Garden, London.

1982
Abba make their final live appearance in Stockholm, Sweden.

1984
Alexis Korner dies aged 55 of lung cancer. Known as 'the founding father of British blues', he was a major force behind the UK 60's R&B scene, and had hits with CCS, including a version of Led Zeppelin's 'Whole Lotta-Love' that became the theme for BBC's *Top Of The Pops*.

1989
Nirvana sign a one-year contract with Sub Pop Records.

1990
New American radio station WKRL in Florida play Led Zeppelin's 'Stairway To Heaven' for 24 hours as a prelude to an all-Zeppelin format.

2002
Welsh singer Shakin' Stevens spends several hours in police custody after being arrested for drink driving.

2007
Queen beat The Beatles as The Greatest British Band of All Time as voted by UK BBC Radio 2 listeners. They pip the Fab Four in a live contest, trouncing other finalists The Rolling Stones, Oasis and Take That.

More than 20,000 vote by e-mail, text and phone.

2009
According to official UK sales figures Duffy's debut album *Rockferry* comes top of the year-end chart, with 1.685 million copies sold.

Take That have the second biggest seller with *The Circus*, Kings of Leon's *Only By The Night* is third. *X Factor* winner Alexandra Burke has the UK's top-selling single after her version of 'Hallelujah' sells 888,000 copies in the last two weeks of the year.

Born on this day:

1936 Roger Miller, singer, guitarist and TV star
1942 Chick Churchill, keyboards (Ten Years After)
1954 Glenn Gones (Parliament, Funkadelic)
1963 Keith Gregory, bass (The Wedding Present)

1969
An entire shipment of John Lennon and Yoko Ono's *Two Virgins* album is seized by authorities in New Jersey due to the nude cover photographs of the couple. The album is eventually housed inside a brown paper outer sleeve for record stores.

Led Zeppelin play the first of four nights at the Whisky A Go-Go, Los Angeles during the band's first North American tour. Support group is Alice Cooper.

1971
George Harrison's *All Things Must Pass* starts a seven week run at No. 1 on the US album chart, making Harrison the first solo Beatle to score a chart-topping LP.

1976
Bad Company, Nazareth, Ronnie Lane's Slim Chance, The Pretty Things and Be-Bop Deluxe all appear at the second day of the Great British Music Festival at London's Olympia. Tickets cost £3.50.

1979
Sex Pistols' bass player Sid Vicious goes on trial in New York accused of murdering his girlfriend Nancy Spungen three months earlier.

1980
Larry Williams is found dead from a gunshot wound in his Los Angeles home, aged 45. Best-known for such early rock'n'roll classics as 'Short Fat Fannie', 'Bony Moronie' and 'Dizzy Miss Lizzy', The Beatles, The Rolling Stones, Dr. Feelgood, Johnny Winter, Little Richard, The Animals, Ritchie Valens and Bill Haley & His Comets were among the artists who covered his songs.

1988
Michael Jackson and Bono share first place in an American poll of The Most Beautiful Lips.

1997
Randy California, guitarist from US group Spirit, is drowned while rescuing his 12-year old son when sucked into a riptide in Hawaii.

2003
50 Cent is arrested by police in New York after his SUV was searched and a loaded .25-calibre handgun and a .45-calibre pistol were found in the vehicle, which had been left in a no-parking zone.

2007
Cristin Keleher, who made headlines in December 1999 by breaking into George Harrison's Hawaii home, is found dead, aged 34, in California. Police said her body had been found in a car with that of a 48-year-old man, both had gunshot wounds to the head after an apparent murder-suicide.

Gnarls Barkley's song 'Crazy' is confirmed as the biggest selling UK single of 2006, selling over 700,000 copies, being the first to reach No. 1 on downloads alone.

The track held off a challenge from *X-Factor* winner, Leon Jackson. Snow Patrol's *Eyes Open* topped the album chart with estimated sales of 1.5 million, while Take That's comeback *Beautiful World* came in just behind. Singles sales had doubled to over 65 million since the download chart was launched in September 2004.

2009
According to official US figures, AC/DC are the biggest album sellers of 2008 with over 3.4 million sold, Lil Wayne was in second place (3.3m), Taylor Swift, third (3.2m), Coldplay, fourth (2.5m) and Metallica, fifth (2.3m).

Born on this day:

January 3

1926 Sir George Martin, record producer
1941 Van Dyke Parks, US songwriter, producer
1945 Stephen Stills, guitar, vocals (Buffalo Springfield, Crosby, Stills, Nash & Young, Manassas)
1946 John Paul Jones, bass (Led Zeppelin & Them Crooked Vultures)

1955
Elvis Presley appears in Boonesville, Virginia. The 20 year-old singer was still a regional star, but by the end of '56 he became a national sensation, playing over 100 concerts, appearing on national television 11 times, and signing a seven-year contract with Paramount Pictures.

1964
The Beatles are seen for the first time on US TV when a clip from the BBC documentary *The Mersey Sound*, showing the group performing 'She Loves You', is broadcast on NBC's *The Jack Paar Show*.

of their first single, 'Hey Joe' and instead launch into Cream's 'Sunshine Of Your Love' as a tribute to the trio who had split a few months earlier.

1973
Bruce Springsteen plays the first of a four-night run at The Main Point, Bryn Mawr, Pennsylvania, opening for comedy rock duo, Travis Shook & The Club Wow.

1976
The Bay City Rollers are at No. 1 on the US singles chart with 'Saturday Night'. At the height of their American success, the Scottish group signed a deal to promote breakfast cereal.

One Bourbon, One Beer', dies aged 52.

1981
David Bowie makes his final appearance as *The Elephant Man* during a Broadway run in New York City.

1987
Aretha Franklin becomes the first woman inducted into the Rock and Roll Hall of Fame.

1992
Simple Minds singer Jim Kerr marries actress Patsy Kensit at Chelsea Registry Office.

2000
Luciano Pavarotti agrees to pay the Italian authorities £1.6 million after losing an appeal against tax evasion charges. It's reported that the singer is worth £300 million.

2002
Zak Foley, bassist with EMF, dies aged 31. The one-hit-wonders had a 1990 hit with 'Unbelievable'.

In *Your Home* magazine, Liam and Noel Gallagher top a readers' poll of celebrities you would least like to live next to, getting 40% of the 'Neighbours From Hell' vote.

1964
The Rolling Stones appear at the Glenlyn Ballroom in Forest Hill, south London, supported by The Detours (later to become The Who).

1967
Having received a US army draft notice, Beach Boy Carl Wilson refuses to be sworn in, saying he is a conscientious objector.

1969
Appearing live on BBC TV's *Happening For Lulu*, the Jimi Hendrix Experience stop performing a version

1979
The Hype (later to be known as U2) appear at McGonagle's in Dublin, Ireland.

1980
American rhythm and blues singer Amos Milburn, renowned for his drinking songs including 'Let Me Go Home, Whiskey' and 'One Scotch,

January 4

1936

Billboard magazine introduces the first ever-pop music chart that ranks records on national sales; big band violinist Joe Venuti is the first No. 1.

1954

Elvis Presley makes his second visit to the Memphis Recording Service and cuts two songs, 'Casual Love Affair' and 'I'll Never Stand In Your Way'. Studio boss Sam Phillips asks Presley to leave his phone number.

1965

The Fender guitar company is bought by CBS for $13 million.

1967

The Jimi Hendrix Experience play the first of what would be over 240 gigs during the year when they appear at the Bromel Club, Bromley.

1968

U.C.L.A. announces that music degrees will include studying the music of The Rolling Stones, saying the group has made an important contribution to modern music.

1969

UK weekly *Disc & Music Echo* reports that The Beatles are to release five new albums; one to be their first ever live album plus four separate LPs, each one the choice of Lennon, McCartney, Harrison and Starr.

1975

Elton John starts a two-week run at No. 1 in the US singles chart with his version of The Beatles' 'Lucy In The Sky With Diamonds', featuring John Lennon on guitar and backing vocals.

1976

Former Beatles' roadie Mal Evans is shot dead by police at his Los Angeles apartment. His girlfriend called the LAPD when she found Evans upset with a rifle in his hand; he pointed the gun at the police who opened fire.

1977

The Sex Pistols shock passengers and airline staff at Heathrow Airport by supposedly spitting and vomiting before boarding a plane to Amsterdam.

1986

Irish singer, songwriter and bassist Phil Lynott, of Thin Lizzy, dies of heart failure and pneumonia after being in a

coma for eight days following a drug overdose. A life-size bronze statue of Lynott was unveiled on Harry Street in Dublin in 2005.

2001

US rapper Vanilla Ice spends the night in Broward County Jail, Fort Lauderdale after allegedly ripping out some of his wife's hair. Born Robert Van Winkle, he explains his actions were to prevent her from jumping out of their moving truck's window. He is released the following morning on $3,500 bail.

Courtney Love files a lawsuit against her alleged stalker claiming that Lesley Barber, the ex-wife of her current boyfriend Jim Barber, drove over her foot. This had forced Love to forfeit her role in a forthcoming film, losing the £200,000 fee that went with it.

2004

Britney Spears has her marriage annulled less than 55 hours after tying the knot at the Little White Wedding Chapel, Las Vegas, with childhood friend Jason Alexander. The couple married on Saturday morning, during a night out in Vegas, but immediately Spears' lawyers filed for an annulment, saying their client "lacked understanding of her actions to the extent that she was incapable of agreeing to the marriage."

2005

AJ Abdallah, the owner of a Detroit recording studio where Eminem recorded his *Slim Shady* album, is found shot dead, aged 36. Discovered by a business colleague at the studio, it was thought Abdallah, who lived in an apartment above the studio on Eight Mile Road, the Detroit street that inspired the title of Eminem's 2002 film *8 Mile*, had been dead for at least two days. Police suggest a robbery may also have taken place.

2006

The rustic house near Nashville, Tennessee where Johnny Cash lived for 35 years is bought by Bee Gees singer Barry Gibb. The house went on the market in June 2005 with an asking price of $2.9m. Gibb said he planned to preserve the house to honour the Cash memory but unfortunately it burns down on April 10, 2007.

Born on this day:

1923 Sam Phillips, founder of Sun Records
1950 Chris Stein, guitar (Blondie)
1969 Brian Warner (Marilyn Manson)

1970 Troy Van Leeuwen, guitarist (Queens Of The Stone Age)
1976 Matthew Walter Wachter, bass (30 Seconds To Mars)

January 5

1967
The Pink Floyd appear at The Marquee Club, London.

1968
Jimi Hendrix is jailed in Stockholm, Sweden on drink charges after destroying his room at the Goteberg Hotel.

1973
Bruce Springsteen releases his debut album, *Greetings From Asbury Park, NJ.*

1979
Prince makes his live debut at the Capri Theatre, Minneapolis.

1989
In the *Melody Maker* Readers Poll, The Mission win Best Band, Best Live Act, Best Single and Best Album; Morrissey – Best Male Singer, Julianne Regan – (from All About Eve) Best Female Singer, and Best New Band is won by The House Of Love. Worst LP goes to Bros with *Push.*

1997
Sonny Bono is killed in a skiing accident at a resort near Lake Tahoe, aged 62. Bono, formerly half of husband and wife duo Sonny & Cher who scored a 1965 UK and US chart-topper with 'I Got You Babe', became a US Republican congressman.

1998
Ken Forssi, bassist with cult LA 60's group, Love, dies of brain cancer aged 55.

2003

Green Day's lead singer Billie Joe Armstrong is arrested on suspicion of drink driving after being stopped in California speeding in a black BMW convertible. He fails a breath test and is taken to Berkeley county jail and later released on $1,053 bail.

2004
Ray Davies is shot in the leg while on holiday in New Orleans. The 59-year-old Kinks singer-songwriter was running after two men who stole his girlfriend's purse at gunpoint. Davies is admitted to the Medical Centre of Louisiana but his injuries are not considered serious. New Orleans police said one person had been arrested, and police were still searching for the second.

2005
New York group Scissor Sisters have the UK's best-selling album of 2004 after overtaking Keane's sales on the last day of the year. Scissor Sisters' self-titled debut CD sells 1,594,259 copies in 2004 - 582 more than Keane's *Hopes and Fears.* Robbie Williams' *Greatest Hits* is the year's third biggest-seller, followed by Maroon 5, Katie Melua and Anastacia.

2008
Josh Groban is at No. 1 on the US album chart with his Christmas album *Noel,* the best selling US album of 2007 selling over 3.5 million copies in 10 weeks.

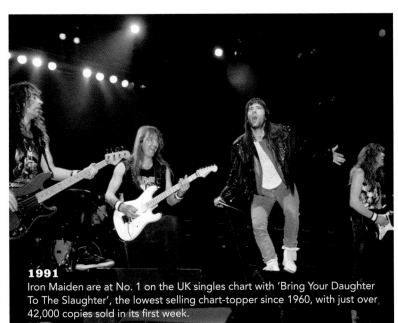

1991
Iron Maiden are at No. 1 on the UK singles chart with 'Bring Your Daughter To The Slaughter', the lowest selling chart-topper since 1960, with just over 42,000 copies sold in its first week.

January 6

Born on this day:

1944 Van McCoy, singer, producer
1946 Syd Barrett, guitar, vocals (Pink Floyd)
1947 Sandy Denny, UK folk singer (Fairport Convention, Fotheringay)

1953 Malcolm Young, guitar (AC/DC)
1964 Mark O'Toole, bass (Frankie Goes To Hollywood)

1956
Elvis Presley performs in the gymnasium at Randolph High School, Mississippi; the last time he ever appears in a small auditorium.

1964
The first night of a 14 date 'Group Scene 1964' UK tour, featuring The Rolling Stones, The Ronettes, Marty Wilde, The Swinging Blue Jeans and Dave Berry and The Cruisers, plays at the Granada Theatre, Harrow-on-the-Hill, Middlesex.

1968
The Beatles *Magical Mystery Tour* starts an eight week run at No. 1 on the US album chart – the group's 11th American chart topping LP.

1970
Crosby, Stills, Nash & Young make their UK live debut at the Royal Albert Hall, London.

1973
Carly Simon's 'You're So Vain' (with Mick Jagger on backing vocals) starts a three week run at No. 1 on the US singles chart.

1977
EMI Records drops The Sex Pistols, giving the band £40,000 to release them from their contract.

1979
The Village People score their only UK No. 1 single with 'Y.M.C.A.' At its peak the single sold over 150,000 copies a day. Within the gay culture from which the group sprang, the song was understood as celebrating the YMCA's reputation as a popular cruising and pick-up spot.

1980
Georgeanna Gordon, singer with Motown girl group The Marvelettes who had a 1961 US No. 1 with 'Please Mr. Postman', dies aged 46.

1987
Eric Clapton starts what will become an annual event by playing six shows at the Royal Albert Hall, London.

1997
Two bronze busts worth £50,000 are stolen from the garden at George Harrison's estate in Henley-on-Thames, Oxfordshire. Thieves had climbed a 10-foot-wall and cut the figures of two monks from their stone plinths.

2001
Pink Floyd guitarist David Gilmour wins the right to his internet identity after taking legal action to reclaim davidgilmour.com. Andrew Herman had registered the URL and was selling Pink Floyd merchandise through the site.

2006
Ms Dynamite is charged in London with assaulting a police officer and disorderly conduct. She had been arrested after allegedly kicking the door to the Paragon Lounge nightclub and was said to have been abusive towards officers who questioned her. The singer allegedly punched a female officer in the face, bruising her nose, while in custody.

A collection of Elvis Presley memorabilia owned by a council worker is to be auctioned off by a High Court receiver to provide compensation for the local authority. Julie Wall, 46, from Rippon Drive, Sleaford, was jailed for three years last October for embezzling nearly £600,000.

2007
US country-rock steel guitar player 'Sneaky' Pete Kleinow, one of the original members of the Flying Burrito Brothers, dies aged 72. He also worked as a session player with John Lennon and Joni Mitchell.

Born on this day:

1942 Danny Williams, singer
1944 Mike McGear, singer, brother of Paul
McCartney (The Scaffold)

1948 Kenny Loggins, singer, songwriter
1959 Kathy Valentine, bass (The Go-Go's)
1974 John Rich, bass, vocals (Lonestar)

January 7

1955
'Rock Around The Clock' by Bill Haley & His Comets, enters the UK chart for the first time.

1964
Harmonica player Cyril Davies dies of leukaemia, aged 32. Davies was a driving force in the early 60's R&B movement, forming Blues Incorporated with Alexis Korner.

1973
David Bowie appears at the City Hall, Newcastle.

1974
Aerosmith play the Michigan Theatre, Detroit, the first date on their 56 concert 'Get Your Wings' North American tour.

1980
Hugh Cornwell of The Stranglers is found guilty of possession of heroin, cocaine and cannabis. He is fined £300 and sentenced to three months in Pentonville prison.

1981
The Police play the first night of a North American tour at the University of Montreal during their 'Zenyatta Mondatta' World Tour.

1993
R.E.M. play a Greenpeace benefit at the 40 Watt Club, Athens, Georgia, for 500 people. The show is recorded on a solar powered mobile recording studio.

1994
Oasis start recording their debut album *Definitely Maybe* at Monrow studios in South Wales.

2003
The Beatles Book Monthly closes down after 40 years. Publisher Sean O'Mahony, who originally set up the magazine in 1963, explains there was nothing more to say as the former Beatles' activities had decreased over the years.

2004
Drummer John Guerin, who worked with Joni Mitchell, Frank Zappa, Linda Ronstadt, Gram Parsons, Todd Rundgren and also played on the original title tune for the TV series *Hawaii Five-O*, dies of pneumonia aged 64.

2006
Paul Gadd (better known as Gary Glitter) is formally charged with committing obscene acts with two girls aged 11 and 12 in Vietnam. The

prosecutor in the southern province of Ba Ria Vung Tau said the charges would carry prison terms of three to seven years. Glitter had been held since November as he tried to flee the country over child sex allegations.

More than 100 guests, including Lisa-Marie Presley, attend Pink's wedding to her motocross racer boyfriend Carey Hart on a beach in Costa Rica. Pink proposed to Hart during one of his races in Mammoth Lakes, California, by holding up a sign that read "Will you marry me?" Hart pulled out of the race to say yes.

January 8

Born on this day:

1935 Elvis Presley	**1959** Paul Hester, drums (Crowded House)
1937 Shirley Bassey	**1969** R. Kelly, singer, writer, producer
1946 Robert Krieger, guitar (The Doors)	**1973** Sean Paul, singer
1947 David Bowie	

1957
Bill Haley & His Comets start the first ever rock & roll tour of Australia, playing two sold-out nights in Sydney.

1966
The Beatles start a six week run at No. 1 on the US album chart with *Rubber Soul* the group's seventh US chart topper, which went on to spend 56 weeks on the chart. The group also started a three week run at No. 1 on the US singles chart with 'We Can Work It Out, The Beatles' 11th US chart-topping single.

1969
Mick Jagger and Keith Richards are barred from the exclusive Hotel Crillen in Lima, Peru for wearing 'op art pants' and nothing else. They were both asked to leave after refusing to change clothes.

1991
Steve Clark, guitarist with Def Leppard, is found dead at his Chelsea flat by his girlfriend, after a night of heavy alcohol consumption combined with prescription drugs.

1994
Jamaican reggae/rap (ragga) duo Chaka Demus and Pliers are at No. 1 in the UK with their version of 60s pop standard, 'Twist And Shout'.

1996
A Los Angeles court finds Robert Hoskins guilty on five counts of stalking, assault and making terrorist threats to Madonna. Hoskins had twice scaled the walls of the singer's estate and had threatened to cut her throat.

2000
After a tip off to the police a £1 million kidnap plot to snatch Spice Girl Victoria Beckham and her baby son, Brooklyn, is foiled. The gang had planned to kidnap the pair when husband David was away playing football.

Christina Aguilera starts a two week run at No. 1 on the US singles chart with 'What A Girl Wants', ending Santana's 12-week run at No. 1 with 'Smooth'.

2001
A woman who believed that Axl Rose communicated with her via telepathy is arrested for stalking the Guns N' Roses singer for a second time.

Police detain Karen Jane McNeil after she is spotted loitering outside his house.

2004
The estate of George Harrison brings a $10 million legal action against Dr. Gilbert Lederman of Staten Island University Hospital, claiming the doctor coerced Harrison into signing souvenirs. The main allegation is that Lederman pushed the cancer stricken ex-Beatle into signing his son's guitar and other items for his two daughters. The case was eventually settled out of court with the guitar in question being destroyed.

1979
Canadian rock band Rush are named the country's official Ambassadors of Music by the Canadian government.

Born on this day:

January 9

1941 Joan Baez, US folk rock singer, songwriter

1944 Jimmy Page, guitarist, producer (The Yardbirds, Led Zeppelin)

1944 Scott Engel, vocals (The Walker Brothers)

1950 David Johansen, vocals (New York Dolls)

1967 Dave Matthews, guitar, vocals (Dave Matthews Band)

1987 Paolo Nutini, Scottish singer, songwriter

1955
Rosemary Clooney is at No. 1 on the UK singles chart with 'Mambo Italiano', the singer's second chart-topper. The song is banned by all ABC owned stations in the US because it "did not reach standards of good taste."

1963
Drummer Charlie Watts joins The Rolling Stones after leaving Alexis Korner's Blues Incorporated.

1973
Mick Jagger is refused a Japanese visa on an account of a 1969 drug conviction, causing The Rolling Stones to cancel a forthcoming tour there.

1979
The Music For UNICEF concert takes place in New York City, featuring Rod Stewart, The Bee Gees, Earth Wind & Fire, Abba and Donna Summer.

1981
Terry Hall and Jerry Dammers from The Specials are both fined £400 after being found guilty of using threatening words during a gig in Cambridge, England.

2000
The chauffeur who drove Puff Daddy and his girlfriend Jennifer Lopez from a night-club after a shooting is reported to be co-operating with prosecutors. Puff Daddy faces up to 15 years in jail for allegedly pulling a gun in a New York club.

2002
Irish singer/songwriter David McWilliams dies of a heart attack at his home in Ballycastle, County Antrim, aged 56. McWilliams' most well-known song, 'The Days Of Pearly Spencer', was successfully revived in 1992 by Marc Almond.

2003
Music producer Robert Johnson and partner Larry Moss sell a grand piano once owned by Elvis Presley for $685,000 to Michael Muzio, chairman of the Blue Moon Group, who is planning to take the piano on a casino-sponsored promotional tour and for it to be put on display at a proposed rock museum at Walt Disney World.

2005
Scissor Sisters are at No. 1 on the UK album chart with their self-titled album. The New York act go on to win Best International Album as well as Best International Group and International Breakthrough Act at the 2005 Brit Awards.

2008
Spice Girl Victoria Beckham is named the Worst Dressed Celebrity in an annual list of fashion disasters. Fashion critic Richard Blackwell, who has compiled the poll every year since 1960, said Beckham stepped out in "one skinny-mini monstrosity after another." Amy Winehouse's trademark beehive and tattoos help earn her second place on the list.

2009
UK singer, turned A&R man, Dave Dee dies at the age of 65, following a three-year battle with cancer. Dave Dee, Dozy, Beaky, Mick & Tich had eight top 10 hits, including a UK number one in 1968 with 'The Legend Of Xanadu', in which Dee famously cracked a whip. The singer (real name: David Harman) was originally a police officer and, as a cadet, he was called to the scene of the car crash that killed Eddie Cochran in 1960.

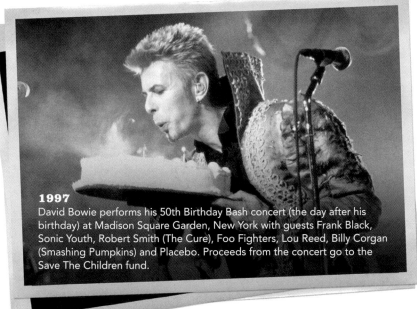

1997
David Bowie performs his 50th Birthday Bash concert (the day after his birthday) at Madison Square Garden, New York with guests Frank Black, Sonic Youth, Robert Smith (The Cure), Foo Fighters, Lou Reed, Billy Corgan (Smashing Pumpkins) and Placebo. Proceeds from the concert go to the Save The Children fund.

January 10

Born on this day:

1917 Jerry Wexler, producer and record company executive
1927 Johnnie Ray, US teen idol singer
1939 Scott McKenzie, singer/songwriter
1943 Jim Croce, US singer/songwriter
1945 Rod Stewart, singer
1948 Donald Fagen, vocals, keyboards (Steely Dan)
1955 Michael Schenker, German guitarist
1986 Alex Turner, guitar, vocals (Arctic Monkeys)

1956
Elvis Presley makes his first recordings for RCA Records at The Methodist Television, Radio & TV Studios in Nashville. 'Heartbreak Hotel' is one of the songs recorded during this session.

1958
Jerry Lee Lewis is at No. 1 on the UK singles chart with 'Great Balls Of Fire'. Lewis is the only major white rock'n'roll star to play piano rather than guitar.

1963
On his second UK visit in less than a month Bob Dylan plays at the Troubadour Club, London.

1964
The Rolling Stones record their third single, 'Not Fade Away' at Regent Sound Studios in London.

1965
John Lennon appears in a pre-recorded comedy skit as well as appearing live in the studio, reading from his book *In His Own Write* in the first episode of the BBC TV show, *Not Only… But Also*, hosted by Dudley Moore.

1969
George Harrison walks out of The Beatles after disagreements with John Lennon and Paul McCartney during rehearsals at Twickenham Film Studios, being filmed for *Let It Be*. He eventually returns after a series of meetings to discuss The Beatles' future.

1976
Blues artist Howlin Wolf (Chester Burnett) dies in hospital of cancer, aged 66. The guitarist, singer and harmonica player's well-known songs included 'Smokestack Lightning', 'Little Red Rooster' and 'Spoonful'.

1981
John Lennon and Yoko Ono's *Double Fantasy* starts an eight-week run at No. 1 on the US album chart. '(Just Like) Starting Over' is at No. 1 on the US singles chart.

1990
Bon Jovi play the first of seven sold-out nights at the Hammersmith Odeon, London, on their 'New Jersey Syndicate' Tour.

1997
Kenny Pickett, singer with 60's band The Creation (who had a minor 1966 hit 'Painter Man'), dies aged 54 of a heart attack.

James Brown receives a star on the Hollywood Walk of Fame.

2001
American guitarist and songwriter and founder member of The Cramps, Bryan Gregory dies after suffering a heart attack aged 46 at Anaheim Memorial Medical Center, California.

2003
A haul of 500 Beatles tapes – known as the 'Get Back' sessions – that were stolen in the 70s, are retrieved after UK police crack a major bootleg operation in London and Amsterdam. Five men are arrested.

2007
Madame Tussauds unveils its fourth waxwork of Kylie Minogue, making the Australian pop star the most modelled celebrity after the Queen. The model became the first scented waxwork, wearing Minogue's Darling perfume.

2008
Radiohead top the US album charts with the official release of *In Rainbows*, originally sold via the internet for a price chosen by fans. The album sells 122,000 copies during its first week on release, giving the band a second US No. 1 following 2000's *Kid A*, which sold an initial 207,000 copies.

2009
Black Eyed Peas singer Fergie marries actor Josh Duhamel at the Church Estates Vineyards in Malibu. Guests include her bandmate Will.i.am and actress Kate Hudson.

Born on this day:

1895 Laurens Hammond, inventor of the Hammond organ
1924 Slim Harpo, blues musician
1942 Clarence Clemons, saxophone (E Street Band)
1958 Vicki Peterson, guitar, vocals (The Bangles)
1968 Tom Dumont (No Doubt)
1971 Mary Jane Blige, American R&B soul singer-songwriter
1971 Tom Rowlands (The Chemical Brothers)
1981 Thomas Meighan, singer (Kasabian)

January 11

1958
The release date for Elvis Presley's single 'Jailhouse Rock' is put back a week after Decca Records' pressing plant in the UK is unable to meet advance orders of 250,000 copies.

1963
The Beatles second single, 'Please Please Me'/ 'Ask Me Why' is released in the UK and becomes the group's first No. 1.

1964
Ring Of Fire by Johnny Cash becomes the first country album to get to No. 1 on the US album chart.

1965
The Righteous Brothers arrive in Britain for a promotional visit to plug their original version of 'You've Lost That Lovin' Feelin'' which is competing in the UK charts against an inferior cover by Cilla Black.

1967
The Jimi Hendrix Experience record 'Purple Haze' and also sign to new label Track Records, run by The Who's managers, Kit Lambert and Chris Stamp.

1978
Elvis Costello & The Attractions appear at the City Hall, Newcastle.

1985
A rock festival held in Rio – featuring Queen, Rod Stewart, AC/DC, Whitesnake, Yes and Iron Maiden – claims to be the biggest ever staged.

1992
On the same day that *Nevermind* reaches No. 1 on the US album chart, Nirvana appear on NBC-TV's *Saturday Night Live*.

1998
Rolling Stone magazine readers pick *Be Here Now* by Oasis as Album Of The Year.

1999
Ex-Mighty Wah singer Pete Wylie appears in a Liverpool court charged with making threats to kill his ex-girlfriend.

2000
Gary Glitter is released from prison after serving half of a four month sentence for possessing child pornography downloaded from the internet. Glitter was told he would have to go on the Sex Offenders Register for seven years.

It is reported that Whitney Houston is under investigation after allegedly trying to smuggle 15.2 grams of marijuana out of Hawaii. A security officer found the drug in the singer's handbag and Houston walked away when he tried to detain her.

2002
Mickey Finn, percussionist and sideman to Marc Bolan in T. Rex, dies of kidney and liver problems, aged 55.

2003
Britain's oldest rockers come out winners in *The Pollstar* listing of The Top 10 Grossing US Tours Of 2002: Paul McCartney $68m, The Rolling Stones $58m, Elton John $47m, The Who $20m, Ozzy Osbourne $18m, Peter Gabriel $10m, Yes $6m, Elvis Costello $5m, The Moody Blues $4m and Jethro Tull $3m.

Girls Aloud singer Cheryl Tweedy is arrested after an alleged attack in a nightclub in Guildford, Surrey. The Popstars Rivals winner was accused of punching a lavatory attendant.

2005
Former Bread guitarist and Academy Award-winning songwriter James Griffin dies at his Nashville home at the age of 61 after suffering from cancer.

2008
Ringo Starr helps launch celebrations for Liverpool's year as European Capital of Culture. He is joined by acrobats who dangle on wires from cranes as the opening party kicks off a year-long programme of more than 350 events. Organisers hope the Capital of Culture tag will attract an extra two million visitors to Liverpool and boost the economy by £100m.

Born on this day:

1941 Long John Baldry, vocals	**1960** Charlie Gillingham, keyboards (Counting Crows)
1946 Cynthia Robinson, vocals (Sly & The Family Stone)	**1963** Guy Chambers, singer, songwriter, producer
1951 Chris Bell, guitarist (Big Star)	**1965** Greg Kriesel, bass (The Offspring)
1954 Felipe Rose, vocals (The Village People)	**1974** Melanie Chisholm (a.k.a. Mel C, Sporty Spice), vocals (The Spice Girls)

1964

The Beatles appear on the ITV show *Sunday Night At The London Palladium* performing 'I Want To Hold Your Hand', 'This Boy', 'All My Loving', 'Money' and 'Twist And Shout'. When The Beatles first appeared on this prestigious British entertainment show on October 13, 1963, their fee was £250, now, just three months later, it has risen to £1,000.

1974

The Steve Miller Band is at No. 1 on the US singles chart with 'The Joker', the first of three No. 1s for them. The song later reaches No. 1 on the UK chart in 1990.

1975

The first night of a UK tour kicks off under the Warner Brothers Music Show banner, featuring Little Feat, Montrose, Tower Of Power, The Doobie Brothers and Graham Central Station. Also released is a sampler album featuring each act, priced at only 69p.

1977

Rolling Stone Keith Richards is fined £750 at Aylesbury Crown Court for possession of cocaine found in his car after the guitarist was involved in a crash the previous May.

The Police, featuring Henri Padovani on guitar, hold their first rehearsal at drummer Stewart Copeland's London flat.

1983

Reebop Kwaku Baah, percussionist with Traffic, who also worked with Eric Clapton, Steve Winwood, Ginger Baker's Air Force, Can and The Rolling Stones, dies from a brain haemorrhage in Stockholm, Sweden.

1992

Bob Geldof is arrested after a disturbance on a Boeing 727 which had been grounded for five hours at Stansted Airport.

1995

Snoop Doggy Dogg is charged in Los Angeles with possession of marijuana and drug paraphernalia.

1996

AC/DC play the first date on their 'Ballbreaker' World Tour in Greensboro, North Carolina. The world tour lasts for 11 months, finishing on November 30 in Christchurch, New Zealand.

2001

British Airways' staff complain about Oasis singer Liam Gallagher's behaviour after he grabs a stewardess' bottom, refuses to stop smoking and throws objects around the cabin during a flight from London to Rio de Janeiro.

2003

Singer-songwriter Maurice Gibb, of The Bee Gees, dies aged 53 in Miami Hospital, Florida following a heart attack during abdominal surgery.

2005

It is announced that the Strawberry Field children's home in Woolton, Liverpool, immortalised by The Beatles, is to close. John Lennon played there as a child.

2007

Toni Braxton files a $10 million lawsuit at the US District Court in Manhattan against former manager Barry Hankerson, alleging "fraud, deception and double dealing." According to Braxton, Hankerson placed his own personal financial interests ahead of hers by using "double-talk" to compromise the relationship between the singer and her former record label, Arista.

1977

EMI Records issues a statement saying it felt unable to promote The Sex Pistols records in view of the adverse publicity the band has generated over the last two months.

Born on this day:

1955 Fred White, drums (Earth Wind & Fire)
1961 Graham McPherson (a.k.a. Suggs), vocals (Madness)
1964 David McClusky, drums (The Bluebells)
1970 Zach de la Rocha, vocals (Rage Against The Machine)

January 13

1962
Chubby Checker's 'The Twist', which first went to No. 1 in September 1960, becomes the only record in American chart history to top the charts on two separate occasions.

1973
Eric Clapton makes his stage comeback, playing two shows at the Rainbow Theatre, London, with Pete Townshend, Ronnie Wood, Stevie Winwood, Rick Grech, Jim Capaldi

already decided the song was not to be played. 'Relax' goes on to become a UK No. 1 for five weeks, spending a total of 48 weeks on the UK chart.

1986
Ex-Sex Pistols John Lydon, Steve Jones and Paul Cook, as well as the mother of Sid Vicious, sue former manager Malcolm McLaren for £1 million. They eventually settled out of court.

2003
Diana Ross appears in a US court charged with driving while twice over the drink driving limit. Tucson police report that Miss Ross could not walk in a straight line, touch her nose or count to 30 after she had been stopped for swerving across the road.

1965
The first day of recording sessions for Bob Dylan's *Bringing It All Back Home* album at Studio A, Columbia Recording Studios, New York City.

1967
Jimi Hendrix plays the second of two nights at the 7 & 1/2 Club near Piccadilly Circus, London.

1968
Johnny Cash plays a show, recorded for a forthcoming live album, at Folsom Prison, near Sacramento, in front of 2,000 inmates.

1969
Elvis Presley begins ten days of recording sessions at American Sound Studios, Memphis – the first time Presley has recorded in his hometown since his Sun Records days in 1956.

1970
Steel Mill (featuring Bruce Springsteen) play The Matrix club in San Francisco. The scheduled headliner Boz Scaggs cancels at the last minute due to illness. Rock critic Philip Elwood ended up writing a highly favorable review of Steel Mill for *The San Francisco Examiner*.

and support from The Average White Band. The concerts were recorded for the *Rainbow Concert* album.

1977
Queen start a 59-date world tour at Dane County Coliseum, Milwaukee. Opening act is Thin Lizzy.

1978
The Police start recording their first album at Surrey Sound Studios with producer Nigel Gray.

1979
Soul singer Donny Hathaway commits suicide by falling from a 15th floor New York hotel window.

1984
BBC Radio 1 announces a ban on 'Relax' by Frankie Goes To Hollywood. DJ Mike Read expressed on air his distaste for both the record's suggestive sleeve and "obscene" lyrics and announced his refusal to play the record, not knowing that the BBC had

2005
A report shows that more songs have been written about Elvis Presley than any other artist. It lists over 220 including 'Graceland' by Paul Simon, 'Calling Elvis' (Dire Straits), 'Happy Birthday Elvis' (Loudon Wainwright III), 'There's A Guy Works Down The Chip Shop Swears He's Elvis' (Kirsty MacColl), 'I Saw Elvis In A UFO' (Ray Stevens), 'Elvis Has Left The Building' (Frank Zappa) and 'My Dog Thinks I'm Elvis' (Ray Herndon).

Born on this day:

1938 Allan Toussaint, US singer, songwriter
1944 Linda Jones, US soul singer
1967 Zakk Wylde, guitarist (Ozzy Osbourne Band)
1968 James Todd Smith (L.L. Cool J)

1969 Dave Grohl, drummer, guitarist, singer (Nirvana, Foo Fighters, Them Crooked Vultures)
1982 Caleb Followill, lead singer, rhythm guitarist (Kings Of Leon)

1964
The Beatles (minus Ringo Starr, who is fog-bound in Liverpool and arrives the next day) depart from London to Paris for an 18-day run at the Olympia Theatre.

1967
Over 25,000 people attend The Human Be-In A Gathering Of The Tribes at San Francisco's Golden Gate Park. The event is a forerunner of major, outdoor rock concerts and features The Grateful Dead, Jefferson Airplane, Quicksilver Messenger Service and Big Brother & The Holding Company.

1970
Diana Ross makes her last appearance with The Supremes at The Frontier Hotel, Las Vegas.

1978
The Sex Pistols play their last gig at Winterland, San Francisco. The original line-up of the band first reformed for a lucrative tour in 1996.

1984
Paul McCartney is at No. 1 on the UK singles chart with 'Pipes Of Peace'. With this release McCartney made chart history by becoming the first artist to have a No. 1 in a group (The Beatles), in a duo (with Stevie Wonder), in a trio (Wings) and as a solo artist.

1992
Jerry Nolan, ex-drummer with New York Dolls, dies from a fatal stroke. The influential American band formed in 1972 and made just two albums, *New York Dolls* (1973) and *Too Much Too Soon* (1974).

1993
US alternative group, The Pixies announce their split. (They re-formed to tour in 2004.)

1996
Oasis are at No. 1 with *(What's The Story) Morning Glory* which spends a total of 145 weeks on the UK album chart.

2003
After discussions with her lawyer, Linda Gail Lewis, the sister of Jerry Lee Lewis, drops a claim of sex discrimination against Van Morrison. Lewis had claimed that Morrison had "publicly humiliated" her on stage and had tried to ruin her life by asking her for sex. Morrison denied all the allegations.

2005
A $100,000 statue honouring the late punk guitarist Johnny Ramone is unveiled by his widow Linda at the Hollywood Forever Cemetery. Johnny died from prostate cancer in September 2004 at the age of 55. Hundreds turned out for the ceremony, including Lisa Marie Presley and Tommy Ramone – the only surviving band member. Joey Ramone died in 2001 of lymphatic cancer and Dee Dee Ramone of a drugs overdose in 2002.

2007
Amy Winehouse starts a two week run at No. 1 on the UK album chart with *Back To Black* (which goes on to become the biggest-selling album of 2007 with sales over 1.5m copies). Nas is at No. 1 on the US album chart with *Hip Hop Is Dead*.

Born on this day:

1893 Ivor Novello, songwriter & actor
1941 Don Van Vliet (Captain Beefheart)
1948 Ronnie Van Zant, vocals (Lynyrd Skynyrd)

1953 Boris Blank (Yello)
1961 Damian O'Neill, guitar (The Undertones)

1961
The Supremes (above) sign a worldwide recording contract with Motown Records.

1965
The Who release their first single, 'I Can't Explain' in the UK. Produced by Kinks producer Shel Talmy, with The Ivy League on backing vocals, it went on to reach No. 8 on the charts.

1967
The Rolling Stones are forced to change the lyrics of 'Let's Spend The Night Together' to "let's spend some time together" when appearing on US TV's *The Ed Sullivan Show* after the producers objected to the content of the lyrics.

1969
George Harrison has a five-hour meeting with John, Paul and Ringo where he makes it clear that he is fully prepared to quit The Beatles for good. Harrison isn't happy with plans for The Beatles to return to live performances.

1972
Don McLean's 'American Pie' starts a four week run at No. 1 in the US singles chart.

1977
The Eagles reach No. 1 on the *Billboard* album chart with *Hotel California*, the band's third US chart-topping LP.

1982
The Police kick off the North American leg of their 119-date 'Ghost In The Machine' world tour in Boston, supported by The Go-Gos.

1983
Men At Work start a four week run at No. 1 in the American singles chart with 'Down Under', the Australian act's second US No. 1, which also reached pole position in the UK.

1992
Dee Murray, bass player with the Elton John band, dies after suffering a stroke, aged 45.

1994
Popular American singer-songwriter Harry Nilsson dies in his sleep of heart failure after spending the previous day in the recording studio.

2002
Adam Ant is admitted to a mental ward 24 hours after being charged by police with pulling a gun on staff in a north London pub.

2006
James Blunt is at No. 1 on the UK album chart with his debut album (and the biggest selling UK album of 2005), *Back To Bedlam*.

2008
Ronnie Wood is recovering following an operation for a hernia after he sustained the injury during the band's recent 'A Bigger Bang' tour. The 60-year-old Rolling Stones guitarist is told to rest for two months after the procedure.

January 16

Born on this day:

1942 Raymond Philips (The Nashville Teens)

1959 Sade (Helen Folasade Adu), singer

1979 Aaliyah, US singer

1981 Nick Valensi, guitar (The Strokes)

1956
Tennessee Ernie Ford is at No. 1 on the UK singles chart with his version of 'Sixteen Tons', written by Merle Travis in 1947 about the miseries of coal mining.

1957
The Cavern Club opens in Liverpool as a jazz club. It went on to become the home of many Liverpool groups including The Beatles who appeared at the venue 292 times.

1964
The Beatles play two shows at the Olympia Theatre, Paris, the first of an 18-night engagement. These first shows are attended mostly by Parisian society dressed in formal evening attire. The French press have little good to say about The Beatles in the next day's reviews, but The Beatles didn't care, because they'd received news that 'I Want to Hold Your Hand' had reached No. 1 in America.

1969
Fleetwood Mac, Creedence Clearwater Revival and Albert Collins appear at the Fillmore West, San Francisco.

1973
Bruce Springsteen appears at Villanova University, Philadelphia to an audience of 25 people.

1977
David Soul, one half of TV cop show *Starsky & Hutch*, is at No. 1 on the UK singles chart with 'Don't Give Up On Us', which also becomes an American chart-topper.

1980
Paul McCartney is jailed for nine days in Tokyo for marijuana possession after being found with 219g on his arrival at Narita Airport. He requests that he be given a guitar in his cell, but this is rejected. McCartney had previously been refused a visa for Japan in 1975 due to a drugs conviction.

1985
David Bowie's schizophrenic half-brother, Terry Burnes, is killed instantly by a passing train, after lying down on railway lines at Coulsdon South station, London. He was 47.

1987
TV presenter Jools Holland is suspended from Channel 4's UK music show *The Tube* for six weeks, after using the phrase "groovy fuckers" during a live trailer broadcast during children's hour.

1988
Former Go-Go's singer Belinda Carlisle scores her first UK No. 1 single with 'Heaven Is A Place On Earth'. The promotional video, directed by Academy Award-winning actress Diane Keaton, features an appearance by Carlisle's husband Morgan Mason, son of actor James Mason.

Tina Turner gets into the record books when she performs in front of 182,000 people in Rio De Janeiro – the largest ever audience for a single artist.

1989
Michael Jackson plays the first of five nights at the Memorial Sports Arena, Los Angeles – the last shows on the singer's 'Bad' World Tour. Jackson donated more than $1m of the final concert's takings to an organisation fighting child cruelty.

1990
Ike Turner, convicted of driving under the influence of cocaine and being under the influence of cocaine, is sentenced to a four year prison sentence in California.

1996
Jamaican authorities open fire on Jimmy Buffett's seaplane, mistaking it for a drug trafficker. U2 singer Bono is also on the plane but neither singer is injured in the incident.

2000
The Coasters singer Will Jones dies, aged 71.

It is reported that Mick Jagger has lost the chance of a knighthood because of his past errant ways. British Prime Minister Tony Blair had second thoughts about the message it would give about family values. Jagger succeeded in getting knighted in December 2003.

2005
Elvis Presley's single 'One Night' makes chart history by becoming the 1,000th UK No. 1. Elvis, who led last week's chart with 'Jailhouse Rock', had now scored more number one UK hits than any other artist with 20 No. 1s, beating The Beatles' tally of 17.

2007
Bob Dylan buys Aultmore House, a mansion in the Scottish Cairngorms National Park, near Nethybridge, Inverness.

2008
Radiohead are forced to abandon an intimate London gig at Rough Trade East's record shop after police raise safety fears. The band move the gig to a nearby club when over 1,500 turn up after the event is announced in the morning, promising tickets to the first 200 fans.

Born on this day:

1945 William Hart, vocals (The Delfonics)
1948 Mick Taylor, guitar (The Rolling Stones)
1955 Steve Earle, US singer, songwriter

1963 Andy Rourke, bass (The Smiths)
1966 Shabba Ranks, singer
1971 Kid Rock, singer
1978 Ricky Wilson, vocals (Kaiser Chiefs)

January
17

1964

The Rolling Stones release their first EP which peaks at No. 15 on the UK singles chart.

1967

The Daily Mail runs a story about a local council survey finding 4,000 holes in the road in Blackburn, Lancashire, inspiring The Beatles song 'A Day In The Life'.

The Jimi Hendrix Experience record a session for Radio Luxembourg's *Ready Steady Radio*. The band run up a bar bill of £2 and 5 shillings (£2.25), which they are unable to pay.

1972

A section of Bellevue Boulevard, Memphis is renamed Elvis Presley Boulevard. The remaining length of the road keeps its original name after protests from the Bellevue Baptist Church.

1974

Dean Martin's son Dino is arrested after attempting to sell two AK-47 machine guns to an undercover agent.

1982

Tommy Tucker, best known for his 1964 US No. 11 hit, 'Hi Heel Sneakers', dies aged 48, after being overcome by poisonous fumes while renovating the floors of his New York home.

1994

Donny Osmond takes part in a charity boxing match held in Chicago against former Partridge Family member Danny Bonaduce, who loses 2-1.

1998

All Saints score their first UK No. 1 single with 'Never Ever'. The track spends a total of twenty-four weeks on the UK chart and is the first of five No. 1 singles for the London based girl group.

1999

Fatboy Slim starts a four-week run at No. 1 on the UK album chart with *You've Come A Long Way Baby*.

2003

Lou Rawls is arrested at Albuquerque Airport, New Mexico after an incident with his companion, Nina Inman. Officers reported that she and Rawls had been talking about their relationship when the conversation escalated into a shoving match, resulting in Rawls being booked on one count of battery on a household member.

2008

The Police play the first show on the Australian and New Zealand leg of their 152-date Reunion tour, at the Westpac Stadium in Wellington.

1970

The Doors appear at the Felt Forum, New York City. The show was recorded for the band's forthcoming *Absolutely Live* album.

Born on this day:

1941 Bobby Goldsboro, US singer
1941 David Ruffin, vocals (The Temptations)
1944 'Legs' Larry Smith, drums (Bonzo Dog Doo Dah Band)

1971 Jonathan Davis, vocals (Korn)
1980 Estelle Swaray, singer

1965

The Rolling Stones record their sixth UK single, 'The Last Time' and 'Play With Fire' at RCA Studios in Hollywood. Not only does it provide the Stones with their third British chart-topper, but it becomes the first Stones single to feature both songs written by Jagger-Richards.

1967

The Jimi Hendrix Experience record an appearance on the BBC's *Top Of The Pops* and later play at the 7½ Club in Mayfair, London.

1974

It is announced that former members of Free (Paul Rodgers & Simon Kirke), Mott The Hoople (Mick Ralphs), and King Crimson (Boz Burrell) have formed Bad Company. The band scored a US No. 1 with their debut album.

1981

Wendy O. Williams of The Plasmatics is arrested on stage in Milwaukee and charged with the offence of simulating sex with a sledgehammer.

1984

Van Halen kick off their 103-date '1984' North American tour at Jacksonville Coliseum, Florida.

1991

During an AC/DC North American tour three fans are killed during a crowd crush at a Salt Lake City gig.

1996

Lisa Marie Presley divorces Michael Jackson after less than two years of marriage.

1997

Songwriter and producer Keith Diamond, who wrote 'Caribbean Queen' and 'Suddenly' for Billy Ocean, and also hits for Donna Summer, James Ingram, Mick Jagger, Sheena Easton and Michael Bolton, dies of a heart attack.

2004

Jennifer Lopez's divorce from her second husband Cris Judd becomes final. Lopez met Judd when filming the video to 'Love Don't Cost A Thing' and they married in 2001 but split the following year. Judd was expected to get a $15 million settlement from the divorce.

2005

Motown producer Norman Whitfield pleads guilty for failing to report to the IRS royalty income on over $2 million he earned from 1995 to 1999. Facing imprisonment over tax evasion, because of health problems, Whitfield is sentenced to six months of house arrest and a $25,000 fine.

2008
Four photographers are arrested for reckless driving after chasing Britney Spears' car on the outskirts of Los Angeles. The cars were following too closely and travelling at an unsafe speed, making several unsafe lane changes, according to police. Each of the men is ordered to post $5,000 bail.

Born on this day:

1935 Johnny O'Keefe, "Australia's king of rock 'n' roll"
1939 Phil Everly, singer, songwriter

1943 Janis Joplin, US singer
1946 Dolly Parton, US singer, songwriter
1949 Robert Palmer, singer, songwriter

January 19

1959
The Platters' 'Smoke Gets In Your Eyes' starts a three week run at No. 1 on the US singles chart.

1967
The Monkees top the UK chart with 'I'm A Believer', the group's only British No. 1.

1971
The Beatles 'White Album' is played in the courtroom at the Sharon Tate murder trial to find out if any of the songs could have incited Charles Manson and his followers to commit murder.

1974
Black Oak Arkansas appear at Kent State University, Ohio. Support act is Bruce Springsteen. Tickets cost $4.00.

1978
Johnny Rotten is fired from The Sex Pistols for "not being weird enough any more."

1980
'Brass In Pocket' gives The Pretenders their first UK No. 1. The band's self-titled debut LP starts a four-week run at the top of the UK album chart.

Pink Floyd's *The Wall* starts a 15-week run at No. 1 on the US album chart. The group's third US chart-topping album, it went on to sell over eight million copies.

1988
Bon Jovi and Motley Crüe manager Doc McGheep pleads guilty to importing more than 40,000lb of marijuana into the US.

1993
Fleetwood Mac reform to perform at Bill Clinton's Inauguration. Their song, 'Don't Stop', was used as the theme for his campaign.

1997
Madonna wins the Best Actress award for her role in *Evita* at the Golden Globe Awards.

1998
American Rockabilly singer-songwriter Carl Perkins dies aged 65 from throat cancer. His classic rock'n'roll song, 'Blue Suede Shoes' was the first Sun record to sell a million copies.

2001
Paul McCartney is said to be worth £725 million and is expected to become the first pop star billionaire after huge sales from *1*, The Beatles hits compilation.

2006
American soul legend Wilson Pickett dies in hospital near his Ashburn, Virginia home of a heart attack, aged 64.

2007
Canadian singer songwriter and former Mamas and Papas singer, Denny Doherty dies at the age of 66 at his home near Toronto, Canada after a short illness.

2008
Singer-songwriter John Stewart, who wrote The Monkees' hit 'Daydream Believer', dies in San Diego, aged 68 after suffering a massive stroke. Stewart was a member of folk group The Kingston Trio and went on to record more than 45 solo albums with his biggest solo success being a US top five single, 'Gold', in 1979.

Born on this day:

1924 Slim Whitman, US country singer
1933 Ron Townson, singer (The 5th Dimension)
1943 Rick Evans, singer (Zager & Evans)
1945 Eric Stewart (The Mindbenders, Hotlegs, 10CC)
1950 Paul Stanley, guitar, vocals (Kiss)
1971 Gary Barlow, singer, songwriter (Take That)
1979 Rob Bourdon, drums (Linkin Park)
1979 Will Young, singer (UK TV's *Pop Idol* winner)

1965
Pioneering American disc-jockey (and the "father of rock and roll"), Alan Freed dies in a Palm Springs, California hospital from uremia and liver cirrhosis brought on by alcoholism, at the age of 43.

1966
The Spencer Davis Group are at No. 1 on the UK singles chart with 'Keep On Running', which replaces The Beatles double A-side, 'We Can Work It Out'/'Day Tripper' at the top.

1968
A reclusive Bob Dylan makes a rare appearance on stage – for the first time since 1966 – as part of the Woody Guthrie Tribute Concert at Carnegie Hall, New York City.

Also appearing are Arlo Guthrie, Odetta, Judy Collins, Richie Havens and Tom Paxton.

1969
Bruce Springsteen has two of his poems published in the Ocean County College Literary Yearbook, *Seascapes*. Springsteen was in his second semester at the Toms River, New Jersey College.

1972
On the first date of a UK tour, Pink Floyd premiere their new album *The Dark Side Of The Moon* at The Dome, Brighton, England.

1982
During an Ozzy Osbourne concert in Des Moines, Iowa, a member of the audience throws an unconscious bat onto the stage. Thinking it was one of his rubber props, Ozzy picked it up and bit off its head. The singer was taken to hospital to be given a rabies injection.

1985
Foreigner have their only UK No. 1 with 'I Want To Know What Love Is'. London-born Mick Jones wrote the song and played guitar with the British-American rock band.

1986
Stevie Wonder and Bob Dylan appear at a concert to celebrate the first Martin Luther King Day in the US.

1996
Bobby Brown is fined $1,000 and sentenced to two years probation and ordered to attend anger management classes after assaulting a security guard.

1997
Ben & Jerry's introduce 'Phish Food', a new flavor of ice cream named after the rock group Phish. The ingredients are chocolate ice  cream, marshmallows, caramel and fish-shaped fudge.

2000
Tourism chiefs in Liverpool are banned from putting up motorway signs reading 'Liverpool, the Birthplace Of The Beatles', because the Highways Agency thought they would distract motorists.

2002
George Harrison has a posthumous UK No. 1 single with the re-release of the 1971 former No. 1 'My Sweet Lord'. Harrison's single replaced Aaliyah's 'More Than A Woman', the only time in chart history that one deceased artist has taken the top spot over from another.

2006
American music executive Johnny Bienstock, owner of Moss Rose Music, who worked with Ernest Tubb, Hank Snow, Elvis Presley, The Bee Gees, Eric Clapton, Del Shannon and Meat Loaf, dies of complications from heart disease aged 83.

Born on this day:

1941 Richie Havens, US singer
1942 Edwin Starr, singer
1950 Billy Ocean, singer
1958 Anita Baker, US soul singer

1976 Emma Bunton (a.k.a. Baby Spice), singer (The Spice Girls)
1980 Benjamin Moody, guitar (Evanescence)

January **21**

1965
Over 3,000 screaming fans greet The Rolling Stones at Sydney Airport when they arrive for a 16-date tour of Australia and New Zealand with Roy Orbison.

1966
George Harrison marries Patti Boyd at the Leatherhead & Esher Register Office, Surrey with Paul McCartney as best man. George had first met Patti on the set of The Beatles movie *A Hard Day's Night* in 1964.

1968
Jimi Hendrix records his version of Bob Dylan's 'All Along The Watchtower' at Olympic Studios, London, overdubbing guitar and bass, due to a dispute with Experience bassist Noel Redding. Rolling Stone Brain Jones and Dave Mason from Traffic both played on the session.

1978
The *Saturday Night Fever* album starts a 24 week run at No. 1 on the US LP charts, going on to sell over 30 million copies worldwide, making it the best selling soundtrack of all time.

1984
Soul singing legend Jackie Wilson dies aged 49. Wilson suffered a massive heart attack while playing a Dick Clark show at the Latin Casino, New Jersey on September 25, 1975,

falling head-first to the stage while singing 'Lonely Teardrops'. He remained in a coma until his death eight years later.

1987
In New York, Bruce Springsteen inducts Roy Orbison into the second annual Rock'n'Roll Hall of Fame.

1992
Billy Idol pleads guilty to assault and battery charges after an incident outside a West Hollywood restaurant. He is fined $2,700 and ordered to appear in a series of anti-drug commercials.

1997
'Colonel' Tom Parker, Elvis Presley's manager and agent, dies of a stroke in Las Vegas, Nevada, at the age of 87. Born Andreas van Kuijk, a Dutch immigrant who changed his name as soon as he arrived in the US, Parker never applied for a green card and feared deportation his entire life. He briefly managed country singers Eddy Arnold and Hank Snow before hooking up with Elvis.

2002
American singer and actress Peggy Lee dies of complications from diabetes and a heart attack at the age of 81.

2003
David Palmer, former keyboard player for Jethro Tull, changes his name to Dee Palmer after a successful sex change operation. Palmer worked with the band (either as arranger or second keyboard player) between 1969 and 1980.

2004
As the third season of *American Idol* is aired on US TV a memo is leaked

showing a list of songs banned from being performed at this year's auditions, including Elton John's 'Candle In The Wind' and 'Fallin' by Alicia Keys. Also songs by Bruce Springsteen, Mariah Carey, No Doubt, R. Kelly, Tom Petty, Korn and Linkin Park are banned over concerns about the cost of securing rights for their use (or the composers not wanting their songs performed on the show).

January 22

Born on this day:
1931 Sam Cooke, US soul singer
1940 Addie Harris, vocals (The Shirelles)
1953 Steve Perry, vocals (Journey)
1962 Michael Hutchence, vocals (INXS)
1965 Steven Adler, drums (Guns N' Roses)

1959
Alone with an acoustic guitar and tape recorder in his New York City apartment Buddy Holly makes his last recordings, including 'Peggy Sue Got Married', 'Crying, Waiting, Hoping', 'That's What They Say', 'What To Do', 'Learning The Game' and 'That Makes It Tough'. The recordings would be overdubbed posthumously and later released by Coral Records.

1966
The Beach Boys record 'Wouldn't It Be Nice', the opening track on their forthcoming *Pet Sounds* album.

1967
Facing criticism over their synthetic nature, The Monkees perform live at The Cow Palace, San Francisco to a sell-out crowd.

1968
During the band's first Australian tour The Who play the first of two nights at Sydney Stadium with The Small Faces and Paul Jones. The venue's revolving stage gets stuck during the first 'house', resulting in a section of the crowd booing.

1969
The Beatles move from Twickenham Film Studios to Apple Studios in London to start recording a new album with Glyn Johns. Organ player Billy Preston (whom The Beatles knew from 1962 when he was a member of Little Richard's backing group in Hamburg) is brought in by George Harrison to augment the sessions as The Beatles were determined to record "live", flaws and all.

1972
David Bowie 'comes out' as bisexual during an interview with Michael Watts in the British music weekly *Melody Maker*.

1975
The Rolling Stones spend a week of auditioning guitarists to replace Mick Taylor. Among those tried out are Rory Gallagher, Jeff Beck, Steve Marriott and Americans Wayne Perkins and Harvey Mandel.

1977
Wings go to No. 1 on the US album chart with *Wings Over America*, Paul McCartney's sixth American chart-topping album after The Beatles break-up.

1980
During their 22-date UK tour The Clash appear at the Apollo Theatre, Glasgow.

1983

The new, 24-hour music video network MTV starts broadcasting to the West Coast after being picked up by Group W Cable, Los Angeles.

1987
One hit wonder Steve 'Silk' Hurley is at No. 1 on the UK singles chart with 'Jack Your Body', the first 'house' record to top the British charts.

1992
Mariah Carey's stepfather goes to court seeking damages, claiming that he had paid for her Manhattan apartment, a car and dental work in her early years on the understanding that she would repay him when she became successful

1993
Metallica start a 77-date 'Nowhere Else To Roam' World Tour at Wings Stadium, Kalamazoo, Michigan.

2004
Ryan Adams fractures a wrist after falling from the stage during a gig at the Royal Court Theatre in Liverpool. A fan said, "One minute he was on the stage and the next he had disappeared. He went down with a thud and we couldn't believe he was trying to continue singing."

2006
The Arctic Monkeys score their second UK No. 1 single with 'When The Sun Goes Down' from their debut album, *Whatever People Say I Am, That's What I'm Not*.

Born on this day:

1889 Leadbelly, blues musician
1910 Django Reinhardt, jazz guitarist
1948 Anita Pointer, singer (The Pointer Sisters)

1950 Danny Federici, keyboards (Bruce Springsteen's E Street Band)
1953 Robin Zander, vocals (Cheap Trick)

January 23

1956
Rock'n'roll fans in Cleveland aged under 18 are banned from dancing in public (unless accompanied by an adult) after Ohio police enforce a law dating back to 1931.

1965
'Downtown' makes Petula Clark the first UK female singer to have a No. 1 on the US singles chart since Vera Lynn in 1952.

1971
George Harrison becomes the first solo Beatle to have a No. 1 with 'My Sweet Lord' at the top of the UK singles chart. The song from Harrison's *All Things Must Pass* album stays at No. 1 for five weeks, and returns to the top of the UK chart in 2002, following his death.

1977
Patti Smith breaks her vertebrae when falling off the stage at a gig in Tampa, Florida.

1978
Terry Kath, guitarist and singer with Chicago, kills himself instantly while cleaning (what he believed) to be an unloaded gun. Kath's last words were "Don't worry it's not loaded" as he put the gun to his head and pulled the trigger.

1988
Nirvana record a 10-song demo with producer Jack Endino. Seattle's Sub Pop Records boss Jonathan Poneman hears the tape and offers to put out a Nirvana single.

1990
Allen Collins, guitarist from Lynyrd Skynyrd, dies of pneumonia after being ill for several months. Collins was one of the founding members, co-writing most of the band's songs (including FM radio staple 'Free Bird'), with late frontman Ronnie Van Zant. He survived a plane crash in 1977 that killed two other band members. Collins was behind the wheel in a car accident in 1986 that killed his girlfriend and left him paralysed from the waist down. He later pleaded no contest to vehicular manslaughter as well as driving under the influence of alcohol.

David Bowie announces his forthcoming and final world tour, 'Sound And Vision 1990', during which he will invite each audience to decide on a 'greatest hits' running order, organised through local radio stations.

1994
Take That go to No. 1 on the UK album chart with *Everything Changes*.

1997
Associates singer-songwriter, Billy MacKenzie commits suicide, aged 39.

2001
An English coroner criticises the rap singer Eminem's lyrics as depressing during an inquest into the death of a 17-year old schoolboy who threw himself in front of a train. The boy had printed out the lyrics to Eminem's 'Rock Bottom' before his death.

2003
R Kelly is arrested on new child pornography charges. The singer was already facing 21 charges relating to producing child pornography and appearing in a video having sex with an underage girl after police said digital pictures were discovered at his home in Florida last June. He is charged with a further 12 counts of possession of child pornography.

2005
One of the biggest charity concerts since Live Aid raises £1.25 million for victims of the tsunami disaster in Asia. The sold-out concert held before 60,000 at The Millennium Stadium, Cardiff, features Eric Clapton, Manic Street Preachers, Keane, Charlotte Church, Snow Patrol, Embrace, Feeder, Craig David and Liberty X.

1986
Ray Charles is inducted into the Rock and Roll Hall of Fame at the first induction dinner, held in New York City.

January 24

Born on this day:

1941 Neil Diamond, singer, songwriter
1941 Ray Stevens, singer, songwriter
1945 Tammi Terrell, singer

1947 Warren Zevon, singer, songwriter
1955 Jools Holland, keyboards (Squeeze), TV presenter

1953

Eddie Fisher is at No. 1 on the UK singles chart with 'Outside Is Heaven'. The father to actress Carrie Fisher, the American singer and entertainer divorced his first wife, Debbie Reynolds to marry his best friend's widow, Elizabeth Taylor, to much unwelcome publicity at the time.

1958

Elvis Presley is at No. 1 on the UK singles chart with 'Jailhouse Rock', which became the first ever single to enter the chart at No. 1 and was Presley's second UK No. 1. It went on to sell over four million copies in the US.

1962

Brian Epstein signs a management contract with The Beatles, entitling him to 25% of the bands gross earnings; the normal management deal being 20%.

1970

James Sheppard, lead singer from The Heartbeats and Shep & The Limelites, who reached No. 2 in the US in 1961 with 'Daddy's Home', is found murdered in his car on the Long Island Expressway, having been beaten and robbed.

1976

Bob Dylan starts a five-week run at pole position on the US album chart with *Desire*, his third US No. 1.

1978

Workers at EMI's record pressing plant refuse to press copies of Buzzcocks forthcoming release 'What Do I Get' because of the title on the B-side 'Oh Shit'.

1979

The Clash release their cover of 'I Fought The Law' (written by Sonny Curtis of Buddy Holly's Crickets), based on the 1966 hit version by The Bobby Fuller Four, as an American single.

1981

Steve Tyler of Aerosmith is hospitalised after being involved in a crash on his motorbike.

1992

Nirvana play their first show in Australia at the Phoenician Club, Sydney. Also on the bill: Tumbleweed and The Meanies.

1995

David Cole (keyboards, C & C Music Factory) dies of meningitis aged 32. His production clients included Mariah Carey, Whitney Houston and Aretha Franklin.

1998

Oasis are top of the UK singles chart with 'All Around The World', boasting the longest running-time for a UK No. 1 with a duration of 9:38. It was one of the first songs to be written by Noel Gallagher, with the band rehearsing it as early as 1992.

2005

57-year-old country singer Lynn Anderson (who had a 1970 Top 5 hit 'Rose Garden') is arrested for shoplifting after being caught stealing a *Harry Potter* DVD from a New Mexico supermarket and punching a police officer during her arrest.

2007

Record producer Dave Shayman (also known as Disco D) is found dead at his home in New York City. 26-year-old Shayman was famous for his production work on hip hop records and was a rising star in the business. His death is being treated as a potential suicide as he was recently diagnosed with manic depression.

2008

Amy Winehouse is admitted into rehab in a battle to kick her drug addiction. A statement from her record company, Universal said she entered the facility "after talks with her record label, management, family and doctors to continue her ongoing recovery against drug addiction."

Born on this day:

1915 Ewan MacColl, singer, songwriter
1931 Stig Anderson, Abba manager, songwriter, producer
1938 Etta James, singer
1954 Robert Finch, vocals (KC & The Sunshine Band)
1956 Andy Cox, bass player (The Beat, Fine Young Cannibals)
1980 Alicia Keys, American R&B and soul singer

January 25

1960
The original cast recording of *The Sound Of Music* starts a 16-week chart-topping run on the US album chart.

1967
The Beatles do a last-minute remix of 'Penny Lane' before the pressing of their next double A-sided single, 'Strawberry Fields Forever'/ 'Penny Lane'. Both songs were originally intended for the forthcoming album *Sgt. Pepper's Lonely Hearts Club Band*.

1971
Grace Slick of Jefferson Airplane gives birth to a daughter, naming her God, although she was later re-named China.

1975
The Carpenters are at No. 1 on the US singles chart with their version of The Marvelettes' 1961 hit, 'Please Mr. Postman'.

1978
Joy Division make their live debut at Pips club in Manchester.

1983
The Allman Brothers bassist Lamar Williams dies of lung cancer age 34. He joined the band in 1972 after the death of original bassist Berry Oakley.

1984
Yoko Ono donates £250,000 to Liverpool old people's home, Strawberry Fields.

1986
Albert Grossman dies of a heart attack while flying on Concorde from New York to London. As well as managing Bob Dylan (between 1962 and 1970), Peter, Paul & Mary, The Band, Janis Joplin and Todd Rundgren, Grossman built the Bearsville Recording Studio near Woodstock in 1969 and a year later founded Bearsville Records.

1989
Bobby Brown is arrested for an overtly sexually suggestive performance after a show in Columbus, Ohio, and is fined $652 under the anti-lewdness ordinance law.

1992
The inaugural Big Day Out festival takes place at the Hordern Pavilion, Sydney. Acts appearing include Nirvana, Beasts of Bourbon, Box The Jesuits, Celibate Rifles, Cosmic Psychos, The Clouds, Club Hoy, Died Pretty, Falling Joys, The Hard Ons with Henry Rollins Hellmen, Massappeal, The Meanies, Smudge, Sound Unlimited Posse, Ratcat, The Village Idiots, Violent Femmes and Yothu Yindi.

2001
Millionaire pop impresario Jonathan King is charged with a further ten offences of sexually abusing children dating back to the 1970s. King is granted bail.

2008
British Sea Power's keyboard and cornet player Phil Sumner ends up in hospital after being knocked unconscious when attempting a stage dive. The crowd at Leeds Irish Centre failed to catch him when he jumped off a 12-foot PA system, landing headfirst. A spokeswoman for the band said: "The impact knocked him out straight away. He was unconscious for three minutes and there was a lot of blood."

January 26

Born on this day:

1948 Corky Laing, drums (Mountain)
1951 David Briggs, guitarist (Little River Band)
1957 Eddie Van Halen, guitarist (Van Halen)

1963 Andrew Ridgeley, vocals (Wham!)
1963 Jazzie B, singer, producer (Soul II Soul)

1961
Elvis Presley achieves his sixth UK No. 1 with 'Are You Lonesome Tonight?' The single includes a spoken passage loosely based on a passage from Shakespeare.

1965
During The Rolling Stones tour of Australia and New Zealand, guitarist Keith Richards has his shirt torn off after 50 fans invade the stage during a show at Brisbane City Hall.

1970
John Lennon writes, records and mixes his next single 'Instant Karma' all in one day.

1977
Former Fleetwood Mac guitarist Peter Green is committed to a mental hospital following an incident when he threatened his accountant Clifford Adams with an air rifle. Adams was trying to deliver a £30,000 royalty cheque to Green.

1980
Prince makes his TV debut on the US ABC show *American Bandstand*.

1989
American singer Donnie Elbert dies of a stroke aged 52.

1991
Cher makes a special video, Cher's Video Canteen, for the troops involved in Desert Storm during the Gulf War, featuring Janet Jackson, Paul Simon, Van Halen and Bonnie Raitt.

Queen achieve their second UK No. 1 with 'Innuendo', at the time, the third longest chart-topping song behind The Beatles 'Hey Jude' and Simple Minds 'Belfast Child'.

2003
Billy Joel is airlifted to hospital after losing control of his Mercedes S500 which skidded for 100 yards before crashing into a tree in The Hamptons, Long Island.

2004
John Lydon is one of ten contestants taking part in the latest *I'm A Celebrity... Get Me Out Of Here* UK reality TV show set in the Australian outback. The former Sex Pistols singer is seen by 11 million viewers on the first night covered in bird seed being pecked by giant ostriches. Lydon, who was paid £25,000 to appear, walked off the jungle set after four days.

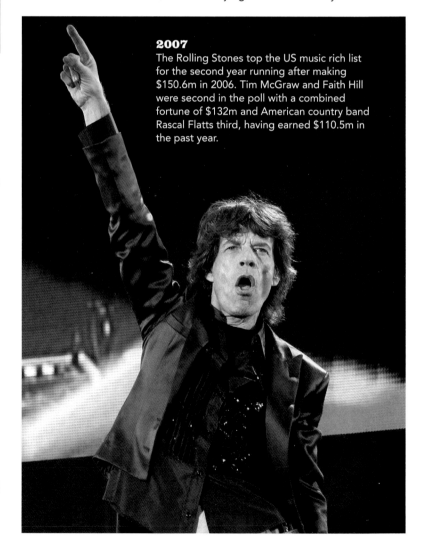

2007
The Rolling Stones top the US music rich list for the second year running after making $150.6m in 2006. Tim McGraw and Faith Hill were second in the poll with a combined fortune of $132m and American country band Rascal Flatts third, having earned $110.5m in the past year.

Born on this day:

1945 Nick Mason, drums (Pink Floyd)
1951 Brian Downey, drums (Thin Lizzy)
1951 Seth Justman, keyboards, vocals (The J. Geils Band)
1961 Gillian Gilbert, keyboards (New Order, The Other Two)
1968 Mike Patton, vocals (Faith No More)
1974 Mark Owen, vocals (Take That)

January 27

1956
Elvis Presley's 'Heartbreak Hotel' is released by RCA Records, who had just purchased Presley's contract from Sun Records for $35,000. The song sells 300,000 copies in its first week and would eventually sell over a million, becoming Elvis' first gold record.

1961
Frank Sinatra plays a benefit show at Carnegie Hall, New York City for Martin Luther King.

1971
David Bowie arrives in the US for the first time; he couldn't play live due to work permit restrictions, but attracts publicity for wearing a dress at a promotional event.

1972
American gospel singer Mahalia Jackson dies in Chicago of heart failure and diabetes complications aged 60. Known as the "Queen of Gospel Music" she recorded over 30 albums.

1977
The Clash sign to CBS Records in the UK for £100,000.

1973
'Superstition' gives Stevie Wonder his second No. 1 single in America, 10 years after his first No. 1.

1980
Def Leppard play the first of two nights at the Marquee Club, London. Tickets cost £2.

1984
Madonna makes her first UK TV appearance when she performs 'Holiday' on Channel 4's *The Tube*, broadcast live from the Hacienda Club, Manchester.

1994
Oasis make their London invite-only live debut when playing The Water Rats pub, King's Cross.

1996
Babylon Zoo start a five-week run at No. 1 on the UK singles chart with 'Spaceman', the fastest selling single (420,000 copies in six days) by a debut artist in the UK. The song, used for a Levi Jeans TV commercial, also went to No. 1 in 23 other countries.

1998
James Brown is charged with possession of marijuana and unlawful use of a firearm after police were called to his South Carolina home. Brown later clamed the drugs were used to help his eyesight.

2002
Beach Boy Brian Wilson plays the first of four sold-out nights at the Royal Festival Hall, London, performing the *Pet Sounds* album in its entirety.

2004
R&B singer Faith Evans and her husband are charged with possession of cocaine and marijuana after being arrested in Atlanta, Georgia. Police pull them over for a suspected licence plate offence.

2006
Gene McFadden, R&B vocalist and songwriter, best known as half of the Philly soul team McFadden & Whitehead, dies of cancer at the age of 56. The duo had the 1979 hit 'Ain't No Stoppin' Us Now', which sold more than eight million copies and was nominated for a Grammy Award.

January 28

Born on this day:

1927 Ronnie Scott, jazz musician, club proprietor
1968 Sarah McLachlan, singer-songwriter

1977 Joseph Fatone (*NSYNC)
1980 Nicolas Carter (Backstreet Boys)

1956
Elvis Presley (with Scotty Moore and Bill Black) makes his first national television appearance on the Dorsey Brothers' *Stage Show* – the first of six Presley appearances on the show in early 1956 and the first of eight performances recorded and broadcast from CBS TV in New York City.

1968
At the end of their Australian tour, The Who, The Small Faces and Paul Jones are arrested when landing in Melbourne, after complaints from a stewardess and pilot. The musicians are accused of "behaving in such a manner as to constitute a risk to the aircraft".

Jim Morrison of The Doors is arrested and charged with public drunkenness after harassing a security guard at a Las Vegas adult movie theatre.

1983
British rock'n'roll singer Billy Fury dies of heart failure, aged 42.

1985
The recording of 'We Are The World', the US equivalent of the Band Aid single. Written by Michael Jackson and Lionel Richie, the all star cast includes Stevie Wonder, Tina Turner, Bruce Springsteen, Diana Ross, Bob Dylan, Ray Charles, Daryl Hall, John Oates, and Cyndi Lauper.

1990
Paula Abdul starts a 10-week run at No. 1 on the US album chart with *Forever Your Girl*. The LP spent 64 consecutive weeks on the *Billboard* Top 200, the longest time for an album to reach the top spot.

1994
Paul and Linda McCartney attend the premiere of *Wayne's World II* in London. The couple then go on to the Hard Rock Café, where actor Mike Myers presents them with a cheque for LIPA (the Liverpool Institute for Performing Arts) for £25,000 from the sale of Linda's vegetarian burgers.

2000
Saxophonist and bandleader Thomas 'Beans' Bowles, who played on many Motown sessions including Marvin Gaye's 'What's Going On', Martha & The Vandellas' 'Heat Wave' and The Supremes' 'Baby Love' and wrote the melody on Stevie Wonder's 'Fingertips Pt. 2', dies of prostate cancer aged 73.

2003
H-Town singer Keven Conner is killed in a car crash in Houston aged 28. Conner died when an SUV ran a red light and crashed into the car he was a passenger in, which had just picked him up from the recording studio.

2005
Ex-Traffic drummer and singer-songwriter Jim Capaldi dies of stomach cancer, aged 60.

2007
Dreamgirls: Music From The Motion Picture is at No. 1 on the US album chart. The musical based on the history of Diana Ross & The Supremes features Jamie Foxx, Beyoncé Knowles, Eddie Murphy, Jennifer Hudson, Anika Noni Rose and Keith Robinson.

2008
According to Forbes.com, Madonna tops the first-ever list focusing on women in the music industry as the richest female musician. It's estimated the 49-year-old banked $72m between June 2006 and June 2007, earning much of that from her 'Confessions' tour – the highest-grossing tour for a female artist – earning $260m worldwide. Barbra Streisand came second with $60 million followed by Celine Dion with $45 million, mainly from her recent concerts at Caesars Palace in Las Vegas.

2009
Lynyrd Skynyrd keyboard player Billy Powell dies aged 56 of a suspected heart attack in Florida, having called police saying he was having trouble breathing. Emergency services try to resuscitate him, but he is pronounced dead an hour later. Powell played piano on Kid Rock's 'All Summer Long' (which sampled the Lynyrd Skynyrd song 'Sweet Home Alabama').

Born on this day:

1933 Sacha Distel, French singer and guitarist

1938 James Jamerson, Motown session bass player (The Funk Brothers)

1944 Andrew Loog Oldham (early Rolling Stones manager)

1947 David Byron, singer (Uriah Heep)

1952 Tommy Ramone, drums (The Ramones)

January 29

1964
The Beatles spend the day at Pathe Marconi Studios in Paris, the group's only recording session for EMI held outside the UK. They record German language versions of 'She Loves You' and 'I Want To Hold Your Hand', after EMI's West German branch persuaded Brian Epstein that they would be unable to sell large quantities of records unless the songs were recorded in the German dialect. The Beatles also record their next single, 'Can't Buy Me Love'.

1965
The Who make their debut appearance on top UK TV show *Ready, Steady, Go!* plugging their first single, 'I Can't Explain'. The studio is full of the group's hip Mod following, who shower their scarves on the group at the song's conclusion.

1972
The triple live album *The Concert For Bangladesh* is at No. 1 on the UK album chart. Hastily organised by George Harrison to raise money for the Bangladesh Relief Fund, the two concerts staged at New York's Madison Square Garden on August 1, 1971, feature Bob Dylan, Ringo Starr, Billy Preston, Eric Clapton, Ravi Shankar, Leon Russell and members of Badfinger.

1979
16-year-old Brenda Spencer kills two people and wounds nine others when she fires shots from a .22-caliber rifle her father had given her for Christmas from her house across the street into the entrance of San Diego's Grover Cleveland Elementary School. When asked why she did it, she answered "I don't like Mondays". The Boomtown Rats go on to write and record a song based on the event.

1983
Australian group Men At Work are at the top of the British and American singles and album charts simultaneously with 'Down Under' and *Business As Usual*. The last artist to achieve this was Rod Stewart in 1971.

1992
American blues singer and guitarist Willie Dixon – a major influence on The Rolling Stones, The Yardbirds, Cream and Led Zeppelin – dies of heart failure.

1994
The Supremes' Mary Wilson is injured when her jeep crashes on a freeway and turns over just outside of Los Angeles. Wilson's 14-year old son is killed in the accident.

2001
A New York based data company issues a chart listing sales of posthumous albums. The idea came about after radio stations wanted to distinguish between proper recordings when the artists were alive and recordings released after their deaths. The Top 5 chart ranked The Doors at No. 5, Eva Cassidy (4), Jimi Hendrix (3), Bob Marley (2) and 2Pac in top position.

2006
The Sheffield-based Arctic Monkeys are at No. 1 on the UK album chart with their debut *Whatever People Say I Am That's What I'm Not*, which becomes the fastest-selling debut in chart history after shifting more than 360,000 copies in its first week of release.

2009
Singer-songwriter John Martyn dies in hospital in Ireland at the age of 60. The folk, blues and funk artist was widely regarded as one of the most soulful and innovative singer-songwriters of his generation and had been cited as an influence by artists as varied as U2, Portishead and Eric Clapton.

Former *American Idol* winner Kelly Clarkson makes the largest ever leap – 96 places – to No. 1 in US chart history with her single, 'My Life Would Suck Without You', after selling 280,000 downloads in the first week. A clip from the single's video is premiered during the commercial break of that week's *American Idol* episode.

Born on this day:

1941	Joe Terranova (Danny & The Juniors)	**1947**	Steve Marriott, guitarist, singer (The Small Faces, Humble Pie)
1942	Marty Balin, vocals (Jefferson Airplane)	**1951**	Phil Collins, drums, piano, vocals (Genesis & solo)

1958

On the first night of a six-date Australian tour, Buddy Holly, Paul Anka, Jerry Lee Lewis, Jodie Sands and Johnny O'Keefe all appear at Sydney Stadium.

1961

The Shirelles become the first girl group to have a US No. 1 with 'Will You Love Me Tomorrow'. The song peaks at No. 4 in the UK.

1969

The Beatles play an impromptu lunchtime gig on the rooftop of their Apple building on London's Savile Row. Lasting just over 40 minutes, before the police closed proceedings down due to noise complaints, it was the last time The Beatles performed live together. Part of the performance can be seen as the finale to The Beatles' *Let It Be* film.

1970

Edison Lighthouse are at No. 1 on the UK singles chart with 'Love Grows (Where My Rosemary Goes)', the group's only Top 40 hit which spent five weeks at the top of the charts. In February 1970, Tony Burrows became the first (and only) person to appear on *Top Of The Pops* fronting three different acts in one show: Edison Lighthouse (who were number one that week), White Plains and The Brotherhood Of Man.

1973

After recently changing their name from Wicked Lester, Gene Simmons, Paul Stanley, Ace Frehley and Peter Criss make their first appearance as Kiss at The Popcorn Club in Queens, New York.

1988

During a court case involving Holly Johnson and ZTT Records it is revealed that Frankie Goes To Hollywood did not play on their hits 'Relax' and 'Two Tribes'. The court is told that top session musicians were used to make the records.

1990

Unhappy with the unauthorised reissue of their first single 'Sally Cinnamon', The Stone Roses trash their former record company Revolver FM's offices and throw paint over cars. The band are arrested and charged with criminal damage.

1999

After spending 11 weeks on the US singles chart Britney Spears starts a two-week run at No. 1 with '...Baby One More Time'. Britney's debut album goes to No. 1 on the US album chart the same day.

2000

Gabrielle is at No. 1 on the UK singles chart with 'Rise', which uses a sample

from Bob Dylan's 'Knocking On Heaven's Door' giving Dylan his third UK No. 1 as a writer, the other two being The Byrds 'Mr. Tambourine Man' (1965) and Manfred Mann's 'The Mighty Quinn' (1968).

Born on this day:

1946 Terry Kath, guitarist (Chicago)
1951 Phil Manzanera, guitar (Roxy Music)
1954 Adrian Vandenburg, guitar (Whitesnake)
1956 John Lydon, singer (Sex Pistols, Public Image Ltd)

1961 Lloyd Cole, vocals, guitar (Lloyd Cole & The Commotions)
1981 Justin Timberlake, singer (*NSYNC & solo)

January 31

1967

The Beatles spend a second day at Knole Park, Sevenoaks, Kent, England, completing filming for the 'Strawberry Fields Forever' promotional video. The film was shot in colour for the benefit of the US market, since British television was still broadcasting in black and white only. Taking time out from filming, John Lennon buys an 1843 poster from an antiques shop which provided him with most the lyrics for The Beatles' song 'Being For The Benefit Of Mr. Kite'.

1978

Greg Herbert, saxophone player with Blood Sweat & Tears, dies aged 30 of an accidental drug overdose in Amsterdam.

1981

Blondie are top of the American singles chart with 'The Tide Is High', the group's third US No. 1 and also a No. 1 in the UK.

third (5.1), Madonna – fourth (5m) and The Beatles – fifth (4.7m).

2007

Jim Morrison is enlisted to help fight global warming more than 35 years after his death. 'Woman In The Window', a previously unreleased poem written and recorded by The Doors frontman shortly before he died in 1971, is being set to music and used to publicise the Global Cool campaign.

2008

Natasha Bedingfield enters the US chart at No. 3 with her album *Pocketful Of Sunshine*, equaling the record set by soul singer Sade in having the highest-ever US chart debut for a UK-signed female. 50,000 copies sell in its first week of release.

1970

The Jackson Five go to No. 1 on the US singles chart with 'I Want You Back'. The song, originally written for Gladys Knight & The Pips, was the first of four American chart-toppers for the group.

1970

American blues musician Slim Harpo dies of a heart attack while recording in London, aged 46. Such British 60s R&B groups as The Rolling Stones, The Pretty Things, The Yardbirds and Them all covered his songs.

1976

Abba's 'Mamma Mia' replaces Queen's 'Bohemian Rhapsody' after a nine-week run at the top of the UK singles chart.

1990

The Stone Roses are granted conditional bail by Wolverhampton Magistrates Court after being arrested for trashing their record company's offices.

2003

Robbie Williams tops a chart based on UK album sales for the past five years. The ex-Take That singer has sold 9.7 million albums, an average of more than 5,000 for each day. The Corrs are in second place with 5.8m, Westlife –

February

Born on this day:

1937 Don Everly, guitar, vocals (The Everly Brothers)
1954 Mike Campbell, guitar (Tom Petty & The Heartbreakers)

1968 Lisa Marie Presley (daughter of Elvis)
1971 Ron Welty, drums (The Offspring)
1975 Big Boi (Antoine Patton), US rapper (Outkast)

February 1

1963

17-year-old Neil Young performs his first professional date at a country club in Winnipeg.

1967

At EMI Studios in London, The Beatles start work on a new song 'Sgt. Pepper's Lonely Hearts Club Band'. It isn't until they have recorded the song that Paul McCartney has the idea to make the song the thematic pivot for their forthcoming album.

1972

Chuck Berry has his first UK No. 1 single with a live recording of a song he'd been playing for over 20 years, 'My Ding-a-Ling'. UK public morality campaigner Mary Whitehouse attempts to have the song banned due to its innuendo-laden lyrics.

1986

Music publisher Dick James dies aged 65 of a heart attack. Best known for having formed Northern Songs as The Beatles' music publishing company, James also signed Elton John and his lyricist Bernie Taupin as unknown artists in 1967 and was the founder of the DJM record label.

1988

The Cars announce they are breaking up after 12 years together.

1995
Manic Street Preachers guitarist Richey James vanishes with no clues to his whereabouts. He checks out of the Embassy Hotel in London at 7am, leaving behind his packed suitcase. His car would be found on the Severn Bridge, outside Bristol, 16 days later.

1992
George Michael and Elton John go to No. 1 on the US singles chart with 'Don't Let The Sun Go Down On Me', also a UK No. 1. All proceeds from the single go to AIDS charities.

2001

An Atlanta museum display of Sir Elton John's private photos, which includes snaps of nude men, is said to be too explicit and is withdrawn. Several school trips to the exhibition were cancelled.

Gerald Cattermole, the 50-year-old father of S Club 7's Paul Cattermole, is jailed for nearly three years for sex acts with two 14-year-old girl fans of the group. He had been warned by police not to get involved with fans who often visited his house.

2004

During a duet with Justin Timberlake at the Superbowl in Houston, Texas, Janet Jackson suffers what was later termed a "wardrobe malfunction" which is broadcast on US TV. Timberlake tears off part of Jackson's top and "accidentally" exposes her right breast.

2008

NASA announce that 'Across The Universe' by The Beatles is to become the first song ever to be beamed directly into space. The track would be transmitted through the Deep Space Network – a network of antennas – on the 40th anniversary of it being recorded, and aimed at the North Star, Polaris, 431 light years from Earth. In a message to NASA, Paul McCartney said the project was an "amazing" feat. "Well done, NASA," he added. "Send my love to the aliens. All the best, Paul."

Born on this day:

1940 Alan Caddy, guitar (The Tornadoes)
1942 Graham Nash, guitar, vocals (The Hollies, Crosby, Stills, Nash & Young)
1946 Howard Bellamy (Bellamy Brothers)
1963 Eva Cassidy, US singer
1971 Ben Mize, drums (Counting Crows)
1977 Shakira, singer

1959

Buddy Holly, Ritchie Valens and The Big Bopper all appear at the Surf Ballroom, Clear Lake, Iowa, as part of the 'Winter Dance Party'. This would be their last ever gig as all three were killed in a plane crash the following day.

1966

The Rolling Stones release '19th Nervous Breakdown', which peaks at No. 2 on the UK singles chart.

1969

Yoko Ono divorces her husband Tony Cox and is granted custody of their daughter Kyoko. John Lennon will marry Yoko on 20 March.

1979

Sex Pistols' bassist Sid Vicious dies of a heroin overdose in New York City following a party to celebrate his release on $50,000 bail pending his trial for the murder of his former girlfriend, Nancy Spungen, the previous October. Party guests say that Vicious took heroin around midnight and an autopsy confirms that he died from an accumulation of fluid in the lungs that was consistent with a heroin overdose. A syringe, spoon and heroin residue are discovered near his body.

2001

Bad Manners' singer Buster Bloodvessel is told he is too overweight to survive an urgently needed operation. Buster collapsed on stage during a show in Italy but doctors felt that his 30 stone frame might not make it through surgery.

2002

The P.P.L. (Phonographic Performance Ltd) launches performersmoney.com for artists to check if they are owed any of the £10 million in unclaimed money the company are holding. It shows that Michael Jackson is owed over £100,000 for 'Say, Say, Say', Stevie Wonder has money owing for 'Ebony And Ivory' and Ray Davies of The Kinks is owed a six-figure fee for 'You Really Got Me'. Director Dominic McGonigal says: "If anyone has seen Rick Astley please let him know he is still earning money for his hits."

2004

TV network CBS apologises for its broadcast of the American Super Bowl entertainment when Janet Jackson's right breast was exposed after Justin Timberlake pulled at her top. CBS quickly cut away from the incident but was flooded with calls from angry viewers. Timberlake insisted it had been an accident saying, "I am sorry that anyone was offended by the wardrobe malfunction during the halftime performance of the Super Bowl."

2007

US keyboard player Joe Hunter, a veteran session musician as one of The Funk Brothers who helped craft the distinctive Motown sound, dies in Detroit, Michigan, aged 79. Hunter performed with such legendary Motown acts as Marvin Gaye, Smokey Robinson and Martha & The Vandellas.

Born on this day:

1943 Dennis Edwards, vocals (The Temptations)
1943 Eric Haydock, bass (The Hollies)
1947 Dave Davies, guitar, vocals (The Kinks)
1947 Melanie, US singer, songwriter
1949 Arthur Kane, bass (New York Dolls)
1990 Sean Kingston, Jamaican-American singer

February 3

1959
Buddy Holly, The Big Bopper and Ritchie Valens die in a plane crash shortly after take-off from Clear Lake, Iowa. The pilot of the single-engine Beechcraft Bonanza is also killed. Holly hired the plane after heating problems developed on his tour bus. All three were traveling to Fargo, North Dakota, for the next show on their 'Winter Dance Party' – covering 24 cities in three weeks to make money after the break-up of Holly's band, The Crickets.

1967
Producer Joe Meek shoots his landlady Violet Shenton and then himself at his north London flat. Meek produced The Tornadoes hit 'Telstar', the first No. 1 in the US by a British group in 1962.

1968
One hit wonders The Lemon Pipers go to No. 1 on the US singles chart with 'Green Tambourine'. The song was a No. 7 hit in the UK.

1973
Elton John starts a three-week run at the top of the *Billboard* charts with 'Crocodile Rock', the first of five US No. 1 singles for Elton.

1990
During a European tour Bob Dylan starts a six-night residency at London's Hammersmith Odeon.

1992
Pearl Jam play their first ever UK show at The Esplanade Club in Southend, Essex to 300 people. The band's first European tour also takes in Norway, Sweden, Holland, France, Spain and Italy.

2003
The controversial documentary *Living With Michael Jackson* is shown on UK television. Reporter Martin Bashir had spent eight months with the star. "Viewers will not believe what they're seeing," says the show's editor.

2004
R. Kelly appears in court and enters a plea of not guilty to 21 charges of child pornography. Kelly, who was free on bail,

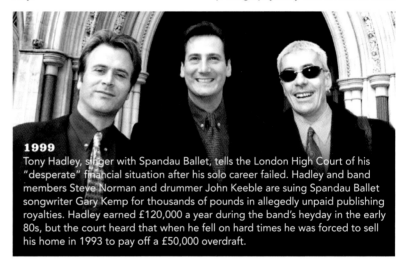

1999
Tony Hadley, singer with Spandau Ballet, tells the London High Court of his "desperate" financial situation after his solo career failed. Hadley and band members Steve Norman and drummer John Keeble are suing Spandau Ballet songwriter Gary Kemp for thousands of pounds in allegedly unpaid publishing royalties. Hadley earned £120,000 a year during the band's heyday in the early 80s, but the court heard that when he fell on hard times he was forced to sell his home in 1993 to pay off a £50,000 overdraft.

did not speak during the brief hearing. Outside the Cook County Criminal Courthouse fans voice their support for the singer, proclaiming his innocence with placards and T-shirts. Kelly had been arrested in Florida after he was indicted by a grand jury in Chicago on 21 counts of child pornography, stemming from a videotape that allegedly showed the star performing sexual acts with a 14-year-old girl.

2007
Razorlight's gig in Lyon is halted mid-set because of an altercation between singer Johnny Borrell and bassist Carl Dalemo. The pair exchange insults before coming to blows onstage. Borrell then storms off, leaving the French crowd amazed and unsure about what is going on.

1979
Blondie celebrate the first of six UK No. 1 singles with 'Heart Of Glass', taken from the band's third album, *Parallel Lines*. 'Heart Of Glass' originally started life in 1975 as 'The Disco Song'.

41

February 4

Born on this day:

1944 Florence Larue, vocals (The 5th Dimension)

1947 Margie and Mary Ann Ganser, vocals (The Shangri-Las)

1948 Alice Cooper (real name: Vincent Furnier), singer

1975 Natalie Imbruglia, actress, singer

1965
The Righteous Brothers are at No. 1 on the UK & US singles chart with the Phil Spector-produced 'You've Lost That Lovin' Feelin'. In 1999 the PRS announced it as The Most Played Song Of The 20th Century.

1968
At EMI Studios in London, The Beatles record 'Across The Universe'. John Lennon and Paul McCartney decide the song needs some falsetto harmonies so they invite two waiting girl fans, Lizzie Bravo, a 16-year-old Brazilian living nearby, and 17-year-old Londoner Gayleen Pease, into the studio to sing on the song.

1978
The Bee Gees start a four-week run at No. 1 on the US singles chart with 'Staying Alive'. From the film soundtrack *Saturday Night Fever*, it gave the Gibb brothers their fifth US No. 1 and was also No. 1 in the UK.

1982
Scottish singer Alex Harvey dies of a heart attack while waiting for a ferry at Zeebrugge, Belgium, after performing a concert with his new band, The Electric Cowboys. Harvey formed the Alex Harvey Big Soul Band in 1959, fronted 60's band Tear Gas and appeared in the London stage version of *Hair*. His Sensational Alex Harvey Band had a 1975 UK No. 7 with a cover of Tom Jones' 'Delilah'.

1983
Karen Carpenter dies, aged 32, of a cardiac arrest at her parents' home in Downey, California. The coroner's report gives the cause of death as imbalances associated with anorexia nervosa.

1984
Stevie Ray Vaughan & Double Trouble kick off their 114-date 'Couldn't Stand The Weather' Tour at the War Memorial Auditorium in Nashville, Tennessee.

1996
Former Milli Vanilli member Rob Pilatus is hospitalised after being hit over the head with a baseball bat in Hollywood, California. Pilatus was attempting to steal his attacker's car at the time.

1998
Former lead singer of East 17, Brian Harvey, is fined £1,000 and ordered to pay prosecution costs of £2,852 after being convicted of kicking a press photographer who was curled up on the ground in a protective ball.

1999
American soul singer Gwen Guthrie, who sang backing vocals for Aretha Franklin, Billy Joel, Stevie Wonder and Madonna, wrote songs for Sister Sledge and Roberta Flack, and had a 1986 R&B No. 1 'Ain't Nothin' Goin' On But The Rent', dies aged 48 of cancer.

2000
Bjorn Ulvaeus confirms that Abba have turned down a $1 billion offer by a British and American consortium to reform. "It is a hell of a lot of money to say no to, but we decided it wasn't for us," Benny Andersson tells the Swedish newspaper *Aftonbladet*.

2003
Courtney Love is arrested at Heathrow Airport for 'endangering an aircraft' on a transatlantic flight. The singer was said to have hurled abuse at the cabin crew on the flight from Los Angeles to London after her nurse, who was in an economy seat, was barred from sitting with Love in the upper class cabin.

2009
Lux Interior (real name: Erick Lee Purkhiser), singer and founding member of The Cramps, dies aged 62 of a heart complaint.

Born on this day:

1935 Alex Harvey, vocals, guitar (The Sensational Alex Harvey Band)
1941 Barrett Strong, US songwriter
1944 Al Kooper, keyboards (The Blues Project, Blood Sweat & Tears)

1948 David Denny, guitar (The Steve Miller Band)
1964 Duff McKagan, bass (Guns N' Roses)
1969 Bobby Brown, singer (New Edition)

February 5

1957

Bill Haley arrives at Southampton from New York on the liner *Queen Elizabeth*, greeted by 5,000 fans. Haley is the first American rock 'n' roll related artist to tour the UK.

1962

Ringo Starr plays two shows with The Beatles, one at the Cavern Club, Liverpool at lunchtime and another in the evening at The Kingsway Club in Southport. Ringo is deputising for an ill Pete Best but he would permanently take over the drum seat in August.

1967

The Sunday tabloid The *News Of The World* prints an article on pop stars and drugs. An undercover reporter had mistakenly identified Rolling Stone Brian Jones as Mick Jagger in a London nightclub and claimed that Jagger had taken drugs. That evening Jagger announces on a live chat show that he is suing the paper for libel.

1983

Def Leppard's album *Pyromania* starts a 92-week run on the US charts, selling over six million copies in America alone, although it doesn't reach the top position, stalling at No. 2.

1999

The members of *NSYNC make a guest appearance on US TV's *Sabrina The Teenage Witch*.

2001

Juliet Peters appears in a London court accused of making death threats to singer Billie Piper. The court listened to tapes of the 13 calls Peters had made to the singer's record company threatening to decapitate and burn her body.

2003

Courtney Love blames her bad language for the alleged air rage incident that led to her arrest at London's Heathrow Airport yesterday. As she leaves Heathrow's police station the singer says: "I cussed at a lady. My daughter always said I had a potty mouth." Asked what it had been like, the singer says: "It was fine. They were wonderful in there. It was like being on *Prime Suspect*."

2006

The Rolling Stones play three songs during half-time coverage of the Super Bowl in Detroit. After the event, the Stones express their displeasure over having Mick Jagger's microphone turned down during the song 'Start Me Up'.

The line "you make a dead man come" is cut short while a barnyard reference to "cocks" in new song, 'Rough Justice', is also cut.

2007

Producer Phil Spector wins $900,000 after settling an embezzlement claim. Spector said former assistant Michelle Blaine removed $425,000 from his pension and did not repay a $635,000 loan. Ms Blaine claimed the loan was a gift and the pension funds were for a film aimed at improving Spector's image. As part of the settlement, she dropped a counter-claim of sexual harassment.

2008

Amy Winehouse is questioned by police in connection with a video apparently showing her smoking crack cocaine. The singer, who was not arrested, was interviewed under caution after the video was posted online by *The Sun* newspaper.

February 6

Born on this day:

1945 Bob Marley, singer/songwriter
1947 Alan Jones, sax (Amen Corner)
1950 Natalie Cole, singer

1962 Axl Rose, singer (Guns N' Roses)
1966 Rick Astley, singer

1958
George Harrison joins Liverpool group The Quarrymen, featuring John Lennon, Paul McCartney, Len Garry, Eric Griffiths and John Lowe. The group is named after Lennon's grammar school.

1960
Jesse Belvin, who scored a 1956 hit with 'Goodnight, My Love', is killed aged 27 in a car accident in Hope, Arkansas. His wife and the car's driver also die from their injuries. The three were trying to make a fast getaway from the first ever mixed race audience concert in the town of Little Rock, after threats had been made against Belvin's life.

1970
Eric Clapton plays the first of two nights at the Fillmore East, New York.

1981
Composer Hugo Montenegro, who had a 1968 UK No. 1 (US No. 2) single, 'The Good The Bad And The Ugly' from the soundtrack to the spaghetti western film of the same name, dies in California. Montenegro worked for RCA Records, producing a series of albums and soundtracks and television themes, including two volumes of *Music From The Man From U.N.C.L.E.*

1982
Kraftwerk are at No. 1 on the UK singles listings with 'The Model'/ 'Computer Love', the first German act to score a UK No. 1 single, which spends 21 weeks on the chart.

1988
Tiffany starts a two week run at No. 1 on the US chart with 'Could've Been', No. 4 in the UK. Tiffany had recorded the song five years ago aged 13.

1989
Legendary Jamaican sound engineer and producer King Tubby, who worked with Robbie Shakespeare, Sly Dunbar

and Carlton Barrett, dies after being shot in the street outside his home.

1996
Former Jam members Bruce Foxton and Rick Buckler reach a High Court settlement with Paul Weller after suing him for more than £100,000, claiming they were owed royalties and group assets.

1998
American singer and guitarist Carl Wilson of The Beach Boys dies aged 51 after a battle with lung cancer, having been diagnosed the previous year.

1998
Austrian singer Falco (Johann Holzel), who had a 1986 UK & US No. 1 single with 'Rock Me Amadeus', making him the first-ever Austrian act to score a chart-topper in both territories, is killed in a road accident after his car collides with a bus.

2001
Guitarist Don Felder is fired from The Eagles. Felder later launched a $50 million law suit against drummer Don Henley and guitarist Glenn Frey, alleging wrongful termination and breach of implied-in-fact contract. Henley and Frey then countersued Felder for breach of contract, alleging that Felder had written and attempted to sell the rights to a "tell-all" book.

Both parties settled out-of-court for an undisclosed amount.

2004
US singer Faith Evans and her husband Todd Russaw agree to enrol in a rehabilitation programme after facing drugs charges for alleged possession of cocaine and marijuana. Prosecutors said the charges would be dropped if the couple successfully completed the 13-week scheme.

2008
A Los Angeles judge issues a restraining order against Britney Spears' manager following a request to the court by her mother. Lynne Spears claims Sam Lutfi, 33, had drugged the troubled pop star and interfered with her finances. In a six-page declaration, Lynne Spears said Lutfi "moved into Britney's home and has purported to take control of her life, home and finances". Her declaration focused on the night of 28 January, a few days before the Grammy-winning star was admitted to hospital for a mental evaluation.

Born on this day:

1948 Jimmy Greenspoon, organ (Three Dog Night)
1962 David Bryan, keyboards (Bon Jovi)

1962 Garth Brooks, country singer
1974 Danny Goffey, drums (Supergrass)
1975 Wes Borland, guitar (Limp Bizkit)

1963
Blues By Six plus The Rolling Stones appear at The Manor House, north London. Tickets cost four shillings (20p).

1964
Pan Am flight 101 is greeted by over 5,000 riotous Beatles fans as it arrives at New York's JFK airport, bringing the Fab Four to the US for the first time.

1967
Robin, Maurice and Barry Gibb of The Bee Gees return to the UK after living in Australia for nine years.

1970
One hit wonders Shocking Blue go to No. 1 on the US singles chart with 'Venus', making them the first Dutch act to top the American charts. The song reaches No. 8 in the UK, as does Bananarama's cover version in 1986.

1976
Bob Dylan starts a five-week run at No. 1 on the *Billboard* album chart with *Desire*, his second US chart-topping LP.

1979
Stephen Stills becomes the first rock performer to record on digital equipment in Los Angeles' Record Plant Studio.

1980
Pink Floyd play the first of seven sold out nights at the Los Angeles Memorial Sports Arena.

1987
George Michael and Aretha Franklin are at No. 1 on the UK singles chart with 'I Knew You Were Waiting (For Me)'. Written by Simon Climie it gave Aretha her first UK No. 1 almost 20 years after her first US hit.

1989
Georgia state representative Billy Randall introduces a bill to make Little Richard's 'Tutti Frutti' the state's official rock song.

1999
Blondie go to No. 1 with 'Maria', giving the group their sixth British chart-topping single, 20 years after

their first. At 54, lead singer Debbie Harry becomes the oldest female to reach the top of the UK singles chart.

2000
The rapper Big Punisher dies of a heart attack, aged 28, weighing 318kg (50 stone). His second album, *Yeeeah Baby*, completed before his death, was issued as scheduled in April 2000 and peaked at No. 3 on the *Billboard* chart.

2005
Michael Jackson's *Thriller* is named the Top Pop Video in a poll of Channel 4 viewers in the UK. The 1983 video, which depicts the singer as a werewolf and a zombie, beats videos by Madonna and Robbie Williams. Animated videos for Peter Gabriel's 'Sledgehammer' and A-Ha's 'Take On Me' are in second and third place respectively. At No. 4 is Queen with 'Bohemian Rhapsody', followed by Madonna's 'Like A Prayer', Robbie Williams' 'Rock DJ', Michael Jackson's 'Billie Jean', The Verve's 'Bittersweet Symphony', Madonna's 'Vogue' and Nirvana's 'Smells Like Teen Spirit'.

1970
Led Zeppelin score their first UK No. 1 album with *Led Zeppelin II*, featuring the US single 'Whole Lotta Love'. The LP stays on the chart for 138 weeks, selling over six million copies in America.

February 8

Born on this day:

1946 Paul Wheatbread (Gary Puckett & The Union Gap)

1961 Vince Neil, vocals (Mötley Crüe)

1977 Dave 'Phoenix' Ferrel, bass (Linkin Park)

1980 Cameron Muncey, guitarist (Jet)

1964
On their first full day in New York, The Beatles (minus George who had a sore throat) are photographed in Central Park. Extra police are called in to keep fans away. Later in the day The Ronettes interview the group for radio station WINS.

1973
Max Yasgur, the owner of the dairy farm in Bethel, New York at which the Woodstock Music & Art Fair was held in August 1969, dies aged 53 of a heart attack.

1975
Bob Dylan goes to No. 1 on the *Billboard* chart with *Blood On The Tracks* – his second US chart-topping album.

1981
R.E.M. have their first ever-recording session at Bombay Studios, Smyrna, Georgia. Tracks include 'Gardening At Night', 'Radio Free Europe' and '(Don't Go Back To) Rockville.'

1983
Winners at the second annual Brit Awards held in London include Paul McCartney (Best British Male Solo Artist), Kim Wilde (Best British Female Solo Artist), Dire Straits (British Group), Yazoo (British Breakthrough Act), and Kid Creole & The Coconuts (International Act). Best Selling Single was Dexy's Midnight Runners 'Come On Eileen' while the Life Achievement Award went to Pete Townshend.

1988
Kenney Jones makes his last appearance as The Who's drummer when the group are given a Lifetime Achievement Award at the Brits. The Who climax the awards show at London's Royal Albert Hall but TV transmission is cut off as it overran into the *9 O'Clock News*. Angry words are exchanged backstage.

1990
Suffering from depression, American singer-songwriter Del Shannon dies of self-inflicted gunshot wounds. Shannon (real name: Charles Westover) had a 1961 UK and US No. 1 with 'Runaway', plus nine other US and 12 other UK Top 40 singles. It had been rumoured he was to join The Traveling Wilburys after Roy Orbison's death in 1988.

1994
Oasis are forced to cancel their first foreign tour after they are deported from Holland. They were involved in a drunken brawl on a cross-channel ferry, resulting in members of the band being arrested and locked in the brig.

2001
Eminem makes his live UK concert debut at the Manchester Arena.

2002
Bob Wooler, the resident DJ and booker at The Cavern Club in Liverpool during the early 1960s when The Beatles appeared there almost 300 times, dies aged 76.

2005
Keith Knudson, drummer with The Doobie Brothers, dies aged 56 of pneumonia.

2006
The 48th annual Grammy Awards are held at the Staples Center, Los Angeles. Madonna opens the awards for a third time. U2 come away with five awards and Mariah Carey wins three of her eight nominations.

2009
R&B singer Chris Brown is questioned over a complaint of assault by Los Angeles police. The 19-year-old had pulled out of his performance at the Grammy Awards, as did his pop star girlfriend Rihanna. Police say Brown argued with an unidentified woman while sitting in a car. Brown walked into a police station and was later released on $50,000 bail.

2005
Kylie Minogue is voted the World's Sexiest Woman in her thirties by UK magazine *Good Housekeeping*. Sade was voted No. 4 in the over forties with Madonna coming in at 7 and Jerry Hall at 8. Sharon Osbourne was voted into third place in the over fifties section.

Born on this day:

1940 Brian Bennett, drums (The Shadows)
1942 Carole King, singer-songwriter
1951 Dennis Thomas (Kool & The Gang)

1960 Holly Johnson, singer (Frankie Goes To Hollywood)

February 9

1961
The Beatles make their lunchtime debut at The Cavern Club in Liverpool. They would go on to make almost 300 further appearances at the club.

1982
George Harrison presents UNICEF with a cheque for $9 million over ten years after the fundraising concert for Bangladesh.

1990
Nirvana set out on a short west coast tour opening for Dinosaur Jr. at the Pine Street Theater, Portland, Oregon.

1993
British broadcaster Bill Grundy dies aged 69 of a heart attack. He was the first television presenter to introduce The Beatles on Granada Television on October 17, 1962, but was more well-known for conducting the infamous Sex Pistols interview on Thames Television on December 1, 1976, when Grundy provoked the band into using obscenities on live TV. The broadcast wrecked Grundy's television career.

1964
The Beatles make their US TV debut on CBS's *The Ed Sullivan Show*, performing five songs including their current American chart-topper, 'I Want To Hold Your Hand'. Over 50,000 applications were received for the available 728 seats in the TV studio and an estimated 73 million people across the States watch the show.

2009
At this year's Grammy Awards held in Los Angeles, Led Zeppelin singer Robert Plant takes home five prizes for his collaboration *Raising Sand* with bluegrass singer Alison Krauss, including Album Of The Year and Record Of The Year (for 'Please Read The Letter'). Coldplay (who won Song Of The Year for 'Viva La Vida'), Adele, Duffy, Radiohead and Peter Gabriel are among the UK acts to be honoured. John Mayer won Best Solo Rock Vocal Performance (for 'Gravity'),

1972
Paul McCartney's new band Wings play a lunchtime show at Nottingham University, the first date of a UK college tour. Over the next fortnight Wings arrive unannounced at ten UK colleges and ask social secretaries if they would like them to perform that evening. Admission is 40p.

1985
Madonna starts a three-week run at No. 1 on the US album chart with *Like A Virgin* (No. 3 in the UK).

1987
Winners at this year's Brit Awards held in London include Peter Gabriel (British Male Solo Artist), Kate Bush (British Female Solo Artist), Five Star (Best British Group), Dire Straits *Brothers In Arms* (British Album), The Housemartins (British Breakthrough Act), Paul Simon (International Solo Artist), The Bangles (Best International Group), Peter Gabriel 'Sledgehammer' (Best British Video) and Pet Shop Boys 'West End Girls' (Best British Single).

Kings Of Leon won best rock performance by a group (with 'Sex on Fire'), Best Rock Song went to Bruce Springsteen (for 'Girls In Their Summer Clothes') and Lil' Wayne won best rap solo performance and best rap album for *Tha Carter III*.

February 10

Born on this day:

1937 Roberta Flack, singer-songwriter
1940 Jimmy Merchant (Frankie Lymon & The Teenagers)
1962 Cliff Burton, bass (Metallica)
1977 Rosanna Tavarez (Eden's Crush)

1967

At EMI's Abbey Road Studios, The Beatles record the orchestral build-up for the middle and end section of 'A Day In The Life'. At the group's request, the orchestra members arrive in full evening dress along with novelty items. One violinist wears a red clown's nose, while another has a fake gorilla's paw on his bow hand. The rest wear funny hats and other assorted novelties. The recording is filmed for a possible *Sgt. Pepper's Lonely Hearts Club Band* television special which is ultimately abandoned. Mick Jagger, Keith Richards, Mike Nesmith and Donovan also attend the session.

1972

David Bowie appears at The Toby Jug, Tolworth, Surrey, on the opening date of his Ziggy Stardust tour.

1974

Record producer Phil Spector is injured in a car crash. He allegedly needs extensive plastic surgery that dramatically alters his looks. Details of the accident are kept secret.

1975

Dave Alexander, the original bassist for The Stooges, dies aged 28 from pneumonia. He was fired from the band in August 1970 after showing up for a gig too drunk to play.

1977

The Clash start recording their debut album at CBS Studios, London.

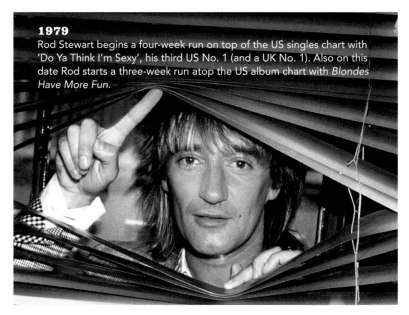

1979

Rod Stewart begins a four-week run on top of the US singles chart with 'Do Ya Think I'm Sexy', his third US No. 1 (and a UK No. 1). Also on this date Rod starts a three-week run atop the US album chart with *Blondes Have More Fun*.

1990

Paula Abdul starts a three-week run at No. 1 on the American singles chart with 'Opposites Attract', her fourth US No. 1 and a No. 2 hit in Britain.

1993

Michael Jackson gives his first TV interview in 14 years, live from his Neverland Valley Ranch, on a special edition of the Oprah Winfrey show.

1997

Brian Connolly, singer with 70's glam rockers Sweet, dies aged 47 of kidney and liver failure. Connolly replaced Ian Gillan (later of Deep Purple and Black Sabbath) in Wainwright's Gentlemen, who became Sweetshop and then shortened their name to Sweet.

1998

Axl Rose is charged with disorderly conduct following a row with a baggage handler at Arizona Airport. Rose was later released on bail.

2004

Diana Ross is sentenced to two days in jail after pleading 'no contest' to a drink driving charge. She is allowed to enter her plea over the telephone from New York; her lawyer said the singer would serve her term at a prison near her Los Angeles home. Ross was arrested in December 2002 after tests indicated she was twice over the drink-drive limit.

2008

Amy Winehouse wins five prizes at this year's Grammy Awards, including Best New Artist, Song Of The Year and Record Of The Year, both for her single 'Rehab'. The UK singer was not at the Los Angeles ceremony to collect the awards due to visa problems. Instead, she makes an acceptance speech by satellite, paying tribute to her husband, Blake Fielder-Civil, who was in custody awaiting trial on charges of attempting to pervert the course of justice and causing grievous bodily harm. Kanye West scoops four Grammy Awards, while Bruce Springsteen wins three. The White Stripes, Justin Timberlake, Carrie Underwood and Mary J Blige all pick up two awards each.

Born on this day:

1935 Gene Vincent, US singer
1963 Sheryl Crow, singer-songwriter
1977 Mike Shinoda, guitar, vocals (Linkin Park)

1979 Brandy, singer
1981 Kelly Rowland, singer (Destiny's Child)
1984 Aubrey O'Day, singer (Danity Kane)

February 11

1956

Elvis Presley appears on American TV's *Stage Show*, performing 'Heartbreak Hotel' and 'Blue Suede Shoes'.

1982

U2 kick off a 32-date North American tour in New Orleans.

1998

The handwritten lyrics to 'Candle In The Wind' by Bernie Taupin are auctioned at Christie's in LA for £278,512.

2008

Paul McCartney and Heather Mills appear at the High Court in London to reach a financial settlement for their divorce. The hearing in the Family Division, which takes place in private, is expected to last five days. The couple, who have a four-year-old daughter, Beatrice, announced the end of their four-year marriage in 2006.

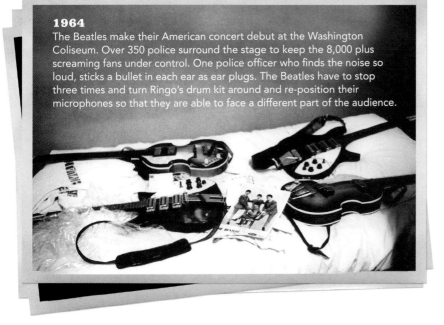

1964

The Beatles make their American concert debut at the Washington Coliseum. Over 350 police surround the stage to keep the 8,000 plus screaming fans under control. One police officer who finds the noise so loud, sticks a bullet in each ear as ear plugs. The Beatles have to stop three times and turn Ringo's drum kit around and re-position their microphones so that they are able to face a different part of the audience.

1967

The Monkees set a new record when their second album *More Of The Monkees* jumps from No. 122 to the top of the US chart. The album then stayed in pole position for 18 weeks.

1985

The Police win Outstanding Contribution to British Music at the fourth annual Brit Awards held in London. Other winners include Prince (Best International Act, Best Soundtrack for *Purple Rain*), Frankie Goes To Hollywood 'Relax' (British Single), Duran Duran 'Wild Boys' (British Video), Neil (actor Nigel Planer) 'Hole In My Shoe' (British Comedy Recording), Sade's *Diamond Life* (British Album), Paul Young (British Male Solo Artist), Alison Moyet (British Female Solo Artist) and Wham! (Best British Group).

1973

A local charity raises over £500 selling bedsheets and pillowcases used by The Rolling Stones during their stay at the Intercontinental Hotel in Auckland, New Zealand.

1992

Mötley Crüe fire their singer Vince Neil after he turned up for rehearsals claiming that he had lost his passion for the band and was now more involved with racing cars.

2009

Ronettes singer Estelle Bennett dies aged 67 at her home in Englewood, New Jersey. Best known for their work with producer Phil Spector, The Ronettes' 1963 hit 'Be My Baby' epitomised Spector's famed "wall of sound" technique.

Februa[ry]

12

Born on this day:

1939 Ray Manzarek, keyboards (The Doors)
1952 Michael McDonald, singer (The Doobie Brothers)
1959 Per Gessle, guitar, vocals (Roxette)

1968 Chynna Phillips (Wilson Phillips)
1970 Jim Creeggan, bass (Barenaked Ladies)

1964

The Beatles return to New York City by train from Washington DC for two performances at Carnegie Hall. Such is the demand for tickets that extra seating is arranged surrounding the stage. Tickets range from $1.65 to $5.50.

1967

A total of 15 police officers raid Redlands, the home of Rolling Stone Keith Richards, and take away various substances for forensic tests. Marianne Faithfull, dressed only in a fur rug, was present with boyfriend Mick Jagger. George and Patti Harrison had left the house earlier in the day.

1970

John Lennon performs 'Instant Karma' on BBC TV's *Top Of The Pops*, becoming the first Beatle to appear live on the show since 1966.

1977

Blondie, Tom Petty & The Heartbreakers and The Ramones all appear at the Whisky a Go Go in Los Angeles, California.

1989

Aretha Franklin loses a court case against Broadway producer Ashton Springer, who sues her for $1 million after Aretha failed to turn up to rehearsals for the stage show *Sing Mahalia Sing*. She blamed her non-appearance on a fear of flying.

1997
David Bowie receives a star on the Hollywood Walk of Fame.

2000

US blues singer Screamin' Jay Hawkins, who recorded the original version of 'I Put A Spell On You' in 1956, dies aged 70. A Golden Gloves boxing champion at 16, he spent two years in jail, was temporary blinded by one of his flaming stage props in 1976, married nine times and is believed to have fathered over 70 children.

2003

Former Doors drummer John Densmore takes legal action against the group's keyboard player Ray Manzarek and guitarist Robby Krieger for breach of contract, trademark infringement and unfair competition. The band had reformed with ex-Cult singer Ian Astbury and former Police drummer Stewart Copeland. Densmore said, "It shouldn't be called The Doors if it's someone other than Jim Morrison singing." As a result the group call themselves The Doors Of The 21st Century.

2004

Eminem's ex-wife Kimberly Mathers is jailed for a month and put on a 90-day drug abuse programme after being found using cocaine while on probation.

2005

The diesel train owned by Cotswold Rail is named after Clash frontman Joe Strummer at a ceremony in Bristol. Strummer died aged 50 in 2002.

2007

During a press conference at West Hollywood's Whisky a Go Go Sting confirms that The Police would be getting back together. The band are set to kick off a lucrative world tour on May 28 in Vancouver, Canada, supported by Fiction Plane, featuring Sting's son Joe Sumner.

2008

Ronald Isley's appeal against a three-year jail term for tax fraud is rejected by a US court. The 65-year-old singer of The Isley Brothers argued against being imprisoned in an Indiana jail on the grounds of age and poor health. The court heard he cashed royalty cheques belonging to his brother O'Kelly, who died in 1996, and spent millions of dollars made from undeclared performances on a yacht and two homes. Isley is ordered to pay more than $3.1m to the US tax service for "pathological" evasion.

1997
U2 hold a press conference in the lingerie department of the Kmart store in Greenwich Village, New York, to announce their Pop Mart world tour. The tour is set to start in Las Vegas on April 25.

Born on this day:

1942 Peter Tork, bass, vocals (The Monkees)
1950 Peter Gabriel, singer, (Genesis, solo)
1956 Peter Hook, bass, (Warsaw, Joy Division, New Order, Revenge)

1972 Robert Harrell, bassist (3 Doors Down)
1974 Robbie Williams, singer (Take That, solo)
1976 Feist, Canadian singer-songwriter

February 13

1961
Frank Sinatra launches his own record label, Reprise Records, later the home of Neil Young, Jimi Hendrix, Joni Mitchell, Randy Newman and The Beach Boys.

1967
The Monkees announce that from now on they will be playing on their own recordings instead of using the work of session musicians. Their first album in this fashion, *Headquarters*, is released in May.

The Beatles' double A-sided single, 'Strawberry Fields Forever'/'Penny Lane' is released by Capitol Records in the US. The single spends ten weeks on the chart, peaking at No. 1. In the UK, it became the first Beatles single since 'Love Me Do' in 1962 not to reach No. 1.

1980
Police raid the Fulham, London home of former Sex Pistol John Lydon who greets them waving a ceremonial sword. The only illegal item they find is a canister of tear gas, which Lydon claims is for defence against intruders.

1982
The Jam become the first band since The Beatles to perform two numbers on the same edition of *Top Of The Pops*, when they play 'A Town Called Malice' and 'Precious', their latest double A-sided No. 1.

The marble slab stolen from the grave of Lynyrd Skynyrd singer Ronnie Van Zant is found two weeks later in a dried up river bed.

1989
Michael Jackson fires his manager, Frank Dileo, who reportedly sought a $60 million settlement to prevent him revealing Jackson's lifestyle to the press.

1993
Founder member of Musical Youth, Patrick Waite, dies aged 24 of a hereditary heart condition, while awaiting a court appearance on drug charges. Musical Youth scored a 1982 UK No. 1 and Grammy-nominated single in 'Pass The Dutchie.'

1996
Take That announce their disbandment in front of the world's press at the Manchester Hilton. They had achieved seven No. 1 singles and two chart-topping albums in the UK. The group reformed in 2005.

1997
Michael Menson of Rebel MC, who had a 1989 UK No. 3 single with 'Street Tuff', dies aged 30 from injuries sustained in a racial attack. Lost on a street in north London, Menson was attacked twice. His killers were determined to burn him alive, throwing fuel at him and setting his back on fire. He suffered terrible burns and died 16 days later.

1998
Police at Manchester Airport arrest former Stone Roses' singer Ian Brown after an incident during a flight from Paris. Brown is found guilty of threatening behaviour in August the same year and jailed for four months. British Airways also ban him from flying with the airline.

2002
American country singer-songwriter Waylon Jennings dies in his sleep after a lengthy fight with diabetes. The tour bassist for Buddy Holly following the break-up of The Crickets, he released a series of duet albums with Willie Nelson in the late 70s. Jennings scored a 1980 US No. 21 single 'Theme From The Dukes Of Hazzard' and was also narrator on the television series. He was a member of The Highwaymen alongside Willie Nelson, Johnny Cash and Kris Kristofferson.

2005
Readers of UK newspaper *The Sun* vote George Michael's 'Careless Whisper' as The Greatest British Pop Single of the past 25 years. As an indictment of the credibility of such polls, at least half of the other singles voted into the Top 10 were released beyond the polling remit including Kate Bush – third with 'Wuthering Heights' (released 1978), The Sex Pistols, sixth with 'God Save The Queen' (released 1977), Queen, seventh with 'We Are The Champions' (1977) and The Undertones tenth with 'Teenage Kicks' (1978).

2007
Rod Stewart is paid $1 million for performing at billionaire Steve Schwarzman's 60th birthday bash held at New York's Park Avenue Armory.

2008
A fan pays $3,000 for a jewelled bra worn by Shakira on her 'Oral Fixation' world tour in 2007, during an auction to raise funds for the singer's children's charity to build a school for poor children in the singer's home country of Colombia. More than $60,000 has been raised so far, with one fan paying $14,100 to meet Shakira. Other items in the auction include a purple wig and Gibson guitar used in the video for 'Las De La Intuicion', which sold for $3,301, and a shiny lavender skirt with turquoise and coral beading that Shakira wore while singing 'Hips Don't Lie' on stage which fetched $1,076.

February 14

Born on this day:

1945 Vic Briggs, guitar (The New Animals)
1947 Tim Buckley, singer-songwriter
1950 Roger Fisher (Heart)
1972 Rob Thomas (Matchbox 20)

1968
Manfred Mann are at No. 1 on the UK singles chart with their version of Bob Dylan's 'The Mighty Quinn', which reached No. 10 in the US.

1986
Frank Zappa appears on an episode of the television series *Miami Vice*, portraying a crime boss named 'Mr. Frankie'.

1998
Celine Dion's 'My Heart Will Go On' sets a new record for the most radio broadcasts in the US with 116 million plays in one week.

1970
The Who appear at Leeds University, England, and record the show for their acclaimed *Live At Leeds* album, released in May. The original LP included just six songs but future editions incorporate more material until, by 2001, the entire show was made available on a double CD.

1999
Elton John appears as himself in an episode of the animated series *The Simpsons* shown on US TV.

2004
Dave Holland, former drummer with Judas Priest, is jailed for eight years for indecent assault and the attempted rape of a 17-year-old boy. The youth, who had learning difficulties, was taking drum lessons from Holland.

1972
John Lennon and Yoko Ono start a week long run as television guest co-hosts on *The Mike Douglas Show* from Philadelphia.

1977
US singer-songwriter Janis Ian receives 461 Valentine's Day cards after indicating in the lyrics of her song 'At Seventeen' she had never received any.

1978
Dire Straits begin recording their first album at Basing Street Studios, London. The whole project cost £12,500 to produce.

1980
Lou Reed marries second wife Sylvia Morales at a ceremony in his Manhattan apartment.

1984
Elton John marries recording engineer Renate Blauer in Sydney, Australia. The couple divorced three years later.

1987
Bon Jovi start a four-week run at No. 1 on the *Billboard* singles chart with 'Livin' On A Prayer', the group's second US No. 1 and a No. 4 hit in the UK.

1990
The Rolling Stones play the first of ten nights at the Korakuen Dome, Tokyo, Japan. The shows are seen by over 500,000 fans, making the band $20 million.

1994
The Grateful Dead's Jerry Garcia marries moviemaker Deborah Koons.

1996
T.A.F.K.A.P. (aka Prince) marries Mayte Garcia in a Minneapolis church. He also composes a special song for his wife, 'Friend, Lover, Sister, Mother, Wife', which she hears for the first time during their first wedding dance.

2005
Kerrang! magazine announces the results of its readers' poll for The Best British Rock Albums Ever. The Top 10 are: 1, Black Sabbath's *Black Sabbath*; 2, Iron Maiden's *Number Of The Beast*; 3 Sex Pistols' *Never Mind The Bollocks*; 4, Led Zeppelin's *IV*; 5, Black Sabbath's *Paranoid*; 6, Muse's *Absolution*; 7, The Clash's *London Calling*; 8, Queen's *Sheer Heart Attack*; 9, Iron Maiden's *Iron Maiden*; 10, Manic Street Preachers' *The Holy Bible*.

2008
Oasis singer Liam Gallagher marries his long-term partner, the ex-All Saints singer Nicole Appleton at a civil ceremony in London. The venue, Westminster Register Office, was where Gallagher married his first wife, Patsy Kensit, in 1997.

Born on this day:

1941 Brian Holland, producer, songwriter
1944 Mick Avory, drums (The Kinks)
1945 John Helliwell, sax (Supertramp)
1959 Ali Campbell, vocals (UB40)

1960 Mikey Craig, bass (Culture Club)
1976 Ronnie Vannucci Jr, drummer (The Killers)

February 15

1961
Singer Jackie Wilson is left with a stomach wound after a female fan, Juanita Jones, went to his New York apartment demanding to see him. Jones' gun went off as he tried to disarm her.

1969
Singer Vickie Jones is arrested on fraud charges for impersonating Aretha Franklin in concert at Fort Myers, Florida. No-one in the audience had asked for their money back.

received threats that the gig would be disrupted.

1991
Kelly Emberg, the ex-girlfriend of Rod Stewart, files a $25 million palimony suit in Los Angeles.

1965
American singer and pianist Nat King Cole dies aged 65 of lung cancer. The father of singer Natalie Cole, in 1956 he became the first black American to host a television variety show.

2000
Sting pulls out of a concert in Vienna in protest at the inclusion of Jorg Haider's far right freedom party in Austria's new government. Lou Reed had also cancelled shows in the country.

1968
US blues harmonica player Little Walter dies from injuries incurred in a fight while taking a break from a performance at a Chicago nightclub. He was the first harmonica player to amplify his harp, giving it a distorted echoing sound. He joined Muddy Waters' band in 1948.

John Lennon and George Harrison arrive in India to study meditation with the Maharishi. Paul McCartney and Ringo Starr arrived four days later. Ringo returned before the others because he disliked the food and compared the experience to staying in a Butlin's holiday camp.

1977
Glen Matlock is fired from The Sex Pistols, being replaced by Sid Vicious. Matlock insists he voluntarily left the band due to personal and musical disagreements with manager Malcolm McLaren and singer Johnny Rotten.

1981
In San Francisco, guitarist Mike Bloomfield is found dead in his car from an accidental heroin overdose. A member of the Paul Butterfield Blues Band and The Electric Flag, he played on Bob Dylan's 1965 album *Highway 61 Revisited*.

1988
After singer Joe Elliot refers to El Paso as "the place with all those greasy Mexicans", Def Leppard are forced to cancel a concert in the town, having

2002
Kerrang! overtakes *New Musical Express* to become the best selling UK weekly music publication. It claims new bands such as Limp Bizkit and Linkin Park have given them a new teenage audience.

2008
A London flat once rented by The Beatles goes up for sale for £1.75m. The group shared the three-bedroom, top floor property at 57 Green Street, Mayfair in the autumn of 1963. A well-known publicity photo of the Fab Four peering over a banister was taken at the top of the property's communal stairwell.

February 16

Born on this day:

1935 Sonny Bono, singer (Sonny & Cher)
1949 Lynn Paul, vocals (The New Seekers)
1956 James Ingram, US singer
1961 Andy Taylor, guitar (Duran Duran)
1972 Taylor Hawkins, drummer (Foo Fighters)

1964
The Beatles make their second live appearance on *The Ed Sullivan Show*, before an audience of 3,500 at the Deauville Hotel in Miami Beach, Florida. The Beatles perform 'She Loves You', 'This Boy', 'All My Loving', 'I Saw Her Standing There', 'From Me To You' and 'I Want To Hold Your Hand'.

1972
Rolling Stones drummer Charlie Watts' wife Shirley is arrested for swearing and hitting customs officials after an incident at Nice Airport.

Led Zeppelin make their Australian live debut when kicking off a six-date tour at the Subiaco Oval, Perth.

1974
Bob Dylan starts a four-week run at the top of the *Billboard* album chart with *Planet Waves*, his first US No. 1.

During a tour of America the members of Emerson, Lake & Palmer are arrested in Salt Lake City after swimming naked in a hotel pool. They are each fined $75.

1975
Cher starts her own weekly hour-long show of music and comedy on CBS-TV. The singer had co-presented *The Sonny & Cher Comedy Hour* with her former husband, Sonny Bono.

1985
Bruce Springsteen goes to the top of the British album chart with *Born In The USA*, his first UK No. 1 LP.

1991
The Simpsons are at No. 1 on the UK singles chart with 'Do The Bartman', written by Michael Jackson and Bryan Lorenand. The Simpsons are the first cartoon characters to make No. 1 since The Archies' hit 'Sugar Sugar' in 1969.

1999
Robbie Williams wins three awards at this year's Brits – Best British Solo Artist, Best Single ('Angels') and Best Video ('Millennium'). Manic Street Preachers win Best British Group, Natalie Imbruglia is Best International Female Artist and Best Newcomer, while Best International Group went to The Corrs.

2002
Thieves break into George Michael's north London home and steal over £100,000 worth of paintings, jewellery and designer clothes before driving off in his £80,000 Aston Martin DB7. They also cause £200,000 worth of damage to the property.

2003
50 Cent is at No. 1 on the US album chart with his debut *Get Rich Or Die Tryin'* (No. 2 in the UK).

2004
US singer Doris Troy, who had a 1963 US No. 10 hit with 'Just One Look' (covered and made a hit by The Hollies in the UK in 1964), performed as a session singer and was signed to the Beatles' Apple label, dies aged 67 in Las Vegas from emphysema.

2005
Kid Rock is arrested for allegedly punching a DJ at a strip club in Nashville, Tennessee. Police are called to the incident but Rock escapes from the club.

Shortly after, he was pulled over by an officer who got the singer's autograph but failed to make him undertake a breath test despite smelling of alcohol. Rock was eventually arrested a few hours later, taken to night court and released on $3,000 bail.

Born on this day:

1905 Orville "Hoppy" Jones, singer (The Ink Spots)

1941 Gene Pitney, singer

1972 Billie Joe Armstrong, guitar, vocals (Green Day)

1981 John Hassall, bassist (The Libertines)

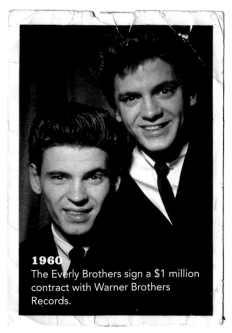

1960
The Everly Brothers sign a $1 million contract with Warner Brothers Records.

1966
Nancy Sinatra (Frank's eldest daughter) is at No. 1 on the UK singles chart with 'These Boots Are Made For Walking'.

1969
Bob Dylan and Johnny Cash record 'Girl From The North Country' in Nashville at CBS Studios. The track appears on Dylan's *Nashville Skyline* album.

1970
Joni Mitchell announces she is retiring from live performances during a concert at London's Royal Albert Hall. Joni was on stage again by year's end.

1971
James Taylor makes his TV debut on *The Johnny Cash Show*. Other guests that week include Neil Young, Linda Ronstadt and Tony Joe White.

1972
As the climax to a 14-date UK tour, Pink Floyd open a four-night run at London's Rainbow Theatre. Tickets cost £1.

1979
The Clash open the US leg of their 'Pearl Harbour '79' North American tour at New York's Palladium.

1989
R.E.M., Hoodoo Gurus and The Go-Betweens all appear at The Hordern Pavilion, Sydney, Australia.

1996
A platinum American Express card once belonging to Bruce Springsteen is sold for $4,500 at a New York memorabilia sale. The singer had given the expired card to a waiter in an LA restaurant by mistake and let them keep it as a souvenir.

1998
Songwriter Bob Merrill, who wrote 'How Much Is That Doggie In The Window' and Barbra Streisand's 'People', commits suicide aged 77.

2000
John Lennon's Steinway piano on which he composed 'Imagine' goes on display at The Beatles Story museum in Liverpool. The piano was set to be auctioned on the internet later in the year and was expected to fetch more than £1 million.

2003
The man behind Backstreet Boys and *NSYNC is being investigated over complaints that aspiring stars paid $1,500 to feature on his website. Lou Pearlman is accused by Florida authorities of getting young actors and models to pay upfront to appear on his Trans Continental company's website by saying he would also help them find work.

2004
Defence lawyers in the murder trial of producer Phil Spector demand that a fingernail overlooked by police investigating Lana Clarkson's shooting should be put forward as evidence. They claim the fingernail, blackened with gunpowder, could indicate that the 40-year old actress killed herself at Spector's Los Angeles mansion. Spector denied murdering Clarkson.

2005
A 1965 Fender Stratocaster guitar belonging to Jimi Hendrix sells for £100,000 at a London auction. Other Hendrix items sold include a poem written two weeks after his appearance at the 1967 Monterey Pop Festival which went for £10,000 and the first Jimi Hendrix Experience's single 'Hey Joe', signed by all three members, which made £2,000.

2008
Welsh singer Duffy starts a five week run at No. 1 on the UK singles chart with 'Mercy', from her debut album *Rockferry*. 'Mercy' was the UK's Best Selling Single of 2008 and won Duffy a Grammy for Best Female Pop Vocal Performance.

February 18

Born on this day:

1933 Yoko Ono, artist, singer	**1954** John Travolta, actor, singer
1952 Randy Crawford	**1955** Brian James, guitar (The Damned,
1953 Robbie Bachman, vocals, guitar	Tanz Der Youth)
(Bachman Turner Overdrive)	**1965** Dr Dre (NWA)

1959
Ray Charles records 'What'd I Say' in New York City. The song, which had evolved in concert as a call-and-response between Charles and his female back-up singers, became Brother Ray's biggest hit to date, reaching No. 1 on the R&B chart and No. 6 on the pop charts.

1962
On weekend leave from marine training, The Everly Brothers appear in full uniform and with regulation cropped hair, singing their new single, 'Crying In The Rain' on *The Ed Sullivan Show*.

1966
Beach Boy Brian Wilson starts recording the backing track for 'Good Vibrations' with LA session musicians. The classic song goes on to become The Beach Boys' third US No. 1 later in the year. As a child, Brian's mother told him that dogs could pick up vibrations from people, which he turned into the general idea for the song.

1969
The Jimi Hendrix Experience make the first of two appearances at the Royal Albert Hall, London, supported by The Soft Machine and Mason, Capaldi, Wood & Frog. The second show, supported by Fat Mattress and Van Der Graaf Generator, took place on 24 February.

1978
Winners at this year's Grammy Awards include Fleetwood Mac (Album Of The Year for *Rumours*), The Eagles (Record Of The Year for *Hotel California*) and The Bee Gees (Best Pop Vocal Performance for 'How Deep Is Your Love').

1980
During a *Rolling Stone* magazine interview Bill Wyman says that he intends leaving the band in 1982 on the group's 20th anniversary. Wyman,

who claimed he was misquoted, didn't leave the Stones until 1993.

1987
Bon Jovi are at No. 1 on the US singles chart with 'Livin' On A Prayer', which made No. 4 in the UK.

1995
American guitarist Bob Stinson from The Replacements dies from a drug overdose. His body was found in his Uptown, Minneapolis apartment.

1998
Noel Gallagher's Epiphone Supernova guitar raises £4,600 in aid of Children In Need at a Bonham's auction held in London.

2000
An American court orders the release of FBI files relating to John Lennon's interests and activities including his alleged support for the Irish Republican Army and the Workers Revolutionary Party. The British Government told the US that it wanted the files to remain secret. MI5 also had files on Lennon which they had passed on to the FBI during the 70s.

2004
A court case in which Marilyn Manson is accused of sexual assault is dismissed after the two sides reach a settlement. Security guard Joshua Keasler had sued Manson after the star allegedly put his legs around

Keasler's neck and gyrated against him on stage at a gig in Detroit, Michigan in 2001. Manson was ordered to pay $4,000 in fines and costs in the criminal proceedings.

2008
Carpenters fans object to plans to have the pop duo's former family home in Downey, south of Los Angeles, knocked down. The current owners of the house say they object to fans looking in the windows and leaving floral tributes. The five-bedroom house was immortalised when it appeared on the cover of The Carpenters' 1973 hit album *Now & Then*.

2009
Welsh singer Duffy wins three trophies at this year's Brit Awards, taking home Best British Female Solo Artist, British Breakthrough Act and British Album Of The Year for her debut *Rockferry*. Kings Of Leon win International Group and International Album for *Only By The Night*, International Male and Female Solo Artists were Kanye West and Katy Perry. British Male Solo Artist went to Paul Weller, Iron Maiden won British Live Act and Elbow won Best British Group. Outstanding Contribution to Music went to Pet Shop Boys.

Born on this day:

1940 Smokey Robinson, singer, songwriter
1948 Toni Iommi, guitar (Black Sabbath)
1957 Falco, singer

1963 Seal (Henry Samuel), singer-songwriter
1975 Daniel Adair, drummer (Nickelback)

February 19

1956
Elvis Presley performs three shows (two matinees and one evening concert) at Fort Homer Hesterly Armory in Tampa, Florida. A full scale riot breaks out when Elvis announces to the 14,000 strong crowd, "Girls, I'll see you backstage." Fans chase Elvis into the dressing room, tearing off his clothes and shoes.

1965
At EMI Studios in London, The Beatles record a new John Lennon song 'You're Going To Lose That Girl' in two takes. The track will be released on the *Help!* album in August.

1972
Harry Nilsson starts a four-week run at No. 1 on the US singles chart with his version of the Badfinger song, 'Without You'.

1976
Rich Stevens, former lead singer with Tower Of Power, is arrested in connection with the drug related murders of three men in San Jose, California. Stevens was found guilty of the charges in November.

1977
Manfred Mann's Earth Band score a No. 1 single in the US with their version of Bruce Springsteen's 'Blinded By The Light'.

1982
Ozzy Osbourne is arrested in San Antonio, Texas for urinating on the Alamo. Osbourne was wearing a dress at the time of his arrest.

1992
During their 'Use Your Illusion' Tour Guns n' Roses play the first of three nights at the Tokyo Dome, Japan.

1994
Mariah Carey has her first UK No. 1 with her version of the Badfinger song 'Without You'. Nilsson also took the song to No. 1 in 1972. Carey's version was released on January 24, 1994, just over a week after Nilsson died following a heart attack. The song's writers, Pete Ham and Tom Evans, committed suicide (Ham in 1975 and Evans in 1983) after an ongoing battle over unpaid royalties.

1995
Mötley Crüe drummer Tommy Lee marries *Baywatch* actress Pamela Anderson on a Cancun beach, with the bride in a white bikini.

1996
Björk attacks a news reporter at an airport in Thailand. News footage captures the singer pulling the female reporter to the floor and banging her head on the ground. Björk later apologised for the attack.

Pulp singer Jarvis Cocker is arrested after invading the stage during an appearance at the Brit Awards by Michael Jackson, who won Artist of a Generation. Cocker was later accused of attacking children who were performing with Jackson but all the charges against him were dropped on 11 March.

2004
The Johnny Cash estate blocks an attempt by advertisers to use 'Ring Of Fire' to promote haemorrhoid-relief products. The idea is said to have been backed by Merle Kilgore, who co-wrote the song with Cash's wife, June Carter Cash. Cash's daughter Rosanne said the family "would never allow the song to be demeaned like that."

2008
Two releases by Oasis are voted The Best British Albums Ever Recorded in a *Q* magazine and HMV poll of 11,000 people. Their 1994 album *Definitely Maybe* came top, while 1995 follow-up *(What's the Story) Morning Glory* was second in the vote. Radiohead's *OK Computer* finished third, followed by The Beatles' *Revolver* and The Stone Roses' self-titled debut. The full list of 50 British albums includes five by The Beatles.

February 20

Born on this day:

1946 J Geils, guitarist (The J. Geils Band)
1950 Walter Becker, guitar, vocals (Steely Dan)
1967 Kurt Cobain, guitar, vocals (Nirvana)
1972 Neil Primrose, drummer (Travis)
1975 Brian Littrell, vocals (Backstreet Boys)
1988 Rihanna (Robyn Rihanna Fenty), R&B singer

1958

Billed as The Big Gold Record Stars, Bill Haley & His Comets, The Everly Brothers, Buddy Holly & The Crickets, Jerry Lee Lewis and Jimmie Rodgers all appear on the first date of a six-day tour of Florida.

1960

Jimi Hendrix makes his stage debut when playing a show at a high school in Seattle.

1963

The Beatles drive through the night from Liverpool to London to appear on the live lunchtime BBC radio show *Parade Of The Pops*, performing 'Love Me Do' and 'Please Please Me', an appearance that lasts just over four minutes. They then drive another 180 miles back north for a performance at Doncaster swimming baths in Yorkshire.

1967

Pink Floyd appear at The Adelphi Ballroom, West Bromwich, England.

1971

Yes appear at Kingston Polytechnic, Surrey, supported by Queen. Tickets cost 50p.

1972

During a tour of Australia, Led Zeppelin play an outdoor show at Kooyong Tennis Courts, Melbourne.

1976

All four members of Kiss have their footprints implanted on the pavement outside Grauman's Chinese Theatre in Hollywood.

Screaming Lord Sutch appears at the College Of Art, High Wycombe, supported by The Sex Pistols.

1977

Winners at this year's Grammy Awards include Stevie Wonder for Best Album with *Songs In The Key Of Life* and Best Vocal Performance for 'I Wish'.

1980

Bon Scott, singer of AC/DC, is pronounced dead on arrival at a London hospital after a heavy night's drinking. Scott was found in the passenger seat of a friend's parked car in East Dulwich, south London. The official coroner's report states that he had "drunk himself to death" after suffocating on his own vomit.

1988

Kylie Minogue is at No. 1 on the UK singles chart with her first hit, 'I Should Be So Lucky'. Minogue had become a household name playing Charlene Ramsey in Australian soap *Neighbours*.

1991

Bob Dylan is awarded a Lifetime Achievement Award at the 33rd Annual Grammy Awards.

2001

Two estate agents are committed to trial at Snaresbrook Crown Court accused of stealing nude photographs of Patsy Kensit, the former wife of Liam Gallagher of Oasis, from the couple's home.

2003

A total of 100 people die after pyrotechnics ignite a club in flames during a gig by Great White in West Warwick, Rhode Island. Great White singer Ty Longley is also killed in the tragedy. Two brothers who own the club are later charged with involuntary manslaughter, along with the group's former tour manager.

2004

Brian Wilson premieres his eagerly awaited, unreleased masterpiece *Smile* – originally referred to by Wilson as his "Teenage Symphony to God" – at London's Royal Festival Hall.

2007

Christina Aguilera kicks off a 42-date North American tour at the Toyota Center in Houston, Texas. The Black Eyed Peas and The Pussycat Dolls are support acts on the tour.

The US salon where pop star Britney Spears shaved her head sets up a website to auction her hair off for more than $1m. The website, buybritneyshair.com, claims to have been set up by salon owner Esther Tognozzi and includes photos of the hair, saying it is "absolutely authentic". As well as the tresses, the winning bidder will also get the clippers Spears used, a blue lighter she left at the salon and the can of Red Bull she was drinking at the time. Meanwhile, Spears has been spotted in Hollywood sporting a short blonde wig.

2008

Winners at this year's Brit Awards in London include Take That who win Best British Live Act and British Single. Arctic Monkeys win Best British Group and Album – both for the second year in a row – and Foo Fighters win Best International Group and Album. Paul McCartney performs some of his hits, including 'Live And Let Die', 'Hey Jude' and 'Lady Madonna' after he was honoured with an Outstanding Contribution Award. The show is presented by Sharon Osbourne.

Born on this day:

1943 David Geffen, record label president
1949 Jerry Harrison, keyboards (The Modern Lovers, Talking Heads)
1961 Ranking Roger, vocals (The Beat)
1969 James Dean Bradfield, guitar, vocals (Manic Street Preachers)

February **21**

1961

The Beatles play three Liverpool gigs in one day. The first is a lunchtime show at the Cavern Club, then in the evening they appear at the Cassanova Club, Liverpool and at Litherland Town Hall, Liverpool.

1964

New York group The Echoes recruit a young piano player named Billy Joel.

1977

Fleetwood Mac release *Rumours*, which goes on to sell more than 15 million copies worldwide and spends 31 weeks at No. 1 on the US chart.

track was first released in 1961 and became a hit in 1987 after being featured in the film *Stand By Me*.

1998

Celine Dion is at No. 1 on the UK singles chart with 'My Heart Will Go On', the theme from the movie *Titanic* and the best selling single of 1998.

1970

Simon & Garfunkel are at No. 1 on the UK album chart with *Bridge Over Troubled Water*. It stays on the chart for over 300 weeks, returning to the top on eight separate occasions, spending a total of 41 weeks at No. 1

2001

Robbie Williams is attacked and thrown from the stage during a concert in Stuttgart, Germany after a man climbed on stage and pushed the singer into the security pit. The attacker is arrested and taken to a secure psychiatric clinic.

2002

Elton John accuses the music industry of exploiting young singers and dumping talented artists for manufactured groups, saying: "There are too many average and mediocre acts, it damages real talent getting airplay. It's just fodder."

2004

Simon Cowell is set to appear in a new episode of *The Simpsons*. The TV *Pop Idol* judge will play a nursery boss who gets punched by Homer Simpson.

1976

Florence Ballard of The Supremes dies aged 32 of cardiac arrest. Ballard had left The Supremes in 1967, lost an $8 million lawsuit against Motown Records and was living on welfare when she died.

1981

Dolly Parton starts a two-week run at No. 1 on the US charts with '9 To 5', her first No. 1, and a No. 47 hit in the UK.

1987

Ben E. King is at No. 1 on the UK singles chart with 'Stand By Me'. The

2008

Britney Spears fails in a court bid to regain visitation rights to her two children. Spears is banned from monitored visits in January of this year after refusing to hand the children back, resulting in a stand-off with police at her house.

February 22

Born on this day:

1938 Bobby Hendricks, vocals (The Drifters)
1943 Louise Lopez, vocals (Odyssey)

1973 Scott Phillips, drums (Creed)
1977 James Blunt, singer, songwriter

1962
Elvis Presley is at No. 1 on the UK singles chart with 'Rock-A-Hula Baby'/ 'Can't Help Falling In Love'. The tracks are from his latest film *Blue Hawaii* and become the singer's tenth chart-topper.

1964
The Beatles arrive back from their first US visit at Heathrow Airport to a welcome from thousands of fans, some who had slept at the airport overnight to get the best vantage positions.

1969
Marc Bolan and Steve Took's duo Tyrannosaurus Rex appear at The Free Trade Hall, Manchester. Support act is David Bowie performing a one-man mime routine.

1975
Scottish group The Average White Band are at No. 1 on the US singles chart with 'Pick Up The Pieces'. Their eponymous album *AWB* also goes to the top of the *Billboard* chart.

1978
The Police appear in a Wrigley's Chewing Gum commercial for US TV, dying their hair blonde for the appearance.

1981
One hit wonder Joe Dolce is at No. 1 on the UK singles chart with 'Shaddap You Face', preventing the Ultravox song, 'Vienna', from reaching the top. 'Shaddap You Face' makes No. 1 in 11 countries with over 35 different foreign language cover versions selling over four million copies.

1987
Andy Warhol, pop artist and producer, dies after a gall bladder operation. A leading light of the Pop Art movement, he produced and managed The Velvet Underground, and designed the 1967 *Velvet Underground And Nico* 'peeled banana' album cover and The Rolling Stones' 1971 *Sticky Fingers* album cover.

1992
New Musical Express writers decide their all time best debut albums. At number one is Patti Smith's *Horses*, followed by Joy Division's *Unknown Pleasures*, MC5's *Kick Out The Jams*, The Jesus and Mary Chain's *Psychocandy* and Television's *Marquee Moon*.

1997
No Doubt go to No. 1 on the UK singles chart with 'Don't Speak', the third single from the band's second album *Tragic Kingdom*.

The Spice Girls start a four-week run at No. 1 on the US singles chart with 'Wannabe', the first UK act to score a chart-topper there for over 18 months.

2000
The engagement ring that Sex Pistol Sid Vicious bought from Camden market in 1977 to give to his girlfriend Nancy Spungen sells at auction for £1,500. Also sold was a pair of John Lennon's jeans for £2,250.

2001
Winners at the 43rd Grammy Awards include U2 (Record Of The Year and Song Of The Year with 'Beautiful Day'), Steely Dan (Album Of The Year for *Two Against Nature*), Macy Gray (Female Pop Vocal for 'I Try'), Sting (Male Pop Vocal for 'She Walks This Earth'), Eminem (Best Rap Album for *The Marshall Mathers LP*), Johnny Cash (Best Male Country Performance for 'Solitary Man'), and Shelby Lynne (Best New Artist).

2002
Drummer Ronnie Verrell, who worked with The Ted Heath Orchestra and The Syd Lawrence Orchestra, and provided the drum licks for Animal in *The Muppet Show*, dies aged 76.

Two middle-aged women spend the first of eight nights sleeping in a car outside Bournemouth International Centre to make sure they are first in the queue for tickets to a Cliff Richard concert.

2004
Norah Jones starts a six-week run at the top of the *Billboard* album chart with *Feels Like Home*, the singer's second US No. 1.

The Sex Pistols' 'Anarchy In The UK' is named The Most Influential Record Of The 1970s in a poll conducted by *Q* magazine. Queen's 'Bohemian Rhapsody' is voted into second place, Donna Summer's 'I Feel Love' – third, T Rex's 'Get It On' – fourth and The Specials' 'Gangsters' came fifth.

Born on this day:

1944 Johnny Winter, guitarist
1946 Rusty Young, pedal steel (Poco)
1952 Brad Whitford, guitar (Aerosmith)
1955 Howard Jones, singer, songwriter
1963 Rob Collins, keyboards (The Charlatans)

1961
Petula Clark has her first UK No. 1 single with 'Sailor'. During her career the former child actress achieved a total of 20 UK Top 40 hits and two US No. 1 singles.

1965
Filming begins on location in the Bahamas for The Beatles follow up to *A Hard Day's Night* with the working title of *Eight Arms To Hold You*.

1972
Elvis Presley and his wife Priscilla are legally separated. The couple had married in 1967.

1978
David Coverdale's Whitesnake make their debut at The Sky Bird Club, Nottingham, England.

1980
U2 appear at The Moonlight Club at The Railway Hotel in West Hampstead, London, with tickets costing £2.

1985
Stevie Wonder is arrested during an anti-apartheid demonstration outside the South African Embassy in Washington. He is released after police questioning.

1988
Michael Jackson plays the first of two nights at Kemper Arena in Kansas City – the opening shows on the second leg of his 'Bad' World Tour.

1989
Isaac Hayes is jailed by an Atlanta judge for owing $346,300 in child support and alimony.

1995
Melvin Franklin of The Temptations dies aged 52 of a brain seizure. In 1978 Franklin was shot in the hand and leg when trying to stop a man from stealing his car.

1998
All the members of Oasis are banned for life from flying Cathay Pacific Airlines after "abusive and disgusting behaviour" during a flight from Hong Kong to Perth, Australia.

2002
The Bee Gees make their last ever concert appearance as a trio at the Love & Hope Ball, Miami Beach, Florida.

2003
Howie Epstein, bassist with Tom Petty & The Heartbreakers, dies aged 47 of a suspected drug overdose in New Mexico. Epstein, who had replaced the band's original bassist Ron Blair, also worked with Bob Dylan, Johnny Cash, Stevie Nicks, Roy Orbison, Carl Perkins, Linda Ronstadt and Del Shannon.

Norah Jones cleans up at the 45th Grammy Awards, held at Madison Square Garden, New York. The singer-songwriter won Album Of The Year and Record Of The Year with *Don't Know Why*, Best New Artist, Song of the Year, and Best Female Pop Vocal for 'Don't Know Why'. Other winners include Best Male Pop Vocal (John Mayer, 'Our Body Is A Wonderland'), Best Male Rock Vocal (Bruce Springsteen, *The Rising*), Best Female Rock Vocal (Sheryl Crow, 'Steve McQueen'), Best Rock Performance By A Group, (Coldplay, 'In My Place') and Best Rap Album (Eminem, *The Eminem Show*).

1985
The Smiths score their first UK No. 1 album with *Meat Is Murder*.

February 24

Born on this day:

1942 Paul Jones, singer, harmonica player, actor, broadcaster (Manfred Mann, The Blues Band)
1947 Rupert Holmes, writer, producer, singer
1959 Colin Farley (Cutting Crew)
1962 Michelle Shocked, singer-songwriter
1974 Chad Hugo, one half of music production duo The Neptunes

---

1957
Buddy Holly records a new version of 'That'll Be The Day', the title coming from a phrase used by John Wayne in the film *The Searchers*.

1963
The Rolling Stones start a Sunday night residency at The Station Hotel, Richmond, Surrey. They are paid £24 for the gig and on the first night 66 people show up.

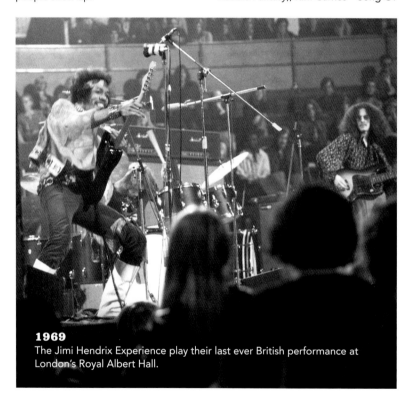

1969
The Jimi Hendrix Experience play their last ever British performance at London's Royal Albert Hall.

1973
Roberta Flack has her second US No. 1 when 'Killing Me Softly With His Song' starts a five-week run at the top. The song was written about US singer-songwriter Don McLean.

1976
The Eagles' *Greatest Hits* becomes the first album to be certified platinum by the R.I.A.A. New platinum certifications represent sales of one million copies for albums and two million for singles.

1982
The Police win Best British Group at the first annual Brit Awards held in London.

Winners at the Grammy Awards include John & Yoko (Album Of The Year with *Double Fantasy*), Kim Carnes – Song Of The Year ('Bette Davis Eyes'), Quincy Jones – Producer Of The Year and Sheena Easton – Best New Act.

1990
American singer Johnnie Ray, who scored over 20 Top 40 singles between 1952 and 1960 including a 1956 UK No. 1 & US No. 2 single, 'Just Walking In The Rain', dies aged 63 of liver failure at Cedars-Sinai Hospital, Los Angeles. Dexys Midnight Runners' name-checked Ray in the lyrics to their 1982 hit 'Come On Eileen'.

1992
Kurt Cobain marries Courtney Love in Waikiki, Hawaii. The press report that the couple are expecting a baby in September of this year.

2000
Carlos Santana wins eight awards at this year Grammy Awards. Before the *Supernatural* album, the guitarist hadn't had a Top 10 album since 1981.

Georgie Fame is banned from driving for a year and fined £350 after being breathalysed the morning after a concert. Police stopped the 56-year-old as he returned to his home in Somerset from a gig in Narberth, Wales.

2004
Estelle Axton, who helped create the legendary US soul music label Stax, dies aged 85 in a Memphis hospital. Stax was home to Otis Redding, Rufus Thomas, Isaac Hayes and Booker T & The MGs. The Stax studio, 'Soulsville USA', was second only to Motown in producing black American hits during its 60s heyday.

2005
Former Orange Juice singer, guitarist and producer Edwyn Collins is rushed to hospital suffering a brain hemorrhage.

2009
The United States Mint launches a new coin featuring American composer, pianist and bandleader Duke Ellington,  making him the first African-American to appear by himself on a US coin.

Born on this day:

1943 George Harrison, guitar, vocals (The Beatles, solo)

1957 Stewart Wood, guitar (Bay City Rollers)

1959 Mike Peters, guitar, vocals (The Alarm)

1971 Daniel Powter, Canadian singer-songwriter

February 25

1963
'Please Please Me' becomes the first Beatles single to be released in the US on the Chicago-based Vee Jay label.

1965
The Seekers are at No. 1 on the UK singles chart with 'I'll Never Find Another You', the Australian folk-pop group's first British chart-topper.

1969
Pink Floyd appear at The Marlowe Theatre, Canterbury, England.

1972
Led Zeppelin appear at Western Springs Stadium, Auckland, New Zealand.

1984
'Jump', by Van Halen starts a five-week run at No. 1 on the US singles chart; No. 7 in the UK.

1985
U2 begin their first full North American arena tour, opening at the Dallas Reunion Arena, Texas.

1995
At a private party for 1,200 select guests on the closing night of the Frank Sinatra Desert Classic golf tournament, Sinatra sings before a

best" and "Wu-Tang is for the children". He was then escorted offstage.

2001
Rapper Lil' Kim claims a shooting that occurred as she was leaving a New York radio station was unconnected to her. One man was wounded in the incident outside the radio station Hot 97 when five men fired 22 bullets. The *New York Daily News* reports the incident was the result of a feud between Lil' Kim and rival rappers Capone-N-Noreaga.

2004
The Rolling Stones top a US Rich List of music's biggest money makers, based on earnings during 2003 when the band played their 'Forty Licks' tour, which grossed $212 million in ticket, CD, DVD and merchandise sales. The three million fans who attended the shows spent an average of $11 each on merchandise. Bruce Springsteen is listed in second place and The Eagles third.

2006
George Michael is found slumped over the wheel of a car in Hyde Park, London. A passerby spots him and calls police who arrest the singer on suspicion of possessing drugs and release him on bail. Michael makes a public statement about the incident, saying: "I was in possession of class C drugs which is an offence and I have no complaints about the police who were professional throughout." He also says that the incident was "my own stupid fault, as usual."

1977
The Jam sign to Polydor Records for £6,000.

1981
Winners at this year's Grammy Awards include Bob Seger (Best Rock Performance for *Against The Wind*), Pat Benatar (Best Female Performance, *Crimes Of Passion*) and Christopher Cross (Best New Artist and Best Song for 'Sailing').

live audience for the very last time. His closing song was 'The Best Is Yet To Come'.

1998
During Shawn Colvin's acceptance speech at the Grammy Awards, Ol Dirty Bastard grabs the microphone and makes various observations such as "Puffy is good, but Wu-Tang is the

2009
Winners at the 2009 *NME* Awards, held at London's O2 Academy, include Oasis who win Best British Band, and Elbow who win Outstanding Contribution to British Music. The Killers take Best International Band, Kings Of Leon win Best Album for *Only By The Night* and The Cure win the Godlike Genius Award.

February 26

Born on this day:

1928 Fats Domino, singer, pianist
1932 Johnny Cash, US country singer/songwriter
1945 Bob 'The Bear' Hite, vocals & harmonica (Canned Heat)
1968 Tim Commerford, bass (Rage Against The Machine)
1979 Corinne Bailey Rae, UK singer, songwriter

1955
Billboard reports that for the first time since their introduction in 1949, 45rpm singles are outselling the old standard 78s.

1964
The Beatles work on the final mixes for 'Can't Buy Me Love' and 'You Can't Do That'. The single, which would be released the following month, tops charts all over the world.

1965
Session guitarist Jimmy Page releases a solo single on Fontana Records entitled 'She Just Satisfies'. It doesn't chart but goes on to become a valuable collectors' item.

1966
David Bowie & The Buzz appear at The Corn Exchange, Chelmsford, Essex.

1969
Peter Sarstedt starts a four-week run at No. 1 on the UK singles chart with 'Where Do You Go To My Lovely?'

1977
Sherman Garnes from Frankie Lymon & The Teenagers, who had a 1956 UK No. 1 and US No. 6 hit, 'Why Do Fools Fall In Love', dies during open-heart surgery.

1979
During a court case between The Sex Pistols and their manager Malcolm McLaren it is revealed that only £30,000 is left of the £800,000 the band had earned.

1980
After seeing U2 play at Dublin's National Boxing Stadium in front of 2,400 people, Rob Partridge and Bill Stewart from Island Records in the UK offer the band a recording contract.

1983
Michael Jackson's *Thriller* goes to No. 1 on the US album chart, becoming the most successful album of all time with sales of over 50 million copies.

1990
Sinead O'Connor is at No. 1 on the UK singles chart with 'Nothing Compares 2 U'. Her version of the Prince song reaches No. 1 in 18 other countries.

1997
American songwriter Ben Raleigh, who co-wrote 'Scooby Doo, Where Are You' and 'Tell Laura I Love Her', dies in a fire in his kitchen after his bathrobe catches light while cooking.

2001
Winners at the Brit Awards include Coldplay (Best British Group and Best British Album for *Parachutes*), Robbie Williams (Best British Male Artist and Best Single for 'Rock DJ'), Sonique (Best British Female Artist) and Best Dance Act went to Fat Boy Slim.

2005
The wife of Status Quo guitarist Rick Parfitt is rushed to hospital after slashing her wrists in a suicide attempt after reading a Sunday newspaper story claiming that Rick had been cheating on her.

2008
Two original members of UK boy band Busted go to court seeking an estimated £10m in unpaid royalties. Ki McPhail and Owen Doyle claim they wrote songs with James Bourne and Matt Willis when the group formed in 2001, but were forced to sign away their rights after "threats" when they were sacked from the band later that year. The songs included 'Year 3000' and 'What I Go To School For' which went on to be hits for the group.

2009
At a ceremony at the White House President Barrack Obama honours Stevie Wonder, his musical hero, with America's highest award for pop music, the Library of Congress' Gershwin prize. The president says the Motown legend had been the soundtrack to his youth and he doubted that his wife would have married him if he hadn't been a fan.

Wonder's song 'Signed, Sealed, Delivered' was the theme song during Obama's presidential campaign.

Born on this day:

1954 Neal Schon, guitar (Journey)
1957 Adrian Smith, guitar (Iron Maiden)
1971 Rozonda Thomas (Chilli), vocals (TLC)

1973 Peter Andre, singer
1981 Josh Groban, US singer

February 27

1964
The Rolling Stones make their second appearance on BBC TV's *Top Of The Pops*, performing their latest single 'Not Fade Away'.

1965
The first date of a 21-twice-nightly UK package tour with Del Shannon, Wayne Fontana & The Mindbenders and Herman's Hermits opens at Sheffield City Hall.

1967
Pink Floyd record their first single 'Arnold Layne' at Sound Techniques Studio, Chelsea, with producer Joe Boyd.

1971
Five months after her death, Janis Joplin starts a nine-week run at No. 1 on the US album chart with *Pearl*.

1980
Winners at the Grammy Awards include The Doobie Brothers (Song Of The Year with 'What A Fool Believes'), Billy Joel (Album Of The Year *52nd Street*), Rickie Lee Jones (Best New Artist), and Gloria Gaynor (Best Disco Record with 'I Will Survive').

1988
George Michael scores his sixth US No. 1 single with 'Father Figure', a No. 11 hit in the UK.

1991
James Brown is paroled after two years of a six-year prison sentence imposed for resisting arrest after a car chase across two US states.

1993
After 14 weeks at No. 1 on the US singles chart, 'I Will Always Love You'

1999
Britney Spears starts a two-week run on top of the UK singles chart with '... Baby One More Time', becoming the biggest-selling single of the year in Britain. The song, also a No. 1 in the US, was originally written for TLC but was submitted too late for inclusion on their third album, *FanMail*.

2004
An employee in a supermarket in Aspen, Colorado alerts police after seeing a man shopping with his face covered by a mask. Police arrive on the scene and identify the man as Michael Jackson who is in town on holiday with his children.

2007
Bobby Brown is sentenced to 30 days in jail over $19,000 in unpaid child support. An arrest warrant was issued in October 2006 after he failed to show up at a hearing on overdue child support for Kim Ward, the mother of two of his children.

1974
Cher files for divorce from Sonny Bono.

1977
Keith Richards is arrested by the Royal Canadian Mounted Police at Toronto's Harbour Castle Hotel, for possession of heroin and cocaine. Bail is set at $25,000.

gives Whitney Houston the longest ever US chart-topper, taking over from Boyz II Men's 'End Of The Road', eventually becoming the second biggest selling single in the US.

Pictures appear in UK papers of Babyshambles singer Pete Doherty making a trip to a zoo in Burford, Oxfordshire, with his model girlfriend Kate Moss. He was blasted by vets after pictures apparently showed Pete throwing a left over cannabis joint to a group of penguins.

February 28

1964
The Yardbirds play on the bill at the Rhythm & Blues Festival at The Town Hall, Birmingham, England.

1966
Police are called after over 100 music fans barricade themselves inside Liverpool's Cavern Club to protest at the club's closure. The club had run up debts of over £10,000.

1968
Frankie Lymon is found dead aged 25 of a suspected drug overdose at his mother's house in New York.

1970
Led Zeppelin are obliged to play a gig in Copenhagen as The Nobs after Eva von Zeppelin, a relative of the airship designer, threatens to sue if the family name was used in Denmark.

David Bowie's just-formed new group, are billed as 'David Bowie's New Electric Band' at the Basildon Arts Lab's experimental music club in Essex.

1974
Singer-songwriter Bobby Bloom, who had a 1970 US No. 8 & UK No. 3 single with 'Montego Bay', shoots himself dead aged 28 at his Hollywood apartment.

1977
At a Los Angeles gig Ray Charles is attacked by a member of the audience who tries to strangle him with a rope.

1984
Michael Jackson wins a record seven Grammy Awards including Album Of The Year for *Thriller*, Record Of The Year and Best Rock Vocal Performance for 'Beat It'; Best Pop Vocal Performance, Best R&B Performance and Best R&B Song for 'Billie Jean', and Best Recording For Children for *E.T The Extra Terrestrial*.

1985
David Byron, singer with hard rock group Uriah Heep, dies aged 38 from an epileptic fit and liver disease.

1996
Grammy Award winners include Alanis Morissette (Album Of The Year) for *Jagged Little Pill*, Best Female Rock Vocal and Best Song ('You Oughta Know'), Nirvana (Best Alternative Album – *Unplugged*) and Coolio (Best Rap Performance – 'Gangsta's Paradise').

1997
Death Row Records' boss Marion 'Suge' Knight is sentenced to nine years in prison for violating his probation for a 1995 assault conviction. Under US law, Knight would not be allowed to run Death Row Records while in prison.

2006
Two stewards are shot during a concert by rapper Kanye West at the N.E.C. in Birmingham, England. Police say the shootings occurred after fans who tried to gain entrance without tickets were escorted from the arena. A man without a ticket entered the foyer and was ejected, but he returned and shot at the stewards, one of whom was in a serious condition after being shot in the face.

2008
Drummer Buddy Miles, who played with Jimi Hendrix in his last regular group, Band Of Gypsys, dies aged 60 at his home in Austin, Texas after struggling with a long-term illness. Born George Allen Miles in Omaha, Nebraska, Buddy's nickname was a tribute to his idol, jazz drummer Buddy Rich. Miles also played with The Delfonics, The Ink Spots, Wilson Pickett, The Electric Flag, Stevie Wonder, David Bowie, Muddy Waters and Barry White. In the 80s, he achieved a certain amount of notoriety in America as the vocalist on the celebrated clay animation California Raisins commercials.

A Rolling Stones album bought for £2 at a car boot sale is sold for £4,000 at auction. The 1976 *Black And Blue* LP was purportedly signed by John Lennon, Yoko Ono, Paul and Linda McCartney and George Harrison as well as members of The Rolling Stones. The seller obtained the album after haggling the price down from £3.

2008
Boy George pleads not guilty to falsely imprisoning a male escort Audun Carlsen by chaining him to a wall. The singer and DJ, who was also accused of assaulting Carlsen during the alleged incident on 28 April 2007, was released on bail until a trial at Snaresbrook Crown Court in November.

Born on this day:

1940 Gretchen Christopher, singer (The Fleetwoods)

1972 Saul Williams, hip-hop artist

1976 Ja Rule (Jeffrey Atkins), US rapper

February 29

1964
The first show of a 29-date twice-nightly tour featuring The Searchers, Booby Vee and Dusty Springfield kicks off at The Adelphi Cinema, Slough.

1980
The glasses worn by Buddy Holly when he died are discovered in a police file in Mason, Iowa. They had been there for over 21 years.

1996
American musician, songwriter and record producer Wes Farrell, one of the writers behind *The Partridge Family* US TV show and who also wrote The McCoys' 1965 hit 'Hang On Sloopy' and The Shirelles' hit 'Boys' (covered by The Beatles), dies aged 56.

Status Quo sue Radio 1 for £250,000 on the grounds that the BBC was breaking the law by not including their new record on the station's playlist.

2000
Eric Clapton loses his license for six months after driving at 45mph in a 30mph zone near his home in Surrey.

1968
The Beatles' *Sgt Pepper's Lonely Hearts Club Band* wins Album Of The Year, Best Cover and Best Engineered and Recorded Album at this year's Grammy Awards.

1972
On the last date of an Australian tour Led Zeppelin play The Festival Hall, Brisbane.

1976
10CC kick off a 30-date UK tour at the Fairfield Hall, Croydon, promoting their new album *How Dare You*. Also this week, 10CC guitarist Eric Stewart is nominated for a Grammy Award in America for his work on *The Original Soundtrack* album.

A special 'Leap Year' concert with The Stranglers, Nasty Pop, Deaf School and Jive Bombers takes place at London's Roundhouse

Two members of Lynyrd Skynyrd are knocked unconscious after a scuffle breaks out between the band and members of the Metropolitan Police boxing team, who are holding a dinner at London's Royal Lancaster Hotel.

1992
U2 kick off the North American leg of the 'Zoo TV' Tour at The Lakeland Civic Centre Arena, Florida.

2000
After 15 minutes Sir Elton John storms out of the opening of his new Broadway musical show, *Aida*, written with Sir Tim Rice complaining that his songs had been ruined.

2008
Mike Smith, lead singer of 1960s British group The Dave Clark Five, dies aged 64 from pneumonia at Stoke Mandeville Hospital in Buckinghamshire, England. The Dave Clark Five, who had 19 UK Top 40 hits including a number one single 'Glad All Over', broke up in the early 70s, having sold over 100 million records.

March

Born on this day:

1944 Mike D'Abo, vocals (Manfred Mann)
1944 Roger Daltrey, vocals (The Who, solo)
1958 Nik Kershaw, singer, songwriter, producer
1973 Ryan Peake, guitar (Nickelback)

March 1

1951
Sam Phillips launches his label Sun Records by releasing 'Drivin' Slow' by saxophonist Johnny London.

1958
Buddy Holly plays the first of 25 dates on his only UK tour at the Trocadero, Elephant & Castle, London. Also on the bill are Gary Miller, The Tanner Sisters, The Montanas, Ronnie Keene & His Orchestra and compere Des O'Connor.

1967
At EMI Studios, Abbey Road, London, The Beatles start recording a John Lennon song, 'Lucy In The Sky With Diamonds'.

1968
Elton John's first single 'I've Been Loving You Too Long' is released on the Philips label but doesn't chart.

1969
Jim Morrison of The Doors is charged with lewd and lascivious behaviour after allegedly showing his penis to an audience during a show in Miami. He is found guilty and sentenced to eight months hard labour. Morrison dies in Paris in 1971 while the sentence is on appeal.

1974
Chris Difford places an advert in a South London shop window: 'Lyricist seeks musician for co-writing'. Glenn Tilbrook answers the ad. The Lennon & McCartney-influenced duo go on to form Squeeze.

1975
Winners at this year's Grammy Awards ceremony include Paul McCartney for Best Pop Vocal on 'Band On The Run', Olivia Newton-John (Record Of The Year with 'I Honestly Love You') and Stevie Wonder (Album Of The Year with *Fulfillingness First Finale*).

1977
Sara Lowndes files for divorce from her singer-songwriter husband, Bob Dylan. The pair had secretly married in 1965.

1979
Manchester band Joy Division appear at The Hope & Anchor, Islington, London. Admission is 75p.

1980
Patti Smith marries ex-MC5 guitarist Fred 'Sonic' Smith "so I won't need to change my maiden name" she quips. Fred Smith passed away on November 4, 1994.

1989
R.E.M. kick off the US leg of their 'Green' World Tour in Louisville, Kentucky.

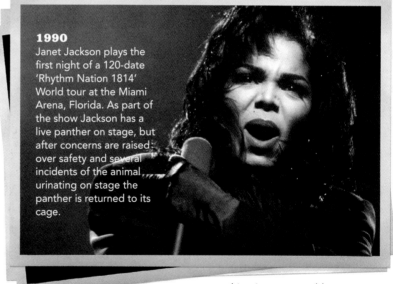

1990
Janet Jackson plays the first night of a 120-date 'Rhythm Nation 1814' World tour at the Miami Arena, Florida. As part of the show Jackson has a live panther on stage, but after concerns are raised over safety and several incidents of the animal urinating on stage the panther is returned to its cage.

1994
Nirvana play their final concert at the 3,000 capacity Terminal Einz, a small airport hanger in Munich, Germany. When the power cuts during the show the band play an impromptu acoustic set including a version of The Cars' 'My Best Friend's Girl'.

1995
Bruce Springsteen's 'Streets Of Philadelphia' wins three Grammys for Song Of The Year, Best Male Vocal Performance and Best Rock Song.

1997
A Motley Crüe fan, Clifford Goldberg, who claimed his hearing had been irreparably damaged after a show in New Jersey, has his lawsuit thrown out of court. The judge decrees that Goldberg knew the risk he was taking by sitting near the front of the stage.

'Bowie Bonds' are issued on the US Stock Exchange. Linked to Bowie's back catalogue, albums with money earned on the bonds via interest from royalties, investors could expect to make an 8% profit in about 10 years.

2004
Michael Jackson unveils a new website, www.mjjsource.com. The site features a celebration of Jackson's music career plus news on his current criminal trial, including short biographies of his attorneys and a calendar listing upcoming court dates.

March 2

Born on this day:

1938 Lawrence Payton, vocals (The Four Tops)

1943 Lou Reed, guitar, vocals (Velvet Underground)

1948 Rory Gallagher, Irish blues guitarist

1950 Karen Carpenter, vocals, drums (The Carpenters)

1962 Jon Bon Jovi, guitar, vocals (Bon Jovi)

1977 Chris Martin, piano, guitar, vocals (Coldplay)

1955
Bo Diddley's first recording session occurs at Universal Recording Studio in Chicago, where he lays down 'Bo Diddley', which tops the US R&B chart the following June.

1960
After completing his national service and flying back to America, Elvis Presley steps on British soil for the first and only time in his life when the plane carrying him stops for refuelling at Prestwick Airport, Scotland.

1964
The Beatles begin filming their first feature film *A Hard Day's Night* at Marylebone station, London.

1974
At this year's Grammy Awards Stevie Wonder wins four awards: Album Of The Year (*Innervisions*), Best R&B Song and Best Vocal for 'Superstition' and Best Pop Vocal Performance for 'You Are The Sunshine Of My Life'.

1975
A policeman who stops a Lincoln Continental for running a red light in Los Angeles is surprised to find Paul McCartney at the wheel with his wife Linda. The cop detects a strong smell of marijuana and on searching the car finds eight ounces of the drug. Linda is arrested for the offence.

1977
The Jam play the first of a five-week Wednesday night run at The Red Cow, Hammersmith, London. The band has just signed a four-year recording contract with Polydor Records.

1985
Wham! start a three week run at No. 1 on the US singles chart with 'Make It Big' which eventually sells over five million copies in America.

1991
Over two decades after its first release 'All Right Now' by Free makes No. 2 in the UK singles chart after being reissued to coincide with its use in a Wrigley's chewing gum TV ad.

French singer and composer Serge Gainsbourg dies of a heart attack. Best known (outside France) for 'Je T'aime... Moi Non Plus', his sensuous 1969 UK No. 1 duet with Jane Birkin, during his career Gainsbourg wrote the soundtracks for more than 40 films. He also famously propositioned Whitney Houston during a televised French TV chat show in 1986.

1996
Oasis score their second UK No.1 single with 'Don't Look Back In Anger'. Taken from the band's *What's The Story Morning Glory* album it is the first Oasis single to feature Noel Gallagher on lead vocals instead of his brother, Liam.

1999
Dusty Springfield dies after a long battle against cancer, aged 59. The much loved British singer had her first UK hit single in 1963 with 'I Only Want To Be With You', which reached No. 4, a 1966 UK No. 1 & US No. 4 single ('You Don't Have To Say You Love Me') plus over 15 other UK Top 40 singles.

2003
Singer-songwriter Hank Ballard dies from throat cancer. Ballard wrote and recorded the original version of 'The Twist', released as a B-side. A year later, Chubby Checker debuted his own chart-topping version of 'The Twist' on Dick Clark's *American Bandstand*, launching a dance craze that prompted the creation of other Twist songs, including 'Twist And Shout' by The Isley Brothers and 'Twistin' The Night Away' by Sam Cooke.

2007
American R&B singer Kelis is arrested in Miami Beach, Florida, after the singer started screaming racial obscenities at two female police officers who were working as prostitutes in an undercover operation on South Beach. Kelis was detained and charged with two misdemeanour charges of disorderly conduct and resisting arrest.

2008
Canadian singer-guitarist, Jeff Healey, dies of cancer. Healey lost his sight to retinoblastoma, a rare cancer of the eyes when he was eight months old, resulting in his eyes being surgically removed. After living cancer-free for 38 years, he developed sarcoma in his legs which spread to his lungs. Healey released over 12 albums, presented a long running radio show and worked with many artists including Stevie Ray Vaughan, Buddy Guy, BB King, ZZ Top, Steve Lukather and Eric Clapton.

2009
Liverpool Hope University launches a Masters degree on The Beatles, popular music and society. The university claims the course, which looks at the studio sound and compositions of The Beatles, is the first of its kind in the UK and "probably the world".

Born on this day:

1944 Jance Garfat, bass (Dr Hook)
1947 Jennifer Warnes, singer

1954 Chris Hughes (Adam & The Ants)
1977 Ronan Keating, vocals (Boyzone)

1966
Neil Young, Bruce Palmer, Stephen Stills and Richie Furay form Buffalo Springfield in Los Angeles.

1973
Slade's 'Cum On Feel The Noize' enters the UK singles chart at No. 1, making Slade the first act to achieve this since The Beatles.

1979
The Bee Gees score their fourth UK No. 1 with 'Tragedy'. Also on this date the Gibb brothers are at the top of the *Billboard* album chart with *Spirits Having Flown*, their second US No. 1 album.

1984
One-hit wonders Nena start a three-week run on top of the UK singles chart with '99 Red Balloons'. Originally sung in their native German, '99 Luftballons' was re-recorded in English and also went on to become a No. 2 hit in the US.

1985
Michael Jackson visits Madame Tussauds waxworks in London to unveil his wax look-alike.

1999
Oasis agree to pay their former drummer Tony McCarroll a one-off sum of £550,000 after he sues the Manchester band for millions in unpaid royalties. McCarroll was sacked from the band in 1995.

2000
Former Bay City Roller Derek Longmuir is released on bail on charges of downloading images of child pornography from the internet and keeping indecent videos in his home.

2003
Ray Jackson, who found fame with Lindisfarne, takes out legal action against Rod Stewart over his 1970s hit song 'Maggie May'. Jackson claims he came up with the worldwide hit's classic mandolin melody and claimed he may have lost at least £1m because he was not credited for the track's distinctive hook. Jackson was paid just £15 for the recording session by Stewart in 1971.

2004
Elton John announces he is planning to marry his long-term partner David Furnish if the new UK Civil Partnership Bill allows it. The couple marry in Windsor on 21 December, 2005.

2005
50 Cent releases *The Massacre*, the follow-up to his platinum debut *Get Rich Or Die Tryin'*. The album sells over one million copies in its first week, going four times platinum in two months. The success of the album gives 50 Cent five Top Five singles in 2005.

2008
Norman Smith, who was the chief engineer on Beatles recording sessions between 1962-65, dies at the age of 85. Nicknamed "Normal Norman" by John Lennon, as an EMI producer he recorded the early Pink Floyd. As Hurricane Smith he had unexpected Top 5 UK hits in 1971 with 'Don't Let It Die' and 'Oh Babe, What Would You Say' the following year.

2009
To celebrate the release of U2's twelfth studio album and their appearance every night for a week on *The Late Show with David Letterman*, New York City Mayor Michael Bloomberg temporarily renames part of 53rd Street in midtown Manhattan, U2 Way.

March 4

Born on this day:

1944 Bobby Womack, soul singer
1948 Chris Squire, bass (The Syn, Yes)
1951 Chris Rea, singer, songwriter, guitarist
1967 Evan Dando, guitar, vocals (The Lemonheads)
1971 Feargal Lawlor, drummer (The Cranberries)

1966
An interview with John Lennon by Maureen Cleave is published in the *London Evening Standard*. Among Lennon's frank answers is the statement: "Christianity will go. It will vanish and shrink. We're more popular then Jesus now... I don't know which will go first, rock 'n' roll or Christianity. Jesus was alright, but his disciples were thick and ordinary. It's them twisting it that ruins it for me." When the remark is taken out of context and reprinted in an American teen magazine, Christian groups in the US are outraged, resulting in some southern states burning Beatles records. Lennon was later forced to apologise.

1967
The Rolling Stones are top of the American singles chart with 'Ruby Tuesday', the group's fourth US No. 1 single. 'Let's Spend The Night Together' was the original A side, but after radio stations ban the song 'Tuesday' became the plug side.

1973
Pink Floyd play the first night on a 19-date North American tour at Dane County Memorial Coliseum, Madison, Wisconsin.

1977
CBS release The Clash's self-titled debut album in the UK. CBS in the U.S. eventually release their own version in 1979, after over 100,000 imported copies of the record make the LP one of the biggest-selling imports of all time.

1979
Randy Jackson of The Jackson 5 is seriously injured in a car crash, breaking both legs and almost dying in the emergency room when a nurse inadvertently injects him with methadone.

1982
Frank Zappa's son Dweezil and his daughter Moon Unit form a band called Fred Zeppelin. Their first single is entitled 'My Mother Is A Space Cadet'.

1986
American songwriter Howard Greenfield dies aged 50 of a brain tumour. Working out of New York's famous Brill Building with Neil Sedaka, Greenfield co-wrote many hits including 'Calendar Girl', 'Breaking Up Is Hard To Do', and 'Crying In The Rain' with Carole King, as well as writing TV themes including *Bewitched*.

1994
Kurt Cobain is rushed to hospital after overdosing in a Rome hotel room during Nirvana's European tour. Cobain had taken 50-60 Rohypnol pills mixed with champagne in a suicide bid; rumours on the internet claim that Cobain is dead.

2001

Village People singer Glenn Hughes, the "biker" character in the disco group, dies aged 50 of lung cancer in New York.

2003
23-year-old Sian Davies is fined £1,000 plus court costs after environmental protection officers raided her flat in Porth, Rhondda, Wales, seizing 15 amplifiers and speakers, plus 135 CDs and cassette tapes. The disc found in her CD player was the Cliff Richard single, 'Peace In Our Time'. A spokesman for the Cliff Richard Organisation said he was delighted to hear of somebody Sian's age owning one of his many recordings but added that Cliff would not want anyone to play his music so that it caused a nuisance.

2007
Take That are at No. 1 on the UK singles chart with 'Shine', their 10th UK chart-topper. The song is featured in several commercials for the relaunched Morrisons supermarkets in the UK and goes on to win Single Of The Year award at the 2008 Brit Awards.

2009
Britney Spears kicks off her first concert tour for five years in New Orleans. The 27-year-old dresses as a ringmaster in the show which features jugglers, acrobats and martial arts dancers.

Born on this day:

1948 Eddy Grant, vocals, guitar (The Equals, solo)

1957 Mark E Smith, vocals (The Fall)

1962 Craig & Charlie Reid (The Proclaimers)

1970 John Frusciante, guitar (Red Hot Chili Peppers)

1982 Russell Leetch, bass guitar (Editors)

March 5

1963
Country singer Patsy Cline is killed in a plane crash at Dyersburg, Virginia, along with The Cowboy Copas and Hawkshaw Hawkins. They were travelling to Nashville to appear at a benefit concert for DJ 'Cactus' Jack Call, who'd died in a car crash. Cline was the first country singer to cross over as a pop artist. Two days later country singer Jack Anglin was killed in a car crash on his way to Cline's funeral.

1965
The Manish Boys release their debut single on Parlophone Records, 'I Pity The Fool', featuring a young David Jones – soon to become David Bowie – on lead vocals.

1971
Led Zeppelin start a 12-date 'Return To The Clubs' tour at the Ulster Hall, Belfast, Northern Ireland as a way of thanking British fans who had supported them from the early days. The band played for their original fees and fans got in for the original admission price.

1973
Michael Jeffrey, the former manager of The Animals and Jimi Hendrix, is one of 68 people killed in a plane crash in Majorca. Jeffery was en route to a court appearance in London related to Hendrix's estate. Some conspiracy theorists believe Jeffrey faked his own death.

1982
Actor, comedian and singer John Belushi dies from an overdose of cocaine and heroin. Belushi was one of the original cast members on US TV's *Saturday Night Live*, played Joliet 'Jake' Blues in *The Blues Brothers* movie and also appeared in the film *Animal House*. His tombstone reads "I may be gone, but rock 'n' roll lives on."

1983
Michael Jackson starts a seven-week run at the top of the US singles chart with 'Billie Jean', his fourth solo US No. 1 and also a chart-topper in the UK. Also on this day Jackson's album *Thriller* went to No. 1 for the first time on the UK album chart, going on to become the biggest selling album of all time with sales over 50 million.

Wham! make their US television debut when they appear on Dick Clark's *American Bandstand*.

1994
Grace Slick is arrested for pointing a shotgun at police at her Tiburon home in California. The singer was later sentenced to 200 hours of community service and three months' worth of Alcoholics Anonymous meetings.

1995
Viv Stanshall, formerly of The Bonzo Dog Doo Dah Band, dies in a fire at his flat in north London.

2000
Former rap artist MC Hammer becomes a preacher at the Jubilee Christian Centre in San Jose. Hammer had been declared bankrupt in 1996 after squandering his $50 million fortune.

2002
The first episode of *The Osbournes* reality show is aired on MTV in America, focusing on the everyday exploits of Ozzy and Sharon Osbourne and two of their children, Jack and Kelly.

2007
Records by Paul Simon and The Rolling Stones are chosen for preservation by the US Library of Congress. The Stones' '(I Can't Get No) Satisfaction' and Simon's *Graceland* album enter the National Recordings Registry, which preserves historic works for future generations.

Other recordings chosen this year include Carl Perkins' 'Blue Suede Shoes', 'Be My Baby' (The Ronettes), 'A Change Is Gonna Come' (Sam Cooke) and the album *The Velvet Underground and Nico*.

2008
Lou Pearlman, the man behind boy bands 'N Sync and The Backstreet Boys, is set to plead guilty to a $300m fraud scheme. The music mogul admits to a Florida court of running scams that defrauded investors and major banks for more than 20 years. The charges carry a maximum of 25 years in prison and a $1m fine.

KING OF POP
MICHAEL JACKSON
THIS IS IT

MICHAELJACKSONLIVE.COM

2009
Michael Jackson personally announces he will perform 10 concerts at London's O2 arena from July 8, 2009. The King of Pop says: "Thank you all. This is it! These will be my final shows in London. And when I say this is it, I mean it, because... I will be performing the songs that my fans want to hear. This is the final curtain call. I will see you in July."

Born on this day:

1944 David Gilmour, guitar, vocals (Pink Floyd)

1944 Mary Wilson, vocals (The Supremes)

1947 Kiki Dee, singer

1970 Betty Boo, singer

1974 Guy Garvey, guitar, vocals (Elbow)

1951
Welsh composer, singer and actor Ivor Novello dies, aged 58. He first became known for the song 'Keep the Home Fires Burning,' which he composed during World War I. The annual British songwriting award is named after him.

1961
UK singing comedian and ukulele player, George Formby, dies aged 57. Formby, who made over 20 films, was made an OBE in 1946.

1970
Awareness Records releases the Charles Manson album *Lie* in the US. Manson was unable to promote the LP due to the fact he was serving a life sentence.

1972
Pink Floyd play the first night of a seven-date Japanese tour at the Tokyo-To Taiikukan.

1973
With Slade at No. 1 in the singles chart with 'Cum On Feel The Noize', Elton John has the chart-topping album with *Don't Shoot Me I'm Only The Piano Player*.

1982
Tight Fit are at No. 1 on the UK singles chart with their version of The Tokens' 1961 hit 'The Lion Sleeps Tonight'. In 2004, a lawsuit brought by the family of the song's writer Solomon Linda against the Disney Corporation claimed that Disney owed $1.6 million in royalties for the use of the song in the film and stage production of *The Lion King*. A settlement was reached for an undisclosed amount in 2006.

1986
Richard Manuel of The Band is found hung from a shower curtain rod in a Florida motel room.

1998
Oasis singer Liam Gallagher appears handcuffed in a Brisbane court, charged with head butting a fan during a gig in Australia. Gallagher is released on bail.

2001
A man who hid for 24 hours in the rafters of a cathedral and secretly filmed the christening of Madonna's baby appears in court. Security staff discovered the man after the ceremony when he made a noise as he climbed down from the rafters.

2004
Diane Richie, the estranged wife of singer Lionel Richie, is in court seeking $300,000 a month in maintenance support. Diane's monthly costs include: $20,000 a year on plastic surgery; $15,000 a month for clothing, shoes and accessories; $5,000 on jewellery; $3,000 on dermatology; $1,000 for laser hair removal and $600 on massages.

David Crosby is charged with criminal possession of a weapon and marijuana after leaving his bag in a New York hotel. The luggage is found by a hotel employee looking for identification who called the authorities. When discovering the luggage missing, Crosby telephoned the hotel to say he would return for it. He was met by police who arrested him.

2005
Stereophonics are at No. 1 on the UK singles chart with 'Dakota', the Welsh band's first No. 1, eight years after their first hit.

2008
A UK charity warns that nine out of ten young people have experienced the first signs of hearing damage after listening to loud music. Experts say prolonged exposure to noise over 85 decibels would harm hearing over time and music played in concerts, bars and clubs was often above this level. The RNID say more people should wear ear plugs to protect their hearing without spoiling their appreciation of music.

Born on this day:

1945 Arthur Lee, guitar, vocals (Love)
1945 Chris White, bass (The Zombies)
1946 Peter Wolf, vocals (The J Geils Band)

1946 Matthew Fisher (Procol Harum)
1952 Ernie Isley (The Isley Brothers)

1962

The Beatles record their first ever radio appearance, at the Playhouse Theatre, Hulme, Manchester, for the BBC radio programme *Teenagers' Turn*. After a rehearsal, The Beatles put on suits for the first time and, along with the other artists appearing, record the show in front of a live audience, some who had travelled from Liverpool.

1967

Working on *Sgt. Pepper's Lonely Hearts Club Band*, The Beatles record additional overdubs for 'Lovely Rita', including harmony vocals, effects, and the percussive sound of comb and paper.

1976

Elton John is immortalised in wax at Madame Tussauds, the first pop music icon to be honoured in this way since The Beatles.

1991

Readers of *Rolling Stone* vote George Michael the best male singer and sexiest male artist.

2001

After a two year high court legal battle, David Balfe, former Teardrop Explodes keyboard player and the man who discovered Blur, wins £250,000 in back royalties accruing after selling his Food Records label to EMI in 1994.

2004

The Smiths' song 'I Know It's Over' tops a poll, 'The Songs That Saved Your Life', held by BBC digital radio station 6 Music. R.E.M.'s 'Everybody Hurts' and Radiohead's 'Fake Plastic Trees' also make the Top 10.

2007

Rhett Hutchence, brother of INXS singer Michael Hutchence, defends his decision to sell some of the late star's belongings online saying he needs money to set up home with his new girlfriend. Items in the auction include lyrics, T-shirts and a fax Michael sent to his then girlfriend Kylie Minogue.

1964
For the first time ever, the UK Top Ten Singles Chart was composed entirely of British acts. Cilla Black holds the No. 1 position with 'Anyone Who Had A Heart'.

1965

During a Rolling Stones gig at The Palace Theatre, Manchester, a female fan falls from the upper circle. Thanks to the crowd below breaking her fall she escapes serious injury with just a few broken teeth.

1966

Tina Turner records her vocal part on the Phil Spector produced 'River Deep, Mountain High'. This classic milestone reaches No. 3 in the UK but only No. 88 on the US chart due to Spector's refusal to pay bribes that would ensure airplay.

1987

The Beastie Boys become the first rap inspired act to have a No. 1 album in the US with their debut, *Licensed To Ill*.

1988

British pedal steel guitar player Gordon Huntley, a member of Matthews Southern Comfort (appearing on their UK No. 1 'Woodstock') and a session player with acts including Elton John, Rod Stewart, The Pretty Things, Cliff Richard and Fairport Convention, dies of cancer.

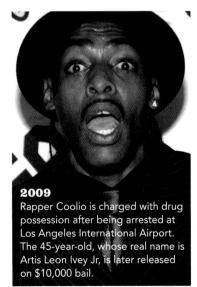

2009
Rapper Coolio is charged with drug possession after being arrested at Los Angeles International Airport. The 45-year-old, whose real name is Artis Leon Ivey Jr, is later released on $10,000 bail.

March 8

Born on this day:

1945 Micky Dolenz, vocals, drums, actor (The Monkees)
1947 Mike Allsup, guitar (Three Dog Night)
1958 Gary Numan, singer (Tubeway Army, solo)
1976 Gareth Coombes, vocals, guitar (Supergrass)
1979 Tom Chaplin, vocals (Keane)

1965
As David Jones, David Bowie appears with The Manish Boys on TV programme *Gadzooks! It's All Happening,* performing their current single 'I Pity The Fool'.

1968
Albert King, Janis Joplin and Tim Buckley appear at the reopened Village Theater in New York, now known as the Fillmore East, promoted by Bill Graham.

1969
The Small Faces split up after four years when singer Steve Marriott announces he is leaving the band. Ronnie Lane, Ian McLagan and Kenney Jones eventually link up with Ron Wood and Rod Stewart to form The Faces.

1973
Paul McCartney is fined £100 for growing cannabis at his farm in Campbeltown, Scotland. McCartney claims some fans sent him the seeds in the mail and that he planted them not knowing what they would grow.

1974
Bad Company, made up of former members from Free (Paul Rodgers, Simon Kirke), Mott The Hoople (Mick Ralphs) and King Crimson (Boz Burrell), kick off their first UK tour at Newcastle City Hall.

1986
Diana Ross is top of the UK singles chart with 'Chain Reaction', written and produced by The Bee Gees who also sang backing vocals. The single becomes her first British No. 1 since 'I'm Still Waiting' in 1971.

1990
In *Rolling Stone,* Cher wins the worst dressed female and worst video awards for 'If I Could Turn Back Time', while Donny Osmond wins the dubious accolade of most unwelcome comeback.

2001
It's reported that US manufacturers Art Asylum plan to ship 100,000 Eminem dolls to UK shops. The lifelike figure has the rapper's tattoos recreated in detail, including the words Cut Here on its neck.

2003
Singer, actor and businessman Adam Faith dies aged 62 in North Staffordshire Hospital of a heart attack.

2008
China is set to impose stricter rules on foreign pop stars after Bjork causes controversy by shouting "Tibet, Tibet" at a Shanghai concert following a powerful performance of her song 'Declare Independence'. Tibetan independence was considered taboo in China, which had ruled the territory since 1951. A spokesperson from the culture ministry said Bjork would be banned from performing in China if there was a repeat performance.

2009
A blue plaque in honour of Keith Moon is unveiled on the site of the Marquee Club in Soho, London, where, in 1964, The Who played a residency. Fans on scooters turn up to pay tribute to the legendary drummer who was 32 when he died of an accidental overdose in 1978. The blue plaque, which means the site is of historic importance, was awarded by the Heritage Foundation.

Born on this day:

1948 Chris Thompson, vocals (Manfred Mann's Earth Band)

1949 Jimmy Fadden (The Nitty Gritty Dirt Band)

1951 Frank Rodriguez (? & The Mysterians)

1958 Martin Fry, vocals (ABC)

1968 Robert Sledge, drums (Ben Folds Five)

1968
Bob Dylan starts a ten-week run at No. 1 on the UK chart with his ninth album, *John Wesley Harding*.

1973
Black Sabbath kick off an eight-date sold out UK tour at Green's Playhouse, Glasgow.

1975
Actor Telly Savalas, famous for his role as US TV cop *Kojak*, is at No. 1 on the UK singles chart with his version of the David Gates song 'If'.

1977
The Jacksons' CBS show airs for the last time on US TV finishing at the bottom of the ratings.

1981
Robert Plant plays a secret gig at Keele University, England with his new band The Honeydrippers.

1985
Dead Or Alive are at No. 1 on the UK singles chart with 'You Spin Me Round (Like A Record)', the first chart-topper for the production team of Stock, Aitken & Waterman who went on to produce over 100 UK Top 40 hits.

1991
'Should I Stay Or Should I Go' gives The Clash their only UK No. 1 single after the track is used for a Levi's TV advertisement. The track was first released in 1982 on the band's *Combat Rock* album.

1996
Oasis guitarist Noel Gallagher walks off stage during a gig at the Vernon Valley Gorge ski resort in New Jersey because his hands are too cold to play.

Take That score their eighth and last UK No. 1 (until re-forming in 2006) with their version of The Bee Gees'

1966
The Beach Boys start recording 'God Only Knows' (off *Pet Sounds*), which becomes a UK No. 2 when released as a single with 'Wouldn't It Be Nice'.

1967
The Small Faces, Family and The Strollers appear on a bill at the Skyline Ballroom, Hull.

'How Deep Is Your Love', from the film *Saturday Night Fever*.

1997
Notorious BIG is gunned down and killed as he leaves a party at the Petersen Automotive Museum, Los Angeles. Born Christopher Wallace, the 24-year-old rapper is pronounced dead on arrival at Cedars Sinai Hospital.

2004
Tom Jones is banned from wearing tight leather pants by his son and manager Mark Jones, who felt it was time for his father to "dress his age", as he was in danger of becoming a laughing stock at 63.

2007
Brad Delp, lead singer of US rock band Boston, commits suicide by carbon monoxide poisoning at his home in the New Hampshire town of Atkinson. Boston had a 1976 US No. 5 single with 'More Than A Feeling' and the US No. 1 single, 'Amanda', 10 years later.

2008
Duffy starts a five-week run at No. 1 on the UK album charts with *Rockferry*, the Welsh singer's debut album.

Born on this day:

1940 Dean Torrence (Jan & Dean)
1947 Tom Scholz, guitar, keyboards (Boston)
1964 Neneh Cherry, singer, songwriter
1966 Dave Krusen, drummer (Pearl Jam)

1971 Timothy Z. Mosley (Timbaland), R&B producer
1973 John Charles LeCompt, guitar (Evanescence)

1960

The UK trade paper *Record Retailer* publishes the first-ever EP (Extended Player) and LP charts. The top EP is *Expresso Bongo* by Cliff Richard & The Shadows and the No. 1 album is *The Explosive Freddy Cannon*.

1973

Pink Floyd's *The Dark Side Of The Moon* is released in America, spending 740 weeks on the album chart over a 14-year period.

1977

At 7am, on a trestle table set up outside Buckingham Palace, The Sex Pistols sign to A&M Records. The contract lasts for all of six days.

1979

Gloria Gaynor starts a three week run at No. 1 on the US singles chart with 'I Will Survive', also a chart-topper in the UK. It was originally released as the B-side to a song first recorded by The Righteous Brothers called 'Substitute'.

1988

Andy Gibb, younger brother of The Bee Gees, dies in hospital, five days after his 30th birthday. His death from myocarditis (inflammation of the heart) resulted from a long battle with cocaine addiction. Gibb was the first male solo artist to chart three consecutive U.S No. 1s with 'I Just Want To Be Your Everything', '(Love Is) Thicker Than Water' and 'Shadow Dancing'.

1995

Former Stone Roses manager Gareth Evans' £10 million lawsuit with the band over alleged wrongful dismissal is settled out of court for an undisclosed sum.

1996
Alanis Morissette wins Best Album and Best Rock Album (for *Jagged Little Pill*), Best Female Singer, Best Songwriter and Best Single at the 25th Juno Awards in Hamilton, Canada.

2000

Chrissie Hynde is arrested for leading an animal rights protest in the Gap store in Manhattan, accusing the clothing store of using leather from cows slaughtered "illegally and cruelly".

2001

TV's *Pop Idol* winner Will Young reveals in an exclusive *News Of The World* interview that he is gay, saying "It's no big deal, its just part of who I am."

2003

Johnny Cash is admitted to Baptist Hospital in Nashville, Tennessee to undergo treatment for pneumonia.

2005

Attending Santa Moria court for his child abuse trial, Michael Jackson arrives in court an hour late dressed in pyjamas after being treated for a back injury.

A survey carried out by Music Choice finds that 'Angels' by Robbie Williams is the song Britons would most like played at their funeral. Frank Sinatra's 'My Way' came second and Monty Python's 'Always Look On The Bright Side Of Life' was voted third.

2009

Tickets for a one-off Paul McCartney gig in Las Vegas sell out seven seconds after going on sale. The former Beatle was booked to perform at the opening of the New Joint at the Hard Rock Hotel and Casino on 19 April in front of 4,000 fans.

Born on this day:

1961 Bruce Watson, guitar (Big Country)
1964 Vinnie Paul, drummer, producer (Pantera, Damageplan)
1968 Lisa Loeb, US singer
1981 LeToya Nicole Luckett, singer (Destiny's Child, solo)

1968

The Otis Redding single '(Sittin' On) The Dock Of The Bay' goes gold in the US three months after the singer was killed in a plane crash.

1970

Winners at this year's Grammy Awards include Joe South for Song Of The Year with 'Games People Play', Crosby Stills & Nash win Best New Artist, and The 5th Dimension have Record Of The Year with 'Aquarius'/'Let The Sun Shine In'.

1971

Jim Morrison arrives in Paris, booking into the Hotel George V. The following week he moved into an apartment at 17 Rue Beautreillis where he lived until his death on 3 July.

1972

Harry Nilsson is at No. 1 on the UK singles chart with his version of the Pete Ham-Tom Evans composition, 'Without You'. First recorded by Badfinger in 1970, the song was also a No. 1 for Mariah Carey in 1994.

1978

French singer Claude Francois is electrocuted changing a light bulb while standing in his bathtub.

1983

Joni Mitchell plays the first night of a 13-date Australian and New Zealand tour at the Capitol Theatre, Sydney.

1989

Debbie Gibson starts a five-week run at No. 1 on the US album chart with *Electric Youth.*

1993

Oasis record their first demos at The Real People's studio in Liverpool, including 'Rock 'n' Roll Star', 'Columbia' and 'Fade Away'.

1995

Van Halen kick off their 131-date 'Balance World Tour' (dubbed the 'Ambulance Tour' by Eddie Van Halen due to his hip surgery and brother, drummer Alex Van Halen wearing a neck brace) at the Pensacola Civic Center, Florida.

1996

Pulp singer Jarvis Cocker walks free from Kensington police station after police fail to charge him with any criminal offence following his 'stage invasion' during Michael Jackson's performance at the Brit Awards on 19 February.

2005

The front door of Ozzy Osbourne's childhood home in Lodge Road, Aston, Birmingham goes up for auction on eBay because the current owner is fed up with fans defacing it. Ali Mubarrat was giving the proceeds to charity.

2006

The soundtrack to The Disney Channel movie, *High School Musical,* is at No. 1 on the US album chart. The album goes on to break all records for a soundtrack, selling over seven million copies worldwide.

2008

Madonna is inducted into the US Rock and Roll Hall of Fame by singer Justin Timberlake at a star-studded ceremony at the Waldorf Astoria Hotel, New York. The 49-year-old thanks her detractors in her acceptance speech, including those "who said I couldn't sing, that I was a one hit wonder."

1978

The debut single from Kate Bush, 'Wuthering Heights', a song inspired by a film of Emily Bronte's novel, starts a four-week run atop the UK singles chart. EMI had originally chosen another track, 'James And The Cold Gun' as the lead-off single from the album *The Kick Inside* but Bush was determined that 'Wuthering Heights' would be the first release.

Born on this day:

1946 Liza Minnelli, singer, actress, dancer
1948 James Taylor, US singer-songwriter
1949 Mike Gibbins, drums (Badfinger)
1957 Marlon Jackson (The Jackson Five)

1969 Graham Coxon, guitar (Blur)
1977 Ben Kenny, bassist (Incubus)
1979 Pete Doherty, guitar, vocals (The Libertines, Babyshambles)

1968
The Rolling Stones start recording their next single 'Jumpin' Jack Flash' with producer Jimmy Miller at Olympic Studios in London.

1969
Paul McCartney marries Linda Eastman at Marylebone Register Office, London. They then hold a reception lunch at The Ritz Hotel. Paul went to the recording studio in the evening to work. George Harrison and his wife Patti are arrested on the same day and charged with possession of marijuana.

1974
John Lennon makes headlines after an incident at the Troubadour Club, Los Angeles. Out on a drinking binge with Harry Nilsson, Lennon hurled insults at the performing Smothers Brothers before being forcibly removed.

1977
Sid Vicious and cronies pick a fight with Bob Harris, presenter of BBC-2's *The Old Grey Whistle Test*, at London's

Speakeasy Club, resulting in one of the TV show's engineers needing 14 stitches to his head. Two days later Harris' solicitors contact Derek Green at A&M, The Sex Pistols' record label.

Green discusses the matter with the company's two founders, Herb Alpert and Jerry Moss, and the decision is made to cancel the Pistols' contract and halt production of their first single for the label, 'God Save The Queen'.

1981
Bow Wow Wow are forced to cancel the first dates of a UK tour after Greater London Council decide that

15-year-old singer Annabella Lwin would be guilty of truancy.

1983
U2 score their first UK No. 1 album with *War*, which spends a total of 147 weeks on the chart. The album features the singles 'New Year's Day' and 'Two Hearts Beat As One'.

1988
Rick Astley starts a two-week run at No. 1 on the US singles chart with 'Never Gonna Give You Up', also a chart-topper in the UK.

1995
The Spin Doctors play a gig at singer Chris Barron's old school in Princeton, New Jersey and raise $10,000 towards a trip to France and the UK for the school choir.

2001
Judy Garland's 'Over The Rainbow' is voted Song Of The Century in a poll published in America. Musicians, critics and fans compile the list by the RIAA. The highest placed UK act is The Rolling Stones '(I Can't Get No) Satisfaction' in 16th place, with The Beatles' 'I Want To Hold Your Hand' at 28.

2009
Hundreds of fans queue at the O2 Arena in London as Michael Jackson tickets go on sale to the public. The 50-year-old pop veteran had confirmed he would be playing a 50-date residency at the venue, beginning on 8 July. Some 360,000 pre-sale tickets had already sold. Organisers say the 'This Is It' tour had become the fastest-selling in history, with 33 seats sold each minute. Prices ranged from £170 to £10,000, but tickets bought directly from the singer's website cost up to £75. Jackson says this will be the last time he will perform in the UK.

March 13

1964
Billboard report that sales of Beatles records currently account for 60% of the US singles market and the album *Meet The Beatles* has reached a record 3.5 million copies sold.

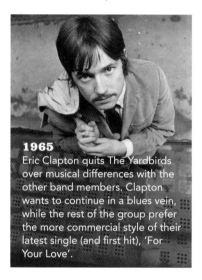

1965
Eric Clapton quits The Yardbirds over musical differences with the other band members. Clapton wants to continue in a blues vein, while the rest of the group prefer the more commercial style of their latest single (and first hit), 'For Your Love'.

1971
Brewer & Shipley enter the US singles chart with 'One Toke Over The Line'. The song, featuring The Grateful Dead's Jerry Garcia on steel guitar, peaks at No. 10 despite being banned by radio stations for its drug references. Brewer & Shipley maintain that the word toke meant token as in ticket, hence the line "waitin' downtown at the railway station, one toke over the line."

1976
The Four Seasons start a three-week run atop the *Billboard* singles chart with 'December 1963 (Oh What A Night)', the group's fifth US No. 1 and also their only UK No. 1.

1977
Iggy Pop (with David Bowie in a low key role as keyboard player) and band kick off a North American tour at Le Plateau Theatre, Montreal, Canada with Blondie as the opening act.

1985
Bob Geldof and Midge Ure receive the Best Selling A-side award for 'Do They Know It's Christmas' at the 30th Ivor Novello Awards.

1987
Bob Seger & The Silver Bullet Band receive a star on the Hollywood Walk of Fame.

1993
This week's edition of Radio One's UK Top 40 Chart Show is in chaos after Gallup, who compiled the chart, got 20 of the 40 entries wrong.

1998
English reggae and ska artist Judge Dread (a.k.a. Alex Hughes) dies after collapsing as he walks off stage in Canterbury, England. Dread achieved 10 UK hit singles during the 70s, was the first white recording artist to have a reggae hit in Jamaica and had the most radio-banned songs of all time.

1999
Cher starts a four-week run at No. 1 on the US singles chart with 'Believe', making her the oldest woman to top the *Billboard* Hot 100 at the age of 53.

2006
The Sex Pistols refuse to attend their own induction into the Rock and Roll Hall of Fame in New York. The Pistols post a handwritten note on their official website, calling the institution "urine in wine", adding, "We're not your monkeys, we're not coming. You're not paying attention."

2008
Michael Jackson refinances his Neverland ranch after being told that if he failed to pay $25m he owed on the California property, it would be auctioned within a week. Jackson bought Neverland in 1987 intending to create a fantasy land for children, naming it after an island in the story *Peter Pan*, where children never grow up.

Born on this day:

1933 Quincy Jones, producer
1945 Walter Parazaider, sax (Chicago)
1946 Jim Pons, bass guitar (The Leaves, The Turtles)
1983 Jordan Taylor Hanson (Hanson)

1955
CBS talent scout Arthur Godfrey turns down the chance to sign Elvis Presley. Instead, at the same audition, he signs Pat Boone.

1963
Cliff Richard & The Shadows are at No. 1 on the UK singles chart with 'Summer Holiday'. Taken from the film of the same name, it becomes Cliff's seventh UK No. 1.

1968
The promotional film for The Beatles' 'Lady Madonna' is broadcast in B&W on BBC's *Top Of The Pops*. The film was shot while the group was recording the track 'Hey Bulldog' in Studio 2, EMI Studios.

1972
Soul singer Linda Jones, who had a 1967 US No. 21 single with 'Hypnotized', dies aged 26 in New York after collapsing into a diabetic coma following a performance at Harlem's Apollo Theater.

1983
Jon Bon Jovi, Richie Sambora and Alec John Such form Bon Jovi.

1985
Dead Or Alive are taken off the UK music television show *The Tube* after admitting they were incapable of playing live. The group had scored a 1985 UK No. 1 with 'You Spin Me Round (Like A Record)'.

1990
Flea and Chad Smith from The Red Hot Chili Peppers are arrested for sexually harassing a woman on Daytona Beach, Florida and each fined $1,000.

1995
With the release of *Me Against The World* Tupac Shakur becomes the first male solo artist to have a No. 1 album on the *Billboard* chart while in prison.

2001
Peter Blake, who designed The Beatles' classic *Sgt. Pepper* album cover, sues the group's record company EMI for more money. Blake was given a one-off payment of £200 in 1967, but was now "cheesed off" that the company had not offered to pay more money.

2006
U2 top *Rolling Stone*'s annual list of 2005's biggest money earners with $154.2m. The Rolling Stones are second with $92.5m and The Eagles third – $63.2m, Paul McCartney fourth – $56m and Elton John fifth – $48.9m.

2008
Peter MacBeth, a member of The Foundations who had UK Top 5 hits with 'Baby, Now That I've Found You' (1967) and 'Build Me Up Buttercup' (1968), is jailed for child sex offences. MacBeth sexually assaulted a young girl on four occasions over the course of six years and downloaded child porn from the internet. Doctors said the 71-year-old cancer sufferer, who was unable to speak due to a tracheotomy, had between three and five years to live.

Born on this day:

1932 Arif Mardin, producer-arranger
1941 Mike Love, vocals (The Beach Boys)
1944 Sly Stone, vocals, guitar (Sly & The Family Stone)

1947 Ry Cooder, guitarist
1962 Terence Trent D'arby, singer
1975 Will.i.am, singer (Black Eyed Peas)

March 15

1955
Elvis Presley signs a management contract with 'Colonel' Tom Parker, who had previously managed country stars Eddy Arnold and Hank Snow, and also the Great Parker Pony Circus with one of the acts being a troupe of dancing chickens.

1964
The Rolling Stones play the Invicta Ballroom in Chatham, Kent.

1969
Tommy Roe starts a four-week run at No. 1 on the US singles chart with 'Dizzy', also a chart-topper in the UK.

1972
DJ Robert W. Morgan jokingly plays Donny Osmond's 'Puppy Love' for 90 minutes on station KHJ in Los Angeles. LAPD mistakenly raid the station studios after receiving numerous calls from listeners but the confused officers leave without making any arrests.

1973
In the US, Roberta Flack is at No. 1 on the *Billboard* singles chart with 'Killing Me Softly With His Song' while Elton John has the No. 1 album with *Don't Shoot Me I'm Only The Piano Player*.

1975

Led Zeppelin top the UK chart with their double album *Physical Graffiti*, the first LP on the band's own Swan Song label. The album spends six weeks at No. 1 on the US chart.

1977
Pink Floyd play the first of six sold-out nights at the Empire Pool, Wembley, London.

1986
The Bangles are at No. 2 on the UK singles chart with 'Manic Monday', a song written by Prince under the pseudonym Christopher. It also makes No. 2 in America, held off the top spot by Prince's own 'Kiss'.

1989
The Rolling Stones sign a $70 million contract to play 50 North American dates – the largest contract in rock history.

1997
The Spice Girls top the UK singles chart with 'Mama', making them the first ever act to have their first four singles reach No. 1 in Britain.

2000
Mick Jagger is ordered to increase his child support payments to Brazilian model Luciana Morad from $5,500 a month to $10,000. Jagger is asked to confirm that he is the father of her child by the court, while Ms Morad is seeking a $10 million settlement. Morad tells the court her monthly expenses: $3,500 for a nanny; $2,500 –3,000 for food and $3,350 to rent her place on New York's Upper West Side.

2002
Yoko Ono unveils a seven-foot bronze statue of John Lennon overlooking the check-in hall of Liverpool John Lennon Airport. The modern re-branding of the airport features a sketch of Lennon's face with the words 'Above Us Only Skies'.

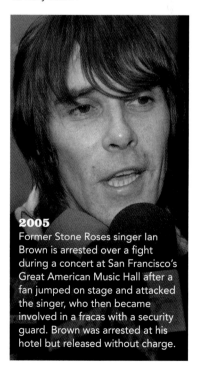

2005
Former Stone Roses singer Ian Brown is arrested over a fight during a concert at San Francisco's Great American Music Hall after a fan jumped on stage and attacked the singer, who then became involved in a fracas with a security guard. Brown was arrested at his hotel but released without charge.

March 16

Born on this day:

1942 Jerry Jeff Walker, US singer, songwriter
1948 Michael Bruce, guitar (Alice Cooper)
1954 Jimmy Nail, UK actor, singer

1954 Nancy Wilson, vocals (Heart)
1959 Flavor Flav (Public Enemy)
1972 Andrew Dunlop, guitar (Travis)
1979 Leena Peisa, keyboards (Lordi)

1959

Doo-wop group The Platters score their only UK and US No. 1 with 'Smoke Gets In Your Eyes'.

1964
The Beatles set a new record for advance sales in the U.S. with 2,100,000 copies of their latest single, 'Can't Buy Me Love'.

1965

The Rolling Stones are at No. 1 on the UK singles chart with 'The Last Time', the group's third UK No. 1 and first A-side for songwriters Mick Jagger and Keith Richards.

1969

Fleetwood Mac, The Move, Amen Corner, Peter Sarstedt, The Tymes, Harmony Grass and Geno Washington all appear at 'Pop World '69' at London's Wembley Empire Pool.

1970

Motown singer Tammi Terrell dies of a brain tumour at the age of 24. Initially Terrell recorded solo but from 1967 onwards she recorded a series of duets with Marvin Gaye. She had collapsed onstage into Gaye's arms on October 14, 1967 during a concert in

Hampton, Virginia. Marvin reacted to her death by taking a four-year hiatus from concert performance and went into self-isolation.

1971

Winners at this year's Grammy Awards include Simon & Garfunkel (Record Of The Year, Song Of The Year and Album Of The Year for *Bridge Over Troubled Water*) and The Carpenters (Best New Act and Best Vocal Performance).

1972

John Lennon lodges an appeal with the US INS office in New York, after he is served with deportation orders arising from a 1968 cannabis possession conviction.

1989

Bez from Happy Mondays is arrested at Manchester Airport moments before boarding a flight to Belfast for a gig, charged with breaking bail conditions set from a previous arrest.

1991

Seven members of country singer Reba McEntire's band and her road manager are among 10 people killed when their private jet crashes in California just north of the Mexican border. McEntire, who had given a private concert in San Diego for IBM employees the night before, was not on the plane.

1992

During a Metallica gig at Orlando Arena fans dangle an usher by his ankles from a balcony as trouble breaks out at the concert. The band is charged $38,000 for repairs and cleaning after the audience trash the building.

2005

Billy Joel checks into a rehabilitation centre for alcohol abuse. A statement from the 55-year-old singer's spokesperson puts his latest problems down to "a recent bout of severe gastrointestinal distress".

Born on this day:

1919 Nat King Cole, singer
1944 John Sebastian, vocals, guitar, harmonica (The Lovin' Spoonful)
1951 Scott Gorham, guitar (Thin Lizzy)
1962 Clare Grogan, vocals (Altered Images)
1967 Billy Corgan, vocals, guitar (Smashing Pumpkins)
1973 Caroline Corr, drums, vocals (The Corrs)
1975 Justin Hawkins, vocals (The Darkness)

March 17

1957

Elvis Presley buys the Graceland mansion in Memphis from Mrs. Ruth Brown-Moore for $102,500. The 23-room, 10,000 square foot home on 13.8 acres of land is expanded to 17,552 square feet of living space before Presley moved in a few weeks later. The original building had at one time been a place of worship, used by the Graceland Christian Church, and was named after the builder's daughter, Grace Toof.

1966

The Walker Brothers score their second UK No. 1 with 'The Sun Ain't Gonna Shine Anymore'.

1967

Otis Redding, Eddie Floyd, Carla Thomas, Sam & Dave and Booker T & The MG's appear at London's Finsbury Park Astoria on the first night of a 17-date UK tour.

1968

The Bee Gees make their US television debut when they appear on *The Ed Sullivan Show*.

1973

Dr Hook's single 'On The Cover Of *Rolling Stone*' peaks at No. 6 on the US chart but is banned in the UK by the BBC due to rules about product placement.

1976

The Heartbreakers, featuring ex-New York Dolls members, guitarist Johnny Thunders and drummer Jerry Nolan, appear at CBGBs, New York.

1978

U2 win £500 and a chance to audition for CBS Ireland in a Dublin talent contest. The Limerick Civic Week Pop '78 Competition was sponsored by *The Evening Express* and Guinness Harp Lager.

1982

Samuel George Jr., lead singer of US group The Capitols, who had a US No. 7 single with 'Cool Jerk', is killed aged 39 after being stabbed during a family argument.

1988

During his 137-date 'Faith World Tour', George Michael plays the first of four sold-out nights at the Sydney Entertainment Centre.

1997

US singer Jermaine Stewart, who had a 1986 UK No. 2 with 'We Don't Have To Take Our Clothes Off' and also worked with Shalamar, The Temptations and Boy George, dies of cancer.

2004

The Kinks' singer and songwriter Ray Davies receives his CBE medal from the Queen at Buckingham Palace for services to the music industry.

2006

The Smiths, who split acrimoniously in 1987, turn down a $5m offer to reform for this year's Coachella US festival.

2008

Ola Brunkert, a 62-year-old Swedish musician who had played on every Abba album and had toured with the group, is found dead with his throat cut after an accident at his home in Majorca, Spain.

March 18

Born on this day:

1938 Charlie Pride, US country singer	**1959** Irene Cara, US singer, actress
1941 Wilson Pickett, US soul singer	**1963** Vanessa Williams, US singer
1950 John Hartman, drums (The Doobie Brothers)	**1979** Adam Levine, guitar, vocals (Maroon 5)

1965

Three of The Rolling Stones, Mick Jagger, Brian Jones and Bill Wyman, are caught urinating against a garage wall in Romford, Essex, after playing the final shows on a UK tour. On July 22 they are each fined £5 for insulting behaviour.

John Lennon gives his friend and ex-Quarryman Pete Shotton £20,000 to open a supermarket at Hayling Island in Hampshire. Lennon, George Harrison and Shotton become joint directors of Hayling Supermarkets Ltd.

1967
At the company's headquarters in Manchester Square, London, Pink Floyd sign to EMI Records.

1972

Neil Young starts a three-week run at No. 1 on the *Billboard* singles chart with 'Heart Of Gold'. Young's only US Top 20 hit as a solo artist reaches No. 10 on the UK chart.

1974

Bruce Springsteen & The E Street Band play the first of eight shows over four nights at Gertie's in Dallas, Texas.

1977

The Clash release their debut single 'White Riot' which peaks at No. 38 on the UK charts.

1982

Driving home from a basketball game in Philadelphia, soul singer Teddy Pendergrass crashes his Rolls Royce and severely injures his spinal cord.

1989

A California radio station arranges to have all of its Cat Stevens records destroyed by steamroller in protest at the singer's support of Ayatollah Khomeni.

1991

U2 pay a fine of £500 on behalf of the Irish Family Planning Association which is found guilty of illegally selling condoms at Dublin's Virgin Megastore.

2001

American singer, guitarist, and songwriter John Phillips, formerly of The Mamas & The Papas, dies aged 65 of heart failure.

Tragedy strikes at an in-store appearance by British boy band A1 in the Indonesian capital of Jakarta after fans stampede. Four girls are killed and two others seriously injured.

2004

Courtney Love exposes her breasts during a TV appearance on David Letterman's talk show. The singer who had her back to the audience flashed at the presenter while singing the song 'Danny Boy'. After the show, Love went on to perform a surprise gig at the Plaid nightclub in Manhattan where she is alleged to have injured a man by throwing a microphone stand into the crowd. Love is charged with assault and reckless endangerment.

2008

Heather Mills' evidence in her divorce case against Sir Paul McCartney is branded "inconsistent", "inaccurate" and "less than candid" by High Court judge Mr. Justice Bennett. Mills is awarded £24.3m, £3.2m per year for herself and the couple's daughter Beatrice, £8m for a home in London and £3m to purchase a home in New York.

The judge found the total value of Sir Paul's assets to be about £400m. Ms. Mills had sought £125m and was offered £15.8m. The full ruling was published a day after Mills was told she could not appeal against its publication.

Born on this day:

1946 Paul Atkinson, guitar (The Zombies)
1946 Ruth Pointer, vocals (The Pointer Sisters)
1952 Derek Longmuir, drums (Bay City Rollers)

1953 Ricky Wilson, guitar (The B-52's)
1959 Terry Hall, vocals (The Specials)

March 19

1958

Big Records release 'Our Song' by a teenage duo from Queens, New York, Tom and Jerry. The duo will become famous in the 60s under their real names, Paul Simon and Art Garfunkel.

1965

Tailor And Cutter magazine runs an article asking The Rolling Stones to start wearing ties. The current fashion did not include wearing ties with shirts and many tie-makers were facing financial disaster. Mick Jagger said of the appeal, "The trouble with a tie is that it could dangle in the soup. It is also something extra on to which a fan can hang when you are trying to get in and out of a theatre."

1974

Jefferson Airplane re-name themselves Jefferson Starship. The new line-up includes Paul Kantner, Grace Slick, David Freiberg, Johnny Barbata, Peter Kaukonen, Cragi Chaquico and Papa John Creach.

1976

After a long history of drug abuse, Paul Kossoff, guitarist with Free and Back Street Crawler, dies aged 25 of heart failure during a flight from Los Angeles to New York.

1982

Ozzy Osbourne's rhythm guitarist and former Quiet Riot member Randy Rhoads is killed in a plane crash. After driving for much of the night, the band had stopped near a small airstrip. The tour bus driver, Andrew Aycock, talked the band's keyboardist, Don Airey, into taking a test flight in a '55 Beechcraft Bonanza. Then Aycock took Rhoads and Rachel Youngblood on another flight and attempts were made to "buzz" the tour bus. The left wing clipped the vehicle, which sent the plane spiraling into a nearby house and bursting into flames. All three bodies were burned beyond recognition and identified by dental records.

1996

The second volume of *The Beatles Anthology* is released. The album features 'Real Love', the second track to be released where the surviving members overdubbed onto an old piano demo recording by John Lennon. The song, first recorded by Lennon in 1977 on a domestic tape recorder at home, originated as part of an unfinished stage play that he and Yoko One were working on at the time entitled *The Ballad Of John And Yoko*.

2001

Former Spice Girl Geri Halliwell's London home is broken into. The intruders scrawl obscene notes on the walls, steal the singer's computer and hi-fi and throw milk and Ribena fruit drink at the walls. They also steal a necklace that used to belong to actress Liz Taylor.

2005

50 Cent becomes the first solo artist to have three singles in the US Top 5; 'Candy Shop' is at No. 1 with 'How We Do' by The Game (a member of his G-Unit group) at No. 4 and 'Disco Inferno' at No. 5.

2006

Shakira is set to become the first pop star to release a single only in the form of a mobile download. The singer's forthcoming release 'Hips Don't Lie' would not be issued in the US as a CD or as a download via the internet but would be available to phone users connected to Verizon.

2007

US soul singer Luther Ingram, who scored a 1972 US No. 2 hit '(If Loving You Is Wrong) I Don't Want to Be Right' and wrote The Staple Singers' hit 'Respect Yourself', dies aged 69 from a heart attack.

March 20

Born on this day:

1951 Carl Palmer, drummer (Crazy World Of Arthur Brown, Atomic Rooster, ELP)

1953 Poison Ivy Rorschach (Kristy Wallace), guitar (The Cramps)

1961 Slim Jim Phantom, drums (The Stray Cats)

1972 Shelly Poole, singer, songwriter (Alisha's Attic)

1972 Alex Kapranos, guitar, vocals (Franz Ferdinand)

1976 Chester Bennington, vocals (Linkin Park)

1960

Elvis Presley starts his first recordings since being discharged from the US Army. A 12-hour session in Nashville produces his next No. 1, 'Stuck On You'. Scotty Moore and Bill Black, who had quit Presley's touring band in 1957, are in the studio with him for the last time.

1965

The first of a twice-nightly UK Tamla Motown package tour kicks off at north London's Finsbury Park Astoria featuring Stevie Wonder, The Miracles, Martha & The Vandellas, The Supremes and The Temptations.

1969

John Lennon marries Yoko Ono at the British Consulate Office in Gibraltar. They spend their honeymoon in Amsterdam campaigning for peace via a week-long 'Bed-In'. Lennon details this period in The Beatles' single, 'The Ballad Of John And Yoko', recorded by just Lennon and Paul McCartney on April 14, 1969.

1971

At their own expense The Rolling Stones place full page advertisements in all the UK music papers disclaiming any connection with the compilation album *Stone Age*, issued by their old record company Decca, saying "in our opinion the content is below the standard we try to keep".

1977

Lou Reed is banned from appearing at the London Palladium because of his supposed punk image.

1982

Joan Jett & The Blackhearts start a seven week run at No. 1 on the US singles chart with 'I Love Rock 'n' Roll'; No. 4 in the UK. The song had previously been a B-side by 70s band, Arrows.

1990

Gloria Estefan's tour bus is rammed by a tractor-trailer on the way to a concert. Emilio Estefan and their son Nayib are injured, while Gloria suffers a serious back injury which requires an operation two days later.

1991

Eric Clapton's four-year-old son, Conor, falls to his death from the 53rd storey of a New York City apartment after a housekeeper who was cleaning the room left a window open. The boy was in the custody of his mother, Italian actress Lori Del Santo, and the pair were visiting a friend's apartment. Clapton was staying in a nearby hotel after taking his son to the circus the previous evening. The tragedy inspired his song 'Tears In Heaven'.

1997

UK police are investigating singer Mark Morrison after they discover he had sent a friend to carry out his community service, a sentence he was given after being involved in a fight.

2001

Jon, Paul and Bradley from pop group S Club 7 are apprehended by police as they walk through Covent Garden, London, openly smoking a marijuana joint. They are taken to Charing Cross police station and held for four hours.

2002

The Daily Mail carries a report that Robbie Williams has become a priest. He was ordained via the Internet by the non-denominational Universal Ministries and officiated the wedding of Billy Morrison from rock band The Cult and Jennifer Holliday.

Born on this day:

1943 Vivian Stanshall, vocals (Bonzo Dog Doo Dah Band)

1946 Ray Dorset, vocals, guitar (Mungo Jerry)

1950 Roger Hodgson, guitar (Supertramp)

1967 Jonas Berggren (Ace Of Base)

1967 Keith Palmer, singer (The Prodigy)

1980 Deryck 'Bizzy D' Whibley (Sum 41)

March 21

1956

Elvis Presley appears at the 4,000 seated YMCA Gymnasium in Lexington, North Carolina. Also on the bill are Mother Maybelle & The Carter Sisters, featuring June Carter, Rod Brasfield, Hal and Ginger. Tickets cost $1 for general admission and $1.50 for reserved seats.

1972

The Grateful Dead play the first of seven nights at the Academy of Music in New York City.

1973

The BBC ban all teenybopper acts from appearing in person on *Top Of The Pops* after a riot following a David Cassidy performance.

1980

Hugh Cornwell of The Stranglers is sent to Pentonville Prison after losing his appeal against a drugs conviction.

1987

U2 score their third UK No. 1 album (also a US No. 1) with *The Joshua Tree*, featuring the singles 'Where The Streets Have No Name' and 'I Still Haven't Found What I'm Looking For'. It becomes the fastest selling album in UK history and the first to sell over a million CDs, spending a total of 156 weeks on the UK chart.

1991

Leo Fender, the inventor of the Telecaster and Stratocaster guitars, dies from Parkinson's disease. He started mass producing solid body electric guitars in the late 40s and when he sold his guitar company in 1965, sales were in excess of $40 million a year.

1997

Snoop Doggy Dog is sentenced to three years probation and fined $1,000 for firearms possession after a handgun was found in his car when being stopped for a traffic violation.

2000

Kurt Cobain and Happy Mondays' singer Shaun Ryder both beat older names such as Keith Richards and Keith Moon in a league of rock'n'roll excess compiled by music weekly *Melody Maker*. Liam Gallagher, Robbie Williams, Courtney Love and Marilyn Manson also feature in the Top 10.

2001

Michael Jackson's interior decorator tells *The Times* that the singer kept 17 fully dressed life size dolls, adult and child sizes, in his bedroom for "company".

2006

Three South African women win a six-year court battle giving them 25% of all past and future royalties from the song 'The Lion Sleeps Tonight', composed in 1939 by their father, Solomon Linda. A cleaner at a Johannesburg record company when he wrote it, Linda received virtually nothing for his work and died in 1962 with just $25 in his bank account. It is estimated that the song, recorded by Pete Seeger, The Karl Denver Trio (as 'Wimoweh'), The Kingston Trio, The Tokens, and R.E.M., had earned $15 million from its use in Disney's *The Lion King* alone.

2008

A five-year legal row over the use of The Beach Boys name is settled by two former members of the group. Mike Love had argued he was the only person allowed to perform under the name and sued Al Jardine, whom he claimed was appearing as an unlicensed Beach Boys act. Jardine's lawyer said "a friendly settlement had been reached that allowed them to focus on the talent and future of this American iconic band".

1985

Bruce Springsteen kicks off the second leg of his 'Born In The USA' World Tour at the Sydney Entertainment Centre, Sydney.

Born on this day:

1943 Keith Relf, vocals (The Yardbirds, Renaissance)

1948 Randy Hobbs, bass (The McCoys, Johnny Winter)

1963 Susanne Sulley, vocals (The Human League)

1979 Aaron Wright North, guitar (Nine Inch Nails)

1980 Shannon Bex, singer (Danity Kane)

1956

While driving to New York for appearances on *The Perry Como Show* and *The Ed Sullivan Show*, Carl Perkins is involved in a car crash, receiving four broken ribs and a broken shoulder and putting Perkins in hospital for several months. His brother Jay is killed in the accident.

1967

The Jimi Hendrix Experience appear at The Guildhall, Southampton, England.

1971

US police arrest all the members of The Allman Brothers Band for heroin and marijuana possession.

1978

The Police sign to A&M Records and go on to score over 15 UK Top 40 hits with the label.

1980

The Jam have their first UK chart-topper with their tenth release, the double A-side 'Going Underground'/'The Dreams Of Children', the first single of the 80s to debut at No. 1.

Pink Floyd's 'Another Brick In The Wall' starts a four week run at No. 1 on the US singles chart. It also reaches the top spot in the UK.

1992

Polygram Records officially announce that Tears For Fears have split up, although Roland Orzabal continues to use the name. The duo reformed in 2004.

1984

Queen film the video for 'I Want To Break Free' at Limehouse Studio in London. Directed by David Mallet, it is a parody of the northern British soap opera *Coronation Street* with the band members dressed in drag. Guitarist Brian May later said the video ruined the band's career in America and was initially banned by MTV.

1994

Singer, songwriter, and producer Dan Hartman dies of a brain tumour in Westport, Connecticut. As a member of The Edgar Winter Group he wrote the band's 1973 hit 'Free Ride', and as a soloist had a 1978 No. 1 dance hit with 'Instant Replay,' wrote 'Relight My Fire' (a UK No. 1 for Take That and Lulu), and collaborated with Tina Turner, Dusty Springfield, Joe Cocker, Bonnie Tyler, Paul Young, James Brown, Holly Johnson and Steve Winwood.

2004

A new book, *The Presley Prophesy*, claims that Elvis Presley's ancestors came from a small village called Lonmay in the north east of Scotland. Author Allan Morrison said he'd found evidence that Elvis' great-great-great-great-great-great grandfather was married in the village 300 years ago.

2009

Lady Gaga starts a three-week run at No. 1 on the UK singles chart with 'Poker Face', her second British chart topper and a No. 1 in over 20 countries.

March 23

1967

At a ceremony held at The Playhouse Theatre in London, The Beatles are awarded three Ivor Novello awards for 1966: Best-Selling British Single ('Yellow Submarine'), Most-Performed Song ('Michelle'), and Next-Most-Performed Song ('Yesterday'). None of The Beatles attend – although a recorded message from Lennon and McCartney is played – and the winning songs are played by Joe Loss and His Orchestra. The lead vocal for 'Michelle' is sung by Ross MacManus, whose son Declan would go on to become Elvis Costello.

1969

During a UK tour Stevie Wonder plays two shows at the Coventry Theatre, with The Foundations, The Flirtations and Emperor Rosko.

1972

The film of *The Concert For Bangladesh* featuring George Harrison, Bob Dylan and Eric Clapton premieres in New York.

1973

John Lennon is ordered to leave the US within 60 days by immigration authorities. Lennon appeals and after a long fight to obtain his Green Card, the ex-Beatle is given permanent resident status on 27 July, 1976.

1977

Elvis Presley appears at the Arizona State University in Tempe, Arizona – the first show of a 49-date US tour lasting over three months and Presley's last-ever tour.

1983

The Smiths make their London debut at The Rock Garden in Covent Garden. The gig is not reviewed in the music press.

1985

Billy Joel marries top fashion model Christie Brinkley on a boat moored alongside the Statue of Liberty. They divorce in 1993.

1991
R.E.M. score their first UK No. 1 album with their seventh LP *Out Of Time* featuring the hit singles 'Losing My Religion' and 'Shiny Happy People'.

1992

Janet Jackson signs with Virgin Records for $16,000,000.

1994

Oasis play at The Angel in Bedford, England and are paid £100 for the gig.

1995

Alan Barton, of one-hit-wonders Black Lace, dies aged 41. 'Agadoo', a 1984 UK No. 2 single, earned the dubious accolade of being voted the worst song of all time by a panel of music writers in Q magazine.

2008

Neil Aspinall, who oversaw the Beatles' Apple Corps business empire from 1968–2007, dies from lung cancer aged 66 at a hospital in New York. A Liverpool school friend of Paul McCartney and George Harrison, he was regarded by many as "the fifth Beatle", becoming the group's road manager in 1961 before working as their personal assistant. In the 80s Aspinall became the head of the Beatles' Apple company and led the legal battle against Apple computers over the use of the Apple name and a royalties dispute between The Beatles and record label EMI. Aspinall had also played background instruments on certain Beatles tracks including 'Magical Mystery Tour', 'Within You, Without You' and 'Being For The Benefit Of Mr. Kite'.

2008
Jack Johnson is top of the US *Billboard* chart with his fifth album *Sleep Through The Static*, which spends three weeks at No. 1, and is also a No. 1 in the UK and Australia.

Born on this day:

1951 Dougie Thompson, bass (Supertramp)
1960 Nena, singer

1970 Mase, vocals (De La Soul)
1970 Sharon Corr, vocals, violin (The Corrs)

1958
At 6.35am, Elvis Presley reports to the Memphis draft board. From there he and 12 other recruits are taken by bus to Kennedy Veterans Memorial Hospital where the singer is assigned army serial number 53310761.

1966
Simon & Garfunkel made their UK singles chart debut with 'Homeward Bound'.

1967
Pink Floyd play the first of two nights at the Ricky Tick Club, Hounslow, London.

1973
During a Lou Reed show in Buffalo, New York, a fan jumps on stage and bites Reed on the bottom. The man is thrown out of the theatre and Reed continues with the show.

1976
Transvestite singer Wayne County appears in court charged with assault after an incident at New York club CBGBs. County had attacked Dictators singer Handsome Dick Manitoba with a mike stand, fracturing his collarbone.

1985
'Easy Lover' by Philip Bailey (a former vocalist with Earth Wind & Fire) and Phil Collins (who produced, drummed and sang on the track) is at No. 1 on the UK singles chart.

1990
Sinead O'Connor is at No. 1 on the UK album chart with *I Do Not Want What I Haven't Got*, featuring the single 'Nothing Compares 2 U'. The album also spent six weeks at No. 1 in America and 13 other countries.

1991
The Black Crowes are dropped as support act on ZZ Top's tour after repeatedly criticising the tour sponsor Miller Beer.

1992
A Chicago court settles the Milli Vanilli class action suit by approving cash rebates of up to $3 to anyone proving they bought the group's music before November 27 1990, the date the lip synching scandal broke. Milli Vanilli had won the 1989 Best New Artist Grammy after hits like 'Blame It On The Rain' and 'Girl, You Know It's True', selling 30 million singles and 14 million albums. But in late 1990, the duo was stripped of the award after it was revealed that neither actually sang on the Milli Vanilli album.

2001
A stretch of road on Highway 19 in Macon, Georgia, is named Duane Allman Boulevard, near where the Allman Brothers guitarist died aged 24 in a motorcycle crash on October 29, 1971.

2002
Gareth Gates, a 17-year-old who won second place on UK TV's *Pop Idol* show, becomes the youngest male solo artist to score a UK No. 1 with his debut release 'Unchained Melody', the fourth time that the song has been at No. 1 in Britain.

2009
Motown drummer Uriel Jones dies aged 74 after suffering complications from a heart attack. Jones played on many Motown classics including 'I Heard It Through The Grapevine', by Marvin Gaye, 'Cloud Nine' by The Temptations, 'I Second That Emotion' by Smokey Robinson & The Miracles and 'For Once In My Life' by Stevie Wonder.

The prosecutor in the Phil Spector murder retrial tells the jury Spector was a "demonic maniac" when he drank and "a very dangerous man" around women. Deputy District Attorney Truc Do urged jurors to find the music producer guilty of murdering Hollywood actress Lana Clarkson in 2003. During her closing argument, she also accused Spector of demonstrating a "conscious disregard for human life".

Born on this day:

1942 Aretha Franklin, singer, pianist
1947 Elton John, singer-songwriter
1949 Nick Lowe, vocals, bass, songwriter, producer (Kippington Lodge, Brinsley Schwarz, Rockpile, solo)

1966 Jeff Healey, Canadian guitarist, singer
1975 Melanie Blatt, vocals (All Saints)

March 25

1966
At a photo session in Bob Whitaker's studio in London, The Beatles pose in white coats using sides of meat with mutilated and butchered dolls for a publicity photo that is used by Capitol in America for the cover of The Beatles' next American album, *Yesterday And Today*. After a public outcry, the LP is pulled from stores and re-issued with a new cover, making the original an instant collector's item.

1967
The Who and Cream make their US concert debuts at the RKO 58th Street Theater, New York City as part of a multi-artist extravaganza promoted by DJ Murray the K.

The Pink Floyd play three gigs in 24 hours: appearing at The Ricky Tick Club in Windsor, then The New Yorker Discotheque, Swindon before an all-night gig at The Shoreline Club, Bognor Regis (in the early hours of 26 March).

1968
The 58th and final episode of *The Monkees* TV series is broadcast on NBC in America.

1969
John and Yoko invite the world's press into their hotel suite at the start of a week long 'Bed-In' at the Amsterdam Hilton. On the first day there is a media scrum to enter the room, thinking that John and Yoko were going to make love in public. Instead they find the newlywed couple in bed, wearing pyjamas and holding hands, promoting the idea of world peace.

1975
Aerosmith play at the War Memorial Coliseum, Fort Wayne, Indiana – the first concert on their 63-date North American 'Toys In The Attic' tour.

1976
US singer-songwriter Jackson Browne's wife Phyllis Major commits suicide.

1983
Motown Records celebrates its 25th anniversary with a concert in Pasadena, featuring The Supremes, Stevie Wonder, The Temptations, The Four Tops, Martha Reeves, Jr. Walker, The Commodores, Marvin Gaye, Smokey Robinson and The Jackson 5.

1989
Madonna is at No. 1 on the UK singles chart with 'Like A Prayer', her sixth UK chart-topper and also No. 1 in America. The song is accompanied by a highly controversial video, which in 2005 was voted the Most Groundbreaking Music Video Of All Time by MTV viewers.

1995
Pearl Jam singer Eddie Vedder is rescued after a riptide carries him 250 feet offshore in New Zealand.

2000
Former Bay City Rollers drummer Derek Longmuir is given 300 hours community service after being caught with a hoard of child pornography, including 150 videos and 73 floppy disks.

2001
The first Britney Spears Pepsi TV commercial is aired on US television. Spears had signed a multi-million dollar deal with Pepsi to sponsor her forthcoming world tour.

2002
R.E.M. guitarist Peter Buck is on trial at Uxbridge Court, accused of attacking two cabin staff and covering them in yoghurt, knocking over a trolley and trying to steal a knife. Bono makes an appearance, telling the court, "I came to court because Peter is actually famously known for being a peaceable person. I once had to twist his arm to get him to a boxing match." Buck is later cleared of all charges.

So Solid Crew singer Asher D is jailed for 18 months after being found guilty of carrying a loaded gun. The 19-year-old singer claimed he bought the gun for his own safety after being constantly threatened by thugs who were jealous of his fame.

The seven-year mystery of missing Manic Street Preachers guitarist Richey Edwards takes a grisly twist when human feet are found near where he vanished in 1995.

2005
Ozzy and Sharon Osbourne are forced to flee their Buckinghamshire mansion after a blaze breaks out while they were sleeping. The couple are roused by a fire alarm and run to safety in the garden, rescuing their pets as they escape.

2008
Bon Jovi guitarist Richie Sambora is arrested on suspicion of drink driving after a police officer noticed his black Hummer weaving in and out of traffic lanes in Laguna Beach, California. He is ordered to appear in court on one count of driving under the influence.

Born on this day:

1917	Rufus Thomas, singer
1944	Diana Ross, singer
1948	Steven Tyler, vocals (Aerosmith)
1950	Teddy Pendergrass, soul singer
1968	James Jonas Iha, guitar (Smashing Pumpkins)
1968	Kenny Chesney, US country singer

1965
Mick Jagger, Brian Jones and Bill Wyman all receive electric shocks from a faulty microphone on stage during a Rolling Stones concert in Denmark. Wyman is knocked unconscious for several minutes.

1969
Marvin Gaye is at No. 1 on the UK singles chart with 'I Heard It Through The Grapevine'. The Norman Whitfield co-written and produced song was first recorded by The Miracles and had

also been a US million seller in 1967 for Gladys Knight & The Pips.

1970
Peter Yarrow of folk trio Peter, Paul & Mary pleads guilty to 'taking immoral liberties' with a 14-year-old girl in Washington D.C. and is sentenced to three months in prison. Ironically, just days earlier, the trio had won a Grammy Award for Best Recording For Children for their album, *Peter, Paul And Mommy*.

1976
One-man British blues band, Duster Bennett, who worked with Alexis Korner, John Mayall, Fleetwood Mac and B.B. King, is killed in a car accident.

1977
Hall & Oates start a three week run at No. 1 on the *Billboard* singles chart with 'Rich Girl', the duo's first US chart-topper but not a hit in the UK.

1983
Duran Duran are at No. 1 for the first time on the UK singles chart with 'Is There Something I Should Know?' On this day the group is on an American promotional trip, being greeted by 5,000 screaming fans at an in-store appearance in New York City.

1985
Radio stations in South Africa ban all of Stevie Wonder's records after he dedicates the Oscar he had won the night before at the Academy Awards to Nelson Mandela.

1988
Michael Jackson starts a two-week run at No. 1 on the US singles chart with 'Man In The Mirror'.

2000
Santana start a two-week run at No. 1 on the UK album chart with *Supernatural*.

2002
Randy Castillo, drummer with Ozzy Osbourne's band during the 80s and early 90s and who also worked with Lita Ford and Motley Crüe, dies aged 51 of cancer.

2004
Jan Berry, of Jan & Dean, dies aged 62, after being in poor health from injuries sustained in a 1966 car crash. The duo's biggest hit was the 1963 US No. 1 (UK No. 26) single 'Surf City', co-written by Beach Boy Brian Wilson.

2005
Australian drummer Paul Hester, formerly of Split Enz, Crowded House and Largest Living Things, commits suicide aged 46 by hanging himself in a park in Melbourne. After leaving Crowded House in 1994, Hester appeared on many TV and radio shows in Australia.

2006
British readers of *Total Guitar* magazine vote Jimmy Page's solo in Led Zeppelin's 'Stairway To Heaven' as The Greatest Guitar Solo Of All Time. The 1971 track was voted ahead of selections by Van Halen, Queen, Jimi Hendrix and The Eagles.

2006
U2's The Edge donates his favourite guitar – a 1975 Gibson Les Paul – to a charity he co-founded to replace instruments lost or destroyed when Hurricane Katrina hit the US.

Born on this day:

1950 Tony Banks, keyboards (Genesis)
1959 Andrew Farriss, keyboards (INXS)
1970 Mariah Carey, singer

1975 Fergie, US R&B singer, songwriter (The Black Eyed Peas)

1958
CBS Records announce the invention of stereophonic records. Although the format would be playable on ordinary record players, when used on the new stereo players, a rich and fuller sound split over two speakers would be heard.

1966
During a UK tour, Roy Orbison falls off a motorbike while scrambling at Hawkstone Park, Birmingham, fracturing his foot. He plays the remaining concert dates sat on a stool and walking on crutches.

1971
Bruce Springsteen & Friendly Enemies open for The Allman Brothers Band at The Sunshine In, Asbury Park in New Jersey. Tickets cost $4.00. Springsteen had just disbanded his group Steel Mill and within a few weeks would form Dr Zoom & The Sonic Boom with Steven Van Zandt.

1973
In New Jersey, Jerry Garcia from The Grateful Dead is arrested after police find cocaine and LSD in his car when busting him for speeding.

Rolling Stone magazine reports that after becoming a disciple of Sri Chinmoy, Carlos Santana had changed his name to 'Devadip', which means "the lamp of the light of the Supreme".

1982
Former Small Faces and Faces bass player Ronnie Lane is admitted to a London hospital for treatment for multiple sclerosis. (Lane eventually dies from the disease in 1997.)

1986
Van Halen kick off their 1986 112-date North American tour – the first with Sammy Hagar on lead vocals – at the Hirsch Memorial Coliseum, Shreveport, Louisiana.

1987
U2 perform from the roof of a store in downtown LA for the video of 'Where The Streets Have No Name', attracting thousands of spectators and bringing traffic to a standstill. The police eventually stop the shoot.

1991
New Kids On The Block's Donnie Wahlberg is arrested after setting fire to carpets (using a bottle of vodka) at The Seelbach Hotel, Louisville, Kentucky. Wahlberg plea bargained the charge down to criminal mischief and was ordered to perform fire safety and anti-drug abuse promos.

2006
Former Village People 'policeman' Victor Willis is arrested in San Francisco, after absconding from a drug and gun trial. Police had charged Willis with being in possession of cocaine and drug paraphernalia in July 2005. Willis would later be sentenced to three years probation after he agreed to enter a treatment program.

2007
The wife of Velvet Revolver singer Scott Weiland is arrested on suspicion of burning over $10,000 of Weiland's belongings outside their home after southern California police find a bin of smouldering clothes. Earlier that day, the couple left two rooms vandalised after an argument at a luxury hotel.

Eminem and his ex-wife Kim Mathers reach a court agreement to stop insulting each other in public. The pair, who divorced for the second time last year, pledge to stop trading insults for the sake of their 11-year-old daughter Hailie. The deal came after the rap star took legal action to stop Kim making "derogatory, disparaging, inflammatory and otherwise negative comments".

2000
Singer, songwriter, poet and actor Ian Dury dies aged 57 after a long battle with cancer.

2008
X Factor winner Leona Lewis becomes the first British woman to top the US pop chart for more than 20 years with her single 'Bleeding Love'. Kim Wilde was the last UK female to top the *Billboard* Hot 100 chart with her 1987 cover version of The Supremes' hit 'You Keep Me Hangin' On'. Petula Clark was the first in 1965 with 'Downtown', while Sheena Easton's 'Morning Train' (released in the UK as '9 To 5') followed in 1981.

March 28

Born on this day:

1945 Chuck Portz, bass (The Turtles)
1948 Milan Williams, keyboards, brass, guitar (The Commodores)
1969 James Atkin, vocals (EMF)
1976 Dave Keuning, guitarist (The Killers)
1986 Lady Gaga, singer, songwriter

1958

Buddy Holly kicks off the first night of a 43-date tour at the Brooklyn Paramount Theatre, New York. The 'Alan Freed's Big Beat Show' also features Jerry Lee Lewis, Chuck Berry, Frankie Lymon, The Diamonds, Billy Ford, Danny & The Juniors, The Chantels, Larry Williams, Screaming Jay Hawkins, The Pastels, Jo-Ann Campbell and Ed Townsend. On most days the acts play two shows.

1967

The Beatles work on the *Sgt. Pepper* track 'Good Morning, Good Morning' at EMI Studios, London. John Lennon, who was inspired to write the song from a Kellogg's cornflake TV commercial, decides he wants to end the song with animal sound effects. Producer George Martin sequences them in such a way that each successive animal is capable of scaring or eating the preceding one.

1974

Delta blues singer and guitarist Arthur 'Big Boy' Crudup, who wrote 'That's All Right (Mama)' covered by Elvis Presley and 'My Baby Left Me', dies aged 69 of a stroke.

1982

After crashing his car on the San Diego Highway, David Crosby is arrested when police find cocaine and a pistol in the vehicle. When an officer asked Crosby why he carried the weapon, his reply was "John Lennon".

1992

Over a $100,000 worth of damage is caused at The Irvine Meadows Amphitheatre, California, when Ozzy Osbourne invites the first two rows of the audience up on stage. When several others take up the singer's offer the band are forced to exit the stage.

1995

Singer Jimmy McShane, who had a 1985 UK No. 3 single and European hit 'Tarzan Boy' with Italian dance outfit Baltimora, dies of AIDS.

1998

Kiss play the first of five sold-out nights on their 'Alive II' World Tour at the Tokyo Budokan, Japan.

2000

Jimmy Page accepts substantial undisclosed libel damages from a magazine which claimed he had caused or contributed to the death of his Led Zeppelin bandmate John Bonham. Page's solicitor, Norman Chapman, told High Court Judge Mr. Justice Morland that the 1999 feature in *Ministry* magazine claimed Page was more concerned with keeping vomit off his bed than saving his friend's life, and that he stood over him wearing Satanist robes and performed a useless spell.

2001

The artist formerly known as both Puffy and Puff Daddy says in an MTV interview that he now wants to be known as P. Diddy. In August 2005, he changes his stage name again to simply 'Diddy'.

2005

After playing a warm-up date the night before at the Los Angeles Sports Arena, U2 kick off their Vertigo tour at the iPay One Center in San Diego. The 131-date world tour would see the band playing in North America, Europe, South America and Japan. By the time it finished, the Vertigo Tour had sold 4,619,021 tickets, grossing $389 million; the second-highest figure ever for a world tour.

2006

Tina Brown, the sister-in-law of Whitney Houston, sells pictures taken in her bathroom to the *National Enquirer* claiming Houston had been taking crack cocaine. The pictures show drug paraphernalia including a crack-smoking pipe, rolling papers, cocaine-caked spoons and cigarette ends strewn across the surface tops of the bathroom.

1976

In Buffalo, New York, Genesis begin their first North American tour since Peter Gabriel left the band, with Phil Collins taking over as lead singer.

Born on this day:

1943 Evangelos Papathanassiou (Vangelis)
1946 Terry Jacks, singer, songwriter
1949 Dave Greenfield, keyboards (The Stranglers)

1959 Perry Farrell, singer (Jane's Addiction, Pornos For Pyros)

March 29

1966
Mick Jagger is injured during a Rolling Stones concert in Marseilles after a fan throws a chair at the stage. The resulting cut requires eight stitches.

Fans mob The Walker Brothers as they enter a hotel in Cheshire resulting in two of the group being concussed.

1975
Led Zeppelin have all of their six albums (to date) in the *Billboard* US Top 100 chart in the same week with their latest album *Physical Graffiti* at No. 1.

1978
David Bowie kicks off his 'Stage' 77-date World Tour at San Diego Sports Arena, California.

1980
Pink Floyd's *The Dark Side Of The Moon* spends its 303rd week on the US album chart, beating the previous record set by Carole King's *Tapestry*.

1983
At the end of a 29-date 'War' UK tour, U2 appear at the Hammersmith Palais, London.

1985
Jeanine Deckers, a.k.a. The Singing Nun, dies aged 52 after taking an overdose of sleeping pills in a suicide pact with a friend. Her 1963 US No. 1 (UK No. 7) single 'Dominique' sold over 1.5 million copies, winning a Grammy Award for the year's Best Gospel Song. Deckers wrote about her financial plight in a suicide note. With great irony, on the very day of her death, unbeknownst to her, the Belgian association that collects royalties for songwriters awarded her $300,000 (571,658 Belgian francs).

1986
Austrian singer Falco starts a three-week run atop the US singles chart with 'Rock Me Amadeus', also a No. 1 in the UK. Falco became the first German-speaking artist to achieve a chart-topper on the US charts.

1999
The David Bowie Internet Radio Network broadcasts its first show for *Rolling Stone* Radio. The show consists of Bowie's favourite songs with Bowie himself introducing each track.

2000
Phil Collins takes out a high court action against two former members of Earth, Wind & Fire. Collins claims his company has overpaid the musicians by £50,000 in royalties on tracks including 'Sussudio' and 'Easy Lover'.

2005
Neil Young is treated for a brain aneurysm at a New York hospital. Doctors expect the 59-year-old to make a full recovery. The aneurysm was discovered when Young's vision became blurred after attending the

Rock and Roll Hall of Fame the previous month.

2007
U2 singer Bono accepts an honorary knighthood at a ceremony in Dublin. Fellow band members The Edge and Adam Clayton join the singer's wife and four children at the British ambassador David Reddaway's official residence. While not entitled to be called Sir because he is not a British citizen, the U2 singer's new title is Knight Commander of the Most Excellent Order of the British Empire (KBE).

March 30

Born on this day:

1942 Graeme Edge, drums (The Moody Blues)

1945 Eric Clapton, guitar, vocals, songwriter (Bluesbreakers, Cream, Blind Faith, solo)

1950 Re Styles, guitar, vocals (The Tubes)

1962 MC Hammer, rapper

1964 Tracy Chapman, singer-songwriter

1968 Celine Dion, French-Canadian singer

1979 Norah Jones, US singer

1963
16-year-old Lesley Gore records her breakthrough hit and US No. 1, 'It's My Party', produced by Quincy Jones.

1967
During an appearance by The Jimi Hendrix Experience on *Top Of The Pops* to plug their latest single, 'Purple Haze', a technician mistakenly puts on the backing track to Alan Price's 'Simon Smith And His Amazing Dancing Bear', to which Hendrix responds, "I don't know the words to this one, man."

in Chalk Farm. Four police cars and a helicopter are required to make the arrest. Their fines totalled £800.

1982
U2 play the second of two nights at the San Francisco Civic Centre, California.

1984
David Gilmour appears as a soloist on the British TV show *The Tube*, broadcast live from Newcastle-upon-Tyne.

been named after him. The singer said he had spent the worst years of his life at the school.

Mungo Jerry singer Ray Dorset is ordered to pay a former employee £620 in back wages after a tribunal heard he had harassed her after she left his company. Dorset told the court he had paid the woman double pay by mistake for 10 months.

1967
The historic photo session for The Beatles' *Sgt. Pepper's Lonely Hearts Club Band* sleeve takes place on a set designed by British pop artist Peter Blake and his wife Jann Haworth and photographed by Michael Cooper at Chelsea Manor Studios, London.

1976
The Sex Pistols play their first show at The 100 Club, London. The band began a weekly residency at the venue in June.

1978
Paul Simonon and Nicky 'Topper' Headon are arrested in Camden Town, London after shooting down racing pigeons with air guns from the roof of their Rehearsal Rehearsal [sic] Studio

1996
The Prodigy start a three-week run at No. 1 on the UK singles chart with 'Firestarter', the first single from their album *The Fat Of The Land*. The wah-wah guitar riff was sampled from The Breeders' track 'S.O.S.'

2000
Mick Jagger makes a nostalgic visit to his old school Dartford Grammar to open the new arts centre that had

2007
A middle-aged man is arrested by police and detained under the Mental Health Act after trying to force his way into Paul McCartney's Sussex home, screaming "I must get to him". The man burst through security patrols and guards who feared an assassination attempt and scrambled to intercept him as he sped towards the front door. He was finally halted by trees and a fence just yards from the property.

Born on this day:

1937 Herb Alpert, bandleader, A&M Records co-founder

1948 Mick Ralphs, guitarist (Mott The Hoople, Bad Company)

1958 Pat McGlynn, guitar (Bay City Rollers)

1959 Angus Young, guitar (AC/DC)

March 31

1949
RCA Victor introduces the 45rpm single record which had been in development since 1940. The 7" disc is designed to compete with the Long Playing record introduced by Columbia a year earlier. Both formats offer better fidelity and longer playing time than the 78rpm record that was currently in use. Advertisements for new record players boasted that with 45rpm records the listener could hear up to ten records with speedy, silent, hardly noticeable changes.

1957
Billed as the nation's only atomic powered singer, Elvis Presley plays two shows (2pm and 6pm) at The Olympia, Detroit, Michigan in front of 24,000 people.

1960
Lonnie Donegan is at No. 1 on the UK singles chart with 'My Old Man's A Dustman', his third chart-topper. The song, recorded live at the Bristol Hippodrome, was a music hall novelty.

1967
On the first night of a 24-date tour featuring a bizarre combination of The Walker Brothers, Cat Stevens and Engelbert Humperdinck, Jimi Hendrix sets fire to his guitar live on stage for the first time while appearing at the Finsbury Park Astoria, north London. The act is designed to get the then little-known Hendrix the attention he deserved as he has been placed low down on the bill.

1972
The Beatles Official Fan Club closes. The *Beatles Monthly* magazine, run in association by Sean O'Mahoney, had ceased publication three years previously.

1974
Television first appear at CBGBs club in New York City.

1984
Kenny Loggins starts a three week run at No. 1 in the US with 'Footloose', the theme from the film of the same name. The single reaches No. 6 in the UK.

1986
O'Kelly Isley, of The Isley Brothers, dies aged 48 of a heart attack. The trio were best known for their 1962 hit version of 'Twist And Shout' (as covered by The Beatles), which had originally been recorded the previous year by The Top Notes.

1990
David Bowie scores his seventh UK No. 1 album with *Changes Bowie*.

1994
Madonna appears on *The Late Show with David Letterman* from New York. The CBS network has to delete 13 offending words from the interview before the show airs. Madonna also hands Letterman a pair of her panties and tells him to sniff them. He declines and stuffs them into his desk drawer.

1995
Jimmy Page escapes being knifed when a man rushes the stage at a Page & Plant gig at Auburn Hills, Michigan, but is stopped by two security guards, whom he wounds instead. After his arrest, the assailant tells police that he wanted to kill Page because of the Satanic music he was playing.

Mexican-American singer Selena is murdered aged 23 by the president of her fan club Yolanda Saldívar. Warner Brothers made a film based on her life, starring Jennifer Lopez, in 1997.

2001
Whitney Houston and husband Bobby Brown are banned for life from Hollywood's Bel Air hotel after their suite was so badly damaged it had to be shut for five days for repairs. Hotel workers said a TV was smashed, two doors were ripped off their hinges and the walls and carpets were stained by alcohol. It was reported that Whitney called in her lawyers to plead with the hotel management not to call the police.

2002
Bee Gee Barry Gibb buys his childhood home in Keppel Road, Chorlton, Manchester. Gibb says he will renovate the house before renting it out and plans to affix a plaque on the outside wall.

2007
A new world record for the longest non-stop concert is set by hundreds of musicians in Japan. The performance begins on the evening of 23 March in the city of Omi, with musicians aged between six and 96 taking turns with over 2,000 tunes being performed over 182 hours. Organisers praise the musicians, one of whom carries on despite a major earthquake during her piano piece. The previous world record was set in Canada in 2001 with 181 hours.

April

Born on this day:

1939 Rudolph Isley, vocals (The Isley Brothers)
1946 Arthur Conley, US soul singer
1946 Ronnie Lane, bass, vocals (The Small Faces, The Faces, Slim Chance)
1948 Jimmy Cliff, Jamaican singer, songwriter
1952 Billy Currie, keyboards (Ultravox)
1954 Jeff Porcaro, drums (Toto)
1961 Mark White, guitar, keyboards (ABC)
1971 Clifford Smith, vocals (Method Man, Wu-Tang Clan)

April 1

1959

On a brief visit to London from Germany where he is stationed with the US Army, Elvis Presley performs at the Half Moon in Putney, accompanying himself on acoustic guitar. He is seen by 11 people and a dog, to whom he dedicates a poignant version of 'Old Shep' which, he tells those present, "was ma mama's favourite ever song".

1961

The Beatles begin a three-month residency at The Top Ten Club, Hamburg, Germany, playing 92 straight nights. The group plays for seven hours a night on weekdays and eight hours at weekends with a 15-minute break every hour. It is during this visit that Astrid Kirchherr cuts Stuart Sutcliffe's hair into the style destined to become known as the "Beatle haircut" which The Beatles later adopt themselves.

1965

The Who fly to Manchester to record an appearance for *Top Of The Pops* at the BBC's Manchester television studio. The group then fly back to London to play a gig supporting Donovan at The Town Hall, Wembley, with Rod Stewart & The Soul Agents also appearing on the bill.

1966

The Troggs record 'Wild Thing' at Pye Studios in Marble Arch, London, produced by Larry Page, with Mick Jagger present as an observer. The song went on to be a No. 1 US and No. 2 UK hit in June.

1969

The Beach Boys announce that they are suing their record label Capitol for $2 million in unpaid royalties.

1972

The three-day Mar Y Sol festival in Puerto Rico features The Faces, Dr. John, The Allman Brothers, Osibisa, Emerson, Lake & Palmer, Alice Cooper and The Mahavishnu Orchestra. Security is simple as the event takes place on an island accessible by ticket only.

1975

The Bay City Rollers' TV series *Shang-A-Lang* premieres on ITV in the UK.

1976
Making their live debut in the UK, AC/DC play at The Red Cow pub in Hammersmith, London.

1984

Marvin Gaye is shot dead by his father at his parents' home in Los Angeles. An argument started after his parents squabbled over misplaced business documents. When Gaye attempted to intervene, his father used a gun Marvin had given him four months before. Gaye Sr. is sentenced to six years probation after pleading guilty to manslaughter. Charges of first-degree murder are dropped after doctors discover Marvin Sr. had a brain tumor.

1985

David Lee Roth quits Van Halen shortly after releasing his solo version of The Beach Boys' 'California Girls', which features Carl Wilson on background vocals. Lee Roth will be replaced by Sammy Hagar later in the year.

2000

Santana start a nine-week run at No. 1 on the US singles chart with 'Maria Maria.'

2004

Paul Atkinson, guitarist with The Zombies, dies aged 58 from liver and kidney disease. Atkinson had also been an A&R executive, working for Columbia and RCA in Britain and America, discovering and signing such acts as Bruce Hornsby, Mr. Mister, Judas Priest and Michael Penn.

2005

During the first leg of their 'Vertigo' World Tour, U2 appear at the Arrowhead Sports Arena, Anaheim, Southern California, with Kings Of Leon as the opening act. By the end of the 131-date tour, 4,619,021 tickets had been sold with a total gross of $389 million.

2007

American indie rock band Modest Mouse are at No. 1 on the US album chart with *We Were Dead Before The Ship Even Sank*. The album features former Smiths guitarist Johnny Marr, who joined the band in May 2006.

Born on this day:

1939 Marvin Gaye, singer, songwriter
1941 Leon Russell, singer, songwriter
1947 Emmylou Harris, country singer, songwriter
1952 Leon Wilkeson, bass (Lynyrd Skynyrd)

1963 Keren Woodward, vocals (Bananarama)
1979 Jesse Carmichael, keyboards, guitar (Maroon 5)

1964
The Beach Boys record their single 'I Get Around', which would become their first US No. 1 over the summer.

1965
The first edition of a new-look *Ready, Steady, Go!* – *Ready Steady Goes Live!* – is shown on certain UK TV stations. Because of increasing criticism from the Musicians Union over artists miming, the show adopts a fresh, 'all-instruments and vocals live' approach. Artists appearing include Manfred Mann and Dionne Warwick.

1966
A charity concert at The Hollywood Bowl, California, features Jan & Dean, Sonny & Cher, The Mamas & The Papas, The Turtles, Otis Redding, Donovan and Bob Lind.

1969
Bruce Springsteen's group Child make their live debut at the Pandemonium Club, Wanamassa, New Jersey.

1971
Janis Joplin is at No. 1 on the US album charts with *Pearl*.

1977
Fleetwood Mac are at No. 1 on the US album chart with *Rumours*. Also on this day the band kick off a seven-date UK tour at the Birmingham Odeon.

1990
At Smart Studios in Madison, Wisconsin, with Butch Vig producing, Nirvana start work on demos of 'In Bloom', 'Dive', 'Lithium', 'Pay To Play', 'Imodium', 'Sappy' and 'Polly'.

1997
Joni Mitchell is reunited with Kilauren Gibb, the daughter she gave up for adoption 32 years earlier.

1998
Rob Pilatus, one half of pop duo Milli Vanilli, is found dead in a Frankfurt hotel room after taking a lethal combination of drugs and alcohol. Milli Vanilli sold 30 million singles and 14 million albums, winning the 1989 Best New Artist Grammy, but in late 1990 the performers were stripped of the award after it was revealed that neither actually sang on their only album.

1999
The Black Crowes play a concert in Knoxville, Tennessee. A year later Joshua Harmon, a teenager sitting in the second row, sues the band for $5,000 claiming significant hearing loss.

2001
Mariah Carey signs a recording deal with Virgin for three albums worth £60m, making it the most lucrative in history. The 31-year old singer had scored 14 US No. 1 singles and sold over 120 million records worldwide to date.

2003
US soul singer Edwin Starr dies aged 61 at his British home in Nottingham. Starr had a 1970 US No. 1 and UK No. 3 with the anti-Vietnam War protest song 'War' (which, according to Starr, was recorded in one take).

2004
Coldplay singer Chris Martin is accused of attacking a photographer after leaving a London restaurant with his wife Gwyneth Paltrow. A Coldplay spokesman said photographer Alessandro Copetti had been running after Paltrow's taxi and tripped. Copetti said he had been taking pictures of the singer and his wife outside a restaurant when Martin kicked him from behind.

2006
A John Lennon schoolbook containing the 12-year-old's drawing of Lewis Carroll's poem *The Walrus And The Carpenter* is sold at auction for £126,500. The poem partly inspired Lennon to write The Beatles' 1967 song 'I Am The Walrus'. Also selling for £12,000 is a ship's log book written by Lennon during a stormy sea trip to Bermuda in 1980, whilst a letter from Paul McCartney to the other Beatles fails to reach its £50,000 reserve price.

Gnarls Barkley starts an eight-week run at No. 1 on the UK singles chart with 'Crazy'. The American duo make chart history by becoming the first ever act to reach No. 1 through computer downloads only. The single is not available to buy in shops until the following week.

Embrace go to No. 1 on the UK album chart with *This New Day*, the band's third UK No. 1 album.

1987
One of the greatest jazz drummers of all time, Buddy Rich dies aged 69 from complications caused by a brain tumour. Rich worked with many acts including Frank Sinatra, Ella Fitzgerald, Louis Armstrong, Dizzy Gillespie, Oscar Peterson and Tommy Dorsey's band.

Born on this day:

1938 Phillippe Wynne, vocals (Detroit Spinners)

1943 Richard Manuel, keyboards, vocals (The Band)

1944 Tony Orlando, singer (Dawn)

1949 Richard Thompson, guitar, vocals (Fairport Convention & solo)

1951 Mel Schacher, bass (Grand Funk Railroad)

1985 Leona Lewis, singer

April 3

1956
Elvis Presley appears on ABC-TV's *The Milton Berle Show* live from the flight deck of the *USS Hancock* in San Diego, California, performing 'Heartbreak Hotel', 'Shake, Rattle And Roll' and 'Blue Suede Shoes'. It was estimated that one out of every four Americans saw the show.

1964
Bob Dylan makes his first entry on the UK singles charts with 'The Times They Are A-Changin'.

1969
The Doors' Jim Morrison turns himself in to the FBI in Los Angeles. He is charged on six counts of lewd behavior and public exposure at a concert in Miami on March 2 and released on $2,000 bail.

1975
Steve Miller is charged with setting fire to the clothes of a friend, Benita Diorio. When police arrived at Miller's house, Diorio was putting out the flames. Miller then got into a fight with some of the policemen and was charged with resisting arrest.

1979
Kate Bush kicks off the 28-date 'Tour Of Life' trek, making her concert debut at Liverpool's Empire Theatre. Bush never undertook another tour again.

1983
After completing a 29-date UK tour, U2 appear on *Top Of The Pops* performing their latest single, 'Two Hearts Beat As One.'

1989
At a Grateful Dead concert at the Pittsburgh Civic Arena, 23 people are arrested after several thousand fans without tickets try to gatecrash the show.

1994
A forthcoming tour by Nirvana and Hole is cancelled amid continuing speculation about Kurt Cobain's drug problems.

1998
Michael Jackson's daughter Paris Michael Katherine Jackson is born.

2002
Influential British avant-garde electronic musician Frank Tovey of Fad Gadget dies aged 45 of heart failure. Tovey was infamous for spreading his naked body in shaving cream onstage and would play various instruments with his head.

2003
Stax Records songwriter Homer Banks, who wrote 'I Can't Stand Up for Falling Down', recorded by Sam & Dave and a 1980 UK hit for Elvis Costello, dies aged 61. Other artists covering Banks' songs include Rod Stewart, The Emotions, Isaac Hayes, Millie Jackson and Johnny Taylor.

2007
Rolling Stones' guitarist Keith Richards denies that he snorted the ashes of his late father during a drugs binge. Jane Rose, Richards' manager, tells MTV News the remarks were made "in jest" and she could not believe they had been taken seriously. Richards had said in an *NME* interview: "He was cremated and I couldn't resist grinding him up with a little bit of blow." But interviewer Mark Beaumont was convinced that Richards was not joking. "He did seem to be quite honest about it. There were too many details for him to be making it up," Beaumont tells BBC News.

2008
Mariah Carey scores the 18th US number one of her career with 'Touch My Body', from her album *E=MC2*. While Carey had now surpassed Elvis Presley's record of 17 American number ones, The Beatles are still in front with 20.

April 4

Born on this day:

1915 Muddy Waters, US blues singer, guitarist

1948 Berry Oakley, bass (The Allman Brothers Band)

1952 Dave Hill, guitarist (Slade)

1952 Gary Moore, guitarist (Skid Row, Thin Lizzy, solo)

1980 Johnny Borrell, guitar, vocals (Razorlight)

1956
Elvis Presley plays the first of two nights at the San Diego Arena, California. The local police chief issues a statement saying that if Elvis ever returned to the city and performed like he did, he would be arrested for disorderly conduct.

1960
RCA Victor Records announces that it will simultaneously release all pop singles in mono and stereo, the first record company to do so.

1964
The Beatles hold the top five places on the *Billboard* US Singles Chart: No. 1 'Can't Buy Me Love', No. 2 'Love Me Do', No. 3 'Roll Over Beethoven', No. 4 'I Want To Hold You Hand', and No. 5 'Please Please Me'. The group also have another nine singles on the chart, bringing their total to 14 singles on the Hot 100.

1968
Jimi Hendrix, B.B. King, Buddy Guy, Joni Mitchell, Al Kooper and Ted Nugent congregate for an all night blues, folk and rock session at The New Generation Club, New York after hearing the news of Martin Luther King's assassination.

1970
Brinsley Schwarz's promotion company sends 133 UK journalists by plane to New York to see the band supporting Van Morrison at the Fillmore East at a cost of £120,000. The event turns into a disaster. The band planned to leave a few days before the show to rehearse, but were denied visas on a technicality. They were finally given visas on the morning of the show and arrived just hours before the concert. The plane carrying the journalists developed a mechanical fault, delaying the flight, and when the journalists arrived in New York 18 hours later they were all exhausted and hungover. Brinsley Schwarz gave

an underwhelming live performance, resulting in a flood of scathing reviews.

1976
The Sex Pistols play the first night of a residency at the El Paradiso club in Soho, London.

1981
Bucks Fizz win the Eurovision Song Contest held in Dublin, Ireland with the UK entry 'Making Your Mind Up'.

1987
U2 enter the US album chart at No. 7 with *The Joshua Tree* making it the highest chart new entry in America for seven years.

1992
Bruce Springsteen scores his third UK No. 1 album with *Human Touch*.

1999
The Corrs album *Talk On Corners* goes to No. 1 on the UK album chart for the 10th time. The Irish group also have the No. 2 position with *Forgiven, Not Forgotten*. Both albums had spent over a year on the chart.

2007
A Swedish couple run into trouble with authorities after trying to name their six-month-old daughter Metallica. Michael and Karolina Tomaro's baby had been baptized with the rock band's name, but tax officials said it was "inappropriate" because under Swedish law, both first names and surnames needed to win the approval of authorities before they could be used.

2008
At London's Court of Appeal, Procol Harum singer/pianist Gary Brooker wins a royalty battle over the band's worldwide hit, 'A Whiter Shade Of Pale', brought by original organist Matthew Fisher. The decision overturned a 2006 ruling that Fisher was entitled to a 40% portion of royalties after he argued he had written the song's organ melody. The court ruled there was an "excessive delay" in the claim being made – nearly 40 years after the song was recorded.

Born on this day:

1929 Joe Meek, producer
1942 Allan Clarke, vocals (The Hollies)
1950 Agnetha Faltskog, vocals (Abba)

1965 Mike McCready, guitar (Pearl Jam)
1973 Pharrell Williams, one half of writing duo (The Neptunes)

1968

The first date of a twice-nightly UK tour, featuring Amen Corner, Gene Pitney, Status Quo, Simon Dupree & The Big Sound and Don Partridge, kicks off at The Odeon Theatre, Lewisham, London.

1975

Minnie Riperton is at No. 1 on the US singles chart (No. 2 in the UK) with the Stevie Wonder produced 'Loving You' – her only US chart hit. Riperton died of cancer on 12 July 1979.

1978

Duran Duran make their live debut at The Lecture Theatre, Birmingham Polytechnic.

1980

R.E.M. play their first ever gig when appearing at St Mary's Episcopal Church, Athens, Georgia.

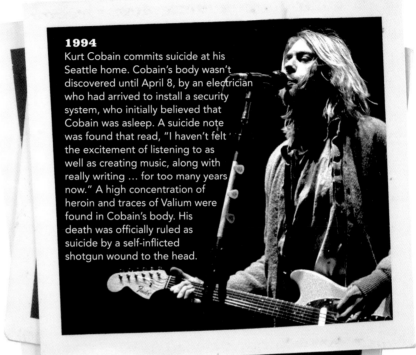

1994
Kurt Cobain commits suicide at his Seattle home. Cobain's body wasn't discovered until April 8, by an electrician who had arrived to install a security system, who initially believed that Cobain was asleep. A suicide note was found that read, "I haven't felt the excitement of listening to as well as creating music, along with really writing … for too many years now." A high concentration of heroin and traces of Valium were found in Cobain's body. His death was officially ruled as suicide by a self-inflicted shotgun wound to the head.

1981
Canned Heat singer and harmonica player, Bob "The Bear" Hite dies aged 36 of a heart attack.

1984

Marvin Gaye's funeral takes place at The Forest Lawn Cemetery, Los Angeles. Smokey Robinson, Stevie Wonder, Quincy Jones, Berry Gordy and other Motown singers, writers and producers attend the service.

1995

Jimi Hendrix's one-time girlfriend Monika Dannerman commits suicide, two days after losing a court battle with another of the guitarist's ex-lovers, Kathy Etchingham.

1998

British drummer Cozy Powell is killed when his car smashes into crash barriers on a motorway in Bristol, England. Powell had worked with Jeff Beck, Whitesnake, Black Sabbath, Rainbow and the ELP spin-off Emerson, Lake, & Powell. The drummer had also played on sessions by Donovan, Roger Daltrey, Jack Bruce, Gary Moore and Brian May.

The Spice Girls perform their first-ever live UK concert before a 9,000 strong audience in Glasgow, Scotland.

2006

Gene Pitney is found dead aged 65 of natural causes in a Cardiff hotel. The American singer was on a UK tour and had shown no signs of illness.

2007

Former Kiss guitarist Mark St. John dies from an apparent brain hemorrhage at the age of 51. St. John was Kiss' third official guitarist, having replaced Vinnie Vincent in 1984 and appeared on the album *Animalize*.

2008

Apple's iTunes becomes the largest music retailer in the US. Market research firm NPD said iTunes had surpassed Wal-Mart in January and February if 12 downloads were considered equal to the sale of one CD album. iTunes had sold more than four billion songs since its launch in 2003.

April 6

Born on this day:

1944 John Stax, bass (The Pretty Things)
1944 Michelle Gilliam (Michelle Phillips), vocals (The Mamas & The Papas)
1947 Tony Connor, drums (Hot Chocolate)
1965 Black Francis, guitarist, vocals (Pixies, Frank Black)

1966
The first session for what would become The Beatles' *Revolver* album starts with the recording of 'Tomorrow Never Knows' at EMI Studios, Abbey Road, London.

1968
It is announced that Pink Floyd founder member Syd Barrett has officially left the group. Barrett suffered from psychiatric disorders compounded by drug use.

1971
Carly Simon is introduced to James Taylor after her show at the Troubadour, Los Angeles. The couple will marry on 3 November, 1972.

1974
The California Jam 1 festival takes place in Ontario, California, featuring The Eagles, Black Sabbath, Deep Purple, Earth Wind & Fire, ELP, Black Oak Arkansas and Seals & Croft. Over 200,000 attend.

Abba win the Eurovision Song Contest in Brighton with 'Waterloo', thus setting them on the road to international success.

1985
UK singer-songwriter Gilbert O'Sullivan wins a lawsuit against his manager Gordon Mills for unpaid royalties and is awarded $2 million.

1998
Wendy O. Williams, former singer of The Plasmatics, dies from self-inflicted gunshot wounds. Williams was known for her wild stage theatrics which included blowing up equipment, near nudity and chain-sawing guitars. In January 1981 police in Milwaukee arrested her for simulating sex on stage. Later that same year in Cleveland, Williams was acquitted of an obscenity charge for simulating sex on stage wearing only shaving cream.

1998
The 'first lady of country music' Tammy Wynette, who scored 12 hit singles, sold over 30 million records worldwide, married five times and once filed for bankruptcy, dies aged 55.

2000
Eighties pop star Steve Strange, ex-singer with Visage, is arrested after stealing a £10.99 Teletubbies doll in Bridgend, south Wales. He was given a suspended jail sentence after being caught on a shoplifting spree stealing cosmetics and clothes from High Street stores. Strange was already on bail for stealing a £15 ladies' jacket from Marks and Spencer in Cardiff when he was arrested.

2004
Guitarist and singer Niki Sullivan dies aged 66 of a heart attack at his home in Independence, Missouri. Sullivan was one of the three original members of Buddy Holly's backing group, The Crickets, and co-wrote and sang back-up vocals on many of Holly's hit songs.

2006
Eminem files for divorce from his wife Kim less than three months after the couple re-married on 14 January. Eminem first married his high school sweetheart Kimberly Scott in 1999 but fantasised about her death in his 2000 hit 'Kim'. Unsurprisingly, their marriage ended the following year. Eminem was seeking joint custody of the couple's 10-year-old daughter Hailie Jade Scott.

2009
The PRS announces that the money made by UK artists overseas increased by £20m in 2008, with British talent earning almost £140m. It said international tours by UK acts including The Police, Coldplay, Elton John and Iron Maiden had boosted income. Four of the top 10 bestselling albums globally were by British artists; Coldplay's *Viva La Vida Or Death And All His Friends* was the bestselling album with 6.8 million copies sold, while Welsh singer-songwriter Duffy was fourth with her debut album *Rockferry*. Leona Lewis and Amy Winehouse were sixth and seventh respectively.

Born on this day:

1937 Charlie Thomas, vocals (The Drifters)
1938 Spencer Dryden, drums (Jefferson Airplane)
1946 Bill Kreutzmann, drums (The Grateful Dead)
1947 Florian Schneider-Esleben, woodwinds (Kraftwerk)

1949 John Oates, singer, guitar (Hall & Oates)
1952 Bruce Gary, drums (The Knack)
1960 Simon Climie, songwriter, producer

1962
While at the Ealing Jazz Club to see Alexis Korner's Blues Incorporated, Mick Jagger and Keith Richards meet Brian Jones for the first time. Jones, originally from Cheltenham, calls himself Elmo Lewis and is sitting in, playing slide guitar, during Korner's set.

1967
Pink Floyd play The Floral Hall in Belfast, Northern Ireland.

1975
Ritchie Blackmore quits Deep Purple to form his own band Rainbow. Tommy Bolin, an American guitarist, replaces Blackmore.

1979
Aerosmith, Van Halen, Cheap Trick, The Boomtown Rats and Ted Nugent appear at the California Music Festival.

1981
The Who's ex-manager and producer, Kit Lambert, dies of a cerebral haemorrhage after falling down a flight of stairs at his mother's home in Fulham, London. The previous evening Lambert had been injured in a beating at a gay nightclub.

Bruce Springsteen and the E Street Band kick off their first full-scale tour outside America, covering 10 countries, in Hamburg, Germany.

1988
During a European tour, Alice Cooper nearly hangs himself when a safety rope snaps during a rehearsal. Cooper dangled for several seconds before a roadie saved him.

1994
Lee Brilleaux, singer and harmonica player with R&B band Dr. Feelgood, dies aged 41 of cancer.

Courtney Love is arrested on drugs and theft charges after a reported overdose. At this time, Love was unaware that her husband Kurt Cobain had died (his body wasn't discovered until April 8).

US soul singer Percy Sledge pleads guilty to income tax evasion after he fails to report $260,000 earned between 1987 and 1989. He was sentenced to serve six months in a halfway house.

1996
Take That go to No. 1 on the UK album chart with their *Greatest Hits* album.

1997
Oasis singer Liam Gallagher marries actress Patsy Kensit at Marylebone Registry Office, London. They divorced three years later.

1998
George Michael is arrested by undercover Beverly Hills police officer Marcelo Rodriguez at The Will Rogers Memorial Park for committing a sex act in a public toilet. The singer later said: "I was followed into the restroom and this cop – well, I didn't know he was a cop at the time obviously – started playing this game. I think it's called 'I'll show you mine, you show me yours, and then when you show me yours, I'm gonna nick you!'" The singer was later fined $810 after being convicted of a "lewd act".

2000
Heinz, bass player and singer with The Tornadoes – whose Joe Meek-produced 1962 UK No. 1 'Telstar', made them the first British group to score a US No. 1 – dies aged 57. Heinz also had a 1963 solo hit 'Just Like Eddie', a tribute to Eddie Cochran

(which featured future Deep Purple guitarist Ritchie Blackmore).

2001
Paul McCartney buys a four-bedroom Beverly Hills home (formerly owned by Courtney Love) for $3.995m. The gated 1930s house has its own swimming pool and 1.5 acres of land.

2002
UK *Pop Idol* runner-up Gareth Gates is at No. 1 on the UK singles chart with his version of 'Unchained Melody', making Gates the seventh act to have a Top 40 hit with the song. Jennifer Lopez is at No. 1 on the US singles chart with 'Ain't It Funny' and Celine Dion has the UK & US No. 1 album *A New Day Has Come*.

2008
Feist win five prizes including Album Of The Year at the Junos, Canada's top music awards. The Canadian singer-songwriter won Single Of The Year for '1234', album and pop album for *The Reminder*, as well as artist and songwriter of the year.

April 8

Born on this day:

1942 Roger Chapman, vocals (Family)
1947 Steve Howe, guitarist (Tomorrow, Yes, Asia)
1962 Izzy Stradlin, guitar (Guns N' Roses)
1971 Darren Jessee, drums (Ben Folds Five)

1964
The Supremes record 'Where Did Our Love Go' at Motown's Detroit Studio. The song would become the first of the female trio's five US No. 1 singles.

1967
The 'Hit The Road Stax' tour featuring Otis Redding, Sam & Dave, Carla Thomas, Eddie Floyd, Arthur Conley and Booker T & The MGs appears at London's Hammersmith Odeon.

In Vienna, Sandie Shaw becomes the first UK female artist to win the Eurovision Song Contest with the song 'Puppet On A String' (which she loathes and declines to ever sing again).

1972
Written after the 'Bloody Sunday' massacre of 13 civilians in Northern Ireland, Paul McCartney & Wings release 'Give Ireland Back To The Irish'. The song is banned by the BBC and the IBA and peaks at 16 in the UK and 21 in the US.

1977
The Damned play at the home of the New York punk scene CBGBs, the first UK punk group to play live dates in the USA.

1979
Aerosmith play the first night on their 38-date 'Night In The Rut' Tour at the Los Angeles Memorial Coliseum.

1982
New Order's bass player Peter Hook is knocked unconscious during a riot at a gig in Rotterdam.

1989
Roxette are at No. 1 on the US singles chart with 'The Look', the duo's first American chart-topper and a No. 7 hit in the UK.

1994
The Recording Industry Association of America announces that Pink Floyd's 1973 album *The Dark Side Of The Moon* has become the fourth biggest-selling album in its history, passing the 13 million mark in US sales. The album has sold more than 25 million copies worldwide.

1995
Take That have their sixth UK No. 1 when the Gary Barlow penned 'Back For Good' goes to the top of the charts, selling over 300,000 in its first week. The song, also a US Top 10 hit, won Best British Single at the 1996 Brit Awards.

1997
American singer-songwriter Laura Nyro dies from ovarian cancer. Nyro wrote 'And When I Die', a hit for Blood, Sweat & Tears, 'Wedding Bell Blues', a hit for The 5th Dimension, and 'Stoney End', which was covered by Barbra Streisand. Suzanne Vega, Phoebe Snow, Rosanne Cash, Frank Sinatra and Linda Ronstadt all covered her songs.

1998
Rolling Stones guitarist Ron Wood is among 12 passengers rescued from a boat off the coast of Brazil. The boat was exploring the islands near Angra Dos Reis, south of Rio de Janeiro, when one of its engines caught fire. Passengers are rescued by nearby journalists and the boat explodes moments after they evacuate.

2002
Marilyn Manson denies claims that he was responsible for the death of a woman after a party at his mansion in 2001. Jennifer Syme, a former girlfriend of actor Keanu Reeves, died when her Jeep Cherokee hit three parked cars. Her mother, Maria St John, was suing the singer for wrongful death, claiming Manson was negligent in "instructing the woman to operate a motor vehicle in her incapacitated condition".

2008
Pete Doherty is jailed for 14 weeks for violating his probation and for using drugs. The ex-Libertines and Babyshambles frontman was given a suspended jail sentence in October 2007 for possession of drugs and driving illegally. Doherty's supervision order required him to make regular visits to court for progress reports, as well as to take part in a drug rehabilitation programme but he missed one probation appointment and had been late for another. The sentence forced Doherty to cancel his biggest gig to date at the Royal Albert Hall scheduled for later in April.

Born on this day:

1932 Carl Perkins
1944 Gene Parsons, drums (The Byrds)
1961 Mark Kelly, keyboards (Marillion)
1977 Gerard Way, vocals (My Chemical Romance)

1978 Rachel Stevens, vocals (S Club 7)
1980 Albert Hammond Jr, guitar (The Strokes)
1987 Jesse McCartney, American singer, actor

April 9

1956
Gene Vincent records the classic rock'n'roll song 'Be Bop-A-Lula', which goes on to be a US & UK Top 20 hit this year.

1966
Cliff Richard's version of 'Blue Turns To Grey', a Mick Jagger-Keith Richards composition, reaches No. 15 on the UK charts.

1973
Newly signed to EMI, Queen play a showcase gig for their record label at London's Marquee Club.

1974
Terry Jacks is at No. 1 on the UK singles chart with 'Seasons In The Sun', originally written in French by Belgian, Jacques Brel, with English lyrics by Rod McKuen. Jacks became the first Canadian to score a No. 1 since Paul Anka in 1957.

1976
American folk singer and songwriter Phil Ochs hangs himself at his sister's home in Queens, New York.

1977
Abba top the US singles chart with 'Dancing Queen', the group's seventh US Top 40 hit (and first No. 1) and also a UK No. 1.

1983
David Bowie is top of the British singles chart (his fourth UK No. 1) with the title track from his latest album *Let's Dance*, featuring blues guitarist Stevie Ray Vaughan. It was also Bowie's first single to reach number one on both sides of the Atlantic.

1988
Dave Prater of '60s Stax soul duo Sam & Dave is killed in a car accident in Syracuse, Georgia, on the way to his mother's house in Ocilla. He was 50.

1989
Rolling Stone Bill Wyman, aged 52, announces his forthcoming marriage to 19-year-old Mandy Smith.

1991
Record producer Martin Hannett, who worked with many Manchester acts including The Smiths, New Order, Joy Division, Happy Mondays, Magazine as well as U2 and The Psychedelic Furs, dies aged 42 of heart failure.

1997
Songwriter Mae Boren Axton, the mother of country singer-songwriter

Hoyt Axton, and known as the 'Queen Mother of Nashville', writing over 200 songs including a co-credit on Elvis Presley's 'Heartbreak Hotel', dies aged 82 after drowning in the bath at her home in Hendersonville, Tennessee after an apparent heart attack.

2000
At 18 years and 11 months Craig David becomes the youngest UK male solo artist to write and sing a UK No. 1 with 'Fill Me In'.

2004
After police search his home, James Speedy, 30, from Seattle, Washington, is charged with stalking Avril Lavigne and is later released on $5,000 bail. Speedy had been under investigation since the previous summer for allegedly sending harassing letters and e-mails to the 19-year-old singer.

2007
Country and western singer Tanya Tucker is sued by her manicurist for $300,000 over claims the star's dog attacked and injured her. Danielle Hobbs stated in court papers that she was bitten at the singer's Nashville home and also claimed that the alleged attack had left her with painful and disfiguring scars on her leg. Hobbs stated that Tucker's assistant told her the dogs were "just babies" and said "they will not hurt you".

2009
Bay City Rollers' manager Tam Paton dies in the bath at his Edinburgh home of a suspected heart attack. The 70-year-old, who had suffered two previous heart attacks and a stroke in recent years, was found dead in his luxury mansion. Paton had made millions through the success of the band in the 70s, but was a far more controversial figure in recent years. He was convicted of sex offences against two boys aged 16 and 17 in 1982, and of drug dealing in 2004 after £26,000 worth of cannabis was found at his home, but was cleared on appeal.

Born on this day:

1948 Fred Smith, bass (Television)
1959 Brian Setzer, guitar, vocals (The Stray Cats)
1959 Katrina Leskanich, singer, songwriter (Katrina & The Waves)
1964 Alan 'Reni' Wren, drums (The Stone Roses)
1979 Sophie Ellis Bextor, singer
1981 Elizabeth Margaret, vocals (Atomic Kitten)

1956
Nat King Cole is attacked on stage by a group of five racial segregationists during a show at the Municipal Hall in Birmingham, Alabama. The men are arrested by police and Cole returns later that night for a second show.

1962
The Beatles' original bass player Stuart Sutcliffe dies aged 22 of a brain haemorrhage in an ambulance on the way to hospital. Sutcliffe had left the group to stay in Hamburg, Germany with his girlfriend photographer Astrid Kirchherr and to pursue his art studies.

1965
A British school in Wrexham, North Wales, asks parents to please keep children in school uniform and not to send them to school in "corduroy trousers like the ones worn by The Rolling Stones".

1968
For his 41st single release Cliff Richard achieves his ninth UK No. 1 with 'Congratulations', the British entry in the 1968 Eurovision Song Contest.

1970
Doors singer Jim Morrison is dragged off stage by keyboardist Ray Manzarek during a concert in Boston, after Morrison asked the audience, 'Would you like to see my genitals?' The venue's management quickly switched off the power. Morrison had been arrested in Miami a year earlier for "lewd and lascivious behavior" during a performance.

Paul McCartney issues a press statement announcing his departure from The Beatles (one week before the release of his first solo album, *McCartney*). John Lennon, who had kept his much earlier decision to leave The Beatles quiet for business reasons, is furious. When a reporter calls Lennon asking him to comment upon McCartney's resignation, Lennon says, "Paul hasn't left. I sacked him."

1976
Peter Frampton is at No. 1 on the US album chart with *Frampton Comes Alive*, the biggest selling live album in rock history.

UK music weekly *Melody Maker* reviews a Sex Pistols gig with the words, "I hope we shall hear no more of them."

1984
Nate Nelson, lead vocalist for The Flamingos on their 1959 hit 'I Only Have Eyes For You', dies of heart disease aged 52, a day after his wife had made a plea to his fans to find a donor heart for her ailing husband.

1985
Madonna kicks off her very first North American tour by playing the first of three nights at the Paramount Theatre in Seattle, Washington. The Beastie Boys open for Madonna on the 40-date 'Virgin' Tour.

1990
Tom Waits takes Doritos Chips to court for using a Waits 'sound-alike' on the company's radio ads. The jury awarded $2.475 million in punitive damages to Waits who commented after the case, "Now, by law, I have what I always felt I had... a distinctive voice."

1994
Over 5,000 fans attend a US public memorial service for Kurt Cobain at Seattle Flag Pavilion.

2001
Eminem is given two years probation and fined $2,500 and $5,000 costs after admitting carrying a concealed weapon. The charges followed an incident outside a club in Warren, Michigan the previous June when Eminem 'pistol whipped' John Guerra after he saw him kissing his wife.

2003
American singer Little Eva dies aged 59 in Kinston, North Carolina. Eva was working as a babysitter for songwriters Carole King and Gerry Goffin who asked her to record the song they'd just written. 'The Loco-Motion' – a 1962 US No. 1 & UK No. 2 single – was also an American No. 1 for Grand Funk Railroad in 1974 and a hit for Kylie Minogue in 1988 (US No. 3 and UK No. 2).

2005
The final episode of *The Osbournes* is aired on MTV in the UK. During its three year run, the show reached a peak audience of eight million. Ozzy was at a loss to explain its popularity, saying, "I suppose Americans get a kick out of watching a crazy Brit family like us make complete fools of ourselves every week."

2006
Actress Gwyneth Paltrow and Coldplay singer Chris Martin announce they have named their second child, a boy, Moses Martin. The couple also had a daughter named Apple.

Born on this day:

1956 Neville Staples, vocals (The Specials, Fun Boy 3)

1958 Stuart Adamson, guitar, vocals (Skids, Big Country)

1966 Lisa Stansfield, singer

1969 Cerys Matthews, vocals (Catatonia)

1987 Joss Stone, singer

April 11

1956
Travelling from Amarillo to Nashville, the plane that Elvis Presley is a passenger on develops engine trouble and is forced to make an emergency landing. The incident creates a fear of flying for Presley.

1961
Bob Dylan plays his first live gig in New York City at Gerde's Folk City, opening for John Lee Hooker.

1965
The Beatles, The Rolling Stones, The Animals, The Kinks and others perform at the New Musical Express poll winners concert, at London's Wembley Empire Pool, England.

1967
During an 18-date European tour The Rolling Stones play two shows at the Olympia Theatre in Paris.

1970
While in Germany Peter Green quits Fleetwood Mac but agrees to finish the band's current European tour to avoid breach of contract.

1977
Alice Cooper plays to an audience of 40,000 in Sydney, Australia, the largest crowd to attend a rock concert in the country's history to date. After the show Cooper is placed under house arrest at his hotel until posting a bond for $59,632 – the amount a promoter claimed to have paid Cooper for a 1975 Australia tour he never fulfilled. The two settled when it was found that the promoter did not meet his part of the agreement either.

1981
Hall & Oates start a three week run at No. 1 on the US singles chart with 'Kiss On My List', the duo's second American chart-topper.

1988
Cher wins an Academy Award for Best Actress for her role in *Moonstruck*.

1991
Paula Abdul holds a press conference in Hollywood to deny allegations that backing vocalist Yvete Marine had sung non-credited lead parts on Abdul's *Forever Your Girl* album.

1992
Pearl Jam appear on US TV show *Saturday Night Live* from New York City.

1994
Oasis release their first single 'Supersonic' which peaks at No. 31 on the UK charts.

2001
At a charity auction, Robbie Williams raises £165,000 in funds for his old school in Stoke to build a performing arts block. The items sold were the singer's personal possessions, including a toilet from a stage show, a Union Jack bikini, Tiger's head briefs, a Millennium jet pack and the handwritten lyrics to 'Angels' which sold for £27,000.

2006
Proof (real name Deshaun Holton), a member of Eminem's rap collective D12, is killed in a Detroit nightclub shooting after an argument broke out at the CCC nightclub on Eight Mile Road, made famous in Eminem's autobiographical film *8 Mile*. Holton was a longtime friend of Eminem and was the rapper's best man at his wedding in January of this year.

1973
The Beach Boys appear at the Omni Coliseum, Atlanta, Georgia. The Beach Boys' popularity was at a low ebb in America and this show proves a financial disaster for the promoter, with less than 3,000 tickets sold for the 16,000 capacity venue. Opening act is Mothers Finest and middle of the bill is Bruce Springsteen who plays a 60-minute set.

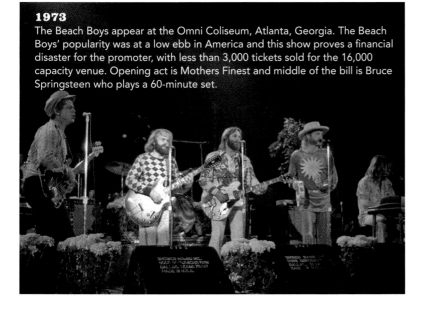

Born on this day:

1944 John Kay, guitar, vocals (Steppenwolf)
1950 David Cassidy, singer, actor
1956 Alexander Briley, vocals (Village People)
1958 Will Sergeant, guitar (Echo & The Bunnymen)
1978 Guy Berryman, bass (Coldplay)

1954
Bill Haley & His Comets record 'Rock Around The Clock' at Pythian Temple studios in New York City. Written by Max C. Freedman and James E. Myers, the song was first recorded by Italian-American band Sonny Dae & His Knights. Considered by many to be the song that put rock 'n' roll on the map around the world, Haley's version was used over the opening titles of the film *Blackboard Jungle* and went on to become a worldwide No. 1 and the biggest selling pop single with sales of over 25 million.

1957
The 'King of Skiffle' Lonnie Donegan is at No. 1 on the UK singles chart with 'Cumberland Gap'.

1963
Bob Dylan performs his first major solo concert at the Town Hall, New York City.

1966
Jan Berry, of Jan & Dean, is almost killed when he crashes his Porsche into a parked truck a short distance from Dead Man's Curve in Los Angeles. Partially paralysed and suffering brain damage, Berry was able to walk again after extensive therapy.

1967
Mick Jagger is punched in the face by an airport official during a row at Le Bourget Airport in Paris. Jagger loses his temper after the Stones entourage was being searched for drugs, resulting in them missing their flight.

1973
The film *That'll Be The Day*, featuring David Essex, Ringo Starr, Keith Moon, and Billy Fury, from a screenplay written by Ray Connolly, premieres in London.

1975
David Bowie announces his second career retirement, saying, "I've rocked my roll. It's a boring dead end, there will be no more rock'n'roll records from me."

During a North American tour, Pink Floyd play the first of two nights at The Cow Palace, San Francisco, California.

1982
David Crosby is arrested when police find him preparing cocaine backstage in his dressing room before a show at Cardi's nightclub in Dallas.

1986
Go-Go's lead singer Belinda Carlisle marries actor Morgan Mason, the son of James Mason.

1989
Two DJs on Los Angeles station KLOS ask "whatever happened to David Cassidy?" The singer calls the station up and the presenters invite him onto their show. Cassidy plays three songs live on air and is subsequently signed by a new record label.

1990
The Astronomical Union's Minor Planet Centre announces that Asteroids 4147-4150, would be named Lennon, McCartney, Harrison and Starr after the four members of The Beatles.

1995
Two weeks after her death, George W. Bush (then the governor of Texas) declares this date "Selena Day" in Texas. Selena, a Mexican American singer, was murdered by the president of her fan club on 31 March.

1997
While on a UK tour, Fun Lovin' Criminals drummer Stephen Borovini receives a police caution after he was arrested on suspicion of making obscene phone calls to women working in gyms in the Leeds area.

2000
The members of Metallica file a suit against Napster, Yale University, The University of Southern California and Indiana University for copyright infringement.

2005
Mariah Carey releases *The Emancipation Of Mimi*, which enters the US chart at No. 1, going six times platinum in less than a year, subsequently becoming the most successful album of 2005.

2008
Day 26, the winners of US TV show *Making The Band*, are at No. 1 on the *Billboard* album chart with their self-titled debut.

Born on this day:

1943 Eve Graham, singer (The New Seekers)
1944 Jack Casady, bass (Jefferson Airplane)
1945 Lowell George, singer, songwriter, guitar (Little Feat)
1946 Al Green, singer
1951 Max Weinberg, drummer (E Street Band)
1962 Hillel Slovak, guitar (The Red Hot Chili Peppers)
1966 Marc Ford, guitar (The Black Crowes)

April
13

1965
The Beatles record the song 'Help!' during an evening recording session at EMI Studios in London.

1967
Nancy and Frank Sinatra are at No. 1 on the UK singles chart with 'Somethin' Stupid', making them the only father and daughter duo to have a chart-topping single.

1970
Genesis appear at the Friars club, Aylesbury, England.

1971
The Rolling Stones release 'Brown Sugar', the first record on their own label, Rolling Stones Records, which introduces the infamous tongue and lips logo.

1974
Paul McCartney & Wings' *Band On The Run* album is at No. 1 on the US album charts – McCartney's third American chart-topping album, which goes on to sell over six million copies worldwide.

1979
Five days into Van Halen's latest tour, David Lee Roth collapses from exhaustion on stage at Spokane Coliseum in Washington.

1993
The first 'Aerosmith Day' is observed in the Commonwealth of Massachusetts after the band is given its very own holiday.

1996
Rage Against The Machine appear on NBC's *Saturday Night Live* but their scheduled two-song performance is cut to one when the band attempt to hang inverted American flags from their amplifiers.

2003
Madonna strikes back at websites who are offering illegal downloads of her new album, *American Life*, by flooding file-sharing networks with decoy files. When the files are opened the voice of Madonna asks, "What the fuck do you think you're doing?" The album had been kept under tight wraps to avoid piracy, with promotional copies being held back from journalists until just before the official release.

2007
Julian Lennon sells a "significant" stake of his share in the songs his father wrote to US music publishing company Primary Wave. The firm would now receive royalty payments when any Lennon compositions were

sold on CD, performed live or played on the radio. The company, who were about to market Julian's new music project, declined to reveal how much the deal was worth but Chief Executive Larry Mestel described it as a "passive" revenue stream that remained under the effective control of Sony/ATV, who owned the majority of the Beatles publishing copyrights

2008
Producer and drummer Clifford Davies, who had worked with Ted Nugent, is found dead aged 59 from a self-inflicted gunshot wound in his home in Atlanta. It was reported that Davies was "extremely distraught" over outstanding medical bills.

2009
Procol Harum's 'A Whiter Shade Of Pale' is the most played song in public places in the past 75 years, according to a chart compiled for BBC Radio 2. Queen's 'Bohemian Rhapsody' was at number two followed by 'All I Have To Do Is Dream' by The Everly Brothers, Wet Wet Wet's 1994 hit, 'Love Is All Around' and Bryan Adams' 1991 hit '(Everything I Do) I Do It For You.'

April 14

Born on this day:

1935 Loretta Lynn, country singer
1942 Tony Burrows, singer-songwriter (Edison Lighthouse, Brotherhood Of Man)
1945 Ritchie Blackmore, guitarist (Deep Purple, Rainbow)
1949 Sonja Kristina, vocals (Curved Air)
1949 Dennis Bryon, drums (Amen Corner, The Bee Gees)

1964

The King Bees (featuring a young David Bowie, then David Jones) play at a wedding reception at The Jack Of Clubs in London.

1967

Polydor Records release The Bee Gees' 'New York Mining Disaster 1941' with a promotional slogan announcing "The most significant talent since The Beatles". The record becomes a Top 20 hit in the UK and US.

1968

Phil Spector marries Ronettes singer and protege Veronica Bennett. The couple divorced in 1973 with Bennett citing several instances of alleged cruelty.

1969

The Beatles' recording of 'The Ballad Of John and Yoko' takes place with just two members, John Lennon and Paul McCartney. Paul plays bass, drums and piano with John on guitars and lead vocals. The song is banned from many radio stations as being blasphemous and on some stations the word 'Christ' was edited to avoid the ban.

1970

Creedence Clearwater Revival make their live UK debut when playing the first of two nights at London's Royal Albert Hall.

1971

The Illinois Crime Commission issues a list of 'drug-oriented records' including 'White Rabbit' by Jefferson Airplane, 'A Whiter Shade Of Pale' by Procol Harum and The Beatles' 'Lucy In The Sky With Diamonds'.

1973

Led Zeppelin start a two-week run on the top of the UK album chart with *Houses Of The Holy*, also a No. 1 in the US. The young girl featured on the cover of the album, climbing naked up Giants Causeway in Northern Ireland, is Samantha Gates who was six at the time of the photo shoot.

1978

Joy Division play at the 'Stiff Test-Chiswick Challenge', at Raffters in Manchester. Future managers Rob Gretton and then journalist Tony Wilson see the band for the first time.

1983

The Pretenders bass player Pete Farndon dies from a drug overdose. He had been sacked from the group on June 14, 1982 (two days before Pretenders guitarist James Honeyman-Scott was found dead of heart failure). Farndon was in the process of forming a new band with former Clash drummer Topper Headon when he died.

1994

Kurt Cobain is cremated at the Bleitz Funeral Home, Seattle. The death certificate listed Cobain's occupation as Poet/Musician and his type of business as Punk Rock.

1995

American actor, writer and folk singer Burl Ives, who had hits with 'Funny Way Of Laughing', 'The Blue Tail Fly' and 'Little Bitty Tear', and won an Academy Award for Best Supporting Actor for his role in the 1958 film *The Big Country*, dies aged 85 of cancer.

2001

Sean Puffy Combs (P. Diddy) is arrested in Miami for riding a scooter in South Beach on a suspended driver's license. He was released 20 minutes later after signing a promise to appear in court.

2003

Alex Conate is arrested, being accused of fabricating a Björk concert then allegedly selling $14,000 worth of tickets at $40 each after persuading a San Diego nightclub owner that Björk had agreed to play there. Conate is accused of fleeing with the money and relocating to Hawaii where he was arrested.

2009

A planned auction of nearly 1,400 items from the former home of Michael Jackson is cancelled in return for Jackson dropping a lawsuit against Juliens Auctions. A public preview of the collection had already begun in Los Angeles, with the exhibition of Jackson's possessions due to stay open until the end of the following week. A last-minute settlement meant Jackson's belongings would now be returned to him.

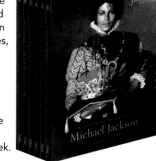

Born on this day:

1944 Dave Edmunds, guitarist, producer (Love Sculpture, Rockpile)

1965 Linda Perry, songwriter, singer (4 Non Blondes)

1967 Frankie Poullain, bass (The Darkness)

1968 Edward John O'Brien, guitarist (Radiohead)

April 15

1966
Buffalo Springfield make their live debut opening for The Byrds at a concert in San Bernardino, California.

1967
The Walker Brothers, Cat Stevens, The Jimi Hendrix Experience and 'Special Guest Star' Engelbert Humperdinck UK package tour appears at the Odeon, Blackpool. Tickets cost 5 or 10 shillings.

1969
Pink Floyd appear at the Royal Festival Hall, London.

1975
Kiss, Rush and The Heavy Metal Kids all appear at the Stanley Theatre in Pittsburgh, Pennsylvania.

1985
During his 'Born In The USA' world tour, Bruce Springsteen and the E Street Band play the fourth of five sold-out nights at Yoyogi Olympic Pool in Tokyo, Japan.

1987
Queen are presented with an award for Outstanding Contribution to British Music at the 32nd Annual Ivor Novello Awards held in London.

1989
American all girl group The Bangles start a four week run at No. 1 on the UK singles chart with 'Eternal Flame'; also a No. 1 in the US and Australia (where it becomes the biggest selling single of 1989).

1996
After a small portion had been scattered in the Ganges River in India 11 days earlier, the rest of Jerry Garcia's ashes are scattered near San Francisco's Golden Gate Bridge. The Grateful Dead leader had died on 9 August, 1995.

2001
Punk pioneer Joey Ramone, singer of The Ramones, dies aged 49 after losing a long battle with lymphatic cancer. On November 30, 2003, a block of East 2nd Street in New York City was officially renamed Joey Ramone Place.

2003
Beyonce is sued by the Wilhemina Artist Agency who claimed she hadn't paid them the commission for her L'Oreal ads. The agency claimed the singer refused to pass on 10 percent of the $1m deal that they had brokered.

2007
Aerosmith, Velvet Revolver, Placebo, Keane and Evanescence all appear at the Quilmes Rock festival at River Stadium, Argentina.

2008
Mayor Antonio Villaraigosa proclaims this day as 'Mariah Carey Day' in Los Angeles.

2009
Former Beatle George Harrison is honoured with a posthumous star on the Hollywood Walk of Fame in Los Angeles. Paul McCartney attends the unveiling outside the landmark Capitol Records building, joining Harrison's widow Olivia and son Dhani. Eric Idle, Tom Petty and actor Tom Hanks also attend the ceremony.

April 16

Born on this day:

1939 Dusty Springfield (Mary O'Brien), singer
1947 Gerry Rafferty, singer-songwriter
1956 Paul Buchanan, vocals, guitar, keyboards (The Blue Nile)
1963 Jimmy Osmond, vocals
1964 Dave Pirner, vocals, guitar (Soul Asylum)

1955
Elvis Presley (with Scotty Moore and Bill Black) perform at the Jamboree at the Sportatorium in Dallas, Texas. Also on the bill are Sonny James, Hank Locklin and Charline Arthur. Admission is 60 cents, half price for children.

1956
Buddy Holly's first single 'Blue Days, Black Nights' is released.

1967
Cream appear on the bill at the *Daily Express* 'Record Star Show' at Wembley's Empire Pool, London.

1969
Elektra Records drop Detroit's MC5 from their label after the band took out an advertisement in a local underground paper that included the company's logo, reading "Fuck Hudsons" in protest at the Michigan department store's refusal to stock their album *Kick Out The Jams*.

1972
The Electric Light Orchestra make their debut at The Fox & Greyhound in Croydon, London.

1973
During his Ziggy Stardust world tour, David Bowie appears at the Kobe, Kobe Kokusai Kaikan, Japan.

1983
Bonnie Tyler is at No. 1 on the UK chart with *Faster Than The Speed Of Night*, her fifth album and only chart-topper.

1985
During the North American leg of their 'Unforgettable Fire' tour U2 play the first of three nights at The Centrum in Worcester, Massachusetts.

1993
David Lee Roth is arrested in New York's Washington Square Park for allegedly buying a $10 bag of marijuana.

1994
Prince has his first UK No. 1 with 'The Most Beautiful Girl In The World' (his 37th single release). It was his first release since changing his stage name to an unpronounceable symbol.

1996
Kiss appear in full make-up at the 38th Grammy Awards, where they use the opportunity to announce a reunion tour. It would mark the first time all four members had appeared together in over 15 years.

1997
Mark Morrison is convicted of threatening a police officer with an illegal 23,000-volt electric stun gun. The singer leaves Marylebone

Magistrates Court in tears after being warned he was likely to be sent to prison.

1998
Janet Jackson plays the first night on her third world tour at The Ahoy in Rotterdam, Netherlands. Support acts on her 'Velvet Rope Tour' include Usher, N Sync and Boyz II Men.

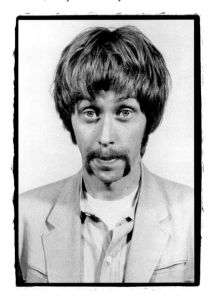

1999
Skip Spence, an original member of Jefferson Airplane and founding member of Moby Grape, dies aged 52 of lung cancer in a San Francisco hospital. He had battled schizophrenia and alcoholism for over 30 years.

2003
Jerry Lee Lewis files for divorce from his sixth wife, Kerrie McCarver Lewis. The 67-year-old singer married Kerrie, who was the president of Lewis Enterprises Inc. fan club, in 1984.

2005
OK Computer by Radiohead is voted the best album of all time in a poll by UK TV station Channel 4. U2 were in second place with *The Joshua Tree* and Nirvana third with *Nevermind*.

1977
David Soul, the blonde Hutch half of popular TV cop show *Starsky & Hutch*, is at No. 1 on the US singles chart with 'Don't Give Up On Us', his only US hit, which was also a No. 1 in the UK.

Born on this day:

1940 Billy Fury, singer
1955 Pete Shelley, guitar, vocals (Buzzcocks)
1967 Matt Chamberlain, session drummer

1974 Victoria Adams (a.k.a. Posh Spice, Victoria Beckham), vocals (The Spice Girls)

April 17

1960

While touring in the UK, 21-year-old US singer Eddie Cochran is killed when the taxi he was travelling in crashed into a lamppost on Rowden Hill, Chippenham, Wiltshire (where a plaque now commemorates the event). Songwriter Sharon Sheeley and singer Gene Vincent survive the crash. Ironically Cochran's current hit at the time was 'Three Steps To Heaven'. The taxi driver, George Martin, is convicted of dangerous driving, fined £50, disqualified from driving for 15 years, and sent to prison for six months.

1965

A reissue of Bob Dylan's second album *The Freewheelin' Bob Dylan* is at No. 1 on the UK LP chart.

1970

Johnny Cash plays at the White House for President Nixon who requested that he perform 'A Boy Named Sue.'

1971

All four Beatles have solo singles in the UK charts: Paul McCartney with 'Another Day', John Lennon ('Power To The People'), George Harrison ('My Sweet Lord') and Ringo Starr ('It Don't Come Easy').

1975

Elvis Presley buys a Convair 880 Jet formally owned by Delta Airlines for $250,000, which he re-christens Lisa Marie. Presley spent a further $600,000 refurbishing the jet to include personal quarters, a meeting area and a dance floor.

1983

Felix Pappalardi, producer and bass player with Mountain, is shot dead by his wife Gail Collins during a jealous rage. Collins was convicted of criminally negligent homicide and sentenced to four years in prison.

1987

Reggae drummer and percussion player Carlton Barrett, formerly of Bob Marley & The Wailers, is shot dead outside his home in Kingston, Jamaica. Barrett was the originator of the one-drop rhythm – a percussive drumming style.

1991

Nirvana appear at the OK Hotel in Seattle, Washington, where they play a new song, 'Smells Like Teen Spirit', live for the first time.

1998
Linda McCartney dies, aged 56, after a battle against cancer.

2007

Bryan Ferry is forced to make an apology after praising Nazi iconography in a German magazine. Talking to *Welt am Sonntag*, he said the Nazis "knew how to put themselves in the limelight and present themselves ... I'm talking about the films of Leni Riefenstahl and the buildings of Albert Speer and the mass marches and the flags. Just amazing – really beautiful." British MPs asked shoppers to think twice about shopping in Marks & Spencer, requesting Ferry be dropped as the face of the M&S Autograph menswear collection. Ferry said he was "deeply upset" by the publicity surrounding the interview.

2009

Morrissey walks off stage during his set at the Coachella festival in California after declaring he could "smell burning flesh". The committed vegetarian took offence to the smell coming from nearby barbecues. Sir Paul McCartney, The Killers and The Cure also appear at the three-day event.

1973
Pink Floyd's *The Dark Side Of the Moon* goes gold in the US. The LP stayed in the US album chart for more than ten years and became the longest charting rock record of all time.

April 18

Born on this day:

1939 Glen D. Hardin, piano (The Crickets)
1942 Mike Vickers, arranger, guitar, woodwinds (Manfred Mann)
1944 Skip Spence, drums, guitar, vocals (Jefferson Airplane, Moby Grape)

1958 Les Pattinson, bass (Echo & The Bunnymen)
1974 Mark Tremonti, guitar (Creed)

1953
Frankie Laine is at No. 1 on the UK singles chart with 'I Believe', staying top of the charts for nine weeks. Laine holds the record for most (non-consecutive) weeks at No. 1 with one single – three chart runs with a total of 18 weeks.

1964
The Beatles pre-recorded appearance on the British comedy programme *The Morecambe and Wise Show* is broadcast on ITV. The Beatles play 'This Boy', 'All My Loving' and 'I Want to Hold Your Hand' and also take part in a comedy sketch with Eric Morecambe and Ernie Wise. The Beatles also hold the UK and US No. 1 positions on this day with 'Can't Buy Me Love'.

1969
Lulu marries Bee Gee Maurice Gibb, with his elder brother Barry as best man. The couple split in 1973.

1970
Steel Mill (featuring Bruce Springsteen) play the Main Gym at Ocean County College, New Jersey. Tickets cost $2.00.

1981
This year's Eurovision Song contest winners Bucks Fizz are at No. 1 on the UK singles chart with 'Making Your Mind Up'.

1984
Michael Jackson undergoes surgery in a Los Angeles hospital to repair damage caused by his hair catching fire during the filming of a Pepsi commercial.

1985
Wham! become the first-ever Western pop act to have an album released in China.

1987
Aretha Franklin and George Michael start a two week run at No. 1 on the US singles chart with 'I Knew You Were Waiting', also a No. 1 in the UK. Aretha set a record for the artist with the longest gap between US No. 1 singles; it had been 19 years and 10 months since 'Respect' in June 1967.

1995
Oasis drummer Tony McCarroll is told by phone that he was to be sacked from the group. McCarroll sued the group for millions in unpaid royalties and in 1996 Oasis agreed to pay him a one-off sum of £550,000.

1996
Bernard Edwards, bass guitarist and producer from Chic, who also worked with ABC, The Power Station, Sister Sledge, Sheila &. Devotion, Diana Ross, Johnny Mathis, Debbie Harry, Air Supply and Rod Stewart, dies of pneumonia in a Tokyo hotel room while touring Japan.

2004
Eamon, an R&B singer from New York, starts a four week run at No. 1 on the UK chart with his debut single, 'Fuck It, (I Don't Want You Back)'. The song earned a listing in the *Guinness Book Of World Records* for "the most expletives in a No. 1 song" with 33.

2005
A UK TV ad featuring US rapper 50 Cent is withdrawn by sports firm Reebok after a London mother Lucy Cope, whose son was shot dead, complained to the Advertising Standards Authority that it glamorised gun crime. The ASA had been investigating 54 other complaints from viewers over a reference to the rapper having been shot nine times.

2006
A line from U2's 1992 hit 'One' was voted the UK's favourite song lyric in a poll of 13,000 people by music channel VH1. The line, "One life, with each other, sisters, brothers" came top. The Smiths' lyric "So you go, and you stand on your own, and you leave on your own, and you go home, and you cry, and you want to die" from the song 'How Soon is Now?' came second in the poll, followed by "I feel stupid and contagious, here we are now, entertain us", from Nirvana's 'Smells Like Teen Spirit' was voted third.

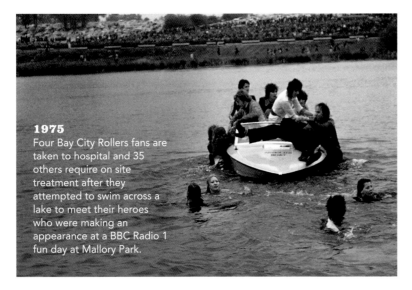

1975
Four Bay City Rollers fans are taken to hospital and 35 others require on site treatment after they attempted to swim across a lake to meet their heroes who were making an appearance at a BBC Radio 1 fun day at Mallory Park.

Born on this day:

1928 Alexis Korner, blues singer, guitarist, broadcaster

1942 Alan Price, keyboards (The Animals, Alan Price Set)

1944 Bernie Worrell, keyboards (Parliament, Funkadelic)

1947 Mark Volman, vocals (The Turtles)

April 19

1965

The film *The T.A.M.I. Show* (Teen Age Music International) featuring a star list of performers including The Rolling Stones, James Brown, The Supremes, The Miracles and Chuck Berry, opens in Britain to limited distribution under the title *Teenage Command Performance*. The movie would not be properly released in the UK until the following year.

1968

John Lennon, George Harrison and their wives leave the Maharishi Mahesh Yogi's ashram in Rishikesh, India two weeks before their study was complete. Ringo and Paul had already left.

1969

Smile (later to be known as Queen) appear at the Revolution Club, London.

1970

Eurovision Song Contest winner Dana, from Ireland, is at No. 1 on the UK singles chart with 'All Kinds Of Everything'.

1974

Bruce Springsteen and the E Street Band appear at the State Theatre, New Brunswick, New Jersey. The gig was unadvertised by the promoter, who gambled that word-of-mouth would be enough to fill the 550-seat venue, but only 250 people attended. Tickets cost $5.50 or $4.50 in advance.

1980

Brian Johnson, 32-year-old English singer with Geordie, replaces the late Bon Scott in Australian rock band AC/DC.

1986

George Michael is at No. 1 on the UK singles chart with 'A Different Corner', the singer's second solo chart-topper, becoming the first solo act in the history of the UK charts to reach No. 1 with his first two releases. The song was also credited with being the second No. 1 (after 'I Just Called To Say I Love You' by Stevie Wonder) to be written, sung, played, arranged and produced by the same person.

1988

Sonny Bono, former singer and one half of Sonny and Cher, is inaugurated as the Mayor of Palm Springs, California.

1995

The Stone Roses play their first gig in five years when appearing at The Rockerfella Club, Oslo, Norway.

2000

Phil Collins wins £250,000 in a high court case over royalties with two former members of his band. The judge ruled that the two musicians had been overpaid in error but because they had no other income they would not have to pay it back.

2002

Police were investigating how tracks from the forthcoming Oasis album *Heathen Chemistry* had been illegally circulated on the Internet. They believed the person responsible had access to the band's private recording sessions.

2003

Conrad Leonard, the oldest working musician in Britain, dies aged 104. Composer and pianist Leonard had worked at the BBC during his career and, until the age of 103, he played the piano each Thursday at lunchtime in the Plantation Cafe at Squire's Garden Centre, Twickenham.

2005

It is announced that two 30-second television commercials designed to attract vacationing families to experience the "real" Elvis Presley at Graceland would air nationally in the US starting in April 2006. It was the first time in the history of Elvis Presley Enterprises, Inc. that the company had used television advertising to promote Graceland tourism.

April 20

Born on this day:

1948 Craig Frost, keyboards (Grand Funk Railroad)
1951 Luther Vandross, soul singer
1971 Mikey Welsh, bass (Weezer)
1972 Carmen Electra, singer (The Pussycat Dolls)

1957
Elvis Presley starts an eight-week run at No. 1 on the US singles chart with 'All Shook Up', selling over two million copies and becoming the biggest single of 1957.

1959
In the US, Goldband Records release 'Puppy Love' by a 13-year old Dolly Parton, a song that was recorded two years earlier when she was just 11 years old. The song didn't chart but was a hit in 1960 for Paul Anka and in 1972 for Donny Osmond.

1968
Deep Purple make their live debut in Tastrup, Denmark.

1979
21-year old lighting director Billy Duffy is killed in an accident during a Kate Bush concert in Southampton, England, falling twenty feet through an open trap door on the stage. Bush held a benefit concert, featuring Peter Gabriel and Steve Harley, on 12 May at London's Hammersmith Odeon for Duffy's family.

1981
John Phillips of The Mamas & The Papas is jailed for five years after pleading guilty to drug possession charges but the sentence was suspended after 30 days. Phillips started touring the US lecturing against the dangers of drugs.

1985
The charity record 'We Are The World' by USA For Africa is at No. 1 on the UK singles chart. The US artists' answer to Band Aid had an all-star cast including Stevie Wonder, Tina Turner, Bruce Springsteen, Diana Ross, Bob Dylan, Daryl Hall, Huey Lewis, Cyndi Lauper, Kim Carnes, Ray Charles, Billy Joel and Paul Simon, plus Michael Jackson and Lionel Richie who composed the track.

1990
Janet Jackson is bestowed with a Hollywood Walk Of Fame star at the start of 'Janet Jackson Week' in Los Angeles.

1991
Steve Marriott, former guitarist and singer with The Small Faces and Humble Pie, dies in a fire at his home in Arkesden, Essex.

1992
A Concert For Life takes place at London's Wembley Stadium as a tribute to Queen singer Freddie Mercury and for AIDS awareness. Acts appearing include Liza Minelli, Elton John, Roger Daltrey, Tony Iommi (Black Sabbath), David Bowie, Mick Ronson, James Hetfield (Metallica), George Michael, Seal, Paul Young, Annie Lennox, Lisa Stansfield, Robert Plant, Joe Elliot and Phil Collen (from Def Leppard), and Axl Rose and Slash (Guns N' Roses).

1993
Aerosmith release *Get A Grip*, becoming their first album to debut at No. 1, selling seven million copies over a two-year timespan in the US alone, 20 million copies worldwide as well as winning the band two Grammy awards.

1997
Michael Jackson attends an unveiling of a wax statue of himself at the Grevin Museum of Wax in Paris, France. Jackson provided one of his own outfits to dress the figure.

2002
In the dispute over who owns the rights to Nirvana's recordings former members Dave Grohl and Krist Novoselic ask a Seattle court to prove that Courtney Love is mentally unstable, telling the court that Love is "irrational, mercurial, self-centered, unmanageable, inconsistent and unpredictable". They also claim a particular contract was invalid because Love was "stoned" at the time.

2006
Babyshambles singer Pete Doherty is arrested in east London on suspicion of possessing drugs only hours after a court appearance. Doherty had earlier admitted to seven charges of drugs possession when appearing before magistrates in east London.

He was given a community order with two years supervision and 18 months drug rehabilitation and was also banned from driving for six months.

Born on this day:

1947 Iggy Pop, singer (The Stooges, solo)
1947 Alan Warner, guitar (The Foundations)

1959 Robert Smith, guitar, vocals (The Cure, The Glove)
1963 Johnny McElhone, guitarist (Altered Images, Texas)

April 21

1963
During their continuing Sunday evening residency, The Rolling Stones appear at The Crawdaddy Club, Station Hotel, Richmond. The band is paid £50 for the gig.

1967
Working at EMI Studios in London, The Beatles complete the sessions for *Sgt. Pepper's Lonely Hearts Club Band* by recording a short section of gibberish which would play in the LP's run-out groove. They record assorted noises and voices, which engineer Geoff Emerick then cut-up, randomly re-assembled and edited backwards. At John Lennon's suggestion, this was preceded by a high-pitch, 15 kilocycle whistle audible only to dogs.

1969
In her only London appearance, Janis Joplin appears at The Royal Albert Hall supported by Yes.

1973
Tony Orlando & Dawn start a four week run at No. 1 on the US singles chart with 'Tie A Yellow Ribbon (Round The Old Oak Tree)', which became the biggest seller of 1973, selling over six million copies. The song is based on a true story of a prisoner who wrote to his wife asking her to tie a yellow ribbon around an oak tree in the town

square of White Oak, Georgia, if she still loved him.

1978
Sandy Denny, former sing of Fairport Convention and Fotheringay, dies aged 31 from a traumatic, mid-brain haemorrhage. Denny had previously been injured in a fall down a staircase, and a month later collapsed at a friend's home, dying four days later in hospital.

1982
Clash frontman Joe Strummer disappears for three weeks, resulting in the group cancelling a tour. The singer is tracked down to Paris, France.

1984
Phil Collins starts a three week run at No. 1 in the *Billboard* singles chart with the theme from *Against All Odds*, Collins' first US No. 1 and a No. 2 in the UK.

1990
Paul McCartney plays to an audience of 184,000 at the Maracana Stadium in

Rio de Janeiro, creating a new world record for the largest crowd attending a rock concert.

1990
Sinead O'Connor starts a four week stay at No. 1 in the US singles chart with her version of the Prince song 'Nothing Compares 2 U'. The track was also a chart-topper in 18 other countries.

2000
Neal Matthews of The Jordanaires, who sang on Elvis Presley's 'Don't Be Cruel' and 'Hound Dog', and also worked with Ricky Nelson, Patsy Cline, Red Foley, Johnny Horton, Jim Reeves, George Jones, Marie Osmond, Tom Jones and Merle Haggard, dies of a heart attack.

2001
R.E.M. guitarist Peter Buck is charged at Heathrow Airport with being drunk on an aircraft and assaulting British Airways crew. Buck was taken into custody after landing on a flight from Seattle and questioned by police for 12 hours.

2006
The Soul2Soul II Tour 2006, a co-headlining tour between country music singers and husband and wife Tim McGraw and Faith Hill kicks off at the Nationwide Arena in Columbus, Ohio, ending after 73 shows on September 3, 2006 in Las Vegas. It became the highest grossing country music tour ever with a take of $90 million.

2007
Doris Richards, the mother of Keith Richards, dies aged 91 of cancer. Doris bought the future Rolling Stone his first guitar for his 15th birthday. Keith learned some chords from her father, Gus Dupree, a musician who instilled in him an early passion for music.

April 22

Born on this day:

1936 Glen Campbell, singer-songwriter
1950 Peter Frampton, guitar, vocals (The Herd, Humble Pie, solo)
1951 Paul Carrack, keyboards, vocals (Ace, Squeeze & solo)
1974 Shavo Odadjian, bass (System Of A Down)
1979 Daniel Johns, guitar, vocals (Silverchair)

1957
Elvis Presley's custom built 'Music Gates' are installed at Graceland, designed by Abe Saucer and built by John Dillars Jr, of Memphis Doors Inc.

1964
The President of The National Federation Of Hairdressers offers a free haircut to the next No. 1 group in the UK pop charts. He says, "The Rolling Stones are the worst. One of them looks as if he's got a feather duster on his head."

1966
Due to a contractual dispute, 'Wild Thing' by The Troggs is released in the US on both the Atco and Fontana labels. The combined sales help to ensure the song reaches No. 1 in the States.

Two dozen local groups perform three songs each at a Battle Of The Bands in Matawan Keyport Roller Drome, New Jersey. The Rogues win first place, second was Sonny & The Starfires, and third place went to The Castiles, featuring Bruce Springsteen on vocals. The three winners are given an opportunity to perform at the Roller Drome the following week as part of a major concert headlined by The Crystals.

1967
In a Most Popular Monkee poll conducted in the UK music paper *Disc & Music Echo*, Davy Jones receives 63% of the votes, Micky Dolenz 22%, Peter Tork 8% and Mike Nesmith 7%.

1969
Fleetwood Mac kick off a 10-date UK tour at the Royal Albert Hall, London. Also on the bill are BB King, Sonny Terry & Brownie McGhee and Duster Bennett.

1977
The Jam release their first single 'In The City', which peaks at No. 40 in the British charts. The trio went on to achieve 17 other Top 40 hits, including four UK No. 1s.

1978
Bob Marley & The Wailers perform at the 'One Love Peace Concert' in Jamaica – Marley's first public appearance in Jamaica since being wounded in an assassination attempt a year and a half earlier.

John Belushi and Dan Aykroyd make their first ever appearance as The Blues Brothers when appearing on US TV's *Saturday Night Live*.

1989
Madonna starts a three-week run on top of the *Billboard* singles chart with 'Like A Prayer', the singer's seventh US No. 1 and also a No. 1 in the UK.

1991
The Dave Matthews Band play their first-ever live show when appearing at the Earth Day Festival in Charlottesville, Virginia.

2001
Destiny's Child are on top of the UK singles chart with their second No. 1, 'Survivor', which won a Grammy Award for Best R&B Performance by a Group. The trio are the first US female band to have more than one British chart-topper.

2003
Songwriter Felice Bryant dies aged 77 of cancer. With her husband Boudleaux Bryant she wrote many hits including The Everly Brothers 'Bye Bye Love', 'All I Have To Do Is Dream', and 'Wake Up Little Susie' and 'Raining In My Heart' for Buddy Holly. Other acts to record their songs include Bob Dylan, Tony Bennett, Simon & Garfunkel, Sarah Vaughan, The Grateful Dead, Dolly Parton, Elvis Presley, The Beach Boys, Roy Orbison, Elvis Costello, Count Basie, Dean Martin, Ruth Brown, Cher, R.E.M. and Ray Charles.

2008
News reports surface in which 50s entertainer Tommy Steele claims to have taken Elvis Presley on a secret sightseeing tour around London in 1958 after the pair struck up a friendship. When the rock legend flew into the capital for a day, Steele apparently took him around famous landmarks such as the Houses of Parliament. For more than 50 years, Presley fans had believed the only time Elvis ever set foot in the UK was during a stop-over at Prestwick Airport in Scotland in March 1960.

April 23

1956

Elvis Presley (with Scotty Moore and Bill Black) plays the first night of a two-week engagement (playing two shows a day) at the New Frontier Hotel, Las Vegas. Presley was not the typical Las Vegas Strip entertainer of the time and his shows are met with a cool reception.

1960

While staying at his aunt's pub The Fox And Hounds in Caversham, Berkshire, Paul McCartney and his friend John Lennon perform acoustically in the pub's taproom as The Nerk Twins.

1971

The Rolling Stones release their classic album *Sticky Fingers*. The album made No. 1 in the UK and the US and was the band's first release to be distributed through Atlantic Records. The cover, showing a pair of jeans with a working zip, was designed by Andy Warhol who was paid £15,000 for his artwork.

1976

The Ramones release their eponymous debut album in the US. On the same date The Sex Pistols play The Nashville Rooms, west London supporting The 101'ers featuring future Clash vocalist Joe Strummer.

1977

Adam & The Ants make their debut at The Roxy Club, London.

1983

David Bowie starts a three week run at No. 1 on the UK album chart with the Nile Rodgers produced *Let's Dance*, featuring the title track which reaches No. 1 on the US and UK singles chart and 'China Girl'.

U2 kick off their 48-date 'War' North American tour at The Carolina Concert For Children benefit, Chapel Hill, Carolina.

1987

Carole King sues record company owner Lou Adler for breach of contract. King claims that she is owed over $400,000 in royalties. She also asks for all rights to her old recordings.

1988

Roy Orbison celebrates his 52nd birthday at a Bruce Springsteen concert, during which the audience sing "Happy Birthday" to him.

1991

Founder member of The New York Dolls, Johnny Thunders, dies in mysterious circumstances in a New Orleans hotel room. Real name John Genzale, from Queens, New York, he renamed himself Johnny Thunders, after a comic book of the same name. The influential New York Dolls formed in 1971 and made just two albums. After leaving the NY Dolls, Thunders and Dolls drummer Jerry Nolan formed The Heartbreakers with ex-Television bassist Richard Hell.

1992

George Michael announces he is donating $500,000 royalties from the sale of 'Don't Let The Sun Go Down On Me' to various British and American charities.

1995

Peter Hodgson, from Liverpool, finds a tape in his attic containing some of The Beatles' earliest recordings made circa 1960. The tape includes 'Hello Little Girl', an early Lennon-McCartney composition that The Beatles never recorded and a cover of Ray Charles' 'Hallelujah, I Love Her So'. The sessions had been made on a reel-to-reel recorder that Hodgson's father had lent to Paul McCartney.

1997

Club boss Paul Donavan is fined over £2,000 after being found guilty of tricking fans into thinking he had Australian pop star Peter Andre appearing at his club in the West Midlands. The act was, in fact, called Peter Andrex, a puppet who threw toilet rolls.

2006

Take That kick off a comeback tour at Newcastle Metro Arena, 10 years after their split.

2008

Bon Jovi guitarist Richie Sambora is sentenced to three years probation after admitting to driving under the influence of alcohol. 48-year-old Sambora, who was not present at the court hearing, would also have to attend first offender alcohol awareness classes.

After an all-day drinking session, Amy Winehouse visits The Good Mixer pub in Camden, north London with Babyshambles guitarist Mik Whitnall. She allegedly punches Mustapha el Mounmi in the face after he refuses to give way to her at the pool table. The singer then left to visit Bar Tok in the early hours. Once at the bar she shouted, "I am a legend, get these people out! I want to take drugs." After leaving the bar, a good Samaritan tried to get her a cab but she reportedly thought he was trying to molest her and allegedly headbutted him in the face.

Born on this day:

1942 Barbra Streisand, singer, actress
1945 Doug Clifford, drums (Creedence Clearwater Revival)
1968 Aaron Comess, drums (The Spin Doctors)
1982 Kelly Clarkson, singer

1955
Perez Prado – known as the 'King of the Mambo' – is at No. 1 on the UK singles chart with 'Cherry Pink And Apple Blossom White'. The instrumental was the theme from the film *Underwater!* and featured in dancing scene with Jane Russell.

1961
Bob Dylan plays harmonica on the track 'Calypso King' on Harry Belafonte's album *The Midnight Special*. The 19-year-old Dylan was paid a $50 session fee for what was his first ever recording appearance.

1965
Wayne Fontana & The Mindbenders are at No. 1 on the US singles chart with 'The Game Of Love', a No. 2 hit in the UK. Wayne took his name from DJ Fontana, Elvis Presley's drummer, while guitarist Eric Stewart went on to form Hotlegs and 10CC.

1968
The Beatles' Apple Publishing company turns down an opportunity to sign David Bowie.

1972
John Lennon's controversial single, 'Woman Is The Nigger Of The World', is released in the US. The song peaks at No. 57, despite virtually every radio station in the country refusing to play it. Yoko Ono had said the phrase during a *Nova* magazine interview in 1968 and Lennon explained that he was making a point that women deserved a higher status in society.

1975
Peter Ham, of Badfinger, commits suicide by hanging himself in the garage of his Surrey home, aged 27. Ham co-wrote 'Without You' with band mate Tom Evans (who also later committed suicide). The song became a hit for Harry Nilsson and won an Ivor Novello award for Song Of The Year in 1973. Ham was a founder member of Welsh group The Iveys, who became Badfinger and were signed to the Beatles' Apple label in 1968. Their first hit, 'Come And Get It', was written by Paul McCartney.

1976
Paul and Linda McCartney, spending the evening with John Lennon at his Dakota apartment in New York, are watching *Saturday Night Live* on NBC. The producer of the show Lorne Michaels makes an impromptu offer on air of $3,000 if The Beatles will turn up and play three songs live. Lennon and McCartney momentarily think about taking a cab to the studio as a joke, but decide against it.

1979
Ray Charles' 'Georgia On My Mind' is proclaimed the state song of Georgia.

1984
Jerry Lee Lewis marries wife number six, 22-year-old Kerrie McCarver.

1984
R.E.M. appear at the Tin Can Club, Birmingham – the first of seven gigs on the band's first full British tour.

1990
In Potsdamer Platz, Berlin, the crew who are constructing the set for Roger Waters' 'The Wall' concert discover an unexploded World War II bomb.

1992
David Bowie marries Somali born model and actress Iman in Switzerland.

1995
Oasis release 'Some Might Say' which gives the band their first UK No. 1 single.

2007
On her website Sheryl Crow proposes that a ban on using too much toilet paper should be introduced to help the environment. The singer suggests using "only one square per restroom visit, except, of course, on those pesky occasions where two to three could be required". Crow made the comments after touring the US in a biodiesel-powered bus to raise awareness about climate change. Crow had also designed a clothing line with what she called a "dining sleeve". The sleeve is detachable and can be replaced with another "dining sleeve" after the diner has used it to wipe his or her mouth.

Born on this day:

1918 Ella Fitzgerald, singer
1945 Bjorn Ulvaeus, guitar, vocals (Abba)
1945 Stu Cook, bass (Creedence Clearwater Revival)
1958 Fish, vocals (Marillion, solo)
1965 Simon Fowler, vocals (Ocean Colour Scene)

April 25

1970
The Jackson Five start a two-week run at No. 1 on the *Billboard* singles chart with 'ABC', the group's second US No. 1 and a No. 8 hit in the UK.

1974
Pamela Courson, the long-term companion of the late Jim Morrison, dies of a drugs overdose. It was Courson who found The Doors singer dead in the bathtub of their apartment in Paris, France, on July 3, 1971.

1977
Elvis Presley makes his last recordings during a concert at the Saginaw Civic Centre, Michigan. Three songs from the show appeared on the posthumously released Presley album, *Moody Blue*.

1979
The Police make their debut on BBC TV's *Top Of The Pops* performing 'Roxanne'.

1980
Stranglers' singer and guitarist Hugh Cornwell is released from a London prison after serving six weeks for possession of drugs.

1982
Paul McCartney & Stevie Wonder are at No. 1 on the UK singles chart with their duet 'Ebony And Ivory', the title inspired by McCartney hearing comedian and neighbour Spike Milligan say, "Black notes, white notes, and you need to play the two to make harmony, folks!"

1987
Madonna goes to No. 1 on the UK chart with 'La Isla Bonita', the fifth and final single from her third studio album, *True Blue*, making Ms. Ciccone the only female artist to score four UK No. 1s. The song had originally been offered to Michael Jackson for his *Bad* album.

1988
Bon Jovi's manager Doc McGee is convicted on drug offences arising from the 1982 seizure of 40,000lb of marijuana smuggled into north Carolina from Colombia. McGee was sentenced to a five-year suspended prison term and given a $15,000 fine.

1990
The Fender Stratocaster that Jimi Hendrix played at the Woodstock festival is auctioned off for a record $295,000.

1994
Adam Horovitz of the Beastie Boys is sentenced to 200 hours of community service for attacking a TV cameraman during the memorial service for actor River Phoenix the previous November.

The Eagles play the first of two reunion shows at Warner Burbank Studios, California before an invited MTV audience. Some of the live songs are used for the *Hell Freezes Over* album. The title was taken from drummer Don Henley's response to the question, "When will the Eagles get back together?"

2003
In this year's *Sunday Times* Rich List, Paul McCartney is confirmed as the world's richest musician with a fortune worth over £760m. Madonna was 4th in the list with £227m, Mick Jagger 6th with £175m and Elton John 7th with £170m. Ozzy Osbourne ranked 24th after earning an estimated £42m from the MTV show *The Osbournes*.

2007
Aides to President George Bush are told they can't book a five star hotel suite at the Imperial Hotel in Vienna, Austria because Mick Jagger had already booked it, splashing out £3,600 a night for the luxury suite, in advance of The Rolling Stones' current world tour.

2009
Richard Monroe Jr. is seeking $22m in damages from Snoop Dogg and others. Monroe tells a court that he received a "brutal" beating from the rapper's security. Jurors are informed that as the performer started his hit 'Gin And Juice' at the White River Amphitheatre, Seattle, Monroe thought there was an open invitation to go up on stage and claimed that Snoop hit him with a microphone as he climbed on stage.

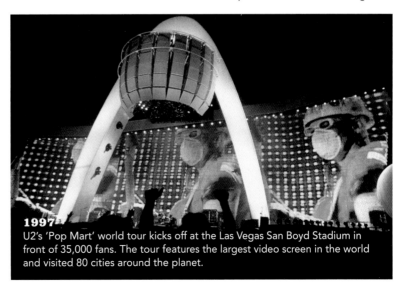

1997
U2's 'Pop Mart' world tour kicks off at the Las Vegas San Boyd Stadium in front of 35,000 fans. The tour features the largest video screen in the world and visited 80 cities around the planet.

April 26

Born on this day:

1938 Duane Eddy, guitar
1940 Giorgio Moroder, producer
1960 Roger Taylor, drums (Duran Duran, The Power Station)
1970 Tionne Watkins (T- Boz), vocals (TLC)
1975 Joey Jordison, drums (Slipknot)

1964
The Beatles and The Rolling Stones are among the headliners at the annual *NME* Pollwinners Concert at the Empire Pool, Wembley.

1966
Dusty Springfield is at No. 1 on the UK singles chart with 'You Don't Have To Say You Love Me', her only British No.1.

1969
During the band's second North American tour Led Zeppelin play the second of two nights at The Winterland Ballroom, San Francisco.

1977
The Grateful Dead appear at The Capitol Theatre, Passaic, New Jersey.

1982
Out on a day's shopping and standing next to his $50,000 Porsche on Hollywood Boulevard, Rod Stewart is mugged by a gunman.

Meat Loaf play the first of four sold-out nights at Wembley Arena, London.

1984
Mike McCartney unveils the £40,000 statue of The Beatles by John Doubleday at the new £8 million Cavern Walks shopping centre in Liverpool. John's first wife, Cynthia, is also in attendance.

1990
New Kids On The Block's Danny Wood injures his ankle while on stage in Manchester when tripping over a toy animal thrown on stage by a fan. He is forced to fly back home to the US for treatment.

Nirvana appear at The Pyramid Club, New York City. The band's label, Sub Pop, film the show and the performance of 'In Bloom' was later used as a promo clip.

1994
Singer Grace Slick pleads guilty to pointing a shotgun at police, claiming she was under stress because her home had burned down the previous year. She was later sentenced to 200 hours of community service.

1995
Courtney Love reportedly turns down an offer of $1m from *Playboy* to pose nude for the magazine.

2001
Destiny's Child are at No. 1 on the UK singles chart with 'Survivor', Janet Jackson is at No. 1 in America with 'All For You' and Shaggy and Ricardo RikRok Ducent have the Australian No. 1 with 'It Wasn't Me'.

2002
TLC member Lisa Lopes is killed aged 30 in a car accident in La Ceiba, Honduras. Seven other people, including Lopes' brother and sister, who were in the Mitsubishi Montero sports utility vehicle when the crash happened, were taken to hospital. Lopes who was driving the car when it crashed had spent the past month in Honduras working on various projects, including a clothing line, a new solo project and a book.

2008
Amy Winehouse spends the night in custody after being arrested on suspicion of assault. Police said Winehouse was "in no fit state" to be questioned when she arrived at the London station and was kept in the cells. The 24-year-old was being questioned about an incident said to have occurred three days earlier after a 38-year-old man claimed he was assaulted.

2008
Leona Lewis is at No. 1 on the *Billboard* chart with her debut album *Spirit*.

Born on this day:

1947 Gordon Haskell, UK singer, songwriter (King Crimson, solo)

1947 Peter Ham, vocals, guitar, piano (Badfinger)

1948 Kate Pierson, vocals (The B-52's)

1951 Paul Frehley, guitar, vocals (Kiss)

1959 Sheena Easton, UK singer

1979 Will Boyd, bass (Evanescence)

April 27

1963

Little Peggy March starts a three week run at No. 1 on the US singles chart with 'I Will Follow Him'. At 15 years, one month and 13 days old, Little Peggy March becomes the youngest female singer to have a US No. 1.

1967

Sandie Shaw is at No. 1 on the UK singles chart with 'Puppet On A String', her third UK No. 1 and the Eurovision Song Contest winner of 1967.

1970

David Bowie & The Hype, Barclay James Harvest, High Tide and The Purple Gang all appear at Stockport Grammar School, England.

1971

The Grateful Dead appear at The Fillmore East in New York City. The Beach Boys also appear on stage with the Dead, who together perform a short set of Beach Boys songs.

1974

A free afternoon event is held in the parking lot of the University of Connecticut, Ice Hockey Arena in Storrs. The four acts appearing are Aerosmith, Bruce Springsteen, Fairport Convention and Fat Back. Springsteen then went on to play another gig that evening at the University of Hartford in Connecticut.

1976

Customs officers on a train at the Russian/Polish Border detain David Bowie after Nazi books and mementoes are found in his luggage. Bowie claims that the material was being used for research on a movie project about Nazi propaganda leader Joseph Paul Goebbels.

1981
Ringo Starr marries American actress Barbara Bach at Marylebone Register Office in London. Paul and Linda McCartney and George and Olivia Harrison are present and the following day's papers are full of pictures of the three Beatles together with their wives and children.

1993

Prince issues a statement saying he is retiring from studio recordings to concentrate on film and other ventures.

1996

Oasis play the first of two nights at Manchester's Maine Road Football Club as a 'thank you' to their fans. The 80,000 tickets sell out in hours.

1999

UK band The Verve announce that they have split. They scored the 1997 UK No. 1 single 'The Drugs Don't Work' and their 1997 UK No. 1 album *Urban Hymns* spent over 100 weeks on the UK chart. Leader of the group Richard Ashcroft went solo scoring the 2000 UK No. 3 single 'A Song For The Lovers' and the 2000 UK No. 1 album *Alone With Everybody*.

2000

American singer Vicki Sue Robinson, who had a 1976 disco hit with 'Turn The Beat Around' and sang back-up vocals on Irene Cara's Top Ten hit single 'Fame', dies, aged 45.

2009

Pearl Jam bassist Jeff Ament is the victim of a robbery outside Southern Tracks Recording studios in Atlanta, where the band are recording. Ament and a band employee had arrived at the rear of the studio when three assailants brandishing knives emerged from the woods wearing black masks and smashed the windows of a rented Jeep. The robbers grabbed Ament's passport, a BlackBerry, $3,000 in cash and $4,320 worth of goods.

Aerosmith announce they are to hold a free concert in Hawaii to placate angry fans who filed a legal case against them, claiming the band had cancelled a sold-out show in Maui two years ago, leaving hundreds of fans out of pocket in favour of a bigger gig in Chicago. Lawyers for the would-be concertgoers said Aerosmith had now agreed to put on a new show and would pay all expenses. Everyone who bought a ticket to the original concert would receive a free ticket.

April 28

Born on this day:

1945 John Wolters, drums (Dr. Hook)
1953 Kim Gordon, bass (Sonic Youth)

1968 Daisy Berkowitz, guitar (Marilyn Manson)
1968 Howard Donald, vocals (Take That)

1958
Alan Feed's Big Beat Show plays two concerts at the Central High School Auditorium in Kalamazoo, Michigan. The tour features Jerry Lee Lewis, Chuck Berry, Frankie Lymon, Buddy Holly, The Diamonds, Billy Ford, Danny & The Juniors, The Chantels, Larry Williams, Screaming Jay Hawkins and The Pastels.

1964
The Beatles record the TV special *Around The Beatles* at Wembley Studios, England. As well as performing songs they also play Act V Scene 1 of Shakespeare's *A Midsummer Night's Dream* with John in the female role of Thisbe. Paul later names his cat Thisbe.

1968
The Broadway musical *Hair* opens at the Baltimore Theatre in New York City. The production ran for 1,729 performances, closing on July 1, 1972.

1979
Blondie score their first US No. 1 single with 'Heart Of Glass', also a chart-topper in the UK.

1981
Former T. Rex bassist, Steve Currie, is killed aged 33 in a car crash returning to his home near Vale de Parra, Algarve, Portugal.

1983
During the second leg of their North American 'War' tour, U2 appear at the Rochester Institute Of Technology Ice Rink, Rochester, New York.

1990
Guns N' Roses leader Axl Rose marries Erin Everly, daughter of Don Everly, at Cupid's Wedding Chapel in Las Vegas. They divorced in January '91 after a stormy nine months of marriage.

1997
Mark Morrison is fined £750 after admitting threatening behaviour during an incident in Leicester when he believed someone had kicked his car.

1999
The tour bus carrying The Clint Boon Experience is involved in a near fatal crash outside Glasgow. Members of the band had to be airlifted to hospital.

2000
A blaze sweeps through James Brown Enterprises, the office that coordinates the superstar's tours. Nobody is injured, but memorabilia and live tapes are destroyed in the blaze. An employee was later arrested and charged with arson.

Paul Atkinson is jailed for three years after being found guilty of stealing more than £25,000 from Rolling Stone Charlie Watts. Atkinson had been the manager of an Arabian stud farm owned by Watts.

2003
Ozzy Osbourne's 17-year-old son Jack goes into rehab at Las Encinas Hospital in Pasadena, California.

2006
Abba star Bjorn Ulvaeus is accused of avoiding paying 87m Swedish kronor in taxes on the band's hit songs and musical *Mamma Mia*. The Swedish government demands he repay the money.

2007
Sugababes singer Amelle Berrabah is arrested and spends the night in a police cell over allegations she assaulted an 18-year-old woman in a Guildford bar. Police confirm a 23-year-old female was arrested following an "incident".

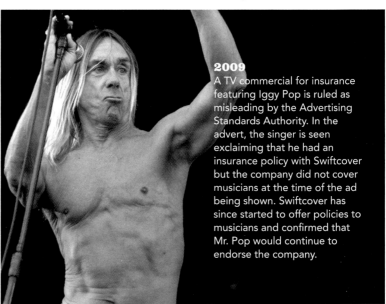

2009
A TV commercial for insurance featuring Iggy Pop is ruled as misleading by the Advertising Standards Authority. In the advert, the singer is seen exclaiming that he had an insurance policy with Swiftcover but the company did not cover musicians at the time of the ad being shown. Swiftcover has since started to offer policies to musicians and confirmed that Mr. Pop would continue to endorse the company.

Born on this day:

1931 Lonnie Donegan, vocals, guitar
1949 Francis Rossi, guitar, vocals (Status Quo)
1968 Carnie Wilson, vocals (Wilson Phillips)

1973 Mike Hogan, bass (The Cranberries)
1981 Tom Smith, bass (Editors)

April 29

1963

Publicist Andrew Oldham and agent Eric Easton sign a management deal with The Rolling Stones after buying the rights to the group's first recordings for £90. Oldham persuades keyboard player Ian Stewart to drop out of the line up and become the band's road manager (while continuing to play piano on the Stones' recordings and, occasionally, on stage).

1965

Jimmy Nicol, the drummer who stood in for Ringo Starr during The Beatles world tour in June 1964, appears in a London Court facing bankruptcy with debts of £4,000.

1967

The 14-Hour Technicolor Dream benefit party for The International Times is held at Alexandra Palace in north London. Seeing the event mentioned on TV, John Lennon attends the show with friend and art dealer, John Dunbar. Coincidentally, Yoko Ono was one of the performers. Other acts to appear include Pink Floyd, The Flies, The Crazy World Of Arthur Brown, The Pretty Things and Suzie Creamcheese.

1976

After a gig in Memphis Bruce Springsteen takes a cab to Elvis Presley's Graceland home and climbs over the wall. A guard assumes he is another crank fan, stops him and throws him out. The incident later becomes one of Springsteen's best known audience 'raps'.

1977

The Grateful Dead play the first of five nights at the New York Palladium.

1981

Elton John pays £14,000 for 232 *Goon Show* scripts broadcast during the 50s at a Christie's auction held in London.

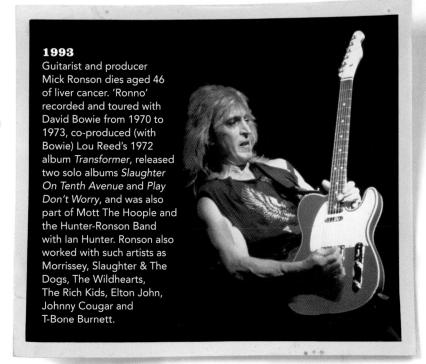

1993

Guitarist and producer Mick Ronson dies aged 46 of liver cancer. 'Ronno' recorded and toured with David Bowie from 1970 to 1973, co-produced (with Bowie) Lou Reed's 1972 album *Transformer*, released two solo albums *Slaughter On Tenth Avenue* and *Play Don't Worry*, and was also part of Mott The Hoople and the Hunter-Ronson Band with Ian Hunter. Ronson also worked with such artists as Morrissey, Slaughter & The Dogs, The Wildhearts, The Rich Kids, Elton John, Johnny Cougar and T-Bone Burnett.

1998

Steven Tyler breaks his knee at a concert in Anchorage, Alaska delaying Aerosmith's 'Nine Lives' tour and necessitating camera angle adjustments in the filming of the video for 'I Don't Want To Miss A Thing'.

2001

Rod Stewart asks for a change in wedding vows, bringing them up-to-date and to be treated more like a dog licence. Stewart says "a change is needed because they've been in existence for 600 years when people used to live until they were only 35."

2003

A $5 million lawsuit brought by a personal injury lawyer claiming that he suffered hearing loss in his left ear from attending a John Fogerty concert is dismissed. The judge says the plaintiff assumed the risk of hearing damage when he attended Fogerty's concert in 1997.

2007

Arctic Monkeys start a three-week run at No. 1 on the UK album chart with their second album *Favourite Worst Nightmare*.

Born on this day:

1933 Willie Nelson, US country singer
1943 Bobby Vee, US singer

1953 Merrill Osmond, singer (The Osmonds)
1971 Chris Henderson, guitar (3 Doors Down)

1960
The Everly Brothers start a seven week run at No. 1 on the UK singles chart with 'Cathy's Clown', giving Warner Bros a No. 1 with their first release.

1965
At Sheffield City Hall, Bob Dylan plays the first night of an eight-date UK tour.

1967
The final night of The Walker Brothers, Cat Stevens, The Jimi Hendrix Experience and Engelbert Humperdinck UK tour takes place at The Granada Theatre, Tooting, south London.

1970
Twiggs Lyndon, the road manager for The Allman Brothers Band, is arrested for murder after he stabs a club manager during an argument over a contract. At the ensuing trial, Lyndon's lawyers argue that he had been temporarily insane at the time of the incident and that touring with the Allman Brothers would drive anyone insane. Lyndon was acquitted.

1977
Led Zeppelin break a new world concert attendance record when playing to 76,229 at the Pontiac Silverdome, Michigan. The Who held the venue's previous record with 75,962 in 1975.

1980
The film *McVicar* with The Who's Roger Daltrey in the title role premieres in London.

1982
Influential American music journalist, author and musician Lester Bangs dies aged 33 of a heart attack. Bangs worked for *Rolling Stone*, *Creem* and *The Village Voice*.

1983
Michael Jackson starts a three-week run at No. 1 on the American singles chart with 'Beat It', his fifth solo US No. 1 and a No. 3 UK hit.

1983
American blues legend Muddy Waters (McKinley Morganfield) dies aged 68 in his sleep at his home in Westmont, Illinois. A major influence on many British blues acts including The Yardbirds, Cream, and Led Zeppelin. The Rolling Stones named themselves after a line in Muddy's song 'Mannish Boy.'

1990
Prince plays a concert at Rupert's nightclub, Minneapolis. The $100 a head ticket proceeds all go to the family of the singer's former bodyguard Charles 'Big Chick' Huntsberry who had died from a heart attack.

1999
Nazareth drummer Darrell Sweet dies aged 52 after suffering a fatal heart attack before a show in New Albany, Indiana.

Three former members of Spandau Ballet lose a court case involving lost royalties worth £1 million against band songwriter and guitarist Gary Kemp. The judge remarks that he had become a fan of the band during the case.

2005
The Dave Matthews Band offer their "deepest apologies" and agree to pay $200,000 compensation to more than 100 boat passengers who were on an architectural tour in Chicago in August

2004 when the band's tour bus dumped human waste on them. Driver Stefan Wohl, who was alone on board the bus at the time the sewage was dumped, was fined $10,000. The band had already donated $100,000 to two groups that protected the Chicago River and its surrounding area.

2008
After meeting while filming the music video for her single 'Bye Bye', Mariah Carey marries 27-year-old actor Nick Cannon in the Bahamas following a whirlwind two-month romance. Carey had previously married Columbia Records executive Tommy Mottola in 1993 but divorced in 1998.

A giant inflatable pig, which floated away during a Roger Waters concert, is recovered in tatters. Two families from La Quinta, California who found what was left of the inflatable, decided to share four life tickets to the Coachella festival that were offered as part of the reward.

1991
Nirvana sign a recording contract with Geffen's DGC label for $290,000.

May

Born on this day:

1944 Rita Coolidge, singer, songwriter
1966 Johnny Colt, bass (The Black Crowes)
1967 Tim McGraw, US country singer

1968 D'arcy Wretsky-Brown, bass (Smashing Pumpkins)
1970 Bernard Butler, guitarist, singer, producer (Suede, solo)

May
1

1955
Leonard Chess signs Chuck Berry to a recording contract after he came highly recommended by Muddy Waters.

1966
The Beatles play a 15-minute live set on stage for the last time in the UK when they appear at the *NME* Poll Winners concert at Wembley Empire Pool.

1967
32-year-old Elvis Presley marries 21-year-old Priscilla Beaulieu, whom he first met in 1959 while stationed in Germany when she was just 14 years old. When Elvis got out of the army in 1960, Priscilla moved into the singer's Graceland mansion with her family's blessing. The wedding ceremony takes place at the Aladdin Hotel in Las Vegas and although the marriage license was only $15, the wedding cake cost $3,500. The couple divorced after five years of marriage on October 9, 1973.

The F.B.I. arrest The Beach Boys' Carl Wilson on charges of avoiding the military draft and refusing to take the Oath of Allegiance. He is later released and joins the rest of the band in Ireland on a British tour.

1969
The Who preview their rock opera *Tommy* live before an invited audience at Ronnie Scott's Club, London.

1974
The Carpenters perform at the White House at the request of President Nixon.

1977
The 'White Riot' tour kicks off at the Roxy in London with The Clash, The Jam and The Buzzcocks.

1979
Elton John becomes the first major pop star to perform in Israel. In three weeks time he will also become the first Western rock performer to tour Russia.

1980
The South African government bans Pink Floyd's single 'Another Brick In The Wall' after black children adopted the song as their anthem in protest against inferior education.

1986
American songwriter and producer Hugo Peretti, who wrote and produced many classic hits, including 'Can't Help Falling In Love', 'Twistin' The Night Away', 'Shout', 'The Hustle' and 'You Make Me Feel Brand New', dies aged 70.

1997
Status Quo guitarist Rick Parfitt has a quadruple heart by-pass operation after visiting his Harley Street doctor complaining of chest pains.

2003
American soul singer Barry White suffers a stroke while being treated for kidney failure. The singer died two months later on July 4, 2003.

2005
Matchbox 20 singer Rob Thomas is at No. 1 on the US album chart with his first solo album *Something To Be*, marking the first time a male artist from a rock group has debuted in the top slot with a solo album since the *Billboard* Top 200 was introduced 50 years ago.

Coldplay become the first British band to have a new entry in the US Top 10 singles chart since The Beatles. Coldplay's latest single 'Speed Of Sound' enters the chart at No. 8, only the second time a UK band has achieved the feat. The Beatles were first with 'Hey Jude' in 1968.

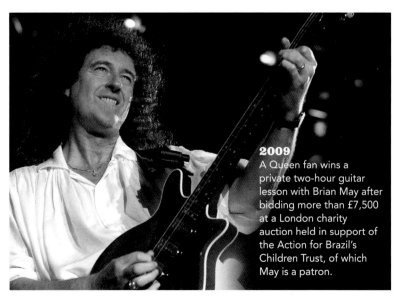

2009
A Queen fan wins a private two-hour guitar lesson with Brian May after bidding more than £7,500 at a London charity auction held in support of the Action for Brazil's Children Trust, of which May is a patron.

Born on this day:

1935 Link Wray, guitar
1946 Lesley Gore, singer
1954 Prescott Niles, bass (The Knack)

1955 Jo Callis, guitar (The Human League)
1967 David McAlmont, singer
1985 Lily Allen, singer

1957

Elvis Presley records the Leiber & Stoller song 'Jailhouse Rock' as featured in his motion picture of the same name.

1963

The Beatles are at No. 1 on the UK singles chart with 'From Me To You', the group's second British chart-topper. The title of the song was inspired from a letters column called From You To Us that ran in the British music newspaper, *New Musical Express*.

1969

Session drummer William 'Benny' Benjamin, one of the original Funk Brothers who played on many Tamla Motown recordings including hits by The Four Tops, The Temptations, Marvin Gaye, The Supremes and Stevie Wonder, dies aged 43 of a stroke. The film *Standing In The Shadows Of Motown*, released in 2003, serves as a tribute to his work.

1970

One hit wonder Norman Greenbaum is at No. 1 on the UK singles chart with 'Spirit In The Sky', also a No. 1 hit for Dr. & The Medics in 1986 and Gareth Gates in 2003.

1980

Joy Division play what will be their last gig when they appear at Birmingham University, England. Singer Ian Curtis committed suicide two weeks later.

1989

A security guard alerts police after a man wearing a wig, fake moustache and false teeth walks into Zales Jewellers, California. Three squad cars arrive and police detain the man, who turns out to be Michael Jackson in disguise.

1991

The video for the R.E.M. song 'Losing My Religion' is banned in Ireland because its religious imagery is seen as unfit for broadcast.

Nirvana book into Sound City Studios in Van Nuys, California for 16 days. On a budget of $65,000 and with Butch Vig producing, the band start recording what would become the *Nevermind* album.

1998

Japanese rock star Hideto Matsumoto is found hanging in the bathroom of his Tokyo apartment and dies in hospital a short time later at the age of 33. His funeral, held on May 7, is attended by over 70,000 people and requires 100 police officers, 170 security guards, police boats and helicopters. 21 people are hospitalised for injuries caused by the massive crowd at his funeral.

2004

Total Guitar magazine's readers vote Guns N' Roses' anthem 'Sweet Child O' Mine' as The Greatest Guitar Riff ever ahead of Nirvana's grunge anthem 'Smells Like Teen Spirit'. Led Zeppelin's 'Whole Lotta Love' came third, followed by Deep Purple's 'Smoke On The Water'. Editor Scott Rowley comments, "To a new generation of guitarists, Guns N' Roses are more thrilling than The Sex Pistols."

2007

Intending to set a new Guinness World Record, almost 2,000 guitarists gather in the market square of Wroclaw, Poland to play 'Hey Joe' by Jimi Hendrix. Organisers say it was the biggest guitar ensemble in recorded history.

2008

Chad Kroeger is banned from driving for a year after being convicted of drink-driving in the Canadian city of Vancouver. The 33-year-old Nickelback singer had almost twice the legal limit of alcohol in his system when he was stopped by police speeding in his Lamborghini.

2009

On a day off from a European tour, Bob Dylan mingles unnoticed with other tourists during a minibus tour to John Lennon's childhood home. He is one of 14 tourists paying £16 for the guided tour to the house to examine photos and documents in the National Trust-owned home, 'Mendips', in Woolton, Liverpool where Lennon grew up with his Aunt Mimi and Uncle George.

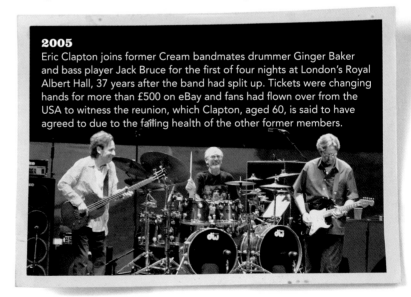

2005

Eric Clapton joins former Cream bandmates drummer Ginger Baker and bass player Jack Bruce for the first of four nights at London's Royal Albert Hall, 37 years after the band had split up. Tickets were changing hands for more than £500 on eBay and fans had flown over from the USA to witness the reunion, which Clapton, aged 60, is said to have agreed to due to the failing health of the other former members.

Born on this day:

1933 James Brown, soul star
1937 Frankie Valli, singer, actor (The Four Seasons, solo)
1950 Mary Hopkin, UK singer

1955 Steve Jones, guitar, DJ (The Sex Pistols)
1981 Farrah Franklin, singer, actress, model (Destiny's Child, solo)

May 3

1968
The Jimi Hendrix Experience record 'Voodoo Chile', featured on the double *Electric Ladyland* album. The song becomes a posthumous UK No. 1 single on 21 November, 1970, two months after Hendrix's death.

1972
Les Harvey, guitarist with Stone The Crows, dies after being electrocuted on stage during a gig at Swansea University, Wales. He was the brother of Scottish singer Alex Harvey and a member of The Alex Harvey Soul Band.

1976
Paul McCartney makes his first US concert appearance in almost a decade when Wings kick off their 31-date 'Wings Over America' tour at the Tarrant County Convention Center, Fort Worth, Texas.

1980
Dexy's Midnight Runners are at No. 1 on the UK singles chart with 'Geno', a song written about UK-based American soul singer Geno Washington.

1997
Michael Jackson is at No. 1 on the British singles chart with 'Blood On The Dance Floor'. The singer's seventh UK No. 1 peaked at 42 on the US charts.

2001
London based bank Coutts & Co. turn down applications from members of Oasis to open accounts on the grounds of the band's bad behaviour.

2004
The US Supreme Court rejects an appeal by two musicians who claim they are owed royalties by Ozzy Osbourne. Bassist Bob Daisley and drummer Lee Kerslake had fought a long-running battle since 1997 with the Osbourne family claiming they were entitled to money from the albums *Blizzard Of Ozz* and *Diary Of A Madman*. Ozzy's wife and manager, Sharon Osbourne, said that the pair had "harassed" her family and that the musicians' contributions had been removed from the albums because of their "abusive and unjust behaviour".

2006
The first edition of Bob Dylan's radio programme *Theme Time Radio Hour* airs on XM Satellite Radio. Tracks played on the show include Blur, Prince, Billy Bragg, Wilco, Mary Gauthier, L.L. Cool J and The Streets.

2008
Rap star Sean 'Diddy' Combs is honoured with a star on Hollywood's Walk of Fame. The 38-year-old dedicated the star to his father, who was shot dead in 1972.

2009
Bob Dylan is at No. 1 on the UK album chart with his 33rd studio album, *Together Through Life*, his seventh British chart-topping album. Dylan, who last topped the UK chart with *New Morning* in 1970, now held the record (previously held by Tom Jones) for the longest gap between solo number one albums.

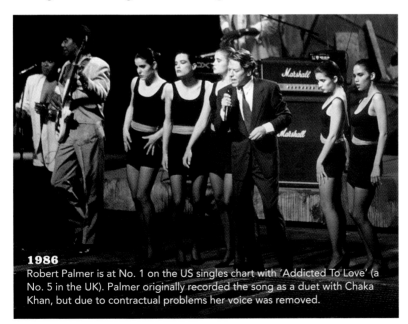

1986
Robert Palmer is at No. 1 on the US singles chart with 'Addicted To Love' (a No. 5 in the UK). Palmer originally recorded the song as a duet with Chaka Khan, but due to contractual problems her voice was removed.

Born on this day:

1942 Ronnie Bond, drums (The Troggs)
1951 Mick Mars, guitar (Mötley Crüe)
1970 Gregg Alexander, US singer-songwriter (New Radicals)

1972 Mike Dirnt, bass (Green Day)
1979 Lance Bass, singer, actor (*NSYNC)

1956

Gene Vincent & His Blue Caps record 'Be Bop A Lula'. The track was written three days before the session. The song becomes a 1956 US No. 7 & UK No. 16 hit single spending 20 weeks on the US chart.

1961

The Beatles perform at The Top Ten Club, during their residency in Hamburg, West Germany.

1967

The Jimi Hendrix Experience appear on UK TV's *Top Of The Pops*, plugging 'The Wind Cries Mary'.

1970

Four students at Kent University are killed and 11 wounded by National Guard troops at a campus demonstration against the escalation of the Vietnam War. The incident inspires Neil Young to compose the protest song, 'Ohio', which is quickly recorded by Crosby, Stills, Nash & Young.

1974

Abba are at No. 1 on the UK singles chart with 'Waterloo', the 1974 Eurovision song contest winner for Sweden and the first of nine UK No. 1 singles for the group. The song was originally called 'Honey Pie'.

1977

The Patti Smith Group, David Johansen, Dead Boys, Blondie, Suicide and Richard Hell & The Voidoids all appear at a Punk Benefit at CBGBs in New York City.

1987

American blues vocalist and harmonica player Paul Butterfield, who fronted The Paul Butterfield Blues Band, dies aged 45 at his home in north Hollywood of drug-related heart failure.

1989

Stevie Ray Vaughan sets out on what would be his last ever tour at the Orpheum Theatre, Vancouver, British Columbia. The guitarist is killed in a helicopter crash on August 27, 1990 after a concert at Alpine Valley Music Theater in Wisconsin, having played 107 of the 110 dates.

1991

Cher scores her first solo UK No. 1 single with 'The Shoop Shoop Song' from the film *Mermaids*. The song had been a hit for Betty Everett in 1964, and gave Cher her first UK No. 1 since 1965's 'I Got You Babe'.

1996

Alanis Morissette starts a six-week run at No. 1 on the UK album chart with *Jagged Little Pill*.

1997

Courtney Love places an advert in *The Seattle Times*, selling the house that she had shared with Kurt Cobain. The five-bedroom, four-bathroom house, built in 1902, is on the market with an asking price of $3 million. The carriage house on the property, where the Nirvana guitarist committed suicide, was demolished during refurbishment.

2008

Madonna's latest album *Hard Candy* goes straight to No. 1 in the UK, giving the singer a chart double, with her song '4 Minutes', featuring Justin Timberlake, on top of the singles chart for a third week. *Hard Candy* is Madonna's 10th number one album.

Thieves break into the childhood home of Motown star Martha Reeves and steal approximately $1 million worth of uninsured recording equipment, including speakers, microphones and karaoke machines. A suspect is arrested at his home later in the day after he tried to sell the goods to a pawnshop for $400.

1973

Led Zeppelin open their 1973 North American tour, billed as the "biggest and most profitable rock & roll tour in the history of the United States". The group gross over $3 million from the dates, flying between gigs in 'The Starship', a rented Boeing 720 passenger jet, including bar, shower room, white fur bedroom and a TV and video in a 30 foot lounge.

Born on this day:

1942 Tammy Wynette, country singer
1948 Bill Ward, drums (Black Sabbath)
1959 Ian McCulloch, singer (Echo & The Bunnymen)

1981 Craig David, UK singer
1988 Adele, UK singer
1989 Chris Brown, US singer

May 5

1956

Elvis Presley scores his first US No. 1 single when 'Heartbreak Hotel' goes to the top of the charts. His self-titled debut album also went to No. 1.

1962

The soundtrack to *West Side Story* is at No. 1 on the US album chart, spending a remarkable 54 weeks at pole position.

1963

On a recommendation from George Harrison, Dick Rowe, head of A&R at Decca Records (notorious as the man who passed on The Beatles) sees The Rolling Stones perform at The Crawdaddy Club in Richmond. The Stones sign a recording deal with the label within a week.

1968

Buffalo Springfield split up. Richie Furay forms Poco and, later in the year, Stephen Stills teams up with David Crosby and Graham Nash to form Crosby, Stills & Nash.

1972

The first day of the three-day Bickershaw Festival in Wigan, England, organised by Jeremy Beadle. The weekend bill features The Grateful Dead, Dr. John, Donovan, The Kinks, Captain Beefheart, Hawkwind, America, Family, Country Joe MacDonald, Wishbone Ash, New Riders Of The Purple Sage, Brinsley Schwarz and The Flamin' Groovies.

1974

Television appear at CBGBs in New York City, supported by The Stillettoes, later to become Blondie, who were playing their first show at the club.

1978

The Buzzcocks, The Slits and Penetration all appear at Liverpool University, England.

1983
The Stranglers 'Golden Brown' is named 'Most Performed Work of 1982' at the 28th Ivor Novello Awards.

1984

Simple Minds' singer Jim Kerr marries Chrissie Hynde in a horse drawn carriage in Central Park, New York.

1990

During a North American tour, Nirvana appear at the Einstein-A-Go-Go club in Jacksonville Beach, Florida.

1992
Radiohead release their first record, 'The Drill EP', in the UK.

1995

Former Guns N' Roses drummer Steven Adler is arrested on a felony count of heroin possession, as well as two misdemeanour drug charges.

1996

Cranberries singer Dolores O'Riordan receives both a public apology and a donation of £7,500 to the War Child charity from *The Sport* newspaper after they ran a story claiming she had performed a gig in Hamburg without wearing any underwear.

2000

Rod Stewart undergoes a one-hour throat operation at Cedar Sinai Medical Centre in Los Angeles to remove a growth on his thyroid which turns out to be benign.

2002

Rick Lewis and Michael Floorwax, two disc jockeys from Denver's KRFX-FM, halt a live radio interview with Detroit rocker Ted Nugent after he used derogatory racial terms for Negroes and Asians. The station received dozens of complaints.

2003

UK holiday camp operators Butlin's introduce a new system of rhyming slang at their bingo halls in an attempt to bring the game up-to-date. Pop stars Jennifer Lopez and Gareth Gates became new catchphrases for the callers, 'Gareth Gates' (8) and 'J-Lo's bum' (71).

Born on this day:

1945 Bob Seger, US singer, songwriter

1950 Robbie McIntosh, drums (Average White Band)

1967 Mark Bryan, guitar (Hootie & The Blowfish)

1971 Chris Shiflett, guitar (Foo Fighters)

1965

In their Clearwater, Florida motel room, Mick Jagger and Keith Richards start writing '(I Can't Get No) Satisfaction', following Richards' purchase of a Gibson fuzz-box earlier that day.

1966

During a four-month world tour, Bob Dylan plays the first night of an 11 UK date tour at the ABC in Belfast, Northern Ireland.

1972

At the height of 'T. Rextasy', a budget priced double album reissue of Tyrannosaurus Rex's first two albums, *My People Were Fair And Had Sky In Their Hair But Now They're Content To Wear Stars On Their Brows* (the longest ever title of an album to date) and *Prophets, Seers And Sages And The Angels Of The Ages* is at No. 1 in the UK.

1978

The soundtrack to *Saturday Night Fever* starts an 18 week run at No. 1 on the UK album chart; also No. 1 in the US. The album, which features seven Bee Gees songs, goes on to sell over 30 million copies worldwide.

1991

Madonna's candid documentary film *Truth Or Dare* (known outside the US as *In Bed With Madonna*) premieres in Los Angeles.

1995

Oasis score their first UK No. 1 single when 'Some Might Say' goes to the top of the UK charts – the first single to be released from the Manchester band's second album *(What's The Story) Morning Glory?* and the last Oasis track to feature original drummer Tony McCarroll.

2002

American songwriter and producer Otis Blackwell, who wrote such classics as 'All Shook Up', 'Return To Sender', 'Don't Be Cruel', 'Great Balls Of Fire' and 'Fever', dies aged 70 from a heart attack. Over the years, Blackwell's songs had sold more than 185 million copies.

'Bohemian Rhapsody' by Queen is voted the UK's favourite single of all time in a poll by the *Guinness Hit Singles* book compilers. 'Imagine' by John Lennon is No. 2, followed by The Beatles' 'Hey Jude' (3), 'Dancing Queen' by Abba (4), and Madonna's 'Like A Prayer' (5).

2004

A sale at Christie's in London becomes the most successful pop auction in the company's history after Beatles memorabilia sells for a record £788,643. The auction includes a leather necklace worn by John Lennon, which sold for £117,250, a signed copy of The Beatles and manager Brian Epstein's management deal (£122,850), a Vox keyboard guitar used by Lennon and Harrison (£100,000), a coloured felt-pen drawing by Lennon (£10,000), a letter with his signature (£5,500), and a pen-and-ink drawing called 'Happy Fish' (£9,500).

2005

US coffee shop chain Starbucks bans the sale of Bruce Springsteen's latest album *Devils And Dust* over concerns about its adult content. The retailer – which stocked CDs at its branches in the US – said it would be promoting other albums instead.

2006

The Go-Betweens singer-songwriter Grant McLennan dies aged 48 in his sleep at his home in Brisbane, Australia. The Australasian Performing Right Association named his 1983 song 'Cattle And Cane' as one of the 30 Greatest Australian Songs Of All Time.

2008

Babyshambles frontman Pete Doherty is released from Wormwood Scrubs prison in west London after serving 29 days of a 14-week sentence for breaching the terms of his probation. The singer told reporters that he was glad to be out and was looking forward to having a drink and spending some time with his pet cats.

2009

A former publicist for Michael Jackson is suing the singer for $44m for his alleged reneging on an agreement. Raymone Bain, who acted as Jackson's publicist during his 2005 trial for child abuse, claimed the singer had agreed to give her 10% of any business deals arranged with her assistance.

1984
Fictional heavy rock group Spinal Tap play a gig at New York's CBGBs.

Born on this day:

1939 Jimmy Ruffin, singer (The Temptations)
1943 Thelma Houston, US soul singer
1945 Christy Moore, Irish singer, songwriter (Planxty, solo)
1946 Jerry Nolan, drums (New York Dolls, The Heartbreakers)
1969 Eagle-Eye Cherry, singer
1986 Matt Helders, drums (Arctic Monkeys)

May 7

1966

The Mamas & The Papas start a three week run at No. 1 on the US singles chart with 'Monday Monday'; No. 3 in the UK. Originally the group reportedly all hated the song, except for its writer John Phillips.

1967

Jimi Hendrix plays two shows at London's Saville Theatre. Ringo Starr, Brian Jones and members of The Beach Boys and The Moody Blues are in the audience.

1972

Reginald Dwight changes his name by deed poll to Elton Hercules John.

1977

The Eagles are at No. 1 on the *Billboard* singles chart with 'Hotel California', the group's fourth US No. 1, reaching No. 8 in the UK.

1978

90,000 tickets are sold in eight hours for Bob Dylan's forthcoming London dates at Earl's Court.

1983

Paul Weller unveils his new group The Style Council at an anti-nuclear benefit gig in London.

1989

Ron Wilson, drummer with US surf group The Surfaris, dies of a brain anueryism.

1991

Wilson Pickett is arrested after running into an 86-year-old man and yelling death threats whilst driving his car over the mayor's front lawn in Englewood, New Jersey. Pickett was charged with having open bottles of alcohol in his car while driving.

1992

A leather jacket worn by John Lennon during the 1960-1963 period is sold at Christies, London, for £24,200.

Nigel Preston, drummer with The Cult, dies aged 32 in London. Preston was a founding member of The Death Cult and also played and recorded with Sex Gang Children, Theatre Of Hate and The Gun Club.

1994
Aerosmith play the first of seven nights at the Nippon Budokan in Tokyo, Japan, during their 245 date 'Get A Grip' world tour.

1998

US singer-songwriter Eddie Rabbitt dies aged 56 of lung cancer. During his career, Rabbitt scored over 20 chart-toppers on the *Billboard* country singles chart including 1981's 'I Love A Rainy Night'. Elvis Presley, Dr. Hook, Tom Jones, Kenny Rogers, Crystal Gayle and Lynn Anderson all recorded his songs.

2000

Britney Spears is at No. 1 on the UK singles chart with 'Oops!... I Did It Again', written and produced by hit-makers Max Martin and Rami Yacoub, who had previously collaborated with Spears on '...Baby One More Time'.

2003

A US surgeon sues 50 Cent over an unpaid medical bill. The doctor claims 50 Cent and his friend turned up at a hospital with multiple gunshot wounds in 2000 but the rapper never paid the $20,000 he owed for treatment despite being asked several times.

2004

A planning inquiry regarding Madonna's appeal to ban ramblers from parts of her £9m country estate hears details of the land's make-up. The pop star claims 100 acres of land at the 1,200-acre Ashcombe House estate had been inaccurately classified as open country. Madonna is appealing against the classification in a hearing. Under the act, people would have the right to access any land registered on the final map as open country – mountain, moor, heath or down.

2009

Trina Johnson-Finn is in custody awaiting trial in Suriname, South America, after being accused of trying to pass herself off as singer Toni Braxton at a concert. The singer was booed off stage in Paramaribo in March and pelted with rubbish when a huge crowd realised she was not the award-winning artist. Johnson-Finn's husband, Raymond Finn, makes a statement saying his wife had been duped by the promoter who had booked and advertised her as the real Braxton.

Born on this day:

1943 Danny Whitten, guitar, singer, songwriter (Crazy Horse)

1947 Rick Derringer, guitar (The McCoys, The Edgar Winter Group)

1951 Chris Frantz, drummer (Talking Heads)

1951 Philip Bailey, vocals (Earth, Wind & Fire)

1955 Alex Van Halen, drums (Van Halen)

1964 Dave Rowntree, drums (Blur)

1972 Darren Hayes, singer, songwriter (Savage Garden)

1976 Martha Wainwright, singer, songwriter

1954

BBC Radio bans the Johnny Ray song 'Such A Night' after listeners complain about its 'suggestiveness'. Ray was famous for his emotional stage act, which included writhing on the floor and crying real tears.

1964

The Beatles have held the No. 1 position on the US singles chart for 14 weeks with three No. 1s in succession: 'I Want To Hold Your Hand' for seven weeks, 'She Loves You' (two weeks) and 'Can't Buy Me Love' (five weeks).

1965

The promotional film for Bob Dylan's 'Subterranean Homesick Blues' (as featured in the movie *Don't Look Back*) is shot at the side of London's Savoy Hotel. The cards that Dylan holds up to the camera were painted by Alan Price and Joan Baez. Standing in the background are Allen Ginsberg and Bob Neuwirth.

1969

John Lennon, George Harrison, and Ringo Starr sign a business management contract with Allen Klein and his company ABKCO, but Paul McCartney refuses to sign, preferring to let his in-laws Lee & John Eastman represent his interests.

1974

British keyboard player Graham Bond commits suicide by throwing himself under a London tube train at Finsbury Park station, aged 36. It took police two days to identify his body which was crushed beyond all recognition. He was briefly a member of Blues Incorporated, a group led by Alexis Korner, before forming the Graham Bond Organisation, with an original lineup of Bond on vocals and organ, Dick Heckstall-Smith (sax), Ginger Baker (drums) and Jack Bruce (bass).

1976

Abba score their third UK No. 1 single with 'Fernando', becoming the group's biggest-selling single, with sales of over 10 million. Also on this day Abba start a nine-week run at No. 1 on the UK album chart with their *Greatest Hits*.

BBC Radio 1 DJ Johnny Walker announces he is quitting the station after being told he must pretend to like The Bay City Rollers.

1982

Neil Bogart dies aged 39 of cancer. With Peter Guber, Bogart was the co-founder of Casablanca Records, home to Donna Summer, The Village People, Kiss, Cher and Joan Jett.

1987

Prince plays the first of three nights at the Isstadion in Stockholm, Sweden at the start of his 37-date 'Sign O' The Times' European tour.

1993

Aerosmith enter the US album chart at No. 1 with *Get A Grip*; No. 2 in the UK. The album went on to sell over 20 million copies worldwide as well as winning the band two Grammy Awards.

Dire Straits' Mark Knopfler receives an honorary music doctorate from the University of Newcastle, England.

1996

A Los Angeles judge rules against Tommy Lee and wife Pamela Anderson in their bid to prevent *Penthouse* magazine publishing stills from an X-rated home movie that was stolen from their home.

2005

Bruce Springsteen is at No. 1 on the US album chart with *Devils And Dust*, his 13th No. 1 studio album.

2006

The Rolling Stones postpone their forthcoming European tour after Keith Richards undergoes emergency brain surgery in New Zealand. The 62 year-old guitarist suffered "mild concussion" when he fell out of a coconut tree while on holiday in Fiji.

Born on this day:

1937 Dave Prater, soul singer (Sam & Dave)
1941 Pete Birrell, bass (Freddie & The Dreamers)
1944 Richie Furay, guitar, vocals (Buffalo Springfield, Poco)
1949 Billy Joel, piano, singer, songwriter
1971 Paul 'Guigsy' McGuigan, bass (Oasis)
1975 Ryan 'Nik' Vikedal, drums (Nickelback)

1964

Gene Vincent & The Shouts appear at The Rhodes Centre, Bishop's Stortford, England. A poster advertises that the first 50 girls would be admitted free; tickets cost six shillings and six (32½p).

Chuck Berry begins his first ever UK tour at The Finsbury Park Astoria Theatre, north London, supported by The Animals, The Swinging Blue Jeans, Karl Denver and The Nashville Teens.

1965

During a UK tour Bob Dylan plays the first of two sold-out nights at London's Royal Albert Hall. All four Beatles watch the concert from a private box.

1966

The Doors play at The Whisky A Go Go, in West Hollywood, California auditioning for the position of the club's house band.

1969

John Lennon and Yoko Ono's *Unfinished Music No. 2: Life With The Lions* and George Harrison's *Electronic Sounds* are released on Apple's short-lived experimental offshoot Zapple Records.

1970

The Guess Who start a three-week run at No. 1 on the US singles chart with 'American Woman', the group's sixth Top 30 hit and only chart topper. The song was born by accident when guitarist Randy Bachman played a heavy riff on stage after breaking a string, and the other members joined in on the jam. A fan in the audience who had recorded the gig presented the tape to the group after the show and they developed it into a full song.

1973

Mick Jagger adds $150,000 of his own money to the $350,000 raised from The Rolling Stones' January benefit concert for victims of the recent Nicaraguan earthquake.

1974

Bonnie Raitt plays two shows at Harvard Square Theatre in Cambridge, Massachusetts. The opening act is Bruce Springsteen and the E Street Band. *Rolling Stone* critic Jon Landau, who would become Springsteen's manager, attended and wrote: "I have seen rock & roll's future and his name is Bruce Springsteen."

1978

Fee Waybill of The Tubes breaks a leg after falling from the stage at the Hammersmith Odeon, London whilst wielding a chainsaw during the band's act.

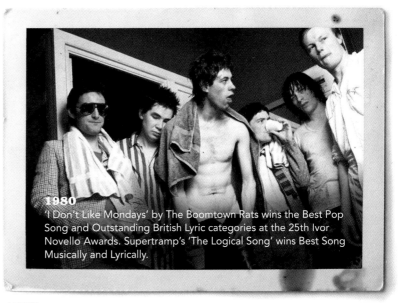

1980
'I Don't Like Mondays' by The Boomtown Rats wins the Best Pop Song and Outstanding British Lyric categories at the 25th Ivor Novello Awards. Supertramp's 'The Logical Song' wins Best Song Musically and Lyrically.

1987

Starship start a four-week run at No. 1 on the UK singles chart with 'Nothing's Gonna Stop Us Now', a song co-written by Albert Hammond and Diane Warren. This made lead singer Grace Slick, at 48, the oldest female to reach No. 1 on the UK chart (later broken by Cher's 'Believe' in 1999).

1992

Bruce Springsteen makes his North American network television debut on *Saturday Night Live* with host Tom Hanks.

1999

The Backstreet Boys score their first UK No. 1 single with 'I Want It That Way', their eighth UK Top 10 hit and a hit in over 25 countries.

2000

Former All Saints manager John Benson is given a £1 million out-of-court settlement after the band sacked him in February 1999.

2008

Foxy Brown avoids a further spell in prison after pleading guilty in a New York court to menacing her neighbour with a BlackBerry phone. The 28-year-old rapper admitted hitting Arlene Raymond during an argument over the volume of her car stereo last July. The incident landed the star in prison for violating the terms of her probation on a separate assault charge.

May 10

Born on this day:

1920	Bert Weedon, guitarist	**1947**	Dave Mason, guitar (Traffic, solo)
1946	Donovan, singer, songwriter	**1957**	Sid Vicious, bass (The Sex Pistols)
1946	Graham Gouldman, singer, songwriter (The Mindbenders, 10CC)	**1960**	Bono, vocals, guitar (U2)

1960

The Silver Beetles (John Lennon, Paul McCartney, George Harrison, Stuart Sutcliffe and Johnny Hutchinson, deputising for absent drummer Tommy Moore) audition before promoter Larry Parnes and singer Billy Fury to secure a slot as Fury's backing group for a tour. Parnes is also looking for backing groups for his lesser-known acts, and The Silver Beetles are selected for singer Johnny Gentle's upcoming tour of Scotland. The group had changed its name from 'The Beatals' to 'The Silver Beetles' after Brian Casser (of Cass & The Cassanovas) remarked that the name 'Beatals' was "ridiculous". He suggested they use the name 'Long John & The Silver Beetles', but John Lennon refused to be referred to as 'Long John'.

1967

Mick Jagger and Keith Richards appear at Chichester Crown Court, Sussex, on drugs charges. They elect to go to trial, pleading not guilty and are both granted £100 bail.

1969

Fleetwood Mac, Pink Floyd, The Move, Status Quo, The Tremeloes, Marmalade, Love Sculpture, and Van Der Graaf Generator all appear at Nottingham County Football Ground, England. Presented by John Peel, tickets were 22/6 (£1.12½) on the gate.

The Turtles give a special performance at the White House as guests of the president's daughter, Tricia Nixon. The group's electronic tuning device is mistaken for a bomb by security and stories abound concerning band members allegedly snorting cocaine on Abraham Lincoln's desk.

Led Zeppelin make their first appearance on the UK album chart when the band's debut album, recorded in 36 hours, reaches No. 6, going on to spend 71 weeks on the British charts. It entered the US chart the following week at No. 10.

1970

David Bowie is awarded an Ivor Novello Award for Best Original Song for 'Space Oddity'.

1974

The Who sell out Madison Square Garden in New York City for four nights with 80,000 tickets sold.

1975

Stevie Wonder plays in front of 125,000 fans at a free concert near the Washington Monument to celebrate Human Kindness Day.

1985

All-girl group The Go-Gos announce they are breaking up. Belinda Carlisle and Jane Wiedlin go on to enjoy solo success, and the group reforms in the late 90s.

1986

Falco is at No. 1 on the UK singles chart with 'Rock Me Amadeus.' Falco is the first-ever Austrian act to score a UK and US chart-topping hit single and the first German speaking artist to achieve a No. 1 on the US charts.

1994

Rapper Tupac Shakur begins serving a 15-day county jail term for attacking director Allen Hughes on a video set.

1999

Shel Silverstein, American singer, songwriter, poet, cartoonist, screenwriter, and author of children's books, dies aged 57 of a heart attack. Silverstein wrote 'A Boy Named Sue' for Johnny Cash (for which Silverstein won a Grammy in 1970) and several songs for Dr Hook, including 'Sylvia's Mother' and 'The Cover Of The Rolling Stone'.

2000

Bobby Brown is arrested at Newark airport, New Jersey for breaking his probation order. He had been wanted in Florida since 1999 when his probation officer reported that a urine test proved positive for cocaine use.

2005

Seal marries German super-model Heidi Klum in a low-key ceremony on a beach in Mexico near the singer's home on the luxurious Costa Careyes.

2007

US hip-hop artist Akon apologises after footage of him dancing provocatively on a nightclub stage with a 14-year-old girl is posted on the internet, resulting in telecommunications company Verizon withdrawing as sponsor of his US tour with Gwen Stefani. In a statement Akon says he didn't know the girl was underage: "I want to sincerely apologise for the embarrassment and any pain I've caused to the young woman who joined me on stage, her family and the Trinidad community for the events at my concert."

Born on this day:

1941 Eric Burdon, singer (The Animals)
1943 Les Chadwick, bass (Gerry & The Pacemakers)

1947 Butch Trucks, drums (The Allman Brothers Band)
1974 Ryan Adams, singer, songwriter
1983 Holly Valance, singer, actress

1963
The Beatles start a 30 week run at No. 1 on the UK album charts with their debut album *Please Please Me*,  making it the longest running chart-topping album by a group ever. The follow up *With The Beatles* replaces it at the top of the charts on December 7, 1963 and stays there for 21 weeks.

1964
During a UK tour The Rolling Stones are refused service in the restaurant at The Grand Hotel, Bristol, because they are not wearing jackets and ties. The following day *The Daily Express* runs the story with the headline: "The Rolling Stones gather no lunch."

1967
The Bee Gees make their *Top Of The Pops* debut performing 'New York Mining Disaster 1941'.

1972
John Lennon and Yoko Ono appear for the second time on Dick Cavett's US television talk show. As well as performing, Lennon reveals he was under surveillance from the FBI.

1974
All of Led Zeppelin attend Elvis Presley's show at the LA Forum, California. After a shaky start to the show, Elvis stops the band and jokingly says: "Wait a minute… if we can start together fellas, because we've got Led Zeppelin out there, let's try to look like we know what we're doing."

1978
At the end of their 46-date 'News Of The World' tour, Queen play three sold-out nights at Wembley Arena, London.

1981
Bob Marley dies aged 36 of lung cancer and a brain tumour in a Miami hospital.

1985
UK producer and keyboard player Paul Hardcastle is at No. 1 on the UK singles chart with '19', the title referring to the average age of American soldiers in the Vietnam War. The song features dialogue by television narrator Peter Thomas, and a strong anti-war message.

1996
Bill Graham, the journalist credited with discovering U2 and the co-founder of Irish music paper *Hot Press*, dies aged 44 of a heart attack. Members of U2, Clannad, Hothouse Flowers and Gavin Friday attend his funeral.

2001
Oasis, The Black Crowes and Spacehog kick off a North American trek, dubbed 'The Tour Of Brotherly Love', at The Hard Rock in Las Vegas. (The tour was so-named as the three bands featured pairs of brothers.)

2003
Ex-Jimi Hendrix Experience bassist Noel Redding dies aged 57 at his home in Ireland. Redding played on the classic Hendrix albums *Are You Experienced*, *Axis: Bold As Love* and *Electric Ladyland* and right up until his death had been taking legal action against the Hendrix estate for payments estimated at £3.26 million for his part in recordings and to receive ongoing royalties.

2004
US songwriter John Whitehead, who co-wrote 'Back Stabbers' for The O'Jays and, as McFadden & Whitehead, wrote and sang 'Ain't No Stopping Us Now' which sold more than eight million copies and was nominated for a Grammy, is killed by a gunman.

2006
George Michael is involved in his second minor car crash in a month after a tabloid photographer found Michael asleep in his parked car in central London. After he woke up the singer crashed into a bollard as he was driving away.

2007
The Game is arrested at his home in connection with an incident where he was alleged to have threatened a person with a gun at a basketball game in south LA in February 2007. The rapper was released the following day after posting $50,000 bail.

May 12

Born on this day:

1928 Burt Bacharach, songwriter, singer, pianist, arranger
1940 Norman Whitfield, songwriter, producer
1942 Ian Dury, singer, songwriter
1945 Ian McLagan, keyboards (The Small Faces, The Faces)
1948 Steve Winwood (The Spencer Davis Group, Traffic, Blind Faith, solo)

1961
The Beatles sign a recording contract with producer Bert Kaempfert in Hamburg, West Germany. That evening they play at The Top Ten Club, Reeperbahn, Hamburg.

1963
Bob Dylan walks out of rehearsals for *The Ed Sullivan Show* after being told he couldn't perform 'Talking John Birch Society Blues' due to it mocking the US military.

1968
On his way to Toronto Jimi Hendrix is arrested by police for possession of hashish and heroin. Hendrix claims the drugs had been planted on him.

Brian Jones makes his final live appearance with The Rolling Stones as the surprise guests at the finale of the *New Musical Express* Poll Winners Concert at the Empire Pool, Wembley.

1971
Mick Jagger marries Bianca Macias at St Tropez Town Hall. The guest list includes the other members of The Rolling Stones, Paul McCartney, Ringo Starr, Eric Clapton and Stephen Stills. The couple separate in 1977 and divorce three years later.

1975
Jefferson Starship give a free concert in New York's Central Park in front of 60,000. The band and concert sponsor, WNEW-FM, are forced to pay $14,000 for cleaning charges and damage done to the park after the event.

1977
Led Zeppelin receive an Outstanding Contribution To British Music award at the Ivor Novello Awards held at the Grosvenor Hotel, London.

1981
Van Halen kick off their 82-date North American 'Fair Warning Tour' at the Halifax Metro Centre in Halifax, Nova Scotia

1983
Meat Loaf files for bankruptcy with debts of over $1 million.

1994
Depeche Mode play the first night on the North American leg of their 159 date 'Exotic Tour' at the Cal Expo in Sacramento, California.

1996
17-year-old Bernadette O'Brien dies a day after being injured bodysurfing at a Smashing Pumpkins gig at The Point, Dublin.

2000
Thieves steal the gates to Strawberry Fields, the Liverpool landmark immortalised by The Beatles song. The 10 foot high iron gates were later found at a local scrap metal dealer.

2001
American singer and TV presenter Perry Como dies aged 88. Como was once the highest-paid performer in the history of television and scored 14 US No. 1 singles from 150 US chart hits and over 25 UK chart hits, including 'Magic Moments' and 'Catch A Falling Star'.

Travis play a gig at singer Fran Healy's local primary school at Weston Park, Crouch End, London. The 150 crowd paid a £1 entry fee to the summer fete.

2004
Barry and Robin Gibb, who had once lived in Manchester, England, are both presented with honorary degrees from Manchester University. They also pick up a posthumous award for their brother Maurice.

2008
Neil Young has a new species of trapdoor spider named after him. *Myrmekiaphila neilyoungi* was discovered in Jefferson County, Alabama, in 2007, by US university biologist Jason Bond who decides to name it after his favourite musician.

Born on this day:

1943 Mary Wells, singer
1945 Magic Dick, harmonica (The J Geils Band)
1950 Stevie Wonder, singer, songwriter, multi-instrumentalist
1964 Lorraine McIntosh, vocals (Deacon Blue)
1966 Darius Rucker, vocals (Hootie & The Blowfish)
1979 Michael Madden, bass (Maroon 5)

May
13

1967
The Monkees second album *More Of The Monkees* goes to No. 1 on the UK charts. In 1967 only four albums reached top position: *The Sound Of Music* (for 17 weeks), The Beatles' *Sgt Pepper's Lonely Hearts Club Band* (25 weeks) and The Monkees first and second albums (9 weeks).

1971
On his 21st birthday Stevie Wonder receives all his childhood earnings. Despite having earned $30 million to date, he receives only $1 million.

1974
Forty-three people are arrested and more than 50 injured after youths start throwing bottles outside a Jackson Five concert at RFK stadium in Washington DC.

1976
Kiss play the first UK date on their current 'Alive World Tour' at the Free Trade Hall in Manchester.

1978
Yvonne Elliman is at No. 1 on the US singles chart with the Gibb brothers' song 'If I Can't Have You'. The song was featured in the current hit film *Saturday Night Fever*.

1981
The Grateful Dead appear at the Providence Civic Center, Rhode Island.

1983
Def Leppard appear at The Mississippi Coast Coliseum, Biloxi, on their 'Pyromania' World Tour.

1985
Bruce Springsteen marries Julianne Phillips at Lake Oswego, Oregon. She files for divorce on August 30, 1988.

1987
U2 play the third of a five-night run at Brendan Byrne Arena, East Rutherford, New Jersey.

1996
Oasis become the fastest-selling group in UK history after all 330,000 tickets priced at £22.50 for their summer shows at Knebworth and Loch Lomand sell out in just nine hours.

2000
Shaun Ryder's Volkswagen Corrado is found abandoned after being used as a getaway car. The former Happy Mondays' singer's car was used in an armed robbery on Harry Ramsden's fish and chip restaurant in Manchester. £7,000 cash was taken in the robbery.

2002
Dionne Warwick is arrested at Miami International Airport for possession of marijuana after authorities find 11 joints in a lipstick case in the singer's hand luggage. The charges are dropped after she completes a drug program and makes a contribution to charity.

2003
Michael Jackson launches a court case against Motown Records. Jacko files the lawsuit in LA, saying he hasn't been paid royalties due from his recordings with The Jackson Five in the 60s and 70s. The singer also claims his music has been used in TV ads without his permission.

2007
Brian May is under 24-hour security watch after a deranged man announced he was setting off to murder him — then disappeared. Police are hunting for a schizophrenic who left a letter behind at his home blaming the Queen guitarist for his illness. In it the man said May was an "impostor" and that *he* was the real rock star. He signed the letter 'Brian May'.

2008
The US Postal Service issues a 42 cent postage stamp in honour of Frank Sinatra. The design shows a 1950s-vintage image of Sinatra wearing a hat.

May 14

Born on this day:

1943 Jack Bruce, bass, vocals (The Graham Bond Organisation, John Mayall's Bluesbreakers, Manfred Mann, Cream, solo)

1952 David Byrne, guitar, vocals (Talking Heads, solo)

1963 Fabrice Morvan, vocals (Milli Vanilli)

1973 Natalie Appleton, singer (All Saints)

1957
Elvis Presley is rushed to a Los Angles hospital after swallowing a porcelain cap from one of his front teeth, which then lodges itself in one of his lungs.

1960
The Silver Beats (John Lennon, Paul McCartney, George Harrison, Stu Sutcliffe and Tommy Moore) perform at Lathom Hall, Seaforth, Liverpool. They play a few songs during the interval to audition for promoter Brian Kelly. Also appearing are Cliff Roberts & The Rockers, The Deltones and Kingsize Taylor & The Dominoes. This is the only occasion on which the group uses the name Silver Beats, quickly changing it back to The Silver Beetles.

1969
During a UK tour, Fairport Convention's van crashes on the M1 motorway on the way home from a gig in Birmingham, killing the group's 19-year-old drummer Martin Lamble and guitarist Richard Thompson's girlfriend Jeannie Franklyn.

1976
Keith Relf, former lead singer of The Yardbirds, is fatally electrocuted while tuning a guitar which was not properly earthed. He was 33. The accident happens in his West London home where he was found by his eight-year-old son, still holding the plugged-in guitar.

1977
Leo Sayer is at No. 1 on the US singles chart with the Albert Hammond-Carole Bayer Sager song 'When I Need You', the singer's second US No. 1, and also a chart-topper in the UK.

1988
Led Zeppelin reunite for Atlantic Records' 40th anniversary party at Madison Square Garden, New York, with Jason Bonham (John Bonham's son) playing drums. Other acts appearing include Foreigner, Crosby, Stills & Nash, Genesis, Emerson Lake & Palmer, Wilson Pickett and Ben E. King.

1993
During an auction at Christies in London the acoustic guitar that Elvis Presley used to make his first recordings, 'That's All Right Mama' and 'Blue Moon of Kentucky' in 1954, sells for £130,285. Four 'Super Hero' costumes worn by the group Kiss sell for £20,000.

1998
George Michael is fined £500 after being convicted of a 'lewd act' in a Los Angeles lavatory. The Los Angeles court also orders him to undergo psychological counselling and carry out 80 hours community service.

2003
Lawyers for Britney Spears and the Skechers footwear company settle a dispute over a deal for the pop star to market a line of roller skates and accessories. Spears had filed a $1.5 million breach of agreement lawsuit against Skechers in December, claiming the company failed to pay her adequately. Skechers responded with a $10 million lawsuit, accusing Spears of fraud and breach of the three-year licensing agreement she signed in January 2002.

2004
Phil Spector is arrested after getting into a scuffle with his chauffeur at the 64-year-old record producer's California mansion. Spector is taken into custody and later released after a court date is set.

2005
A judge in Springfield, Massachusetts, orders rapper 50 Cent to stay clean of drugs and take an anger management course to avoid spending time in jail. The rapper appeared in court charged with assaulting three women at a concert in 2004 after leaping into the crowd.

2008
Metallica start a 26-date North American and European tour at the Wiltern Theatre, Los Angeles, California.

Born on this day:

1932 Baba Oje, Arrested Development
1948 Brian Eno, keyboards, producer
        (Roxy Music, solo)

1953 Mike Oldfield, multi-instrumentalist,
        producer
1959 Andrew Eldritch, vocals (The Sisters
        Of Mercy)

May
15

1961

Floyd Cramer is at No. 1 on the UK singles chart with 'On The Rebound', the US singer's only British chart-topper. The Nashville pianist played on many Elvis Presley hits.

1967

Paul McCartney meets American photographer Linda Eastman for the first time at a Georgie Fame gig at the Bag O'Nails club in London.

1973

Bob Marley & The Wailers play the first of four sold-out nights at The Speakeasy club in London as part of their 'Catch A Fire' UK tour.

1974

Frank Zappa and his wife Gail announce the birth of their third child, a boy named Ahmet Rodan, after the Japanese movie monster that lived off a steady diet of 707 planes.

1981

Former Sex Pistol John Lydon's band PIL (Public Image Ltd) perform a show at New York's Ritz Club posing behind a video screen while the music is played from tapes. They are showered with missiles and eventually booed off stage.

1992

Barbara Lee of The Chiffons, who had a 1963 US No. 1 single 'He's So Fine', dies from a heart attack the day before her 45th birthday.

1997

Oasis become one of the first artists to attempt to exert censorship over the Internet. The group work with label Sony to put an end to unofficial websites carrying lyrics, sound files and photographs of the band.

1998

American singer and actor Frank Sinatra dies at the Cedars-Sinai Medical Center, Los Angeles aged 82, after suffering a heart attack.

1999

Rob Gretton, manager of Joy Division and New Order, dies aged 46. Gretton was also a partner in Factory Records, proprietor of the Rob's Records label and a co-founder, along with Tony Wilson, of The Hacienda nightclub in Manchester.

2000

It is reported that Britney Spears has been crowned the queen of America's fastest growing youth movement, the teenage celibates. Spears tells a German magazine that she intends to abstain from sex until her wedding night.

2003

Country singer June Carter Cash, the second wife of Johnny Cash, dies in Nashville, Tennessee, of complications following heart valve replacement surgery, aged 73.

2008

Neil Diamond reaches the top of the US *Billboard* album chart for the first time in his career with *Home Before Dark,* the 67-year-old singer's 29th studio album.

His previous highest chart position was in 1973 when the soundtrack to the film *Jonathan Livingston Seagull* peaked at No. 2. At the age of 67, Diamond becomes the oldest artist to have a US number one. The record was previously held by Bob Dylan in 2006 with *Modern Times*, released when Dylan was 65.

147

Born on this day:

1946 Robert Fripp, guitar (King Crimson)
1947 Darrell Sweet, drums (Nazareth)
1951 Jonathan Richman, guitar, vocals (The Modern Lovers, solo)
1964 Boyd Tinsley, violinist (Dave Matthews Band)
1965 Krist Novoselic, bass (Nirvana)
1966 Janet Jackson, singer

1963
The Beatles appear live on the national BBC TV children's program *Pops and Lenny* at Television Theatre, Shepherd's Bush Green, London, in front of an live audience. The Beatles perform 'From Me to You' and a shortened version of 'Please Please Me.'

1965
The limousine taking The Rolling Stones away from a gig at the Civic Hall, Long Beach, California, is besieged by fans who stand on the roof, caving it in. The band members attempt to hold the roof up while their chauffeur drives off with bodies falling onto the road.

1966
The Beach Boys release *Pet Sounds* in the US. Although now regarded as one of the best and most influential albums in popular music, the album fails to sell as well as previous Beach Boys product in America, only reaching No. 10. It fares better in the UK where its genius was instantly recognised, reaching No. 2.

1969
Jack Casady of Jefferson Airplane is busted for possession of marijuana and receives a two and a half year suspended sentence.

At the Fillmore East in New York City, Roger Daltrey and Pete Townshend unwittingly assault a plain clothes police officer who runs uninvited on to the stage during their first show that evening to warn that the neighbouring building is on fire. While the charges against Daltrey were later dropped, The Who guitarist was fined $30 for the offence.

1974
Brian May collapses in New York while Queen are on a US tour. He is flown back to England suffering from hepatitis.

1976
Patti Smith makes her UK concert debut at The Roundhouse, north London.

1981
Kim Carnes starts a nine-week run at No. 1 on the US singles chart with 'Bette Davis Eyes', the singer's only American No. 1 and a No. 10 hit in the UK.

1984
Ozzy Osbourne is arrested in Memphis, Tennessee for 'staggering drunk' down Beale Street.

1987
U2's 'With Or Without You' starts a three-week run at No. 1 on the US singles chart, the group's first American chart-topper.

1992
Kiss kick off the European leg of their 'Revenge World Tour' at the Glasgow SEC, Scotland.

1993
US soul singer Marv Johnson, who had a US Top 10 single in 1960 with 'I Love The Way You Love' and a 1969 UK No. 10 with 'I'll Pick A Rose For My Rose', dies aged 54 of a stroke. Johnson's recording of Berry Gordy's song 'Come To Me' became Motown Records first-ever single release in May 1959.

1998
Keith Richards falls and breaks several ribs while reaching for a book of nude art in the study of his Connecticut home, causing The Rolling Stones to postpone dates on their 'Bridges To Babylon' tour.

2004
Frankee starts a three-week run at No. 1 on the UK singles chart with 'F.U.R.B. (F U Right Back)'. The song is a "reply" to the No. 1 by Eamon that it replaces, 'Fuck It (I Don't Want You Back)'. This is the first time that a record and its reply have both made No 1. R&B singer Eamon earned a listing in the *Guinness Book of World Records* for "the most expletives in a No. 1 song" with 33.

Born on this day:

1948 Bill Bruford, drums (King Crimson, Yes)

1960 Simon Fuller, record producer, manager

1961 Enya Ni Bhraonain, vocals (Clannad)

1965 Trent Reznor, singer, songwriter (Nine Inch Nails)

1970 Jordan Knight, singer (New Kids On The Block)

1974 Andrea Corr, vocals, tin whistle (The Corrs)

May
17

1963
The first Monterey Folk Festival in California is held over three days and features Joan Baez, Bob Dylan and Peter Paul & Mary.

1966
During his notorious 'electric' UK tour, Bob Dylan appears at The Free Trade Hall, Manchester. At one point, a member of the audience shouted out "Judas", unhappy at Dylan's move from acoustic folk to rock. Dylan replies with a mumbled, "I don't believe you. You're a liar". For years only unofficially available as a bootleg recording, the concert was eventually released by Sony as part of Dylan's *The Bootleg Series* in 1999.

1969
It is reported that for the first time ever album sales have overtaken

singles sales in the UK. 49,184,000 albums were produced during 1968 compared with 49,161,000 singles.

1971
Dawn are at No. 1 on the UK singles chart with 'Knock Three Times', the trio's first of two British chart-toppers. Singer Tony Orlando had retired from singing when he was persuaded to front Dawn for studio recordings.

1975
Elton John is awarded a Platinum Record for sales of a million copies of the LP *Captain Fantastic & The Brown Dirt Cowboy*, the first album ever to be certified Platinum on the day of its release.

1979
The Police appear at the Santa Monica Civic Auditorium, California.

1986
The Sunday night UK TV satirical puppet show *Spitting Image* starts a three-week run at No. 1 on the British singles chart with 'The Chicken Song'.

1987
A fire destroys Tom Petty's Los Angeles home, causing an estimated $800,000 worth of damage.

1989
Rolling Stone Bill Wyman opens his first Sticky Fingers restaurant in Kensington, west London.

1990
Nirvana plays the last date of a North American tour at the Zoo in Boise, Idaho. This was drummer Chad Channing's final gig with the band; Dave Grohl replaced him in September after Grohl's band Scream split up.

1996
US blues guitarist Johnny 'Guitar' Watson dies aged 61 of a heart attack while on tour in Yokohama, Japan. According to eyewitness reports, he collapsed mid-guitar solo, his last words reportedly "ain't that a bitch."

2002
US songwriter Sharon Sheeley, who composed 'Poor Little Fool', a US No. 1 for Ricky Nelson in 1958 and 'Somethin' Else' for Eddie Cochran, dies aged 62 of a cerebral haemorrhage at Sherman Oaks Hospital. Sheeley survived the car crash that killed her boyfriend Cochran during a 1960 UK tour.

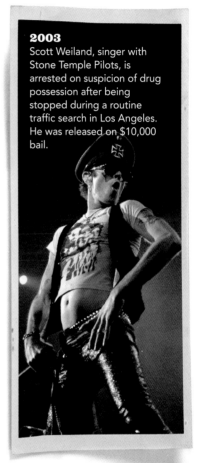

2003
Scott Weiland, singer with Stone Temple Pilots, is arrested on suspicion of drug possession after being stopped during a routine traffic search in Los Angeles. He was released on $10,000 bail.

2006
Paul McCartney and his second wife Heather Mills admit that after four years of marriage, they are going their separate ways.

2008
Amy Winehouse and Pete Doherty post a two-minute clip of themselves playing with newborn mice on Youtube. The video shows Doherty and Winehouse in a bare room, making rambling comments, picking up the mice and talking to them.

Green Day go to No. 1 on the UK album chart with their eighth studio album *21st Century Breakdown*.

Born on this day:

1942 Albert Hammond, singer, songwriter
1949 Rick Wakeman, keyboards (Strawbs, Yes, solo)
1952 George Strait, US country singer, songwriter
1954 Wreckless Eric (aka Eric Goulden), singer, songwriter
1969 Martika, US singer
1975 Jack Johnson, singer, songwriter

1966

The Castiles (with Bruce Springsteen on vocals) make their first recordings at Mr. Music Inc. in Brick Town, New Jersey, cutting two Springsteen songs, 'Baby I' and 'That's What You Get'. The songs are cut directly to disc, of which seven or eight test pressings are made.

1967

The Beatles are selected to represent Britain for the first-ever global-wide satellite broadcast *Our World* on June 25. The group agreed to be shown in the studio recording a song written especially for the occasion. With the satellite programme being broadcast to many non-English-speaking countries, the BBC requested The Beatles to "keep it simple".

1974

Ray Stevens starts a three week run at No. 1 on the US singles chart with the novelty song 'The Streak' which capitalises on the then popular craze of streaking. It is also No. 1 in the UK.

1975

Five times married US country singer Tammy Wynette is at No. 1 on the UK singles chart with 'Stand By Your Man'. Originally recorded by Wynette and released as an American single in 1968, it proved to be the most successful record of her career and is one of the most covered songs in the history of country music.

1980

Joy Division singer and guitarist Ian Curtis hangs himself in the kitchen of his house in Macclesfield, England at the age of 23. Curtis had the Iggy Pop album *The Idiot*, playing on his stereo and left a note that said, "At this very moment, I wish I were dead. I just can't cope anymore.

1993

Sister Lovers, 18 Wheeler, Boyfriend and Oasis appear on a bill at King Tut's club in Glasgow, Scotland. Creation Records' boss Alan McGee had missed a train at nearby Queen Street station, and decided to head to Tut's to kill time before the next one. After seeing Oasis, McGee declares, "I've found the greatest rock 'n' roll band since The Beatles" and signs them to his Creation label.

1997

Blur win the Music Industry Soccer Six, pop music's equivalent of the FA Cup, at Fulham's FC's ground Craven Cottage, beating off competition from Robbie Williams, My Life Story and The Prodigy.

2000

Madonna's boyfriend Guy Ritchie is arrested after attacking a fan outside the superstar's London home. Ritchie is said to have kicked and punched the man after the couple returned home from a night out.

2003

The Isley Brothers are at No. 1 on the US album chart with 'Body Kiss', the group's first US No. 1 in over 30 years.

2004

Clint Warwick, the original bass player with The Moody Blues, dies from liver disease at the age of 63. Warwick left the band in 1966 after playing on the group's only No. 1 hit, 'Go Now'.

Born on this day:

1945 Pete Townshend, guitar, songwriter, keyboards, vocals (The Who, solo)
1947 Greg Herbert, saxophone (Blood Sweat & Tears)
1949 Dusty Hill, bass (ZZ Top)
1952 Grace Jones, singer, model
1952 Joey Ramone, singer (The Ramones)
1954 Philip Rudd, drums (AC/DC)
1970 Stuart Cable, drums (Stereophonics)

May 19

1958
The soundtrack to *South Pacific* is at No. 1 on the US album chart.

1960
American DJ Alan Freed is indicted along with seven others for accepting $30,650 in payola from six record companies. Two years later, he was convicted and given a suspended sentence and a $300 fine.

1961
The Everly Brothers launch their own record label, Calliope.

1967
The Beatles hold a press party at manager Brian Epstein's London home for the launch of the *Sgt Pepper's Lonely Hearts Club Band* album. Linda Eastman is among the photographers present.

1973
Paul Simon releases the single 'Kodachrome' which becomes a hit in the US, but was banned from airplay in the UK because it is a brand name.

1976
Keith Richards crashes his car near Newport Pagnell, Buckinghamshire, after falling asleep at the wheel. Marijuana and cocaine are found by the police, resulting in another fine for the Rolling Stones guitarist.

1978
Dire Straits release their first major label single 'Sultans Of Swing', recorded on a £120 budget.

1979
Eric Clapton holds a party at his Surrey home, celebrating his recent marriage to Patti Boyd. Clapton sets up a small stage in the garden and as the evening progresses Paul McCartney, George Harrison and Ringo Starr end up jamming live together (for the first time since 1969) along with Clapton, Ginger Baker and Mick Jagger. The all-star band run through old Little Richard and Eddie Cochran songs.

1980
Ringo Starr and his future wife Barbara Bach are involved in a car crash less than half a mile from where Marc Bolan was killed. The car is a write-off but Starr and Bach are not seriously injured.

1981
Sting is named Songwriter of the Year at the 26th Ivor Novello Awards.

1984
Bob Marley & The Wailers start a 12-week run at No. 1 on the UK album chart with the compilation album *Legend*, released to commemorate the third anniversary of Marley's death.

1988
James Brown is arrested for the fifth time in 12 months, following a car chase near his home. He is charged with assault, resisting arrest and being in charge of illegal weapons, and was given a six-year jail sentence.

2001
Mike Sammes, founder of The Mike Sammes Singers, dies aged 73. The Mike Sammes Singers worked with Tom Jones, Cliff Richard and The Beatles, being featured on 'I Am The Walrus' and 'The Long And Winding Road'.

2007
Lawyers for Michael Jackson drop an effort to block an auction of the star's personal belongings and other Jackson family items. An agreement is reached with representatives of an auctioneer, who is the current owner of the materials, and a New Jersey man who claims to own a warehouse full of Jackson memorabilia after a failed business venture wound up in the bankruptcy court.

1990
Madonna starts a three-week run at No. 1 on the US singles chart with 'Vogue'. Originally planned as a B-side, it becomes the singer's eighth American chart-topper and seventh UK No. 1 hit.

May 20

Born on this day:

1944 Joe Cocker, singer
1946 Cher, singer, actor
1958 Jane Wieldin, guitar, vocals (The Go-Gos, solo)

1963 Brian Nash, guitar (Frankie Goes To Hollywood)

1960
The Silver Beetles (John Lennon, Paul McCartney, George Harrison, Stu Sutcliffe, and Tommy Moore) play the first night of a short Scottish tour backing singer Johnny Gentle at Alloa Town Hall in Clackmannanshire. Three of the Silver Beetles adopt stage names: Paul McCartney becomes Paul Ramon, George Harrison is Carl Harrison, and Stuart Sutcliffe is Stuart de Stael.

1964
Rudy Lewis of The Drifters dies aged 28 under mysterious circumstances the night before the group is set to record 'Under The Boardwalk'. Former Drifters' backup singer Johnny Moore is brought back to perform lead vocals for the recording session.

1966
After growing tired of waiting for John Entwistle and Keith Moon to arrive for The Who's gig at the Corn Exchange in Newbury, Berkshire, Pete Townshend and Roger Daltrey start the gig with the rhythm section from the local support band. When Moon and Entwistle finally arrive in the middle of the set, a fight breaks out, with Townshend hitting Moon on the head with his guitar. Moon quits the group but rejoins a week later.

1967
The Young Rascals start a two week run at No. 1 on the US singles chart with 'Groovin', which made No. 8 in the UK.

1968
BBC-2 TV air a short play called *The Pistol Shot*, featuring a young mime artist called David Bowie.

1969
While watching a baseball game at Dodger Stadium, Los Angeles, Peter Cetera of Chicago is set upon by four Marines because they object to the length of his hair. Cetera's jaw is broken, resulting in the singer spending two days in intensive care.

1972
T. Rex are at No. 1 on the UK singles chart with 'Metal Guru', the group's fourth and final British chart-topper. They also have the UK No. 1 album with *Bolan Boogie*.

1978
The Buddy Holly Story film premieres in Holly's hometown of Lubbock, Texas.

1981
Bruce Springsteen appears at Bingley Hall, Stafford, England during his European tour.

1989
Paula Abdul starts a two-week run at No. 1 on the US singles chart with 'Forever Your Girl', her second US No. 1 and a No. 24 hit in the UK.

1995
Don Henley from The Eagles marries model Sharon Summerall. Guests included Glenn Frey, Joe Walsh, Timothy B. Schmit, David Crosby, Randy Newman, Jimmy Buffett, Jackson Browne, Billy Joel, Sting and Sheryl Crow.

1997
U2 cause chaos in Kansas City, Missouri after they pay for traffic control to close down five lanes so they can shoot the video for 'Last Night On Earth'. Apart from causing major traffic jams, a passing Cadillac crashes into a plate glass window trying to avoid a cameraman.

1998
Tommy Lee from Mötley Crüe is sentenced to six months jail after being found guilty of spousal abuse.

Frank Sinatra's funeral is held at The Church of the Good Shepherd in Beverly Hills.

Black Sabbath drummer Bill Ward is taken to hospital in London after suffering a heart attack during a band rehearsal.

2005
Kylie Minogue has a cancerous lump removed from her breast at St Frances Xavier Cabrini Hospital in Melbourne, Australia. The singer had been due to begin the 20-date Australian leg of her current worldwide 'Showgirl' Tour in Sydney.

2007
Rihanna featuring Jay-Z starts a 10-week consecutive run at No. 1 on the UK singles chart with 'Umbrella' making it the longest running chart-topping single since Wet Wet Wet's cover of 'Love Is All Around'.

2009
Michael Jackson delays the opening four nights of his 'This Is It' UK tour at London's O2 Arena. Concert promoters AEG Live say the delay is necessary because the singer needs more time for dress rehearsals. The first show, on 8 July, is pushed back by five nights. Three other July dates will now not take place until March 2010.

May 21

1966

The Castiles (with Bruce Springsteen on vocals) appear at Freehold Regional High School, New Jersey. All five members of the band are Juniors at Freehold High School.

1967

The Jimi Hendrix Experience signs with Reprise Records on the US Warner Brothers label.

1968
Rolling Stone Brian Jones appears on a charge of possession of marijuana at Great Marlborough Street Magistrates Court, London. He is released on £200 bail.

1974

Two would-be concert promoters are arrested by police in America on fraud charges in connection with selling mail order tickets for a forthcoming Elten (*sic*) John show. Police take away over $12,000 in cheques.

1977

Rod Stewart is at No. 1 on the UK singles chart with the double A-sided single 'I Don't Want To Talk About It' / 'The First Cut Is The Deepest'.

1980

Joe Strummer of The Clash is arrested at a problematic gig in Hamburg, Germany, after smashing his guitar over the head of a member of the audience. He is released after an alcohol test proved negative.

1982

The Hacienda Club opens in Manchester, England. Many local acts, including The Stone Roses, Oasis, Happy Mondays, The Smiths, The Charlatans, and James, will all play at the club. Madonna makes her UK TV debut when Channel 4 music show *The Tube* is broadcast live from the club. The Hacienda closes in 1997.

1983

David Bowie is at No. 1 on the US singles chart with 'Let's Dance', featuring blues guitarist Stevie Ray Vaughan. It was Bowie's first single to reach No. 1 on both sides of the Atlantic.

1994

All 4 One start an 11-week run at the top of the US singles chart with 'I Swear' (a No. 2 hit in the UK), previously a No. 1 country hit for John Montgomery in 1994.

2003

Soul singer James Brown is pardoned for his past crimes in the US state of South Carolina. Brown had served a two-and-a-half-year prison term after an arrest on drug and assault charges in 1988 and was granted a pardon by the State Department of Probation, Parole and Pardon Services. Brown, who appeared before the board, sang 'God Bless America' after the decision.

2008

Lou Pearlman, the music mogul who created The Backstreet Boys and 'N Sync, is sentenced to 25 years in federal prison over a decades-long scam that swindled thousands of investors out of their life savings. Many victims were Pearlman's relatives, friends and retirees who lost everything.

2009

Natalie Cole, 59-year-old daughter of Nat King Cole, decides to postpone her summer tour, set to begin in June, as she recovers from undergoing a kidney transplant.

Born on this day:

1924 Charles Aznavour, French singer
1950 Bernie Taupin, songwriter
1954 Jerry Dammers, singer, songwriter (The Specials)

1959 Morrissey, singer, songwriter (The Smiths, solo)
1979 Russell Pritchard, bass (The Zutons)

1958
Jerry Lee Lewis arrives at London's Heathrow Airport to begin his first British tour, along with his new bride, 14-year-old third cousin Myra. Although advised against it, Lewis answers all questions about his private life. The public's shock over the rock'n'roll pianist's marriage marks the start of a controversy leading to his British tour being cancelled after just three of the scheduled 37 performances.

1964
The Beatles score their second US No. 1 album with *The Beatles Second Album* which displaces *Meet The Beatles* from the top of the *Billboard* charts.

1968
Gary Puckett & The Union Gap are at No. 1 on the UK singles chart with 'Young Girl'. The song, about the perils of having sex with a minor, is the American act's only British chart-topper.

1971
The Rolling Stones' *Sticky Fingers* starts a four-week run at the top of the US charts, the group's second US No. 1 album.

1976
Wings start a five-week run at the top of the US singles chart with 'Silly Love Songs', Paul McCartney's fifth US No. 1 since leaving The Beatles. It makes No. 2 in the UK.

1980
U2 start a 23-date '11 O'Clock Tick Tock' tour at The Hope & Anchor, London.

1989
The Stone Roses appear at Dingwalls, London. Tickets cost £5.

1991
Will Sinnott from The Shamen drowns while swimming off the coast of La Gomera. The Shamen were in Tenerife filming a video for their new single, 'Move Any Mountain'.

1997
Radiohead play the first of two sold-out nights at Zeleste, Barcelona, Spain.

2000
Robbie Williams sets up a children's charity Give It Sum with the £2m seed money he earned from a Pepsi deal. Beneficiaries will include UNICEF and Jeans For Genes.

2002
Adam Ant (real name: Stuart Goddard) appears at The Old Bailey in London charged with possession of an imitation firearm. Goddard had been arrested on January 12 after an altercation at The Prince Of Wales pub in north London when the singer pulled a starting pistol on some patrons who had made fun of his appearance. He threatened to shoot them if they didn't move back.

2003
Soul singer Ruben Studdard wins the second series of talent show *American Idol* after 24 million viewers vote in the final. Studdard beats fellow finalist Clay Aiken in a tense live showdown.

2005
The Dave Matthews Band are at No. 1 on the US album chart with *Stand Up*, which enters the chart at No. 1 with sales of 465,000.

2009
White Stripes' drummer Meg White marries Jackson Smith, the son of Patti Smith, at ex-husband and bandmate Jack White's Nashville home. The event is part of a double wedding, which also sees bassist Jack Lawrence, Jack White's musical compatriot in The Raconteurs and The Dead Weather, marry Jo McCaughey.

Born on this day:

1934 Robert Moog, inventor of the synthesizer
1967 Junior Waite (Musical Youth)
1967 Philip James Selway, drums (Radiohead)

1974 Jewel, US singer-songwriter
1975 KT Tunstall, guitar, singer-songwriter

May 23

1960

The Everly Brothers start a five week run at the top of the US singles chart with 'Cathy's Clown'. The song spent seven weeks at No. 1 in the UK.

1967

Pink Floyd record their second single 'See Emily Play', written by original frontman Syd Barrett, which reached No. 6 in the UK.

1970

Grateful Dead play their first gig outside the US at The Hollywood Rock Music Festival in Newcastle-under-Lyme, England.

1973

Jefferson Airplane are prevented from giving a free concert in Golden Gate Park after San Francisco authorities pass a resolution banning electronic instruments. As Starship, the group later wrote 'We Built This City' about the ban.

1978

Bruce Springsteen and the E Street Band kick off their 117 show 'Darkness' Tour at Shea's Buffalo in Buffalo, New York.

1979

Due to a record company dispute, Tom Petty is forced to file for bankruptcy owing $575,000. A long-running battle with his record company MCA followed.

1982

The UK Musicians' Union move a resolution to ban synthesizers and drum machines from sessions and live concerts fearing that their use will put musicians out of work.

1991

Photographer Michael Lavine takes what would become the publicity shots for Nirvana's *Nevermind* album at Jay Aaron Studios in Los Angeles. The idea for the front cover shot of the baby swimming came after Kurt

Cobain and Dave Grohl saw a TV documentary on water babies. Several children were used; five-month old Spencer Eldon's photo taken by Kirk Weddle coming out best.

1992

A statement issued by Freddie Mercury's lawyers says that Mercury has bequeathed the majority of his estate (£10 million) to his long-time friend Mary Austin.

2000

Noel Gallagher walks out on Oasis during a European tour. The move was put down to a series of bust-ups with his brother Liam. The band draft in replacement guitarist Matt Deighton for the rest of the European dates.

2002

Up For Grabs opens at London's Wyndham's Theatre featuring Madonna in the lead role. The first night crowd complains that the singer is lacking in vocal power and strains to hear her lines.

2006

The king of Sweden presents Robert Plant, Jimmy Page and John Paul Jones and the daughter of late drummer John Bonham with the Polar Music Prize in Stockholm, recognising Led Zeppelin as "great pioneers" of rock music. Previous winners include Sir Paul McCartney, Bruce Springsteen and producer Quincy Jones. The Polar Music Prize was founded in 1989 by Stig Anderson, manager of Swedish pop group Abba, who named it after his record label, Polar Records. Zeppelin recorded their 1979 album *In Through The Out Door* at Polar Studios.

2009

Amy Winehouse cancels a concert to celebrate the 50th anniversary of Island Records. Winehouse's management say her appearance, scheduled to take place on 31 May at London's Shepherd's Bush Empire, had now been cancelled completely.

1975

Led Zeppelin start a five-night run at Earl's Court, London. Tickets cost £1.00 – £2.50

Born on this day:

1941 Bob Dylan
1945 Dave Peacock, bass, vocals (Chas & Dave)

1947 Albert Bouchard, drums (Blue Öyster Cult)
1969 Rich Robinson, guitar (The Black Crowes)

1963
US Delta blues guitarist and singer, Elmore James, dies aged 45 of a heart attack. Known as 'The King Of The Slide Guitar', James influenced (among others) BB King, Jimi Hendrix, Fleetwood Mac, The Rolling Stones and Led Zeppelin.

1966
Captain Beefheart & The Magic Band appear at The Whisky A Go Go, West Hollywood, California, supported by Buffalo Springfield and The Doors.

1969
Bob Dylan scores his fourth No. 1 UK album with *Nashville Skyline*.

1974
American composer, pianist, and bandleader Duke Ellington, dies aged 75 of lung cancer and pneumonia.

In 2009 the United States Mint launched a new coin featuring Duke Ellington on the reverse side.

1980
Genesis fans turning up at The Roxy club box office in Los Angeles to buy tickets for a forthcoming gig are surprised to find the band members Phil Collins, Tony Banks and Mike Rutherford selling the tickets themselves.

1991
Gene Clark, founder member of The Byrds, dies aged 49 of a heart attack.

1997
The Spice Girls are at No. 1 on the US album chart with *Spice*, making them the first ever UK girl group to achieve this feat and only the third all-female group to do so after The Supremes and The Go-Gos.

1999
Freddie Mercury is featured on a new set of millennium stamps issued by the Royal Mail to mark his contribution to the Live Aid charity concert in 1985. The Queen frontman, who died in 1991, was featured on the 19p stamp. The singer was a keen stamp collector, and his collection was bought by the Post Office in 1993.

2000
Andrea and Sharon Corr from The Corrs both collapse in the midday sun while shooting their new video in the Mojave Desert, California. After being treated in hospital for heat exhaustion the pair are back on the set within 24 hours.

2003
Paul McCartney makes his first-ever live performance in Russia when appearing in front of 20,000 fans in Red Square.

2004
Madonna kicks off the North American leg of her 'Re-invention' World Tour by playing three sold out nights at the Los Angeles Forum. The tour becomes the top grossing of the year, with ticket sales of nearly $125 million and over 900,000 fans attending the 60-date tour. As a follower of the Kabbalah, Madonna didn't play any Friday gigs as the teaching of the religion forbid it.

2009
Billy Joel is sued by his former drummer for hundreds of thousands of dollars in unpaid royalties. Liberty Devitto, who was Joel's drummer from 1975 until 2005, claimed that Joel hadn't paid him proper royalties for 10 years of work. "People get fired, they get severance or insurance for a certain period of time," said Devitto. "I didn't even get a phone call. It was cold."

Born on this day:

1921 Hal David, songwriter, pianist
1926 Miles Davis, jazz trumpeter, composer

1958 Paul Weller, singer, guitarist, keyboards (The Jam, Style Council, solo)
1975 Lauryn Hill, singer (The Fugees, solo)

1965

Blues harmonica player, singer and songwriter Rice Miller (better known as Sonny Boy Williamson) dies in his sleep. Miller was billed as Sonny Boy Williamson by King Biscuit radio sponsor Max Moore, apparently in an attempt to profit from the fame of the more renowned Chicago-based harmonica player and singer John Lee Williamson, who recorded as Sonny Boy Williamson. The 'second' Sonny Boy proved to be a major influence on the emergent 60s British R&B scene with The Animals and The Yardbirds (as an example) backing him during a UK tour as well as covering his songs.

1967

Pink Floyd appear at the Gwent Constabulary ('A' Division) Spring Holiday Barn Dance, held at The Barn, Grosmont Wood Farm in Cross Ash, Wales.

1969

A benefit concert is held at The Roundhouse, north London to raise money for the families of Fairport Convention drummer Martin Lamble and clothes designer Jeannie Franklyn who were both killed in an accident driving back from a gig (Franklyn was also Fairport guitarist Richard Thompson's girlfriend). Also on the bill are Family, The Pretty Things, Soft Machine and DJ John Peel.

1973

Carole King plays a concert in New York's Central Park, attracting an audience of 100,000.

1978

Paul McGuinness sees The Hype (soon to become U2) at the Project Arts Centre, Dublin and becomes their manager.

1985

Dire Straits score their second UK No. 1 album with *Brothers In Arms*, also No. 1 in the US and 24 other countries.

It went on to sell over 20 million copies worldwide, mainly on the newly introduced compact disc format.

1990

Fleetwood Mac play the first of 42 North American dates on their 'Behind The Mask' World Tour at the PNE Coliseum in Vancouver, Canada. Squeeze are the opening act.

1992

Khalil Rountree, tour manager of Boyz II Men, is killed by gunfire after a scuffle in an elevator on the 26th floor of a Chicago hotel. Their assistant tour manager is also injured.

1995

The earliest known recording of Mick Jagger and Keith Richards from 1961, when they were known as Little Boy Blue & The Blue Boys, is sold at Christies auction house in London for £50,250. The buyer is reputed to be Jagger himself.

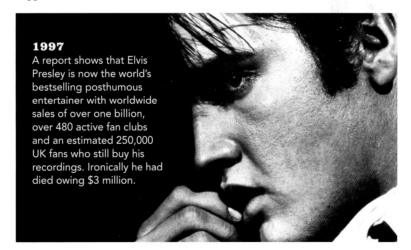

1997

A report shows that Elvis Presley is now the world's bestselling posthumous entertainer with worldwide sales of over one billion, over 480 active fan clubs and an estimated 250,000 UK fans who still buy his recordings. Ironically he had died owing $3 million.

2000

UK Supermarket chain ASDA decide to cancel a planned signing tour to promote Boyzone's Mikey Graham's debut solo single 'Like An Angel' after Graham admitted that he'd used cannabis and had gone on alcohol binges with his fellow Boyz.

2004

Madonna cancels three shows in Israel after terrorists threaten to kill her and her children. A spokesperson said the singer was targeted because she symbolised the West and not because she practised the Jewish faith Kabbalah.

2007

Former 60s pop star Wayne Fontana is remanded in custody after admitting pouring petrol over a bailiff's car and setting light to it. The judge criticised the eccentric former lead singer of The Mindbenders for arriving at Derby Crown Court dressed as the Lady of Justice. He had to hand his sword and scales to guards but still wore a crown, cape and dark glasses, claiming "justice is blind."

2009

Jay Bennett, who was suing the band Wilco over a royalties claim, dies aged 45 at his home in Illinois. Bennett worked as a sound engineer and played with Wilco between 1994 and 2001. Bennett filed his legal action against lead singer Jeff Tweedy at the beginning of May, claiming $50,000 for five albums he made with the group.

Born on this day:

1943 Levon Helm, drums, vocals (The Band)
1948 Stevie Nicks, singer (Fleetwood Mac, solo)

1949 Mick Ronson, guitarist, producer (The Rats, The Spiders From Mars, Mott The Hoople, The Hunter-Ronson Band, solo)
1964 Lenny Kravitz, singer, guitarist, producer

1964
Marianne Faithfull records the Mick Jagger-Keith Richards composition 'As Tears Go By', accompanied by future Led Zeppelin members Jimmy Page on guitar and John Paul Jones on bass.

1968
US blues artist Little Willie John, who co-wrote and was the first to record 'Fever' (covered by Peggy Lee in 1958) and 'Need Your Love So Bad', covered in 1968 by Fleetwood Mac, dies in prison after being convicted of manslaughter.

1969
In Room 1742 of The Hotel La Reine Elizabeth, Montreal, Canada, John Lennon and Yoko Ono begin an eight-day 'Bed-In' to promote world peace. On June 1, the 'Plastic Ono Band' (consisting of whoever was in the room at the time) record 'Give Peace A Chance'. Among the choristers were Timothy and Rosemary Leary, Allen Ginsberg, Petula Clark and Derek Taylor.

1972
On the verge of splitting up, Mott The Hoople are offered two songs by their fan David Bowie, 'Suffragette City' and 'All The Young Dudes', the latter of which they record. The song gives the group a No. 3 UK and US Top 40 hit, and a new lease of life.

1973
The Edgar Winter Group, featuring ex-McCoys guitarist Rick Derringer, are No. 1 on the US singles chart with 'Frankenstein', the band's only American chart-topper, which reached No. 18 in the UK.

1974
Tragedy strikes at a David Cassidy concert at London's White City when over 1,000 fans have to be treated by first aid workers due to the frenzied excitement. One fan, Bernadette Whelan, dies from heart failure four days later.

1977
Billy Powell, singer with The O'Jays, dies aged 35 of cancer. Originally known as The Triumphs, and then The Mascots, they took the name The O'Jays in tribute to Philadelphia radio disc jockey Eddie O'Jay.

1982
The Rolling Stones kick off a 23-date UK and European tour at The Capital Theatre, Aberdeen, Scotland.

1994
Michael Jackson marries Lisa Marie Presley, daughter of Elvis Presley. The couple will divorce in 1995.

1996
A fire at Eric Clapton's house in Chelsea, London, causes over £1.5m worth of damage. Firemen arrive on the scene to find Clapton braving the blaze to save his collection of guitars.

1997
Bob Dylan is admitted to a Malibu hospital with chest pains, causing all of his summer tour to be cancelled.

2000
Mötley Crüe drummer Tommy Lee is jailed for five days for drinking alcohol. Lee appeared in front of an LA court charged with violating his probation by consuming alcohol, an act that directly contravened the terms of his parole.

2002
The first episode of *At Home With The Osbournes* is shown on MTV in the UK.

2009
A US judge ends a bitter two-year battle over James Brown's estate. Judge Jack Early ruled half of his assets will go to a charitable trust, a quarter to his wife and young son, and the rest to his six adult children. Brown's family and wife Tomi Rae Hynie Brown had fought over his fortune since the soul legend died of heart failure in 2006.

Born on this day:

1956 Neil Finn, singer, songwriter (Split Enz, Crowded House, solo)
1957 Siouxsie Sioux, vocals (Siouxsie & The Banshees, The Creatures)
1971 Lisa Lopes (Left-Eye), vocals (TLC)
1975 Dre (Andre Benjamin), US rapper (Outkast)

May 27

1957
Buddy Holly and the Crickets release their first record, 'That'll Be The Day', a UK No. 1 and US No. 3 hit.

1964
Eleven boys are suspended from a school in Coventry, England for having Mick Jagger haircuts.

1967
Pink Floyd appear at The Civic Hall, Nantwich, England.

1977
The Sex Pistols single 'God Save The Queen' is released in the UK. Banned by TV and radio, high street shops and pressing plant workers refuse to handle the record. It sold 200,000 copies in one week and 'officially' peaked at No. 2 on the UK charts the week of 11 June, although according to reports it outsold that week's officially listed No. 1, Rod Stewart's 'I Don't Want To Talk About It'.

1988
Def Leppard kick off the third leg of their North American 'Hysteria' World Tour at George M. Sullivan Arena, Anchorage, Alaska.

1989
Cliff Richard releases his 100th single, 'The Best Of Me', which becomes his 26th Top 3 UK hit.

1990
The Stone Roses play at Spike Island, Cheshire, England to a capacity crowd of 30,000.

1994
The Eagles play their first show in 14 years at the Burbank Studios, California. The two-and-a-half-hour concert ends with two encores, closing with 'Desperado'.

1997
Oasis singer Liam Gallagher is left with cuts and bruises after a scuffle with a youth at the Tower Thistle Hotel in east London. Members of the band had been drinking at the bar when the fight broke out.

1999
Winners at the Ivor Novello Songwriting Awards include Rod Stewart (who wins a Lifetime Achievement Award), Robbie Williams and Guy Chambers (Songwriters Of The Year) and Chrissie Hynde (Outstanding Contribution To British Music).

2000
Paula Yates is awarded £400,000 in an out-of-court settlement from her boyfriend Michael Hutchence's fortune. INXS singer Hutchence was found dead aged 37 in his hotel suite in Sydney in 1997.

2007
Saatchi & Saatchi are fired by Dr Martens for running an advertising campaign featuring dead rock icons such as Kurt Cobain and Sid Vicious wearing the brand's boots in heaven. David Suddens, the chief executive of Dr Martens' parent company Airwear, said the brand had not commissioned the series of four print ads.

2008
Paul McCartney is awarded an honorary Doctor of Music degree from Yale University in the United States. Yale's president, Richard Levin, said the former Beatle had "awakened a generation, giving a fresh sound to rock and roll and to rhythm and blues." A band played 'Hey Jude' as 65-year-old McCartney walked on stage to accept his degree.

2009
American Express file court papers in Los Angeles against Courtney Love,

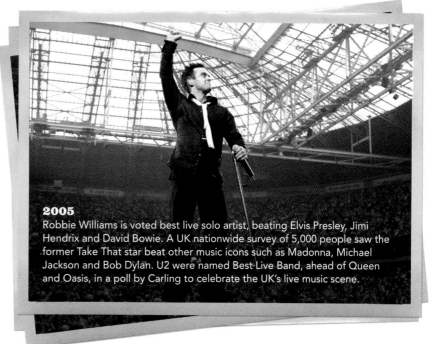

2005
Robbie Williams is voted best live solo artist, beating Elvis Presley, Jimi Hendrix and David Bowie. A UK nationwide survey of 5,000 people saw the former Take That star beat other music icons such as Madonna, Michael Jackson and Bob Dylan. U2 were named Best Live Band, ahead of Queen and Oasis, in a poll by Carling to celebrate the UK's live music scene.

claiming she owes more than $350,000. The company said it had suspended Love's Amex Gold card after she "failed and refused" to make payments.

May 28

Born on this day:

1916 Papa John Creach, violin (Jefferson Airplane, Jefferson Starship)
1944 Gladys Knight, singer
1945 John Fogerty, guitar, vocals (Creedence Clearwater Revival, The Blue Ridge Riders, solo)

1949 Wendy O. Williams, singer (The Plasmatics)
1962 Roland Gift, singer (Fine Young Cannibals)
1968 Kylie Minogue, singer, actress

1964
The BBC receive over 8,000 postal applications wanting tickets for The Rolling Stones panel appearance on *Juke Box Jury* on June 27.

1966
Herb Alpert & The Tijuana Brass go to No. 1 on the US album chart with *What Now My Love*, setting a new American record with four albums in the US Top Ten (the other three being *South Of The Border*, *Going Places* and *Whipped Cream And Other Delights*).

Love appear at the Whisky A Go Go, West Hollywood, supported by The Doors.

1969
Mick Jagger and Marianne Faithfull are arrested at their London home and charged with possession of cannabis. They are released on £50 bail.

1973
Ronnie Lane leaves The Faces to form his own band Slim Chance.

1977
Sting, Stewart Copeland and Andy Summers play together for the first time as part of Mike Howlett's band, Strontium 90, at the Circus Hippodrome, Paris.

1982
Promoter Bill Graham stages a special Vietnam Veterans Benefit Concert in San Francisco starring Jefferson Starship, The Grateful Dead and Country Joe.

1983
Actress and singer Irene Cara starts a six-week run at No. 1 on the US singles chart with 'Flashdance ... What A Feeling', taken from the film *Flashdance*, a No. 2 hit in the UK. Cara had also appeared in TV's *Roots* and *The Next Generation*.

The four-day US Festival '83, featuring The Clash, U2, David Bowie, The Pretenders, Van Halen, Stray Cats, Men At Work, Judas Priest, Stevie Nicks, Willie Nelson, INXS, Joe Walsh, Mötley Crüe and Ozzy Osbourne, starts in California. Over 750,000 fans attend the festival.

1988
Aerosmith singer Steven Tyler marries second wife Teresa Barrick in her hometown of Tulsa, Oklahoma.

1996
Depeche Mode singer Dave Gahan is rushed to Cedars Sinai Hospital, Los Angeles after an apparent drug overdose. The singer is later arrested for possession of cocaine and heroin.

2000
Britney Spears is at No. 1 on the US album chart with *Oops!... I Did It Again*.

2004
Derek Frigo, guitarist from 80s glam band Enuff Z' Nuff, dies aged 36 of a drug overdose.

2007
The Police kick off their 152-show reunion tour at General Motors Place in Vancouver, Canada, before 22,000 fans.

1995
Hootie & The Blowfish start a four-week run at No. 1 on the US album chart with *Cracked Rear View*, going on to sell over 15m copies.

160

Born on this day:

1945 Gary Brooker (The Paramounts, Procol Harum)
1956 La Toya Jackson, singer
1958 Marie Fredriksson, singer (Roxette)
1967 Noel Gallagher, guitar, singer, songwriter (Oasis)
1975 Melanie Brown (a.k.a. Mel B), singer (The Spice Girls)

May 29

1942
Bing Crosby records the Irving Berlin song 'White Christmas', which will go on to become the biggest-selling single of all time, with sales of over 30 million, until overtaken in 1997 by Elton John's 'Candle In The Wind'.

1959
The Drifters, Jimmy Reed, Ray Charles and BB King all appear at the Herndon Stadium in Atlanta, Georgia.

1962
Chubby Checker wins a Grammy Award for Best Rock and Roll Recording for 'Let's Twist Again' and Ray Charles wins Best Rhythm & Blues Recording for 'Hit The Road Jack'.

1965
The Beach Boys start a two-week run at No. 1 on the US singles chart with 'Help Me Rhonda', the group's second American chart-topper. It only reaches No. 27 in the UK.

1967
The Move, Cream, The Jimi Hendrix Experience, Zoot Money and Pink Floyd all appear at the Tulip Bulb Auction Hall in Spalding, Lincolnshire, England. Tickets cost £1.

1971
Three dozen Grateful Dead fans are treated for bad trips after they unwittingly drink apple juice spiked with LSD served at a gig at San Francisco's Winterland.

1977
Manchester band Warsaw, later to become Joy Division, make their live debut supporting The Buzzcocks at The Electric Circus, Manchester, England.

1982
Paul McCartney starts a three-week run at No. 1 on the *Billboard* album chart with *Tug Of War*.

1983
American schoolboy band New Edition (who include Bobby Brown) are at No. 1 on the UK singles chart with 'Candy Girl'. Songwriter and producer Maurice Starr, who discovered New Edition performing at a local talent show, went on to produce and write for New Kids On The Block.

1991
After just completing the recording of the *Nevermind* album, Nirvana play a last-minute show at the Jabberjaw in Los Angeles. In the audience are Iggy Pop and L7 bassist Jennifer Finch who brought along her best friend, Courtney Love.

1992
Concerned that some pupils are overly identifying with Freddie Mercury, the Sacred Heart School in Clifton, New Jersey decides not to use the Queen song 'We Are The Champions' at their graduation ceremony.

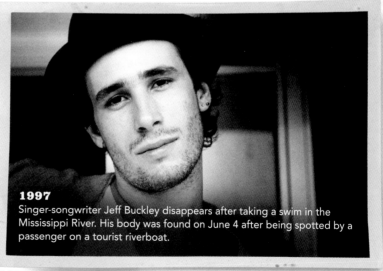

1997
Singer-songwriter Jeff Buckley disappears after taking a swim in the Mississippi River. His body was found on June 4 after being spotted by a passenger on a tourist riverboat.

1999
Skeletal remains are found by photographers looking for old car wrecks to shoot at the bottom of Decker Canyon near Malibu, California. Based on forensic evidence the remains belong to Philip Kramer, former bassist with rock group Iron Butterfly, who had disappeared on his way home from work on February 12, 1995. His death was ruled as a probable suicide.

2002
A 16ft by 6ft mosaic designed by John Lennon goes on display at The Beatles Story museum in Liverpool. The mosaic had been built into Lennon's swimming pool at his Kenwood home in Surrey where he lived between 1964 and 1968.

2009
The 69-year-old producer Phil Spector is sentenced to 15-years-to-life for second-degree murder and an additional four years for personal use of a gun after being found guilty the previous month of shooting and murdering actress Lana Clarkson at his California home in 2003. Spector had pleaded not guilty to the second-degree murder during a five-month retrial in Los Angeles. His lawyers say he will appeal.

Born on this day:

1944 Lenny Davidson, guitar (The Dave Clark Five)

1955 Nicky 'Topper' Headon, drums (The Clash)

1964 Tom Morello, guitar (Rage Against The Machine)

1968 Tim Burgess, vocals (The Charlatans)

1964
The Beatles are at No. 1 on the US singles chart with 'Love Me Do', the group's fourth American chart-topper in five months. When released as their first British single in October 1962, the song only got as high as No. 17.

1966
The Who top an all-star bill including The Kinks, The Small Faces, The Yardbirds and Dave Dee, Dozy, Beaky, Mick & Tich at Sincil Bank Football Ground, Lincoln, England – one of the earliest prototypes of the outdoor, one-day rock festival.

The Doors appear at The Hullabaloo Club, West Hollywood, California.

1969
Led Zeppelin play the first of two nights at The Fillmore East, New York.

1976
The Sex Pistols appear at Reading University, Berkshire.

1980
Carl Radle, bass player with Derek & The Dominoes and Eric Clapton's band, dies aged 38 of kidney failure. Radle also worked with Gary Lewis & The Playboys, George Harrison, Joe Cocker, Dave Mason and Delaney and Bonnie.

1987
Adam Horovitz from The Beastie Boys is arrested while on a UK tour after a beer can hit a fan during a disturbance in Liverpool.

David Bowie kicks off his 87-date Glass Spider World Tour at the Feynoord Stadium, Rotterdam, Holland.

1993
Sun Ra, avant-garde jazz composer, bandleader, keyboards player, poet and philosopher known for his "cosmic philosophy", musical compositions and performances, dies aged 79 in Birmingham, Alabama. As well as his eclectic music, Sun Ra's unorthodox beliefs led him to claim that he was not from Earth but from Saturn.

2002
Diana Ross voluntarily enters a Malibu drug and alcohol rehabilitation centre called Promises to "clear up some personal issues" before setting out on a summer concert tour.

2003
Mickie Most, who produced hits for The Animals, Herman's Hermits, Donovan, Lulu and Jeff Beck and ran his own record label RAK in the 1970s, having success with Kim Wilde, Hot Chocolate, Suzi Quatro and Mud, dies aged 64.

2005
Coldplay's new album is illegally leaked on the internet a week before its UK and US release and on the day copies were sent to UK radio stations and the day before it went on sale in Japan. Security measures around the release include hosting album playbacks at Abbey Road studios for journalists instead of sending them copies of the album, and any CDs that were sent out were labelled with a false name – The Fir Trees – to throw would-be pirates off the scent.

2007
Britney Spears said she "truly hit rock bottom" when she went to rehab earlier this year. In a message on her website, the singer wrote "I genuinely did not know what to do with myself" following her split from husband Kevin Federline. The 25-year-old singer entered a Malibu treatment facility in February after months of partying which ended with the singer shaving off all her hair.

2009
A news story claims that Mick Jagger offered to buy an ice cream van but was turned down by its owner who'd promised his daughter he would drive her to her wedding in the vehicle. Guiseppe Della Camera had spent 10 years restoring the rusting van after he spotted it being used as a chicken shed on a farm. The restoration was such a success that Jagger offered to buy the vehicle when he saw it at a show on Wandsworth Common. "Jagger told me he'd really fallen in love with my van and asked me if I would consider selling it," Camera said. "I was stunned when he offered me £100,000."

Ozzy Osbourne announces he is suing Black Sabbath's guitarist Tony Iommi over royalty payments. The 60-year-old former Sabbath vocalist accused Iommi of falsely claiming to have sole rights to the band's name which had cost him royalties from merchandise sales and was seeking unspecified damages, lost profits and a declaration he was half-owner of the trademark. Iommi claimed Osbourne legally relinquished rights to the band's name in the 1980s. Osbourne said he believed all four original members of the band should have equal shares in Black Sabbath's name.

May 31

1961
Chuck Berry opens Berry Park, an amusement complex near St Louis, which has its own zoo, golf course and ferris wheel.

1968
During a session for what will become 'The White Album', The Beatles work on 'Revolution'. After numerous overdubs have been added, the final six minutes of the song are removed to form the basis of the experimental 'Revolution 9', while the first half becomes the slow version of 'Revolution' (known as 'Revolution 1').

1970
Peter Green leaves Fleetwood Mac.

1973
In Los Angeles, during the birthday celebrations of Led Zeppelin's John Bonham at a private home, George and Patti Harrison are thrown fully clothed into the swimming pool.

1975
During a press conference held at the 5th Avenue Hotel in New York City to announce The Rolling Stones' forthcoming American tour, the Stones themselves come down the street playing live from the back of a flatbed truck.

1976
The Who's concert today at Charlton Athletic Football Ground, south London enters *The Guinness Book of Records* as the loudest recorded performance by a rock band, measured at 120 decibels.

1977
The BBC announces a ban on The Sex Pistols single 'God Save The Queen' saying it was "in gross bad taste". The IBA issue a warning to all radio stations that playing the single would be in breach of Section 4:1:A of the Broadcasting Act.

1998
Geri Halliwell announces she has quit The Spice Girls, saying, "This is because of differences between us. I am sure the group will continue to be successful and I wish them all the best."

2000
US soul singer Johnnie Taylor dies of a heart attack in a Texas hospital shortly after his 62nd birthday. Taylor had been a member of The Highway QCs and The Five Echoes and in 1957 replaced Sam Cooke in The Soul Stirrers. He scored the 1976 US No. 1 'Disco Lady.'

2003
UK police announce that thousands of people attending pop festivals this summer would be subjected to a computerised drug test. Individuals are to be asked to provide swab samples from their hands, which will be inserted into a drug detection machine. It is to be a voluntary test but anti-drug officers could search anyone who refused.

2004
US guitarist Robert Quine, who worked with Richard Hell, Lou Reed, Brian Eno, Lloyd Cole, Marianne Faithfull, Tom Waits and They Might Be Giants, is found dead aged 61 of a heroin overdose in his New York City home.

2005
Former East 17 singer Brian Harvey is in a critical condition in a London hospital after falling under the wheels of his Mercedes convertible. The accident happened outside Harvey's home in Walthamstow when he reversed from an access road into the street. The singer suffered a broken leg, pelvis and a crushed abdomen and ribs.

2008
Death Cab For Cutie are at No. 1 on the US album chart with their sixth release *Narrow Stairs*.

June

Born on this day:

1947 Ron Wood, guitar (The Birds, Jeff Beck Group, The Faces, The Rolling Stones)

1959 Alan Wilder, keyboards, vocals (Depeche Mode)

1960 Simon Gallup, bass (The Cure)

1963 Mike Joyce, drums (The Smiths)

1974 Alanis Morissette, Canadian singer-songwriter

June 1

1959
The first edition of *Juke Box Jury* airs on the BBC. The host, David Jacobs, leads a revolving panel of four guests who predict whether records will be a hit or a miss.

1963
Lesley Gore begins a two week run at No. 1 on the US singles chart with 'It's My Party', produced by Quincy Jones, a staff producer for Mercury Records. Dave Stewart and Barbara Gaskin score a UK No. 1 in 1981 with their version of the song.

1964
The Rolling Stones arrive on BOAC flight 505 at Kennedy Airport for their debut US tour. The first date is on June 5 in San Bernardino, California.

1966
During a 12-hour session at EMI Studios, The Beatles add overdubs to 'Yellow Submarine', with John Lennon blowing bubbles into a bucket of water and shouting "Full speed ahead Mr. Bosun!" The group's roadie Mal Evans plays a bass drum strapped to his chest, marching around the studio with The Beatles following behind (conga-line style) singing, "We all live in a yellow submarine."

1967
The British release date for The Beatles' *Sgt Pepper's Lonely Hearts Club Band*. Costing £25,000 to produce, the album was recorded at London's EMI Studios using 700 hours of studio time. It spends 27 weeks at No. 1 in the UK and 15 weeks at No. 1 in the American *Billboard* chart.

1968
Simon & Garfunkel reach No. 1 on the US singles chart with 'Mrs Robinson', which was featured in the popular contemporary film *The Graduate*, starring Dustin Hoffman and Anne Bancroft. The song was also a UK hit for The Lemonheads in 1992.

1971
The two-room shack in Tupelo, Mississippi where Elvis Presley was born on January 8, 1935 is opened to the public as a tourist attraction.

1972
Pink Floyd begin recording *The Dark Side Of The Moon* at Abbey Road Studios in London.

1973
Former Soft Machine drummer Robert Wyatt breaks his spine after falling three stories from a window, leaving him permanently disabled and confined to a wheelchair.

1975
The Rolling Stones kick off their biggest ever US tour – taking in 45 shows in 26 cities – at Louisiana State University. Guitarist Ron Wood joins the Stones on tour for first time, as then-temporary replacement for Mick Taylor.

1977
Bob Marley & The Wailers play the first of four nights at London's Rainbow Theatre. Six nights were booked at the Rainbow but the last two shows were cancelled due to a serious toe injury Marley received in a football game. The tour's second leg in the United States is postponed and then cancelled.

1978
U2 appear at Mount Temple Comprehensive School in Dublin, Ireland.

1981
The first issue of heavy metal magazine *Kerrang!* is published as a special pull-out by UK music weekly *Sounds*. AC/DC are on the cover and Motörhead, Girlschool and Saxon are featured inside.

1985
Bruce Springsteen kicks off the European leg of his 'Born In The USA' World Tour at Slane Castle in Dublin, Ireland.

1991
American soul singer David Ruffin, formerly of The Temptations, dies aged 50 of a drug overdose at a Philadelphia hospital. His solo hits included the 1975 US No. 9 & UK No. 10 single 'Walk Away From Love'.

Sting appears on the first airing of a new Soviet TV rock show, *Rock Steady*.

2000
The movie *Honest*, directed by ex-Eurythmics Dave Stewart, starring three of All Saints, is pulled by cinemas after a disastrous showing at the box office. The three singers play sisters who turn to crime in the late '60s.

2005
White Stripes singer/guitarist Jack White marries his girlfriend, British model Karen Elson, in a canoe on the Amazon in Brazil.

2006
The 1994 debut album by Oasis, *Definitely Maybe*, is voted the Greatest Album of All Time in a survey to mark 50 years of the Official UK Albums Chart. The Beatles are in second and third place with *Sgt Pepper's Lonely Hearts Club Band* and *Revolver, OK Computer* by Radiohead is fourth and *(What's The Story) Morning Glory?* by Oasis is fifth.

Born on this day:

1941 Charlie Watts, drums (The Rolling Stones)
1959 Michael Steele, bass, vocals (The Runaways, The Bangles)
1960 Tony Hadley, vocals (Spandau Ballet)
1976 Tim Rice-Oxley, piano (Keane)
1980 Fabrizio Moreti, drummer (The Strokes)

1962
Owen Gray's 'Twist Baby' becomes the first single released on the UK-based Island Records.

1966
The Who kick off a ten-date European tour at the Grona Lund in Stockholm, Sweden.

1967
David Bowie releases his self-titled debut album on the Deram label, but the LP fails to make the UK charts.

1973
The Electric Light Orchestra begin their first US tour in San Diego, California.

1981
Prince makes his live British debut at The Lyceum Ballroom, London, but he does not play the UK again for five years.

1984
Wham! have their first UK No. 1 with 'Wake Me Up Before You Go Go', written and produced by George Michael. Inspiration for the song was a scribbled note left by Michael's Wham! partner Andrew Ridgeley for Ridgeley's parents, originally intended to read "wake me up before you go" but with "up" accidentally written twice, so Ridgeley wrote "go" twice on purpose.

1989
Rolling Stone Bill Wyman marries 19-year-old Mandy Smith at Bury St. Edmunds Registry Office. Wyman's 28-year-old son Stephen is best man. The other four Stones and their wives attend the blessing at the Church of St. John the Evangelist in London three days later. The marriage lasts 17 months.

1993
Aerosmith appear at The Landon Arena in Kansas, the first night on their 169-date 'Get A Grip' World Tour.

1999
Junior Braithwaite of Bob Marley & The Wailers is shot dead aged 46.

2002
It is reported that Paul McCartney has thrown his fiancée Heather Mills' engagement ring out of a hotel window during a row. Guards at Miami's Turnberry Isle Resort comb the grounds using metal detectors and later find the £15,000 ring.

2003
A painting of Kylie Minogue wearing gold hot pants causes tempers to fray among drivers in Brighton. Artist Simon Etheridge put up the almost life-size picture in his own Art Asylum gallery as part of a festival and motorists have been causing regular traffic hold-ups as they stop to take a second look.

2008
US guitarist and singer Bo Diddley dies aged 79 of heart failure at his home in Archer, Florida. The legendary singer and performer, renowned for his "shave and a haircut" rhythm and homemade square guitar, influenced artists from Buddy Holly to Bruce Springsteen, The Rolling Stones and U2.

2005
Franz Ferdinand's frontman, Alex Kapranos, is detained by Russian police after being suspected of spying. Kapranos was attempting to board a plane in Moscow when the altercation took place. Travelling under his actual surname, Huntley, Kapranos was accused of being an MI6 agent who was previously suspected of stealing information on Russian weaponry. Unfortunately for the singer, the surname Huntley was also used by actual former MI6 agent Richard Tomlinson who did steal secrets in the early 90s. The singer is freed after he points out that the Huntley they were so concerned about was 13 years older than him.

Born on this day:

1939 Ian Hunter, vocals, guitar (Mott The Hoople, Hunter-Ronson Band, solo)

1942 Curtis Mayfield, US singer, songwriter, guitar (The Impressions, solo)

1943 Michael Clarke, drums (The Byrds, Flying Burrito Brothers, Firefall)

1946 John Paul Jones, bass, keyboards, producer (Led Zeppelin)

1952 Billy Powell, keyboards (Lynyrd Skynyrd)

1974 Kelly Jones, vocals, guitar (Stereophonics)

1949

Elvis Presley receives an 'A' in language but only a 'C' in music on his 8th grade report card at Humes High School, Memphis, Tennessee.

1964

During a photo session Ringo Starr is taken ill suffering from tonsillitis and pharyngitis, the day before a Beatles world tour is about to start. After a last-minute phone call from George Martin, session drummer Jimmy Nicol rushes over to EMI Studios where he and The Beatles run through six songs from their tour repertoire in a quick rehearsal. Nicol subsequently becomes a Beatle for 11 days.

1967

Aretha Franklin goes to No. 1 on the US singles chart (No. 10 in Britain) with her version of Otis Redding's 'Respect'. Aretha scores her first UK No. 1 20 years later with 'I Knew You Were Waiting', a duet with George Michael.

1968
Valerie Solanas shoots Andy Warhol and art critic and curator Mario Amaya at Warhol's studio in New York City. Solanas had been to see Warhol after asking for the return of a script which had apparently been misplaced. Warhol is seriously wounded in the attack and barely survives.

The Doors 'Light My Fire' is released in the US and goes on to be No. 1 on the singles chart two months later.

1970

Ray Davies is forced to make a 6,000-mile round trip from New York to London to re-record one word in a song. Due to a British advertising ban, Davies has to change the word 'Coca' in Coca Cola to Cherry Cola on The Kinks' forthcoming single 'Lola'.

1972

The Rolling Stones kick off their seventh North American tour at the Pacific Coliseum, Vancouver, Canada. The 32-date tour grosses $4 million, making it the richest rock tour in history at that time.

1983

US session drummer Jim Gordon murders his mother by pounding her head with a hammer. A schizophrenic, it was not until Gordon's trial in 1984 that he was properly diagnosed. Because his attorney is unable to use the insanity defense, Gordon is sentenced to 16 years-to-life in prison. A Grammy Award winner for co-writing 'Layla' with Eric Clapton, Gordon also worked with The Beach Boys, John Lennon, George Harrison and Frank Zappa among many other artists.

1995

Bryan Adams starts a five-week run at No. 1 on the US singles chart with 'Have You Ever Really Loved A Woman'. Taken from the film *Don Juan De Marco* it becomes Adams third US solo No. 1; a No. 4 hit in the UK.

2002

Paul McCartney, Sting, Elton John, Brian Wilson, Cliff Richard, Ozzy Osbourne, The Corrs, Will Young, Atomic Kitten and S Club 7 all appear at The Queen's Jubilee concert at Buckingham Palace, London.

2003

Barry Manilow suffers a broken nose after he accidentally walks into a wall at his home in Palm Springs, California and knocks himself unconscious.

June 4

Born on this day:

1944 Roger Ball, sax (Average White Band)
1952 Jimmy McCulloch, guitar (Thunderclap Newman, Stone The Crows, Wings)
1956 Reeves Gabrels, guitar (Tin Machine)
1974 Stefan Lessard, bass (Dave Matthews Band)

1942
Glenn Wallichs launches Capitol Records in the US. The label becomes home to such artists as Frank Sinatra, The Beatles, The Beach Boys, Eddie Cochran, Gene Vincent, Bobby Darin, Dean Martin, Glen Campbell, The Steve Miller Band, Dr. Hook, Bob Seger, Tina Turner, Heart and countless others. Wallichs invented the art of record promotion by sending copies of new releases to disc jockeys.

1967
Procol Harum, The Jimi Hendrix Experience and Denny Laine all appear at The Saville Theatre in London. Hendrix performs the song 'Sgt. Pepper's Lonely Hearts Club Band', which had only just been released a few days earlier, impressing Paul McCartney who was in the audience.

1969
Hundreds of people in Glenrowan, Australia, sign a petition protesting against the casting of Mick Jagger in the role of Australian folk hero, Ned Kelly.

1970
Elvis Presley begins five days of recording at RCA's Studio B in Nashville, Tennessee, starting each day at 6pm and working until dawn.

1974
David Bowie kicks off his 73-date 'Diamond Dogs' Tour at the Forum, Montreal, Canada.

1976
At CBGBs club live recordings are made of performances by Blondie, Mink DeVille, Talking Heads, Laughing Dogs and Tuff Darts. The tracks feature on the album *Live At CBGBs New York*.

1983
The Police start a four-week run at No. 1 in the UK with 'Every Breath You Take', the group's fifth and final chart-topping single, taken from their album *Synchronicity*. Sting wins Song Of The Year and The Police win Best Pop Performance for the song at the 1984 Grammy Awards.

1984
Bruce Springsteen releases *Born In The USA* which goes on to top the US album chart for seven weeks and spawn seven Top 10 singles.

1985
Elton John begins a high court battle with Dick James Music, seeking the rights to early songs and recordings plus damages estimated at more than £30 million . The singer loses the six-month court battle to recover the copyright to 169 songs but the court orders Dick James to cough up millions in unpaid royalties.

1990
American punk rock singer Stiv Bators of The Dead Boys and The Lords Of The New Church dies after being hit by a taxi in Paris. Bators was out drinking when he was hit while crossing the road; he was taken to hospital but left before seeing a doctor. He died in his sleep as the result of a concussion.

1992
The US Postal Service announces the results of a poll conducted to see which picture of Elvis Presley should be used on a commemorative stamp. The young Elvis beats the (older and larger) Vegas-era Elvis.

1993
Kurt Cobain is arrested after a dispute, allegedly concerning the Nirvana's guitarist's collection of firearms, at his house in Seattle.

1994
Wet Wet Wet start a 15-week run at No. 1 on the UK singles chart with 'Love Is All Around', from the film *Four Weddings And A Funeral*. The song, written by Reg Presley, was a former Top 10 hit for Reg's group, The Troggs, in 1967.

2002
George Michael is jeered and heckled by the audience of a CNN news show during a phone interview. Michael is defending the content of the video to his new single 'Shoot The Dog' in which US President George W Bush is shown in bed with UK Prime Minister Tony Blair. George maintains it was an attack on Blair and not President Bush.

Wyclef Jean is arrested protesting against cuts to education following an attempt to perform, which is forbidden by the event's permit. The rally is to protest a proposed $1.2 billion cut to New York's public education system.

2004
Nathan Moore, former singer with Brother Beyond and Worlds Apart, appears at Highbury Corner Magistrates Court and pleads guilty to a charge of kerb crawling in central London. He is fined £250 and ordered to pay £50 costs. The former pop singer was arrested on May 27 in the King's Cross area after he approached a woman he thought was a prostitute and requested a sexual favour. He then rode away on his moped before being arrested.

Born on this day:

1946 Freddie Stone, guitar (Sly & The Family Stone)
1947 Tom Evans, bass, vocals (Badfinger)
1956 Richard Butler, vocals (Psychedelic Furs)
1971 Mark Wahlberg (Marky Mark), vocals, actor (New Kids On The Block, solo)

1959
Robert Zimmerman graduates from high school in Hibbing, Minnesota. Because of his long sideburns and leather jacket, Zimmerman – who will change his name to Bob Dylan in 1960 – was known as a greaser to classmates in the remote rural community,

1964
The Rolling Stones play their first-ever live date in America at the Swing Auditorium, San Bernardino, California.

1966
At London's Marquee Club, 'The Bowie Showboat', a lunchtime performance from David Bowie, offers "three hours of music and mime", plus a Top Ten disco. Admission is 3 shillings (15p).

1968
The Jimi Hendrix Experience appear on Dusty Springfield's TV show, *It Must Be Dusty*, filmed at the ATV Studios, Boreham Wood. Jimi and Dusty perform a duet on the Inez & Charlie Foxx hit, 'Mockingbird'.

1971
Grand Funk Railroad smash the record held by The Beatles when they sell out New York's Shea Stadium in 72 hours.

1976
The Who, The Sensational Alex Harvey Band, Little Feat, The Outlaws and Streetwalkers appear at Celtic Football Club, Glasgow. Tickets cost £4.
It was the second of three 'Who Put The Boot In' shows at British football stadiums.

1977
Alice Cooper's boa constrictor, a co-star of his live act, suffers a fatal bite from a rat it is being fed for breakfast. Cooper holds auditions for a replacement and a snake named 'Angel' gets the gig.

1979
Blues legend Muddy Waters (aged 64) marries Marva Jean Brooks on her 25th birthday.

1983
During a 48-date North American tour U2 play at the Red Rocks Amphitheater near Denver. The show is recorded and released as *U2 Live At Red Rocks: Under A Blood Red Sky*.

1990
American drummer Jim Hodder, who was the original drummer with Steely Dan and also worked with Sammy Hagar and David Soul, drowns aged 42 in his swimming pool.

1993
Country singer Conway Twitty (real name: Harold Lloyd Jenkins), who had a 1958 US & UK No. 1 single with 'It's Only Make Believe', dies aged 59 from an abdominal aortic aneurysm. Until 2000, Twitty held the record for the most No. 1 singles of any country act with 45. He lived in Hendersonville, Tennessee, just north of Nashville, where he built a country music entertainment complex called Twitty City.

Mariah Carey marries the President of Sony Music, Tommy Mottola, in a Manhattan ceremony. Guests include Billy Joel, Bruce Springsteen, Barbra Streisand and Ozzy Osbourne. The couple separate in 1997.

1997
Oasis guitarist Noel Gallagher marries Meg Matthews at the Little Church of The West in Las Vegas (where Elvis and Priscilla Presley wed). They divorce in 2001.

Ex-Small Faces and Faces bassist and Slim Chance leader Ronnie Lane dies aged 51 after a 20-year battle with multiple sclerosis.

2003
R. Kelly is banned from travelling to LA for a video shoot. He isn't allowed to leave Chicago after being charged with 21 child porn offences, including a video which allegedly shows him having sex with an underage girl.

A grandfather who set up his own pirate radio station in Wakefield, Yorkshire, is under investigation by local broadcasting authorities. The man, known as Ricky Rock, erected a 32ft transmitter in his garden and has been playing hits by The Beatles, The Beach Boys and Elvis Presley. Ricky says he set up the station because the "talentless boy bands and dance music" featured on local stations did not cater to the tastes of his generation.

2007
Jurors in the murder trial of music producer Phil Spector are shown the bloody revolver that was found at the feet of Lana Clarkson, the actress he is accused of killing at his home in the early hours of February 3, 2003. She had accompanied Spector to his Alhambra, California mansion after meeting him at her job as a hostess at the House of Blues just hours earlier.

Paul McCartney releases his 21st solo album, *Memory Almost Full*, on the new Hear Music Starbucks label. It is later announced that all copies sold through the UK Starbucks chain would not be eligible for the British charts as the 533 stores were not registered with the Official Chart Company. The album is played non-stop in more than 10,000 Starbucks outlets across 29 countries.

June 6

Born on this day:

1936 Levi Stubbs, vocals (The Four Tops)
1944 Clarence White, guitar (Kentucky Colonels, The Byrds)

1960 Steve Vai, guitar (Frank Zappa, David Lee Roth, Whitesnake)
1978 Carl Barat, guitar, vocals (The Libertines)

1960
Bing Crosby is presented with a Platinum disc to commemorate his 200 millionth record sold. The sales figures are a combined total of 2,600 recorded singles and 125 albums. Crosby's global lifetime sales on 179 labels in 28 countries totaled 400 million records.

1962
The first Beatles recording session takes place at EMI Studios, Abbey Road, London. The group (with Pete Best on drums) record four tracks, one of which is 'Love Me Do', and are paid £7.10 each for the session.

1966
Roy Orbison's 25-year-old wife, Claudette, is killed when a truck pulls out of a side road and collides with the motorbike that she and her husband are riding on in Gallatin, Texas.

1968
Screaming Lord Sutch appears at the Freehold Hullabaloo in Freehold, New Jersey. Sutch was touring the East Coast in an old, custom-painted Rolls Royce hearse. Support band is The Castiles, featuring Bruce Springsteen on vocals.

1971
John Lennon & Yoko Ono jam on stage with Frank Zappa & The Mothers Of Invention during the encore of Zappa's gig at The Fillmore East, New York. The recording is later released on the couple's 1972 album *Some Time In New York City*.

1979
Def Leppard play at Crookes Working Man's Club, Sheffield, Yorkshire. The gig is reviewed in UK music paper *Sounds* and leads to a recording contract with Phonogram Records.

1982
Stevie Wonder, Bob Dylan, Crosby Stills & Nash, Tom Petty, Stevie Nicks and Jackson Browne all appear at The Rose Bowl, Pasadena, California to a crowd of 85,000 fans.

1987
Michael Jackson announces that he is breaking all ties with the Jehovah's Witnesses. Jackson had been raised as a Jehovah's Witness and would don disguises and go door-to-door with the Watchtower message in cities where he was performing.

1996
William Palmer, the inventor of the magnetic tape recorder, dies. Before this music had been cut direct to record.

1999
Plans are announced for Elvis Presley to tour the UK almost 23 years after his death. A virtual version of 'the King' will perform with a live orchestra and members of his band.

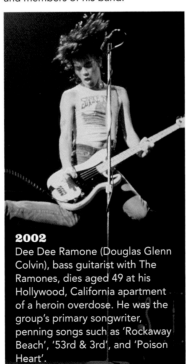

2002
Dee Dee Ramone (Douglas Glenn Colvin), bass guitarist with The Ramones, dies aged 49 at his Hollywood, California apartment of a heroin overdose. He was the group's primary songwriter, penning songs such as 'Rockaway Beach', '53rd & 3rd', and 'Poison Heart'.

2003
A High Court judge in London rules that rap lyrics should be treated as a foreign language after admitting that he was unsure of the meaning of 'shizzle my nizzle' and 'mish mish man'. The court battle was over a copyright issue between the Ant'ill Mob and The Heartless Crew who had used the lyrics on a remix.

2006
Billy Preston dies aged 59 of kidney failure in Scottsdale, Arizona. The Grammy-winning keyboard player collaborated with some of the greatest names in the music industry including The Beatles, The Rolling Stones, Nat King Cole, Little Richard, Ray Charles, George Harrison, Ringo Starr, Elton John, Eric Clapton and Bob Dylan.

2008
Ki McPhail and Owen Doyle, former band members from Busted, lose a £10m royalties battle. The pair claim they wrote songs with the two other band members, James Bourne and Matt Willis, including 'Year 3000' and 'What I Go To School For', but were forced to sign away their rights before being sacked from the band in October 2001. The judge in the case, Mr. Justice Morgan, criticises the evidence they give and dismisses the claims.

Born on this day:

1940 Tom Jones, Welsh singer
1957 Paddy McAloon, guitar, vocals (Prefab Sprout)
1958 Prince, singer, songwriter, multi-instrumentalist
1967 David Navarro, guitar (Jane's Addiction)
1985 Charlie Simpson, guitar, vocals (Busted)

June 7

1964
During their first ever US tour The Rolling Stones are booed at a gig in San Antonio, Texas. Some performing monkeys who had been the act on before the group were brought back on stage for another performance.

1968
Peter Green's Fleetwood Mac, The Grateful Dead and Jefferson Airplane all appear for the first of a three-night run at The Carousel Ballroom, San Francisco, California.

1969
Blind Faith, featuring Steve Winwood, Eric Clapton, Ginger Baker and Ric Grech, make their live debut at a free concert in London's Hyde Park.

Bob Dylan and Joni Mitchell appear as guests on the first ABC TV *Johnny Cash Show* from the Ryman Auditorium in Nashville. Cash duets with both artists.

1975
Elton John's *Captain Fantastic & The Brown Dirt Cowboy* is top of the US album chart, the first LP ever to enter the *Billboard* chart at No. 1.

1980
Bob Marley & The Wailers, The Average White Band, Joe Jackson and The Q-Tips all appear at the Summer Of '80 Garden Party, Crystal Palace, south London. Tickets cost £7.50.

1985
The Smiths play the first date of a US tour at Chicago's Aragon Ballroom.

1987
On his 'Glass Spider' tour, David Bowie plays a concert in West Berlin in front of the Reichstag with the speakers pointing towards the nearby Berlin Wall where thousands of young East Berliners stand and listen.

1990
The Black Crowes play their debut UK gig at London's Marquee Club.

1991
During their 'Use Your Illusion' Tour, Guns N' Roses play the first of two nights at the CNE Stadium, Toronto, Canada.

1995
Radiohead guitarist Johnny Greenwood is admitted to hospital after his ear leaks blood. The problem is diagnosed as resulting from his arm movement during continuous guitar thrashing.

1997
Hanson start a three-week run at No. 1 on the UK singles chart with 'MMMbop', one of the biggest debut singles of all time, reaching No. 1 in 27 countries. Originally called The Hanson Brothers, lead singer Zak Hanson was just 13-years-old at the time.

1998
Songwriter-producer Wally Gold, originally a member of late 50s group The Four Esquires, and who wrote the Lesley Gore hit 'It's My Party' and 'It's Now Or Never', a hit for Elvis Presley, dies aged 70 in a New Jersey hospital.

2001
During 'The Tour of Brotherly Love', Oasis, The Black Crowes and Spacehog play the first of three nights at Radio City Music Hall in New York City.

2002
Virgin Records announce they have dropped Victoria Beckham after her debut solo album, which cost over £3 million to make, sells only 50,000 copies.

1977
Led Zeppelin play the first of six sold out nights at Madison Square Garden, New York.

Born on this day:

1940 Nancy Sinatra, US singer, actress
1942 Chuck Negron, vocals (Three Dog Night)

1960 Mick Hucknall, vocals, songwriter (Simply Red)
1977 Kayne West, US rapper, producer

1963
The Crystals' 'Da Doo Ron Ron' peaks at No. 3 on the US singles chart. Produced in Los Angeles by Phil Spector, who used multi-track recording to achieve a result that becomes known as a "wall of sound", the backing musicians include Glen Campbell on guitar, Leon Russell on piano, Hal Blaine on drums and Nino Tempo on sax.

1967
Procol Harum are at No. 1 on the UK singles chart with 'A Whiter Shade Of Pale', the group's only UK No. 1. In 2004 the song was named the most played record of the past 70 years and more than 900 recorded versions by other artists are known.

1969
In a press statement it is announced that founder member Brian Jones is leaving The Rolling Stones. A quote attributed to Jones says that he no longer sees "eye to eye" with the rest of the band over musical direction.

1970
After mistakenly driving too close to the border, Deep Purple's van and equipment is impounded by East German police during a European tour.

1974

Dolly Parton is at No. 1 on the US country chart with 'I Will Always Love You'. The Parton-penned song later became a worldwide hit for Whitney Houston in 1992.

1985
Tears For Fears start a two-week run at No. 1 on the *Billboard* singles chart with 'Everybody Wants To Rule The World', the group's first US No. 1.

1987
Yogi Horton, a session drummer with Luther Vandross, jumps to his death from a 17th floor hotel window, having told his wife he was tired of living in the shadow of the soul singer. Horton also worked with The B-52s, Diana Ross and Debbie Harry.

1989
At a Greenpeace Rainbow Warrior's press conference, vegetarian Chrissie Hynde is alleged to have told people to boycott and damage McDonald's restaurants. The following day a branch of the fast food chain in Milton Keynes, England is firebombed and Hynde is threatened with a police charge of "incitement to criminal damage".

1991
Bruce Springsteen marries singer Patti Scialfa at their Beverly Hills home.

1996
The Fugees score their first UK No. 1 with their version of the Roberta Flack 1973 hit 'Killing Me Softly (With His Song)'. The song, composed by Charles Fox and Norman Gimbel in 1971, was inspired by Lori Lieberman's poem 'Killing Me Softly With His Blues', written after having seen a performance by US singer-songwriter Don McLean.

2001
AC/DC, The Offspring, Queens Of The Stone Age and Megadeth all appear at the Milton Keynes Bowl, England. Tickets cost £28.50.

2002
Months of secrecy surrounding Paul McCartney's remarriage are blown when John Leslie, the owner of the 17th century Castle Leslie in Co Monaghan, lets slip to reporters that McCartney has booked the castle for his marriage to Heather Mills.

2003
Led Zeppelin top the *Billboard* chart with the 3-CD live set *How The West Was Won*, the band's seventh US No. 1 album.

2007
George Michael is sentenced to 100 hours of community service and banned from driving for two years at Brent Magistrates Court, north London. The 43-year-old was arrested last October after being found slumped at the steering wheel of his car. He pleads guilty to driving while unfit, blaming "tiredness and prescribed drugs" for the offence.

2008
Rolling Stone magazine publishes a list of the Top 50 Guitar Songs of All Time. No. 5 is 'Brown Sugar' by The Rolling Stones, 4, 'You Really Got Me' The Kinks, 3, 'Crossroads', Cream, 2, 'Purple Haze', Jimi Hendrix and 1, 'Johnny B Goode', Chuck Berry.

Born on this day:

1915 Les Paul, guitarist and designer of the Gibson Les Paul guitar

1934 Jackie Wilson, US soul singer

1941 Jon Lord, keyboards (The Artwoods, Deep Purple, Whitesnake)

1947 John 'Mitch' Mitchell, drums (The Riot Squad, Georgie Fame & The Blue Flames, Jimi Hendrix Experience)

1967 Dean Felber, bass (Hootie & The Blowfish)

1963

On the last night of their tour with Roy Orbison, The Beatles perform at King George's Hall, Blackburn, Lancashire. It is during this tour that their fans start throwing jelly babies at the stage while the group is performing, after an off-the-cuff remark in an interview that George Harrison enjoyed eating them.

1964

During an evening session Bob Dylan records 'Mr. Tambourine Man' at Columbia Recording Studios, New York.

1967

The Monkees play at the Hollywood Bowl in Los Angeles, California. During his solo spot, Micky Dolenz leaps into the fountain separating the audience from the stage.

1972

Elvis Presley makes entertainment history by performing four sold-out shows at New York's Madison Square Garden. George Harrison, David Bowie, Bob Dylan and Art Garfunkel are among the music stars that attend the shows which are recorded for the album *Elvis As Recorded At Madison Square Garden*.

Bruce Springsteen signs with Columbia Records and re-assembles the E Street Band from various Asbury Park musicians who have played with him in the past.

1975

Windsor Davies and Don Estelle are at No. 1 on the UK singles chart with 'Whispering Grass'. It is a spin-off from the BBC TV sitcom *It Ain't Half Hot Mum*. Originally recorded by The Ink Spots in 1940.

1978

Joy Division appear at The Russell Club, Manchester, England.

1984
Cyndi Lauper starts a two-week run at No. 1 on the US singles chart with 'Time After Time', a No. 3 hit in the UK.

1990

M.C. Hammer's debut album starts a record breaking 21-week stay at the top of the US album charts, making it the longest uninterrupted run since the *Billboard* charts started.

Bailiffs repossess the mansion owned by the group 5 Star after non-payment of mortgage fees. The group had achieved 15 top 20 hits over five years.

Wilson Phillips go to No. 1 in the US with 'Hold On', 25 years to the day Wendy and Carnie's father Brian Wilson had been at No. 1 with The Beach Boys' 'Help Me Rhonda'.

1994

After an argument TLC singer Left Eye sets fire to her boyfriend's Atlanta mansion, worth $2 million, burning it to the ground. She is charged with arson and fined $10,000 with five years probation.

1998

The Ronettes appear in the Supreme Court of New York for their lawsuit against producer Phil Spector. The trio, whose hits included 'Be My Baby' and 'Walking In The Rain', claim that Spector had breached a 34-year-old contract by paying the members no royalties since 1963. Although The Ronettes go on to win the case, the New York State Court of Appeals overturns the decision in October 2002, saying that the contract the girls signed with Spector in 1963 was still binding.

2007

George Michael becomes the first music artist to perform at the rebuilt Wembley Stadium in London when he plays the first of two shows there during his '25 Live Tour'.

2009

Three men ambush the former S Club 7 singer Rachel Stevens as she enters her flat near Regents Park, north London, and steal her engagement ring, a necklace and her watch.

June 10

Born on this day:

1922 Judy Garland, singer, actress
1944 Rick Price, bass (The Move, Wizzard)
1961 Kim Deal, bass, vocals (Pixies, The Breeders)
1964 Jimmy Chamberlin, drums (Smashing Pumpkins)

1964
The first edition of the official *Rolling Stones Monthly* book is issued, priced at one shilling and sixpence. Also on this day, the Stones record 'It's All Over Now' during their first session at Chess studios in Chicago.

1972
The Rolling Stones double LP *Exile On Main Street* goes to No. 1 on the British chart, becoming the band's seventh UK No. 1 album.

1974
The Who begin a four-night, sold-out run at Madison Square Garden in New York City.

1976
Wings set a new world record when they perform in front of 67,100 fans at the Kingdome, Seattle – the largest attendance for an indoor crowd.

1977
Joe Strummer and Nick 'Topper' Headon from The Clash are each fined £5 by a London court for spray-painting "The Clash" on a wall.

1982
Addie Harris from The Shirelles, who had a US No. 1 and UK No. 4 single with 'Will You Love Me Tomorrow' in 1961, becoming the first all-girl group to have a No. 1 single on the *Billboard* Hot 100, dies of a heart attack after a show in Atlanta.

1983
Chris Sievey of UK group The Freshies releases the first computer game single. When played on a Sinclair ZX 81 computer via a record deck the lyrics of the song appear on the screen.

1986
Jerry Garcia of The Grateful Dead goes into a five-day diabetic coma, resulting in the band withdrawing from their current tour.

1991
While attending the funeral of fellow group member David Ruffin in Detroit, Eddie Kendricks of The Temptations is arrested on charges of owing $26,000 in child support.

1993
Irish singer Sinead O'Connor takes out a full-page ad in the *Irish Times* asking the public to "stop hurting me please". She blames her troubles on abuse she suffered as a child. O'Connor was still attracting criticism for ripping up a picture of the Pope during a *Saturday Night Live* appearance the previous October.

2004
Legendary US singer-songwriter Ray Charles (real name: Ray Charles Robinson) dies aged 73 of liver cancer.

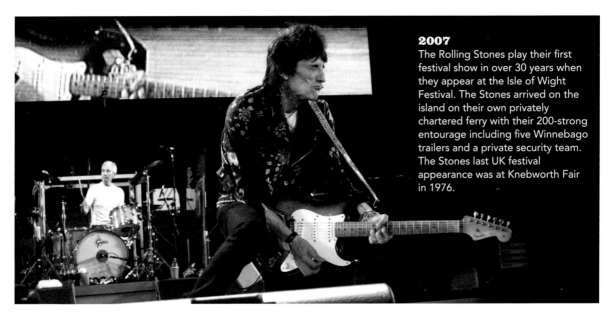

2007
The Rolling Stones play their first festival show in over 30 years when they appear at the Isle of Wight Festival. The Stones arrived on the island on their own privately chartered ferry with their 200-strong entourage including five Winnebago trailers and a private security team. The Stones last UK festival appearance was at Knebworth Fair in 1976.

Born on this day:

1940 Joseph DiNicola (Joey & The Starlighters)
1947 Glenn Leonard, vocals (The Temptations)
1948 Alan Skipper, drums (The Pretty Things)
1949 Frank Beard, drums (ZZ Top)

1964

The Beatles touch down at Mascot Airport, Sydney, at the start of their first (and only) Australian tour. Despite the torrential rain and strong winds, the group agree to parade themselves before waiting fans (many who'd camped out overnight) on the back of a flatbed truck.

1966

European radio stations mistakenly report that The Who's lead singer Roger Daltrey has been killed in a car crash. Actually, it was guitarist Pete Townshend who had been involved in a car accident two weeks earlier.

1967

Appearing in this week's music weekly *Melody Maker* is an ad reading: 'Freaky lead guitarist, bass and drummer wanted for Marc Bolan's new group. Also any other astral flyers like with car's amplification and that which never grows in window boxes, phone Wimbledon 0697.'

1969

The Beatles are at No. 1 on the UK singles chart with 'The Ballad Of John And Yoko', the group's 18th (and final) British chart-topper. Only two Beatles played on the track, John Lennon and Paul McCartney.

1976

AC/DC appear at Glasgow City Hall, Scotland, on the first night of their 'Lock Up Your Daughters' 19-date UK tour.

1977

Joe Strummer and Topper Headon are detained overnight in prison in Newcastle-upon-Tyne after failing to appear at Morpeth Magistrates Court on May 21. Both Clash members were to answer a charge relating to the theft of a Holiday Inn pillowcase. They are both fined £100.

As Britain celebrates the Queen's Silver Jubilee, The Sex Pistols reach No. 2 in the singles chart with 'God Save The Queen'. It is widely believed that the charts were rigged to prevent them reaching No. 1.

1988

Nelson Mandela's 70th birthday tribute takes place at Wembley Stadium, London, featuring Whitney Houston, Phil Collins, Dire Straits, Stevie Wonder, Tracy Chapman, George Michael, Eric Clapton, UB40, Eurythmics and Simple Minds. The event is broadcast live to 40 countries with an estimated audience of one billion.

1997

Simply Red singer Mick Hucknall receives a Master of Science Degree at UMIST, Manchester for his fund-raising work following an IRA bombing in the city the previous year.

2001
Paul McCartney marries Heather Mills at St Salvator Church, Ireland. Guests include Ringo Starr, David Gilmour, Jools Holland and Chrissie Hynde. Heather walks down the aisle clutching a bouquet of 11 'McCartney' roses. The couple divorced in 2008.

2003

Adam Ant is arrested after going berserk and stripping off in a London cafe. The former 80s pop star had thrown stones at nearby houses, smashing windows before going to the Curly Dog Café, north west London.

2008

The American Federation of Musicians file a federal lawsuit against the producers of *American Idol*, claiming musicians are underpaid because the show's live music was re-recorded for re-runs. The union files the suit seeking unspecified damages in the US District Court in Los Angeles, alleging that American Idol Productions Inc. and its subsidiary Tick Tock Productions Inc. violated a collective bargaining agreement.

2009

Peter Doherty is released on £50,000 bail to await trial accused of driving dangerously after a gig. The Babyshambles frontman was stopped after police saw a car being driven erratically in Gloucester. The 30-year-old had appeared at Stroud Magistrates' Court, pleading guilty to possessing heroin and to having no driving licence or insurance.

Born on this day:

1941 Roy Harper, UK singer-songwriter
1943 Reg Presley, vocals (The Troggs)
1951 Brad Delp, guitar, vocals (Boston)
1952 Pete Farndon, bass (The Pretenders)

1959 John Linnell, vocals, accordion (They Might Be Giants)
1979 Robyn, Swedish singer

1964

The Beatles arrive in Adelaide, Australia and are greeted by an estimated 300,000 fans (the biggest welcome they would ever receive), who line the 10-mile route from the airport to the city centre. That night, the group gave their first shows in Australia, playing two shows at the Centennial Hall. Temporary drummer Jimmy Nicol was standing in for Ringo, who was recovering from tonsillitis.

1966

The Dave Clark Five make a record 12th appearance on US TV's *The Ed Sullivan Show*.

1976

The Who, The Sensational Alex Harvey Band, Little Feat, The Outlaws and Streetwalkers all appear at Swansea City Football Club, Swansea, Wales. Tickets cost £4.

1979

The Police appear at The Locarno, Bristol, England supported by The Cramps.

1982

Bruce Springsteen, James Taylor, Jackson Browne, Linda Ronstadt and Gary 'US' Bonds all appear at a rally for nuclear disarmament in Central Park, New York to over 450,000 fans.

1989

The Elvis Presley Autoland Museum, containing over 20 cars which were owned by Presley, opens at Graceland, Memphis, Tennessee.

1990

David Bowie appears at Deer Creek, Indianapolis, on the North American leg of his 'Sound & Vision' Tour.

1999

It is reported that Oasis have paid Gary Glitter an out-of-court settlement of £200,000 after being accused of lifting the chanted lyric, "Hello, hello, it's good to be back" for their song 'Hello' from Glitter's 1973 hit 'Hello! Hello! I'm Back Again'.

2000

Sinead O'Connor announces that she is a lesbian. The mother of two tells the American magazine *Curve* that she had been in the closet for years saying, "I am a lesbian. I haven't been very open about that, I've gone out with blokes because I haven't necessarily been terribly comfortable about being a lesbian."

2002

Clive Calder, the man credited with discovering Britney Spears, sells his record company Zomba to BMG Music for $2 billion. Calder started Zomba in 1975 and had hits with Billy Ocean, Sam Fox and Tight Fit.

2006

Prince receives a Webby Lifetime Achievement Award in recognition of his "visionary" use of the internet. Prince was the first major artist to release an entire album, 1997's *Crystal Ball*, exclusively in cyberspace.

2008

Amy Winehouse performs an exclusive gig at a Moscow art gallery for Chelsea FC owner Roman Abramovich and his girlfriend Daria Zhukova. It is reported that the singer was paid £1m for her services at the launch of The Garage gallery, which has been set up by Ms Zhukova.

2005

Pink Floyd announce they will reunite with estranged former bassist Roger Waters, who left the band in 1985, for the Live 8 London concert on July 2. This will be the first time the four members of the band have played together since 'The Wall' Tour in 1981.

Born on this day:

1934 Uriel Jones, Motown session drummer
1949 Dennis Locorriere, guitar, vocals
         (Dr Hook)
1963 Robbie Merrill, bass (Godsmack)
1968 David Gray, UK singer, songwriter

1969
The Rolling Stones hold a photo call in Hyde Park to introduce new guitarist Mick Taylor.

1970
Grand Funk Railroad, supported by Steel Mill (featuring Bruce Springsteen), appear at the Ocean Ice Palace in Bricktown, New Jersey. Tickets $5.00.

1972
Clyde McPhatter, original lead vocalist with The Drifters, dies of a heart attack in New York. Joining Billy Ward & the Dominoes in 1950, he formed The Drifters in 1953, had several solo hits including 1962 'Lover Please' and was posthumously inducted into the Rock and Roll Hall of Fame in 1987.

1975
In New York, John Lennon makes his last ever TV appearance, performing 'Slippin And Slidin' and 'Imagine' on the variety show, *Salute To Sir Lew Grade*.

1981
Smokey Robinson is top of the UK singles chart (his first solo No. 1) with 'Being With You', a song he wrote in the late 60s.

1988
The biggest charity rock concert since Live Aid three years earlier takes place at London's Wembley Stadium, denouncing South African apartheid. Among the performers are Sting, Stevie Wonder, Bryan Adams, George Michael, Whitney Houston and Dire Straits. Half the money raised goes towards anti-apartheid activities in Britain, the rest being donated to children's charities in southern Africa.

1995
Alanis Morissette releases *Jagged Little Pill*, which goes on to sell over 30 million copies worldwide making Morissette the first female Canadian to score a US No. 1 album.

2000
37-year-old Susan E. Santodonato collapses and dies of a heart attack outside New York radio station

Star 105.7 after a Britney Spears impersonator left the building. A crowd had gathered after a DJ claims Britney Spears is in the studio.

2003
The elder statesmen of music are rewarded in this year's Queen's Birthday Honours list for their services to music. Sting is awarded a CBE, Gerry Marsden an MBE, Errol Brown an MBE and Pink Floyd's Dave Gilmour a CBE.

2005
At the end of a 16-week hearing in Santa Maria, California, Michael Jackson is cleared by a jury of eight women and four men of all 10 charges of child abuse including abusing a 13-year-old boy, conspiracy to kidnap and supplying alcohol to a minor to assist with a felony.

2000
While appearing in a Florida court, singer Bobby Brown admits he is an alcoholic, saying, "I have a disease, I am an addict, I am an alcoholic."

Born on this day:

1945 Rod Argent, keyboards (The Zombies, Argent)

1949 Jim Lea, bass, piano, violin (Slade)

1961 Boy George, singer, DJ (Culture Club, solo)

1963 Chris De Garmo, guitar (Queensryche)

1953
Elvis Presley graduates from IC Hulmes High School in Memphis; his graduation photo shows him to have a split curl in the middle of his forehead, later to become his trademark.

1964
Touring Australia, The Beatles arrive in Melbourne and are greeted at the airport by over 5,000 fans. Another 200,000 line the route from the airport to the city. Army and navy units are brought in to help control the crowds outside the Southern Cross hotel; cars are crushed, hundreds of girls faint and over 50 people are admitted to hospital with injuries.

The Manish Boys, featuring David Bowie, audition for the UK television talent show *Opportunity Knocks*.

1967
The Doors appear at Steve Paul's Scene, New York City. Jimi Hendrix is among the audience.

1970
Derek & The Dominoes play their first gig at London's Lyceum.

1972
Led Zeppelin play the first of two nights at Nassau Coliseum on Long Island, New York.

1980
Billy Joel starts a six-week run at No. 1 on the *Billboard* album chart with *Glass Houses*, his second US No. 1 album.

Peter Gabriel scores his first UK No. 1 album with his third solo release *Peter Gabriel*.

1984
On his 23rd birthday a model of Boy George from Culture Club is unveiled at Madame Tussaud's waxworks in London.

1986
Three fans die after falling from a balcony during an Ozzy Osbourne gig at Long Beach Arena, California.

1987
Madonna plays the first date on her 'Who's That Girl' World Tour at the Osaka Stadium, Osaka, Japan. The tour becomes the highest-grossing tour ever, generating over $20 million.

1991
Nirvana appear at The Hollywood Palladium, California.

1994
Composer Henry Mancini, who wrote the music to 'Moon River', which was originally sung in the movie *Breakfast At Tiffany's*, and was also the theme song for the Andy Williams television show, dies aged 70. Mancini recorded over 90 albums, contributed music to over 100 movies, including the theme from *The Pink Panther*, and had a US No. 1 single in 1969 with 'Love Theme from *Romeo And Juliet*'.

2000
Noel Gallagher from Oasis is voted into first place in *Melody Maker*'s annual 'Un-coolest People in Rock' survey. Marilyn Manson comes second and Robbie Williams is third.

2002
Mick Jagger becomes a Sir when he is knighted in the Queen's Birthday Honours. His lifelong compatriot, Keith Richards, is unimpressed. "I kneel for no-one," he says.

2006
Shakira kicks off her 99-date Oral Fixation world tour in Zaragoza, Spain. Attended by over two million, the tour grosses over $98 million.

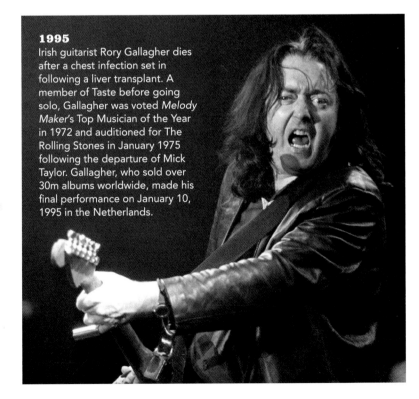

1995
Irish guitarist Rory Gallagher dies after a chest infection set in following a liver transplant. A member of Taste before going solo, Gallagher was voted *Melody Maker*'s Top Musician of the Year in 1972 and auditioned for The Rolling Stones in January 1975 following the departure of Mick Taylor. Gallagher, who sold over 30m albums worldwide, made his final performance on January 10, 1995 in the Netherlands.

Born on this day:

1941 Harry Nilsson, US singer, songwriter
1943 Muff Winwood, guitar, songwriter, producer (The Spencer Davis Group)
1943 Johnny Halliday, French singer

1946 Noddy Holder, guitar, vocals (Slade)
1976 Gary Lightbody, guitar, vocals (Snow Patrol)
1985 Nadine Coyle, vocals (Girls Aloud)

June 15

1958

The first episode of Jack Good's teenage music show, *Oh Boy!* is broadcast over the ITV network in the UK.

1963

Kyu Sakamoto starts a three-week run at No. 1 on the US singles chart with 'Sukiyaki', the first-ever Japanese song to do so.

1967

Guitarist Peter Green quits John Mayall's Bluesbreakers. Green goes on to form Fleetwood Mac, named after drummer Mick Fleetwood and bass player John McVie.

1974

Elvis Presley starts an 18-date US tour at the Tarrant County Center, Forth Worth, Texas – the first of four nights at the venue.

Bo Donaldson and the Heywoods start a two week run at No. 1 on the US singles chart with 'Billy Don't Be A Hero'. The song is also a UK No. 1 for Paper Lace.

1977

The Sex Pistols hold a Jubilee party on a boat as it sails down the River Thames in London. The Pistols perform 'Anarchy In The UK' outside the Houses Of Parliament resulting in members of the party, including Pistols' manager Malcolm McLaren, being arrested when the boat docks later that night.

1985

Dire Straits start a nine-week run at No. 1 on the US album chart with *Brothers In Arms*.

1988

During Bruce Springsteen's stay in Rome while on a world tour a paparazzi takes a shot of him in his underpants sharing an intimate moment with his backing singer Patti Scialfa. The picture confirms rumours that he and Scialfa are having an affair.

1989

Nirvana's debut album *Bleach* is released in the US. The title for the album came from a poster 'Bleach Your Works' urging drug users to bleach their needles.

1996

US jazz singing legend Ella Fitzgerald – the 'First Lady of Song' – dies, aged 79, in Beverly Hills, California. Already blinded by the effects of diabetes, Fitzgerald had both her legs amputated in 1993.

2002

An autographed copy of The Beatles' album *Sgt. Pepper's Lonely Hearts Club Band* sells at auction for £34,000, more than five times the estimated price.

2005

Coldplay go straight to No. 1 on the US *Billboard* chart with their third album *X&Y*, having already entered at No. 1 in the UK. It goes on to top over 30 global charts. The last time a British artist had a simultaneous US and UK No. 1 album was in November 2000 with *1*, a compilation of hits by The Beatles. The last contemporary album to reach No. 1 on both sides of the Atlantic was Radiohead's *Kid A* in October 2000.

2008

Liverpool is voted England's most musical city in a national campaign set up by the Arts Council. The home of (among others) The Beatles, Frankie Goes To Hollywood, OMD and The Zutons took 49% of the vote in an online poll set up by the funding body. Sheffield – which brought the world Arctic Monkeys and Pulp – is second, while Manchester with Oasis, Stone Roses, The Fall and The Smiths comes third.

June 16

Born on this day:

1941 Lamont Dozier, Motown producer, songwriter

1950 James Smith, vocals (The Stylistics)

1954 Gerry Roberts, guitar (The Boomtown Rats)

1971 Tupac Amaru Shakur, rapper

1962

The Konrads, featuring Dave Jay (later to become David Bowie), make their live debut at Bromley Technical School in Kent, England.

1964

The Rolling Stones pay £1,500 in return air fares from America to honour a booking made a year earlier for £100 at Magdalen College, Oxford.

1965

Bob Dylan records 'Like A Rolling Stone' at Columbia Recording Studios in New York City.

1966

The Beatles make a surprise live appearance on the UK television programme *Top Of The Pops* performing both sides of their new single, 'Paperback Writer' and 'Rain'.

1967

The first of the three-day Monterey Pop Festival takes place in California. All proceeds go to charity as all the artists agree to perform for free. The festival sees the first major US appearances by The Who, Jimi Hendrix and Janis Joplin. Also on the bill are The Byrds, Grateful Dead, Otis Redding, Simon & Garfunkel, The Steve Miller Band, Canned Heat, The Mamas & The Papas, Jefferson Airplane, Buffalo Springfield and The Electric Flag. Tickets cost $3.50–6.50.

1970

Mungo Jerry are at No. 1 on the UK singles chart with 'In The Summertime', which goes on to become the best selling British single of 1970, spending seven weeks at No. 1 and is a hit in 26 other countries. The UK release was a maxi-single playing at 33 rpm (whereas singles generally played at 45 rpm).

1976

The Jackson 5's four-week summer variety show premieres on CBS TV featuring the Jackson brothers with their sisters La Toya, Rebbie and Janet.

1982

Pretenders' guitarist James Honeyman-Scott dies following sustained cocaine and heroin addiction.

1984

Frankie Goes To Hollywood have their second UK No. 1 with 'Two Tribes', which stays at the top for nine weeks, making Frankie Goes To Hollywood the second band after Gerry & The Pacemakers – also from Liverpool – to have their first two singles go to the top of the UK chart. During this run the group's previous single 'Relax' climbs back up the charts to No. 2.

1990

Roxette start a two-week run on top of the *Billboard* singles chart with 'It Must Have Been Love'. The song, taken from the film *Pretty Woman*, becomes the Swedish duo's third US No. 1 and a No. 3 hit in the UK.

1999

The singer turned politician Screaming Lord Sutch is found dead aged 58 after hanging himself. Sutch was the first long-haired pop star, boasting tresses over 18 inches long, and the self-styled lord (real name David Sutch) was Britain's longest-serving political leader, standing in nearly 40 elections for the Monster Raving Loony Party.

2000

On the first night of his 'Up In Smoke' tour in Chula Vista, Snoop Dogg's tour bus is stopped at the Temecula border checkpoint in San Diego after the border patrol smells marijuana wafting from the tour bus. A member of the crew is arrested.

2007

Rod Stewart marries girlfriend, model Penny Lancaster on the Italian Riviera just outside the resort of Portofino. The 62-year-old singer was previously married to models Alana Hamilton and Rachel Hunter and has seven children by three women.

Born on this day:

1930 Cliff Gallup, guitar (Gene Vincent & His Blue Caps)

1943 Barry Manilow, singer, songwriter

1947 Glenn Buxton, guitar (Alice Cooper Band)

1947 Paul Young, vocals (Sad Café, solo)

June 17

1954

Guitarist Danny Cedrone dies of a broken neck after falling down a staircase, 10 days after he recorded the lead guitar break on 'Rock Around The Clock' with Bill Haley & His Comets. Session player Cedrone was paid $21 for his work, as at that time Haley chose not to hire a full-time guitarist for his group.

1955

After a month of booking gigs in larger venues in Dallas and Houston, Colonel Tom Parker arranges a meeting with Elvis Presley's manager, Bob Neal, resulting in an agreement that saw the Colonel handle Presley's gigs and career strategy from then on.

1965

At EMI Studios in London, work is completed on a new Paul McCartney-written Beatles song, 'Yesterday', with the overdubbing of an additional vocal track by McCartney and a string quartet scored by George Martin.

The Kinks and The Moody Blues make their US concert debut at the Academy of Music in New York City.

1971

Carole King goes to No. 1 on the US album chart with *Tapestry* for the first of 15 consecutive weeks. The album contains the hits 'It's Too Late', 'I Feel The Earth Move', 'Will You Love Me Tomorrow?' and 'You've Got A Friend'.

1972

Don McLean has his first UK No. 1 single with 'Vincent.' The song was written about the 19th century artist Vincent Van Gogh and is played daily at the Van Gogh Museum in Amsterdam.

1977

After Jimmy Helms pulls out of a gig at Shoreditch College in Egham, Surrey, the members of the social committee decide to call upon famous local resident, Elton John, to ask if he would perform. Elton does the gig in return for two bottles of wine.

1978

Andy Gibb becomes the first solo artist in the history of the US charts to

have his first three releases reach No. 1, when 'Shadow Dancing' hits the top of the chart. Spending seven weeks at No. 1 it becomes the best selling US single in 1978.

1987

Florida real estate agent Vittoria Holman sues Mötley Crüe and their concert promoter for hearing loss allegedly incurred at a concert in December 1985. Holman and her daughter had front row seats less than 10 feet from the speakers. The case is settled out of court with the band's insurance company paying Holman over $30,000.

1999

A teenage girl is crushed to death during a gig by Hole at the Hultsfred Festival, Sweden.

2005

Babyshambles singer Pete Doherty and girlfriend Kate Moss are thrown off a yacht after being found smoking crack cocaine. The couple had been invited onto the yacht by Moss' friend Davinia Taylor but were asked to leave and were dropped off in Porto Cervo.

2008

In London, Welsh singer Duffy's single 'Mercy' is named song of the year at the *Mojo* magazine awards. Best Breakthrough Act goes to The Last Shadow Puppets, the side project of Arctic Monkeys singer Alex Turner. Other acts honoured at the reader-voted *Mojo* honours include Led Zeppelin, Paul Weller, The Sex Pistols and Genesis. Ska band The Specials are welcomed into the *Mojo* Hall of Fame and former Creedence Clearwater Revival frontman John Fogerty wins the Inspiration Award for his contribution to rock music.

June 18

Born on this day:

1942 Paul McCartney, bass, vocals (The Beatles, Wings, solo)

1942 Carl Radle, bass (Derek & The Dominoes, Eric Clapton Band)

1957 Tom Bailey, vocals, keyboards (The Thompson Twins)

1971 Nathan Morris, Boyz II Men

1948

Columbia Records start the first mass production of the 33rpm long player. The new format can contain a maximum of 23 minutes of music per side as opposed to the three minutes that could be squeezed on to a 78rpm disc.

1955

Jimmy Young is at No. 1 on the UK singles chart with his version of 'Unchained Melody' (a theme for the obscure prison film *Unchained* and a hit for the Righteous Brothers in 1965). Young went on to become one of the UK's favourite radio DJs.

1964

Touring Australia, The Beatles play at Sydney Stadium. It is Paul McCartney's 22nd birthday and after the show his guests include 17 girls who were winners of the local *Daily Mirror*'s "Why I would like to be a guest at a Beatle's birthday party" competition.

1976

Abba give a special live performance in Stockholm for Sweden's King Carl XVI Gustaf and Silvia Sommerlath on the eve of their wedding.

1983

Swiss band Yello release the first three-dimensional picture disc, complete with 3-D glasses.

1988

'Doctorin' The Tardis' by The Timelords (a.k.a. Scottish duo Bill Drummond and Jimmy Cauty, who formed KLF) is at No. 1 on the UK singles chart. The song was a mash-up of the *Doctor Who* theme music, Gary Glitter's 'Rock And Roll (Part Two)' and sections from 'Blockbuster' by Sweet.

1993

Over 30 years on, A&M Records chairman Jerry Moss and vice-chairman Herb Alpert announce they are leaving the company they founded, having sold A&M to Polygram in 1990 for $500 million. The label, started by Moss and Alpert in the garage of Alpert's Los Angeles home in 1962, was home to such acts as Joe Cocker, The Flying Burrito Brothers, Joan Baez, The Carpenters, Supertramp, The Police, Bryan Adams, and Herb Alpert & The Tijuana Brass.

1997

During a North American tour U2 play the first of two nights at Oakland Coliseum, San Francisco, supported by Oasis.

2003

Pop Idol creator Simon Fuller becomes the first British manager since The Beatles' Brian Epstein to hold the top three positions in the US singles chart. Fuller, who steered such fabrications as the Spice Girls and S Club 7 to success, was also in charge of such bestselling acts as Clay Aiken and Ruben Studdard.

2008

A Los Angeles hotel files a lawsuit against Phil Spector for failing to pay more than $100,000 in outstanding bills for lawyers and expert witnesses in his murder trial. The Westin Bonaventure Hotel claims that by the time Spector's trial ended with a hung jury, the defendant owed the hotel more than $104,000.

1977

Fleetwood Mac are at No. 1 on the US singles chart with 'Dreams', the band's first and only US No. 1, which made 24 in the UK.

Born on this day:

1936 Tommy DeVito, vocals (The Four Seasons)

1948 Nick Drake, guitar, singer, songwriter

1951 Ann Wilson, vocals (Heart)

1963 Paula Abdul, singer, dancer, *American Idol* judge

June 19

1965

The Who, Manfred Mann, Long John Baldry, The Birds, Solomon Burke, Zoot Money and Marianne Faithfull are among the artists appearing at the Uxbridge Blues Festival.

The Four Tops go to No. 1 on the US singles chart with 'I Can't Help Myself'. Lead singer Levi Stubbs wasn't satisfied with his vocal performance and was promised that he could re-record it the following day, but no other session ever took place. The track that became the hit was the second take of the song.

1967

In an ITN interview Paul McCartney clarifies remarks he made in a *Life* magazine interview by admitting that he has taken the drug LSD.

1968

The Rolling Stones score their seventh UK No. 1 single with 'Jumpin Jack Flash'.

1969

The Doors appear at the PNE Garden Auditorium, Vancouver, Canada.

1974

The Jackson 5 play two shows at the Glasgow Apollo, Scotland.

1976

Future Smiths' singer Steven Morrissey has a letter published in this week's issue of music magazine *Record Mirror & Disc* asking the editor why the paper has not included any stories on The Sex Pistols.

1980

US singer Donna Summer becomes the first act to be signed by David Geffen to his new Geffen record label.

1987

Guns N' Roses make their sold out UK live debut at London's Marquee Club.

1990

Prince plays the first of 12 sold-out nights at London's Wembley Arena on his 'Nude' European tour.

1992

The Greenpeace 'Stop Sellafield' campaign concert takes place at the G-Mex in Manchester, England with U2, Big Audio Dynamite II, Public Enemy and Kraftwerk.

2000

Eminem is immortalised in animation with a cartoon series, which will be hosted on a new web site. Some 26 weekly 'webisodes' will be broadcast on the site, with Eminem providing all the voices.

2003

G-Man from So Solid Crew is jailed for four years for possessing a loaded handgun, dumped during a police chase in London last November. The 24-year-old always denied it, as well as denying any knowledge about 11 other bullets that were found in a south London flat. The jury in London's Southwark Crown Court hears evidence that DNA found on the weapon matched his own and finds him guilty.

2007

Darren Hayes, formerly of Australian pop duo Savage Garden, marries his boyfriend Richard Cullen in a civil partnership ceremony in London. Hayes was previously married to make-up artist Colby Taylor between 1997 and 1999.

Law firm Lavely and Singer, acting for Britney Spears, demand Florida radio station WFLZ immediately remove banners featuring pictures of the singer with a shaved head. The "offensive" billboards included the slogans "Total Nut Jobs", "Shock Therapy" and "Certifiable" running across the images. (Spears had been photographed shaving her own head in a Californian hair salon earlier this year.)

June 20

Born on this day:

1924 Chet Atkins, guitarist
1942 Brian Wilson, bass, keyboards, singer, songwriter (The Beach Boys, solo)
1949 Lionel Richie, singer (The Commodores, solo)
1960 John Taylor, bass (Duran Duran)
1966 Stone Gossard, guitar (Pearl Jam)

1948
Toast Of The Town, which would later be called *The Ed Sullivan Show*, is premiered on CBS-TV. The first show is produced on a budget of $1,375. Only $375 is allocated for talent and $200 of that is shared by the young stars of that night's programme, Dean Martin and Jerry Lewis.

1963
Gerry & The Pacemakers are at No. 1 on the UK singles chart with 'I Like It', the group's second chart-topper.

1969
David Bowie records 'Space Oddity' at Trident Studios, London, with Gus Dudgeon producing after Bowie's normal producer, Tony Visconti, declined. The track went on to become a UK No. 1 when re-released in 1975.

1969
The first day of a three-day festival in Newport, California, featuring Ike & Tina Turner, Marvin Gaye, Creedence Clearwater Revival, The Byrds, The Rascals, Steppenwolf, The Jimi Hendrix Experience, Janis Joplin, Johnny Winter, Eric Burdon and Love. A three-day ticket costs $15. Hendrix receives a fee of $125,000 – at the time the highest ever paid to a rock act for a single appearance.

1973
Neil Diamond appears on the 20th anniversary show of US TV's *American Bandstand*, which also features Little Richard, Cheech & Chong, Paul Revere & The Raiders and Three Dog Night.

1985
The Smiths' guitarist Johnny Marr marries long-time girlfriend Angela Brown in San Francisco.

1987
Aerosmith appear at the Cotton Bowl in Dallas, Texas – the first night of their 'Permanent Vacation' 147-date world tour.

1992
Mariah Carey scores her sixth American No. 1 with 'I'll Be There', a No. 2 hit in the UK. The song was also a US No. 1 for the Jackson 5 in 1970.

1995
Jeff Buckley plays the first night of a UK tour at The Queens Hall, Edinburgh.

1997
Lawrence Payton of The Four Tops dies aged 59 from liver cancer.

1998
Black Sabbath, Foo Fighters, Korn, Pantera, Soulfly, Slayer, Fear Factory, Coal Chamber, Life Of Agony, Limp Bizkit, Entombed, Human Waste Project, Neurosis and Pitchshifter all appear at Ozzfest at the Milton Keynes Bowl.

2000
The Ronettes are awarded $2.6 million in "back earnings" from Phil Spector. New York judge Paula Omansky rules that the legendary producer has cheated them out of royalties due.

2004
Organisers of a Paul McCartney gig in Petersburg, Russia, hire three jets to spray dry ice into the clouds so it won't rain during the concert. The gig is estimated as being McCartney's 3,000th concert appearance. He had performed 2,535 (known) gigs with The Quarrymen and The Beatles, 140 gigs with Wings and 325 solo shows.

2008
American singer songwriter Jimmy Buffett announces that his Margaritaville Holdings has partnered with New York gambling company Coastal Marina to buy the Trump Marina Hotel Casino for $316 million. Buffet's vast business empire also includes tequila, beer, frozen food, footwear, restaurants, a resort, a record label and a recording studio. In 2006, *Rolling Stone* magazine estimated Buffett's earnings at $44 million.

Born on this day:

1944 Ray Davies, guitar, vocals, songwriter (The Kinks, solo)

1948 Joey Molland, guitar, vocals (Badfinger)

1950 Joey Kramer, drums (Aerosmith)

1953 Nils Lofgren, guitar, singer (solo, E Street Band, Neil Young)

1981 Brandon Flowers, vocals, keyboards (The Killers)

1955
Elvis Presley plays two shows in Beaumont, Texas, with bassist Bill Black and guitarist Scotty Moore.

1966
Reg Calvert, manager of The Fortunes, Screaming Lord Sutch and the owner of offshore pirate radio station Radio City, is shot dead by business rival William Smedley during a confrontation. Smedley, the owner of rival pirate station Radio Caroline, was later cleared of the murder on the grounds of self-defence.

Jimmy Page makes his live debut with The Yardbirds at London's Marquee Club.

At EMI Studios in London, The Beatles record from start to finish a new John Lennon song 'She Said, She Said', the last track to be recorded for their *Revolver* album. The song was reportedly based on a bizarre conversation that Lennon had with Peter Fonda while John and George Harrison were tripping on LSD the previous year.

1968
The Who appear at Durham University, Durham – their last British show before a gruelling two month American tour.

1972
On their North American tour, Led Zeppelin appear at Denver Coliseum, Denver.

1975
Guitarist Ritchie Blackmore quits Deep Purple to form his own group Rainbow.

1976
Touring the US for the first time, Wings play the last dates of their 31-date 'Wings Over America' tour with the first of three nights at the Los Angeles Forum.

1977
Sex Pistol Johnny Rotten is attacked in a brawl outside the live music venue Dingwalls in Camden, north London.

1980
After a concert at Nice University, police arrest The Stranglers for allegedly starting a riot.

German orchestra leader and songwriter Bert Kaempfert dies aged 56. Kaempfert released over 50 albums and both Frank Sinatra

('Strangers In The Night') and Elvis Presley ('Wooden Heart') covered his songs. In 1961, he hired The Beatles to back Tony Sheridan on recording sessions for German label Polydor. These were The Beatles' first commercial recordings.

1994
George Michael loses his lawsuit against Sony Records. Michael claimed that his 15-year contract with Sony was unfair because the company could refuse to release albums it thought would not be commercially successful. Michael vowed he would never record for Sony again but re-signed with the company in 2003.

1998
Bobby Brown is arrested on charges of sexual battery after an incident at the Beverly Hills Hilton Hotel, Los Angeles.

2000
Karen McNeil, a 39-year-old who claimed she is the wife of Axl Rose and communicates with him telepathically, is jailed for one year for stalking the singer.

2001
John Lee Hooker, legendary American blues singer and guitarist and a major influence on the British 60s blues boom, dies aged 83 in his sleep.

Born on this day:

1936 Kris Kristofferson, US singer, songwriter, actor

1948 Todd Rundgren, US guitarist, singer, producer

1949 Alan Osmond, vocals (The Osmonds)

1953 Cyndi Lauper, US singer

1962 Bobby Gillespie, drums, vocals (The Jesus & Mary Chain, Primal Scream)

1970 Steven Page, guitar, vocals (Barenaked Ladies)

1956
Elvis Presley starts a three-day run playing 10 shows at the Paramount Theater in Atlanta, Georgia. The stage manager is told: "Pull all white lights, Presley works all in color, Presley act has no encore. When he leaves the stage, immediately close curtains."

1963
13-year old Stevie Wonder first enters the US singles chart as Little Stevie Wonder with 'Fingertips (Parts 1 and 2)'.

1964
The Beatles play their first show in New Zealand at Wellington Town Hall. At the first show the microphones provided are extremely poor, prompting John Lennon to bitterly complain afterwards. Support act Johnny Devlin fixes the problem for the second show and his reward is a photo taken with the group.

1968
Herb Alpert starts a four-week run on top of the US singles chart with 'This Guy's In Love With You', his first No. 1, the first No. 1 for the A&M label and also the writers Bacharach and David's first chart-topper. It was a No. 3 hit in the UK.

1969
American singer and actress Judy Garland dies aged 47 of a barbiturate overdose on the floor of her rented Chelsea home in London.

1970
Led Zeppelin make their only Icelandic appearance at the Laugardalsholl Hall in Reykjavik. During this visit, Robert Plant was inspired to write the lyrics for 'Immigrant Song' on *Led Zeppelin III*.

1971
In England, Melanie, Quintessence, The Edgar Broughton Band, Pink Fairies, Terry Reid, Gong, David Bowie, Hawkwind, Arthur Brown, Brinsley Schwarz, Fairport Convention and Family all appear at the second Glastonbury Festival.

1978
The Boomtown Rats, supported by Matt Vinyl & The Decorators, appear at the Odeon Theatre, Edinburgh, Scotland.

1981
Mark David Chapman pleads guilty to murdering John Lennon in December 1980. He is later sentenced to 20 years to life and remains in jail indefinitely despite applications for his release.

1988
American session guitarist Jesse Ed Davis dies aged 43 of a heroin overdose after collapsing in a laundry room in Venice, California. He worked with Taj Mahal, Conway Twitty, Eric Clapton, John Lennon, George Harrison, Leonard Cohen, Keith Moon, Jackson Browne, Steve Miller, Harry Nilsson and The Faces.

1992
Nirvana's Kurt Cobain is rushed to hospital suffering from acute stomach pains brought on by ulcers after a gig in Belfast, Northern Ireland.

1996
Arthur Ross, the brother of singer Diana Ross, and his wife are murdered by suffocation in the basement of their rented Detroit home. The badly decomposed bodies are discovered after neighbors complain of a foul odour coming from the house. Two men were later charged with murder and robbery. Arthur Ross had written songs for Marvin Gaye, The Miracles and Madonna.

2000
After giving himself various new identities during the 1990s, 'The Artist Formally Known As Prince' announces he wants to be known as Prince again.

2002
U2 guitarist The Edge marries his girlfriend of ten years Morleigh Steinberg in Eze in the south of France. The couple first met when she was a belly dancer on the band's Zoo TV tour. Guests include Bono, Dave Stewart and Lenny Kravitz.

2008
Coldplay go to No. 1 on the UK singles chart for the first time with 'Viva La Vida'. History was made by this single as it had no physical CD single release in Britain, being available by internet download only. The song won a Grammy Award for Song of the Year in 2009.

Born on this day:

1929 June Carter Cash, country singer, songwriter

1937 Nikki Sullivan, guitar, vocals (The Crickets)

1940 Stuart Sutcliffe (The Beatles' original bassist)

1965 Paul 'Bonehead' Arthurs, guitar (Oasis)

1984 Duffy, Welsh singer

June 23

1957

Lonnie Donegan is top of the UK singles chart with 'Gamblin' Man'/ 'Putting On The Style', the singer's second UK No. 1. It was the last British chart-topper to be released on 78rpm as well as a 7" vinyl record.

1962

Ray Charles starts a 14-week run at No. 1 on the US album chart with *Modern Sounds In Country And Western Music*.

1970

Chubby Checker is arrested in Niagara Falls after police discover marijuana and other drugs in his car.

1973

George Harrison starts a five-week run at No. 1 on the *Billboard* album chart with *Living In The Material World*, his second US No. 1.

1975

During his 'Welcome To My Nightmare' tour in Vancouver, Canada, Alice Cooper falls from the stage and breaks six ribs.

1984

Duran Duran start a two week run on top of the *Billboard* singles chart with 'The Reflex', the group's first US No. 1, and also a British chart-topper

1989

George Michael receives the Silver Clef Award for Outstanding Achievements to British Music.

1990

Keith Sorrentino (13) files a $500,000 lawsuit against Madonna, claiming he suffered nightmares and bed-wetting problems after an incident outside Madonna's home when she allegedly flung him to the ground.

Buddy Holly's Gibson acoustic guitar is sold for £139,658 at a Sotheby's auction. The guitar was in a tooled leather case made by Holly himself.

1995

Drummer Alan White makes his live debut with Oasis at Glastonbury Festival. Also, former Take That singer Robbie Williams appears on stage with the band during the show.

2000

The Experience Music Project is unveiled in Seattle by Paul Allen, co-founder of Microsoft. The £150m museum contains over 80,000 items of Hendrix memorabilia, including a smashed guitar from the 1967 Monterey Pop Festival.

2002

The top music earners from US sales during 2001 are listed by *Rolling Stone* magazine as: 1, U2 with $61.9m; 2, Dr. Dre – $51.9m; 3, The Beatles – $47.9m: 4, Dave Matthews Band – $43.4m: 5, Madonna – $40.8m.

2004

Bob Dylan is awarded an honorary degree by the University of St. Andrews, Scotland's oldest university, and made a "Doctor of Music".

2009

Chris Brown pleads guilty to one count of assault on his former girlfriend, Rihanna. The 19-year-old R&B singer is sentenced to five years probation and ordered to do six months community service. Brown had faced charges of assaulting Rihanna, 21, during a row in February. The last-minute plea deal came before a hearing at a Los Angeles court at which Rihanna was due to give evidence. The Los Angeles County Superior Court judge also orders Brown and Rihanna to stay at least 50 yards from each other, except at entertainment industry events when the distance is reduced to 10 yards.

2003

Diana Ross appears in court and testifies that she was coerced and felt intimidated into taking a breath test that showed her blood alcohol level was 0.2 (well over the 0.08 limit). The singer says, "If I didn't take the breath tests, I was either going to go to the hospital or to jail." After the hearing, Ross asked the judge if it would be possible to have court paperwork processed using her married name of Diana Naess. The City Magistrate said he thought it was "a little late" for that now.

June 24

Born on this day:

1944 Chris Wood, sax, flute (Traffic)
1944 Jeff Beck, guitar (The Yardbirds, Jeff Beck Group, Beck, Bogert & Appice, solo)
1944 Mick Fleetwood, drums (The Cheynes, John Mayall's Bluesbreakers, Fleetwood Mac)

1957 Jeff Cease, guitar (The Black Crowes)
1959 Andy McCluskey, vocals, guitar, keyboards (OMD)
1961 Curt Smith, vocals, bass (Tears For Fears)

1964
The Beatles nearly the miss the first of two concerts at the Auckland Town Hall, New Zealand, because the local Chief Constable refuses to provide a police escort from the group's hotel, claiming "The Beatles are not royalty".

1965
John Lennon's second book of poetry and drawings, *A Spaniard In The Works*, is published. The book consists of nonsensical stories and drawings similar to the style of his 1964 book *In His Own Write*.

1966
The Rolling Stones kick off their fifth North American tour at the Manning Bowl, Lynn, Massachusetts. Support acts include The McCoys and The Standells.

1967
The Monkees go to No. 1 on the US album charts with *Headquarters*, the group's third chart-topper.

1969
The Doors appear at The Roach, New Orleans, Louisiana.

1977
The Jacksons are at No. 1 on the UK singles chart with 'Show You The Way To Go'. The Jacksons were the Jackson Five, including Michael, but Jermaine had temporarily quit.

1978
Genesis, Jefferson Starship, Jeff Beck, Tom Petty & The Heartbreakers, Devo, Brand X and The Atlanta Rhythm Section all appear at this year's Knebworth Festival at Knebworth Park, Hertfordshire. Tickets cost £6.

1988
UB40 bass player Earl Falconer is sent to prison for six months, with a further 12 suspended, after admitting causing his brother's death in a car accident.

1989
Richard Marx scores his second US No. 1 single with 'Satisfied'.

1990
New Kids On The Block's Donnie Wahlberg spends two days in hospital after falling through an unlocked trapdoor mid-concert in Saratoga Springs, New York

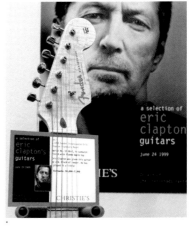

1999
Eric Clapton puts 100 of his guitars up for auction at Christie's in New York City to raise money for his drug rehab clinic, the Crossroads Centre in Antigua, which he founded in 1998. His 1956 Fender Stratocaster named 'Brownie', which was used to record the electric version of 'Layla', sells for a record $497,500. The auction helps raise nearly $5 million for the clinic.

2003
A man who was deported from Sweden for stalking Abba singer Agnetha Faeltskog is arrested near the singer's island retreat. Gert van der Graaf, 37, had been the singer's boyfriend from 1997 to 1999, but had been given a restraining order barring him from seeing or talking to her in 2000.

2005
The Thrills, The Zutons, Doves, The Killers, White Stripes, Kaiser Chiefs, Ash, The Coral, Keane, New Order, Coldplay, James Blunt, Brian Wilson, Garbage, Primal Scream and Basement Jaxx all appear at this year's UK Glastonbury Festival.

2007
The White Stripes go to No. 1 on the UK album chart with *Icky Thump*, the duo's sixth studio album.

1973
The Grateful Dead appear at the Portland Memorial Coliseum, Portland, Oregon.

Born on this day:

1945 Carly Simon, US singer, songwriter
1946 Allen Lanier, guitar, keyboards (Blue Öyster Cult)
1952 Tim Finn, singer, songwriter (Split Enz, Crowded House, solo)
1963 George Michael, singer, songwriter (Wham!, solo)
1972 Mike Kroeger, bass (Nickelback)

June 25

1964
Roy Orbison is at No. 1 on the British singles chart with 'It's Over', his second UK No. 1. Orbison becomes the first American artist to score a UK No. 1 in the past 47 weeks.

1966
The Beach Boys, The Byrds, Love, Captain Beefheart, The Lovin' Spoonful and Percy Sledge all appear on a bill at The Hollywood Bowl, Hollywood, California.

Jackie Wilson is arrested for inciting a riot and refusing to obey a police order at a nightclub in Port Arthur, Texas. Wilson has a crowd of 400 whipped into a frenzy and refused to stop singing when requested to do so by police. He was later convicted of drunkenness and fined $30.

1967
During a North American tour The Jimi Hendrix Experience give a free afternoon concert in Golden Gate Park, San Francisco. They then play another two shows that evening at the Fillmore Auditorium.

Some 40 million people see The Beatles perform 'All You Need Is Love', live via satellite as part of the TV global link-up, *Our World*. Mick Jagger, Keith Richards, Eric Clapton, Graham Nash, Keith Moon and Gary Leeds are among the guests providing backing vocals.

1977
Marvin Gaye goes to No. 1 on the *Billboard* singles chart with 'Got To Give It Up', his third US No. 1.

1980
Billy Joel appears at Madison Square Garden, New York City.

1983
The Police score their fourth UK No. 1 album with *Synchronicity*, also a Billboard chart-topper in the US,

featuring the singles 'Every Breath You Take' and 'Wrapped Around Your Finger'.

1987
Songwriter Boudleaux Bryant dies. With his wife Felice he wrote The Everly Brothers hits, 'Bye Bye Love', 'All I Have To Do Is Dream' and 'Wake Up Little Susie' plus 'Raining In My Heart', a hit for Buddy Holly. Other acts who recorded their songs include Bob Dylan, Tony Bennett, Simon & Garfunkel, Sarah Vaughan, Grateful Dead, Dolly Parton, Elvis Presley, The Beach Boys, Roy Orbison, Elvis Costello, Count Basie, Dean Martin, Ruth Brown, Cher, R.E.M. and Ray Charles.

1988
Hillel Slovak, original guitarist and founding member of The Red Hot Chili Peppers, dies from a heroin overdose shortly after the band return from a European tour. Slovak recorded two albums with the Chili Peppers, *Freaky Styley* and *The Uplift Mofo Party Plan*.

Debbie Gibson goes to No. 1 on the US singles chart with 'Foolish Beat', making Debbie (aged 17) the youngest female to write, produce and record a US No. 1 single.

1993
Bruce Springsteen is a surprise guest on David Letterman's final show as host of NBC's *Late Night*.

1995
Pink Floyd are on top of the *Billboard* album chart with *Pulse*, their fifth US No. 1.

2006
Turkish-American music producer and arranger Arif Mardin dies aged 74 from pancreatic cancer. The winner of 11 Grammy Awards, Mardin worked at Atlantic Records for over 30 years before moving to EMI, and produced records by Aretha Franklin, Bette Midler, Roberta Flack, Wilson Pickett, Ringo Starr, The Average White Band, The Bee Gees, Barbra Streisand and Norah Jones.

2009
Michael Jackson dies at the age of 50 after suffering heart failure at his home in Beverly Hills. Jackson is credited with transforming the music video into an art form, and four of his solo albums – *Off The Wall* (1979), *Bad* (1987), *Dangerous* (1991) and *HIStory* (1995) – are among the world's best-selling records, while 1982's *Thriller* is the world's best-selling record of all time with sales of over 50 million. *The Guinness Book Of World Records* lists Jackson as one of the Most Successful Entertainers of All Time, with 13 Grammy Awards and 13 No. 1 singles. Prior to his death, Jackson had been scheduled to perform 50 sold-out concerts to over one million people at London's O2 Arena from July 13, 2009 to March 6, 2010.

June 26

Born on this day:

1943 Georgie Fame, UK singer, songwriter, organist

1955 Mick Jones, guitar, vocals (The Clash, BAD, Carbon: Silicon)

1956 Chris Isaak, US singer, songwriter, actor

1969 Colin Greenwood, bass (Radiohead)

1979 Nathan Followill, drums (Kings Of Leon)

1955

Elvis Presley, with Scotty Moore and Bill Black, play the first of three nights at the Keesler Air Force Base in Biloxi, Mississippi. The local paper runs a preview which reads: "A good looking youngster who has become a juke-box favorite with his 'That's Alright, Mama' and 'Blue Moon Of Kentucky', Presley is expected to repeat some of his hit tunes at the Airmen's Club show in addition to mixing up a few country tunes with some 'bop' and novelty numbers."

1965

The Byrds are at No. 1 on the US singles chart with their version of Bob Dylan's 'Mr Tambourine Man'. Roger McGuinn is the only member of the band to play on the song, the rest being LA session musicians.

1969

Joni Mitchell appears on ABC TV's *Mama Cass Television Program* from Los Angeles, California.

1973

Rolling Stone Keith Richards and his girlfriend Anita Pallenberg are arrested at their home on Cheyne Walk, Chelsea, London, on drugs and gun charges.

1974

Cher divorces Sonny Bono after 10 years of marriage. Four days later, Cher marries guitarist Gregg Allman but the couple split up 10 days later, get back together and split again. They did stay married for three years, producing a son, Elijah Blue Allman.

1981

Bob Dylan plays the first of five nights at Earl's Court, London during his current European tour.

1982

American singer and one hit wonder Charlene is at No. 1 on the UK singles chart with 'I've Never Been To Me'. The song, recorded in 1976, was reissued by Motown Records in 1982, by which time Charlene had moved to England and was working in a sweet shop in Ilford, east London.

1999

Elton John is reported to be in talks with a City finance house to secure a £25 million loan, using his back catalogue of hits as security. It has been reported that Elton is spending £250,000 a week on credit cards.

2001

The Archbishop of Canterbury George Carey causes uproar among theologians after rejecting an application from a former rock musician for a degree course on religious grounds. Former Cockney Rebel member Andrew Brown, who is now a minister of the Unitarian Church, wanted to complete a MA in theology but Carey rejected his application because Brown did not belong to a mainstream church.

2005

Tickets for a forthcoming Rolling Stones gig at the Hollywood Bowl are set to become the most expensive in rock'n'roll history. Fans will have to pay up to £249 for a seat – £2 per minute – to watch the Stones.

2008

Total Guitar magazine votes Celine Dion's rendition of the AC/DC track

'You Shook Me All Night Long' as the world's worst ever cover version. The magazine's editor Stephen Lawson says Dion's cover was "sacrilege". In the best cover versions list, Jimi Hendrix is voted into first place with his version of Bob Dylan's 'All Along The Watchtower,' The Beatles' rendition of 'Twist And Shout' (first recorded by The Top Notes) was in second place, followed by Guns N' Roses' version of the Wings song 'Live And Let Die'.

1977
Elvis Presley makes his last ever live stage appearance at the Market Square Arena in Indianapolis. The last two songs he performs are 'Hurt' and 'Bridge Over Troubled Water'. Before the show Elvis is presented with a plaque commemorating the two billionth record to come out of RCA's pressing plant.

June 27

Born on this day:

1935 Doc Pomus, US songwriter
1944 Bruce Johnson, vocals, bass, keyboards (The Beach Boys)
1976 Leigh Nash, singer (Sixpence None The Richer)
1983 Evan David Taubenfeld, guitar (Avril Lavigne Band)

1967
Mick Jagger is found guilty of illegal possession of two amphetamine pills discovered in his jacket at a house party given by Keith Richards. He is remanded overnight at Lewes jail, England (prisoner number 7856). Jagger requests books on Tibet and modern art and two packs of Benson & Hedges cigarettes.

1968
Elvis Presley appears on an NBC TV show *Elvis* billed as his "comeback special". The undoubted highlight of the show features 'the King' performing on a small, square stage, surrounded by a mostly female audience. Presley was outfitted in black leather and performed many of his early hits.

1970
The Bath Festival of Blues and Progressive Music starts at Shepton Mallet, England, tickets £1.10s (£1.50). Appearing are Led Zeppelin, Pink Floyd, The Byrds and many other top bands. Rain on the Sunday evening causes Jefferson Airplane to abandon their set but The Byrds, who follow, play acoustically.

The Trans-Continental Pop Festival (better known as the Festival Express) sets off. The tour is unique in that rather than flying to each city, most of the acts travel on a chartered CN train. The Grateful Dead, Janis Joplin, The Band, The Flying Burrito Brothers and the Buddy Guy Blues Band all travel together on the train, playing shows in Toronto, Winnipeg, Saskatoon and Calgary.

1987
Whitney Houston becomes the first woman in US history to enter the album chart at No. 1 with *Whitney*, and also becomes the first woman to top the singles chart with four consecutive releases when 'I Wanna Dance With Somebody' gets to No. 1.

1992
Michael Jackson plays the first night on his 'Dangerous' World Tour at the Olympic Stadium in Munich, Germany. The tour consists of 69 concerts before approximately 3.9 million fans across three continents. All profits from the tour are donated to various charities including the Heal The World Foundation, which is Jackson's principal reason for doing the tour.

1994
Aerosmith become the first major rock band to let fans download a new track free from the internet.

1998
After spending 30 weeks on the UK album chart The Corrs are at No. 1 with *Talk On Corners*, which goes on to become the best selling UK album of 1998, spending 142 weeks on the chart.

1999
Brian O'Hara, original guitarist with The Fourmost, hangs himself aged 56. Managed by Brian Epstein, the Liverpool group's biggest hit was a 1964 UK No. 6 with 'A Little Loving'.

2003
Rapper Mystikal pleads guilty to charges that he forced his hairstylist to perform sex acts on him and two bodyguards. Mystikal (real name: Michael Tyler) was charged with aggravated rape. He agrees to plead guilty and is sentenced to five years' probation.

2008
The first day of this year's Glastonbury Festival. The line-up at the three-day event includes Kings of Leon, The Fratellis, Editors, The Gossip, The Feeling, KT Tunstall, Kate Nash, Jay Z, Amy Winehouse, The Raconteurs, James Blunt, Crowded House, Seasick Steve, Martha Wainwright, The Verve, Leonard Cohen, The Ting Tings, Goldfrapp, Neil Diamond, Pete Doherty, Scouting For Girls, Mark Ronson, Duffy, The Zutons, Groove Armada and John Mayer.

2002
One day before the scheduled first show of The Who's 2002 US tour, bass player John Entwistle dies aged 57 in his hotel room at the Hard Rock Hotel and Casino in Las Vegas. Entwistle had spent the night with a showgirl who woke at 10am to find him cold and unresponsive. The Las Vegas medical examiner determined that death was due to a heart attack induced by an undetermined amount of cocaine.

June 28

1959

Bobby Darin is top of the UK singles chart with 'Dream Lover'. It was also the American singer's first No. 1 and featured Neil Sedaka on piano.

1966

The Small Faces appear at The Marquee Club in Wardour Street, London. Admission costs 7/6 (37½p).

1969

Fleetwood Mac, Led Zeppelin, The Nice, John Mayall, Ten Years After, Taste, Liverpool Scene and Chicken Shack all appear during The Bath Festival of Blues where the DJ is John Peel. Tickets cost 18/6.

1975

The Eagles start a five-week run at No. 1 on the US album chart with *One Of These Nights*.

American singer-songwriter Tim Buckley completes the last show of a tour in Dallas, Texas, playing to a sold-out crowd of 1,800 people. This was Buckley's last ever show: he died the following day aged 28 of a heroin and morphine overdose.

1977

Elton John achieves a life long ambition when he becomes the Chairman of Watford FC.

1980

Paul McCartney's 'Coming Up' becomes one of the few live recordings to reach the top of *Billboard*'s Hot 100. American disc jockeys prefer it to the studio version on the flip side of the record. (The studio version was the 'hit' side in the UK.)

1985

Sister Sledge reach No. 1 on the British singles chart with 'Frankie', the sisters only UK No. 1. Nile Rodgers from Chic produced the hit for the soul trio from Philadelphia.

1986

Wham! are at No. 1 on the UK singles chart with their fourth and final British chart-topper, 'The Edge Of Heaven'. Also on this day the duo play their farewell concert in front of 80,000 fans at London's Wembley Stadium.

1997

Puff Daddy and Faith Evans start a three-week run at No. 1 on the UK singles chart with 'I'll Be Missing You'. Released in memory of fellow Bad Boy Records artist Notorious B.I.G., who was murdered on March 9, the song samples the melody of The Police's 1983 hit 'Every Breath You Take'.

Pink Floyd's *The Dark Side Of The Moon* spends its 1,056th week on the US album chart. A bizarre connection arises from hardcore fans that if the album is played while watching *The Wizard Of Oz* film in mute, starting exactly when the MGM lion roared the third time during the movie's intro, the music somehow soundtracks the scenes in the film.

2007

Benno Goldewijk, from Holland, and Spaniard Alfredo Pecina Matias are killed and two other men injured during an accident dismantling the stage after a Rolling Stones concert in Madrid. Three of the workers fell 10m from a metal structure and landed on a fourth. The Stones are currently on the European leg of their 'A Bigger Bang' world tour.

2007

The Spice Girls confirm they will reform for a world tour during December 2007 and January 2008 with the original line-up who had not performed on stage together since Ginger Spice Geri Halliwell quit in May 1998. The 11 dates announced include a London show on 15 December, eight days after the first show in Los Angeles. Other dates included Cologne, Madrid, Beijing, Hong Kong, Sydney and Cape Town. The tour is being put together by Simon Fuller, whose 19 company masterminded the group's global success more than a decade earlier.

Born on this day:

1948 Ian Paice, drums (Deep Purple)
1953 Colin Hay, guitar, vocals (Men At Work)

1978 Nicole Scherzinger, singer (Pussycat Dolls)
1979 Tim McCord, bass (Evanescence)

1961
Del Shannon is at No. 1 on the UK singles chart with 'Runaway', his only British No. 1 and the first of 14 UK Top 40 hits.

1967
Rolling Stone Keith Richard is found guilty of allowing his house to be used for the illegal smoking of cannabis. He is sentenced to one year in jail and a £500 fine (prison number 5855). Mick Jagger is also fined £100 and given three months in jail on drug charges. Jagger and Richards are both released the following day after being granted bail of £7,000.

1968
Pink Floyd play the first ever free concert in Hyde Park by a rock group, promoted by Blackhill Enterprises. Also on the bill are Jethro Tull and Roy Harper.

1969
American soul singer Shorty Long, who had a 1968 US No. 8 single with 'Here Comes The Judge', and acted as an MC for many of the Motown Revue shows and tours, drowns aged 29 after his boat capsizes on the Detroit River in Michigan.

The Jimi Hendrix Experience play their last ever concert at the Denver Pop Festival. The show ends in a riot with the police overreacting by firing tear gas into the audience, while the band escape locked in the back of their equipment truck.

1973
Deep Purple singer Ian Gillan quits the band at the end of a tour of Japan.

1978
Peter Frampton breaks his arm and cracks several ribs when involved in a car crash in the Bahamas.

1979
American singer-songwriter, multi-instrumentalist and producer Lowell George dies, aged 34, of a heart attack. The Little Feat front man is found dead at the Key Bridge Marriott Hotel in Arlington, Virginia.

1984
Bruce Springsteen kicks off the first leg of his 'Born In The USA' tour with a three-night run at the Civic Center in St. Paul, Minnesota. Springsteen will play a total of 156 shows on the tour, ending on October 2, 1985 in Los Angeles.

1985
David Bowie and Mick Jagger record a version of Martha & The Vandellas' 1964 hit 'Dancing In The Street' for the forthcoming Live Aid fundraising event. The single went on to become a No. 1 UK hit.

John Lennon's 1965 Rolls-Royce Phantom V limousine, with psychedelic paintwork, sells for a record sum of $2.2 million, at a Sotheby's auction in New York.

1988
Nirvana, Mudhoney and Tad all appear at the Moore Theatre, Seattle.

Brenda Richie, the wife of Lionel Richie, is arrested in Beverly Hills, California after allegedly hitting the singer and a young woman after she found them in bed together. She is released on $5,000 bail and charges against her are eventually dropped.

1996
In this year's honours list, record producer George Martin receives a knighthood and Van Morrison an OBE, while music promoter Harvey Goldsmith becomes an MBE.

1999
Michael Jackson suffers severe bruising after falling over 50 feet when a bridge collapses during a concert at Munich's Olympic Stadium. Jackson was singing 'Earth Song' at the time of the accident.

2000
Eight men are trampled to death during Pearl Jam's performance at The Roskilde Festival, near Copenhagen. Police say the victims had all slipped or fallen in the mud at the front of the stage.

Eminem's mother goes to court claiming defamation of character in a $10 million civil suit, after taking exception to the line "My mother smokes more dope than I do" from her son's single 'My Name Is'.

2004
Courtney Love is reprimanded by Los Angeles Judge Melissa Jackson for turning up five hours late to a hearing. Love pleads guilty to a single charge of disorderly conduct and is given a discharge on condition she pays the victim's medical bills, joins a drug programme and stays out of trouble.

2007
Lily Allen is questioned by police over an alleged assault in March on a photographer outside the Wardour Club in Soho, London. She is freed on police bail.

Born on this day:

1943 Florence Ballard, vocals (The Supremes)
1951 Stanley Clarke, jazz bass player
1962 Julianne Regan, vocals (All About Eve)
1979 Andrew Burrows, drums (Razorlight)

June 30

1966
The Beatles play the first of five concerts at the Nippon Budokan Hall, Japan. The concert is filmed with The Beatles wearing black suits. The following day's first performance was also filmed, with The Beatles wearing white suits. There is a strict police presence with 3,000 police observing each concert in front of 10,000 fans.

1967
An advertisement appears in the London *Evening Standard* stating that "The Who consider Mick Jagger and Keith Richards have been treated as scapegoats for the drug problem, and as a protest against the savage sentences imposed on them at Chichester yesterday, The Who are issuing today the first of a series of Jagger/Richards songs to keep their work before the public until they are again free to record themselves."

1973
George Harrison knocks Paul McCartney from the top of the *Billboard* singles chart with 'Give Me Love, Give Me Peace On Earth', his second US No. 1 and a No. 8 hit in the UK.

1975
The Jackson 5 announce they are leaving Motown Records for Epic Records. The brothers are forced to change their name to The Jacksons because Motown own the J5 name.

1976
Police raid the home of Neil Diamond searching for drugs, finding less than one ounce of marijuana.

Stuart Goddard (Adam Ant) places the following ad in the classified section of the *Melody Maker*: "Beat on a bass, with the B-Sides." Andy Warren answers the ad and the pair go on to form Adam & The Ants.

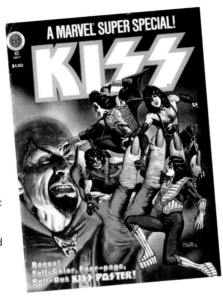

1977
Marvel Comics launch a comic book based on the rock group Kiss.

1978
United Artists release Buzzcocks' 'Love You More'. At one minute and 29 seconds it is the second shortest single ever released. Maurice Williams & The Zodiacs' 1960 hit 'Stay' was the shortest hit at one minute 28 seconds.

1984
Huey Lewis & The News are at No. 1 on the US album chart with *Sports*.

1989
The Stone Roses play at Leeds Polytechnic in England. The gig almost doesn't occur after a security man refuses singer Ian Brown entry into the gig.

1995
American soul singer Phyllis Hyman commits suicide aged 45 by overdosing on pentobarbital and secobarbital in her New York City apartment. She was found hours before she was scheduled to perform at the Apollo Theatre in New York.

2001
American guitarist and producer Chet Atkins, who recorded over 100 albums during his career, produced records for Perry Como, Elvis Presley, Don Gibson, Jim Reeves and Waylon Jennings, and was a major influence on George Harrison and Mark Knopfler, dies aged 77 in Nashville.

Beach Boy Al Jardine goes to court in a bid to sue his former band mates, claiming he has been frozen out of the group. The $4 million suit is filed against Mike Love, Brian Wilson, the Carl Wilson Trust and Brother Records Incorporated in a New York Superior Court. In 1998 a US judge temporarily barred Jardine from performing under the name "Beach Boys Family And Friends" after representations from Mike Love and Brother Records. Jardine lost the case in 2003.

2004
Kinks founder member Dave Davies is left paralysed on the right-hand side of his body after suffering a stroke. The 57-year-old guitarist and brother of fellow Kink Ray Davies had been promoting his solo material when he collapsed.

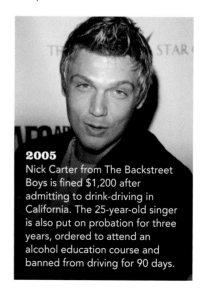

2005
Nick Carter from The Backstreet Boys is fined $1,200 after admitting to drink-driving in California. The 25-year-old singer is also put on probation for three years, ordered to attend an alcohol education course and banned from driving for 90 days.

Born on this day:

1915 Willie Dixon, blues singer, guitarist
1945 Deborah Harry, singer, actress (Blondie, solo)
1956 Phil Solem, singer, songwriter (The Rembrandts)
1971 Missy Elliott, singer

July 1

1956
Elvis Presley appears on NBC-TV's *The Steve Allen Show* performing 'Hound Dog' to a live hound on a stool. US TV critic John Crosby panned Presley's performance, calling him an "unspeakable, untalented and vulgar young entertainer."

1963
The Beatles record their fourth single in less than four hours at EMI Studios, London. Released in August, 'She Loves You' (backed with 'I'll Get You') went on to become The Beatles' first million-selling single.

1969
John Lennon, Yoko Ono and their respective children, Julian and Kyoko, are involved in a car accident in Golspie, Scotland. Both John and Yoko need hospital treatment. The Lennons later had the car crushed into a cube and exhibited it on the lawn at their home in Tittenhurst Park, Ascot.

1973
Slade, supported by The Sensational Alex Harvey Band, appear at Earl's Court, London, with tickets costing £1.00-£2.00. Special 'Slade' trains run from Brighton, Bristol, Birmingham and Manchester to take fans to the show.

1975
10CC are at No. 1 on the UK singles chart with 'I'm Not In Love'. The instrumental break features the repeated spoken phrase: "Be quiet, big boys don't cry...", which was spoken by Kathy Warren, the receptionist at Strawberry Studios, Stockport, Cheshire where the band recorded the track.

1977
During a North American tour Pink Floyd play the first of four sold-out nights at Madison Square Garden, New York.

1981
Rushton Moreve, bass player with Steppenwolf who co-wrote their hit 'Magic Carpet Ride', is killed aged 32 in a motorcycle accident in Santa Barbara, California.

1982
The Dead Kennedys appear at Fairmont Hall, San Diego, California.

1983
A New Jersey-based rock quintet calling themselves Bon Jovi sign to Phonogram's Mercury Records.

1989
Lou Reed, Joe Jackson, Elvis Costello, The Robert Cray Band, Nick Cave & The Bad Seeds, Tanita Tikaram, The Pixies, R.E.M. and Texas all appear at the Rock Torhout Festival, Torhout, Belgium.

1999
American singer Guy Mitchell, who had a 1957 UK & US No. 1 single with 'Singing The Blues' plus over 10 other UK Top 40 singles, dies aged 72 at Desert Springs Hospital in Las Vegas. Mitchell also appeared as George Romack in the 1961 NBC western detective series *Whispering Smith*.

Jamaican reggae singer Dennis Brown dies aged 42, the official cause of his death given as a collapsed lung. During his career, he recorded more than 75 albums and had the 1979 UK No. 14 single 'Money In My Pocket'. Bob Marley cited Brown as his favourite singer, naming him "The Crown Prince of Reggae".

2000
Kylie Minogue is at No. 1 on the UK singles chart with 'Spinning Around', the singer's fifth chart-topper which was co-written by Paula Abdul (it was originally intended for Abdul's 'comeback' album). 'Spinning Around' makes Minogue one of three artists (the others being Madonna and U2) to have had a No. 1 in the 80s, 90s and 2000s.

2005
Four Tops singer Renaldo 'Obie' Benson dies aged 69 in a Detroit hospital from lung cancer. He was diagnosed after having a leg amputated due to circulation problems. The Four Tops sold over 50 million records, and had hits including 'I Can't Help Myself' (1965) and 'Reach Out (I'll Be There)' (1966). Benson also co-wrote 'What's Going On' which became a No. 2 hit in 1971 for Marvin Gaye.

2008
Whitesnake guitarist Mel Galley, who also played with Trapeze, Glenn Hughes, Cozy Powell and The Blue Jays, dies aged 60 from cancer of the oesophagus.

2009
Cliff Richard is ordered to demolish a £30,000 conservatory at his home in Surrey after the local council rules that it should never have been built. The planning committee say the building contravenes policy on green belt areas because it adds more than 30% extra floor space.

July 2

Born on this day:

1949 Roy Bittan, piano, organ (Bruce Springsteen & The E Street Band)
1952 Johnny Colla, guitar, sax (Huey Lewis & The News)
1954 Pete Briquette, bass, vocals (The Boomtown Rats)
1974 Rocky Gray, drummer (Evanescence)

1956
Elvis Presley records 'Hound Dog' at RCA Studios, New York. This is the first time The Jordanaires have worked with Presley and Take 31 was the version released.

1962
Jimi Hendrix is honourably discharged from the 101st Airborne Paratroopers, after breaking his ankle during his 26th and final parachute jump.

1965
The Beach Boys and Sam The Sham & The Pharoahs appear at the Community Concourse, San Diego, California.

1966
David Bowie & The Lower Third appear at The Lion Hotel in Warrington, Lancashire, receiving a fee of £30 for the gig.

1969
Bassist Noel Redding quits the Jimi Hendrix Experience after the band appeared at the three-day Denver Pop Festival. Hendrix and drummer Mitch Mitchell would later team with bassist Billy Cox to form the short-lived Gypsy Sun & Rainbows, playing at the forthcoming Woodstock Music & Art Fair.

1980
Bob Weir and Mickey Hart from The Grateful Dead are arrested on suspicion of starting a riot at the San Diego Sports Arena after trying to intervene in a drugs bust.

1982
Nicky 'Topper' Headon of The Clash is remanded on bail, charged with stealing a bus stop worth £30 from Fulham Road, London.

1988
Michael Jackson becomes the first artist to achieve five No. 1 singles from one album (*Bad*) when 'Dirty Diana' goes to the top of the US *Billboard* charts. The other four are the title track, 'I Just Can't Stop Loving You', 'The Way You Make Me Feel' and 'Man In The Mirror'.

1991
Axl Rose causes a riot to break out during a Guns N' Roses concert after leaping into the crowd to remove a camera from a fan at the Riverpoint Amphitheatre, Maryland Heights. Over 50 people are injured and 15 fans arrested.

LiverpoolJohn LennonAirport
a b o v e   u s   o n l y   s k y

2001
Liverpool Airport at Speke is renamed John Lennon Airport. Yoko Ono is present to unveil a new logo that includes the late Beatle's famous self-portrait and the words 'Above Us Only Sky' taken from his song 'Imagine'.

2005
The world's biggest music stars unite in concerts around the world to put pressure on political leaders ahead of the G8 summit to tackle poverty in Africa. Concerts in 10 cities, including London, Philadelphia, Paris, Berlin, Johannesburg, Rome and Moscow, play to hundreds of thousands of people. A TV audience of several hundred million watched the gigs. The London concert is headlined by a Pink Floyd reunion featuring the classic line up of Roger Waters, David Gilmour, Richard Wright and Nick Mason, who had not performed together for over 20 years.

Two years after suffering a major stroke, American R&B, soul singer-songwriter and record producer Luther Vandross dies aged 54 at the JFK Medical Centre, New Jersey. Vandross worked with Diana Ross, Carly Simon, Chaka Khan, Donna Summer, Barbra Streisand, Mariah Carey and David Bowie, and had won four Grammys for his final album *Dance With My Father*.

2008
Cheshire police confirm the memorial gravestone of former Joy Division singer Ian Curtis has been stolen from his burial plot in Macclesfield Cemetery. Officers are appealing for anyone with information on its whereabouts. Detectives said the stone had the inscription 'Ian Curtis 18-5-80' and the words 'Love Will Tear Us Apart'.

1973
Roxy Music's synthesiser player Brian Eno quits the band after a personality clash with singer Bryan Ferry.

Born on this day:

1929 David Lynch (The Platters)
1930 Thomas Tedesco, American session
      guitarist

1943 Judith Durham, vocals (The Seekers)
1960 Vince Clarke, keyboards (Depeche
      Mode)

1967

A private party is thrown at the Speakeasy Club in London by Vic Lewis for NEMS Enterprises to celebrate The Monkees' successful concerts at Wembley Empire Pool. Guests include all of The Monkees (except Davy Jones), all of The Beatles (except Ringo Starr), Dusty Springfield, Eric Clapton, Lulu and members of Manfred Mann, The Who and Procol Harum.

1969

Brian Jones drowns while taking a midnight swim at his home at Cotchford Farm, Hartfield, East Sussex. He was 27. His body was found at the bottom of the swimming pool by his Swedish girlfriend Anna Wohlin. The coroner's report stated

death by misadventure, and noted his liver and heart were heavily enlarged by drug and alcohol abuse. To this day rumours persist that foul play was involved in Jones' death.

1970

The three-day Atlanta Pop Festival takes place, featuring The Allman Brothers, Jimi Hendrix, Jethro Tull, Johnny Winter, Mountain, Procol Harum and Rare Earth. Over 200,000 music fans attend.

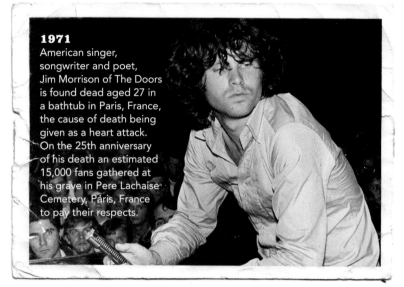

1971

American singer, songwriter and poet, Jim Morrison of The Doors is found dead aged 27 in a bathtub in Paris, France, the cause of death being given as a heart attack. On the 25th anniversary of his death an estimated 15,000 fans gathered at his grave in Pere Lachaise Cemetery, Paris, France to pay their respects.

1973

Laurens Hammond, the inventor of the Hammond organ, dies aged 73. Many rock artists, including Procol Harum, The Nice, Led Zeppelin, The Doors, The Allman Brothers and The Faces, featured the sound of the Hammond. He also invented a silent spring-driven clock and during World War Two Hammond helped design guided missile systems.

1975

Chuck Negron, singer from Three Dog Night, is arrested at his Louisville hotel room on the opening night of a US tour and charged with possession of cocaine.

1982

The Human League start a three-week run at No. 1 on the US singles charts with 'Don't You Want Me', also a UK No. 1.

1986

U2 crew member Greg Carroll, from New Zealand, is killed in a motorcycle accident in Dublin while running an errand for Bono. The song 'One Tree Hill' (named after the highest of the volcanic hills that overlook Auckland) on the band's album *The Joshua Tree* is dedicated to Carroll.

1996

When rain stops play at the Wimbledon Lawn Tennis Championships, Cliff Richard launches into a spontaneous concert, leading spectators through some of his old hits. It is later revealed that Cliff had planned the moment as a publicity stunt.

2002

Session violinist Bobby Valentino serenades a High Court judge during a copyright battle worth an estimated £100,000 over The Bluebells' 'Young At Heart'. Valentino won his case as joint owner of the song.

Three diners at a newly opened Britney Spears-owned restaurant suffer food poisoning. The three students who had eaten wild striped bass at the New York restaurant make official complaints and vow never to eat there again.

2003

Libertines' singer and guitarist Pete Doherty is arrested after breaking into band member Carl Barat's flat and stealing a laptop computer and a guitar.

Born on this day:

1938 Bill Withers, singer
1954 John Waite, singer (The Babys)
1958 Kirk Pengilly, guitar, vocals (INXS)

1971 Andy Creeggan, piano (Barenaked Ladies)
1972 William Goldsmith, drums (Foo Fighters)

1958
The Everly Brothers hold the UK No. 1 position with 'All I Have To Do Is Dream', the duo's first chart-topping single.

1964
The Beach Boys start a two-week run on top of the US singles chart with 'I Get Around', the group's first No. 1.

1966
The Beatles play two shows at the Rizal Memorial Football Stadium, Manila, to over 80,000 fans. Earlier that day The Beatles failed to appear at a palace reception hosted by President Marcos. The Philippines media misrepresented this as a deliberate snub, and when manager Brian Epstein tried to make a statement on local television, his apology was mysteriously disrupted by static. The next day as The Beatles make their way to the airport, the Philippines government retaliate by withdrawing police protection for the group, and they are greeted by an angry mob.

1969
The first day of the two-day Atlanta Pop Festival, held in Byron, Georgia, featuring Janis Joplin, Led Zeppelin, Johnny Winter, Delaney & Bonnie, Creedence Clearwater Revival, Canned Heat, Joe Cocker, Blood Sweat & Tears, Chuck Berry, Spirit, Chicago and Paul Butterfield.

1973
Slade drummer Don Powell is badly injured in a car crash in which his 20-year-old girlfriend Angela Morris is killed.

1976
The Clash make their live debut supporting The Sex Pistols at The Black Swan, Sheffield, Yorkshire.

1985
Dire Straits play the first of ten consecutive nights at London's Wembley Arena.

1990
Paul Stanley from Kiss sustains neck and back injuries when he is involved in a car crash in New Jersey.

1993
In London, The Smashing Pumpkins play an acoustic show at the Soho strip club Raymond's Revue Bar.

1999
Victoria 'Posh Spice' Adams marries footballer David Beckham at Luttrellstown Castle, Ireland. The couple had signed a deal worth £1million for *OK* magazine to have the exclusive picture rights.

2000
A man falls 80 feet to his death during a Metallica concert at Raven Stadium, Baltimore.

2005
At Dublin's Circuit Court, Judge Matthew Deery orders U2's former stylist Lola Cashman to return several items of memorabilia including a Stetson hat and earrings which the band accused her of stealing. The judge says he found the version of events given by Cashman, who had written an unauthorised book called *Inside The Zoo*, to be doubtful, particularly her description of Bono running around backstage in his underpants.

2007
At a court in Albuquerque, New Mexico former laboratory worker Devon Townsend admits stalking Chester Bennington, lead singer with US band Linkin Park. The court is told how Townsend travelled to Arizona solely for the purpose of trying to see the singer and used government computers to obtain Bennington's personal information, accessing his e-mail account and mobile phone voicemail.

2003
American record producer, soul singer-songwriter and five-time Grammy Award-winner Barry White dies aged 58 from kidney failure.

Born on this day:

1920 Smiley Lewis, R&B singer
1943 Robbie Robertson, guitar, vocals (The Band)

1950 Huey Lewis, singer (Huey Lewis & The News)
1985 Nick O'Malley, bass (Arctic Monkeys)

July 5

1954
Working for the first time in a recording studio with Scotty Moore and Bill Black, Elvis Presley fools around during a break with an up-tempo version of 'That's All Right'. Producer Sam Phillips has them repeat the jam and records it. It becomes Presley's first release on Sun Records.

1966
On the recommendation of Rolling Stone Keith Richards' girlfriend Linda Keith, Chas Chandler from The Animals goes to see Jimi Hendrix play at The Cafe Wha in Greenwich Village, New York City. Chandler suggests that Hendrix should come to London, which Jimi agrees to.

(a US No. 2 in 1957), dies aged 55 of cancer.

1999
At a press conference on the Greenpeace boat 'Rainbow Warrior', moored on the River Thames in London, Eurythmics announce their first world tour in over a decade, saying that all profits will be donated to charity.

2000
Michael 'Cub' Koda, founder member of Brownsville Station, who wrote their million-selling 1974 hit 'Smokin' In The Boys Room' (later covered by Mötley Crüe), dies aged 51 of complications from kidney failure.

2003
The Daily Star runs a front-page story claiming that the body of Manic Street Preachers' guitarist Richey Edwards, who has been reported missing since February 1995, has been found. Fishermen in an angling contest had discovered bones half buried in mud on the riverbank near Avonmouth.

2005
Pink Floyd's David Gilmour said artists who had seen album sales soar after the Live 8 concerts should donate their profits to charity. UK sales figures released two days after the London concert showed Pink Floyd's *Echoes: The Best Of Pink Floyd* had risen by 1343%, The Who's *Then And Now* by

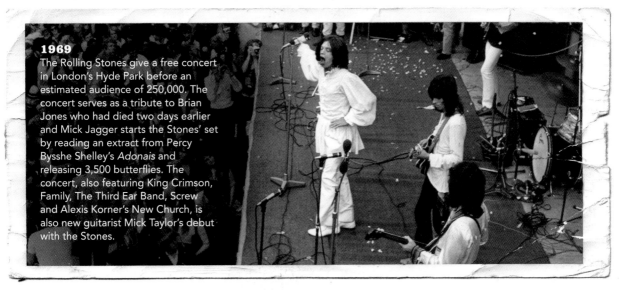

1969
The Rolling Stones give a free concert in London's Hyde Park before an estimated audience of 250,000. The concert serves as a tribute to Brian Jones who had died two days earlier and Mick Jagger starts the Stones' set by reading an extract from Percy Bysshe Shelley's *Adonais* and releasing 3,500 butterflies. The concert, also featuring King Crimson, Family, The Third Ear Band, Screw and Alexis Korner's New Church, is also new guitarist Mick Taylor's debut with the Stones.

1975
Pink Floyd, Captain Beefheart, The Steve Miller Band and Roy Harper appear at the Knebworth Festival.

1982
Sun Records' musical director Bill Justis, who worked alongside Sam Phillips with Johnny Cash, Elvis Presley, Roy Orbison, Charlie Rich and Jerry Lee Lewis and had rock 'n' roll's first instrumental hit with 'Raunchy'

He took his nickname from Cubby on television's *Mickey Mouse Club*.

2002
It is reported that Dr Dre has become the richest music star after earning £62m in the last year; £37m from his own earnings plus £25m from his record label Aftermath.

863% and Annie Lennox-Eurythmics *Greatest Hits* by 500%.

2007
Lyricist Hy Zaret, who wrote the words for the song 'Unchained Melody', dies aged 99 at his home in Westport, Connecticut. Zaret co-wrote the song, which has been recorded over 300 times, with film composer Alex North for the 1955 prison film *Unchained*.

July 6

1957

John Lennon and Paul McCartney meet for the first time at the Woolton Parish Church Fete where Lennon's skiffle group The Quarry Men are appearing. Having already played during the afternoon, The Quarry Men are setting up for their evening performance when an eager-to-impress McCartney picks up a guitar and plays Eddie Cochran's 'Twenty Flight Rock' and Gene Vincent's 'Be-Bop-A-Lula'. Lennon is swayed, even more so when McCartney shows him and Eric Griffiths how to tune their guitars. After Lennon deliberates for several days, McCartney is invited to join The Quarry Men two weeks later.

1968

The two-day Woburn Music Festival starts at Woburn Abbey, Bedfordshire featuring Donovan, Fleetwood Mac, Pentangle, The Jimi Hendrix Experience, Alexis Korner, Family and Tyrannosaurus Rex. Tickets are priced at £2.

1971

American jazz trumpeter, singer, bandleader and actor, Louis Armstrong dies aged 69. Nicknamed Satchmo, Armstrong made frequent use of laxatives as a means of controlling his weight. This resulted in him appearing in humorous advertisements for a laxative product Swiss Kriss, which bore a picture of Armstrong sitting on a toilet, with the slogan "Satch says, 'Leave it all behind ya!'"

1975

During The Rolling Stones' US tour, Keith Richards is arrested by the highway patrol in Arkansas on charges of reckless driving and possessing an offensive weapon, namely a seven-inch hunting knife.

1979

American singer, songwriter and producer, Van McCoy, who had a US No. 1 single with 'The Hustle' in 1975, and who worked with Gladys Knight & The Pips, The Stylistics, Aretha Franklin and David Ruffin, dies from a heart attack in Englewood, New Jersey.

1984

The Jacksons kick off their North American 'Victory' tour at Arrowhead Stadium, Kansas City. Over two million people attend the 55 concerts which gross over $75 million. Michael Jackson donates $5 million to various charities.

1992

The day before his 52nd birthday, Ringo Starr plays his hometown for the first time in 26 years when he and the All-Starr Band perform at Liverpool's Empire Theatre. The show is filmed for a Disney Channel documentary, *Ringo Starr: Going Home*.

1999

Michael Wallace, keyboard player with Third World, who had a 1978 UK No. 10 single with 'Now That We've Found Love', is shot dead aged 43 in Kingston, Jamaica.

2001

Offers over £20,000 are invited for a pair of Elton John's Salvatore Ferragamo sandals – set to become the most expensive shoes in history when going under the hammer in a charity auction to raise funds for the singer's AIDS Trust.

2005

Grammy Award winning rap star Lil' Kim (real name: Kimberley Jones), convicted of perjury and conspiracy back in March, is sentenced to a year in prison for lying to a grand jury to protect friends, and is also fined $50,000. Charges were brought against her after a gunfight erupted outside a New York radio station in 2001 as a rival rap group arrived.

2007

Britney Spears apologises for attacking a photographer's car with an umbrella earlier in the year. Pictures of the singer lashing out appeared in several newspapers shortly after having her head shaved in an LA hair salon. In a message on her website, she says, "I apologise to the pap for a stunt that was done four months ago." Spears says she got "carried away" preparing for a film part, adding that she did not get the role.

Born on this day:

1940 Richard Starkey (Ringo Starr), drums, vocals, actor (The Beatles, solo)

1950 David Hodo, vocals (The Village People)

1952 Lynval Golding, guitar (The Specials, Fun Boy 3)

July 7

1966
The Kinks are at No. 1 on the UK singles chart with 'Sunny Afternoon', the group's third and last British chart-topper.

1969
At Abbey Road in London, George Harrison records 'Here Comes The Sun' with just two other Beatles, Paul McCartney and Ringo Starr. John Lennon is absent recovering from a car crash in Scotland.

1971
26-year-old Swedish pop star Bjorn Ulvaeus and 21-year-old Agnetha Faltskog marry in Verum, Sweden. 3,000 fans assemble and in the chaos a police horse steps on the bride's foot, causing her slight injury.

1978
Grateful Dead play the first of four nights at the Red Rocks Amphitheatre in Denver, Colorado.

1980
Led Zeppelin play their last ever concert with drummer John Bonham at the Eissporthalle, West Berlin at the end of a European tour.

1984
Bruce Springsteen is at No. 1 on the *Billboard* chart with *Born In The USA*. The album goes on to spend a total of 139 weeks on the US chart and is also one of three albums (the others being Michael Jackson's *Thriller* and Janet Jackson's *Rhythm Nation 1814*) to produce seven Top 10 US singles.

1989
It is announced that for the first time compact discs are outselling vinyl albums. This week's UK No. 1 album is *Emergency On Planet Earth* by Jamiroquai.

2000
Eminem's wife, Kimberly Mathers, is hospitalised after slitting her wrists

following her husband's show at Detroit's Joe Louis Arena as part of the 'Up In Smoke' Tour.

2001
Janet Jackson plays the first night on her 'All For You' World Tour at the Rose Garden Arena in Portland, Oregon. The 72-date tour grossed over $55 million.

2006
Syd Barrett, singer, songwriter, guitarist, artist and one of the founding members of Pink Floyd, dies at 60 from complications arising from diabetes. Barrett was active as a rock musician for only about seven years before going into self-imposed seclusion lasting more than 30 years, with his mental deterioration blamed on schizophrenia exacerbated by drug use.

2007
Ozzy Osbourne becomes the first artist to receive a star on Birmingham's own Hollywood-style Walk of Fame. The singer, from Aston, tells more than 1,000 fans assembled on Broad Street that the brass paving star meant more to him than any Hollywood accolade. Organisers name other local pop stars who might be similarly honoured, including Duran Duran, Jamelia, Robert Plant and UB40.

The Live Earth concerts, organised by former US Vice-President Al Gore as part of his campaign to "heal the planet", take place around the world with The Police closing the day's events in New Jersey. Concerts are also held in Washington, Rio de Janeiro, Johannesburg, London, Hamburg, Tokyo, Shanghai and Sydney.

2009
Michael Jackson's family and fans bid farewell to the pop superstar at an emotional memorial service. The singer's coffin is placed in front of the stage during the event at the Staples Center in Los Angeles after an earlier private funeral. Jackson's daughter Paris, 11, fights back tears to describe him as "the best father you could ever imagine". Stevie Wonder, Lionel Richie and Mariah Carey pay tribute before the family join a sombre finale on stage. Motown boss Berry Gordy, who originally signed the Jackson 5, ends his tribute with the words: "Michael, thank you for the joy, thank you for the love. You will live in my heart forever."

July 8

Born on this day:

1945 Ricky Wolf, vocals (The Flowerpot Men)

1961 Graham Jones, guitar (Haircut 100)

1970 Beck, singer, songwriter, guitarist

1985 Jamie Cook, guitarist (Arctic Monkeys)

1954
Producer Sam Phillips takes an acetate recording of Elvis Presley singing 'That's All Right' to Memphis radio station WHBQ DJ Dewey Phillips. When Dewey plays the song just after 9.30 that evening, the phone lines light up asking the DJ to play the song again.

1965
The Dave Clark Five's film *Catch Us If You Can*, directed by John Boorman, premieres in London. The film is renamed *Having A Wild Weekend* for its US release.

1967
The Monkees begin a 29-date US tour with The Jimi Hendrix Experience among the support acts.

1969
Marianne Faithfull is found in a coma after taking a near fatal overdose of sleeping tablets at her Sydney hotel. She and Jagger had arrived in Australia two days earlier to work on Tony Richardson's *Ned Kelly* film. As a result, Marianne's part is taken by actress Diane Craig.

1971
A minor riot occurs during a Mott The Hoople gig at the Royal Albert Hall, London. Some fans are injured and two boxes are damaged causing a temporary ban on rock gigs at the venue. The band pay £1,467 for damages to property.

1978
Joe Strummer and Paul Simonon from The Clash are arrested (and later fined) for being drunk and disorderly after a gig at Glasgow's Apollo.

1987
U2 appear at Vorst National, Brussels, Belgium on their 'Joshua Tree' World Tour.

1989
Fine Young Cannibals score their second US No. 1 with 'Good Thing'.

1995
TLC start a seven-week run on top of the American singles chart with 'Waterfalls', the group's second US No. 1 and a No. 4 hit in the UK.

1999
Take That's former manager Nigel Martin Smith starts a new business as an undertaker. He was reportedly unhappy with a funeral service he had used so he decided to buy a local firm in Manchester.

2002
Speaking at a civil rights meeting in New York, Michael Jackson claims there was a "conspiracy" among record companies, especially towards black artists, alleging that the business was rife with racism. A spokesman for Jackson's record label Sony says the remarks were "ludicrous, spiteful and hurtful."

2004
Mark Purseglove, known as 'the world's biggest bootlegger', was sentenced to three years and six months jail by Blackfriars Crown Court. Purseglove had built up a £15 million pirate CD empire from bootlegging unauthorised recordings by acts including The Beatles, David Bowie and Pink Floyd.

2007
Prince is forced off stage by police halfway through his set at the First Avenue nightclub during a late-night gig in his home town of Minneapolis. The club is only allowed to stay open until 3am but Prince takes to the stage at 2.45am. Prince had already played two concerts in Minneapolis before his late-night club appearance; his first performance was at a department store where he promoted his new cologne with a nine-song, 45-minute set.

Born on this day:

1946 Bon Scott, singer (The Valentines, AC/DC)

1959 Jim Kerr, vocals (Simple Minds)

1964 Courtney Love, guitar, vocals (Babes In Toyland, Hole)

1975 Jack White, guitar, vocals (The White Stripes, The Raconteurs, The Dead Weather)

1975 Isaac Brock, singer, guitarist (Modest Mouse)

July 9

1954
Elvis Presley records 'Blue Moon Of Kentucky', the B-side of his first single, 'That's All Right' (recorded four days earlier) at Sun Studio in Memphis, Tennessee.

1955
Bill Haley & His Comets are at No. 1 on the US singles chart with 'Rock Around The Clock', staying in the top slot for eight weeks.

1962
Bob Dylan records 'Blowin' In The Wind' at Columbia Recording Studios in New York City during an afternoon session.

1967
On a US tour supporting The Monkees, The Jimi Hendrix Experience appear at the Convention Hall, Miami, Florida. After it becomes plainly apparent that the group is not suited to teenybopper audiences, the tour's promoter Dick Clark and Hendrix's manager Chas Chandler concoct a story saying that the conservative Daughters of the American Revolution group had complained at Jimi's act and so the Experience left the tour after just six shows.

1969
Working at Abbey Road studios in London The Beatles record 'Maxwell's Silver Hammer.' John Lennon returns to the studio after recovering from a car crash in Scotland, and a bed is installed in the Abbey Road studio for Yoko, who is pregnant and had been more seriously injured in the car accident.

1972
Paul McCartney & Wings kick off a 26-date 'Wings Over Europe' tour at the outdoor Theatre Antique in the French town of Chateau Vallon. The band (and families) travel between shows on a double-decker London bus with psychedelic interior.

1974

Crosby, Stills, Nash & Young kick off a reunion tour at the Seattle Coliseum in front of 15,000 fans, with an incredible four-and-a-half show. After this performance, to save their voices, the show was cut down to around three hours.

1976
The Pretty Things, Supercharge and third-on-the-bill The Sex Pistols all appear at The Lyceum, London, England. Tickets are £1.75.

1977
Elvis Costello quits his day job at Elizabeth Arden Cosmetics to become a full time musician.

1983
Wham! go to No. 1 on the UK album chart with their debut release *Fantastic!*, which spends 116 weeks on the chart.

1989
New Edition's production manager is charged with criminal homicide after allegedly shooting the support act's security man after they ran over their stage time.

1999
A statement is issued by Jerry Hall's lawyers saying that she has formally agreed to separate from husband Mick Jagger. The couple married in a ceremony of questionable validity in Bali, Indonesia on 21 November, 1990.

Elton John has a pacemaker fitted in an operation at a London hospital following reports about his ill health, forcing the cancellation of a series of concerts.

2004
David Bowie is forced to cancel a string of European shows after emergency heart surgery, originally attributed to a shoulder injury. The 57-year-old singer had an operation the previous month in Germany, while on tour, to treat "an acutely blocked artery."

2006
Lily Allen scores her first UK No. 1 single with 'Smile', the organ riff being a sample of Jackie Mittoo playing keyboards on 'Free Soul' by The Soul Brothers. Lily's actor father, Keith Allen, was part of Fat Les who had a football novelty hit with 'Vindaloo' in 1998.

2007
Happy Mondays' frontman Shaun Ryder faces a £50 fine after smoking several cigarettes on stage during a concert at The Ritz, Manchester, flouting the smoking ban which had been introduced in Britain on 1 July. Performers were only exempt from the smoking ban in enclosed public places if the "artistic integrity" of their act required it.

July 10

Born on this day:

1947 Arlo Guthrie, US singer-songwriter
1949 Ronnie James Dio, vocals (Rainbow, Black Sabbath, Dio)
1954 Neil Tennant, vocals (Pet Shop Boys)

1959 Sandy West, drummer (The Runaways)
1970 Jason Orange, vocals (Take That)

1964

Over 200,000 Liverpudlians take to the streets to celebrate The Beatles return to Liverpool for the Northern premiere of their first film *A Hard Day's Night*. The group are honored in a public ceremony at the Town Hall and as they stand on the balcony looking out at the large crowd, John Lennon gives a few mock 'Sieg Heil' salutes.

1965

The Rolling Stones start a four-week run at No. 1 on the *Billboard* singles chart with '(I Can't Get No) Satisfaction', the group's first American chart-topper.

1966

Johnny Tillotson, The Jive Five, The Tymes, The Shangri-La's and local band The Castiles (with Bruce Springsteen on vocals) all appear at the Surf 'n' See Club in Seabright, New Jersey.

1968

Eric Clapton announces that Cream will break-up after their current US tour.

The Nice are banned from appearing at London's Royal Albert Hall after burning an American flag on stage.

1969

The funeral of Rolling Stone Brian Jones takes place in his home town of Cheltenham. More than 500 people gather at Cheltenham Parish Church to pay their respects. During the service, Canon Hugh Evan Hopkins repeated Brian's message to his parents after being busted for drug possession, "Please don't judge me too harshly". Bill Wyman and Charlie Watts are the only Stones to attend the funeral.

1974

David Bowie plays the first of five dates at The Tower Theatre in

Philadelphia, the recordings of which will make up the *David Live* album released later that year.

1979

Chuck Berry is sentenced to five months in jail after being found guilty of income tax evasion.

1987

Legendary producer, record company executive and music writer John Hammond, who brought Bob Dylan, Aretha Franklin, Leonard Cohen, Bruce Springsteen and Stevie Ray Vaughan to Columbia Records, and worked as a producer with Bessie Smith, Billie Holiday, Benny Goodman and Count Basie, dies aged 76 after a series of strokes.

2008

The drum skin used on the cover of The Beatles' *Sgt. Pepper* album sells for £541,250 at Christie's memorabilia auction in London. Other items sold include John Lennon's lyrics for 'Give Peace A Chance' (£421,250) and a pair of tinted prescription sunglasses which Lennon wore on the cover of the 'Mind Games' single (£39,650). A rare 1/4 inch reel-to-reel master tape recording of the Jimi Hendrix Experience performing at the Woburn Music Festival in 1968 goes for £48,050, a Marshall amplifier used by Hendrix in concert fetches £25,000 and a pair of his stripy flared trousers make £20,000.

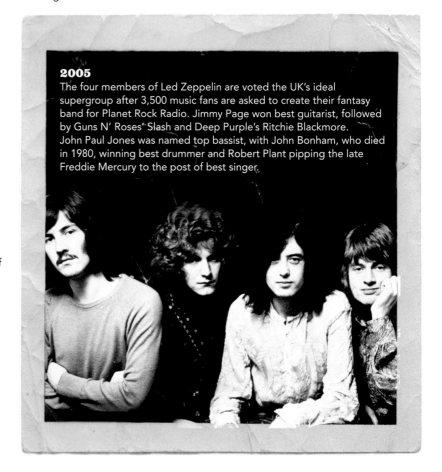

2005

The four members of Led Zeppelin are voted the UK's ideal supergroup after 3,500 music fans are asked to create their fantasy band for Planet Rock Radio. Jimmy Page won best guitarist, followed by Guns N' Roses' Slash and Deep Purple's Ritchie Blackmore. John Paul Jones was named top bassist, with John Bonham, who died in 1980, winning best drummer and Robert Plant pipping the late Freddie Mercury to the post of best singer.

Born on this day:

1951 Bonnie Pointer, singer (The Pointer Sisters)
1959 Richie Sambora, guitar (Bon Jovi)
1959 Susanne Vega, US singer-songwriter
1975 Lil' Kim, US singer

July
11

1969

'Space Oddity' by David Bowie was first released in the UK, timed to coincide with the Apollo moon landing. The single initially only gets as far as 48 before being re-promoted later in the year, where it reaches the Top 5. The song became an unexpected number one when reissued again in Britain in 1975. ('Space Oddity' reached No. 15 in America in 1973.)

1971

The Bruce Springsteen Band open for Humble Pie at The Sunshine Inn, Asbury Park, New Jersey. After the show Pie guitarist Peter Frampton is impressed enough to tell Springsteen and the band he'd like to have them open for Humble Pie on a national basis. Frampton also says he will arrange to get the band an audition with Humble Pie's record label, A & M Records. For no logical reason Springsteen's manager, Tinker West, declines both offers on the spot.

1977

The opening night of The Vortex Club, Wardour Street, London with Siouxsie & The Banshees, Adam & The Ants, The Slits and Sham 69.

1981

The Specials have their second and final UK No. 1 single with 'Ghost Town'. Despite being a song about Coventry, the band chose to film the video of themselves driving a Vauxhall Cresta at night around empty London streets.

1987

Heart start a three-week run at No. 1 on the US singles chart with 'Alone'.

1992

A range of eight ties designed by Jerry Garcia of The Grateful Dead goes on sale in the US. The collection will gross millions in the US by the end of the year and even forthcoming President Bill Clinton bought a set.

1996

Jonathan Melvoin, keyboard player with the Smashing Pumpkins and the brother of Susannah and Wendy Melvoin of Prince and the Revolution, dies aged 34 from a drug overdose in New York City. Smashing Pumpkins drummer Jimmy Chamberlin, who was with Melvoin, tried but failed to revive him after Chamberlin was allegedly advised by 911 operators to put Melvoin's head in the shower. Several songs are inspired by his death, including Sarah McLachlan's hit single 'Angel.'

1998

At 15, Billie becomes the second youngest female in chart history to reach No. 1 on the UK singles chart (with 'Because We Want To'); Helen Shapiro was the youngest at 14 with the 1961 No. 1, 'You Don't Know'.

1999

Ricky Martin starts a three week run at No. 1 on the UK singles chart (US No. 1 for 5 weeks) with 'Livin' La Vida Loca'. The song is the first chart-topper to be recorded, edited, and mixed on a DAW (Digital Audio Workstation).

2002

More than 200 mourners attend the funeral of The Who's bass player, John Entwistle at the 12th century church St. Edward in Stow-on-the-Wold in the Cotswolds. Both Roger Daltrey and Pete Townshend are present.

2004

The Darkness replace David Bowie at this year's T In The Park Scottish festival following Bowie's heart operation. Other acts appearing include Muse, Franz Ferdinand, Faithless, Scissor Sisters, Black Eyed Peas and Pink.

2008

It is announced that Ron Wood has left Jo, his wife of 23 years, and moved in with 18-year-old Russian cocktail waitress Ekaterina Ivanova.

The 61-year-old dad-of-four had met the teenager while out drinking after the London premiere of The Rolling Stones film *Shine A Light* in April and had taken her off to his home in Ireland.

2009

The Black Eyes Peas 'I Gotta Feeling' starts a 14-week run at No. 1 on the US singles chart, ending the 12-week run of the band's previous single 'Boom Boom Pow'. It makes the band only the fourth to replace themselves at No. 1 in chart history, following The Beatles, Boyz II Men and OutKast.

July 12

Born on this day:

1943 Christine McVie, keyboards, vocals (Chicken Shack, Fleetwood Mac)

1947 Wilko Johnson, guitar (Dr Feelgood, Solid Senders)

1950 Eric Carr, drums (Kiss)

1977 Dominic Howard, drums (Muse)

1954
19-year-old Elvis Presley signs a recording contract with Sun Records. He also gives his notice in at his day job at The Crown Electric Company. Sam Phillips from Sun Records originally wants to use Elvis to make demos of songs meant for other artists but soon realises that he has a singer and performer who can bridge the gap between white and black artists.

1962
The Rolling Stones make their live debut at the Marquee Jazz Club, London, filling in for Alexis Korner's Blues Incorporated who had an important BBC radio engagement, with Dick Taylor on bass and Mick Avory (later of The Kinks) on drums. The band are billed as The Rollin' Stones and are paid £20 for the gig.

1964
The Beatles appear at the Hippodrome Theatre, Brighton with support acts The Fourmost and The Shubdubs (whose drummer, Jimmy Nicol, had recently filled in for an ill Ringo Starr on The Beatles' world tour). On the way to the gig George Harrison is involved in a minor crash in his brand new E-Type Jaguar on King's Road, Fulham. Passing pedestrians reportedly collect bits of broken glass as souvenirs.

1969
One hit wonders Zager and Evans start a six-week run at No. 1 on the US singles chart with 'In The Year 2525'.

1976
The Grateful Dead play the first of six nights at The Orpheum Theatre, San Francisco, California.

1979
American singer-songwriter Minnie Riperton dies aged 31 of cancer. Minnie worked at Chess Records, singing backup for artists such as Etta James, Fontella Bass, Bo Diddley, Chuck Berry and Muddy Waters, and sang lead for the experimental rock/soul group Rotary Connection. She was also a member of Wonderlove in 1973, a backup group for Stevie Wonder, who produced her hit 'Loving You', a US No. 1 in 1975.

1980
Olivia Newton-John and the Electric Light Orchestra are at No. 1 with 'Xanadu', taken from the film of the same name. It gave Olivia Newton-John her third UK No. 1 single.

1983
Former Traffic member Chris Wood dies aged 39 of liver failure after a lengthy illness. As well as playing flute and saxophone and occasionally contributing keyboards and vocals, Wood co-wrote several of Traffic's early songs. In addition, Wood appeared on Jimi Hendrix's *Electric Ladyland* album in 1968.

1988
At the Brighton Centre in East Sussex, Paul McCartney appears in person to receive the title of Honorary Doctorate from the University of Sussex.

1996
Smashing Pumpkins' drummer Jimmy Chamberlin is charged with drug possession after the death of the band's keyboard player Jonathan Melvoin in his New York Hotel room.

2003
The first day of the two-day T In The Park festival in Scotland. Artists appearing include R.E.M., The White Stripes, Idlewind, The Cardigans, The Proclaimers, The Music, The Charlatans, Coldplay, Supergrass, The Darkness, Turin Brakes, The Coral and Feeder.

2008
American singer Earl Nelson (Earl Lee Nelson), one half of the duo Bob & Earl, who recorded 'Harlem Shuffle' in 1963, dies aged 79 in Lake Charles, Louisiana. Nelson also sang background vocals on 'Rockin' Robin', a US No. 2 for The Jackson 5 in 1972.

Born on this day:

1942 Roger McGuinn, guitar, vocals (The Byrds, solo)

1942 Stephen Jo Bladd, drums (The J Geils Band)

1961 Lawrence Donegan, bass (Lloyd Cole & The Commotions)

1964
The Animals are at No. 1 on the UK singles chart with 'The House Of The Rising Sun'. Recorded in one take, it was the first UK No. 1 single to have a playing time of more than four minutes.

1968
Black Sabbath play their first gig at a small backstreet blues club in Birmingham, England.

1976
The first issue of UK punk fanzine *Sniffin' Glue* is published, with features on The Stranglers, Ramones and Blue Öyster Cult. Former bank clerk Mark Perry was the editor.

1991
Bryan Adams goes to No. 1 on the UK singles chart with '(Everything I Do) I Do It For You', which stays at the top for a record-breaking 16 weeks. It is also a No. 1 in the US for seven weeks.

1996
Over 2,000 guitar players, including Chet Atkins and Jeff 'Skunk' Baxter, set a new world record for the longest ever jam session when they play 'Heartbreak Hotel' for 75 minutes at Nashville's Riverfront Park. The previous record was set in Vancouver, Canada on May 7, 1994, when Randy Bachman led 1,322 amateur guitarists in a performance that lasted 68 minutes.

2004
Arthur 'Killer' Kane, bass player with The New York Dolls, dies aged 55 after checking himself in to a Los Angeles emergency room, complaining of fatigue. He is quickly diagnosed with leukemia and dies within two hours. The influential American band formed in 1972 and made just two albums, *New York Dolls* (1973) and *Too Much Too Soon* (1974). Arthur's estranged wife wanted to honour her late husband's wishes and bury him next to his former Dolls bandmates Johnny Thunders and Jerry Nolan in Mount St Mary's cemetery in Brooklyn, New York, but officials at the morgue refused to release the body for burial because it had laid in a morgue for over a month.

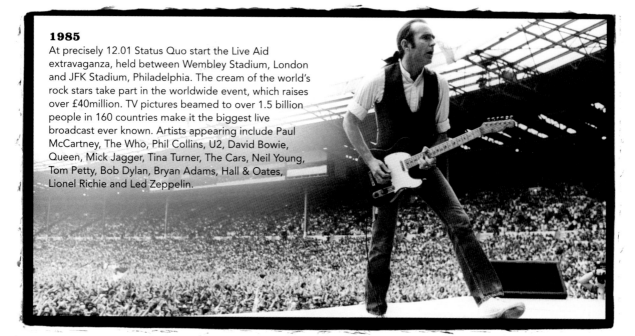

1985
At precisely 12.01 Status Quo start the Live Aid extravaganza, held between Wembley Stadium, London and JFK Stadium, Philadelphia. The cream of the world's rock stars take part in the worldwide event, which raises over £40million. TV pictures beamed to over 1.5 billion people in 160 countries make it the biggest live broadcast ever known. Artists appearing include Paul McCartney, The Who, Phil Collins, U2, David Bowie, Queen, Mick Jagger, Tina Turner, The Cars, Neil Young, Tom Petty, Bob Dylan, Bryan Adams, Hall & Oates, Lionel Richie and Led Zeppelin.

1987
Representatives from 50 of America's largest record retailers are guests at Michael Jackson's home in Encino, California to preview his new album, *Bad*. The LP will go on to sell over 30 million copies worldwide.

1997
A trial against John Denver for drink driving ends in a hung jury deadlocked 3-3. Denver's defence attorney argues that the singer suffers from a thyroid condition that has distorted blood alcohol tests.

2007
Rod Stewart collects his CBE from Prince Charles at Buckingham Palace. The singer, who was honoured for his services to music, wears a skull and crossbones tie, white trousers and a striped shirt instead of the conventional morning suit.

July 14

Born on this day:
1912 Woody Guthrie, US folk singer
1952 Chris Cross, bass, synth (Ultravox)
1971 Nick McCabe, guitar (The Verve)
1975 Taboo (Black Eyed Peas)
1978 Ruben Studdard, singer

1962
The Beatles play their first ever gig in Wales at The Regent Dansette in Rhyl. Tickets cost five shillings (25p).

1964
The Rolling Stones are at No. 1 on the UK singles chart with 'It's All Over Now', the group's first British chart-topper.

1967
The Who begin their first full North American tour as support band to Herman's Hermits on 55 dates.

1971
The Byrds, James Taylor, Steeleye Span, Sandy Denny, Tom Paxton and The Incredible String Band all appear at the UK Lincoln Folk Festival. Tickets cost £2.00.

1973
A drunk driver kills ex-Byrds guitarist Clarence White while he is loading equipment after a gig in Palmdale, California.

During a concert at the John Wayne Theatre in Hollywood, California, Phil Everly smashes his guitar and storms off stage. Don finishes the set solo and announces that The Everly Brothers have split.

1977
Elvis Costello & The Attractions make their live debut supporting Wayne County & The Electric Chairs at The Garden, Penzance, Cornwall.

1982
The movie version of Pink Floyd's *The Wall* has its premiere in London.

1984
Phillippe Wynne, lead singer with The Detroit Spinners, dies aged 43 of a heart attack while performing at Ivey's nightclub in Oakland, California.

1988
Michael Jackson gains a place in *The Guinness Book Of World Records* when playing the first of five nights at London's Wembley Stadium. The shows on his 'Bad' World Tour set a new attendance record with a total of 504,000, beating the previous record of four sold-out nights held by Genesis.

1997
Walkers 'Spice Girls' Crisps go on sale in the UK, selling over 16 million bags by the end of the year.

2006
Primal Scream singer Bobby Gillespie sustains two black eyes and a broken nose when he is attacked in a hotel bar in Madrid, Spain. The singer has to temporarily postpone a *Top Of The Pops* recording due to his injuries.

2007
A pair of glasses worn by John Lennon sparks a bidding war after being offered for sale online. Anonymous rival bidders push the price for the circular sunglasses, worn by Lennon during the Beatles 1966 tour of Japan where the band played some of their last ever live dates, as high as £750,000 at online auction house 991.com.

2009
Michael Jackson fans from all over the world congregate at London's O2 arena, where the star had been due to begin his run of 50 concerts. Fans leave messages on a wall of tributes, conduct Jackson sing-a-longs and hold a minute's silence at 18.30 BST to mark the time when the doors to the concert would have opened.

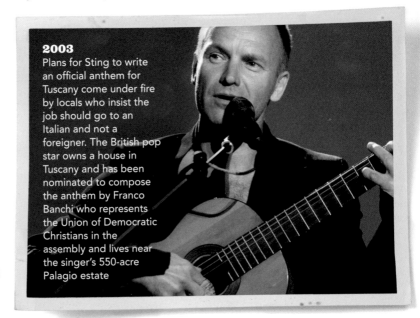

2003
Plans for Sting to write an official anthem for Tuscany come under fire by locals who insist the job should go to an Italian and not a foreigner. The British pop star owns a house in Tuscany and has been nominated to compose the anthem by Franco Banchi who represents the Union of Democratic Christians in the assembly and lives near the singer's 550-acre Palagio estate

Born on this day:

1946 Linda Ronstadt, US singer, songwriter
1948 Artimus Pyle, drums (Lynyrd Skynyrd)
1949 Trevor Horn, vocals, producer (Yes, Buggles)
1952 Johnny Thunders, vocals, guitar (The New York Dolls, The Heartbreakers, solo)
1956 Ian Curtis, guitar, vocals (Warsaw, Joy Division)
1977 Ray Toro, lead guitar (My Chemical Romance)

July 15

1952
At eight years of age, Gladys Knight wins $2,000 on US television show *Ted Mack's Amateur Hour* after performing the song 'Too Young'.

1958
John Lennon's mother Julia is killed by a car driven by Eric Clague, an off-duty drunken police officer who was later acquitted of the offence. John is 17 at the time and lives with his Aunt Mimi, Julia's sister.

1966
David Bowie & The Buzz appear at Loughton Youth Centre, Loughton, Essex.

1967
The Doors and The Jefferson Airplane play an afternoon and evening show to over 8,000 fans at the Anaheim Convention Center, California.

1973
The Edgar Winter Group, Sly & The Family Stone, Canned Heat, Lindisfarne and The Kinks all appear at The Great Western Express festival at White City, west London. With his wife having recently walked out of their marriage, taking their young children with her, Ray Davies of The Kinks announces from the stage that he is sick of the whole thing and is retiring. He then walks into a local hospital and collapses from an overdose of tranquillizers.

1978
The Rolling Stones start a two-week run on top of the *Billboard* album chart with *Some Girls*, the group's seventh US No. 1 album.

1981
Joe Walsh appears at the SDSU Open Air Theatre, San Diego, California.

1985
Nude photos of a pre-fame Madonna taken in 1977 appear in this month's editions of *Playboy* and *Penthouse* magazine.

1998
Aerosmith are forced to cancel a forthcoming US tour after Joey Kramer is admitted to hospital with second-degree burns sustained in a freak accident. The drummer's car caught on fire and was completely destroyed as he was filling it up with petrol.

2000
Former Sad Cafe singer and Mike & The Mechanics member Paul Young dies aged 53 of a heart attack at his Manchester home.

A Manchester judge reprimands Happy Mondays' singer Shaun Ryder after he turns up a day late in court to give evidence. Ryder tells the court he had been on "a bender". The accused man is cleared of dangerous driving and assaulting Ryder.

2002
Paul McCartney is named the highest-earning music star of the year so far after selling tickets worth £33.9m during his recent US tour.

2004
U2 call in police after thieves steal a CD preview of the band's latest album *Vertigo* during a U2 photo shoot in the south of France.

2005
Victor Edward Willis, the original 'policeman' in the Village People, is arrested after police find a gun and drugs in his convertible in Daly City, south of San Francisco. Willis also has an outstanding $15,000 felony warrant for possession of narcotics.

2007
Over 10,000 people apply for a job with P Diddy after the rapper posts an advert on Youtube looking to find a new personal assistant. He warns applicants that the job will be far from easy and will involve everything from getting him ready for the red carpet to aiding in billion dollar deals to helping him jump out of planes in movies.

2007
The Enemy go to No. 1 on the UK album chart with their debut album 'We'll Live And Die In These Towns.'

Born on this day:

1940 Tony Jackson, bass, vocals (The Searchers, Tony Jackson Group)
1941 Desmond Dekker, Jamaican singer

1947 Thomas Boggs, drums (The Box Tops)
1952 Stewart Copeland, drummer (Curved Air, The Police)

1962
The Beach Boys sign to Capitol Records in the US.

1988
Steve Cayter, a road crew technician with Def Leppard, dies of a brain

1993
The first of the three day Phoenix festival in England starts featuring Sonic Youth, Faith No More, The Black Crowes, Julian Cope, Pop Will Eat Itself, Radiohead, Living Colour, Manic Street Preachers and Pulp.

1966
The formation of the first supergroup Cream, featuring Jack Bruce, Ginger Baker (both formerly with the Graham Bond Organisation) and ex-Yardbirds and John Mayall Bluesbreakers' guitarist, Eric Clapton, is announced.

1995
Wayne Osmond from The Osmonds undergoes a brain tumour operation at Duke University Medical Center, North Carolina.

Rap singer Queen Latifah is the victim of a car-jacking attempt that goes wrong, leaving her bodyguard shot and wounded.

2000
The Corrs present a petition to the European Commission demanding legislation to end piracy on the internet. The Manic Street Preachers and The Spice Girls add their names to the petition.

2007
The White Stripes play the shortest live show ever at George Street, St. John's, Newfoundland, Canada. Jack White played a single C# note accompanied by a bass drum/crash cymbal hit from Meg White, following which Jack announces, "We have now officially played in every province and territory in Canada." The pair then leave the stage and perform a full show later that night in St John's.

1967
Joni Mitchell, Leonard Cohen, Judy Collins, Janis Ian, David Blue, Mike Settle, Tom Paxton and Eric Andersen all appear at the Newport Folk Festival in Newport, Rhode Island.

haemorrhage on stage before a show at the Alpine Valley Music Theatre in East Troy, Wisconsin.

2009
A stage being built in France for a concert by Madonna collapses, killing two workers and injuring six others. Technicians were setting up the stage at the Velodrome stadium in Marseille when the partially-built roof falls in, bringing down a crane. Madonna was performing on her 'Sticky And Sweet' tour in Udine, Italy, when she received news of the incident and was said to be "devastated".

1981
US singer-songwriter Harry Chapin, who had success in the 70s with 'Taxi', 'W-O-L-D' and a No. 1 with 'Cat's In The Cradle', is killed aged 38 suffering a cardiac arrest while driving on a New York expressway. His car is hit from behind by a tractor-trailer, causing the gas tank to explode.

1989
Tom Jones loses a paternity suit and is ordered by Judge Judy Sheindlin to pay $200 a week in child support to 27-year-old Katherine Berkery, of New York. Further terms of the settlement are agreed upon a couple of months later.

Born on this day:

1939 Spencer Davis, guitar, harmonica (The Spencer Davis Group)

1947 Wolfgang Flur, electronic drums (Kraftwerk)

1949 Terry 'Geezer' Butler, bass (Black Sabbath)

1949 Mick Tucker, drums (Sweet)

July 17

1959

After years of alcohol abuse Billie Holiday dies aged 43 from cirrhosis of the liver in a New York City hospital while under arrest for heroin possession, with police officers stationed at the door to her room. In the final years of her life, she was progressively swindled out of her earnings and had just 70 cents in the bank at the time of her death.

1967

The Beatles single 'All You Need Is Love' / 'Baby You're A Rich Man' is released in the US, becoming The Beatles 14th American No. 1.

1972

Angry fans throw bottles and rocks after 3,000 tickets for The Rolling Stones show in Montreal turn out to be fakes. A bomb exploded under the band's equipment van is believed to be the work of French separatists.

1975

Bob Marley & The Wailers play the first of two nights at The Lyceum Theatre, London. Both nights are recorded for the *Live* album, released in November, featuring the single 'No Woman No Cry'.

1982

Irene Cara is at No. 1 on the UK singles chart with 'Fame', which is based on the hit TV series about a New York drama school. Cara (who played the role of Coco Hernandez in the original movie) won an Academy Award for Best Original Song and the Golden Globe Award for the same.

1987

The Ozzy Osbourne Band start a 16-week tour of US prisons.

1992

The first night of a North American tour by Guns N' Roses, Metallica and Faith No More opens at RFK Stadium, Washington DC.

1995
Robbie Williams officially leaves Take That. While he was with the 'boy band', they scored six UK No. 1 singles and two chart-topping albums.

1996

Chas Chandler dies, aged 57, at Newcastle General Hospital, where he was undergoing tests related to an aortic aneurysm. He had been the bass player with The Animals and manager/producer of The Jimi Hendrix Experience and Slade.

1999

Kevin Wilkinson, drummer with Howard Jones, and who also worked with China Crisis, Holly & The Italians, Squeeze and The Waterboys, commits suicide aged 41 by hanging.

2004

Half of the 4,500 people in the audience walk out of Linda Ronstadt's show at the Aladdin Resort & Casino in Las Vegas after the singer dedicates an encore of 'Desperado' to filmmaker Michael Moore and urges the crowd to see his film *Fahrenheit 9/11*.

2005

Jamaican musician Laurel Aitken, 'the Godfather of Ska', dies. His 1958 'Boogie In My Bones' became the first release on the Island Records label in Jamaica and was No. 1 on the Jamaican charts for 11 weeks.

2008

Ageing rock stars and session musicians will now keep receiving royalties for their old recordings for the rest of their lives under a European Union scheme for copyright on recordings to last for 95 years. Performers currently risk losing the rights to their recordings after 50 years. Veteran artists like Cliff Richard and Roger Daltrey are among those who campaigned for it to be extended.

July 18

Born on this day:

1939 Dion Di Mucci, US singer, actor
1941 Martha Reeves, soul singer
1950 Glenn Hughes, singer (Village People)

1975 Daron Malakian, guitar (System Of A Down)

1953
Elvis Presley makes his first ever recording when paying $4 at the Memphis Recording Service to sing two songs, 'My Happiness' and 'That's When Your Heartaches Begin', as a present for his mother Gladys.

1960
Brenda Lee, the 4' 11" singer nicknamed Little Miss Dynamite, is at No. 1 on the US singles chart with 'I'm Sorry', which reaches No. 12 in the UK.

1964
The Four Seasons start a two-week run at No. 1 on the US singles chart with 'Rag Doll', the group's fourth No. 1 and a No. 2 hit in the UK. Co-writer Bob Gaudio said that he got the inspiration for the song from a young girl in tattered clothes that cleaned his car windows at a stop light.

1966
Bobby Fuller, leader of The Bobby Fuller Four, who had a 1966 US No. 9 with 'I Fought The Law', written by Sonny Curtis of Buddy Holly's Crickets and later covered by The Clash, is found dead aged 23 in his car parked outside Fuller's West Hollywood apartment. Fuller died from gasoline asphyxiation, and while police call it a suicide, the possibility of foul play involving the Mafia has always been rumoured.

1970
Pink Floyd, Roy Harper, Kevin Ayers, and the Edgar Broughton Band all appear at a free concert held in Hyde Park, London.

1972
Members of Sly & The Family Stone are arrested after police find two pounds of marijuana in the group's motor home.

1973
Bruce Springsteen plays the first of four nights at Max's Kansas City in New York, supported by Bob Marley & The Wailers who were on their first ever North American tour.

1978
Def Leppard make their live debut at Westfield School, Sheffield, in front of 150 students.

1988
Nico (real name: Christa Päffgen) dies aged 49 after suffering a cerebral haemorrhage while cycling in intense heat on holiday with her son in Ibiza, Spain. The German born singer worked as a fashion model and actress, appearing in Fellini's *La Dolce Vita*. As part of the Andy Warhol set she appeared in the film *Chelsea Girls* as well as being the visual foil and occasional vocalist with The Velvet Underground. She spent her final years recording and performing while in the grips of heroin addiction.

In Santa Monica, California Ike Turner is sentenced to one year in jail for possessing and transporting cocaine. Police had stopped Turner in August 1987 for driving erratically and found about six grams of rock cocaine in his car.

1992
Bobby Brown marries Whitney Houston at her New Jersey estate. Those in attendance include Stevie Wonder, Gloria Estefan, Natalie Cole, Patti LaBelle and Freddie Jackson. After years of making tabloid headlines, Houston would file for divorce in September 2006.

2001
Kiss add another product to their ever-growing merchandising universe: the 'Kiss Kasket'. The coffin features the faces of the four founding members of the band, the Kiss logo and the words: Kiss Forever. Pantera guitarist Dimebag Darrell is buried in one after he was shot and killed on stage in December 2004.

2007
Sting and his wife, Trudie Styler, are ordered to pay their former chef compensation after losing a sexual discrimination case. Jane Martin, 41, was awarded £24,944 at an employment tribunal in Southampton after she was sacked by Miss Styler from the couple's estate in Wiltshire because she fell pregnant.

Paul Simon files a lawsuit against Rhythm USA Inc., a Georgia-based subsidiary of a Japanese firm, claiming the company doesn't have his permission to sell wall clocks that play 'Bridge Over Troubled Water'. The suit claims that a proper licensing agreement would earn Simon at least $1 million.

Born on this day:

1947 Bernie Leadon, guitar (The Flying Burrito Brothers, The Eagles)

1947 Brian May, guitarist (Queen, solo)

1947 Keith Godchaux, keyboards (The Grateful Dead)

1952 Allen Collins, guitar (Lynyrd Skynyrd)

July 19

1958
The manager of The Drifters, George Treadwell, sacks the entire group and hires the unknown Ben E King and The Five Crowns as their replacements.

1967
Elvis Presley begins work on his latest (and 27th) movie *Speedway*, co-starring Nancy Sinatra, at the MGM soundstage, Hollywood.

1968
Bo Diddley plays the first of two nights at the Hippodrome, San Diego, supported by Frumious Bandersnatch.

1972
Mick Jagger and Keith Richards are arrested in Warwick, Rhode Island on assault charges after a fight breaks out with a photographer at the airport.

1975
Paul McCartney & Wings are at No. 1 on the *Billboard* singles chart with 'Listen To What The Man Said', McCartney's fourth US chart-topper and a No. 6 hit in the UK. Wings also have the No. 1 album with *Venus And Mars*, McCartney's fourth US chart-topping album since The Beatles.

1976
Deep Purple split up at the end of a UK tour. David Coverdale goes on to form Whitesnake, Jon Lord and Ian Paice join up with Tony Ashton, while newcomers Glenn Hughes returns to Trapeze and Tommy Bolin puts together his own band (but dies soon after). The classic line up of Gillan, Blackmore, Glover, Lord and Paice reformed in 1984.

1981
On Roy Orbison Day in Odessa, Texas, Orbison is given the keys to the city and performs for the first time in Odessa in 15 years.

1987
Bruce Springsteen plays his first ever show behind the Iron Curtain in East Berlin in front of 180,000 people. The show is broadcast on East German TV.

1989
James Brown changes accommodation behind bars after $40,000 in cash and cheques are discovered in his medium security cell at the Stevenson Correctional Institute in Columbia, South Carolina. The Godfather of Soul was given a six year sentence the previous December after several run-ins with the law, including illegal gun possession, resisting arrest, assault and leading the authorities on a number of car chases.

2001
Wu Tang Clan rapper ODB (Russell Jones) is sentenced to spend between two and four years behind bars after being found guilty of drug possession. He was arrested in July 1999 when police found cocaine and marijuana in his car after he was pulled over for driving through a red light. The rapper was later sent to a Los Angeles rehabilitation centre but went on the run from authorities the previous October.

2005
Singer-songwriter James Blunt is at No. 1 on the UK singles chart – for the first of five weeks – with 'You're Beautiful', from his debut album *Back To Bedlam*.

1991
Steven Adler, ex-drummer with Guns N' Roses, files a suit in Los Angeles county court alleging that he was fraudulently removed from the group and that the band introduced him to hard drugs.

Born on this day:

1945 John Lodge, bass, vocals (The Moody Blues)

1945 Kim Carnes, singer-songwriter

1947 Carlos Santana, guitar (Santana)

1956 Paul Cook, drums (The Sex Pistols, The Professionals)

1964 Chris Cornell, vocals, guitar (Soundgarden, Audioslave)

1940

The first comprehensive record chart is published in *Billboard* with the first No. 1 song being 'I'll Never Smile Again' by Frank Sinatra and the Tommy Dorsey Orchestra. The magazine had previously published best-seller lists submitted by the individual record companies, but the new chart combines the top sellers from all major labels.

1954

The Blue Moon Boys, featuring Elvis Presley, Scotty Moore and Bill Black, make their live debut appearing off a flatbed truck outside a new drug store in Memphis. The band's name was taken from a song they had recorded just two weeks previously, 'Blue Moon Of Kentucky'.

1963

Jan And Dean start a two-week run at No. 1 on the US singles chart with 'Surf City', written by Beach Boy Brian Wilson, with the other Beach Boys on backing vocals.

1968

Iron Butterfly's second album, *In-A-Gadda-Da-Vida*, enters the *Billboard* album chart for the first time. The album, containing the 17-minute title track that filled the second side of the LP, goes on to sell over four million copies in the US alone.

1971

The Carpenters' TV show *Make Your Own Kind Of Music* starts a six-week run on NBC-TV.

1975

Bruce Springsteen & The E Street Band play the opening night on their Born To Run Tour at The Palace Theatre, Providence, Rhode Island. This gig also sees the live debut of Steven Van Zandt (Miami Steve) as a member of The E Street Band.

1976

The Buzzcocks make their live debut supporting The Sex Pistols and The Damned at The Lesser Free Trade Hall, Manchester. The audience includes Bernard Sumner, Peter Hook, Steven Morrissey and Mark E Smith. Tickets cost £1.

1986

Carlos Santana celebrates his 39th birthday, and 20th anniversary in the music business, with a concert in San Francisco. Previous group members are assembled for the event, and 17 of them perform together on stage.

1990

Madonna plays the first of three sold-out nights at London's Wembley Stadium on her 57-date 'Blond Ambition' World Tour.

1999

Church groups in middle America claim that pictures of Britney Spears printed in *Rolling Stone* magazine encourage child pornography.

2000

The Evergreen Ballroom in Lacey, Washington is destroyed by a fire. During the ballroom's heyday in the 1950s, 60s and 70s, many of music's greats played there including Elvis Presley, Johnny Cash, Duke Ellington, Chuck Berry, Little Richard, Ike & Tina Turner and Fats Domino. Glen Campbell had lived in the kitchen at the venue for a time before he became famous.

2003

A tooth said to have been pulled out of Elvis Presley's mouth after an injury fails to sell on the auction site eBay. The tooth, also accompanied by some of the singer's hair, had been put on a 10-day sale with a reserve price of £64,100.

2008

Rapper DMX (real name: Earl Simmons) is arrested at a shopping centre in Phoenix on suspicion of giving a false name to get out of paying for hospital medical expenses. County Sheriff Joe Arpaio says the star told Mayo Clinic in Arizona that his name was Troy Jones and failed to pay a $7,500 bill in April.

Born on this day:

1946 Barry Whitwam, drums (Herman's Hermits)

1947 Cat Stevens (Steven Georgiou, now Yusef Islam), singer-songwriter

1955 Howie Epstein, bass (Tom Petty & The Heartbreakers)

1961 Jim Martin, guitar (Faith No More)

July 21

1967
The Jimi Hendrix Experience play the first of three nights at the Cafe-au-Go-Go in the basement of 152 Bleecker Street, Greenwich Village, New York.

1977
The video for The Sex Pistols' 'Pretty Vacant', shot in London's Marquee Club, is shown on BBC TV's *Top Of The Pops.*

1982
Queen play the first night on a 32-date 'Hot Space' North American tour at the Forum, Montreal, Canada.

1990
Roger Waters' *The Wall* is staged at the Berlin Wall in Potsdamer Platz, Berlin. Over 200,000 people attend the event which is broadcast live worldwide. Van Morrison, Bryan Adams, Joni Mitchell, Marianne Faithfull, The Scorpions, Cyndi Lauper, and Sinead O'Connor are among the artists who take part.

1994
Oasis play their first ever American gig as part of the New Music Seminar at Wetlands in New York City.

1995
A judge in Los Angeles throws out a lawsuit against Michael Jackson by five of his former security guards. The guards had claimed they were fired for knowing too much about night-time visits by young boys to Jackson's estate.

1996
Arriving at a UK festival, the tour bus carrying members of Terrorvision inadvertently runs over sleeping festivalgoer Daniel Duffy as he lay in his tent, breaking his hip.

2001
Madonna kicks off the North American leg of her 47-date 'Drowned' World Tour at the First Union Center in Philadelphia, Pennsylvania. It is the singer's first world tour in eight years, following 'The Girlie Show' in 1993. Over 730,000 people attend the shows throughout North America and Europe and the tour grosses over $75 million.

2002
Producer Gus Dudgeon, who worked with artists including Elton John, David Bowie, The Beach Boys, Kiki Dee, The Bonzo Dog Doo-Dah Band, The Strawbs, XTC and Joan Armatrading, is killed aged 59 in a car accident near Reading, together with his wife Sheila. They had been driving along the M4 motorway on their way home from a party when Gus fell asleep at the wheel of the Jaguar XK8 convertible, crashing down an embankment at speed and ending up in a ditch.

2003
Chris Martin is charged with malicious damage in Australia after he allegedly attacked the car of a photographer who had taken pictures of Martin surfing at Seven Mile Beach. The Coldplay singer admitted he had lost his temper due to the constant harassment by the journalist, and consequently smashed his windscreen and let the air out of his tyres.

2005
UK singer Long John Baldry dies aged 64 of a chest infection. He was one of the founding fathers of British R&B in the early 60s performing with Blues Incorporated and Cyril Davies' R&B All Stars. When Davies died in January 1964, Baldry took over leadership and changed the name to Long John Baldry & The Hoochie Coochie Men, with Rod Stewart on second vocals. He then formed Steam Packet, featuring Stewart and Julie Driscoll on vocals and Brian Auger on organ. Baldry's later backing group Bluesology included pianist Reg Dwight (later to be known as Elton John). Baldry also narrated *Winnie The Pooh* recordings for Disney and was the voice for Robotnik on the *Sonic The Hedgehog* computer game.

2008
Amy Winehouse's husband, 26-year-old Blake Fielder-Civil, is jailed for 27 months for attacking a pub landlord and perverting the course of justice. Fielder-Civil, of Camden, north London, admitted assaulting 36-year-old James King at the Macbeths pub in Hoxton, east London, in June 2006.

The Police play the first of two nights at the Red Rocks Amphitheatre in Denver, Colorado during the final leg of their 152-date world reunion tour. The tour becomes the third highest grossing tour of all time, with revenues reaching over $340 million.

2009
Liam Gallagher walks off stage during an iTunes Festival gig at the Roundhouse in Camden, north London, after pints of beer are thrown at him. The 36-year-old Oasis singer storms off after snarling, "I hope you feel as uncomfortable as I feel." His brother Noel, who carries on with the set, says, "I think someone's in a bad mood." Liam returns to the stage after an absence of almost half an hour.

July 22

1965

Mick Jagger, Brian Jones and Bill Wyman are each fined £5 at East Ham Magistrates Court, London after being found guilty of insulting behaviour at a Romford Road service station on 18 March. The three Rolling Stones had all urinated against a wall.

1971

John Lennon and Yoko Ono spend the day making a promotional film for 'Imagine' at their mansion in Tittenhurst Park Ascot, England. The footage shows the couple walking along the driveway on the grounds through the mist and Lennon miming 'Imagine' at his white piano in the white music room.

1972

While on tour, Paul and Linda McCartney are arrested in Sweden for possession of marijuana.

1977

Stiff Records releases *My Aim Is True*, the debut album from Elvis Costello in the UK.

1979

Little Richard, now known as the Reverend Richard Penniman, tells his congregation about the evils of rock'n'roll music, declaring, "If God can save an old homosexual like me, he can save anybody."

1989

Former actress Martika starts a two week run at No. 1 on the US singles chart with 'Toy Soldiers', a No. 5 hit in the UK.

1996

Donovan is forced to postpone a comeback tour of the US because of a 30-year-old marijuana conviction in the UK. American authorities delay granting him a waiver to enter the country.

2004

French singer and jazz guitarist Sacha Distel, who worked alongside Dizzy Gillespie and Tony Bennett, dies aged 71 after a long battle with deteriorating health.

2004

American singer, songwriter and producer Arthur Crier, a member of The Chimes and who had worked with Little Eva, Gene Pitney, The Four Tops, The Temptations, Ben E. King, Johnny Nash and The Coasters, dies aged 69 of heart failure.

2005

Research by a car insurance company shows that listening to the wrong sort of music when driving could lead to aggression and distraction. Dr. Nicola Dibben, a music psychologist says "singing while driving stimulates the mind." Songs she recommends include Pulp's 'Disco 2000' and 'Hey Ya' by Outkast, but the likes of The Prodigy's 'Firestarter' are to be avoided.

2006

Johnny Cash is at No. 1 on the US album chart with *American V: A Hundred Highways*. Released posthumously on July 4, the vocal parts were recorded before Cash's death, but the instruments were not added until 2005.

2007

Ja Rule and Lil' Wayne are arrested separately after a concert in Manhattan on charges of carrying illegal firearms. Rule was stopped for speeding when a weapon was discovered in his car and officers who arrested Wayne for smoking marijuana also found a pistol in his car.

Born on this day:

1947 Tony Joe White, US singer-songwriter
1965 Slash, guitar (Guns N' Roses, Velvet Revolver)
1973 Fran Healy, vocals, guitar (Travis)
1980 Steve 'Stevo 32' Jocz (Sum 41)

1955
Slim Whitman is at No. 1 on the UK singles chart with 'Rose Marie', which stays at the top of the charts for 11 weeks. Whitman held the record for the most consecutive weeks at No. 1 (11 weeks) until Bryan Adams broke the record in 1991 with '(Everything I Do) I Do It For You'.

1964
The Beatles are at No. 1 on the UK singles chart with 'A Hard Day's Night', the group's sixth British chart-topper.

1969
The Rolling Stones are at No. 1 on the UK singles chart with 'Honky Tonk Women', the group's eighth and last UK No. 1.

1977
Who drummer Keith Moon joins Led Zeppelin on stage during a gig at The Forum, Inglewood, Los Angeles, playing a tympani alongside drummer John Bonham.

1979
Keith Godchaux, keyboard player with The Grateful Dead, dies aged 32 after being involved in a car accident. He co-wrote songs with Lowell George (of Little Feat) and was a member of The New Riders Of The Purple Sage.

1983
The Police are top of the US album chart with *Synchronicity*, which spends a total of seventeen weeks at No. 1. Also today the band kick off the North American leg of their 107-date 'Synchronicity' world tour at Comiskey Park, Chicago, Illinois.

1988
After 49 weeks on the US album chart, *Hysteria* by Def Leppard gets to the No. 1 position.

1989
Ringo Starr kicks off his first solo tour since the break-up of The Beatles with a show in Dallas, Texas. His backup All-Starr Band includes guitarists Joe Walsh and Nils Lofgren, organist Billy Preston and Bruce Springsteen's sax man Clarence Clemons.

1996
Rob Collins, keyboard player with The Charlatans, dies aged 29 in a car crash. Collins had been recording keyboard parts for the band's fifth album *Tellin' Stories* at a studio in Wales. An investigation into the accident shows that Collins had consumed a sizable amount of alcohol and was not wearing a seatbelt. He dies from head injuries on the roadside shortly after the accident having been thrown through the windscreen.

2000
Farrah Franklin leaves Destiny's Child after only five months with the group. The remaining trio of Beyonce, Kelly, and Michelle said that Farrah was not kicked out, but all had agreed that Farrah and Destiny's Child should part ways.

2003
James Brown announces his separation from his fourth wife using an advertisement featuring the Disney character Goofy. The 70-year-old places the notice in *Variety* magazine, which features a picture of himself, his wife Tomi Rae and their two-year-old son, James Joseph Brown II, posing with Goofy at Walt Disney World.

2005
Queen's 1985 Live Aid performance is voted The Best Rock Concert Ever by over 7,000 UK Sony Ericsson music fans. Radiohead are voted The Best Festival Act for their 1997 Glastonbury performance and Bob Dylan's 1966 Manchester Free Trade Hall concert won The Best Ever Solo Gig.

2008
Kid Rock is sentenced to a year on probation and fined $1,000 for his part in a fight in an Atlanta waffle restaurant in 2007. The 37-year-old also receives 80 hours community service and six hours of anger management counselling. The rapper pleads no contest to one count of battery and four other assault charges are dropped. Kid Rock had been performing at a gig in Atlanta before stopping off in his tour bus in the early hours of the morning. The fight took place when an argument broke out with another customer at the restaurant.

July 24

Born on this day:

1942 Heinz Burt, bass, vocals (The Tornados, solo)
1947 Alan Whitehead, drummer (Marmalade)
1961 Gary Cherone, vocals (Extreme)
1970 Jennifer Lopez, singer, actress

1965
The Byrds are at No. 1 on the UK singles chart with their version of Bob Dylan's 'Mr Tambourine Man', the first Dylan-composed song to reach No. 1.

1967
All four Beatles and manager Brian Epstein sign a petition printed in *The Times* newspaper calling for the legalisation of marijuana.

1972
Bobby Ramirez, drummer with Edger Winter's White Trash, is killed aged 23 after becoming involved in a brawl in a Chicago bar. The fight started after comments were made about the length of his hair.

1976
After 16 Top 40 hits, Elton John scores his first UK No. 1 with 'Don't Go Breaking My Heart', a duet with Kiki Dee. It was written by Elton without Bernie Taupin under the pseudonym 'Ann Orson and Carte Blanche'.

1982
Survivor (below) start a six-week run at No. 1 on the US singles chart with 'Eye Of The Tiger', taken from the film *Rocky III*.

1984
The Rev. C.L. Franklin (father of soul singer Aretha Franklin) dies aged 69. An American Baptist minister as well as a civil rights activist, Franklin had been in a coma since 1979 after being shot by burglars at his Detroit home.

1993
UB40 start a seven week run at No. 1 on the US singles chart with a cover of 'Can't Help Falling In Love'. Elvis Presley had the first hit with the song in 1961.

1997
Police give Oasis singer Liam Gallagher a formal caution after he admitts criminal damage following an incident with a cyclist in Camden, north London. Gallagher had grabbed the rider from the window of his chauffeur driven car and broken the man's Ray-Bans sunglasses.

1999
Phil Collins marries for the third time. The 48-year-old drummer weds marketing consultant Orianne Cevey in Lausanne, Switzerland. Guests include Elton John, Eric Clapton and Mark Knopfler.

2002
Garden centre Clifton Nurseries, of Maida Vale, West London is sued over claims it killed a collection of the late singer Freddie Mercury's prized koi fish. Mercury's former partner, Mary Austin, who inherited the collection, claims 84 fish died when the electricity powering a temporary pond was accidentally turned off by a worker. One koi could be worth up to £250,000 and at the time of Mercury's death he had amassed one of the best collections of the fish in the UK.

2005
Bad Beat singer Patrick Sherry dies after a stage dive went wrong during a gig at the Warehouse in Leeds, England. Sherry leapt towards the crowd at the end of the band's set and tried to grab a lighting rig from the ceiling but missed and hit the floor.

2008
At Yeovil Magistrates Court Pete Doherty pleads guilty to causing criminal damage after smashing a photographer's camera and is ordered to pay £918.27 in compensation. The 29-year-old lost his temper with news agency employee Catherine Mead when she followed him around Crewkerne, Somerset, in August 2007.

Rapper 50 Cent is suing Taco Bell claiming the US fast food chain used his name and image without permission in an advertising campaign. New York court papers say the advertisement, part of Taco Bell's 'Why Pay More?' campaign, which promoted items for under a dollar, featured the star being encouraged to change his name to 79 Cent, 89 Cent or 99 Cent. The rapper accuses the chain of "diluting the value of his good name".

Born on this day:

1925 Benny Benjamin, drummer ('The Funk Brothers' session man)

1943 Jim McCarty, drums (The Yardbirds, Renaissance, Box Of Frogs)

1951 Verdine White, bass, vocals (Earth, Wind & Fire)

1958 Thurston Moore, guitar, vocals (Sonic Youth)

1960
Roy Orbison reaches No. 2 on the US singles chart with 'Only The Lonely', his first hit. The song was turned down by The Everly Brothers and Elvis Presley so Orbison decided to record it himself.

1965
In a controversial appearance, Bob Dylan plays three songs with an electric band live for the first time at The Newport Folk Festival in Newport, Rhode Island and is booed by sections of the audience.

1969
Neil Young appears with Crosby, Stills & Nash for the first time at The Fillmore East, New York. Young was initially asked only to help out at concerts but ended up joining the group on and off for the next 40 years.

1970
The Carpenters start a four-week run at No. 1 on the US singles chart with '(They Long To Be) Close To You', the first of three US No. 1s and 17 other Top 40 hits for the family duo. The song was written in 1963 by Hal David and Burt Bacharach and was first offered to Herb Alpert, who didn't feel comfortable singing the line "so they sprinkled moon dust in your hair".

1984
Willie Mae 'Big Mama' Thornton, who had a No. 1 R&B hit in 1953 with 'Hound Dog' (later covered by Elvis Presley) and who also wrote and recorded 'Ball 'n' Chain', which Janis Joplin covered, dies aged 58 in Los Angeles of heart and liver complications.

1990
Bruce Springsteen becomes a father when partner Patti Scialfa gives birth to a boy, Evan James.

1995
Grammy Award winning country singer-songwriter Charlie Rich, who began as a rockabilly artist for Sun Records in Memphis in 1958, dies aged 62 in his sleep. Rich scored a 1974 US No. 1 & UK No. 2 single with 'The Most Beautiful Girl' and a No. 1 country hit with 'Behind Closed Doors'.

1999
The Woodstock 30th Anniversary Festival ends with riots, resulting in 120 people being arrested. Three people die during the three-day event in unrelated incidents and many are hospitalised after drinking polluted water.

2002
Two former members of Destiny's Child settle out of court over the lyrics to the hit single 'Survivor', which they claim are libellous. LeToya Luckett and LaTavia Roberson, who left the group in 2000, say that the song broke an agreement which stopped both sides making any public comment of a disparaging nature concerning one another. The line in question said, "You thought that I'd be stressed without you, but I'm chillin'. You thought I wouldn't sell without you, sold nine million."

2003
Erik Braunn, from American psychedelic rock band Iron Butterfly, dies aged 52 of cardiac failure. Braunn was just 16-years-old when he joined Iron Butterfly, who had a 1968 US No. 14 single 'In-A- Gadda-Da-Vida'.

2006
George Michael phones the UK daytime TV *Richard And Judy* chat show to talk about the recent story when the singer was caught 'cruising' for sex and being photographed kissing and groping a stranger.

Born on this day:

1941 Neil Landon, vocals (The Flowerpot Men, Fat Mattress)
1941 Darlene Love, vocals (The Crystals)
1943 Mick Jagger, vocals (The Rolling Stones, solo)

1949 Roger Taylor, drums, vocals (Queen)
1980 Dave 'Brown Sound' Baksh, guitar, vocals (Sum 41)

1968
The Jackson 5 sign a one-year contract with Motown Records.

1970
Jimi Hendrix plays in his home town of Seattle for the last time when he appearing at Sick's Stadium.

1974
The Allman Brothers appear at Boston Garden, Massachusetts with The Eagles as support band.

1977
Led Zeppelin cut short a US tour after Robert Plant's six year-old-son Karac dies unexpectedly of a stomach virus at home in England.

1980
Rainbow, Judas Priest, Scorpions, Saxon, April Wine and Riot appear at The Monsters Of Rock Festival, Donington Park, England. Tickets cost £7.50.

1990
Brent Mydland, keyboard player from The Grateful Dead, is found dead aged 37 on the floor of his home from a drug overdose.

1992
American singer and Motown artist, Mary Wells, referred to as The First Lady of Motown and who had a 1964 US No. 1 and UK No. 5 single 'My Guy', dies aged 49 of laryngeal cancer. Forced to give up her career and with no health insurance, Wells had to sell her home. Her old Motown friends, including Diana Ross, Mary Wilson, The Temptations and Martha Reeves, along with Dionne Warwick, Rod Stewart, Bruce Springsteen, Aretha Franklin and Bonnie Raitt, personally pledge donations in support.

2001
Paul McCartney announces his engagement to Heather Mills, the anti-landmine campaigner and former model. The couple married in 2002 and divorced in 2006.

2006
The Rex acoustic guitar on which Paul McCartney learned his first chords sells for £330,000 at an auction at London's Abbey Road Studios.

The final edition of *Top Of The Pops* is recorded at BBC Television Centre in London. Just 200 members of the public are in the audience for the show, co-hosted by veteran disc jockey Jimmy Savile, who was the show's very first presenter. Past performances from The Spice Girls, Wham, Madonna, Beyonce Knowles and Robbie Williams feature in the show alongside The Rolling Stones, who were among the artists that appeared in the first edition broadcast New Year's Day 1964.

Jeffrey Borer and Arvel Jett Reeves plead guilty to secretly videotaping Michael Jackson as he flew to Santa Barbara, California, to surrender in a child-molestation investigation. The two men admit they installed two digital video recorders to record Jackson and his lawyer as the pair travelled on a private jet from Las Vegas to Santa Barbara in November 2003.

1986
Peter Gabriel is at No. 1 on the US singles chart with 'Sledgehammer', a No. 4 hit in the UK.

Born on this day:

1943 Alan Ramsey, guitar (Gary Lewis & The Playboys)
1944 Bobbie Gentry, US singer-songwriter
1949 Rory MacDonald, bass, vocals (Runrig)
1962 Karl Mueller, bass (Soul Asylum)

July 27

1958

Fans of rock'n'roll are warned that tuning into music on their car radio could cost them more money. Researchers from the Esso gas company say the rhythm of rock'n'roll could cause the driver to be foot heavy on the pedal, making them waste fuel.

1968

Bee Gee Robin Gibb collapses from nervous exhaustion as the group are about to set out on their first US tour. The dates are postponed.

1974

John Denver starts a two-week run at No. 1 on the US singles chart with 'Annie's Song', the singer's second American chart-topper. The song is a tribute to his wife and was written in 10 minutes while Denver was on a ski lift.

Paul McCartney & Wings start a seven-week run at No. 1 on the UK album chart with *Band On The Run*, which goes on to sell over six million copies worldwide.

1976

After a four-year legal fight, John Lennon is awarded his much-sought Green Card at the INS offices in New York, allowing him permanent residence in the US.

1986

Queen become the first Western act since Louis Armstrong in 1964 to perform in eastern Europe when the band played at Budapest's Nepstadion, Hungary. The gig was filmed and released as *Queen Magic In Budapest*.

1991

Bryan Adams starts a seven-week run at No. 1 on the US singles chart with '(Everything I Do) I Do It For You'.

1992

Michael Jackson sues the British tabloid *The Daily Mirror* over photos and an article that said he was left a "scar face" from numerous plastic surgeries. The suit was later settled out of court.

1994

Jeff Buckley and Jewel both appear at Hahn Cosmopolitian Theatre, San Diego, California.

1996

The Spice Girls score their first UK No. 1 with 'Wannabe', which becomes the best-selling single by a female group, spending seven weeks in the top slot and selling over six million copies worldwide.

1997

Jason Caulfield and James Hunt, both roadies for Primal Scream, are arrested for possessing drugs during a festival in Tullinge, Sweden.

2001

Leon Wilkeson, bass player with Lynyrd Skynyrd and also a member of The Rossington-Collins Band, is found dead aged 49 in a hotel room in Florida.

2002

Mariah Carey checks herself into an undisclosed hospital suffering from "extreme exhaustion" and cancels all public appearances, including her headlining appearance at MTV's 20th birthday party. Her record company denies tabloid reports that Carey tried to commit suicide, saying she did have cuts on her body, but the injuries were unintentional after breaking some glasses and dishes.

Born on this day:

1945 Rick Wright, keyboards, vocals (Pink Floyd)

1949 Peter Doyle, singer (The New Seekers)

1949 Simon Kirke, drums (Free)

1949 Steve Took, percussion (Tyrannosaurus Rex)

1954

The first press interview with 19-year-old Elvis Presley is published in The *Memphis Press-Scimitar*.

1956

Gene Vincent makes his first appearance on national TV in the US on *The Perry Como Show*. Vincent had released 'Woman Love' the previous month but it was the B-side, 'Be-Bop-A-Lula', that eventually made the Top 10. The song had been purchased from a fellow hospital patient when Vincent was recovering from leg injuries.

1969

Police in Moscow report that thousands of public phone booths have been vandalised by thieves stealing parts of the phones to convert their acoustic guitars to electric. A feature in a Russian youth magazine had shown details on how to do this.

1973

Thin Lizzy appear at The Marquee Club, London.

The Watkins Glen outdoor summer jam is held outside Watkins Glen, New York with The Allman Brothers, The Grateful Dead and The Band. With over 600,000 attending, many historians claim the event was the largest gathering of people in American history. 150,000 tickets were sold for $10 each, but for all others it was a free concert. The crowd was so huge that a large part of the audience was not able to see the stage.

1979

'I Don't Like Mondays' gives The Boomtown Rats their second UK No. 1 single. Singer Bob Geldof wrote the song after reading a report on 16-year-old Brenda Ann Spencer, who fired indiscriminately at children playing in a school playground across the street from her home in San Diego, California. She killed two adults and injured eight children and one police officer. Spencer showed no remorse for her crime, and her full explanation for her actions was "I don't like Mondays, this livens up the day."

1982

Queen play the second of two nights at Madison Square Garden, New York.

1991

Almost 100 arrests are made when an estimated 2,000 youths riot after a MC Hammer concert in Penticon, Canada.

1996

Marge Ganser from The Shangri-Las dies aged 48 of breast cancer. The New York girl group scored over ten hits during the 60's including a 1964 US No. 1, 'Leader Of The Pack'.

2002

The Dave Matthews Band are at No. 1 on the US album chart with *Busted Stuff*.

2003

The wine made on Cliff Richard's Algarve estate starts a UK supermarket battle. Fans are asking when the wine would go on sale, with the Tesco chain saying they will be first although Waitrose have been selling the red at £8.49 a bottle for the past week.

2004

In Santa Monica, California, Justin Timberlake obtains a restraining order against photographer Artemus Earl Lister who allegedly stalked him.

2006

Prince's second wife Manuela Testolini Nelson files for divorce. His first marriage, to dancer Mayte Garcia, took place in 1996 but only lasted two years.

2008

Amy Winehouse is rushed to hospital after she starts to have fits at her home in Camden, north London. A spokesman says it appears the singer had suffered a reaction to medication she was taking to help her off hard drugs.

Born on this day:

1953 Geddy Lee, bass, vocals (Rush)
1953 Patti Scialfa, US singer (Bruce Springsteen & The E Street Band)
1959 John Sykes, keyboards (Thin Lizzy, Whitesnake)
1973 Wanya Morris, vocals (Boyz II Men)

July 29

1963
With the US charts full of Hot Rod songs, Capitol Records sends disc jockeys a list of car terms and phrases to help promote The Beach Boys' latest release 'Little Deuce Coupe'.

1966
Eric Clapton, Jack Bruce and Ginger Baker made their low-key live debut as Cream at The Twisted Wheel, Manchester.

Bob Dylan suffers a broken neck vertebra when he crashes his Triumph 55 motorbike near his home in Woodstock, New York.

American teen magazine *Datebook* reprints part of Maureen Cleave's infamous John Lennon interview in which he said, "We're bigger than Jesus now." American Christians in the Southern Bible Belt react with outrage, organising Beatle bonfires while radio stations boycott the group's records.

1967
The Doors start a three-week run on top of the *Billbaord* singles chart with their first US No. 1, 'Light My Fire'. It only reached number 49 on the UK chart, but when reissued in 1991 to coincide with Oliver Stone's Doors biopic the song got as high as seven.

1968
The first recording session for The Beatles' seven-minute epic 'Hey Jude' takes place at EMI Studios, London. Paul McCartney was inspired to write the song for John Lennon's son Julian in the wake of his parents' separation.

1972
While publicising his forthcoming London gigs, Screaming Lord Sutch is arrested in London after jumping from a bus in Downing Street with four nude women.

1973
While in town to play two Madison Square Garden concerts in New York, Led Zeppelin lose $180,000 in cash taken from a safe deposit box at The Drake Hotel.

1974
Former Mamas & The Papas singer Mama Cass Elliot dies in her sleep aged 32 from a heart attack after playing a sold out show in London, England. She was staying at Harry Nilsson's London flat at the time. The building was to claim another rock star fatality four years later when Keith Moon died in the same flat.

1978
The film soundtrack to *Grease*, featuring John Travolta and Olivia Newton-John, goes to No. 1 on the US album chart.

1987
Michigan state governor James Blanchard declares an annual statewide Four Tops Day, honouring the group for its contribution to American music.

1988
American record producer and pedal steel guitar player Pete Drake, who worked with Elvis Presley, George Harrison and Ringo Starr, and played on such hits as Lynn Anderson's 'Rose Garden', Charlie Rich's 'Behind Closed Doors', Bob Dylan's 'Lay Lady Lay' and Tammy Wynette's 'Stand By Your Man', dies aged 55 of lung disease.

1990
Elton John checks into a Chicago clinic to cure bulimia and an addiction problem, taking over a year off from touring and recording.

2006
Pamela Anderson marries for the second time to US rapper Kid Rock on a yacht off the French resort of St Tropez. The 39-year-old former *Baywatch* star, divorced from rock star Tommy Lee in 1998, had recently got back together with Kid Rock after a brief engagement ended in 2003. Anderson and Rock split after four months of marriage.

2007
Heart problems force Kiss singer and guitarist Paul Stanley to abandon a show in California. Paramedics stop and restart his heart to give it a regular rhythm after his heart spontaneously jumped to 190 plus beats per minute.

Born on this day:

1941	Paul Anka, singer, songwriter
1946	Jeffrey Hammond-Hammond, bass (Jethro Tull)
1957	Rat Scabies, drums (The Damned)
1958	Kate Bush, singer, songwriter
1968	Sean Moore, drums (Manic Street Preachers)

1954

Slim Whitman, Billy Walker, Sugarfoot Collins, Sonny Harvelle, Tinker Fry, Curly Harris and a young Elvis Presley appear at The Hillbilly Hoedown, Overton Park Shell, in Memphis. Elvis is so nervous he stands up on the balls of his feet and shakes his leg in time with the music. When he comes offstage he asks why people are yelling at him. Someone tells him it was because he was shaking his leg, which with Elvis' baggy pleated pants, created a wild gyrating effect in time with the music.

1963

The Rolling Stones appear at The Ricky Tick Club, Windsor, Berkshire.

1966

The Troggs start a two-week run at No. 1 on the US singles chart with 'Wild Thing'.

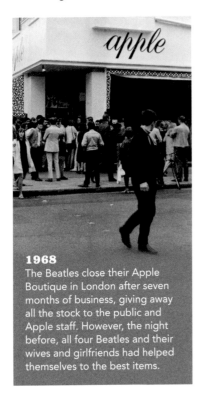

1968

The Beatles close their Apple Boutique in London after seven months of business, giving away all the stock to the public and Apple staff. However, the night before, all four Beatles and their wives and girlfriends had helped themselves to the best items.

1974

Bruce Springsteen & The E Street Band play The Troubadour in Los Angeles, on a double bill with Roger McGuinn from The Byrds.

1978

Fleetwood Mac and The Steve Miller Band appear at JFK Stadium, Philadelphia.

1986

Boy George is fined £250 by a London court for possession of heroin.

Variety magazine report that RCA has dropped John Denver from its roster after the release of his single 'What Are We Making Weapons For'. The report says the song upset the record company's new owner, General Electric, one of the largest defense contractors in America.

1991

A police officer is forced to tear up a traffic ticket given to the limousine that Axl Rose was travelling in after it made an illegal turn. Rose threatened to cancel that night's Guns N' Roses gig if the ticket was issued.

1997

A judge in Los Angeles rules that Michael Jackson and members of his family are not liable for losses incurred by the producers of the failed 1994 *Jackson Family Honors* TV special.

1998

Jamiroquai are at No. 1 on the UK singles chart with 'Deeper Underground', the first single from the album *Synkronized*. It is included on the soundtrack of the movie *Godzilla*.

2003

Sam Phillips, the legendary founder of Sun Records and discoverer of Elvis Presley, who worked with Carl Perkins, Johnny Cash, Roy Orbison, Ike Turner, B.B. King and Jerry Lee Lewis, dies aged 80 of respiratory failure at St. Francis Hospital, Memphis. In the 1940s, Phillips worked as a DJ for Muscle Shoals, Alabama radio station WLAY, and recorded what some consider to be the first rock 'n' roll record, 'Rocket 88' by Jackie Brenston and his Delta Cats in 1951.

The Rolling Stones, AC/DC, Rush, The Guess Who, Justin Timberlake, The Flaming Lips, Sass Jordan and The Isley Brothers play a benefit concert in Toronto, Canada, to prove that the city is safe from the SARS virus. With 450,000 spectators, it is the largest concert in Canadian history.

2005

A new Jimi Hendrix biography, *Room Full Of Mirrors* by Seattle writer Charles R. Cross, published to mark the 35th anniversary of the guitarist's death, claims Jimi pretended to be gay in order to get discharged from the army.

2006

British gay magazine *Attitude* listed the 'Top 10 Gay Albums' of all time. No. 1 was *Scissor Sisters* – Scissor Sisters, 2, *Arrival* – Abba, 3, *Vauxhall And I* – Morrissey, 4, *Light Years* – Kylie Minogue, 5, *Older* – George Michael, 6, *Welcome To The Pleasuredome* – Frankie Goes to Hollywood, 7, *Erotica* – Madonna, 8, *I Am A Bird Now* – Antony & The Johnsons, 9, *Bad Girls* – Donna Summer and No. 10, *The Man Who Sold the World* – David Bowie.

2009

Procol Harum organist Matthew Fisher wins a legal battle to be recognised as co-writer of the band's 1967 hit 'A Whiter Shade Of Pale'. Law Lords rule that Fisher, who claimed he wrote the song's organ melody, is entitled to a share of future royalties. In 2006, the High Court ruled he was entitled to 40% of the copyright, but the Court Of Appeal overturned the ruling in 2008 saying he waited too long to bring the case to court.

July **31**

1964

Country singer Jim Reeves is killed aged 41 in a plane crash when the single engine aircraft flying him from Arkansas to Nashville crashes in thick fog. Reeves was the first country singer to successfully cross over into the pop market.

1966

The Doors appear at The Fifth Estate, Phoenix, Arizona.

1967

Mick Jagger is given a conditional discharge for possessing two pep pills and Keith Richards' conviction for permitting his house to be used for the purpose of smoking cannabis resin is quashed by the appeal court.

1969

Elvis Presley kicks off a four-week run at the Las Vegas International Hotel, his first live shows since 1961, for which he reportedly nets $1.5m. On the menu is a Presley special: Polk salad with corn muffins and honey.

1971

James Taylor goes to No. 1 on the US singles chart with the Carole King song 'You Got A Friend', which goes on to win the 1971 Grammy Award for Best Pop Vocal Performance, Male. Taylor scores nine other solo US Top 40 hits during the 70s.

1979

AC/DC appear at The Allen County War Memorial Coliseum, Fort Wayne, Indiana on their 'If You Want Blood' Tour.

1980

John Phillips of The Mamas & The Papas is apprehended by FBI narcotics agents for possession of cocaine. Phillips is later sentenced to 250 hours community service, giving anti-drug lectures with his actress daughter Mackenzie.

1992

Michael Jackson makes an unscheduled appearance on his hotel balcony in London after a man threatens to jump from an apartment building across the street. 28-year-old Eric Herminie told police he would leap to his death if he didn't see Jackson, who was in Britain for a series of concerts. Jackson spends a couple of minutes waving to Herminie, who then climbs back into the building.

1999

Christina Aguilera scores her first US No. 1 single with 'Genie In A Bottle', also No. 1 in the UK. The song spent five weeks on top of the US singles chart and won Aguilera the Best New Artist Grammy for the year.

2000

Eighties pop maestro Mike Stock, one third of 80's hit factory Stock, Aitken & Waterman, is declared bankrupt. He had been involved in several court battles over copyright issues.

2001

BBC producer John Walters dies aged 63. Having played trumpet with The Alan Price Set in the 60s, Walters joined the BBC in 1967 and became producer on Radio 1 DJ John Peel's *Top Gear* show two years later, going on to broadcast some of the most groundbreaking music of the era.

2002

Otis Ferry, the son of Roxy Music singer Bryan Ferry, is arrested by armed police outside Prime Minister Tony Blair's home as Ferry tries to stage a demonstration by placing posters supporting animal hunts on the walls of Blair's County Durham house. Ferry had gone through security gates and was arrested when he refused to give his name.

2004

Mark Morrison is arrested after a fracas at Leicester's After Dark night-club in which his platinum and diamond medallion were stolen.

Morrison said he was the victim and complained of wrongful arrest, unlawful imprisonment and police assault. A £20,000 reward for the return of the pendant was offered by the singer's record label.

August

Born on this day:

1942 Jerry Garcia, guitar, vocals (Grateful Dead)

1953 Robert Cray, singer, blues guitarist

1959 Joe Elliott, vocals (Def Leppard)

1964 Adam Duritz, vocals (Counting Crows)

1963
The first issue of *The Beatles Monthly Book* is published. Devoted entirely to the group, whether collectively or as individuals, the magazine continues until December 1969 and at its peak sells over 350,000 copies a month worldwide.

1964
US singer Johnny Burnette is killed aged 30 in a boating accident on Clear Lake, California. He had a 1961 US No. 8 & UK No. 3 single with 'You're Sixteen'.

1965
The Rolling Stones appear at the London Palladium supported by The Walker Brothers, The Fourmost, Steampacket (featuring Long John Baldry, Rod Stewart and Julie Driscoll) and Sugar Pie Desanto with The Shevelles.

1969
The three-day Atlantic City Pop Festival begins, featuring BB King, Janis Joplin, Santana, Joni Mitchell, Three Dog Night, Dr John, Procol Harum, Arthur Brown, Little Richard and Canned Heat.

1980
Def Leppard make their US live debut in New York City, opening for AC/DC. It is also Def Leppard singer Joe Elliott's 21st birthday.

1987
Bob Seger scores his first US No. 1 single with 'Shakedown', taken from the film *Beverly Hills Cop II*.

MTV Europe is launched – the first video played being 'Money For Nothing' by Dire Straits which contains the appropriate line 'I Want My MTV'.

1990
UB40 are deported from the Seychelles after police discover marijuana in their hotel rooms.

2000
Madonna's forthcoming single 'Music' has its release date brought forward by two weeks after the track is made available as an illegal MP3 file on the internet.

2002
A new book, *Show The Girl The Door*, written by a former tour manager, discloses some strange demands by female acts. It reveals that Shania Twain travels with a sniffer dog in case of bombs, Jennifer Lopez likes her dressing room to be all white, including carpets, flowers and furniture, Cher has high security rooms for her wigs, Janet Jackson has a full medical team on standby, including a doctor, nurse and throat specialist, and Britney Spears demands her favourite Gummie Bear soft sweets.

2007
Prince kicks off a series of 21 sold out UK shows at London's O2 Arena. Tickets for the events cost £31.21 – the same figure used by the singer as a name for his album, website and perfume. After completing the 21 nights the Jehovah's Witness was planning to take time out to study the Bible.

Eminem's publishing company is seeking more than $75,000 for copyright infringement and unfair competition against computer firm Apple for allegedly selling his music on iTunes without permission. Apple are paying Eminem's record label for each download – but Eight Mile Style argue it had not approved the deal.

John Lennon's sunglasses are snapped up by a British collector at auction. The sunglasses, from one of the last Beatles concerts, were expected to fetch around £1m, but auction bosses refuse to say what the actual figure is. Lennon gave the gold-rimmed glasses to his Japanese interpreter in Tokyo in 1966, and the translator removed the lenses when Lennon died.

1971
The Concert For Bangladesh, organised by George Harrison to aid victims of famine and war in Bangladesh, takes place at New York's Madison Square Garden. As well as Harrison, performers appearing include Bob Dylan, Ringo Starr, Eric Clapton, Billy Preston, Ravi Shankar and members of Badfinger. Harrison has to shell out his own money to maintain the fund after legal problems froze all proceeds. The triple album release (the second in a row by Harrison) hit No. 1 in the UK and 2 in the US and received a Grammy Award for Album of the Year.

August 2

Born on this day:

1937 Garth Hudson, organ, saxophone (The Band)

1951 Andrew Gold, singer, songwriter

1957 Butch Vig, producer, drummer (Garbage)

1962 Lee Mavers, guitar, vocals (The La's)

1962
Robert Allen Zimmerman legally changes his name to Robert Dylan.

1970
Elvis Presley is at No.1 on the UK singles chart with his version of 'The Wonder Of You', his 16th chart-topper. Ray Peterson recorded the original version in 1959 which gave him a Top 30 hit.

1973
The Mamas & The Papas file a lawsuit against their record label Dunhill for a million dollars in unpaid royalties.

1975
The Eagles are at No. 1 on the *Billboard* singles chart with 'One Of These Nights', the group's second US No. 1 single and the first to chart in the UK where it peaked at No. 23.

1977
Sex Pistol Sid Vicious is fined £125 by a London court after he was found carrying a knife at the 100 Club Punk Festival last September.

1980
The Clash release their single 'Bank Robber' after it was only available as an import. The band's record company CBS didn't want to release the record, claiming it was insufficiently commercial.

1986
Chris de Burgh is top of the UK singles chart with 'The Lady In Red', his first No. 1 after 24 single releases.

1987
David Martin, bass player with Sam The Sham & The Pharaohs, dies aged 50 of a heart attack. Martin co-wrote the group's 1965 US No. 2 & UK No. 11 single 'Wooly Bully'.

1997
Sarah McLachlan enters the US album chart at No. 2 with *Surfacing*, for which the singer-songwriter also won two Grammys.

2000
Jerome Smith from KC & The Sunshine Band dies after being crushed by a bulldozer he was operating.

Liverpool music store Rushworth & Dreaper closes down after 150 years of trading. The store became famous after supplying The Beatles and other Liverpool groups with musical instruments.

2001
New Orleans International Airport is re-named Louis Armstrong Airport in honour of the New Orleans born trumpet player, singer and bandleader.

2004
Eric Clapton buys a 50% share in Cordings to save the historic gentleman's outfitters from closure. The store, based in London since 1839, had run into financial difficulties. The guitarist says he had been fond of the shop since a window display caught his eye when he was 16, and had become a regular customer. Cordings was the originator of the Covert coat and the Tattersall shirt and made riding boots for the Queen Mother, the Duke of Windsor and Mrs. Simpson.

2005
Brandon Flowers from The Killers marries Tana Munblowsky in a private ceremony held in Hawaii.

1983
Motown bass player James Jamerson, who played on nearly 30 No. 1 hits, dies aged 47 in Los Angeles of complications stemming from cirrhosis of the liver, heart failure and pneumonia. As one of The Funk Brothers he was the uncredited bassist on most of Motown Records' hits in the 1960s and early 1970s, including songs by Stevie Wonder, The Temptations, Martha & The Vandellas, Marvin Gaye, The Four Tops and The Supremes.

Born on this day:

1926	Tony Bennett, American singer	**1966**	Shirley Manson, vocals (Garbage)
1951	John Graham, guitar (Earth Wind & Fire)	**1966**	Dean Sams, keyboards (Lonestar)
1963	James Hetfield, guitar, vocals (Metallica)		

August 3

1963

The Beatles play their last ever gig at the Cavern Club in Liverpool. Their fee for their first appearance at the Cavern was £5, but they receive £300 for this final performance.

The Beach Boys release 'Surfer Girl', the first song Brian Wilson ever wrote and the first one he produced.

1967

The Jimi Hendrix Experience play the first of five nights at the Salvation Club in New York City.

1968

The Doors start a two-week run at No. 1 on the US singles chart with 'Hello I Love You', the group's second American chart-topper.

1971

Paul McCartney announces the formation of his new group Wings featuring wife Linda and former Moody Blues guitarist and singer, Denny Laine.

1985

'Drive' by The Cars is re-released following its dramatic use on TV during the Live Aid concert coverage. All royalties from the record go to the Band Aid trust.

Madonna scores her first UK No. 1 single with 'Into The Groove', taken from the movie *Desperately Seeking Susan* which stars Madonna and Rosanna Arquette. 'Into The Groove' remains Madonna's best selling single in the UK, having sold over 850,000 copies.

Tears For Fears start a three week run on top of the American singles chart with 'Shout', the duo's second US No. 1.

1986

The News Of The World prints an exclusive interview with 16-year-old model Mandy Smith, who reveals she has been having an affair with Rolling Stone Bill Wyman, now aged 49, for the past two and a half years.

1991

Metallica hold a playback party to launch their self-titled album at Madison Square Garden in New York City. Kurt Cobain and Chris Novoselic from Nirvana both attend.

1996

Los Del Rio start a 14-week run at No. 1 on the *Billboard* singles chart with 'Macarena', a No. 2 hit in the UK.

2000

Maurice Kinn, the UK publisher who launched *New Musical Express* in 1953, instigated the first charts based on record sales, and organised the annual *NME* poll winners concerts, dies aged 76.

2006

Arthur Lee, singer and guitarist of the influential 1960s band Love, dies aged 61 in Memphis following a battle with acute myeloid leukaemia.

2007

Brian May hands in his astronomy PhD thesis – 36 years after abandoning it to join Queen. May had recently carried out observational work in Tenerife, where he studied the formation of "zodiacal dust clouds".

2008

Kid Rock is at No. 1 on the UK singles chart with 'All Summer Long'. The song is based on Warren Zevon's 'Werewolves Of London' and Lynyrd Skynyrd's 'Sweet Home Alabama'.

Born on this day:

1901 Louis Armstrong, singer, bandleader, trumpeter
1936 Elsberry Hobbs, singer (The Drifters)
1947 Klaus Schulze, synthesizer (Tangerine Dream)
1947 Paul Layton, singer (The New Seekers)
1952 Marie Ni Bhraonain, singer, songwriter (Clannad)

1962
The Rolling Stones play the first of 22 weekly shows at Ealing Jazz Club in West London. They are known as The Rollin' Stones during this early period.

1963
UK music weekly *NME* reports that The Beatles could score their first US hit with 'From Me To You' as the single was 'bubbling under' on the charts at No. 116.

1966
The Troggs reach No. 1 on the British singles chart with 'With A Girl Like You', the group's only UK No. 1 single. Simultaneously, The Troggs are top of the US singles chart with 'Wild Thing'.

1967
A female Monkees fan stows away on the band's plane between shows in Minneapolis and St. Louis. The girl's father threatens to bring charges for transporting a minor across state lines.

1968
The two-day Newport Pop Festival in California begins, featuring Canned Heat, Sonny & Cher, Steppenwolf, The Byrds, The Grateful Dead, Tiny Tim, Iron Butterfly and Jefferson Airplane. Over 100,000 fans attend the festival.

1980
John Lennon begins recording what will become his final album, *Double Fantasy*, at The Hit Factory, New York.

1984
Prince starts a 24-week run at the top of the US album charts with *Purple Rain*, which goes on to sell over 10 million copies.

1990
During a New Kids On The Block concert in Montreal, Canada, three armed robbers steal merchandise sales proceeds of $260,000.

1996
Oasis play the first of two sold out nights at Balloch Castle Country Park, Loch Lomand, Scotland to over 80,000 fans. The concerts are marred by the death of roadie James Hunter, who was crushed between a fork-lift truck and a lorry during the shows.

2000
Craig David scores his second UK No. 1 single with '7 Days'. At the age of 19, he becomes the youngest male artist to score two chart-toppers since Donny Osmond in 1973.

2001
Dave Stewart marries fashion photographer Anouska Fisz on a private beach on the French Riviera. Guests include Elton John, Mick Jagger, Oasis brothers Liam and Noel Gallagher and Stewart's former Eurythmics partner Annie Lennox.

Mariah Carey hires a private eye to spy on her ex-husband, Sony Records boss Tommy Mottola. Investigator Jack Palladino tells the press that Mariah believes her ex-husband is conducting a smear campaign against the singer.

2007
US singer-songwriter Lee Hazlewood dies aged 78 of cancer in his home near Las Vegas. Hazlewood wrote and produced many of Nancy Sinatra's most well-known hits, including 'These Boots Are Made For Walkin'', 'Jackson' and 'Did You Ever?' He also produced Duane Eddy and Gram Parsons and 'Something Stupid', the duet Nancy recorded with her father Frank in 1967.

1979
A benefit concert is held at the Los Angeles Forum for Little Feat guitarist and singer Lowell George, featuring members of his band plus Jackson Browne, Linda Ronstadt, Emmylou Harris and Bonnie Raitt.

Born on this day:

1942 Rick Huxley, guitar (Dave Clark Five)
1946 Jimmy Webb, US singer, songwriter
1959 Pete Burns, vocals (Mystery Girls, Dead Or Alive)

1960 Stuart Croxford-Neale, keyboards (Kajagoogoo)

August 5

1957
American Bandstand is broadcast for the first time on US TV. Dick Clark had replaced Bob Horn the previous year when the show was still called *Bandstand*. Clark went on to host the show until its final season in 1989.

1965
Jan Berry of Jan & Dean is accidentally knocked off a camera car and breaks his leg on the first day of filming a movie called *Easy Come, Easy Go*. Several other people are also hurt, causing Paramount to cancel the movie entirely. The film is resuscitated by the company in 1967 as an Elvis Presley film.

1966
The Beatles' seventh album *Revolver* is released in the UK, reaching No. 1. When released in the US three days later the LP also peaked at pole position, spending 77 weeks on the *Billboard* chart.

1968
American country guitarist Luther Perkins, who worked with Johnny Cash and The Carter Family and featured on the live album *Johnny Cash At Folsom Prison*, dies at the age of 40 as a result of severe burns and smoke inhalation. Perkins fell asleep at home in his den with a cigarette in his hand. He was dragged from the fire unconscious with severe second and third degree burns but he never regained consciousness.

1969
George Harrison has his new Moog synthesizer brought from his home into EMI Studios for The Beatles to use in finishing their forthcoming album *Abbey Road*.

1972
Aerosmith sign to CBS Records for $125,000 after record company boss Clive Davis sees them play at Max's Kansas City in New York.

1975
Led Zeppelin singer Robert Plant and his wife Maureen are badly injured in a car crash while on holiday in Rhodes.

1979
Def Leppard sign to Phonogram Records with an advance of £120,000, giving them a 10% royalty on 100% of sales for the first two years.

1983
David Crosby is sentenced to five years in jail in Texas for drug and firearms offences. Crosby had slept through most of his trial.

1986
Culture Club keyboard player Michael Rudetsky is found dead at Boy George's London home in Hampstead.

1992
Jeff Porcaro, drummer from Toto, dies age 38. His death has been the subject of controversy: some say the attack was caused by an allergic reaction to garden pesticide, while others say Porcaro's heart was weakened by smoking and cocaine use. As a session drummer Porcaro worked with many acts including Sonny & Cher, Roger Waters, Eric Clapton, Paul McCartney, Steely Dan, Paul Simon and Boz Scaggs.

1995
Take That play the first of ten sold out nights at The Nynex Arena,

Manchester – their first shows without Robbie Williams who had quit the group on July 17.

2005
Bob Dylan's 'Like A Rolling Stone' tops a poll of rock and film stars to find the music, movies, TV shows and books that changed the world. The 1965 single beat Elvis Presley's 'Heartbreak Hotel' into second place in a survey for *Uncut* magazine. Paul McCartney, Noel Gallagher, Robert Downey Jr, Keith Richards and Lou Reed are among those who give their opinions.

2007
Beatles fans fear the misuse of the Fab Four's music has hit rock bottom following the decision to license 'All You Need Is Love' for use in a nappy advert. Procter & Gamble had purchased the rights to use the song from Sony/ATV Music Publishing, which now owns Northern Songs. The ad featured a baby jumping on a teddy bear in a disposable nappy which offered "ultimate leak protection".

2008
American singer-songwriter Robert Hazard, who wrote Cyndi Lauper's 'Girls Just Wanna Have Fun' and fronted Robert Hazard & The Heroes in the 80s, dies after surgery for pancreatic cancer.

2009
Mark McLeod, a 53-year-old who claims he is secretly engaged to Miley Cyrus, is arrested and charged with stalking the US singer after trying to contact the *Hannah Montana* actress on a film set near Savannah, Georgia. McLeod claims he had met Cyrus 18 months earlier and that she had accepted his marriage proposal. He tells police that Cyrus' father, country singer Billy Ray Cyrus, approved of their relationship and that Cyrus had sent him "secret messages" through her TV show.

August 6

Born on this day:

1929 Mike Elliot, tenor sax (The Foundations)

1938 Isaac Hayes, singer

1969 Elliot Smith, US singer-songwriter

1972 Geri Halliwell, vocals (The Spice Girls)

1960
Chubby Checker appears on US TV show *American Bandstand,* performing 'The Twist'. The song went to No. 1 on the US chart and again 18 months later in 1962 – the only song to go to the top of the American charts on two separate occasions.

1965
Decca in the UK release The Small Faces' debut single, 'Whatcha Gonna Do About It'.

1969
During a North American tour, Led Zeppelin appear at the Memorial Auditorium, Sacramento, California.

1970
The 10th National Jazz, Blues and Pop four day Festival begins at Plumpton Racecourse in Sussex, England. The weekend bill features Family, The Groundhogs, Cat Stevens, Deep Purple, Fat Mattress, Yes, Caravan, The Strawbs, Black Sabbath, The Wild Angels, Wishbone Ash and Daddy Longlegs.

1973
Stevie Wonder is seriously injured when the car he is riding in crashes into a truck on I-85 near Winston-Salem, North Carolina leaving him in a coma for four days. The accident also leaves him without any sense of smell.

1977
The Police appear at The Red Cow pub, Hammersmith, London. Admission is 60p.

1981
Stevie Nicks releases her first solo album *Bella Donna* which contains four Top 40 US hits: 'Stop Draggin' My Heart Around' (with Tom Petty), 'Leather And Lace' (with Don Henley), 'Edge Of Seventeen' and 'After The Glitter Fades'.

1988
Guns N' Roses debut album *Appetite For Destruction* goes to No. 1 in the US, after spending 57 weeks on the chart and selling over five million copies. The singles from the album – 'Sweet Child O' Mine', 'Welcome To The Jungle' and 'Paradise City' – are all US Top 10 hits.

1989
Adam Clayton of U2 is arrested at The Blue Light Inn car park in Dublin for marijuana possession and intent to supply the drug to another person. His conviction is waived in exchange for paying £25,000 to the Dublin Woman's Aid Centre.

1994
Lisa Loeb starts a three-week run at No. 1 on the US singles chart with 'Stay (I Missed You)', a No. 6 hit in the UK. The song is featured in the film *Reality Bites* after Loeb's friend, actor Ethan Hawke, asked her to provide a song for the movie.

2001
Whitney Houston becomes one of the highest-paid artists in the world after signing a new deal with Arista Records, said to be worth more than $100m.

2004
Rick James, known as 'The King of Punk-Funk', who scored a 1981 US No. 3 album *Street Songs* and No. 16 single 'Super Freak Part 1', is found dead, aged 56, at his Los Angeles home. In the late 60s James worked with a Toronto band, The Mynah Birds, featuring Neil Young, who recorded an unreleased album for Motown. James also worked as a songwriter and producer for Motown. Addicted to cocaine, he once admitted to spending $7,000 a week on drugs for five years.

2007
Marilyn Manson is being sued by a former band member who says he is owed $20m in shared profits. Stephen Bier, who played keyboards under the stage name Madonna Wayne Gacy, claims he was not paid properly over a period of almost two decades. In legal papers filed in Los Angeles, Bier claims Manson falsely told him the band was not making much money yet managed to buy a $2m home and collect Nazi memorabilia, including coat hangers used by Adolf Hitler.

August 7

1954

Elvis Presley appears at The Eagles Nest in Memphis, Tennessee (the first of 12 shows at the venue during this year). The advertisement in the local paper reads: See and hear Elvis singing 'That's All Right' and 'The Blue Moon Of Kentucky'.

1957

The Quarry Men play at The Cavern Club in Liverpool (without Paul McCartney who is away at Boy Scout summer camp). The Cavern is still a jazz club, but skiffle is tolerated. However, when John Lennon dared to play 'Hound Dog' and 'Blue Suede Shoes', the club owner sends a note to the stage saying, "Cut out the bloody rock!"

1964

The first night of the fourth Richmond Jazz Festival is held over three days in Richmond, England. The Rolling Stones, Manfred Mann, The Yardbirds, Ronnie Scott, Tubby Hayes and Mose Allison are among the artists appearing.

1970

The first day of the Goose Lake International Music Festival, which is held over three days in Leoni, Michigan, and attended by over 200,000. Acts appearing include Jethro Tull, Ten Years After, Mountain, Chicago, Bob Seger, John Sebastian, The James Gang, The Stooges, Brownsville Station, MC5, The Faces and The Flying Burrito Brothers.

1982

Dexy's Midnight Runners score their second and last UK No. 1 with 'Come On Eileen', which becomes the best selling single of 1982 and wins Best British Single at the 1983 Brit Awards.

1984

American soul singer Esther Phillips dies aged 48 from liver and kidney failure in Carson, California.

1997

Garth Brooks plays to the largest ever crowd at a concert in New York's Central Park. An estimated one million people attend with an additional 14.6 million viewing live on HBO.

2002

Three members of Oasis are injured when the taxi they are travelling in is involved in a crash during a US tour in Indianapolis. Noel Gallagher, Andy Bell and Jay Darlington are taken to hospital and treated for cuts and bruises.

2003

The Osmonds receive a star on the Hollywood Walk of Fame.

2007

Pete Doherty is warned by a judge that he could face jail or a community order over drugs offences. In July, the 28-year-old Babyshambles frontman pleaded guilty to driving illegally while in possession of crack cocaine, heroin, ketamine and cannabis. The judge says, "What I have in mind is a community order or prison... if he does not show his motivation, it's prison – it's as simple as that." The singer volunteers to show the position of an implant in his stomach designed to help him give up drugs.

2008

Elvis Presley's peacock jumpsuit fetches $300,000, making it the most expensive piece of Elvis memorabilia ever sold at an auction. The white outfit with a plunging V-neck and high collar featured a blue-and-gold peacock design, hand-embroidered on the front and back and along the pant legs.

2009

Willy DeVille dies aged 58 following a battle with pancreatic cancer. His band, Mink Deville, who appeared at CBGBs in New York in the 70s, scored a 1977 UK Top 20 hit with 'Spanish Stroll'. Doctors discovered he had cancer earlier this year as he was preparing to undergo treatment for hepatitis C.

August 8

Born on this day:

1927 Andy Warhol, pop artist, producer
1950 Andy Fairweather-Low, guitar, singer, songwriter (Amen Corner, solo)

1961 The Edge (real name: Dave Evans), guitar, vocals (U2)
1973 Scott Stapp, singer, songwriter (Creed)

1960
Decca Records scrap 25,000 copies of Ray Peterson's 'Tell Laura I Love Her' because they feel the song, which recounts the last thoughts of a teenager dying from a car accident, was "too tasteless and vulgar". A cover version by Ricky Valance went to No. 1 on the UK charts a month later.

1966
In response to John Lennon's misquoted remark about The Beatles being bigger than Jesus, the South African Broadcasting Corporation announce a ban on playing all Beatles records.

1969
The photo session for the cover of The Beatles' *Abbey Road* album takes place on the Abbey Road pedestrian crossing near EMI Studios. Balanced on a step-ladder in the middle of the road, photographer Iain McMillan takes six shots of John, Ringo, Paul, and George walking across the zebra crossing while a policeman holds up waiting traffic.

1970
Janis Joplin buys a headstone for the grave of her greatest influence, Bessie Smith (below), at the Mont Lawn Cemetery in Philadelphia. Blues singer Smith died in 1937 after being refused admission to a 'whites only' hospital.

1971
Tim Buckley and Tom Waits both appear at the In The Alley club, San Diego, California.

1980
The GLC (Greater London Council) ban The Plasmatics from blowing up a car on stage during their UK live debut at London's Hammersmith Odeon.

1986
David Crosby is released from prison after serving three years for drug and weapons possession. His conviction would be overturned by a Texas appeals court in November 1987.

1991
On A Friday (later to become known as Radiohead) appear at The Jericho Tavern, Oxford, England. The band had met while attending Abingdon School, a boys-only public school. 'On A Friday' referred to the band's usual rehearsal day in the school's music room.

1992
A riot breaks out during a Guns N' Roses and Metallica gig at Montreal Stadium when Metallica's show is cut short after singer James Hetfield is injured by pyrotechnics. Guns N' Roses then take the stage but frontman Axl Rose claims that his throat hurt, causing the band to leave the stage early. The cancellation led to a riot by the audience who overturn cars, smash windows, loot local stores and start fires.

1996
Kiss appear at the Riverfront Coliseum, Cincinnati, Ohio on their 192-date 'Alive' World Tour. During the show a fan throws his prosthetic leg on stage, which all the members sign and pass back to him.

1987
U2 score their second US No. 1 single from their *Joshua Tree* album with 'I Still Haven't Found What I'm Looking For'.

2002
The UK's biggest undertakers Co-Op Funeral Services report that bereaved families prefer pop songs to hymns at funerals. Top of the list is 'Wind Beneath My Wings' by Bette Midler. Other songs include 'Angels' by Robbie Williams and 'My Heart Will Go On' by Celine Dion. The company also report some unusual choices, including Queen's 'Another One Bites The Dust' and 'Wake Me Up Before You Go-Go' by Wham!

Born on this day:

1946 Marinus Gerritsen, bass (Golden Earring)

1954 Bruce Thomas, bass (Quiver, Elvis Costello & The Attractions)

1955 Benjamin Orr, bass, vocals (The Cars)

1963 Whitney Houston, US singer

1963

The first ever edition of UK TV's most influential pop show, *Ready, Steady, Go!* is shown. Introduced by Keith Fordyce, this pilot show features Billy Fury and Brian Poole & The Tremeloes. Originally 30 minutes long, it expands to 50 minutes the following year and soon attracts the most popular artists, including The Beatles, The Rolling Stones, Dusty Springfield, Donovan, The Who and many others. The final show was in December 1966.

1967

Scott McKenzie is at No. 1 on the UK singles chart with 'San Francisco (Be Sure To Wear Some Flowers In Your Hair)', his only UK Top 40 hit, written by John Phillips of The Mamas & The Papas.

The Small Faces enter the singles chart with 'Itchycoo Park'. The single peaks at No. 3 in the UK chart.

1969

During a North American tour Led Zeppelin appear at the Anaheim Convention Center in California. Support act, Jethro Tull, are currently at No. 1 on the UK album chart with their second LP, *Stand Up*.

1975

The Bee Gees start a two-week run at the top of the *Billboard* singles chart with 'Jive Talkin', the group's second US No. 1.

1980

Abba score their eighth UK No. 1 with 'The Winner Takes It All', taken from the *Super Trouper* album. By this time, both couples in the group are divorced.

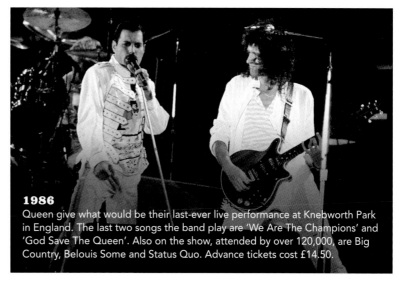

1986

Queen give what would be their last-ever live performance at Knebworth Park in England. The last two songs the band play are 'We Are The Champions' and 'God Save The Queen'. Also on the show, attended by over 120,000, are Big Country, Belouis Some and Status Quo. Advance tickets cost £14.50.

1994

During an Oasis gig at The Riverside in Newcastle-upon-Tyne, England, Noel Gallagher is hit in the face by a man who jumps on stage. The guitarist refuses to carry on playing and after leaving the stage a mob of over 300 people attack the band's bus as they are leaving.

1995

Jerry Garcia, guitarist and singer from Grateful Dead, dies aged 53 from a heart attack at the Serenity Knolls rehabilitation clinic in San Francisco.

2005

The Magic Numbers walk out of an appearance on UK music show *Top Of The Pops* in protest at the "derogatory, unfunny remarks" of presenter Richard Bacon, who said the band had been put in a "fat melting pot of talent".

2007

Amy Winehouse cancels a series of European shows after being admitted to hospital suffering from "severe exhaustion". The 23-year-old singer is taken to London's University College Hospital and later discharged. Over the past few weeks she has pulled out of Glasgow's T In The Park festival, Liverpool's Summer Pops event and concerts in Norway and Denmark for the same reason.

Jennifer Lopez wins $545,000 in a case against her first husband, who planned to publish a book claiming she had several affairs. Lopez claims Ojani Noa had violated a previous legal settlement preventing him from revealing private details about their relationship. The star claims Noa offered not to publish the book in return for $5 million.

August 10

Born on this day:

1909 Leo Fender, inventor of the Telecaster and Stratocaster guitars
1940 Bobby Hatfield, singer (The Righteous Brothers)
1947 Ian Anderson, flute, vocals (Jethro Tull)
1947 Ronnie Spector, singer (The Ronettes, solo)
1961 Jon Farriss, drums (INXS)

1959
Four members of The Platters are arrested following a gig in Cincinnati after being found with four 19-year-old women (three of them white) in various stages of undress. The scandal results in radio stations across America removing Platters records from their playlists.

1963
13-year-old Little Stevie Wonder starts a three week run at No. 1 on the US singles chart with 'Fingertips Part 2', making him the youngest singer to top the charts.

1964
Mick Jagger is fined £32 in Liverpool for driving without insurance and breaking the speed limit. His solicitor explains that Jagger was on "an errand of mercy", driving to see two fans injured in a car crash.

1968
Deep Purple, Tyrannosaurus Rex, Ten Years After, The Nice, Ginger Baker and Arthur Brown all appear at the National Jazz & Blues Festival, Kempton Park Racecourse, Sunbury-on-Thames, England.

1970
Simon & Garfunkel's album *Bridge Over Troubled Water* is at No. 1 on the UK album chart, The Beatles are second with *Let It Be* and Bob Dylan is third with *Self Portrait*.

1976
Elton John plays the first of seven sold-out nights at Madison Square Garden in New York City. The $1.25 million generated from the shows break the record set by The Rolling Stones the year before.

1985
Simon Le Bon from Duran Duran is air lifted to safety when his boat 'Drum' overturns while racing off the English coast. Le Bon was trapped under the hull with five other crew members for 20 minutes, until being rescued by the Royal Navy.

1992
Def Leppard kick off the North American leg of their 248-date 'Seven Day Weekend' World Tour at Madison Square Garden in New York City.

1993
A gig by The Dave Matthews Band at The Flood Zone in Richmond, Virginia is recorded, with some of the songs ending up on the band's first album, *Remember Two Things*.

1999
It is announced that Oasis rhythm guitarist Paul 'Bonehead' Arthurs has quit the band after finishing his guitar parts on their new album.

2002
Lisa Marie Presley marries actor Nicolas Cage in Hawaii. The marriage is Presley's third.

2007
Anthony Wilson, the UK music mogul behind some of Manchester's most successful bands, dies aged 57 after suffering from kidney cancer. The TV presenter and entrepreneur founded Factory Records – the label that signed Joy Division, New Order and Happy Mondays – and was also famous for setting up The Hacienda nightclub in Manchester.

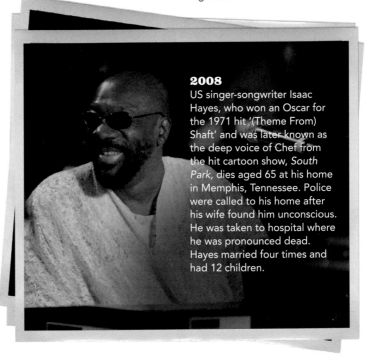

2008
US singer-songwriter Isaac Hayes, who won an Oscar for the 1971 hit '(Theme From) Shaft' and was later known as the deep voice of Chef from the hit cartoon show, *South Park*, dies aged 65 at his home in Memphis, Tennessee. Police were called to his home after his wife found him unconscious. He was taken to hospital where he was pronounced dead. Hayes married four times and had 12 children.

August 11

1964

The Beatles start recording their fourth album (*Beatles For Sale*, not yet titled), at EMI studios in London, England.

1966

At a press conference held on the 27th floor of The Astor Towers Hotel in Chicago, John Lennon is forced to apologise for his misquoted remarks that The Beatles were "more popular than Jesus". Lennon told reporters, "I wasn't saying The Beatles are better than God or Jesus, I said 'Beatles' because it's easy for me to talk about The Beatles. I could have said TV or cinema, motorcars or anything popular and would have got away with it..."

1967

The first day of the weekend Windsor Jazz & Blues Festival. The event features The Small Faces, The Move, The Marmalade, Paul Jones, Pink Floyd, Amen Corner, Donovan, Zoot Money, Cream, Jeff Beck, John Mayall, Peter Green's Fleetwood Mac and The Crazy World Of Arthur Brown. An advance ticket costs £2. During his set, Arthur Brown's trademark flaming helmet burns out of control so organiser Harold Pendleton's father-in-law has to douse the flames with a pint of beer.

1969

350 special guests are invited to see Motown Records new signings The Jackson 5 play at The Daisy Club in Beverly Hills, California.

1979

Led Zeppelin play their last ever UK show at Knebworth Park, England. Also on the bill are The New Barbarians (featuring Ron Wood and Keith Richards), Todd Rundgren, Southside Johnny & The Asbury Dukes, Chas & Dave and Fairport Convention.

1982

The Police appear at the McGill Stadium, Montreal, Quebec, Canada on their 'Ghost In The Machine' Tour.

1984

Ray Parker Jr. starts a three-week run at No. 1 on the US singles chart with the theme from the film *Ghostbusters*. Parker, who had been a session guitarist for Stevie Wonder and Marvin Gaye, was accused of plagiarising the melody from Huey Lewis & The News' song 'I Want A New Drug', resulting in Lewis suing Parker. The pair settled out of court in 1985.

1989

Three members of L.L. Cool J's crew are arrested and charged with raping a 15-year-old girl. The incident took place after a concert when the girl had won a backstage pass on a radio contest.

1999

Kiss arrive on Hollywood Boulevard to unveil their star on the Walk Of Fame. The band had released over 30 albums and sold over 80 million records worldwide.

2000

Madonna gives birth to a baby boy, Rocco Ritchie, at The Cedars-Sinai Hospital, Beverly Hills.

2001

Black Sabbath, Linkin Park, Slipknot and Marilyn Manson all appear at the Ozzfest at PNC Bank Arts Centre, New Jersey.

2002

Bruce Springsteen starts a two week run on top of the *Billboard* album chart with 'The Rising', the singer's fifth US No. 1.

2008

Karl Wiosna from Graig, near Pontypridd in Wales has his stereo equipment and music collection destroyed after being served with a noise abatement notice, which he later admitted breaching. Environmental health officers were alerted by neighbours who complained about the unacceptable volume Wiosna was playing his Cher and U2 records. Two tape and record decks, a radio and CDs were seized and destroyed by the council. Wiosna was also fined £265.

August 12

Born on this day:

1949 Mark Knopfler, guitar, vocals, songwriter (Dire Straits, solo)

1950 Ronald David Mael, keyboards (Sparks)

1961 Roy Hay, guitar, vocals (Culture Club)

1968 Paul Tucker, keyboards (Lighthouse Family)

1966
The Beatles perform two shows at the International Amphitheatre in Chicago, Illinois – the first stop on what would turn out to be the group's final US tour. Support acts are The Remains, Bobby Hebb, The Cyrkle and The Ronettes.

1967
The Jimi Hendrix Experience appear at The Ambassador Theatre, Washington DC.

1968
Jimmy Page, John Paul Jones, Robert Plant and John Bonham play together for the first time, rehearsing at a studio in Lisle Street in London's West End. The first song they play is a version of Johnny Burnette's 'The Train Kept A-Rollin'.

1971
John & Yoko donate £1,000 to the Clyde Shipbuilders Scottish Union fighting fund who are refusing to stop work at the Glasgow site after being made redundant.

1972
Alice Cooper is at No. 1 on the UK singles chart with 'School's Out'.

1973
The Eagles, Joni Mitchell and Neil Young & The Santa Monica Flyers all appear at The Corral Club in Topanga, California.

1977
Henri Padovani, guitarist with The Police, quits the group after nine months, leaving them as a trio.

1978
The Commodores start a two week run at No. 1 on the US singles chart with 'Three Times A Lady', also a chart-topper in the UK. It becomes Motown's biggest British selling single. Lionel Richie wrote the song about his love for his wife, mother and grandmother hence "Once, twice, three times a lady."

1985
Kyu Sakamoto is killed aged 43 in a plane crash when JAL Flight 123 – a 747 – crashes and burns on a thickly wooded mountain about 60 miles northwest of Tokyo. Sakamoto had a 1963 US No. 1 & UK No. 6 single with 'Sukiyaki', the first Japanese artist to hit the top of the US singles chart.

1989
A two-day Moscow Music Peace Festival is held at The Lenin Stadium in Moscow, Russia. Western acts who appear include Mötley Crüe, Ozzy Osbourne, Bon Jovi, Skid Row and The Scorpions. This is the first time that an audience has been allowed to stand up and dance at a stadium rock concert in the Soviet Union. Previous to this, all concerts had to be seated.

1996
The Spice Girls are at No. 1 on the UK singles chart with 'Wannabe', while Los Del Rio are top of the US singles chart with 'Macarena'.

Alanis Morissette appears at the Darien Lake Performing Arts Center, Buffalo, New York, with Radiohead as support.

2000
During an outdoor gig in Mancos, California, as 38.Special are mid-set, the wind takes hold of an overhead canopy and brings down ten tons of equipment onto the stage. The drum kit is completely crushed but no one is seriously injured.

2006
LeToya is at No. 1 on the US album chart with her solo debut *LeToya*, released six years after her dismissal from Destiny's Child.

2009
Guitarist Les Paul dies aged 94 from severe pneumonia in hospital at White Plains, New York. Paul contributed to the birth of rock by developing one of the first solid-body electric guitars, which went on sale in 1952, and also other influential recording innovations such as multi-track recording and overdubbing. The Gibson 'Les Paul' guitar is favoured by many top players. In the early 50s, Paul and his wife Mary Ford had a string of hits including 'Mockin' Bird Hill', 'How High The Moon' and 'Vaya Con Dios'.

Born on this day:

1951   Dan Fogelberg, US singer-
        songwriter
1958   Feargal Sharkey, singer (The
        Undertones, solo)

1959   Danny Bonaduce, vocals, actor (The
        Partridge Family)
1982   LeAnn Rimes, US singer

August 13

1964

The Supremes record 'Baby Love', which becomes the group's first UK No. 1 and second US chart-topper.

1966

In the UK, The Beatles' *Revolver* starts a seven-week run at No. 1, spending a total of 34 weeks on the UK chart.

1967

Peter Green's Fleetwood Mac make their live debut when appearing at the National Jazz and Blues Festival in Windsor.

1971

King Curtis is stabbed to death by a vagrant on the front steps of his New York home. The saxophonist, whose distinctive work can be heard on such Coasters hits as 'Yakety Yak' and 'Charlie Brown', had recently worked with John Lennon on his *Imagine* album.

John Lennon flies from Heathrow Airport to New York in a continuation of his and wife Yoko's custody battle for Yoko's eight-year-old daughter, Kyoko. Lennon never set foot on British soil again.

1980

Four masked robbers break in to Todd Rundgren's New York house and steal hi-fi equipment and paintings after tying the musician up. It is reported that one of the intruders had been humming Rundgren's hit 'I Saw The Light'.

1982

American soul singer Joe Tex dies aged 49 at his home in Navasota, Texas, following a heart attack.

1992

Neil Diamond plays the first of six sold-out nights at New York's Madison Square Garden. Diamond brings in over $40 million from touring this year – the second highest in the music industry.

1994

Members of Oasis and The Verve are arrested after smashing up a hotel bar and breaking into a church to steal communion wine. Both bands were appearing at the Hulsfred Festival in Sweden.

Woodstock '94, featuring Green Day, Nine Inch Nails, Aerosmith and Red Hot Chili Peppers, is held in Saugerties, New York. Over 350,000 fans attend and tickets cost $135.00.

1999

Slash is arrested by Los Angeles County sheriff's deputies and released on bail. The ex-Guns N' Roses guitarist is accused of assaulting his girlfriend at his Sunset Boulevard recording studio.

Mick Jagger's marriage to model Jerry Hall is declared null and void at the London High Court. Neither Jagger nor Hall are present for the 30-minute hearing before Mr. Justice Connell.

After hearing evidence on behalf of 43-year-old Hall the judge rules their 1990 marriage in Bali was not valid either in Indonesia or under English law and a decree of nullity is granted to Hall. The annulment avoids what had been expected to be a long and costly court battle, in which Hall was reportedly seeking a £30m share of Jagger's wealth.

2000

Melanie C goes to No. 1 on the UK singles chart with 'I Turn To You'. It gives the former Spice Girl her second UK No. 1.

2004

'Angels' by Robbie Williams is voted the Best Single Which Should Have Been A Number One But Never Was in a poll for music channel VH1. The ballad, which reached No. 4 in December 1997, beat Savage Garden's 'Truly, Madly, Deeply' and Aerosmith's 'I Don't Want To Miss A Thing'. Other songs said to have deserved a top placing include Madonna with 'Ray Of Light', 'Beautiful Stranger', 'Crazy For You' and 'Material Girl', Bon Jovi with 'Always' and Oasis with 'Wonderwall' and 'Live Forever'. Cliff Richard's hit 'Millennium Prayer' was voted the worst No. 1 single of all time.

Born on this day:

1941 David Crosby (The Byrds, Crosby, Stills, Nash & Young, solo)

1946 Larry Graham, bass guitar (Sly & The Family Stone)

1965 Mark Collins, guitar (The Charlatans)

1966 Tanya Donelly, singer, guitarist (Throwing Muses, Belly)

1958

Elvis Presley's mother, Gladys, dies. At her funeral two days later Presley is so overcome with grief he is unable to stand and has to be supported. Over 500 police are at the service to keep the gigantic crowd at bay.

1962

Unhappy with drummer Pete Best's role in The Beatles, the other three members decide to sack him. Ringo Starr, who was nearing the end of a three-month engagement with Rory Storm & The Hurricanes at a Butlin's holiday camp in Skegness, receives a telephone call from John Lennon, asking him to join The Beatles.

1965

Sonny & Cher start a three-week run at No. 1 on the US singles chart with 'I Got You Babe'.

1970

Stephen Stills is arrested and later freed on bail on suspected drugs charges while staying at a San Diego hotel after being found crawling along a corridor in an incoherent state.

The first day of the three-day Folk, Blues & Jazz Festival at Krumlin, Yorkshire, featuring Atomic Rooster, The Kinks, Elton John, Mungo Jerry, Alan Price, Georgie Fame, Juicy Lucy, The Pretty Things and The Groundhogs. Weekend tickets are £3. The Who were originally advertised as appearing but due to the exclusive nature of their contract with the organisers of that year's Isle of Wight Festival are unable to do so.

1976

Funded by a £400 loan from Dr. Feelgood singer Lee Brilleaux, 'So It Goes' by Nick Lowe becomes the first record released on Stiff Records. Lowe plays all the instruments on the single which cost £45 to record.

1985

Michael Jackson outbids Paul McCartney and Yoko Ono to secure the ATV Music Publishing catalogue. At $47.5m Jackson gains the rights to more than 250 songs written by John Lennon and Paul McCartney.

1988

US guitarist Roy Buchanan dies aged 48 after hanging himself by his own shirt in Fairfax County Jail, Virginia after being arrested for drunkenness. Buchanan released over 15 solo albums and Jeff Beck dedicated his version of the Stevie Wonder song 'Cause We've Ended As Lovers' to Buchanan on his 1975 *Blow By Blow* album.

1993

Freddie Mercury has his first solo (posthumous) UK No. 1 single with a remixed version of 'Living On My Own'. The song had originally been a minor hit in 1985 when released from Mercury's solo album *Mr. Bad Guy*.

2002

Dave Williams, original lead singer of American heavy rock band Drowning Pool, is found dead aged 30 on the band's tour bus during Ozzy Osbourne's Ozzfest tour in Manassas, Virginia. The autopsy concludes that he suffered from a form of heart disease. The band's debut album, *Sinner*, had sold over one million copies in the US since its release in June 2001.

2003

One True Voice, a boy band formed alongside Girls Aloud from the ITV pop talent show *Popstars: The Rivals*, split up. One True Voice are later voted Britain's Worst Group in a poll just a day after their tour was cancelled due to poor ticket sales.

2006

Boy George is seen sweeping streets in New York as part of a five-day community service sentence. The former Culture Club frontman is moved into a fenced-off area after only 30 minutes when he is mobbed by the media. The 45-year-old singer was found guilty of wasting police time earlier this year and was threatened with jail if he failed to complete the court-imposed sentence.

Born on this day:

1933 Bill Pinkney, vocals (The Drifters)
1942 Pete York, drums (The Spencer Davis Group, Hardin-York)
1950 Tommy Aldridge, drums (Whitesnake)

1967 Adam Yauch, vocals (The Beastie Boys)

August 15

1965
The Beatles set a new world record for the largest attendance at a pop concert when they play in front of 55,600 fans at Shea Stadium in New York City, grossing $304,000.

1969
During a North American tour Led Zeppelin appear at the Hemisfair Arena in San Antonio, Texas. Jethro Tull and Sweet Smoke are also on the bill. During the show Zeppelin receive abuse from locals due to the length of their hair.

The first day of the three-day Woodstock Music and Art Fair, held on Max Yasgur's 600 acre farm in Bethel outside New York. Attended by over 400,000 people, the free event features Jimi Hendrix, Joe Cocker, Crosby Stills Nash & Young, Santana, The Who, Creedence Clearwater Revival, Grateful Dead, Janis Joplin, The Band, Canned Heat, Joan Baez, Santana, Melanie,

Ten Years After, Sly & The Family Stone, Johnny Winter, Jefferson Airplane, Ravi Shanker, Country Joe & The Fish, Blood Sweat & Tears, Arlo Guthrie, and Joe Cocker. Over the weekend there are three deaths, two births and four miscarriages. Joni Mitchell, who was booked to appear but pulled out due to being booked for a TV show, wrote the song 'Woodstock', based on reports of the event.

1979
The futuristic satire film, *Americathon*, featuring Meat Loaf, premieres in Los Angeles. The soundtrack includes songs by The Beach Boys, Nick Lowe and Elvis Costello.

1987
Michael Jackson achieves his third UK No.1 with 'I Just Can't Stop Loving You', a duet with Siedah Garrett – originally intended to be a duet between Jackson and either Barbra Streisand or Whitney Houston. Session singer Garrett also worked with Madonna.

1991
Paul Simon plays a free concert in New York's Central Park before an audience of three quarters of a million.

1992
Jamaican singer-songwriter Jackie Edwards dies aged 54. Edwards worked as a singer and songwriter for Island Records and wrote both No. 1 singles, 'Keep On Running' and 'Somebody Help Me' for The Spencer Davis Group.

1995
The Clarence, the Dublin hotel owned by U2, is damaged by a fire which takes over three hours to control. Also 'The Kitchen' nightclub in the same building is evacuated after being affected by the fire.

2002
A memorial to John Lennon is unveiled in the remote Scottish village of Durness where Lennon had spent his holidays from age seven to 15. The lyrics from 'In My Life' are inscribed on three stones.

2008
Record producer Jerry Wexler, who coined the term 'rhythm and blues' while writing for *Billboard* magazine in the late 1940s and influenced the careers of many singers including Aretha Franklin, Ray Charles and Bob Dylan, dies aged 91 at his home in Sarasota, Florida.

August 16

Born on this day:

1949 Scott Asheton, drums (The Stooges)	**1958** Madonna, singer, actress
1957 Tim Farriss, guitar (INXS)	**1972** Emily Erwin, singer (Dixie Chicks)

1938

American blues musician Robert Johnson dies at the age of 27, probably poisoned by a jealous husband. His recordings, from 1936–1937, influenced generations of musicians including Muddy Waters, Bob Dylan, Jimi Hendrix, The Rolling Stones and Led Zeppelin.

1962

Little Stevie Wonder (aged 12) releases his first single, 'I Call It Pretty Music (But The Old People Call It The Blues)', featuring Marvin Gaye on drums.

1965

The official stage name of R&B singer, David Jones, from Bromley, Kent, becomes David Bowie.

1968

The Jackson 5 make their formal debut with Diana Ross & The Supremes at the Great Western Forum, California.

Bruce Springsteen's new band Earth make their live debut at the Off Broad Street Coffee House in Red Bank, New Jersey.

1969

During a North American tour Led Zeppelin appear at the Convention Hall in Asbury Park, New Jersey, with Joe Cocker as support. Zeppelin had been asked to perform at Woodstock, but due to this gig commitment they were unable to attend. Down the road Bruce Springsteen's band Child are playing the first of two shows over two days at the Student Prince, Asbury Park. Springsteen is also unable to attend Woodstock due to these gigs.

1977

Manchester punk band Buzzcocks sign to EMI's United Artists label.

1977
Elvis Presley is found by his girlfriend Ginger Alden lying on the floor of his bathroom at his Memphis home Graceland, dead of heart failure at the age of 42. News of his death makes headlines throughout the world.

1988

Kiss play at London's Marquee Club on their current 129-date 'Crazy Nights' World Tour.

1997

On the 20th anniversary of Elvis Presley's death over 30,000 fans descend on Memphis, Tennessee for a 10-minute mourning circuit around his grave. A poll found that almost a third of the fans are keeping an eye out in case the singer is actually still alive and somewhere in the crowd.

2005

On her 47th birthday, Madonna suffers three cracked ribs, a broken collarbone and a broken hand in a horse-riding accident on her Ashcombe House country estate on the border of Wiltshire and Dorset.

P Diddy appears on the US TV *Today* show and announces that he is altering his stage name again, dropping the 'P' and referring to himself simply as 'Diddy'. The name change upsets Richard 'Diddy' Dearlove, a London based DJ who takes out court proceedings against P Diddy over the use of the name. An out-of-court settlement of £110,000 is agreed and as a result the rapper is no longer able to use the name Diddy in the UK.

2007

A fan of the 80s pop band Wham! is silenced after becoming the first noise nuisance to be prosecuted by Newcastle city council's night watch team. Brian Turner, of Sandyford, Newcastle-upon-Tyne, had tormented neighbours by playing the duo's hit song 'Last Christmas' all night at full volume from 1am onwards. Magistrates fine Turner £200 and order him to pay £215 costs.

Born on this day:

1953 Kevin Rowland, vocals (Dexy's Midnight Runners)

1958 Belinda Carlisle, vocals (The Go-Go's, solo)

1965 Steve Gorman, drums (The Black Crowes)

1969 Donnie Wahlberg, vocals (New Kids On The Block)

1960

The Beatles begin their first Hamburg engagement at The Indra, on the Grosse Freiheit, Hamburg, West Germany, playing the first of 48 nights at the club. The Beatles are lodged in a single room behind the screen of a nearby movie house.

1964

Glasgow Council announces that all boys and men with Beatle-styled haircuts will have to wear bathing caps after a committee is told that hair from 'Beatle-cuts' is clogging the pools' filters.

1968

The Doors start a four-week run at No. 1 on the US album chart with *Waiting For The Sun.*

1973

Former Temptations singer Paul Williams is found dead aged 34 in his car after shooting himself. He owed $80,000 in taxes and his celebrity boutique business had failed.

1979

The *New York Post* tabloid reports that Anita Pallenberg, the common law wife of Keith Richards, is linked to a witches' coven in South Salem, New York where Richards owns a house. A policeman claims he was attacked by a flock of black-hooded, caped people and a local youth claims he had been invited by Pallenberg to take part in "pot smoking sex orgies". Locals also claim they found "ritualistic stakes" and small animals that had been "sacrificed" near the house.

1987

Session drummer Gary Chester, who played on many major hits including 'Brown Eyed Girl', 'Under The Boardwalk', 'Walk On By' and 'It's My Party', dies aged 62 of cancer.

1991

Nirvana shoot the video for 'Smells Like Teen Spirit' at GMT Studios in Culver City, California. The clip costs less than $50,000 to make and features real Nirvana fans as the audience.

1995

Depeche Mode singer Dave Gahan is rushed to Cedars-Sinai Medical Centre after an apparent suicide attempt. Police found him at his Los Angeles home with a two-inch laceration on his wrist.

1999

Former Bay City Rollers drummer Derek Longmuir appears at the Edinburgh Sheriff Court accused of child porn and drugs offences. Longmuir, 48, denies the charges. He is later sentenced to 300 hours community service.

2008

Jackson Browne is suing US Republican presidential candidate John McCain for using one of his songs without permission. Browne claims the use of his song 'Running On Empty' in an advertisement was an infringement of copyright and would lead people to conclude he endorsed McCain. Browne is seeking more than $75,000 in damages.

2009

An arrest warrant is issued for singer Bobby Brown after he fails to appear at a court hearing involving child maintenance payments. Judge Christina Harms orders that Brown be arrested next time he is in the state of Massachusetts. The singer had allegedly fallen $45,000 behind in payments for two teenage children he had with former girlfriend Kim Ward.

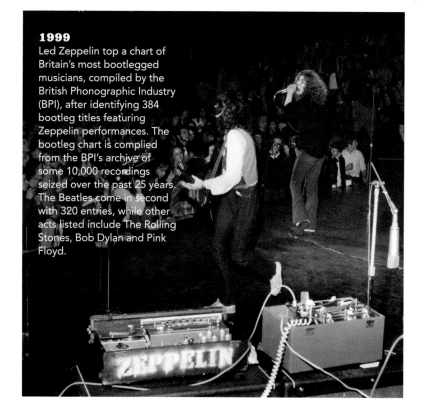

1999
Led Zeppelin top a chart of Britain's most bootlegged musicians, compiled by the British Phonographic Industry (BPI), after identifying 384 bootleg titles featuring Zeppelin performances. The bootleg chart is compiled from the BPI's archive of some 10,000 recordings seized over the past 25 years. The Beatles come in second with 320 entries, while other acts listed include The Rolling Stones, Bob Dylan and Pink Floyd.

Born on this day:

1944 Carl Wayne, vocals (The Move)
1950 Dennis Elliott, drums (Foreigner)
1951 John Rees, bass (Men At Work)
1983 Mika, UK singer

1958
The Kalin Twins are at No. 1 on the UK singles chart with 'When'. The brothers become the first twins to score a chart-topping record.

1962
Ringo Starr plays his debut gig with The Beatles at the local Horticultural Society Dance, in Port Sunlight, Birkenhead, England, having had a two-hour rehearsal in preparation.

1966
Paul Jones leaves Manfred Mann just as their latest single 'Pretty Flamingo' is climbing the US charts.

1969
Mick Jagger is accidentally shot in the hand during filming of *Ned Kelly* in Australia.

1973
Diana Ross scores her second US No. 1 single with 'Touch Me In The Morning'.

1977
The Police make their live debut as a three-piece band when playing at Rebecca's Birmingham, England.

1979
AC/DC, Nils Lofgren, The Stranglers and The Who appear on a one-day show at Wembley Stadium, London.

1982
The City of Liverpool names four streets after the fab four: John Lennon Drive, Paul McCartney Way, George Harrison Close and Ringo Starr Drive.

1984
George Michael is top of the UK singles chart with his first solo single, 'Careless Whisper', making Michael the first person to reach No. 1 as a solo artist and a member of a band in the same year. The song gives Epic Records UK their first British million seller and is No. 1 in over 20 countries, selling over six million copies worldwide.

Nick Rhodes of Duran Duran marries American model Julie Anne at Marylebone Registry Office, London.

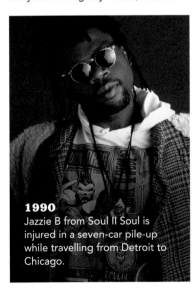

1990
Jazzie B from Soul II Soul is injured in a seven-car pile-up while travelling from Detroit to Chicago.

1991
Poster and album sleeve artist Rick Griffin dies aged 46 after being forced off the road by a van he was attempting to pass on his Harley Heritage Softail motorbike.

1992
Kurt Cobain becomes a father when his wife Courtney Love gives birth to a daughter, Frances Bean.

2003
Tony Jackson, original bass player with 60s group The Searchers, dies aged 65 of cirrhosis of the liver.

2005
Kanye West calls for an end to homophobia in the hip-hop community during an MTV interview saying "hip-hop was always about speaking your mind and about breaking down barriers, but everyone in hip-hop discriminates against gay people. Not just hip-hop, but America just discriminates, I wanna just to come on TV and just tell my rappers, just tell my friends, 'Yo, stop it'."

2006
US film-maker Adam Muskiewicz sets up elviswanted.com as part of a documentary exploring the myth that the singer is still alive and offers a $3m reward for anybody who finds him. The film was due for release in August 2007, to coincide with the 30th anniversary of Presley's death.

Born on this day:

1939 Ginger Baker, drums (The Graham Bond Organisation, Cream, Blind Faith, Ginger Baker's Airforce)
1940 Johnny Nash, singer

1945 Ian Gillan, vocals (Deep Purple)
1951 John Deacon, bass (Queen)

August 19

1964
The High Numbers (The Who) play The Scene club in Soho, London.

1967
The Beatles score their 14th US No. 1 single with 'All You Need Is Love'. Mick Jagger, Keith Richards, Eric Clapton, Keith Moon, Graham Nash, Mike McGear and ex-Walker Brother Gary Leeds are all among the backing chorus on the track.

1969
Joni Mitchell, David Crosby, Stephen Stills and Jefferson Airplane appear on ABC TV's *The Dick Cavett Show* from Television Center in New York City, most having come direct from the Woodstock festival that had just concluded.

1971
Led Zeppelin kick off their North American tour at Pacific Coliseum, Vancouver, Canada, playing to a sold out crowd of over 17,000 fans. Another 3,000 ticketless fans outside the venue start a battle with local police.

1972
David Bowie plays the first of two nights at the Rainbow Theatre, north London on his current Ziggy Stardust tour.

1977
The Sex Pistols start an undercover UK tour as The Spots (an acronym for Sex Pistols On Tour Secretly).

1988
'Crazy' by Patsy Cline and Elvis Presley's 'Hound Dog' are declared the most played jukebox songs of the first 100 years since its invention. The jukebox had been around since 1906, but earlier models had been seen in 1889.

1999
Lauryn Hill wins New Artist Of The Year and Album Of The Year at the US 'Source Hip Hop Music Awards' in Los Angeles. R. Kelly won R&B Artist of The Year, DMX won Artist Of The Year and Solo and Live Performer Of The Year.

2003
Steven Hindley, a 41 year-old from Nottinghamshire who sent threatening emails to S Club singer Tina Barrett, is jailed for six months. Hindley showered the singer with roses, chocolates and teddy bears, but when the messages went ignored he began to issue threats, including a potential sniper attack. One email begged Barrett to visit Hindley at his home, claiming he was the victim of an incurable brain tumour and had just three weeks to live.

2005
A life-size bronze statue of Phil Lynott designed by Paul Daly is unveiled on Harry Street in Dublin. The ceremony is attended by Lynott's former Thin Lizzy band members Gary Moore, Brian Robertson and Scott Gorham.

2008
Saxophonist LeRoi Moore, a founding member of the Dave Matthews Band, dies aged 46 from injuries sustained in a vehicle accident in June on his Virginia farm.

August 20

Born on this day:

1948	Robert Plant, singer (Led Zeppelin, solo)
1949	Phil Lynott, bass, singer, songwriter (Thin Lizzy)
1966	Dimebag Darrell, guitar (Pantera)
1971	Fred Durst, vocals (Limp Bizkit)
1979	Jamie Cullum, jazz pianist, singer, songwriter

1955
Bo Diddley appears at the Apollo Theater, Harlem, New York.

1965
The Rolling Stones' manager Andrew Loog Oldham and his partner Tony Calder unveil Immediate Records. Mick Jagger, Eric Clapton and actress and model Nico (later to join The Velvet Underground) all attend the launch party. The label's first release is The McCoy's US hit, 'Hang On Sloopy', and becomes the home of Chris Farlowe, The Small Faces, The Nice, Amen Corner and a young producer-guitarist, Jimmy Page.

1966
Touring America for the last time, The Beatles are forced to cancel and reschedule their performance to the following day at Cincinnati's open-air stadium, Crosley Field. Heavy rain (with no cover provided) make electrocution a virtual certainty if The Beatles had attempted to perform.

1968
The University of Tennessee reports that a guinea pig subjected to days of rock music played at 120 decibels has suffered acute hearing damage.

1973
Bruce Springsteen plays the first of a seven-night run at Oliver's in Boston, Massachusetts performing two hour-long sets each night.

1980
During a North American tour, Queen appear at the Civic Center, Hartford, Connecticut.

1983
Madness, Joan Jett, The Police and R.E.M. all appear at JFK Stadium, Philadelphia.

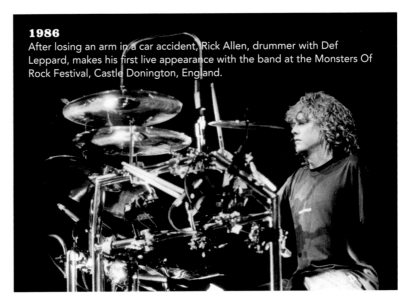

1986
After losing an arm in a car accident, Rick Allen, drummer with Def Leppard, makes his first live appearance with the band at the Monsters Of Rock Festival, Castle Donington, England.

1988
Steve Winwood is at No. 1 on the US album chart with *Roll With It*.

1992
An American doctor files a $35m lawsuit against the Southwest Bell phone company. He alleges that his wife died because he could not reach 911 due to all the lines being jammed with demand for Garth Brooks concert tickets.

2003
Madame Tussauds in London opens an interactive *Pop Idol* display with a speaking waxwork of judge Simon Cowell that makes comments such as: "That was extraordinary – unfortunately, extraordinarily bad", "Do you really think that you could become a Pop Idol? Well then you're deaf" and "Thank you, goodbye and that was the worst performance I've ever seen".

2004
In a divorce case, Rob Tinsley, from Stoke-on-Trent, England, names Bryan Adams as the 'other man' in his court papers after years spent trying to cope with his wife's obsession. Tinsley says he had to live with posters of the singer on their bedroom wall, as well as a 6ft cut-out which stood at the foot of the bed.

2008
Rosanne Cash, the daughter of late country star Johnny Cash, calls the use of her father's name to endorse a US Republican presidential candidate John McCain 'appalling'. According to media reports, while appearing at a rally in Florida, country star John Rich implied the Man In Black would have backed McCain. Writing on her website, Rosanne calls the remarks "presumptuous". "Even I would not presume to say publicly what I 'know' he thought or felt," she added.

Born on this day:

1952   Joe Strummer, singer, songwriter (The 101'ers, The Clash, solo)

1957   Budgie, drums (Big In Japan, The Slits, Siouxsie & The Banshees, The Creatures)

1957   Kim Sledge, vocals (Sister Sledge)

1971   Liam Howlett, keyboards (The Prodigy)

August 21

1961
Patsy Cline records the classic Willie Nelson song 'Crazy'. Cline is still on crutches after going through a car windshield in a head-on collision two months earlier.

1967
The Doors start recording their second album *Strange Days* at Sunset Sound Studios, Hollywood, California.

1968
Tommy James & The Shondells return to the UK No. 1 position for the second time with the single 'Mony Mony'.

1971
Arthur Brown's Kingdom Come, Hawkwind, Duster Bennett, Brewers Droop, Indian Summer, Graphite and (second from the bottom of the bill) Queen all appear at the Tregye Festival, Truro, Cornwall, England.

1972
Jack Casady of Jefferson Airplane is arrested after a fight breaks out on stage during a concert in Akron at which the police are called "pigs". Grace Slick is maced and another band member is injured at the show.

1982
U2 singer Bono marries Alison Stewart, his girlfriend since 1975, at All Saints Church, Raheny in Ireland. U2 bassist Adam Clayton acts as best man.

1983
Ramones guitarist Johnny Ramone undergoes a four-hour brain surgery operation after being found unconscious on a New York street where he had been involved in a fight.

1997
Ex-Stone Roses drummer Alan Wren is jailed for seven days after being rude to a Manchester magistrate. 'Reni' was before the court for having no car insurance and loses his temper after being quizzed about his earnings.

Oasis' third album *Be Here Now* becomes one of the fastest-selling albums ever, shifting over a million copies on the first day of release.

2002
Atomic Kitten are facing legal action after sacking fellow Liverpudlian Andy McCluskey, the songwriter who wrote the band's first No. 1, 'Whole Again'. The female trio were about to be dropped by Innocent Records when they recorded the song that became a huge hit. The girls then wanted a bigger share of royalties, which McCluskey had turned down. Under the original deal each girl got 4p from the sale of one single.

2005
Robert Moog, inventor of the synthesizer, dies aged 71, four months after being diagnosed with brain cancer. Dr Moog built his first electronic instrument, a theremin, aged 14 and made the MiniMoog, "the first compact, easy-to-use synthesizer" in 1970. He won the Polar prize, Sweden's "music Nobel prize", in 2001. Wendy Carlos' 1968 Grammy award-winning album, *Switched-On Bach*, brought Moog to prominence.

2006
A man surfing the internet in America foils three men who broke into a shop in Liverpool, England. The man, who had logged onto a site streaming live footage of Mathew Street and a forthcoming Beatles festival, saw the men smashing the window of a shop and climbing inside. He phoned Merseyside police who arrested them.

2008
Drummer Buddy Harman dies of congestive heart failure, aged 79. Harman worked with Elvis Presley ('Little Sister'), Patsy Cline ('Crazy'), Roy Orbison ('Pretty Woman'), Johnny Cash ('Ring Of Fire'), Tammy Wynette ('Stand By Your Man'), as well as Dolly Parton, Chet Atkins, Willie Nelson, Perry Como and Reba McEntire. He was the first house drummer for The Grand Ole Opry and can be heard on over 18,000 recordings.

Born on this day:

1920	John Lee Hooker, blues singer, guitarist	**1961**	Roland Orzabal, singer, guitarist (Tears For Fears)
1945	Ron Dante, singer, songwriter (The Archies)	**1963**	Tori Amos, singer, songwriter
1961	Debbie Peterson, drums (The Bangles)		

1956

Elvis Presley begins work on his first movie. In the drama set during and just after the Civil War, Elvis plays Clint Reno, the youngest of four brothers. The original title for the movie – *The Reno Brothers* – is changed to take advantage of the song 'Love Me Tender' recorded for the film.

1962

The first Beatles television footage is shot by Manchester based Granada TV, at a lunchtime session at The Cavern Club, Liverpool, with new drummer Ringo Starr.

1969

The Beatles assemble at John Lennon's Tittenhurst Park home in Ascot, England for their last ever photo session.

1970

Creedence Clearwater Revival start a nine-week run at No. 1 on the US album chart with *Cosmo's Factory*.

1978

Sex Pistol Sid Vicious makes his last live stage appearance when appearing with drummer Rat Scabies from The Damned, former Sex Pistol bassist Glen Matlock and Vicious' girlfriend Nancy Spungen at London's Electric Ballroom. The audience includes Elvis Costello, Blondie, Joan Jett, The Slits and Captain Sensible.

1987

Madonna goes top of the *Billboard* singles chart with 'Who's That Girl', her sixth US No. 1 and also a chart-topper in the UK.

1997

U2 play the first of two sold-out nights at London's Wembley Stadium on their 'Pop Mart' tour.

2003

Kjell Henning Bjoernestad, a Norwegian Elvis Presley impersonator, sets a world record by singing the rock'n'roll legend's hits non-stop for over 26 hours. The previous record was set by British Elvis fan Gary Jay who sang for 25 hours, 33 minutes and 30 seconds.

2005

50 Cent is suing a US car dealer for allegedly using his name in an advert without permission. Modestly describing himself in the legal action as a "hugely successful" artist "known for his good looks, 'gangsta' image and hard knocks success story", the rapper is seeking more than £1m from Gary Barbera Enterprises for a Dodge Magnum advert with the line "Just Like 50 Says" alongside a photo of 50 Cent.

2007

Savage Garden singer Darren Hayes is arrested and released on bail pending further inquiries on suspicion of racially abusing a member of staff at a Thai restaurant in Soho, London.

2009

Soul singer Johnny Carter, who was a member of doo-wop groups The Dells and The Flamingos, dies aged 75. Carter, who was famed for his falsetto vocals, was one of very few artists to be inducted into the US Rock and Roll Hall of Fame with two acts.

Born on this day:

1946 Keith Moon, drums (The Who)
1959 Edwyn Collins, singer, songwriter (Orange Juice, solo)

1962 Shaun Ryder, vocals (Happy Mondays, Black Grape)
1978 Julian Casablancas, guitar, vocals (The Strokes)

August 23

1965
Security guards at a Manchester TV studio hose down 200 Rolling Stones fans after they break down barriers while waiting for the group to arrive for a television performance.

1967
Joni Mitchell plays her first ever UK show when opening for The Piccadilly Line at The Marquee Club in London.

1970
Lou Reed and The Velvet Underground perform together for the last time at the New York Club Max's Kansas City. Reed works as a typist for his father for the next two years, at $40 per week.

1975
Joy Division singer Ian Curtis marries Deborah Woodruff, whom he met while still at school, when he was 19 and she was 18. They remained married until his death when he hung himself in the kitchen of his house in Macclesfield, England at the age of 23.

1980
David Bowie is at No. 1 on the UK singles chart with 'Ashes To Ashes', his second British chart-topper. From the *Scary Monsters (And Super Creeps)* album the song continues the story of Major Tom from Bowie's 1969 hit 'Space Oddity'. The accompanying video was one of the most iconic of the 80s, costing £250,000, at the time the most expensive music video ever made.

1985
Aerosmith play the first night of their 89-date 'Done With Mirrors' tour at the Alpine Valley Music Theatre in East Troy, Wisconsin.

1991
The first day of the annual Reading Festival in Berkshire, England. Iggy Pop, Sonic Youth, Pop Will Eat Itself, Dinosaur Jr, Chapterhouse, Nirvana, Silverfish, Babes In Toyland, James, The Fall, De La Soul, Blur, Teenage Fanclub, Flowered Up, The Fat Lady Sings, Kingmaker, Mercury Rev, The Sisters Of Mercy and Ned's Atomic Dustbin appear over the three-day event.

2004
Queen become the first UK rock band to receive official approval in Iran, where Western music is strictly prohibited. Lead singer Freddie Mercury, who died of AIDS in 1991, was of Iranian ancestry and pirated Queen albums had been available there for years.

2005
Les McKeown, lead singer of The Bay City Rollers, appears in court charged with drug offences. McKeown, aged 49, is accused of conspiring with four other people, including the band's current drummer Pat McGlynn, to supply cocaine. He was arrested in Dalston, east London, in June as part of a major police operation.

2007
Comedy writer Buddy Sheffield sues Disney, alleging that he originally came up with the idea for *Hannah Montana* but was never compensated by the company. In the lawsuit, Sheffield claims that he pitched an idea for a TV series called *Rock And Roland*, with the plot involving a junior high student who lives a secret double life as a rock star, to The Disney Channel in 2001.

2008
At the Millennium Stadium in Cardiff, Wales, Madonna kicks off her 86-date 'Sticky & Sweet' Tour, becoming at $280 million the highest grossing tour by a solo artist, breaking the previous record Madonna achieved with her 2006 'Confessions' Tour.

August 24

Born on this day:

1938 David Frieberg, bass, guitar, vocals (Quicksilver Messenger Service, Jefferson Starship)

1944 Jim Capaldi, drums, vocals, songwriter (Traffic, solo)

1948 Jean-Michel Jarre, French instrumentalist

1951 Michael Derosier, drums (Heart)

1963
Little Stevie Wonder becomes the first artist ever to score a US No. 1 album and single in the same week. Wonder is top of the album chart with *Little Stevie Wonder/The 12 Year Old Genius* and has the chart-topping single 'Fingertips Part 2', also the first ever live recording to reach pole position.

1966
The Doors start recording their debut album for Elektra at Sunset Sound Recording Studios, West Sunset Boulevard, Los Angeles, California.

1967
17-year-old New Jersey singer and guitarist Bruce Springsteen joins a group called Earth.

1969
During a North American tour Led Zeppelin appear at the Veterans Memorial Coliseum in Jacksonville, Florida.

1975
Queen start recording 'Bohemian Rhapsody' at Rockfield Studios in Monmouth, Wales. Freddie Mercury has mentally prepared the song beforehand and directs the band throughout the sessions that take place over three weeks. Mercury, May and Taylor sing their vocal parts continually for up to 12 hours a day, resulting in 180 separate overdubs.

1977
Singer and songwriter Waylon Jennings is arrested and charged with possession of cocaine. Jennings had recently been named an honorary police chief.

1980
Iron Maiden, Whitesnake, Def Leppard, UFO, Gillan, Pat Travers Band and Rory Gallagher appear at the 20th National Rock Festival Reading Rock '80, England. Advance tickets £12.50.

1981
Mark Chapman is given a 20 years to life jail sentence for the murder of John Lennon on December 8, 1980. He has yet to be released.

1983
After less than three months of marriage Shawn Michelle Stevens, the fifth wife of Jerry Lee Lewis, is found dead at their Mississippi home of a methadone overdose. Jerry Lee would marry again in 1984 to 22 year-old Kerrie McCarver but the couple divorce in 2004.

1989
To mark the 20th anniversary of its release, The Who perform *Tommy* for charity at the Universal Amphitheatre, Los Angeles, with special guests Steve Winwood, Elton John, Phil Collins, Patti LaBelle and Billy Idol.

1996
Oasis singer Liam Gallagher fails to turn up for the recording of the band's MTV *Unplugged* session at London's Royal Festival Hall in front of 400 fans. Liam eventually arrives and sits in the audience watching his brother Noel take over the vocals.

2004
Al Dvorin, the announcer who popularised the phrase "Elvis has left the building", dies aged 81 in a car crash on his way home from an Elvis Presley convention in California. In the early 70s, Colonel Parker asked Dvorin to inform fans at a gig that Presley would not be appearing for an encore. He took the stage and announced: "Ladies and gentlemen, Elvis has left the building. Thank you and goodnight." Dvorin was never paid for recordings of his words, and was bitter towards the multi-million pound Elvis Presley Enterprises. At the time of the accident Dvorin was in a car driven by Elvis photographer Ed Bonja who was treated at a hospital and released.

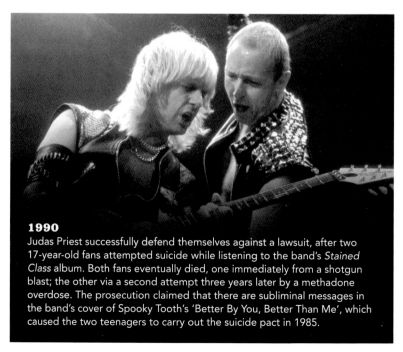

1990
Judas Priest successfully defend themselves against a lawsuit, after two 17-year-old fans attempted suicide while listening to the band's *Stained Class* album. Both fans eventually died, one immediately from a shotgun blast; the other via a second attempt three years later by a methadone overdose. The prosecution claimed that there are subliminal messages in the band's cover of Spooky Tooth's 'Better By You, Better Than Me', which caused the two teenagers to carry out the suicide pact in 1985.

Born on this day:

1949 Gene Simmons, bass, vocals (Kiss)
1951 Rob Halford, vocals (Judas Priest)
1955 Elvis Costello, singer, songwriter
1961 Billy Ray Cyrus, US singer
1962 Vivian Campbell, guitar (Dio, Whitesnake, Def Leppard)

August 25

1957
Canadian singer-songwriter Paul Anka is top of the UK singles chart with 'Diana' (written about his brother's babysitter). His only British chart-topper, Anka was the first teenage solo act to reach No. 1.

1962
Little Eva is at No. 1 on the US singles chart with 'The Loco-motion'. After offering it to Dee Dee Sharp ('Mashed Potato Time') who turned it down, writers Carole King and Gerry Goffin had their babysitter Eva Boyd record the song instead.

1967
After a two-year hiatus Brian Wilson returns to perform live with The Beach Boys in Honolulu, Hawaii. The shows are recorded and filmed.

1970
Elton John makes his US live debut at The Troubadour club in Los Angeles. In the audience are Quincy Jones, Leon Russell and Don Henley. Elton's latest single 'Border Song' has just debuted at No. 92 on the *Billboard* chart.

1979
The Knack start a five-week run at No. 1 on the US singles chart with 'My Sharona', the band's only US chart topper and a No. 6 hit in the UK. Lead singer Doug Fieger says he was inspired to write the tune by Sharrona Alperin, a 17-year-old senior at Los Angeles' Fairfax High.

1981
R.E.M. appear at The Scorpio, Charlotte, North Carolina, on a show billed as 'Charlotte's First Gay New Wave Disco and Costume Party', with the $3 ticket charge benefitting various gay charities.

1993
Snoop Doggy Dogg is released on $1 million bail after being accused of

involvement with the murder of a member of the By Yerself gang during a shooting in Los Angeles. Snoop was acquitted of the charges in 1996.

1994
Take That kick off a 36-date sold out UK tour with three nights at the Glasgow SECC. During the tour, the group play nine sold out nights at London's Wembley Arena.

Jimmy Buffett crashes his Grumman G-44 Widgeon seaplane upon take-off in Nantucket, Massachusetts. Buffett swims away from the wreckage.

1997
A deranged man who plans to set fire to the stage that Michael Jackson is performing on in Finland is arrested before he is able to light the gasoline he'd put there. The man had escaped from a mental institution near Helsinki.

1999
Robert Fisher from Climie Fisher dies aged 39 of cancer. With Simon Climie, he scored a 1988 UK No. 2 single with 'Love Changes Everything' and wrote songs for Rod Stewart, Milli Vanilli, Fleetwood Mac and Jermaine Jackson.

2000
Jack Nitzsche, Academy Award-winning film score composer and recording engineer/producer who worked with Phil Spector, The Walker Brothers, The Rolling Stones and Neil Young and Crazy Horse, dies aged 63 of a heart attack.

2001
American singer/actress Aaliyah is killed aged 22 in a plane crash in the Bahamas. The small Cessna plane crashes a few minutes after take off, killing everyone on board. Aaliyah had been filming a video for her latest release 'Rock The Boat' on the island.

2005
Two former members of Guns N' Roses are suing singer Axl Rose for allegedly naming himself sole administrator of the US rock band's copyrights. Slash and Duff – otherwise known as Saul Hudson and Michael McKagan – accuse Rose of "arrogance and ego". The legal action claims the singer "was no longer willing to acknowledge the contributions of his former partners."

2006
Aerosmith bassist Tom Hamilton is undergoing treatment for throat cancer, causing him to sit out the first half of the band's 'Route of All Evil' Tour, the first time he's missed any shows in the band's history.

2008
Jimmy Page accompanies Leona Lewis singing Led Zeppelin's 'Whole Lotta Love' during the closing ceremony of the Beijing Olympic Games.

August 26

Born on this day:

1948 Jet Black, drums (The Stranglers)
1966 Dan Vickrey, guitar (Counting Crows)
1967 Jeff Tweedy, singer, songwriter, guitarist (Wilco)
1969 Adrian Young, drummer (No Doubt)

1967
The Small Faces, The Move, The Gass, Tomorrow, Denny Laine, The Jeff Beck Group, Eric Burdon & The Animals and Marmalade all appear on the first day of the three-day non-stop happening 'Festival of the Flower Children' at Woburn Abbey, England. DJ's John Peel and Tommy Vance host the event and day tickets cost £1.

1970
The first day of the third Isle of Wight Pop Festival. The five-day event features Jimi Hendrix (in his last ever UK appearance), The Who, The Doors, Joan Baez, Joni Mitchell, Donovan, Jethro Tull, Miles Davis, Arrival, Cactus, Family, Taste, Mungo Jerry, ELP, Spirit, The Moody Blues, Chicago, Procol Harum, Sly & The Family Stone and Free. Weekend tickets cost £3.

1973
At the start of a UK tour 10CC make their live debut at the Palace Lido, Isle of Man.

1978
Frankie Valli is at No. 1 on the *Billboard* singles chart with the Barry Gibb song 'Grease' which goes on to sell over two million in the US.

1981
Ottawa City Council name Paul Anka Day to celebrate the singer's 25th anniversary in show business. The council also name a street Paul Anka Drive in his honour. The Canadian singer-songwriter has written over 900 songs including the standard 'My Way'.

1987
Sonny Bono, who once said that he never voted until he was 53, announces that he was running for mayor of Palm Springs, California. He won the election in 1988 and went on to win a seat in Congress in 1996.

1993
A double sided acetate of The Beatles performing 'Some Other Guy' and 'Kansas City' in 1962 at The Cavern in Liverpool sells for £16,500 – a world record price for a recording – at Christie's, London.

1994
Scottish singer Frankie Miller suffers a massive brain haemorrhage in New York, while writing material for a new band he and Joe Walsh had formed.

1995
Blur score their first UK No. 1 single with 'Country House' and win a media battle with Oasis for the top position. Both acts release their new singles on the same day; 'Country House' sells 270,000 copies, compared to 220,000 achieved by Oasis' 'Roll With It' which entered the chart in second position.

1997
Chad Smith of the Red Hot Chili Peppers is admitted to hospital after crashing his motorbike while driving down Sunset Boulevard.

2003
Rolling Stone magazine name Jimi Hendrix as the greatest guitarist in rock history. Eric Clapton, Jimmy Page, Keith Richards, Chuck Berry, Stevie Ray Vaughan and Ry Cooder also make the Top 10 list.

2004
Laura Branigan, who had a 1982 US No. 2 & UK No. 6 single with 'Gloria' and a 1984 US No. 4 & UK No. 5 with 'Self Control', dies aged 47 of a brain aneurysm.

2005
US President George Bush signs a federal bill to rename the post office near the Los Angeles studio where Ray Charles recorded much of his music after the R&B legend. Brother Ray died in June 2004 at the age of 74 from acute liver disease.

2007
Police who raid the home of US rap star DMX find 12 neglected pit bull terrier dogs and a number of guns. The bodies of three more dogs had been buried. The rapper, who had launched his own range of dog clothing including caps, scarves and raincoats for canines, also featured a pit bull straining at the leash on the cover of his latest album, *Year Of The Dog... Again.*

Born on this day:

1942 Daryl Dragon, keyboards (The Beach Boys, The Captain & Tennille)

1953 Alex Lifeson, guitar (Rush)

1970 Tony Kanal, bass (No Doubt)

1977 Mase, US male rapper

August 27

1965

On the last night of a five-day break during their North American tour, The Beatles meet Elvis Presley at his mansion in Beverly Hills. It is an awkward meeting, leaving The Beatles with the impression that Presley's personality is decidedly "unmagnetic". John Lennon remarked in later years, "It was like meeting Engelbert Humperdinck."

1966

The Beach Boys' 'God Only Knows' peaks at No. 2 on the UK singles chart.

1967

Brian Epstein dies aged 32 from an accidental overdose of prescribed tablets at his home in Belgravia, London.

The Beatles receive the news while at the Maharishi's transcendental meditation seminar at Bangor, Wales. The indoctrination is cut short as they make their way back to London.

1982

Queen appear at City Myriad, Oklahoma City, Oklahoma.

1988

'Monkey' gives George Michael his eighth US No. 1 single of the 80s, a record only beaten by Michael Jackson.

1990

Stevie Ray Vaughan is killed aged 35 when the helicopter he was flying in hit a man-made ski slope while trying to navigate through dense fog. Vaughn and his band Double Trouble had played a show at Alpine Valley Music Theatre, East Troy, Wisconsin with Eric Clapton and Robert Cray & The Memphis Horns. Vaughan was informed by a member of Clapton's crew that three seats were open on a helicopter returning to Chicago. However, it turned out there was only one seat left; Vaughan requested it from his brother, who obliged. Three members of Clapton's entourage are also killed in the accident. In 2003, *Rolling Stone* magazine ranked Stevie Ray Vaughan seventh in its list of the 100 Greatest Guitarists Of All Time.

1992

John Lennon's handwritten lyrics to The Beatles song 'A Day In The Life' sell at a Sotheby's auction in London for £48,400.

1994

Boyz II Men start a 14-week run at No. 1 on the US singles chart with 'I'll Make Love To You', a No. 5 hit in the UK. The record-breaking stay came to an end when they knocked themselves from the top with 'On Bended Knee'.

2003

Singer-songwriter Janis Ian marries her lesbian partner, Patricia Snyder, in Toronto. It was the second marriage for both.

P Diddy is being sued for $5m by a woman who claims she was assaulted by a bouncer outside his New York restaurant. Stephanie Grieso said she was arguing outside Justin's in August 2002 when a bouncer grabbed her by the neck and pushed her down on the pavement, causing leg injuries.

2004

The first day of the annual UK Carling Weekend is held in both Reading and Leeds, England. Green Day, The Darkness, The White Stripes, Morrissey, The Libertines, Franz Ferdinand, The Hives, 50 Cent (who is booed off stage after being greeted by a rain of bottles thrown at him and his G-Unit crew), The Streets, The Vines, Soulwax, Dogs Die In Hot Cars, The Offspring, Ash, Placebo and Lostprophets all appear.

2007

Kevin Federline's lawyers ask Britney Spears to pay some of her former husband's legal expenses in their divorce case. Federline's legal team say he had "no net income" after various expenses, and that Ms Spears is "clearly the monied party" in the dispute. According to legal documents filed in Los Angeles, the pop star's average monthly income is $737,868. The couple had married in October 2004 but filed for divorce in November 2006.

August 28

Born on this day:

1939 Clem Cattini, drums (The Tornadoes)

1942 Sterling Morrison, guitar (The Velvet Underground)

1943 Ann 'Honey' Lantree, drums (The Honeycombs)

1949 Hugh Cornwell, guitar, vocals (The Stranglers, solo)

1951 Wayne Osmond, vocals (The Osmonds)

1961
Tamla Records release The Marvelettes first single, 'Please Mr. Postman'. The song goes on to sell over a million copies and becomes the group's biggest hit, reaching the top of both the *Billboard* Pop and R&B charts.

1964
After playing a show at Forest Hills Tennis Stadium, New York, The Beatles meet Bob Dylan for the first time at The Delmonico Hotel. Dylan and mutual journalist friend Al Aronowitz introduce the Fab Four to marijuana.

1965
Bob Dylan plays Forest Hills Tennis Stadium in New York City on the first night of a 40-date North American tour. Dylan plays the first set solo and for the second is backed by a band consisting of Robbie Robertson, Levon Helm, Harvey Brooks and Al Kooper. This format – one acoustic and one electric set – is kept throughout the tour.

1970
During the last night of Elvis Presley's four-week engagement at The International Hotel in Las Vegas, a hotel security guard receives a phone call saying that Elvis would be shot on stage. The person demands $50,000 to reveal the name of the potential killer. Later that day a menu was found amongst the singer's mail on which Presley's face was destroyed and a gun had been drawn pointing to his heart. The threats are taken seriously but Elvis plays the show without any incident.

1972
Alice Cooper is at No. 1 on the UK singles chart with 'School's Out'.

1981
Producer Guy Stevens dies aged 38 from a heart attack. A former DJ at the influential Scene club in Soho, Stevens was once president of the UK Chuck Berry Appreciation Society and he brought Berry to the UK for his first tour in 1964. He gave Procol Harum and Mott the Hoople their distinctive names and also produced Mott and The Clash, including the latter's *London Calling* album.

1984
The Jacksons' 'Victory' Tour breaks the record for concert ticket sales after surpassing the 1.1 million mark in two months.

1988
Kylie Minogue sets a new record when her debut album *Kylie* becomes the biggest selling album by a female artist in Britain with sales of almost two million.

1993
Billy Joel starts a three-week run at No. 1 on the US album chart with *River Of Dreams*. Joel claims most of the music came to him in his sleep, hence the title. The singer's second wife, one time model Christie Brinkley, painted the album cover which was later voted Worst Album Cover Of The Year.

2005
Art Garfunkel is charged by police with marijuana possession after a joint is allegedly found in the ashtray of his car. Garfunkel had pleaded guilty the previous year to possession of marijuana in upstate New York.

Justin Timberlake accepts "substantial" libel damages for a fabricated story that he had an affair behind girlfriend Cameron Diaz's back. A *News Of The World* tabloid article in July 2004 alleged Timberlake had sexual relations with model Lucy Clarkson. The singer's solicitor, Simon Smith, told London's High Court that Clarkson had admitted lying to the newspaper. Timberlake donates the damages awarded to charity.

2009
Noel Gallagher quits Oasis, saying he can no longer work with his brother Liam. Noel, the group's lead guitarist and chief songwriter, had recently been involved in a series of rows with front man Liam, and admits he and his brother rarely speak, do not travel together and only see each other on stage. The guitarist says: "It's with some sadness and great relief to tell you that I quit Oasis tonight."

Born on this day:

1958 Michael Jackson, singer, songwriter (The Jackson 5, solo)

1958 Elizabeth Fraser, vocals (Cocteau Twins)

1959 Eddi Reader, singer, songwriter (Fairground Attraction)

1975 Kyle Cook, guitar (Matchbox 20)

August 29

1964

Roy Orbison's 'Oh, Pretty Woman' is released in the US. It goes on to reach No. 1 four weeks later.

1966

The Beatles play their last concert before a paying audience at Candlestick Park in San Francisco to a sold-out crowd of 25,000. John and Paul, knowing that this would be the last concert, bring cameras on stage and take pictures between songs. During this tour, The Beatles have not played a single song from their latest album, *Revolver*. They finish their career as a live band with a version of Little Richard's 'Long Tall Sally'.

1976

Jimmy Reed dies in San Francisco following an epileptic seizure just before his 51st birthday. Reed was a major influence on such British 60s R&B groups as The Rolling Stones, The Animals and The Pretty Things.

1977

Three people are arrested in Memphis after trying to steal Elvis' body. As a result, his remains will be moved to his Graceland mansion.

1981

The two-day Rock On The Tyne festival begins in Gateshead, England, features Ian Dury, Elvis Costello, U2, Rory Gallagher, Doll By Doll, Wang Chung, Becket, Dr Feelgood, The Ginger Nutters (featuring Ginger Baker), Trimmer & Jenkins and Lindisfarne.

1986

A mini dress worn by Kim Wilde is sold at Christie's rock memorabilia auction for £400.

1987

Def Leppard score their first UK No. 1 album with *Hysteria*, which also tops the US chart in July the following year after spending 49 weeks working its way to the top.

1987

Rick Astley's debut hit 'Never Gonna Give You Up' starts a five-week run at No. 1 on the UK singles chart, becoming the Biggest Selling Single of 1987 and winning Best British Single at the 1988 Brit Awards.

1990

Elton John checks into a rehab centre in Chicago to receive treatment for bulimia, alcoholism and drugs.

1991

At 7pm, DJ Kurt St. Thomas from radio station WFNX in Boston gives Nirvana's *Nevermind* its world premiere by playing the album from start to finish.

1994

Oasis release their debut album *Definitely Maybe*, which goes on to spend 177 weeks on the UK chart.

2000

Slipknot cause chaos at this year's *Kerrang!* Awards, smashing glasses, setting fire to their table, throwing a monitor off the stage and destroying a microphone. The band pick up three awards including Best Single and Best Live Act.

2008

US rapper DMX pleads guilty to attempting to buy cocaine and cannabis in Miami. The 37-year-old singer, real name Earl Simmons, enters the plea in a Florida court and is sentenced to time served. Simmons was still in custody awaiting extradition to the state of Arizona on outstanding drug and animal cruelty charges.

Organisers of a French music concert threaten legal action after Amy Winehouse pulls out of her performance. Winehouse failed to travel to the three-day Rock En Seine festival in Paris where the line-up included The Raconteurs, The Streets and Kate Nash.

2009

The Los Angeles coroner confirms Michael Jackson's death was homicide, primarily caused by the powerful anaesthetic Propofol. The singer suffered a cardiac arrest at his Los Angeles home in June, aged 50. The report says Propofol and the sedative Lorazepam were the "primary drugs responsible for Jackson's death", but four further drugs were also found.

Born on this day:

1935 John Phillips, vocals, guitar
(The Mamas & The Papas, solo)

1939 John Peel, BBC radio DJ and TV
presenter

1958 Martin Jackson, drummer
(Magazine, Swing Out Sister)

1986 George Ryan Ross III, guitar, singer
(Panic At The Disco)

1969
Two weeks after Woodstock, the second Isle of Wight festival takes place in the UK. Over 150,000 turn up over the three days to see Bob Dylan, The Band, Blodwyn Pig, Blonde On Blonde, Bonzo Dog Band, Edgar Broughton Band, Joe Cocker, Aynsley Dunbar Retaliation, Family, Fat Mattress, Julie Felix, Free, Gypsy, Richie Havens, The Moody Blues, The Nice, Tom Paxton, Pentangle, The Pretty Things, Third Ear Band and The Who. Tickets cost 25 shillings (£1.25). Celebrities who come to watch Dylan's first full-gig in three years include John Lennon & Yoko Ono, George Harrison, Ringo Starr, Keith Richards, Charlie Watts, Jane Fonda, Richard Burton and Elizabeth Taylor.

1972
John Lennon, Yoko Ono and Elephant's Memory headline two shows at Madison Square Gardens to raise money for the One to One charity. Stevie Wonder, Sha Na Na and Roberta Flack also appear at the event. Lennon personally buys $60,000 worth of tickets which are given to volunteer fund-raisers. Several of the performances are later included on the posthumous Lennon release *Live In New York City* album and video.

1975
Paul Kossoff, guitarist with Back Street Crawler, 'dies' for 35 minutes in hospital after being taken ill. Kossoff eventually succumbs to heart failure on March 19, 1976 after a history of drug abuse.

1988
Bruce Springsteen's wife Julianne files for divorce after newspapers publish photos of her husband and backing singer Patti Scialfa together.

1989
Billy Joel fires his manager and former brother-in-law Frank Weber after an accounting audit reveals discrepancies. Joel takes Weber to court and sues him for $90 million.

Izzy Stradlin, from Guns N' Roses is arrested for making a public disturbance on a US domestic flight. Stradlin urinated on the floor, verbally abused a stewardess and smoked in the non-smoking section of the aircraft.

1995
Sterling Morrison, a founder member of The Velvet Underground, dies of cancer at his home in New York City two days after his 53rd birthday. The guitarist left the group in August 1971 and re-joined in 1993 for the band's European reunion tour. Having earned a PhD in mediaeval studies, during the 80s Morrison became the captain of a Houston tugboat.

Carly Simon and James Taylor play their own solo sets before performing live together in front of 10,000 fans at Martha's Vineyard, Massachusetts, to raise money for the local agricultural society. It is the first time the former couple have appeared live on the same stage since 1979.

1997
Members from The Wu-Tang Clan are arrested after the alleged assault on a record promotions manager following a show in Chicago.

2007
Rap star Lil' Wayne is sued for $1m by a woman who claims she was crushed at an October 2006 gig in Maryland, after a large amount of cash was thrown into the audience. Tyrique Layne, then 17, says she lost consciousness after being trampled by the crowd and has suffered memory loss and severe headaches.

Born on this day:

1945 Van Morrison, singer, songwriter, harmonica, sax (Them, solo)

1957 Gina Schock, drums (The Go-Go's)

1957 Glenn Tilbrook, guitar, vocals (Squeeze, solo)

1977 Del Marquis, guitar (Scissor Sisters)

August 31

1957

Elvis Presley appears at the Empire Stadium in Vancouver, Canada – only the third time Presley has ever performed outside North America – and the last. 26,000 fans attend the show with tickets costing $1.50, $2.50 and $3.50.

1963

The Ronettes first enter the US singles chart with 'Be My Baby', the girl group's only Top 10 hit. Lead singer, Veronica Bennett, later marries the record's Wall of Sound producer Phil Spector.

1968

The Move, The Pretty Things, The Crazy World Of Arthur Brown, Orange Bicycle, Jefferson Airplane, Fairport Convention and Tyrannosaurus Rex all appear at the first Isle Of Wight Festival held over two days. Tickets cost 25 shillings (£1.25).

1969

During a North American tour, Led Zeppelin appear at the Texas International Pop Festival in Lewisville. Also on the bill are BB King, The Incredible String Band, Sam & Dave and Janis Joplin.

1974

Traffic make their last live performance at the annual Reading Festival. Other acts appearing include Alex Harvey, 10cc, Focus, Steve Harley and Procol Harum. A weekend ticket cost £5.50.

1976

George Harrison is found guilty of "subconscious plagiarism" of The Chiffons' 'He's So Fine' when writing his 1970 hit 'My Sweet Lord'. Earnings from the song are awarded to writer Ronnie Mack's estate. The Chiffons later record their own version of 'My Sweet Lord'.

1984

Prince's *Purple Rain* film opens at cinemas across the UK with special late night previews.

1985

Brothers In Arms by Dire Straits starts a nine-week run at No. 1 on the US album charts. The album also tops the charts in 25 other countries and goes on to sell over 20 million worldwide.

1987

The largest pre-order of albums in the history of CBS Records occurs as 2.25 million copies of Michael Jackson's *Bad* are shipped to American record stores. The album, which went on to sell over 13 million copies, follows *Thriller*, the biggest Jackson seller of all time with over 35 million sold.

1991

Metallica start a four-week run at No. 1 on the *Bilboard* album chart with *Metallica*. The album, featuring the singles 'Enter Sandman', 'Sad But True', 'The Unforgiven' and 'Nothing Else Matters', goes on to sell over 10 million copies in the US alone.

1994

Aaliyah and R. Kelly secretly marry at the Sheraton Gateway Suites, Rosemont, Illinois. Aaliyah never admits being married, though *Vibe* magazine published a copy of the marriage certificate. Unfortunately, she was only 15 at the time, so the marriage was later annulled.

2002

NASA announce that Lance Bass, singer with *NSYNC, is to become the first celebrity astronaut. His $23.8 million place on a Russian Soyuz module will make him at 23 the youngest person to go into orbit. Bass ended up not taking part in the flight after failing to pay for his $20 million ticket on the craft.

2007

Hilly Kristal (left), founder of the New York punk club CBGBs, dies aged 75 from complications arising from lung cancer. Kristal's club, credited with discovering The Patti Smith Group, Television and The Ramones, became a breeding ground for punk rock. The venue, whose full title CBGB-OMFUG stood for Country, Bluegrass, Blues and other music for uplifting gourmandisers, was originally launched to showcase country music.

September

Born on this day:

1946 Barry Gibb, singer, songwriter, producer (The Bee Gees)

1955 Bruce Foxton, bass, vocals (The Jam)

1957 Gloria Estefan, singer (Miami Sound Machine, solo)

1976 Babydaddy, bass (Scissor Sisters)

September 1

1955
After complaints from his neighbours, rock 'n' roll fan Sidney Adams is fined £3 and 10 shillings (£3.50) by a London Court after playing Bill Haley's 'Shake, Rattle And Roll' all day at full volume.

1957
'The Biggest Show Of Stars' package tour kicks off at the Brooklyn Paramount featuring Buddy Holly & The Crickets, The Drifters, The Everly Brothers and Frankie Lymon. On some dates certain artists are unable to play because of segregation laws.

1966
The Byrds play the first of an 11-night run at the Whisky A Go Go, Hollywood, California.

1967
The Beatles hold a meeting at Paul McCartney's London house to decide upon their next course of action following the death of manager Brian Epstein on 27 August. They decide to postpone their planned trip to India and to begin the already-delayed production of the *Magical Mystery Tour* film. They have two songs already recorded for the soundtrack, 'Magical Mystery Tour' and 'Your Mother Should Know'.

David Bowie releases the single 'Love You Till Tuesday' which fails to reach the charts.

1973
Elton John and Steely Dan appear at Balboa Stadium, San Diego, California.

1977
Blondie sign their first major record company contract with Chrysalis Records.

1979
U2 release their very first recording, an EP entitled 'U2-3', through CBS Ireland.

1980
Fleetwood Mac end a nine-month world tour with a performance at the Hollywood Bowl. Lindsay Buckingham announces on stage, "This is our last show for a long time."

1984
After a 25-year career, Tina Turner achieves her first solo No. 1 single in the US with 'What's Love Got To Do With It?'

1990
The Cure broadcast a four-hour pirate radio show from a secret London location to premiere their latest album, *Mixed Up*.

1996
Kim Wilde marries actor Hal Fowler who she met while working on the West End musical production of The Who's *Tommy*.

2004
Former Libertines' frontman Pete Doherty is given a suspended four month jail sentence after admitting possession of a flick knife. The singer was found with the weapon by police as he drove to his London home on 18 June.

2005
Barry Cowsill, former bass guitarist with The Cowsills, dies aged 51 from injuries sustained in Hurricane Katrina. His body is not recovered until December 28, 2005, from the Chartres Street Wharf, New Orleans.

2007
Supergrass are forced to put all plans on hold after band member Mick Quinn breaks his back. The bass player and vocalist sleepwalked out of a first floor window of a villa where he was staying in the south of France. Quinn was rushed to a specialist spinal unit in Toulouse where surgeons operate to repair two broken vertebrae as well as a smashed heel.

2009
Jake Brockman, former keyboard player with Echo & The Bunnymen, is killed when his motorbike is in collision with a converted ambulance on the Isle of Man. In 1989 the band's original drummer Pete De Freitas also died in a motorcycle accident.

September 2

Born on this day:

1943 Rosalind Ashford, vocals (Martha & The Vandellas, Ashford & Simpson)
1951 Mik Kaminski, violin (Electric Light Orchestra)
1957 Steve Porcaro, keyboards (Toto)
1987 Spencer James Smith, drums (Panic At The Disco)

1965
The Doors record their first demos, cutting six Jim Morrison originals at World Pacific Jazz Studios in Los Angeles, California.

1971
Grateful Dead's former manager is arrested after disappearing with over $70,000 of the band's money.

1972
The Erie Canal Soda Pop Festival is held over three days on Bull Island, near Griffin, Indiana. The promoters expected 50,000 but over 200,000 attend the festival. Many bands pull out as the festival steadily drifts into anarchy. Bands that did appear include Flash Cadillac & The Continental Kids, Black Oak Arkansas, Cheech & Chong, Foghat, Albert King, Brownsville Station, Canned Heat, Flash, Ravi Shankar, Rory Gallagher, Lee Michaels & Frosty, The Eagles, The Amboy Dukes and Gentle Giant. Three concert goers drown in the Wabash River and as the festival ends the remaining crowd burn down the stage.

1988
The 'Human Rights Now!' world tour – taking in five continents and claiming to be the most ambitious rock tour in history – kicks off at Wembley Stadium, London with Sting, Bruce Springsteen, Peter Gabriel, Tracy Chapman and Youssu n'Dour.

1989
Ozzy Osbourne is charged with threatening to kill his wife Sharon. Ozzy is released on the condition that he immediately goes into detox. The case is later dropped when the couple decide to reconcile.

1995
Michael Jackson is at No. 1 on the US singles chart with a song written by R. Kelly, 'You Are Not Alone'. It holds a Guinness World Record as being the first song in the 37-year history of the *Billboard* Hot 100 to debut in the pole position.

2002
Thieves break into the London home of Icelandic singer Björk and steal valuable recording equipment. The 36-year-old singer is asleep in the flat at the time of the incident.

2005
Mariah Carey becomes only the fifth act ever to hold the top two positions in the *Billboard* Hot 100 singles chart. The singer's 'We Belong Together' notches a tenth consecutive week at No. 1 while 'Shake It Off' jumps two places to second. 'We Belong Together' was Carey's 16th chart-topper, giving her the third highest number of US chart-toppers behind The Beatles and Elvis Presley.

Kanye West criticises President Bush's response to Hurricane Katrina during a televised benefit concert in New York. The show, to raise funds for relief efforts, features Leonardo DiCaprio, Richard Gere, Glenn Close, Harry Connick Jr and Wynton Marsalis. Appearing alongside comedian Mike Myers for a 90-second segment, West tells the audience: "George Bush doesn't care about black people." The comment goes out live on the US east coast, but is cut from a taped version seen on the west coast.

2009
Guy Babylon, keyboard player with the Elton John Band, dies of a heart attack while swimming in his pool at his home in Los Angeles, California.

1984
U2 play the second of two nights at the Logan Campbell Centre, Auckland, New Zealand during their 'Unforgettable Fire' World Tour. While in New Zealand, they employ local roadie, Greg Carroll, who impresses the band so much they offer to relocate him to Ireland to work for them.

Born on this day:

1942 Al Jardine, guitar, vocals (The Beach Boys)

1944 Gary Leeds, drums, vocals (The Walker Brothers, Gary Walker & The Rain)

1948 Donald Brewer, drums (Grand Funk Railroad, Bob Seger)

1980 Jay 'Cone' McCaslin, bass (Sum 41)

September 3

1965
A Rolling Stones gig in Dublin, Ireland ends in a riot after 30 fans jump onto the stage. Jagger is knocked to the floor as the rest of the band flee into the wings.

1966
Donovan is at No. 1 on the US singles chart with 'Sunshine Superman', a No. 2 hit in the UK. The track, recorded at EMI Studios in December 1965, features future Yardbirds and Led Zeppelin guitarist Jimmy Page.

1970
Alan Wilson, guitar player with Canned Heat, is found dead aged 27 of a drug overdose in fellow band member Bob Hite's garden in Topanga Canyon, Los Angeles.

Arthur Brown is arrested at the Palermo Pop '70 Festival in Italy after he sets fire to his helmet (during the performance of his hit 'Fire') and strips naked on stage during the performance.

It is reported that the Bob Dylan bootleg *Great White Wonder* has sold over 350,000 copies.

1977
The month after his death, Elvis Presley has 27 albums and nine singles in the UK Top 100. *Moody Blue* was the No. 1 album while 'Way Down' was top single.

1982
The first day of the US Festival is held in San Bernardino, California. The three-day event features Tom Petty, Fleetwood Mac, The Police, The Cars, Talking Heads, The Kinks, Ramones, B52's, The (English) Beat, Gang Of Four, The Grateful Dead, Pat Benatar, and Jackson Browne. Apple Computers founder Steven Wozniak bankrolls the festival.

1991
Ike Turner is released from prison having served 18 months of a four-year prison term. In an interview with *Variety* Turner, who had been arrested on 10 previous occasions, claims to have spent over $11 million on cocaine.

1999
The largest music bootleg bust in American history is made. It is estimated that this single operation alone is responsible for $100 million in lost revenues. Recording equipment valued at $250,000 is confiscated along with almost one million CDs and tapes.

2003
Libertines' singer Pete Doherty is sentenced to six months imprisonment after being found guilty on burglary and drug possession charges. His sentence is reduced on appeal to two months.

2004
Songwriter, record producer and advertising executive Billy Davis, who co-wrote Jackie Wilson's 'Reet Petite' and the jingle 'I'd Like To Buy The World A Coke', dies aged 72 in New York after a long illness. Aretha Franklin, James Brown, Marvin Gaye, The Supremes and Gladys Knight also recorded Davis' songs.

2005
Fats Domino is rescued from New Orleans shortly after Hurricane Katrina hits the city. The 77-year-old singer had been reported missing since the storm in New Orleans which had flooded the city, leaving thousands feared dead.

2006
Hundreds of Paris Hilton albums are tampered with in record stores in Bristol, Brighton, Birmingham, Newcastle, Glasgow and London in the latest stunt by Banksy. The "guerrilla artist" replaces Hilton's CD with his own remixes and gives them titles such as 'Why Am I Famous?', 'What Have I Done?' and 'What Am I For?'. He also changes pictures of her on the CD sleeve to show the US socialite topless and with a dog's head.

2008
Heavy metal band Slipknot score their first US No. 1 album – but only after a recount put them ahead of rapper The Game's latest release. Slipknot top the *Billboard* chart with their fourth studio album *All Hope Is Gone* which, according to analysts Nielsen SoundScan, sells 239,516 copies – 1,134 more than The Game's album.

September 4

Born on this day:

1951 Martin Chambers, drums (The Pretenders)

1971 Ty Longley, guitar, vocals (Great White)

1974 Carmit Bachar, vocals (Pussycat Dolls)

1975 Mark Ronson, producer

1981 Beyonce Knowles, singer, actress (Destiny's Child, solo)

1954

To coincide with the release of his second Sun single, 'Good Rockin' Tonight', Elvis Presley, along with Bill Black and Scotty Moore, make their first appearance at The Grand Ole Opry. The audience reaction is so poor, the Opry's manager Jim Denny tells Elvis that he should go back to driving a truck.

1962

The Beatles first recording session with Ringo Starr on drums takes place at EMI's Studios, Abbey Road, north west London. Producer George Martin was unhappy with the group's first session on June 6, so he called The Beatles back into the studio to try again. They run through six songs, of which two – 'How Do You Do It' and 'Love Me Do' – are recorded; the latter becomes the version released as the A-side of the Beatles' debut UK single on October 5.

1968

The Bee Gees achieve their second UK No. 1 single with 'I've Gotta Get A Message To You'.

1976

The Sex Pistols make their television debut when appearing live on the Manchester based Granada TV programme, *So It Goes*, hosted by Tony Wilson.

1979

Grateful Dead play the first of three nights at Madison Square Garden, New York.

1982

The Steve Miller Band start a two week run at No. 1 on the US singles chart with 'Abracadabra', which is the group's third US No. 1 and a No. 2 hit in the UK.

1984

U2 play the first of five nights at Sydney Entertainment Centre in Australia during their 'Unforgettable Fire' World Tour.

1987

Mike Joyce, drummer with The Smiths, quits the band saying that his "present role within the group had been fulfilled."

1995

Blur, Oasis, Radiohead, Paul Weller, Manic Street Preachers and The Stone Roses all record tracks for the *War Child* charity album, which is released five days later. All profits will go to children caught up in the current war in former Yugoslavia.

1996

Oasis stir things up at the MTV Awards held at New York's Radio City Music Hall. During the band's performance of 'Champagne Supernova', singer Liam Gallagher spits on stage and throws a beer into the crowd.

2000

Former Spice Girl Mel C starts a 21-date UK tour at The Assembly Rooms, Derby.

2005

Ex-Badfinger drummer Mike Gibbins dies aged 56 in his sleep at his Florida home. Originally called The Iveys and signed to The Beatles' Apple label, Badfinger had a 1970 UK No. 4 & US No. 7 single with the Paul McCartney-penned 'Come And Get It'.

McFly go to No. 1 on the UK album chart with *Wonderland,* the group's second No. 1 album.

2007

The Police play the opening UK date on their reunion tour with the first of two nights at the National Indoor Arena in Birmingham, England.

2008

The first Fender Stratocaster burned on stage by Jimi Hendrix, at the end of a 1967 show at the Finsbury Park Astoria, north London, sells for £280,000 at a London auction of rock memorabilia. The sale also includes The Beatles' first management contract, signed in 1962 by all four members of the group and manager Brian Epstein, which sells for £240,000.

1971

Paul and Linda McCartney are at No. 1 on the US singles chart with 'Uncle Albert/Admiral Halsey', McCartney's first US solo chart-topper. The single had been extracted from the McCartneys' album *Ram* for the American market but is not released in the UK.

Born on this day:

1945 Al Stewart, UK singer-songwriter
1946 Buddy Miles, drums (The Electric Flag, Band Of Gypsys)
1946 Freddie Mercury, singer (Queen, solo)
1946 Loudon Wainwright III, Canadian singer-songwriter
1968 Brad Wilk, drums (Rage Against The Machine)

September 5

1964

The Animals start a three week run on top of the US singles chart with 'The House Of The Rising Sun'. When first released the group's American record company MGM printed the time of the song on the record as three minutes, feeling that the real time of four minutes was too long for radio airplay.

1967

At EMI Studios, London, in their first session since Brian Epstein's death, The Beatles begin recording John Lennon's new song 'I Am the Walrus'.

1968

During their first visit to the UK The Doors appear on *Top Of The Pops* miming their US No. 1 'Hello I Love You'.

1976

Lynyrd Skynyrd guitarist Gary Rossington is seriously injured in a car crash in Florida.

1978

Joe Negroni from Frankie Lymon & The Teenagers dies of a brain haemorrhage.

1981

Soft Cell are at No. 1 on the UK singles chart with their version of 'Tainted Love.' The song had been a hit for Gloria Jones in 1964. (Jones, who became Marc Bolan's girlfriend, was the driver of the car that crashed and killed Bolan on 16 September, 1977. Jones also nearly died in the accident.)

1987

Ian Astbury of The Cult is arrested after a Vancouver show ends in a riot. Staff at the concert claim they were assaulted by Astbury, who spends the night in the local police cells.

1990

Ian Dury & The Blockheads drummer Charley Charles dies of cancer.

1994

Oasis appear at The Hacienda in Manchester to celebrate the launch of their debut album *Definitely Maybe*.

1998

Aerosmith score their first US No. 1 single with the Diane Warren written song 'I Don't Want To Miss A Thing'.

2006

Arctic Monkeys win this year's UK Mercury Prize for their album *Whatever People Say I Am, That's What I'm Not*. The Sheffield-based band's album became the fastest-selling debut in chart history after shifting more than 360,000 copies in its first week of release in February 2006.

2008

A worldwide study of more than 36,000 people concludes that musical tastes and personality type are closely related. The research, carried out by Professor Adrian North of Heriot Watt University, Edinburgh in the UK suggests classical fans are shy, heavy metallers are gentle and at ease with themselves, indie fans have low self-esteem and are not hard working, rap fans have high self-esteem and are outgoing, country & western fans are hardworking and outgoing, reggae fans are creative but not hardworking, and chart pop fans have high self-esteem, are not creative, but are hardworking and outgoing.

1998

Manic Street Preachers score their first UK No. 1 single with 'If You Tolerate This Your Children Will Be Next', the band's 19th hit and the first Welsh act to have a No. 1 since Shakin' Stevens in 1985. The song enters *The Guinness Book of World Records* as the longest title for a chart-topping single without brackets.

September 6

Born on this day:

1925 Jimmy Reed, blues singer, guitar, songwriter

1944 Roger Waters, bass, vocals (Pink Floyd, solo)

1961 Pal Waaktaam, guitar (A-Ha)

1971 Dolores O'Riordan, singer (The Cranberries)

1963
Cilla Black signs a management contract with Beatles manager Brian Epstein. Cilla changed her name to Black (it was White) after a misprint in the music paper *Mersey Beat*.

1968
At EMI Studios in London, The Beatles record overdubs onto George Harrison's 'While My Guitar Gently Weeps'. George records his lead vocal and uncredited guest Eric Clapton adds the distinctive guitar solo.

1970
Jimi Hendrix makes his final live appearance at the Isle Of Fehmarn in Germany. The guitarist dies in London 12 days later.

1974
The 101 All Stars (featuring Joe Strummer) make their debut at The Telegraph, Brixton Hill, south London.

1975
Glen Campbell starts a two-week run on top of the American singles chart with 'Rhinestone Cowboy', his first No. 1 after 13 US Top 40 hits.

1978
Tom Wilson, who produced various albums including Bob Dylan (*The Times They Are A-Changin'*, *Another Side Of Bob Dylan* and *Bringing It All Back Home*),Frank Zappa (*Freak Out!*), Simon & Garfunkel (*Wednesday Morning, 3 A.M.*) and The Velvet Underground (*White Light/White Heat*) dies, aged 47 of a heart attack in Los Angeles.

1980
U2 kick off the first leg of their 29 date UK 'Boy' tour at The General Woolfe in Coventry, England.

1985
Desperately Seeking Susan, the movie starring Madonna and Rosanna Arquette, goes on general release in the UK.

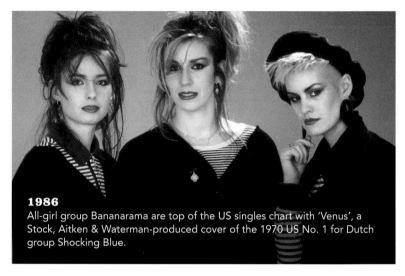

1986
All-girl group Bananarama are top of the US singles chart with 'Venus', a Stock, Aitken & Waterman-produced cover of the 1970 US No. 1 for Dutch group Shocking Blue.

1990
Tom Fogerty, former guitarist with Creedence Clearwater Revival, dies aged 49, due to complications from AIDS acquired during a blood transfusion.

1994
Highly respected English session musician Nicky Hopkins dies aged 50 in Nashville, Tennessee, of complications from intestinal surgery. Hopkins played piano on recordings by The Beatles, The Rolling Stones, The Who, The Jeff Beck Group (of whom he was briefly a member), The Kinks, The Small Faces, John Lennon, George Harrison and Quicksilver Messenger Service.

1997
Elton John records his newly written version of 'Candle In The Wind (1997)' after performing it live at Diana, Princess of Wales' funeral to a record UK television audience of 31.5 million. The track goes on to become the biggest selling single of all-time.

2001
Earth, Wind & Fire announce that Viagra will sponsor their forthcoming 30th anniversary American tour.

2004
Jamiroquai singer Jay Kay is banned for six months and fined £750 after being clocked driving at 100mph. His lawyers argue that Kay needs his licence so he can have "respite" from his busy professional life.

2005
Sir Bob Geldof is awarded the freedom of his native Dublin after the City Council votes in favour of giving him the accolade in honour of his campaign against world poverty and alleviating debt in Africa.

2008
US rock band Great White, whose pyrotechnics sparked a fire that killed 100 people, agree to pay $1m to survivors and victims' relatives. The blaze began at The Station nightclub in the US state of Rhode Island in 2003 when the group's tour manager shot off pyrotechnics at the start of the concert. One band member, guitarist Ty Longley, was killed in the fire. Tour manager Daniel Biechele pleaded guilty in 2006 to 100 counts of involuntary manslaughter and was given parole in March after serving less than half of his four-year prison sentence. More than 200 people were also injured in the blaze.

September 7

1959

Craig Douglas is at No. 1 on the UK singles chart with his version of Sam Cooke's hit 'Only Sixteen'. Real name Terence Perkins, Douglas was employed as a milkman before becoming a professional singer and was known as the 'Singing Milkman'.

1968

On their UK visit The Doors play the first of two sold out nights at The Roundhouse, London, performing two shows per evening. Granada TV films the gigs (later shown as *The Doors Are Open*), with fellow American band, Jefferson Airplane, sharing the bill.

Billed as 'Yard Birds', Jimmy Page, Robert Plant, John Paul Jones and John Bonham make their live debut at The Teen Club Box 45 in Gladsaxe, Denmark.

1978
Who drummer Keith Moon dies aged 32 of an overdose of Heminevrin tablets prescribed to combat alcoholism. A post-mortem confirms there were 32 tablets in his system, 26 of which were undissolved. The night before, Moon had attended a party organised by Paul McCartney to launch *The Buddy Holly Story* movie. *Who Are You*, the last Who album on which Moon played, was released two weeks before his death.

1976
Abba are at No. 1 on the UK singles chart with 'Dancing Queen', the group's fourth British chart-topper and their only US No. 1. The song is also No. 1 in over a dozen countries, including the Swedish charts for 14 weeks.

1985

John Parr starts a two-week run at No. 1 on the US singles chart (No. 6 in the UK) with 'St Elmo's Fire', taken from the film of the same name.

1987

As part of their 'Hysteria' World Tour, Def Leppard play the first of three nights at London's Hammersmith Odeon.

1996

Michael Jackson plays the first concert on the 82-date 'HIStory' World Tour, Jackson's third world concert tour, at Letna Park, Prague in the Czech Republic. The tour will be attended by approximately 4.5 million fans, beating Jackson's previous 'Bad' Tour with 4.4 million, and grossing a total of over $163.5 million.

2001

Michael Jackson is reunited onstage with The Jackson 5 in New York's Madison Square Garden, ending Jackson's 11-year hiatus from performing in the US. Jackson is also joined by Eminem, Whitney Houston, Gladys Knight, Britney Spears and Destiny's Child to celebrate the 30th anniversary of his singing career.

2003

US singer-songwriter Warren Zevon dies in Los Angeles aged 56 of cancer. Zevon, who worked as a session musician and was piano player and band leader for The Everly Brothers, recorded over 15 solo albums, some featuring guest appearances from Jackson Browne, The Eagles and Linda Ronstadt. He had a US No. 21 single in 1978 with 'Werewolves Of London'.

2007

A report shows that two-thirds of young people who regularly use MP3 players face premature hearing damage. The Royal National Institute for Deaf People said its findings were alarming, with research showing that 72 out of 110 MP3 users tested in the UK were listening to volumes above 85 decibels. Some MP3 players at full volume registered at 105 decibels, an aircraft taking off measured at 110 decibels.

September 8

Born on this day:

1897 Jimmie Rodgers, singer, songwriter
1932 Patsy Cline, country singer
1945 Ron 'Pigpen' McKernan, organ (The Grateful Dead)
1975 Richard Hughes, drums (Keane)
1979 Pink, US singer

1952
After Atlantic Records buys Ray Charles' contract from Swingtime, he records his first four-song session for the Atlantic label.

1957
'Reet Petite' by Jackie Wilson is originally released, becoming a UK chart-topper 29 years later.

1966
John Lennon is on location near Hanover, Germany, filming his role as Musketeer Gripweed in *How I Won The War*, directed by Richard Lester, the man behind The Beatles' films *A Hard Day's Night* and *Help!* The part requires Lennon to get his hair cut short and don National Health specs – which he continues to wear for the rest of his life.

1967
The Doors appear at the Lagoon Park Patio Gardens, Farmington, Salt Lake City, Utah.

1968
Led Zeppelin appear at Raventlow Parken, Nykobing Lolland, Denmark, supported by The Beatnicks and The Ladybirds (who were an all-girl, topless go-go dancing outfit!).

1973
Marvin Gaye starts a two-week run on top of the *Billboard* singles chart with 'Let's Get It On', his second US No. 1.

1977
It is announced that guitarist Jimmy McCulloch has left Wings to join the re-formed Small Faces. McCulloch has played with Paul McCartney's band since 1974. He died aged 26 of a drug overdose in 1979.

1984
Stevie Wonder achieves his first solo UK No. 1 with 'I Just Called To Say I Love You', taken from the film *Lady In Red*, some 18 years after his UK chart debut in 1966.

1989
Robert Wiggins from Grandmaster Flash & The Furious Five dies of a heart attack.

1993
At a show in Hollywood, Kurt Cobain and Courtney Love appear on stage together performing a song they wrote called 'Penny Royal Tea'.

1997
Derek Taylor, the long-serving Beatles publicist who also did PR for The Beach Boys, The Byrds, Paul Revere & The Raiders and Captain Beefheart, dies aged 67 of cancer. In 1967, together with Lou Adler and John Phillips, Taylor helped organise the Monterey Pop Festival. He also worked for Warner Brothers in the 70s and The Beatles' Apple organisation up until his death.

1999
Sean Puffy Combes and his bodyguard Paul Offered both plead guilty to harassment in a New York Court. The pair face charges of assaulting record company executive Steve Stoute with a champagne bottle, a chair and a telephone.

2003
David Bowie performs the first interactive concert in London when his 'Reality' performance is beamed live into 21 cinemas worldwide. Members of the audience talk to Bowie via microphones linked to ISDN lines and he takes song requests from fans.

2004
Led Zeppelin frontman Robert Plant is guest of honour at the unveiling of a statue of 15th century rebel leader, Owain Glyndwr, at Pennal church, near Machynlleth in Wales. Plant, who owns a farmhouse in the area, had donated money towards a bronze sculpture of the Welsh prince.

2007
Foxy Brown is sent to jail for a year in New York for violating her probation terms after she travels outside New York without the court's permission and misses anger management classes. The rapper (real name: Inga Marchand) was arrested for allegedly assaulting a neighbour and in October 2006 she was put on probation for allegedly assaulting two nail salon workers in August 2004.

2002
Iron Maiden singer Bruce Dickinson starts his new job as an airline pilot. The heavy metal singer qualified as a £35,000 salaried first officer with Gatwick based airline Astraeus which services Portugal and Egypt.

Born on this day:

1940 Joe Negroni, vocals (Frankie Lymon & The Teenagers)
1941 Otis Redding, soul singer
1952 Dave Stewart, guitar, keyboards, songwriter (The Tourists, Eurythmics, solo)

1970 Macy Gray, US singer
1975 Michael Bublé, Canadian singer

September 9

1956
Elvis Presley makes his first appearance on CBS TV's *The Ed Sullivan Show*, performing 'Don't Be Cruel', 'Love Me Tender' and 'Ready Teddy'.

1965
US trade newspaper *The Hollywood Reporter* runs the following advert: "Madness folk & roll musicians, singers wanted for acting roles in new TV show. Parts for 4 insane boys." The audition process eventually leads to *The Monkees*.

1968
At EMI Studios, The Beatles record 'Helter Skelter'. John Lennon plays bass and honks amateurishly on a saxophone, while roadie Mal Evans tries his best playing trumpet. Paul McCartney records his lead vocal and George Harrison runs around the studio holding a flaming ashtray above his head in the style of Arthur Brown and his flaming helmet.

1972
Slade are at No. 1 on the UK singles chart with 'Mama Weer All Crazee Now', the group's third UK No. 1.

1977
David Bowie appears on Marc Bolan's ITV show, *Marc*, singing 'Heroes' as well as a duet with Bolan, 'Standing Next To You', which is prematurely terminated when Bolan falls from the stage, much to Bowie's amusement. After the show the pair record demos together which are never finished because Bolan is killed in a car crash a week later.

1978
U2 appear at The Top Hat Ballroom, Dublin, Ireland.

1989
Sonic Youth, supported by Nirvana, appear at The Cabaret Metro, Chicago.

1992
Nirvana's Krist Novoselic knocks himself unconscious during the MTV Awards after being hit on the head with his bass guitar which he threw up in the air.

2004
US guitar maker Ernie Ball dies after a long illness. In the late 50s Ball opened the first music store in Tarzana, California to exclusively sell guitars. He developed thin gauge guitar strings called 'Slinkys' specifically designed for playing rock on electric guitar.

2005
An international conference devoted to the life, work and influence of Bruce Springsteen is held at Monmouth University, New Jersey. The festivities include various live acts, as well as keynote addresses by rock critics and figures from the music industry. More than 150 papers are presented to the course including Springsteen and American Folklore, Springsteen and Dylan's American Dreamscapes, Springsteen's Musical Legacy, 'Born To Run' at 30-Years-Old, Springsteen and New Jersey and the Boss and the Bible.

2006
50 Cent is stopped by police for alleged unsafe driving in New York and receives citations for an unsafe lane change, driving with an expired permit, and driving without insurance or vehicle registration. A crowd gathers, taking photos, jeering the police and cheering the rap star after he is pulled over in his silver open-topped Lamborghini.

2008
A man is charged with assault after an attack on Oasis guitarist Noel Gallagher during the band's set at the V Festival in Canada. Gallagher is admitted to hospital after a man runs on stage and pushes him over while he plays guitar. Toronto police say Daniel Sullivan, 47, was charged over the incident. A band statement said the guitarist "fell heavily on to his monitor speakers."

September 10

Born on this day:

1945 Jose Feliciano, guitar, singer, songwriter

1950 Joe Perry, guitar (Aerosmith)

1957 Carol Decker, vocals (T'Pau)

1957 Siobhan Fahey, vocals (Bananarama)

1984 Matthew Followill, guitar (Kings Of Leon)

1963

During a chance meeting between Rolling Stones manager Andrew Oldham and John Lennon and Paul McCartney, the two Beatles play the Stones, who are rehearsing at the club Studio 51 in Soho, a partly finished song 'I Wanna Be Your Man'. When the Stones give their approval, the pair finish writing the song there and then and it becomes the Stones' second single and first Top 20 hit.

1964

The Kinks third single, 'You Really Got Me', is at No. 1 on the UK singles chart.

1965

The Byrds begin recording their third single, a cover of Pete Seeger's 'Turn! Turn! Turn!' based on a Bible passage from the Book of Ecclesiastes. The song becomes the group's second (and last) US No. 1 hit.

1967

Elvis Presley records 'Guitar Man' at RCA Studios, Nashville, Tennessee.

1974

The New York Dolls split up. The influential American band formed in 1972 and made just two albums, *New York Dolls* (1973) and *Too Much Too Soon* (1974).

1983

Former Stevie Wonder guitarist Michael Sembello starts a two-week run at No. 1 on the US singles chart with 'Maniac', from the film *Flashdance*.

1988

Guns N' Roses start a two-week run on top of the *Billboard* singles chart with 'Sweet Child O' Mine', their first US No. 1.

1991

Nirvana's single 'Smells Like Teen Spirit' is released in the US.

1994

R.E.M. are at No. 9 on the UK singles chart with 'What's The Frequency, Kenneth?', the song inspired by a bizarre incident when a US newsreader was attacked.

1996

Music journalist Ray Coleman dies aged 59 of cancer. Coleman had been editor-in-chief of the UK music weekly papers *Melody Maker* and *Disc* throughout the 60s and 70s and was friends with such musical greats as The Beatles and The Rolling Stones. In the 80s he wrote official biographies of Eric Clapton and Bill Wyman, as well as a two-volume biography of John Lennon.

2001

Jamiroquai singer Jay Kay pleads not guilty to assault charges after being accused of hitting a photographer and destroying camera equipment outside a London night club.

2005

The 1967 Beatles track 'A Day In The Life' from *Sgt Pepper's Lonely Hearts Club Band* is voted the Best British Song of All Time in a survey by *Q* magazine, who called the track "the ultimate sonic rendition of what it means to be British". The Kinks' song 'Waterloo Sunset' came second while 'Wonderwall' by Oasis was voted third.

2007

Pamela Anderson's ex-husband Kid Rock is involved in an alleged assault on drummer Tommy Lee (who was previously married to the actress). Police interview witnesses to a tussle involving the pair at the MTV Music Video Awards in Las Vegas. Lee is removed from the ceremony while Rock is allowed to remain.

2007

Girls Aloud break the record for the most consecutive Top 10 hits in the UK singles chart by a female act. The girls' latest, 'Sexy! No No No', enters the chart at No. 5, giving them a run of 16 Top 10 hits.

Born on this day:

1957 Jon Moss, drums (Culture Club)
1958 Mick Talbot, keyboards (The Style Council)
1965 Moby, producer, singer

1971 Richard Ashcroft, guitar, vocals (The Verve)
1977 Jonny Buckland, guitar (Coldplay)

September 11

1956
Police are called to break up a crowd of rowdy teenagers following the showing of the film *Rock Around The Clock* at the Trocadero Cinema in London. The following day, *The Times* prints a reader's letter that says: "The hypnotic rhythm and the wild gestures have a maddening effect on a rhythm loving age group and the result of its impact is the relaxing of all self control." The film is quickly banned in several English cities.

1964
A 16-year-old youth wins a Mick Jagger impersonation contest at The Town Hall, Greenwich. The winner turns out to be Mick's younger brother Chris.

1967
Filming begins on The Beatles' *Magical Mystery Tour*, with no script, nor a very clear idea of exactly what is to be accomplished. The 'Magical Mystery Tour' bus sets off for the West Country in England, stopping for the night in Teignmouth, Devon where hundreds of fans greet The Beatles at their hotel.

1968
Larry Graham, bass player from Sly & The Family Stone, is busted for cannabis possession as the band arrive in London to start a UK tour.

1971
The animated *Jackson 5* series premieres on ABC-TV in the US.

1976
KC & The Sunshine Band are at No. 1 on the *Billboard* singles chart with '(Shake Shake Shake), Shake Your Booty', the group's third US No. 1.

1982
John 'Cougar' Mellencamp becomes the only male artist to have two singles – 'Jack And Diane' at No. 4, 'Hurts So Good' at No. 8 – in the US

Top Ten as well as the No. 1 album *American Fool* – at the top for the first of nine weeks.

1988
Michael Jackson appears at Aintree Racecourse in Liverpool, England on his 'Bad' World Tour. Over 3,000 fans are treated by the St. John Ambulance service for fainting, hysteria and being crushed among the crowd of 125,000 – the largest concert on the 123-date world tour.

1993
Mariah Carey starts an eight-week run at No. 1 on the US singles chart with 'Dreamlover'. This same day her fourth album, *Music Box*, goes to No. 1 in the UK.

1996
Noel Gallagher walks out on Oasis half way through an American tour after a fight with his brother Liam in a hotel in Charlotte, North Carolina. Noel flies back to London the following day.

2003
Tommy Chong, one-half of the comedy team of Cheech & Chong, is sentenced to nine months in federal prison and fined $20,000 for selling drug paraphernalia over the internet. The 65 year-old Chong pleaded guilty to the charges last May.

2006
A study from the University of Leicester finds that more than a quarter of classical music fans have tried cannabis. Researchers are trying to find out what people's taste in music reveal about their lifestyles. The UK study also reveals that blues buffs are the most likely to have received a driving penalty, while hip hop and dance music fans are more likely to have multiple sex partners and are among the biggest drug-takers surveyed. More than 2,500 people were interviewed for the study, which was published in the scientific journal *Psychology of Music*.

2001
Walking to work as a comic book illustrator in New York, Gerard Way witnesses the 9/11 attacks on the World Trade Center. The day's events inspire him to start a band, which becomes My Chemical Romance with Way as their lead singer.

Born on this day:

1944 Barry White, soul singer, producer
1952 Neil Peart, drums (Rush)

1956 Barry Andrews, keyboards (XTC, Shriekback)
1966 Ben Folds, US singer, songwriter, keyboards

1954
The first 'teen idol', Frank Sinatra, is at No. 1 on the British singles chart with 'Three Coins In The Fountain,' the singer's first UK No. 1. The song wins an Academy Award for Best Original Song of 1954.

1964
The Supremes, The Shangri-Las, Marvin Gaye, Dusty Springfield, The Ronettes, Millie Small, The Temptations, The Miracles and Little Anthony & The Imperials all appear at The Fox Theatre, Brooklyn, New York.

1968
During their first ever overseas tour Led Zeppelin appear at the Stora Scenen in Stockholm, Sweden.

1970
Judy Collins, Tom Paxton, Richie Havens, Joan Baez and Peter Fonda are among those taking part in a Woody Guthrie Memorial Concert held at the Hollywood Bowl in Los Angeles, California.

1980
During a North American tour, Queen appear at Kemper Arena, Kansas City.

1986
Public Image Ltd guitarist John McGeoch needs 40 stitches in his face after a two-litre wine bottle is thrown at the stage during a PIL gig in Vienna.

1987
Michael Jackson starts a five-week run at No. 1 on the UK album chart with *Bad*, his follow up to *Thriller*. *Bad* stays top of the US chart for six weeks.

1988
Pogues singer Shane MacGowan is admitted to a Dublin hospital suffering from nervous exhaustion.

1990
Stevie Nicks and Christine McVie from Fleetwood Mac announce they are leaving the band at the end of their current tour.

1997
Stig Anderson, songwriter, producer, founder of the Polar Music record label and Abba's manager, dies aged 66 of a heart attack. Anderson co-wrote some of Abba's biggest hits, including 'Waterloo', 'Mamma Mia', 'S.O.S', 'Fernando', 'Dancing Queen', 'Knowing Me, Knowing You' and 'The Name of the Game'. His funeral is broadcast live on Swedish television – an honour otherwise reserved only for distinguished statesmen or royalty.

2002
Sean Stewart, the 22-year-old son of Rod Stewart, is sentenced to 90 days in jail and ordered to undergo drug rehabilitation after pleading no contest to attacking a man outside a Malibu, California restaurant. Stewart was arrested on December 5, 2001, after he was seen kicking the man in the face and stomach. He is also sentenced to five years probation and ordered to pay $5,600 to the victim.

2004
American drummer and arranger Kenny Buttrey, who worked with Neil Young, (*After The Gold Rush*, *Harvest*), Bob Dylan (*Blonde On Blonde*, *John Wesley Harding*, *Nashville Skyline*), Bob Seger, Elvis Presley, Donovan, George Harrison, Joan Baez, Dan Fogelberg, Kris Kristofferson, Jimmy Buffett, Chuck Berry and Area Code 615, dies aged 59 of cancer in Nashville, Tennessee,

2007
The surviving members of Led Zeppelin announce they will reform for a star-studded tribute concert to Atlantic Records' founder Ahmet Ertegun who died on 14 December, 2006. On the drums will be Jason, the son of John Bonham, who died in 1980. The one-off concert, the trio's first full-scale performance for 19 years, will take place at the O2 Arena in London on November 26 with tickets costing £125. All profits from the show will go towards scholarships in Ertegun's name in the UK, the USA and Turkey, the country of his birth.

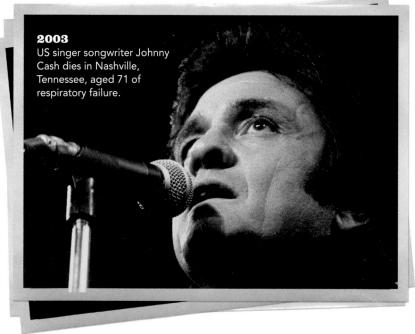

2003
US singer songwriter Johnny Cash dies in Nashville, Tennessee, aged 71 of respiratory failure.

Born on this day:

1944 Peter Cetera, vocals (Chicago)
1952 Randy Jones, vocals (Village People)
1963 Dave Mustaine, guitar, vocals (Metallica, Megadeth)
1965 Zak Starkey, drums (The Icicle Works, The Who, Oasis)
1983 James Bourne, singer, songwriter (Busted)

September 13

1960

A campaign is started in the UK to ban Ray Peterson's American hit 'Tell Laura I Love Her'. The song, telling of a lovesick youngster who drives in a stock car race to win the hand of his sweetheart but crashes and, just before dying, utters the words of the title, is denounced in the press as likely to inspire a teen-age "glorious death cult".

1963

Graham Nash falls out of The Hollies' van after a gig in Scotland. Nash checked to see if the door was locked, it wasn't and he fell out as it was travelling at 40 mph.

1964

During a UK tour two dozen rugby players are hired as a human crash barrier at a Rolling Stones gig at the Liverpool Empire. The human chain disappears under a wave of 5,000 fans as the Stones take to the stage.

1967

The Beatles form an electronics company called Fiftyshapes, Ltd. They appoint an acquaintance of John Lennon, John Alexis Mardas (Magic Alex) as the company's director. Alex claims he can build a 72-track tape machine, instead of the four-track used at Abbey Road. One of his more outrageous plans is to replace the acoustic baffles around Ringo Starr's drums with an invisible sonic force field. Unsurprisingly none of this ever materialises. George Harrison later said that employing Mardas was "the biggest disaster of all time".

1969

John and Yoko with the Plastic Ono Band fly to Canada to perform at the Rock & Roll Revival Show in Toronto. The band – featuring Eric Clapton, Klaus Voormann and drummer Alan White – are put together so late that they have to rehearse on the plane from London. Also appearing at the

concert are Chuck Berry, Gene Vincent, Bo Diddley, The Doors and Alice Cooper. Lennon later releases the Plastic Ono Band's performance as the *Live Peace In Toronto 1969* album.

1971

During their North American tour, Led Zeppelin appear at Berkeley Community Theatre, Berkeley, California.

1986

Berlin are at No. 1 on the US singles chart with the Giorgio Moroder written and produced 'Take My Breath Away'. On the B-side is The Righteous Brothers' 'You've Lost That Lovin' Feelin'. Both songs are featured in the film *Top Gun*.

1991

Geffen Records host a party to launch Nirvana's single 'Smells Like Teen Spirit.' The band end up being thrown out of their own party after starting a food fight.

1996

Tupac Amaru Shakur (right) dies aged 25 after 13 bullets are fired into his BMW while he was driving through Las Vegas. The incident is blamed on East versus West Coast Gang wars. Shakur was a convicted sex offender, guilty of sexual abuse. After serving eleven months of his sentence he was released from prison on an appeal financed by Marion "Suge" Knight, the CEO of Death Row Records.

2000

Elton John throws a tantrum at a sell-out show at the Estoril Casino near Lisbon. Elton is unhappy after the audience was slow to leave a VIP dinner before the concert. The singer storms out of the building and flies home on his private jet without playing a note.

2005

The home where Jimi Hendrix grew up in Seattle is saved from demolition at the last minute. The James Marshall Hendrix Foundation and the City of Seattle agree to renovate the building into a community centre opposite the cemetery where the guitarist was buried in 1970.

September 14

Born on this day:

1949   Steve Gaines, guitar (Lynyrd Skynyrd)
1950   Paul Kossoff, guitar (Free, Back Street Crawler)
1959   Morten Harket, vocals (A-Ha)
1981   Ashley Roberts, singer (Pussycat Dolls)
1983   Amy Winehouse, singer, songwriter

1955

Little Richard enters a New Orleans studio to begin two days of recording. Things don't go well and, during a break, Richard and his producer Bumps Blackwell go to the local Dew Drop Inn for lunch. Richard starts playing the piano in the bar like crazy, singing a loud and lewd version of 'Tutti Frutti'. With only 15 minutes left of the session, Richard records the song and coins the phrase "a-wop-bop-a-loo-bop-a-lop-bam-boom".

1968

Roy Orbison's house in Nashville burns down killing his two eldest sons. Orbison is on tour in the UK at the time of the tragic accident.

1969

In the UK Smile (later to become Queen) appear at PJ's Club in Truro, Cornwall.

1974

Crosby Stills Nash & Young, Joni Mitchell, The Band, Jesse Colin Young and Joe Walsh all appear on a one-day show at London's Wembley Stadium.

1988

Prince plays the first night of the North American leg on his 'Lovesexy' 84-date world tour at the Met Center, Minneapolis, Minnesota.

1994

US singer Steve Earle is sentenced to a year in jail after being found guilty of possession of crack cocaine.

1997

Over 2,000 people watch as Pete Townshend unveils an English Heritage Blue Plaque at 23 Brook Street, Mayfair, London, to mark where Jimi Hendrix lived in 1968-69. Hendrix is the first deceased rock star to be given such an honour. 18th century classical composer George Frideric Handel had once lived in the neighbouring property.

1999

It is reported that George Michael is being sued for $10m by the policeman who arrested the singer in a public lavatory. Marcelo Rodriguez claims he was mocked in the video 'Outside', leaving him in physical distress.

2002
No Doubt singer Gwen Stefani marries Gavin Rossdale of Bush in St. Paul's Church, London

2005

HMV stores in Canada remove Bob Dylan CDs from their shelves in protest at the singer's decision to sell his new album only through Starbucks after signing an exclusive contract with the coffee giant. The chain had previously boycotted CDs by Alanis Morissette and The Rolling Stones because of exclusive deals.

2006

Whitney Houston files for divorce from singer Bobby Brown, after 14 years of marriage.

2008

Kings Of Leon start a three-week run at No. 1 on the UK singles chart with 'Sex On Fire', taken from the band's fourth studio album *Only By The Night*.

Iron Maiden singer Bruce Dickinson is one of the pilots who flew specially chartered flights to rescue 85,000 tourists stranded in the US, the Caribbean, Africa and Europe after Britain's third-largest tour operator went into administration. The singer, who had worked for the airline Astraeus for seven years, took up flying during a low point in his solo career after temporarily quitting the band in 1993.

1979
The film *Quadrophenia* is released. Based on The Who's 1973 album it features Phil Daniels, Toyah Willcox, Ray Winstone, Michael Elphick and Sting.

1961

A group from Hawthorne, California called The Pendletones attend their first real recording session at Hite Morgan's studio in Los Angeles. The band record 'Surfin', a song that will help shape their career as The Beach Boys.

1962

The Four Seasons start a five-week run at No. 1 on the US singles chart with 'Sherry', which made No. 8 in the UK. They become the first American group to have three chart-toppers in succession.

1968

The Doors are forced to perform as a trio in Amsterdam after singer Jim Morrison collapses while dancing during support act Jefferson Airplane's performance.

1970

Black Sabbath and The Dog That Bit People appear at The Marquee, London.

1979

Bob Dylan releases *Slow Train Coming*, an album of religious songs written after Dylan's conversion to Christianity, including the Grammy Award winning single, 'Gotta Serve Somebody'. The album alienates many of his long time fans.

1984

Frankie Goes To Hollywood's 'Relax' becomes the longest running chart hit since Engelbert Humperdink's 'Release Me', spending 43 weeks on the UK singles chart.

1990

The Steve Miller Band have a UK No. 1 with 'The Joker', 16 years after its first release. The track was featured in a TV ad for jeans.

1994

A crudely recorded reel-to-reel tape of The Quarry Men appearing at St Peter's Parish Church garden party, Liverpool on July 6, 1957 – the day John Lennon met Paul McCartney – sells for £69,000 at a Sotheby's auction.

1997

A 34-year-old man is awarded more than £20,000 by a French court after he lost his hearing after standing too close to loudspeakers at a U2 concert in 1993.

2003

Abba tribute acts overtake Elvis impersonators in the battle of British covers singers, according to a survey. The Swedish group jump from third most copied act in 2001 to top in 2002 with imitators like Bjorn Again, Abba Fever and Voulez Vous putting on Abba shows. Elvis drops to number two while The Beatles drop to three.

2004

Ramones guitarist Johnny Ramone (real name: John Cummings) dies aged 55 in Los Angeles after a five-year battle with prostate cancer.

2008

Pink Floyd keyboard player and founder member Richard Wright dies aged 65 from cancer. Wright appeared on all of the group's recordings until being forced from the band by Roger Waters in 1980. He rejoined the line-up as an auxiliary member after Waters departure. In 2005, the full band reunited – for the first time in 24 years – for the Live 8 concert in London's Hyde Park. Wright also contributed vocals and keyboards to David Gilmour's 2006 solo album *On An Island*. Gilmour pays tribute to Wright, saying: "He was such a lovely, gentle, genuine man and will be missed terribly by so many who loved him."

Born on this day:

1925	B.B. King, US blues guitarist
1948	Kenney Jones, drums (The Small Faces, The Faces, The Who)
1952	Ron Blair, bass (Tom Petty & The Heartbreakers)
1963	Richard Marx, singer, songwriter
1984	Katie Melua, singer, songwriter

1963

The Beatles' 'She Loves You' is first released by Swan Records in America. Although the song is currently No. 1 in the UK, 'She Loves You' is ignored in the US until 1964 when it reached the top of the *Billboard* chart.

1970

Led Zeppelin win the Best Group award in the *Melody Maker* Readers Poll. It is the first time in eight years that The Beatles haven't won the award.

Jimi Hendrix joins Eric Burdon on stage at Ronnie Scott's club in London for what would become the guitarist's last ever informal musical appearance.

1979

The first 'old skool' rap single, The Sugarhill Gang's 'Rapper's Delight', is released on New York-based Sugarhill Records.

1988

Former Clash drummer Topper Headon is released from jail after serving 10 months of a 15-month sentence on a narcotics charge.

1989

In Australia, U2 jam with B.B. King on a boat rented for the blues legend's 64th birthday on Sydney Harbour.

1996

Pearl Jam play the first night of their 'No Code' tour at the Key Arena in Seattle, Washington. Because of the band's refusal to play in Ticketmaster venue areas, they are forced to use alternate ticketing companies for the shows which fans complain are out-of-the-way and hard to get to.

1998

At a Sotheby's auction a notebook belonging to former Beatles roadie Mal Evans containing the lyrics to 'Hey Jude' sells for £111,500, a two-tone denim jacket belonging to John Lennon fetches £9,200 and the Union Jack dress worn by Spice Girl Ginger Spice raises £41,320.

1977

Marc Bolan is killed instantly when the car driven by his girlfriend, Gloria Jones, leaves the road and hits a tree on Barnes Common in south west London. Bolan was 29. The couple were on the way back to their home in Richmond after a night out at a Mayfair restaurant. A local man who witnessed the crash said, "When I arrived a girl was lying on the bonnet and a man with long dark curly hair was stretched out in the road – there was a hell of a mess." The site of the accident has since become a shrine to Bolan.

2006

Bob Dylan's *Modern Times* enters the US album chart at No. 1, making it Dylan's first album to reach that position since 1976's *Desire*, 30 years prior. At 65, Dylan becomes the oldest living musician to top the *Billboard* album chart. The record also reaches No. 1 in Australia, Canada, Denmark, Ireland, New Zealand, Norway and Switzerland.

Born on this day:

1923 Hank Williams, US country singer, songwriter

1947 Jim Hodder, drums (Steely Dan)

1950 Fee Waybill, vocals (The Tubes)

1968 Anastacia, US singer

1969 Keith Flint, vocals (The Prodigy)

1956
The BBC announce the removal of Bill Haley & His Comets' 'Rockin' Through The Rye' from its playlist because they feel the song goes against traditional British standards. The record, based on an 18th century Scottish folk tune, is at No. 5 on the UK charts.

1964
Police arrive at a Rolling Stones gig at the ABC Theatre in Carlisle, England, after trouble breaks out among the 4,000 fans at the concert.

1967
The Doors are banned from *The Ed Sullivan Show* after Jim Morrison breaks an agreement with the show's producers who had requested a change to the lyric "Girl, we couldn't get much higher" in 'Light My Fire'. Morrison said before the live transmission that he wouldn't sing the words but did anyway. The Doors also perform their new single, 'People Are Strange'.

1973
Def Leppard, Mötley Cröe, Eddie Money and Uriah Heep all appear at Jack Murphy Stadium, San Diego, California.

1976
The Sex Pistols play a gig for the inmates at Chelmsford Prison, Essex.

1991
Rob Tyner, ex-lead singer with the American rock band MC5, dies aged 46 after suffering a heart attack in the seat of his parked car in his hometown of Berkley, Michigan.

Over four million copies of Guns N' Roses albums *Use Your Illusion I* and *Use Your Illusion II* are simultaneously released for retail sale, making it the largest ship-out in rock history in the US.

1996
A bomb is found at a South London sorting office addressed to Icelandic singer Bjork. Police in Miami alert the post office after finding the body of Ricardo Lopez who had made a video of himself making the bomb and then committing suicide.

2000
Television presenter Paula Yates is found dead from a suspected drug overdose. Yates had presented the UK music TV show *The Tube* during the 80s, married Bob Geldof and was the girlfriend of INXS singer Michael Hutchence at the time of his death in 1997.

2003
Moore and Bode Cigars are suing P Diddy after film footage of their "secret" production process turned up in his latest video. The company claim an unidentified cameraman filmed their "unique method of rolling cigars" which was then used in the rappers 'Shake Ya Tailfeather' video without permission.

2004
Israeli police arrest two of Madonna's bodyguards after they assault photographers waiting for the singer outside her hotel. Madonna is in Israel with 2,000 other students of Kabbalah, the Jewish mystical cult.

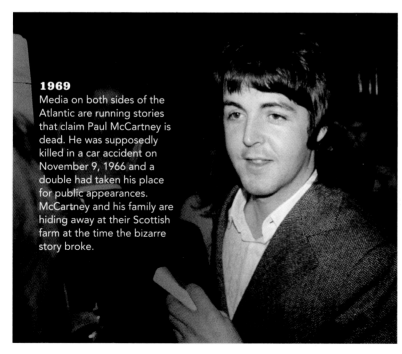

1969
Media on both sides of the Atlantic are running stories that claim Paul McCartney is dead. He was supposedly killed in a car accident on November 9, 1966 and a double had taken his place for public appearances. McCartney and his family are hiding away at their Scottish farm at the time the bizarre story broke.

September 18

Born on this day:

1950 Mike Hossack, drums (The Doobie Brothers)

1952 Dee Dee Ramone, bass (The Ramones)

1962 Joanne Catherall, vocals (The Human League)

1966 Mike Heaton, drums (Embrace)

1960
On his 21st birthday, Frankie Avalon is given $600,000 that he earned as a minor from such hits as his 1959 US No. 1 'Venus'.

1961
Bobby Vee starts a two-week run at No. 1 on the US singles chart with 'Take Good Care Of My Baby'.

1970
Jimi Hendrix is pronounced dead on arrival at St. Mary Abbot's Hospital in London at the age of 27 after choking on his own vomit. His final hours at an apartment in Notting Hill Gate are still a subject of morbid speculation. Hendrix's German girlfriend, Monika Dannemann, who was with him at the time but was unable to rouse him, committed suicide in 1996.

1971
The Who score their first and only UK No. 1 album with *Who's Next*.

1976
One hit wonders Wild Cherry start a three-week run at No. 1 on the US singles chart with 'Play That Funky Music', which started life as a B-side. It is the group's only hit in the UK, peaking at No. 7.

1983
Kiss appear without their make-up for the first time during an MTV interview.

1984
David Bowie wins Video Of The Year for 'China Girl' at the first MTV Video Awards.

1993
Garth Brooks is at No. 1 on the US album chart with *In Pieces*. The album, which spends 25 weeks on the chart and sells over six million copies, peaks at No. 2 on the UK chart.

1996
At Sotheby's in London, Julian Lennon successfully bids just over £21,000 for the recording notes to the song Paul McCartney wrote for him, 'Hey Jude'.

At the same event, John Lennon's scribbled lyrics to 'Being For The Benefit Of Mr. Kite' sell for £57,500.

2004
Britney Spears marries dancer Kevin Federline during a private ceremony in Los Angeles. Federline has two daughters from his previous relationship with actress Shar Jackson.

2006
Police stop 73-year-old country singer Willie Nelson's tour bus near Lafayette, Louisiana. Four members of his band are charged with drug possession after marijuana and magic mushrooms are found on the bus by police.

Echo & The Bunnymen singer Ian McCulloch is convicted of committing a breach of the peace by shouting, swearing and threatening Gary Duncan and his girlfriend Juliet Sebley backstage at Glasgow Barrowlands in Scotland. The court was told that McCulloch had lost his temper when he discovered the two fans in a toilet cubicle inside his private dressing room.

Cliff Richard unveils a plaque to mark where the tiny basement 2I's coffee bar opened on London's Old Compton Street, 50 years ago. The Tornados, Tommy Steele, The Shadows and Adam Faith are among the stars who started out at the club, which was the birthplace of British rock'n'roll.

2007
Britney Spears is dropped by her management company, one month after employing their services. Los Angeles-based The Firm said: "We have terminated our professional relationship with Britney Spears. We believe she is enormously talented, but current circumstances have prevented us from properly doing our job."

Born on this day:

1940	Bill Medley, singer (The Righteous Brothers)	**1947**	Lol Creme, vocals, guitar (10CC)
1941	Cass Elliott, singer (The Mamas & The Papas, solo)	**1951**	Daniel Lanois, producer
		1963	Jarvis Cocker, singer (Pulp)
		1977	Ryan Dusick, drums (Maroon 5)

1960

Former Philadelphia chicken plucker Chubby Checker is at No. 1 on the US singles chart with 'The Twist'.

1963

The Detours (later to be called The Who) appear at The Oldfield Hotel, Greenford, England.

1969

Creedence Clearwater Revival score their only UK No. 1 single with 'Bad Moon Rising', a US No. 2 hit. Also on this day the group start a four-week run on top of the US album chart with *Green River*.

1970

The first UK Glastonbury Festival takes place featuring Marc Bolan, Ian Anderson, Keith Christmas, Quintessence, Amazing Blondel and Sam Apple Pie.

1973

Country rock singer-songwriter, Gram Parsons, formerly of The Byrds and The Flying Burrito Brothers, dies aged 26 under mysterious conditions in Joshua Tree, California. His death is attributed to heart failure but later it

was officially announced as a drug overdose. His coffin was stolen by two of his associates, manager Phil Kaufman and Michael Martin, a former roadie for The Byrds, and taken to the Joshua Tree Monument and Cap Roc in the California desert, where it was set alight, in accordance with Parson's wishes. The two were later arrested by police.

1979

The No Nukes concert is held at New York's Madison Square Garden. Performers include Stephen Stills, David Crosby, Jackson Browne, Bonnie Raitt, The Doobie Brothers, Poco, Tom Petty, Carly Simon, James Taylor and Bruce Springsteen.

1981

Simon & Garfunkel reunite for a concert in New York's Central Park. Over 400,000 attend the show and the performance is recorded for a record and video release.

1992

The Shamen start a four-week run at No. 1 on the British singles chart with 'Ebeneezer Goode', one of the most controversial UK chart toppers due to its perceived subliminal endorsement of recreational drug use. The song is initially banned by the BBC.

Radiohead film the video for their new single 'Creep' during a show at The Venue, Oxford, England.

1995

P.M. Dawn's DJ JC Eternal is arrested on charges of sexual assault and child abuse after an alleged affair with his 14 year-old cousin. He is released on $10,000 bail.

2002

James Brown is being sued by his own daughters for more than £650,000 of song royalties they claim they are owed. Deanna Brown Thomas and Dr. Yamma Brown Lumar, a Texas

physician, say Brown has withheld royalties on 25 co-written songs. The lawsuit claims that Brown has held a grudge against his daughters since 1998, when Ms Thomas had her father committed to a psychiatric hospital to be treated for addiction to painkillers.

2005

Research published by Guinness World Records shows that Status Quo have achieved more hit singles than any other band in UK chart history. The band have scored 61 chart successes, dating from 'Pictures Of Matchstick Men' in 1968 to 'You'll Come Around' in 2004. Queen come second with 52 hits, with The Rolling Stones and UB40 having 51 hits each.

2008

American jazz session drummer Earl Palmer, who worked with scores of artists including Little Richard ('Tutti Frutti'), Ike And Tina Turner ('River Deep, Mountain High'), Fats Domino ('I'm Walkin') and The Righteous Brothers ('You've Lost That Lovin' Feelin'), dies aged 83.

September 20

Born on this day:

1945 Sweet Pea Atkinson (Was Not Was)
1949 Chuck and John Panozzo, bass and drums (Styx)
1959 Alannah Currie, vocals, sax (The Thompson Twins)
1960 Robert Wiggins (Grandmaster Flash & The Furious Five)

1969
Based on the comic-book TV series Archie and his friends The Archies start a four-week run at No. 1 on the US singles chart with 'Sugar Sugar'. It goes on to become the longest running one hit wonder in the UK after spending eight weeks at the top of the charts.

UK music paper *Melody Maker* Readers Poll results are published. Winners include Eric Clapton who wins Best Musician, whilst Bob Dylan wins Best Male Singer and best album for *Nashville Skyline*. Best group is The Beatles, Best Single goes to Simon & Garfunkel for 'The Boxer' and Janis Joplin wins Best Female Singer.

During a meeting in London between John Lennon, Paul McCartney and Ringo Starr, Lennon announces he is leaving The Beatles.

1970
Jim Morrison of The Doors is acquitted on charges of lewd and lascivious behavior, but is found guilty of exposing himself during a concert at The Dinner Key Auditorium in Coconut Grove a year and a half earlier. At his trial at the Dade County Courthouse in Miami, Judge Goodman sentences Morrison to six months hard labor and a $500 fine for public exposure and 60 days hard labor for profanity. The sentence is appealed but Morrison is never brought to trial, as he dies in Paris, France on July 3, 1971.

1973
On his way to perform his second concert of the day, US singer-songwriter Jim Croce is killed with five others when his chartered aircraft hits a tree on take off in Louisiana.

1975
'Fame' gives David Bowie his first No. 1 in the US. The song was co-written with John Lennon and Bowie's guitarist Carlos Alomar.

1976
The first of the two-night 100 Club Punk Festival, Oxford St, London, featuring The Sex Pistols, The Clash, Subway Sect, Suzie (*sic*) And The Banshees, The Buzzcocks, Vibrators and Stinky Toys. Admission: £1.50.

1980
Queen start a five-week run on top of the US album chart with *The Game*, the group's only US No. 1 album.

1993
Just back from a tour of Japan, The Charlatans keyboard player Rob Collins and an old friend stop at an off-licence. Collins' friend goes in, half-jokingly saying he could rob the place. The police arrest the pair the next day and charge them both with attempted robbery and possession of a firearm (it was a replica gun).

1994
The Dave Matthews Band release *Under The Table And Dreaming*. The album is dedicated to Matthews' older sister Anne, who was killed by her husband in 1994 in a murder-suicide.

1997
Elton John starts a six-week run at No. 1 on the UK singles chart with 'Something About The Way You Look Tonight' and 'Candle In The Wind 97', a re-write of his 1973 song about Marilyn Monroe with new lyrics that relate to Diana, Princess of Wales. This version raises funds for Diana's charity following her death in Paris, and goes on to become the biggest selling single in the world ever.

Pearl Jam's 'Jeremy' video is cited as one of the reasons American teenager Barry Loukaitis snapped into a violent rage that left three people dead. Defence attorneys take the unprecedented step of playing the video in a Washington court.

2005
Canadian JD Fortune beats two other finalists to become the new lead singer with INXS after a worldwide search to replace the late Michael Hutchence. INXS held auditions in six continents as part of a reality TV series.

2007
Stereophonics singer Kelly Jones is admitted to hospital after being injured during an altercation with a member of a west London club's security team. The band had gone there after appearing at the Vodafone Live Music Awards.

Born on this day:

1934 Leonard Cohen, Canadian singer, songwriter, poet

1947 Don Felder, guitar, vocals (The Eagles)

1972 Liam Gallagher, vocals (Oasis)

1977 Sam Rivers, bass (Limp Bizkit)

September 21

1968

Madame Tussaud's waxwork museum in London give The Beatles their fifth image change of clothes and hair in four years.

1971

The first edition of the BBC TV music show *The Old Grey Whistle Test* is aired. The show includes film clips of Jimi Hendrix from the Monterey Pop Festival playing 'Wild Thing', Bob Dylan performing 'Maggie's Farm' (from the *Don't Look Back* film), plus America and Lesley Duncan live in the studio.

1974

One hit wonder Carl Douglas is at No. 1 on the UK singles chart with 'Kung Fu Fighting'. The song, recorded in 10 minutes, had started out as a B-side and went on to sell over 10 million copies.

1980

During a North American tour, Bob Marley collapses while jogging in New York's Central Park. After hospital tests he is diagnosed as having cancer. Marley played his last ever concert two nights later at the Stanley Theater in Pittsburgh, Pennsylvania.

1981

Adam And The Ants are at the top of the UK singles chart with their second No. 1 'Prince Charming.'

1985

Madonna scores her first UK No. 1 album with *Like A Virgin*, 10 months after its release. The album spends a total 152 weeks on the UK chart.

1986

The *National Enquirer* magazine features a picture of Michael Jackson in an oxygen chamber with a story claiming that Jackson has a bizarre plan to live until he is 150 years old.

1987

American jazz bassist Jaco Pastorius, who was a member of jazz fusion outfit Weather Report and worked with various acts including Joni Mitchell and Herbie Hancock, dies aged 35 from injuries sustained in a fight. Pastorius was trying to enter the Midnight Bottle Club in Wilton Manors, Florida (where he'd been banned) and became involved in a fight with a bouncer. Pastorius fell into a coma and was put on life support. In 2006, Pastorius was voted The Greatest Bass Player Who Has Ever Lived by readers of *Bass Guitar* magazine.

1989

U2 play the first of three nights at Perth Entertainment Centre in Australia during their 'Lovetown' World Tour.

1991

Status Quo put themselves into the *Guinness Book Of World Records* by appearing at four venues in Sheffield, Glasgow, Birmingham and London within a 12-hour period.

1996

The Fugees score their second UK No. 1 single with 'Ready Or Not' – the song's chorus based on 'Ready Or Not Here I Come (Can't Hide From Love)' by The Delfonics. The Fugees previous single, 'Killing Me Softly', was so successful that the track was 'deleted' while still in the Top 20 to make way for 'Ready Or Not'.

2007

Snoop Dogg is sentenced to three years probation and 160 hours of community service after pleading guilty to carrying a collapsible baton. The rapper was arrested in September 2006 after the baton was found in his bag at John Wayne Airport in Orange County, California. In April 2007 he was given five years probation and 800 hours community service after pleading no contest to gun and drug charges in a Californian court.

Born on this day:

1949 David Coverdale, vocals (Deep Purple, Whitesnake)

1957 Nick Cave, Australian singer, songwriter, writer

1960 Joan Jett, guitar, vocals (The Runaways, solo)

1975 Mystikal (Michael Tyler), US rapper

1958
After receiving special permission from the US Army, Elvis Presley gives one last press conference at the Military Ocean Terminal in Brooklyn. He then joins the rest of the 3rd Armored Division on the USS General Randall en route to Bremerhaven, Germany.

1962
The Springfields, featuring Dusty Springfield, her brother Tom and their friend, Tim Feld, enter the US Top 20 with 'Silver Threads And Golden Needles', becoming the first British vocal group to chart that high in America.

1965
San Francisco band The Great Society, featuring Grace Slick and her husband Darby, make their live debut at The Coffee Gallery, North Beach, California.

1969
A new weekly TV show The Music Scene airs on ABC in the US for the first time. Stevie Wonder, Crosby Stills Nash & Young, Tom Jones, Cass Elliot, James Brown, Janis Joplin and Sly & the Family Stone are all booked to appear on the show.

1972
David Bowie kicks off the North American leg of his 'Ziggy Stardust' world tour at the Music Hall in Cleveland, Ohio.

1974
The Sonny Bono Comedy Revue is shown for the first time on ABC-TV in the US.

1979
Def Leppard receive their first major live review when UK music weekly Melody Maker covers the band's Wolverhampton gig. With a 15 year-old drummer they have just released their debut three-track single.

1981
American composer Harry Warren, who wrote over 800 songs including 'I Only Have Eyes For You' (a hit for The Flamingos and Art Garfunkel), 'You Must Have Been A Beautiful Baby', 'Jeepers Creepers', 'That's Amore' and 'Chattanooga Choo Choo', dies aged 88. Warren's songs have been featured in over 300 films.

1985
Joni Mitchell, Willie Nelson, Neil Young, Bob Dylan and Tom Petty all appear at the first Farm Aid concert – an event to help small farmers in America – at the Memorial Stadium at the University of Illinois, Champaign.

1986
The Smiths sign to EMI Records for £1 million.

1990
Garth Brooks' album No Fences enters the US album chart, going on to become the biggest selling country album of all time, selling over 13m copies in the first five years of release.

1990
Nirvana play their biggest gig to date at the Motor Sports International Garage, Seattle. Drummer Dave Grohl, who would audition for the band in a few days time, is among the audience of 15,000.

1992
Def Leppard are forced to cancel two US shows after their sound equipment truck is found abandoned after one of the band's drivers had attempted to rob a store. The driver is later charged for drug possession and criminal damage.

1999
Diana Ross is arrested on Concorde after an incident at Heathrow Airport. The singer claims that a female security guard touched her breasts while frisking her. Ross retaliated by rubbing her hands down the security guard.

2001
'A Tribute To Heroes', a programme organised to raise money following the terrorist attacks on the Pentagon and New York's World Trade Center, is aired live, commercial free, on most of the major US TV networks. Neil Young, Tom Petty, Paul Simon, Billy Joel, U2, Limp Bizkit, Bruce Springsteen and Pearl Jam all perform. Manning the telephones to take pledges are celebrities, including Jack Nicholson, Jim Carrey, Whoopi Goldberg, Goldie Hawn, Robin Williams, Meg Ryan, Cuba Gooding Jr., Kurt Russell, Adam Sandler and many others.

2007
The Game is given a conditional discharge at Manhattan's Criminal Court after being charged with impersonating a police officer. Police say the rapper told a cab driver he was an undercover officer, ordering him to run several red lights. The Game (real name: Jayceon Taylor) claims the cab driver noticed they were being followed and asked who was in the car. He says he told the driver they were the hip-hop police, and the driver decided on his own to run the traffic signals.

1930   Ray Charles, singer, songwriter
1939   Roy Buchanan, US guitarist

1943   Julio Iglesias, Spanish singer
1949   Bruce Springsteen, US singer, songwriter

September
23

1957
The Crickets are at No. 1 on the US singles chart with 'That'll Be The Day', the title being taken from a phrase used by John Wayne in the film *The Searchers*.

1965
The Walker Brothers are at No. 1 on the UK singles chart with Burt Bacharach & Hal David's 'Make It Easy On Yourself', the trio's first of two UK chart-toppers.

1966
The 12-date 'Rolling Stones 66' UK tour kicks off at London's Royal Albert Hall. Support acts are The Yardbirds, Ike & Tina Turner and Peter Jay & The New Jaywalkers. The show has to be stopped several times during the Stones set when frenzied fans invade the stage.

1967
The Mothers Of Invention make their UK live debut at London's Royal Albert Hall.

1971
Led Zeppelin play the first of two nights at The Budokan Hall, Tokyo, Japan.

1974
Robbie McIntosh, founder member of the Average White Band, dies aged 24 of a heroin overdose at a Hollywood party. AWB scored a No. 1 single 'Pick Up The Pieces', which was nominated for a Grammy Award in 1975.

1978
10CC have their third and final UK No. 1 single with 'Dreadlock Holiday'. The lyrics, about a white man lost in Jamaica, are based on a true event that happened to Moody Blues vocalist Justin Hayward and Eric Stewart from 10CC in Barbados.

1980
Bob Marley collapses on stage during a concert at the Stanley Theater in Pittsburgh, Pennsylvania. Marley had collapsed in New York's Central Park while jogging two days before and was told to immediately cancel his US tour, but flew to Pittsburgh for one final performance. This was the last time Marley ever appeared on stage. He died of cancer in May 1981.

1995
Jamaican Ragga singer Shaggy scores his second UK chart-topper when 'Boombastic' goes to the top of the charts for one week. The song is also a US No. 1.

2001
Kylie Minogue starts a five-week run at No. 1 on the UK singles chart with 'Can't Get You Out Of My Head'. The Australian singer's sixth chart-topper was written and produced by Cathy Dennis and former Mud guitarist Rob Davis for which the pair won an Ivor Novello Award for the Most Performed Song of the Year. 'Can't Get You Out Of My Head' charts at No. 1 in 40 countries.

2004
Slipknot's Corey Taylor issues a statement denying he is dead. Rumours started after a shock jock in Des Moines broadcast the announcement that the singer had died of a drug overdose, which then became a fatal car crash.

A bodyguard for rapper Lil' Kim is sentenced to 12 years in prison after admitting firing at least 20 times in a shoot-out with a rival gang. The judge sentencing Suif Jackson says society needs protection from a gun-toting man with five convictions. The shooting took place when the entourages of Lil' Kim and Capone-N-Noreaga crossed at a New York radio station.

2006
At 60, Neil Young is named Artist of the Year at the Americana Honors and Awards at the fifth annual event in Nashville, Tennessee.

2006
Beyonce is at No. 1 on the US album chart with her second solo album 'B'Day.'

September 24

Born on this day:

1933   Mel Taylor, drums (The Ventures)
1941   Linda McCartney, photographer, keyboards, vocals

1942   Gerry Marsden, guitar, vocals (Gerry & The Pacemakers)
1971   Peter Salisbury, drums (The Verve)

1965
Bob Dylan plays the first night of a 36-date North American tour at Austin Municipal Auditorium, Austin, Texas.

1966
Jimi Hendrix arrives in London with manager Chas Chandler on a flight from New York City. He only has the clothes he is wearing, having sold his other belongings to pay a hotel bill in New York.

1975
Rod Stewart is at No. 1 on the UK singles chart with a cover of Sutherland Brother & Quiver's 'Sailing'. Rod's version became a hit after it was used in a TV documentary series.

1980
The mixing of the forthcoming John and Yoko album *Double Fantasy* moves from The Hit Factory in New York City to Record Plant East. During this session, John Lennon gives an interview to rock journalist Lisa Robinson.

1988
Bobby McFerrin starts a two week run at No. 1 on the US singles chart with 'Don't Worry Be Happy', the first a-cappella record to be a chart-topper.

The Hollies are at No. 1 in the UK with 'He Ain't Heavy, He's My Brother' after the song was revived for a UK TV beer commercial. The song was originally a hit for the group in 1969 and featured a young Elton John on piano.

1991
Nirvana's album *Nevermind* is released in America, entering the chart at No. 144 on its first week; it peaked at No. 1 in January 1992.

1995
The Charlatans are arrested by 24-armed police when landing in New York. The band are accused of trying to disrupt the plane's flight path, and passengers complain of the group being drunk, spitting and interfering with the in-flight TV sets.

2003
Singer-songwriter Matthew Jay dies aged 24 after falling from a seventh-storey window in London. He had released the 2001 album *Draw* and toured with The Doves, Stereophonics, Dido and Starsailor.

The Dave Matthews Band play New York City's Central Park in front of almost 100,000, the band's largest audience to date. The show is later released as an album.

2006
Scissor Sisters top the UK album and singles charts. The New Yorkers' second album, *Ta-Dah*, enters in the top spot while the single 'I Don't Feel Like Dancin'' spends a third week at number one.

1984
Culture Club achieve their second UK No. 1 single with 'Karma Chameleon', which stays at the top of the charts for six weeks, becoming the best-selling single of 1983. The harmonica part is played by Judd Lander who had been a member of Merseybeat group The Hideaways in the 60s.

Born on this day:

1945 Owen 'Onnie' McIntyre, guitar (The Average White Band)

1946 Bryan MacLean, guitar, vocals (Love)

1955 Steve Severin, bass (Siouxsie & The Banshees)

1974 Richie Edwards, bass (The Darkness)

1964

The Temptations begin recording 'My Girl' which went on to be their first US No. 1 and the first of 15 US Top 10 hits.

1965

The Beatles cartoon series premieres on ABC TV in the US. The first story is titled 'I Want To Hold Your Hand' and has the group exploring the ocean floor in a diving bell where they meet a lovesick octopus. The rights to the cartoon series are subsequently bought by Apple, The Beatles' own company, which has effectively suppressed them.

1970

The first episode of *The Partridge Family* is shown on US TV, featuring Shirley Jones, David Cassidy, Susan Dey and Danny Bonaduce.

1971

David Bowie and America both appear at Friars in Aylesbury, England. Tickets cost 50p.

1975

Jackie Wilson has a heart attack while performing live on stage at the Latin Casino, New Jersey. Wilson collapses into a coma, suffering severe brain damage. Ironically, he was in the middle of singing one of his biggest hits, 'Lonely Teardrops', and was two words into the line "... my heart is crying" when he collapsed to the stage, striking his head heavily. Wilson died aged 49 on 21 January, 1984. Van Morrison wrote the song 'Jackie Wilson Said', later covered by Dexy's Midnight Runners, as a tribute to Wilson.

1976

Wings play a charity concert in St Marks Square, Venice to raise funds for the historic city. The night is a success but the weight of the equipment used by the group causes more damage to the square.

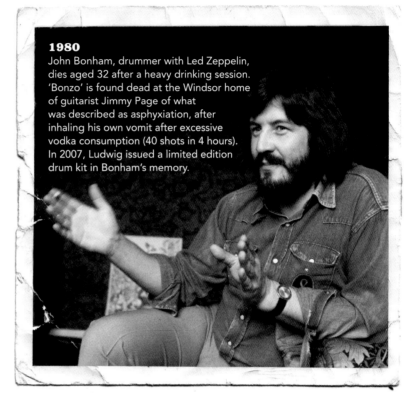

1980

John Bonham, drummer with Led Zeppelin, dies aged 32 after a heavy drinking session. 'Bonzo' is found dead at the Windsor home of guitarist Jimmy Page of what was described as asphyxiation, after inhaling his own vomit after excessive vodka consumption (40 shots in 4 hours). In 2007, Ludwig issued a limited edition drum kit in Bonham's memory.

1982

Queen make a guest appearance on US TV's *Saturday Night Live*, where they perform 'Crazy Little Thing Called Love' and 'Under Pressure'.

1990

Drummer Dave Grohl auditions for Nirvana and is instantly given the job. Grohl's last band Scream had recently split-up.

1992

Two fans are stabbed and 20 arrests are made after trouble breaks out at a Ozzy Osbourne gig in Oklahoma City. The sale of alcohol at the concert is blamed for the incident.

1993

Madonna plays the first of two sold-out shows at London's Wembley Stadium, the first night of her 39-date 'Girlie Show' World Tour.

1995

Courtney Love is given a one-year prison sentence, suspended for two years, fined $1000 and ordered to attend an anger management course after being found guilty of assaulting Bikini Kill singer Kathleen Hanna.

1999

Oasis singer Liam Gallagher is stopped by customs officials at Heathrow Airport and made to pay £1,300 for not declaring a fur coat he had bought in America.

2000

Ozzy Osbourne formally requests that Black Sabbath be removed from the nomination list for the Rock and Roll Hall of Fame. Calling the inclusion "meaningless", Osbourne stated, "Let's face it. Black Sabbath have never been media darlings. We're a people's band and that suits us just fine."

Born on this day:

1945 Bryan Ferry, singer (Roxy Music)	**1962** Tracey Thorn, vocals (Everything But The Girl)
1948 Olivia Newton-John, singer, actress	**1965** Cindy Herron, vocals (En Vogue)
1954 Craig Chaquico, guitar (Jefferson Starship)	**1972** Shawn Stockman (Boyz II Men)

1937
American blues singer Bessie Smith dies aged 43 after being involved in a car accident while travelling along Route 61 outside Memphis, Tennessee. Her 1923 song, 'Downhearted Blues' was inducted into the Grammy Hall of Fame in 2006.

1961
The Greenbriar Boys start a two-week residency at Gerde's Folk Club in New York. The opening act is Bob Dylan.

1964
Roy Orbison starts a three-week run at No. 1 on the US singles chart with 'Oh Pretty Woman'.

1965
At the end of a European tour Roger Daltrey knocks out Keith Moon and is sacked from The Who. The band were playing two shows in one night in Denmark when an argument breaks out between all four band members. Daltrey is reinstated the following week.

1968
Rolling Stone Brian Jones is fined £50 with 100 guineas cost after being found guilty of possession of cannabis.

1969
The Beatles release *Abbey Road* in the UK, the final studio recordings from the group.

1970
Pink Floyd kick off their third North American tour at The Electric Factory, Philadelphia.

1980
U2 appear at The Cedar Ballroom, Birmingham, England on their 'Boy' tour.

1981
The Go-Go's start a six-week run at No. 1 on the US album chart with 'Beauty And The Beat'.

1981
Bruce Dickinson, who had been the vocalist with Samson, joins UK heavy metal band Iron Maiden.

1987
Michael Jackson starts a six-week run at No. 1 on the US album chart with *Bad*.

1992
Nirvana appear at The Castaic Lake Amphitheatre, Castaic, California.

1996
Police find drugs hidden in a Smarties tube when raiding the London home of Paula Yates and INXS singer Michael Hutchence. The couple are absent in Australia at the time of the raid.

2003
Robert Palmer, who had a 1986 US No. 1 & UK No. 5 with 'Addicted To Love' and the 1988 hit 'Simply Irresistible', dies of a heart attack aged 54 in Paris, France. Palmer was a member of Vinegar Joe and The Power Station (with Duran Duran members Andy Taylor and John Taylor and former Chic member Tony Thompson).

A report is published on backstage requirements by musicians and reveals that Limp Bizkit insist all the lamps in their rooms be dimmable, Mariah Carey will only drinks from 'bendy' straws not straight ones, Van Halen insists that backstage celery is trimmed and not peeled, Red Hot Chili Peppers require a meditation room and a selection of aromatherapy candles, and Barry Manilow requests that the air temperature in the auditorium be kept at a regular 65 degrees.

2004
Green Day score their first UK No. 1 album with A*merican Idiot*, the band's seventh release.

2007
A charitable foundation set up by singer Shakira donates $40 million to help victims of natural disasters. The money will go towards repairing damage caused by an earthquake in Peru and a hurricane in Nicaragua. A further $5 million will be spent on health and education in four Latin American countries.

1943 Randy Bachman, guitar, vocals (The Guess Who, Bachman Turner Overdrive)

1947 Meat Loaf, US singer, actor

1953 Greg Ham, saxophone, keyboards (Men At Work)

1978 Brad Arnold, singer (3 Doors Down)

1984 Avril Lavigne, Canadian singer

1963

The Rolling Stones appear at the Floral Hall Ballroom in Morecambe, Lancashire on a bill with The Merseybeats, Dave Berry & The Cruisers and The Dooglebugs.

1964

The Beach Boys make their US TV debut on *The Ed Sullivan Show*.

1968

Pink Floyd appear at The Queens Hall in Dunoon, Scotland.

1972

Rory Storm, singer from Liverpool group Rory Storm & The Hurricanes, dies aged 32 after taking an overdose of sleeping pills in a suicide pact with his mother. Ringo Starr played drums with the group before joining The Beatles.

1979

Scottish guitarist Jimmy McCulloch, formerly of Thunderclap Newman, Stone The Crows and Wings, dies aged 26 from a heroin overdose in his flat in Maida Vale, London.

1987
Dolly Parton's TV show *Dolly* is shown for the first time on American network ABC.

1990

Dee Dee Ramone of the Ramones is arrested for possession of marijuana during a drug bust in New York's Greenwich Village.

Marvin Gaye's name is added to Hollywood Boulevard's 'Walkway Of Fame' in Los Angeles.

2000

U2 play a show from the rooftop of the self-owned Clarence Hotel in Dublin. Over 4,000 fans gather on the streets below.

2003

Kylie Minogue calls in police to investigate a series of threatening letters, which started as ordinary fan mail but became increasingly aggressive. The singer has received 700 letters at her home and office.

2008

Pink Floyd's former manager Bryan Morrison dies after spending over two years in a coma. Morrison, who suffered severe brain injuries in a polo accident at the Royal Berkshire Polo Club, England in 2006, and never recovered, also once managed The Pretty Things and was a prominent music publisher.

1986

Metallica bass player Cliff Burton is crushed to death after the band's tour bus crashes between Stockholm and Copenhagen. During a European tour members from the band drew cards for the most comfortable bunk on the tour bus. Burton won the game with the Ace of Spades and was asleep when the tour bus ran over a patch of black ice and skidded off the road. He was thrown through the window of the bus which fell on top of him.

Born on this day:

1902	Ed Sullivan, TV host	**1946**	Helen Shapiro, UK singer
1938	Ben E King, singer (The Drifters, solo)	**1984**	Melody Thornton, singer (The Pussycat Dolls)
1943	Nick Nicholas, bass (Steppenwolf)		

1962

The Beatles perform a lunchtime show at the Cavern Club, Liverpool. That night they perform aboard the vessel *MV Royal Iris* on the River Mersey. It's The Beatles' third and final 'Riverboat Shuffle'.

1968

American radio DJ Dewey Phillips, one of rock 'n' roll's pioneering disc jockeys, dies of heart failure aged 42. In July 1954, he was the first DJ to play the young Elvis Presley's debut record, 'That's All Right'/'Blue Moon Of Kentucky'.

Bruce Springsteen and a local folk rock group The Founders appear at the Off Broad Street Coffee House in Red Bank, New Jersey.

1974

Bad Company are at No. 1 on the US album chart with their self-titled debut album. Before the group formed in 1973, Paul Rodgers and Simon Kirke were in Free, while Mick Ralphs had played guitar with Mott The Hoople and Boz Burrell was bass player for King Crimson. The band produce six albums together before disbanding in 1983.

1976

A&M Records sues George Harrison for $6 million over non-delivery of a new album after he missed the contract deadline by two months.

1980

The Police are at No. 1 on the UK singles chart with 'Don't Stand So Close To Me', the group's third chart-topper and the best selling single of 1980.

1987

U2 play the first of two nights at Madison Square Garden in New York City during their 'Joshua Tree' World Tour.

1991

American jazz trumpeter, bandleader, and composer Miles Davis, considered one of the most influential musicians of the 20th century, dies aged 65 of a stroke and pneumonia.

1991

On the week their album *Nevermind* is released, Nirvana make an appearance at the Tower Records store and then play a show at The Marquee Club in New York City. Their single 'Smells Like Teen Spirit' also enters the US Top 20 this week.

1994

R&B singer Bobby Brown witnesses a fatal drive-by-shooting in Roxbury, New Jersey. His sister's fiancé is killed in the incident.

2000

As part of their UK 'Under A Big Top Tour', Radiohead play the first of two nights at Glasgow Green in Scotland.

2002

Tina Turner's hometown, made famous in her song 'Nutbush City Limits', names a stretch of State Highway 19, the Tina Turner Highway. Turner lived in Nutbush, a small town about 50 miles northeast of Memphis, until she was 17.

2004

Producer Phil Spector is charged in Los Angeles with the murder of 40-year-old actress Lana Clarkson in an unsealed indictment. Spector is in court as the indictment about the slaying of Clarkson is read. He remains free on $1 million bail.

2007

An ad for P Diddy's Unforgivable Woman perfume range, featuring a lingerie-clad model cavorting with the rapper in a New York hotel stairwell, is shown on Channel 4 in the UK. The ad is banned in the US by the Federal Communications Commission for being too sexually explicit for American audiences.

2009

Adam Goldstein (DJ AM), American club DJ and musician, dies aged 36 of an accidental drug overdose at home in New York City. He had worked with Blink 182, Crazy Town and Madonna. Goldstein had survived a plane crash along with Blink 182 drummer Travis Barker in September 2008.

2002

Madonna is voted the Greatest Female Singer of All-Time by 75,000 music fans in a VH1 poll. However, critics and music fans are unhappy that Kylie Minogue is voted into second place, beating Diana Ross (12) and Annie Lennox (14). The highest placed UK artist is Kate Bush who is voted tenth.

September 29

Born on this day:

1935 Jerry Lee Lewis, piano, singer, songwriter

1939 Tommy Boyce, US singer, songwriter

1948 Mark Farner, guitar, vocals (Grand Funk Railroad)

1968 Matt & Luke Goss, vocals (Bros)

1956
Bill Haley has five songs in the UK Top 30: 'Rockin Through The Rye', 'Saints Rock n' Roll', 'Rock Around The Clock', 'Razzle Dazzle', and 'See You Later Alligator'.

1960
One hit wonder Ricky Valance is at No. 1 on the UK singles chart with 'Tell Laura I Love Her', making him the first Welsh singer to top the charts.

1963
The first night of a 30-date UK package featuring The Everly Brothers, Bo Diddley, The Rolling Stones, Mickie Most and The Flintstones kicks off at the New Victoria Theatre, London. The tour plays two shows each night.

1973
Grand Funk Railroad are at No. 1 on the US singles chart with 'We're An American Band', the group's first of two American chart-toppers.

1976
Enjoying his own birthday celebrations, singer Jerry Lee Lewis accidentally shoots his bass player Norman Owens in the chest. Lewis had been blasting holes in an office door. Owens survives but sues his boss.

1979
The Police have their first UK No. 1 single with 'Message In A Bottle', the group's third Top 20 hit.

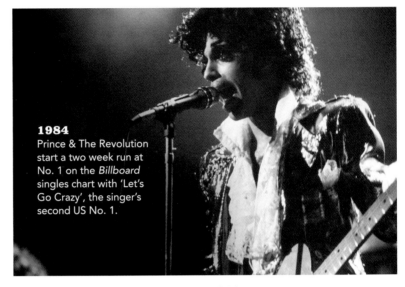

1984
Prince & The Revolution start a two week run at No. 1 on the *Billboard* singles chart with 'Let's Go Crazy', the singer's second US No. 1.

1989
While travelling on his motorbike from Los Angeles, Bruce Springsteen calls in at Matt's Saloon in Prescott, Arizona and jams with the house band for an hour. He also donates $100,000 to a barmaid's hospital bill.

1991
Metallica kick off their 138-date 'Wherever We May Roam' World Tour at the Civic Center in Peoria, Illinois.

1999
The Manic Street Preachers are given a bill for £28,000 after smashing up equipment during their show at Scotland's T In The Park festival.

2004
Part of Keith Moon's Premier drum kit, custom made for The Who drummer in 1967, sells for £120,000 in London to an American collector, setting a world auction record for a set of drums.

The Sun reports that Michael Jackson has a secret fourth child who is now 19. The story claims that Norwegian Omar Bhatti was born after a one night stand and had stayed with Jackson at his Neverland home in California.

2007
US rapper 50 Cent is beaten by rival rap star Kanye West in the stand-off to claim the best-selling album in the US. West's *Graduation* shifted 957,000 copies in its first week of sales while 50 Cent's album, *Curtis*, only sold 691,000. Before the albums went on sale 50 Cent vowed he would retire from making solo albums if he was outsold by West. 50 Cent axes his forthcoming European tour and a performance at London's MOBO Awards, the Vodafone Live Music Awards in London, as well as an MTV show in Germany.

Born on this day:

1935 Johnny Mathis, US singer
1942 Frankie Lymon, singer (Frankie Lymon & The Teenagers)
1947 Marc Bolan, guitarist, singer, songwriter (John's Children, T Rex, solo)
1964 Robby Takac, bass (Goo Goo Dolls)

September 30

1967
BBC Radio 1 is launched in the UK. Former Radio Caroline DJ Tony Blackburn is the first presenter on air, playing The Move's 'Flowers In The Rain' as the first record.

1972
David Cassidy, star of the US TV series *The Partridge Family*, is at No. 1 on the UK singles chart with a cover of The Young Rascals' 1967 US hit, 'How Can I Be Sure'.

1974
Police are called to a Lynyrd Skynyrd and Blue Öyster Cult concert after a fight breaks out between two sound engineers. The Skynyrd roadie claims that the sound had been deliberately turned off during the band's set.

1977
Mary Ford, one-half of the husband-and-wife musical team, Les Paul & Mary Ford, dies from cancer aged 53 after being in a diabetic coma for 54 days. Between 1950 and 1954 the couple had 16 top-ten hits; in 1951 alone, they sold six million records.

1984
The music division of Thorn EMI, said to be the greatest recording organisation in the world, reports a worldwide loss of almost $5 million during the last six months.

1992
US singer Steve Earle is arrested in Nashville after he fails to report for jury service.

1993
Kate Pierson from The B-52's is charged with criminal mischief and trespassing during an anti-fur protest at *Vogue*'s New York City offices.

1994
T.A.F.K.A.P. (aka Prince) launches music channel VH1 in the UK with the first airing of his new video for 'Dolphin'.

1995
Mariah Carey makes chart history when she starts an eight week run at No. 1 on the US singles chart with 'Fantasy', making her the first female act to enter the chart in pole position.

1999
Chris de Burgh's website is closed down after countless obscene messages are posted on the guestbook. One message consists entirely of two four-letter words repeated 3,500 times.

2003
An auction of the contents of Sir Elton John's London home raises more than £1.4 million. An oil painting, entitled Madison Square Park, sells for £67,200, and a 19th Century portrait of Lieutenant George Dyer, painted by James Northcote in 1817, fetches £55,200. Elton is selling off the items so he can redecorate his home in a more modern style.

2007
Country music singer Keith Urban crashes his motorcycle on the way to an Alcoholics Anonymous meeting. The 39-year-old, who is not injured, said he was being followed by a photographer when the accident happened near his home in Sydney, Australia.

1978
John Travolta and Olivia Newton-John score their second UK No. 1 from the film *Grease* with 'Summer Nights'.

BRITNEY GOES MAD ON COKE

Stroppy star soaks snapper with cola

U.F.O. Fes

MOVE
Saturday

PINK FLOW
Friday & Satur

TOMORROW
with KEITH WEST
Friday

SOFT
MACH
Saturda

ALSO: THE NACK, FAIRPORT
Friday & Saturday, 10 p.m.–6 a.m.
OPEN TO THE PUBLIC FRIDAY
MEMBERS (15/-) and GUESTS (2
FOR THE BENEFIT

October

MAD

SHE SAYS:
He's lazy
tightwad
who prefers
the pub to
his family

RITCHIE
GET BITC

olid Crew gun
r gets 30 years

similar to scenes in Wild West
films. Both men drew their
and Morgan fired four

christina aguilera
genie in a bottle

Security staff bar Dylan
from his own concert

From Nicholas Wapshott
in New York

ISON and TITO BURNS present

"HOLE IN MY SHOE"
"PAPER SUN"

TRAFFIC

Born on this day:

1945 Donny Hathaway, US soul singer
1947 Rob Davis, guitarist, songwriter (Mud)
1948 Cub Koda, guitarist, songwriter
(Brownsville Station)

1959 Youssou N'dour, Senegalese singer,
percussionist

October 1

1956

After test audiences gave a negative reaction to his death at the end of the film *Love Me Tender*, Elvis Presley is called back to re-shoot a new ending where the hero lives.

1965

Bob Dylan appears at Carnegie Hall in New York City and introduces his new touring band made up of guitarist Robbie Robertson, organist Garth Hudson, bassist Rick Danko, pianist Richard Manual and drummer Levon Helm. They later become known simply as The Band.

1966

An unknown Jimi Hendrix, having only been in the UK for a week, jams with Cream at their gig at London Polytechnic.

1967

Thieves break into Mick Jagger's London flat and steal jewellery and furs belonging to his then girlfriend Marianne Faithfull.

1970

Jimi Hendrix is buried at The Greenwood Cemetery at the Dunlop Baptist Church, Seattle. Among the mourners are Miles Davis, Eric Burdon, Johnny Winter and members of Derek & The Dominoes.

1975

Al Jackson, drummer with Booker T. & The MGs, is shot and killed aged 40 by an intruder at his Memphis home.

1977

Elton John becomes the first musician to be honoured in New York City's Madison Square Hall Of Fame.

1982

John Cougar is at No. 1 on both the US album and singles chart with *American Fool* and 'Jack And Diane' respectively.

1983

The Swedish Post Office issues an Abba stamp.

1990

Forbes magazine lists New Kids On The Block as the fifth highest earning entertainers in the US with an income of $78 million.

2004

The Lord Mayor of Melbourne officially opens AC/DC Lane in honour of the veteran rockers. The Lord Mayor erects the sign to cheers while bagpipes play the band's song 'Long Way To The Top'. The City of Melbourne has extra copies of the sign made, in anticipation of fans stealing them.

an operation in Telford. A Babyshambles gig in Norwich planned for the following night is cancelled.

2007

Radiohead's official website crashes after the band announce that their new album *In Rainbows* would only be available to order via www.radiohead.com. Fans could pre-order the download at any price they chose or pay £40 for a 'discbox', which includes two CDs, two records, plus artwork and booklets.

The Spice Girls' London reunion concert sells out in 38 seconds after fans are notified tickets had gone on sale. More than one million people in

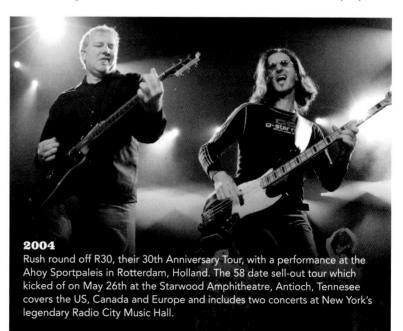

2004

Rush round off R30, their 30th Anniversary Tour, with a performance at the Ahoy Sportpaleis in Rotterdam, Holland. The 58 date sell-out tour which kicked of on May 26th at the Starwood Amphitheatre, Antioch, Tennesee covers the US, Canada and Europe and includes two concerts at New York's legendary Radio City Music Hall.

2005

During a police drugs operation Pete Doherty is arrested and held overnight in Shrewsbury where his band Babyshambles had been playing. Police say a man and a woman were arrested for possession of Class A drugs and 17 others searched during

the UK register for the concert on December 15 at the O2 Arena. Tickets cost £55-75. Three more London dates are added to the world tour which is scheduled to start in Vancouver on December 2.

October 2

Born on this day:

1945 Don McLean, US singer, songwriter
1949 Richard Hell, vocals (The Voidoids)
1950 Mike Rutherford, guitar (Genesis)
1951 Sting, singer, songwriter (The Police, solo)
1955 Phil Oakey, vocals (The Human League)
1971 Tiffany, US singer

1961
Phil Spector and partner Lester Sill release The Crystals' 'Oh Yeah Maybe Baby', the first single on their new Philles label. A little over a year later, the label (and The Crystals) have a No. 1 with 'He's A Rebel'.

1965
The McCoys are at No. 1 on the US singles chart with 'Hang On Sloopy' (No. 5 in the UK when released on Andrew Oldham's new Immediate label). The song was first released by The Vibrations and called 'My Girl Sloopy'.

1971
Rod Stewart starts a five-week run at No. 1 on the US singles chart with 'Maggie May'/'Reason To Believe', his first solo chart-topper. Stewart's album *Every Picture Tells A Story* also starts a four-week run on this day at No. 1 on the UK and US chart.

1977
The body of Elvis Presley and his mother Gladys are moved from the cemetery where they are buried to Elvis' home Graceland after an unsuccessful attempt is made to snatch the body from the coffin.

1980
Leaveil Degree from the soul group The Whispers starts a two-year prison sentence in Boron California for his part in a diamond robbery.

1982
Musical Youth – a group made up of Birmingham schoolboys, aged 11-16 – are at No. 1 on the UK singles chart with 'Pass The Dutchie'. The song is a cover of The Mighty Diamonds song, 'Pass The Kutchie', a slang term for a cannabis smoking pipe, but the word is changed to prevent the song being banned for drug reference.

1983
Abba singer Agnetha Faltskog is taken to hospital suffering from concussion after being involved in a car crash in Skane, Sweden.

Welsh singer Bonnie Tyler is top of the *Billboard* singles chart with the Jim Steinman written and produced track, 'Total Eclipse Of The Heart', making her the only Welsh artist to score a US No. 1.

1995
Oasis release their second album *(What's The Story), Morning Glory* which enters the UK chart at No. 1.

2002
Adam Ant escapes a prison sentence after a judge rules that an incident in which he threatened drinkers with a replica pistol in a London pub was a result of mental illness. The 80's pop star has been having voluntary psychiatric treatment since the incident.

Robbie Williams signs the most lucrative British record deal in history with EMI Records for £80m. Asked what he was going to do with the money, Williams said, "I'm going to count it all."

2003
Police are called to a suspected burglary at the Los Angeles house of Courtney Love's former boyfriend and ex-manager Jim Barber in the early hours. Love is picked up in the street outside and detained, with officers noting "Miss Love's behaviour was consistent with being under the influence of a controlled substance." Shortly after her arrest, Love is taken to hospital with a suspected drug overdose.

2007
Britney Spears is ordered to hand over her two young children to former husband Kevin Federline by a Los Angeles judge. The court rules that Federline will be given custody of two-year-old Sean Preston and one-year-old Jayden James until further notice. Last month Judge Scott Gordon said Ms Spears showed "a habitual, frequent and continuous use of controlled substances and alcohol." The singer is ordered to undergo random drug and alcohol tests twice a week as part of her child custody dispute with Federline.

1998
America's singing cowboy Gene Autry, who scored 25 successive Top 10 country hits, dies aged 91. In 1995 it was estimated Autrey was worth $320 million.

Born on this day:

October 3

1938 Eddie Cochran, guitar, singer, songwriter

1941 Chubby Checker, US singer

1947 Lindsey Buckingham, guitar, vocals (Fleetwood Mac, solo)

1954 Stevie Ray Vaughan, guitar, singer

1962 Tommy Lee, dummer (Mötley Crüe)

1969 Gwen Stefani, singer (No Doubt, solo)

1978 Jake Shears, singer (Scissor Sisters)

1945

A 10-year-old Elvis Presley comes second in a talent contest at the Mississippi Alabama Dairy Show, singing 'Old Shep' – his first ever-public appearance.

1958

The 'Biggest Show Of Stars 1958' Tour featuring Buddy Holly, Frankie Avalon, Bobby Darin, The Olympics, Dion & The Belmonts, Bobby Freeman, The Elegants, Jimmy Clanton, The Danleers, Duane Eddy, Clyde McPhatter, and The Coasters kicks off at The Worcester Auditorium in Worcester, Massachusetts.

1967

American folk singer and songwriter Woody Guthrie dies aged 55 from Huntington's Chorea disease. Guthrie was a major influence on Bob Dylan and American folk music and the film *Bound For Glory* is based on his life. Many of Guthrie's songs are archived in the Library of Congress, and his best-known song, 'This Land Is Your Land', is regularly sung in American schools.

1978

Aerosmith bail 30 fans out of jail after they are arrested for smoking pot during an Aerosmith concert at Fort Wayne Coliseum, Indiana.

1987

M/A/R/S are at No. 1 on the UK singles chart with 'Pump Up The Volume', the first British-made house hit which heavily sampled other recordings, resulting in litigation.

1991

M.C. Hammer offers a $50,000 reward for the return of Michael Jackson's white glove, which had been stolen from the Motown Museum. It is returned to the museum two days after the theft.

Texas governor Ann Richards proclaims October 3 to be Stevie Ray Vaughan Day. An annual motorcycle ride and concert in central Texas benefits the Stevie Ray Vaughan Memorial Scholarship Fund.

1997

A court battle starts between Garth Brooks and Warren G over the trademark of the letter 'G' which both artists use. The dispute is settled out of court the following year.

2000

Benjamin Orr, singer and bass player with The Cars who sang lead vocals on the band's hits 'Just What I Needed', 'Let's Go' and 'Drive', dies aged 53 of cancer at his Atlanta home.

2002

Darryl DeLoach, original guitarist and vocalist from American psychedelic rock band Iron Butterfly, dies aged 56 of liver cancer.

2008

Singer, producer and songwriter Johnny J (Johnny Jackson), who produced Tupac Shakur's albums *All Eyez On Me* and *Me Against The World*, as well as many of Shakur's subsequent posthumous albums, dies after jumping from a tier in a Los Angeles jail while serving a sentence for driving under the influence.

2000

John Lennon's assassin Mark David Chapman is denied parole after serving 20 years in prison. Chapman was interviewed for 50 minutes by parole board members who conclude that releasing Chapman would "deprecate the seriousness of the crime." He is denied parole at four subsequent hearings in 2002, 2004, 2006 and 2008.

October 4

Born on this day:

1942 Helen Reddy, Australian singer, songwriter

1959 Chris Lowe, keyboards (Pet Shop Boys)

1961 Jon Secada, US singer

1984 Katina Sergeevna, singer (Tatu)

1961
Bob Dylan plays a showcase at New York City's Carnegie Hall to 53 people.

1962
The Tornados are at No. 1 on the UK singles chart with the instrumental, 'Telstar', named after the communications satellite. The track becomes the first major hit from a UK act to reach No. 1 on the American chart.

1963
The Beatles make the first of three appearances on the UK ITV pop show *Ready, Steady, Go!*

1969
The Beatles' *Abbey Road* is at No. 1 on the UK album chart. The cover supposedly contains clues that add to the 'Paul Is Dead' phenomenon: Paul is barefoot and the car number plate 'LMW 281F' supposedly referred to the fact that McCartney would be 28 years old if he was still alive. 'LMW' was said to stand for 'Linda McCartney Weeps', and the four Beatles represent the priest (John, dressed in white), the undertaker (Ringo, in a black suit), the corpse (Paul, in a suit but barefoot) and the gravedigger (George, in jeans and a denim work shirt).

1970
Janis Joplin is found dead at The Landmark Motor Hotel, Hollywood from an accidental heroin overdose.

1971
Pink Floyd film at the Roman Amphitheatre, Pompeii, Italy, for their *Live In Pompeii* movie.

1980
Winners in the *Melody Maker* Readers Poll include Kate Bush who won Best Female Singer, Peter Gabriel – Best Male Singer, Ritchie Blackmore – Best Guitarist, Phil Collins – Best Drummer, Genesis – Band Of The Year, Pink Floyd – Best Single for 'Another Brick In The Wall' and Saxon – Brightest Hope.

1982
The Smiths make their live debut at The Ritz, Manchester.

1986
Paul Simon starts a five-week run at No. 1 on the UK album chart with *Graceland*.

1997
Boyz II Men are at No. 1 on the US singles chart with '4 Seasons Of Loneliness', the group's fifth American chart-topper and a No. 10 hit in the UK.

1999
It is reported that the half-sister of Jimi Hendrix is planning to exhume the guitarist's body and move it to a pay-to-view mausoleum. Other plans for the new site include a chance for fans to buy one of the burial plots around the guitarist's proposed new resting-place.

2004
Canadian bassist Bruce Palmer, a member of The Mynah Birds, The Buffalo Springfield and who also worked with Crosby, Stills, Nash & Young and Neil Young, dies aged 58 of a heart attack in Belleville, Ontario.

2007
The Rolling Stones set a new record for the top grossing tour of all time with their 'A Bigger Bang' tour, which ran from late 2005 to August 2007, earning the band £247m with the Stones playing to over 3.5 million people at 113 shows. The previous high was set by U2's 2005-6 'Vertigo' tour, earning £220m.

Born on this day:

1943 Steve Miller, guitar, singer (Steve Miller Band)

1947 Brian Johnson, singer (Geordie, AC/DC)

1951 Bob Geldof, singer (Boomtown Rats, solo)

1961 David Bryson, guitar (Counting Crows)

1978 James Burgon Valentine, guitar (Maroon 5)

October 5

1958
Cliff Richard & The Shadows play their first gig together at The Victoria Hall, Hanley, England.

1962
The Beatles' debut single 'Love Me Do' is released in the UK, spending 18 weeks on the chart peaking at No. 17 on its initial release.

1965
Johnny Cash is arrested crossing the Mexican border into El Paso, Texas. Customs officials find hundreds of pills in his guitar case. He receives a suspended jail sentence and a $1,000 fine.

1966
The Jimi Hendrix Experience – Jimi Hendrix, Noel Redding and Mitch Mitchell – play together for the first time.

1974
Mike Oldfield's *Tubular Bells* is at No. 1 on the UK chart, 15 months after being released. The album goes on to sell over 10 million copies worldwide.

1975
Stevie Wonder appears at the Wonder Dream Concert in Kingston, Jamaica, a Jamaican Institute for the Blind benefit concert. The three original

Wailers – Bob Marley, Peter Tosh and Bunny Wailer – perform together for the last time.

1987
Ex-Smiths' guitarist Johnny Marr begins rehearsals with The Pretenders in preparation for the band supporting U2 in America.

1991
Guns N' Roses start a two-week run at No. 1 on the US album chart with *Use Your Illusion II*.

1992
Eddie Kendricks of The Temptations dies aged 52 of lung cancer, a year after having his lung removed. Kendrick's distinctive falsetto lead voice can be heard on 'The Way You Do The Things You Do', 'Get Ready' and 'Just My Imagination' and as a solo artist. He recorded several hits of his own during the 70s, including the US No. 1 'Keep On Truckin'.

1996
American group Deep Blue Something are at No. 1 on the UK singles chart with 'Breakfast At Tiffany's'. The song references the classic 1961 Audrey Hepburn film of the same name.

1999
Roger Daltrey announces that The Who are to reform as a stripped down band of five, making their first performance in Las Vegas on October 29. The show, also broadcast live on the internet, was later released on DVD as *The Vegas Job*.

2000
British TV show *Top Of The Pops* issues a Top 40 chart based on singles that have spent the longest time on the UK chart. In third place is 'My Way' by Frank Sinatra, The Beatles' 'She Loves You' was second and 'Relax' by Frankie Goes To Hollywood comes first.

2006
Reggae legend Bob Marley is honoured with a heritage plaque at his former north London home at 34 Ridgmount Gardens, Camden. The event was part of Black History Month, a season of events celebrating the contribution of London's African-Caribbean communities.

Jeffrey Borer, who admitted secretly videotaping Michael Jackson on a private jet, is sentenced to six months of home detention and fined $10,000. Borer, who was the owner of private jet firm XtraJet, had instructed an employee to buy and install two video recorders on the plane.

2007
Isaac Hanson, guitarist from US pop band Hanson, has surgery to remove a blood clot from his lungs after being diagnosed with the potentially fatal Paget-Schroetter Syndrome. He is expected to make a full and speedy recovery.

Born on this day:

1949 Bobby Farrell, vocals (Boney M)
1949 Thomas McClary, guitar (The Commodores)
1960 Richard Jobson, guitar, vocals, broadcaster (The Skids)
1966 Tommy Stinson, bass (The Replacements)

1959
One hit wonder Jerry Keller is at No. 1 on the UK singles chart with 'Here Comes Summer'. Keller goes on to become a vocalist for TV jingles throughout the 1970s and 80s.

1964
The Beatles spend the afternoon recording 'Eight Days A Week' at EMI Studios in London. The evening is spent at The Ad Lib Club partying with The Ronettes, Cilla Black and Mick Jagger.

1973
Cher starts a two-week run on top of the *Billboard* singles chart with 'Half-Breed', the singer's second US No. 1.

1978
Australia's 'King of rock'n'roll' Johnny O'Keefe, the first Australian rock'n'roll performer to tour the United States, and Australia's most successful chart performer, with 29 Top 40 hits between 1958 and 1974, dies aged 43 of a heart attack. O'Keefe's 1958 hit, 'Real Wild Child', is covered by Iggy Pop in 1986.

1979
Buzzcocks, supported by Joy Division, appear at The Odeon Theatre, Edinburgh, Scotland. Tickets cost £2.50.

1980
The Bee Gees sue their record company Polygram and the band's manager Robert Stigwood for fraud.

1984
David Bowie scores his sixth UK No. 1 album with *Tonight*, featuring the single 'Blue Jean'.

1991
At Michael Jackson's Neverland Ranch, Jackson gives away the bride at Elizabeth Taylor's seventh wedding. The groom is construction worker Larry Fortensky, whom Taylor would divorce in 1997.

1996
Celine Dion is at No. 1 on the US album chart with *Falling Into You*.

1998
A music industry poll is published by London magazine *Time Out*, naming the top stars from the past 30 years. In fifth place was Marvin Gaye, fourth – James Brown, third – Bob Marley, second – The Beatles, while first place goes to David Bowie.

1999
Winners at The MOBO Awards include Kele Le Roc – Best Newcomer and Best Single, Shanks & Bigfoot – Best Dance Act, TLC – Best Video 'No Scrubs', Lauryn Hill – Best International Act, while Tina Turner wins a Lifetime Achievement Award.

2000
Manhattan Supreme Court sentences rapper Busta Rhymes to five years probation after pleading guilty to a gun possession charge.

2004
Britney Spears throws a full cup of Coca-Cola over a photographer who is waiting to take pictures of the singer and her new husband outside a Subway takeaway shop in Malibu, California.

2005
While touring to promote their latest album *A Bigger Bang*, The Rolling Stones are forced to halt eight songs into a show at Scott Stadium at the University of Virginia after police receive a bomb threat targeting the stage area. A 45-minute sweep of the area finds nothing unusual, and the band complete the show.

2007
Bruce Springsteen is being sued for $850,000 by Todd Minikus who claims The Boss backed out of a contract to buy a horse. Springsteen and his wife Patti Scialfa are both named in legal documents filed in Florida. Minikus claims the couple pulled out of a deal to pay $650,000 for a horse named Pavarotti.

Born on this day:

1945 Kevin Godley, drums, singer (10CC)
1951 John Cougar Mellencamp, guitar, singer, songwriter
1953 Tico Torres, drums (Bon Jovi)
1959 Simon Cowell, *Pop Idol* and *American Idol* judge
1967 Toni Braxton, US singer
1968 Thom Yorke, vocals, guitar, keyboards (Radiohead)
1976 Taylor Hicks, US soul singer, songwriter

October 7

1963
The Rolling Stones record the Lennon & McCartney penned song 'I Wanna Be Your Man' as the group's second single at Kingsway Studios, London.

1966
Johnny Kidd, who had a 1960 UK No. 1 single with 'Shakin' All Over', is killed aged 27 in a car crash while on tour in Radcliffe, Manchester.

New Orleans R&B singer Smiley Lewis, who wrote 'One Night' covered by Elvis Presley and 'I Hear You Knocking', a 1955 US No. 2 for Gale Storm plus a UK No. 1 & US No. 2 in 1970 for Dave Edmunds, dies aged 53 of stomach cancer.

1967
Cass Elliot from The Mamas & The Papas spends the night in a London jail after being accused of stealing from a hotel. A TV and concert appearance at the Royal Albert Hall has to be cancelled.

1978
US music magazine *Billboard* reports that Marvin Gaye had twice filed bankruptcy papers earlier in the year with debts of $7 million.

1982
Led Zeppelin's Jimmy Page is given a 12-month conditional discharge after being found guilty of possessing cocaine.

1989
Paula Abdul is at No. 1 on the US album chart with *Forever Your Girl*. Abdul spent 64 consecutive weeks on the *Billboard* 200 before hitting No. 1, making it the longest time for an album to reach the top spot.

1995
Alanis Morissette is at No. 1 on the US album chart with *Jagged Little Pill*, which went on to become the biggest selling album ever by a female artist with sales of over 30m.

1999
It is reported that four musicians who claimed they worked on Lauryn Hill's *Miseducation* album are suing for unpaid royalties as co-writers and producers.

2002
Mick Jagger donates £100,000 to his old grammar school in Dartford to help pay for a music director and buy musical instruments. The new centre is also named after Jagger.

2004
53-year-old Mötley Crüe guitarist Mick Mars has a hip replacement operation in an LA hospital.

2005
Boy George is arrested in New York on a drug charge. George had called the authorities after he thought somebody was breaking into his apartment. When police arrive and make a search they find traces of cocaine on a computer table.

2007
25-year-old hip-hop artist Lil' Wayne is arrested after a concert in Idaho on a warrant stemming from a drug possession charge. Because of the nature of the charge, the rapper – real name Dwayne Michael Carter Jr – is not eligible for bail.

Bruce Springsteen is at No. 1 on the UK chart with *Magic*, the Boss' 15th studio album and seventh UK No. 1; also a US No. 1.

1975
John Lennon is awarded his 'Green Card' – permanent residency status – at a hearing in New York which overturns previous efforts by the US Government to deport him. Two days later Yoko gives birth to his son Sean.

October 8

Born on this day:

1940 George Bellamy, guitar (The Tornados)
1945 Ray Royer, guitar (Procol Harum)
1945 Butch Rillera, drums (Redbone)

1949 Hamish Stewart, guitar, vocals (The Average White Band, Paul McCartney's band)
1951 Johnny Ramone, guitar (The Ramones)
1968 Leeroy Thornhill, dancer (Prodigy)

1964
Working at EMI Studios, London, The Beatles record 'She's A Woman', the B-side of their next single, in seven takes plus overdubs. From start to finish it takes five hours to complete. The lyrics are completed that morning on the way to the studio.

1965
The Florescents, supported by The Castiles, featuring a young singer called Bruce Springsteen, appear at The IB Club in Howell, New Jersey. This was The Castiles first publicly advertised nightclub appearance. Admission is $1.00.

1966
Cream drummer Ginger Baker collapses during a gig at Sussex University, Brighton, England after playing his drum solo on 'Toad'. He recovers in a local hospital.

1967
The Jimi Hendrix Experience, The Crazy World of Arthur Brown, The Herd and Eire Apparent appear performing two shows at the Saville Theatre in London.

1976
Rainbow appear at the Luxor Theater, Hoensbroek, Holland supported by AC/DC.

1977
One half of TV cop show *Starsky & Hutch* David Soul is at No. 1 on the UK chart with 'Silver Lady', his second and last British chart-topping single.

1982
R.E.M. appear at The Peppermint Lounge, New York City, supported by The Fleshtones.

1987
The three members from ZZ Top make advance bookings for seats on the first passenger flight to the moon. (They are still waiting for confirmation of the trip.)

1988
On their twelfth single release, U2 score their first UK No. 1 (US No. 3) with 'Desire', which is taken from their album *Rattle And Hum*.

Pink Floyd's *The Dark Side Of The Moon* finally leaves *Billboard*'s Hot 200 Album Chart after a record breaking 741 weeks.

1992
The US Postal Service issues a set of commemorative stamps to celebrate pop music legends. The stamps include Elvis Presley, Bill Haley, Buddy Holly, Otis Redding, Ritchie Valens, Clyde McPhatter and Dinah Washington.

2000
Radiohead start a two-week run at No. 1 on the UK album chart with *Kid A*, also a chart-topper in the US.

2003
Coldplay singer Chris Martin's lawyer Megan Cusack asks Australian police to drop a charge of malicious damage after her client (who was not present in

court at Byron Bay, New South Wales) allegedly attacked a photographer's car. Martin was charged in July for breaking a windscreen with a rock after being photographed surfing.

2004
Britney Spears splits with Larry Rudolph, the manager who had guided her career since she was 13 years old. Rudolph says he and Spears had "mutually agreed not to renew their nine-year management relationship."

2007
Arctic Monkeys are named the best act in the world at this year's *Q* Awards held in London. Best album goes to Amy Winehouse's *Back To Black*; Muse – Best Live Act; Manic Street Preachers – the year's top track for 'Your Love Alone Is Not Enough'; and 'Ruby' by Kaiser Chiefs won Best Video. Top Breakthrough Artist was Kate Nash. Icon Of The Year is Paul McCartney, Kylie Minogue is named Idol of 2007, former Blur frontman Damon Albarn takes the prize for inspiration, Classic Songwriter Award goes to Billy Bragg, Innovation In Sound Award to Sigur Ros and Lifetime Achievement Award to Johnny Marr. The late Tony Wilson, founder of Manchester's Factory Records, is named *Q*'s hero.

October 9

1961
Ray Charles starts a two-week run at No. 1 on the US singles chart with 'Hit The Road Jack', which reaches No. 6 on the UK chart.

1965
The Beatles start a four-week run at No. 1 on the American singles chart with the Paul McCartney ballad 'Yesterday', giving the group their tenth US No. 1.

1969
For the first time in the history of the show, the BBC's *Top Of The Pops* producers refuse to air the No. 1 song, 'Je T'aime... Moi Non Plus', the erotic French language love song by Serge Gainsbourg and actress Jane Birkin. The song, an instrumental with the voices of Gainsbourg and Birkin apparently recorded in the act of love and superimposed over the top, caused such a stir in Britain that the original label, Fontana, drop the record despite it being No. 2 on the charts. A small record company, Major Minor, buys the rights and sees the song climb to the top, the first French language song to ever do so.

1971
Rod Stewart is top of the British singles chart with 'Maggie May' (originally released as a B side to 'Reason To Believe'). The first of six UK No. 1's for Stewart, it spent five weeks at the top of the chart.

The Who play a small, low-key show at the University of Surrey, Guildford, with guest John Sebastian joining in on harmonica on 'Magic Bus' – the only outside musician to jam with The Who on stage. Backstage, the group celebrate John Entwistle's 27th birthday.

1973
Elvis and Priscilla Presley divorce after six years of marriage. Priscilla is awarded property, $725,000 cash and $4,200 a month support.

1976
The Sex Pistols sign to EMI Records for £40,000. The contract is terminated just three months later with the label stopping production of the Pistol's first single, 'Anarchy In The UK', and deleting it from its catalogue. EMI later issue a statement saying it felt unable to promote The Sex Pistols in view of the adverse publicity the band had generated over the last few months.

1978
Belgian singer-songwriter Jacques Brel dies aged 49 of cancer. Artists who recorded his songs include Scott Walker, Alex Harvey, Ray Charles, Frank Sinatra, Dusty Springfield, David Bowie, Nina Simone and Terry Jacks.

1981
During a North American tour The Rolling Stones play the first of two nights at the Los Angeles Memorial Coliseum. Support act is Prince who, dressed in controversial bikini briefs and trench coat, runs off stage after 15 minutes when the crowd boos and throws beer cans at him.

1990
All four members of The Stone Roses are each fined £3,000 after being found guilty of criminal damage at their former record company's offices.

2001
Joseph Johnson wrecks a $300,000 Lamborghini Diablo sports car owned by hip-hop star Missy Elliott after losing control of the 550-horsepower vehicle, crashing into a traffic sign and a tree. Johnson, who took the car without permission from the garage where it was being stored, is later sentenced to three years in jail and ordered to pay $170,000.

2003
Ambrose Kappos, 37, of New York, is charged with three counts of stalking and harassing singer Sheryl Crow. Kappos is arrested after being accused of sneaking into New York's Hammerstein Ballroom then trying to get into Crow's limousine as she left the venue. Kappos' brother said he was harmless but "infatuated" with the singer.

1985
Marking what would have been John Lennon's 45th birthday, Yoko Ono formally opens a three and a half acre garden in New York's Central Park that will be known as Strawberry Fields. Thanks to a $1 million donation from Yoko, the area is planted with trees, shrubs and flowers gathered from across the world.

Born on this day:

1955 David Lee Roth, vocals (Van Halen)
1955 Midge Ure, guitarist, singer, songwriter (Slik, Rich Kids, Ultravox)
1959 Kirsty MacColl, UK singer, songwriter
1961 Martin Kemp, bass (Spandau Ballet)

1956

Elvis Presley's 'Love Me Tender' enters the US chart for a 19-week stay, peaking at No. 1 for 5 weeks. The song, from Presley's first film of the same name, was adapted from the tune 'Aura Lee', written in 1861.

1959

The Quarry Men play at The Casbah Coffee Club, Liverpool. Guitarist Ken Brown, suffering from a heavy cold, is unable to appear and after the show, an argument starts when Paul McCartney says that Brown should not get a share of the group's fee since he had not performed. Lennon and Harrison side with McCartney and Brown quits The Quarry Men.

Berry Gordy's first release on the newly established Motown Records, 'Bad Girl' by The Miracles, enters the *Billboard* Pop chart.

1964

During a UK tour The Beatles play two shows at the De Montfort Hall, Leicester. Ringo Starr takes delivery of a brand new Facel Vega, apparently reaching speeds of 140mph on the M6 motorway.

1970

The Carpenters are at No. 2 on the US singles chart with 'We've Only Just Begun'. The song was originally written for a bank commercial.

1978

Joe Perry and Steve Tyler from Aerosmith are injured after a cherry bomb is thrown on stage during a gig in Philadelphia. The group perform behind a safety fence for the rest of the tour.

1980

The funeral takes place of Led Zeppelin's drummer, John Bonham. 'Bonzo' was found dead at guitarist's Jimmy Page's house of what was described as asphyxiation, after inhaling his own vomit following excessive vodka consumption (40 shots in four hours) aged 32.

1987

Whitesnake are at No. 1 on the US singles chart with 'Here I Go Again'.

1992

R.E.M. score their second UK No. 1 album with *Automatic For The People*, featuring the singles 'Drive', 'Everybody Hurts', 'Man On The Moon' and 'The Sidewinder Sleeps Tonight'.

1999

American singer, songwriter and actor Hoyt Axton, whose songs were recorded by artists including Elvis Presley, Three Dog Night, John Denver, Ringo Starr and Glen Campbell, dies aged 61 of a heart attack in Victor, Montana. His mother Mae Boren Axton wrote 'Heartbreak Hotel'.

A charity auction selling Elvis Presley's belongings is held at The Grand Hotel, Las Vegas. A wristwatch sells for $32,500, a cigar box $25,000, an autographed baseball $19,000, and a 1956 Lincoln Continental $250,000.

2002

Protesters dressed in monkey costumes picket outside the north Wales holiday home of former Stone Roses' singer Ian Brown. The 12 demonstrators are upset that Brown is selling the five-bedroom house, in the small village of Llithfaen on the Llyn Peninsula for an inflated price – £150,000 – which local people cannot afford. The outfits reference the name of Brown's recent solo album *Unfinished Monkey Business.*

2007

Sting tops a list of the worst lyricists ever, for such alleged sins as name-dropping Russian novelist Vladimir Nabokov in The Police song 'Don't Stand So Close to Me', naming a song after a Volvo bumper sticker ('If You Love Someone Set Them Free') and co-opting the works of Chaucer, St. Augustine and Shakespeare. The survey in *Blender* magazine placed Rush drummer Neil Peart at 2, Creed frontman Scott Stapp at 3 and Oasis guitarist Noel Gallagher at 4, saying Gallagher "seemed incapable of following a metaphor through a single line, let alone a whole verse."

2009

Boyzone singer Stephen Gately dies suddenly at the age of 33 while on holiday in Majorca. Spanish police say there are no signs of suspicious circumstances. Gately was on holiday with his long-term partner Andy Cowles.

Born on this day:

1946 Gary Mallaber, drums (Steve Miller Band)

1949 Daryl Hall, singer, songwriter (Hall & Oates, solo)

1950 Andrew Woolfolk, sax (Earth, Wind & Fire)

1957 Blair Cunningham, drums (Haircut 100, Echo & The Bunnymen)

October 11

1955
Elvis Presley, Carl Perkins and Johnny Cash kick off an 11-date tour of the Southern US states in Abilene, Texas.

1962
The Beatles make their first appearance in the UK singles chart with 'Love Me Do' backed by 'P.S. I Love You'.

1966
Pink Floyd (who are paid £15 for the gig) and The Soft Machine appear at the launch of the underground newspaper *International Times* at north London's Roundhouse venue in Chalk Farm. Among the 2,500 people who attend are Paul McCartney (disguised as an Arab), Marianne Faithfull (who wore a nun's habit that barely covered her) and actress Monica Vitti. Legend has it that the sugar cubes given away at the entrance were coated with LSD, although many brought their own.

1967
The Doors appear at Danbury High School, Danbury, Connecticut. Before the group come on stage an announcer tells the audience not to leave their seats during the performance or they will be escorted from the venue. A beauty pageant precedes The Doors' appearance.

1976
Pussycat start a four week run at No. 1 on the UK singles chart with 'Mississippi', making them the first Dutch act to top the British chart.

1978
Siouxsie & The Banshees, supported by Spizz Oil and The Human League, appear at The Pavilion, Hemel Hempstead, England.

1980
The Police score their second UK No. 1 album with *Zenyatta Mondatta*.

1986
Madonna achieves her third UK No. 1 with the title track from her album *True Blue*. The title comes from a favorite expression of her then husband, actor Sean Penn, and was a direct tribute to him.

1988
Former Beatle Ringo Starr and his wife Barbara Bach start treatment for alcohol abuse at a clinic in Tucson, Arizona.

1990
Drummer Dave Grohl plays his first gig with Nirvana when they appear at the North Shore Surf Club in Olympia, Washington.

1995
Tupac Shakur is released from Clinton Correctional Prison on $1.4m bail which was posted by Suge Knight. In return 2Pac signs a three-album deal with Knight's Death Row Records.

1997
Elton John is at No. 1 on the US singles chart with 'Candle In The Wind '97', a re-write of his 1973 song about Marilyn Monroe to raise funds for the Diana, Princess of Wales charity. It went on to become the biggest selling worldwide single ever.

1999
Deborah Rowe, the wife of Michael Jackson, files for divorce after three years of marriage. The couple met when Rowe was working as a nurse at his plastic surgeon's office.

Mötley Crüe drummer Tommy Lee is released on $5,000 bail after facing charges relating to a riot at a 1997 gig in North Carolina. Lee allegedly incited the crowd to attack a guard and had also poured a drink over the man's head.

2003
Mojo magazine readers vote the studio session for Elvis Presley's debut single 'That's All Right' as the most pivotal moment in rock history. Bob Dylan's switch from acoustic to electric guitar in 1965 comes second, and 'White Riot', the debut single by The Clash released in 1977, is voted third.

2005
Freddie Mercury's 1974 Rolls Royce is offered for auction on eBay by his family. The Silver Shadow luxury vehicle had already attracted bids of up to £8,400. It comes with an unused box of tissues the singer always stored in the car.

2006
Madonna adopts a one-year-old boy in Malawi, Africa. The boy's father, Yohane Banda, tells reporters, "I know he will be very happy in America." The boy's mother had died a week after he was born.

2009
Barbra Streisand goes to the top of the US album charts with *Love Is The Answer*. It is her ninth No. 1 album, making her the only artist to have a No. 1 album in America in five different decades.

October 12

Born on this day:

1935 Sam Moore, singer (Sam & Dave)
1942 Melvin Franklin, vocals (Temptations)
1948 Rick Parfitt, vocals, guitar (Status Quo)

1969 Martie Erwin, multi-instrumentalist (Dixie Chicks)

1967
The Doors appear at The Surf Club, Nantasket Beach, Massachusetts, supported by Ultimate Spinach.

1968
Big Brother & The Holding Company are at No. 1 on the US album chart with *Cheap Thrills*.

1971
Gene Vincent dies aged 36 from a perforated ulcer. In 1960, while on tour in the UK, Vincent and songwriter Sharon Sheeley were seriously injured in the car crash that killed Sheeley's boyfriend, Eddie Cochran.

1974
The Bay City Rollers are at No. 1 on the UK album chart with their debut LP *Rollin'*.

death in their room at the Chelsea Hotel, New York City. Vicious is arrested, charged with murder and placed in the detox unit at a New York prison.

1982
The Who appear at Shea Stadium, New York City, the first of two shows on consecutive nights, supported by The Clash.

1985
Ricky Wilson, guitarist with The B-52s, dies aged 32 of complications from AIDS.

Jennifer Rush is top of the British singles chart with 'The Power Of Love', which stays at No. 1 for five weeks, becoming the biggest selling single of the year and the biggest

1991
Simply Red's fourth album *Stars*, featuring the singles 'Thrill Me', 'For Your Babies' and the title track, is at No. 1 on the UK chart for the first of five times. The album becomes the biggest seller of 1991 and '92 in the UK, spending 134 weeks on the chart.

1992
Tupac Shakur is released from prison pending an appeal for sexual assault on $1.4m bail.

1997
US singer songwriter John Denver is killed aged 53 when the light aircraft he is piloting crashes into Monterey Bay, California.

1999
Adrian Young, drummer with No Doubt, proposes to his girlfriend Nina during a gig in San Francisco. Young comes on stage before the band's encore and gets down on bended knee with a ring. She accepts.

2005
Mötley Crüe drummer Tommy Lee is treated at a local hospital for minor burns sustained from a pyrotechnics explosion which occurred during a concert in Casper, Wyoming when Lee was suspended from a wire 30 feet above the stage.

Singer and Live Aid co-founder Midge Ure receives an honorary degree from Dundee's University of Abertay. "Having left school at the age of 15, I never expected to receive such an accolade," Ure says.

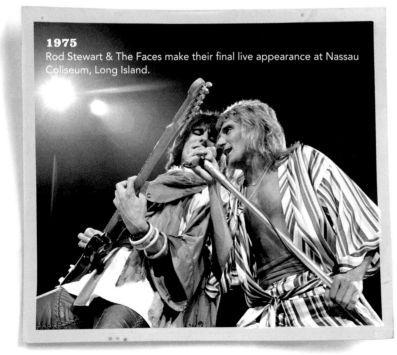

1975
Rod Stewart & The Faces make their final live appearance at Nassau Coliseum, Long Island.

1978
Sex Pistol Sid Vicious calls the police to report that someone has stabbed his girlfriend Nancy Spungen to

single ever for a woman in the UK. Celine Dion also enjoys a No. 1 US hit with her version in 1993.

Born on this day:

1941 Paul Simon, singer, songwriter
1944 Robert Lamm, vocals, keyboards (Chicago)
1947 Sammy Hagar, vocals (Montrose, Van Halen)
1980 Ashanti, singer

October 13

1962
Don Everly collapses during rehearsals on stage at the Prince of Wales Theatre in London on the eve of a 22-date Everly Brothers UK tour. He is flown back to America for treatment and the tour continues with brother Phil performing solo.

1975
Neil Young undergoes an operation at a Los Angeles hospital to remove an object from his vocal cords.

1979
Reggatta De Blanc, the second album by The Police which cost only £6,000

For Time', his sixth US solo chart-topper.

2000
UK newspaper *The Daily Mirror* reports that Toni Braxton has pulled out of this year's MOBO Awards after one of her breast implants had exploded. A spokesman at her record label Arista says, "We don't comment on our artistes' personal lives."

2002
UK rock band Muse take legal action against Celine Dion after she announces her forthcoming Las Vegas show would be called 'Muse'. Singer Matt Bellamy says, "We don't want anyone to think we're Celine Dion's backing band."

2004
The US Internal Revenue Service charge 63-year-old Ronald Isley, lead singer of the Isley Brothers, with tax evasion for failing to report income from royalties and performances by the band between 1997 and 2002. He is later found guilty and sentenced to three years in prison.

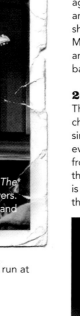

1963
The Beatles make their bill-topping debut on ITV's *Sunday Night At The London Palladium*, transmitted live to an audience of 15 million viewers. The group perform 'From Me To You', 'I'll Get You', 'She Loves You' and 'Twist And Shout'.

1965
The Who record 'My Generation' and 'The Kids Are Alright' at IBC Studios, London. When released as a single 'My Generation' reaches No. 2 on the UK chart, held off the top position by The Seekers' 'The Carnival Is Over'.

1974
TV host Ed Sullivan, whose Sunday night CBS TV show from New York City ran from June 20, 1948 to June 6, 1971, dies aged 73 of cancer. The Beatles' *Sullivan* appearance on February 9, 1964, considered a milestone in American pop culture and the beginning of The British Invasion in music, drew an estimated 73 million viewers.

to record, starts a four-week run at No. 1 in the UK.

1984
U2 score their second UK No. 1 album with *The Unforgettable Fire*, produced by Brian Eno and Daniel Lanois and featuring the single 'Pride (In The Name Of Love)'.

1987
David Bowie plays the first of two nights at the Los Angeles Memorial Sports Arena on the North American leg of his 'Glass Spider' Tour.

1990
George Michael is at No. 1 on the *Billboard* singles chart with 'Praying

Born on this day:

1940 Cliff Richard, UK singer
1946 Justin Hayward, guitar, vocals (Moody Blues)
1974 Natalie Maines, singer, songwriter (Dixie Chicks)

1975 Shaznay Lewis, vocals (All Saints)
1978 Usher, singer

1957

Elvis Presley's 'Jailhouse Rock' is released, becoming his ninth US No. 1 single, staying on the *Billboard* chart for 19 weeks. Elvis stages his own choreography for the song's sequence in the *Jailhouse Rock* film, which some historians consider to be the first rock video.

1988

Def Leppard become the first act in chart history to sell seven million copies of two consecutive LPs, *Pyromania* (released in 1983) and *Hysteria*.

Bruce Springsteen appears at Estadio Mundialista, Mendoza, Argentina to a crowd of over 30,000. The concert is also aired on Chilean TV.

2004

Eric Clapton is suspended from driving in France after being caught speeding at 134mph in his Porsche 911 Turbo near Merceuil. He is given a 750 euro fine and his UK license is confiscated. After paying the fine Clapton poses for photographs with French police and then leaves the scene in his Porsche – with his secretary behind the wheel.

2006

Freddy Fender, the Tex-Mex singer known for the country standards, 'Before The Next Teardrop Falls' (a US No. 1 in 1975) and 'Wasted Days And Wasted Nights', dies aged 69 of complications from lung cancer.

1967

The second series of *The Monkees* TV show starts in the UK. Plans for the shows to be screened in colour on BBC 2 are dropped, and it appears in black and white on BBC 1.

1969

Police in New Jersey issue a warrant for the arrest of Frank Sinatra in relation to his alleged connections with the Mafia.

1972

Michael Jackson is at No. 1 on the US singles chart with 'Ben', his first solo chart-topper (No. 7 in the UK).

1976

Aerosmith start their first ever UK tour at Liverpool's Empire Theatre.

1990

Multi-Emmy and Grammy award-winning American composer, pianist and conductor Leonard Bernstein dies aged 72 of pneumonia. Bernstein conducted the New York Philharmonic at the age of 25 and wrote three symphonies, two operas, five musicals (including *West Side Story*) and numerous other pieces.

1996

Madonna gives birth to her first child, Lourdes Maria Ciccone Leon.

2007

US rapper TI is arrested and charged with weapons offences just hours before he is due to perform and collect two awards at the BET hip-hop gala in Atlanta. The 27-year-old is held in a car park on suspicion of collecting machine guns and silencers bought for him by his bodyguard. His award for CD of the Year is accepted by rapper Common, who wins the prize jointly with TI.

2008

Illustrator and rock cartoonist Ray Lowry dies aged 64. Lowry contributed illustrations for *NME*, *Punch*, *Private Eye* and *The Guardian* and designed the artwork for The Clash's 1979 album *London Calling*.

Born on this day:

1938 Marv Johnson, US singer
1946 Richard Carpenter, keyboards, vocals (Carpenters)
1947 Chris De Burgh, singer, songwriter
1953 Tito Jackson, vocals (Jackson 5)

October 15

1955

Buddy (Buddy Holly) & Bob open for Elvis Presley at the Big D Jamboree, at Lubbock's Cotton Club, Texas. Nashville talent scout Eddie Crandall is in the audience and arranges for Holly to audition and record demos for the Decca label.

1965

Jimi Hendrix signs his first recording contract – a three-year deal with Ed Chalpin for PPX Inc. in New York. Hendrix receives $1 and a one per cent royalty on all of his recordings.

1966

The Who play a ballroom date at The Corn Exchange, Chelmsford, Essex.

1972

Lieutenant Pigeon is at No. 1 on the UK singles chart with 'Mouldy Old Dough'. Keyboard player Rob Woodward has his mum play piano on the single, making them the only mother and son act to score a UK No. 1. The song is recorded in the front room of their semi-detached house.

1973

Keith Richards is found guilty of trafficking cannabis by a court in Nice, France. He is given a one-year suspended sentence and a 5,000 franc fine. Additionally, the Rolling Stones guitarist is banned from entering France for two years.

1979

Abba play their first North American concert in Vancouver, Canada.

1988

Bon Jovi start a four-week run at No. 1 on the US album chart with *New Jersey*.

UB40 are at No. 1 on the *Billboard* singles chart with their version of Neil Diamond's 'Red Red Wine', also a chart-topper in the UK.

1997

Michael Jackson plays the last date on the HIStory Tour at King's Park Rugby Stadium, Durban, South Africa. During the tour, Jackson performs 82 concerts in 58 cities to over 4.5 million fans, visiting five continents and 35 countries.

2000

The 56 year-old Welsh rocker Dave Edmunds has a triple heart bypass operation at LA's Cedars Sinai Hospital.

2006

Sugababes are named as the most successful UK all-female act of the 21st century, according to new figures. Since their chart debut in 2000, they have scored 16 hits, beating the likes of Madonna and Britney Spears. The trio first made UK chart history in 2002 when 'Freak Like Me' made them the youngest female group to top the chart.

2007

Britney Spears visits a Los Angeles police station to be photographed and fingerprinted ahead of her hit-and-run court case. The 25-year-old singer spends about 30 minutes at the station after a judge orders her to submit to the procedure. Spears was charged last month for allegedly crashing into a parked car while driving without a valid licence.

2008

Jon Bon Jovi becomes the latest musician to disapprove of the use of a song in John McCain's US presidential campaign. (Foo Fighters, Heart and Jackson Browne had all asked McCain to stop using their tracks in his presidential bid.) The Bon Jovi song 'Who Says You Can't Go Home' was used during rallies held by Republican vice presidential candidate Sarah Palin. A Democrat supporter, Bon Jovi threw a $30,000 per person, fund-raising dinner for Democrat candidate Barack Obama at his New Jersey home in September.

307

October 16

Born on this day:

1938 Nico, model, singer, actress (Velvet Underground, solo)

1943 Fred Turner, bass, vocals (Bachman Turner Overdrive)

1947 Bob Weir, guitar (Grateful Dead)

1959 Gary Kemp, guitar, keyboards (Spandau Ballet)

1962 Flea, bass, vocals (Red Hot Chili Peppers)

1977 John Mayer, US singer, songwriter

1951
Richard Penniman, an 18-year-old from Georgia who is already using the stage name Little Richard, makes his first recordings at the studios of Atlanta radio station WGST.

1962
The first night of a two month Motown Records package tour – featuring Marvin Gaye, The Supremes, Mary Wells, The Miracles and 12-year-old Stevie Wonder – starts in Washington DC.

1965
At EMI Studios, London, The Beatles record 'Day Tripper' in three takes, completing the song by adding vocals and other overdubs.

1969
Leonard Chess, record company executive and founder of the Chess record label, home to John Lee Hooker, Chuck Berry, Bo Diddley, Little Walter, The Moonglows, The Flamingos, Jimmy Reed and Sonny Boy Williamson among other greats, dies aged 52 of a heart attack.

1974
The Grateful Dead play the first of five nights at the Winterland Arena, San Francisco, California.

1976
One hit wonder Rick Dees & His Cast Of Idiots are at No. 1 on the US singles chart with 'Disco Duck (Part One)'. Dees was an American TV and radio presenter.

1986
Keith Richards, Eric Clapton and Robert Cray join other artists on stage in St Louis for Chuck Berry's 60th birthday concert, organised by Richards and directed by Taylor Hackford for the film *Hail! Hail! Rock & Roll*.

1992
Bob Dylan's 30th anniversary (of his recording debut) tribute concert takes place at Madison Square Garden in New York City. Guest performers include Neil Young, Eric Clapton, George Harrison, Roger McGuinn, Tom Petty, Ron Wood and Dylan himself.

2001
Two security guards are sacked after refusing to allow Bob Dylan into his own concert at the Jackson County Exposition Center, Oregon. Dylan, who had demanded that security on his 'Love And Theft' tour should be tighter than ever, didn't have a pass when he arrived backstage.

2006
CBGBs, the legendary New York punk club credited with discovering Patti Smith and The Ramones, closes after a final gig by Smith herself. Blondie and Talking Heads also found fame after performing at the club that helped launch US punk music. The venue first opened in December 1973, its full name CBGB OMFUG standing for "country, bluegrass, blues and other music for uplifting gormandizers".

2007
French rock star Bertrand Cantat is freed from jail after serving half of an eight-year sentence for killing his actress girlfriend Marie Trintignant. Cantat, singer with Noir Desir, was jailed for manslaughter after a violent row with Trintignant in a Lithuanian hotel in July 2003. She died after spending days in a coma.

2007
Madonna signs a groundbreaking recording and touring contract with concert promoter Live Nation, becoming the first major star to choose an all-in-one agreement with a tour company over a traditional record contract. The deal, reported to be worth $120m over 10 years, will give Live Nation rights to all her music-related projects – including new albums, tours, merchandise, websites, DVDs, sponsorship, TV shows and films.

Born on this day:

1935 Michael Eavis, Glastonbury Festival organiser
1946 Jim Tucker, guitar (The Turtles)

1972 Eminem, US rapper
1972 Wyclef Jean, singer (The Fugees, solo)

October
17

1962

In between their lunchtime and evening shows at The Cavern Club in Liverpool, The Beatles travel to the Granada TV Centre in Manchester to make their television debut, appearing live on the local magazine programme *People And Places*. The group perform two songs, 'Some Other Guy' and 'Love Me Do'.

1964

Manfred Mann start a two-week run on top of the US singles chart with 'Do Wah Diddy Diddy', possibly the first No. 1 with a nonsense song title. Also a No. 1 in Britain, the song was first recorded by the American group The Exciters.

1969

Paul Kantner of Jefferson Airplane is busted for marijuana possession in Honolulu and fined $350.

1970

The Jackson 5 start a five-week run at No. 1 on the US singles chart with 'I'll Be There', the group's fourth chart-topper of 1970, making No. 4 in the UK. Motown claims the group sold over 10 million records during this year.

1987

The Bee Gees become the only group to have a British chart-topper in each of three decades (1960s, '70s & '80s) when 'You Win Again' goes to the top of the UK singles chart, the brothers' fifth and final No. 1.

1991

American singer and television presenter Tennessee Ernie Ford, who had a 1955 US & UK No. 1 with his version of the Merle Travis song, 'Sixteen Tons' dies aged 72 of liver failure. In the '60s he hosted a daytime ABC television talk show, *The Tennessee Ernie Ford Show*.

1992

During a UK tour The Frank And Walters appear at The Junction, Cambridge with Radiohead as support.

1995

During an interview with *The Observer* magazine (published today) Noel Gallagher from Oasis states he wished Damon Albarn and Alex James of Blur would die from AIDS. He later retracts his statement.

Sting's former accountant Keith Moore is sentenced to six years in jail after being found guilty of embezzling £6m from the singer's 108 bank accounts.

1998

UK newspaper *The Daily Star* runs a story claiming that R.E.M. singer Michael Stipe has admitted that he is gay during an MTV interview shown in the US. Stipe was actually voicing his disgust at the killing of a young gay student in America.

1999

It is reported that Michael Jackson had played a secret gig at a martial arts exhibition in Barnstaple, England. The man who had arrived in the white stretch limo was Navi, a Londoner who claimed to be the world's number one 'Jacko' impersonator.

Thomas Durden, who wrote the lyrics to 'Heartbreak Hotel', dies aged 79. Durden had read a newspaper account of a suicide where the man had left a note saying, "I walk a lonely street".

2000

A flat in Montague Square, London, which was once rented in 1965 by Ringo Starr, goes on the market for £575,000. The two bedroom, two-story property was also home to Jimi Hendrix and John & Yoko during the late '60s.

2008

Four Tops' singer dies aged 72 at his Detroit home. Stubbs had been in ill health since being diagnosed with cancer in 1995 and a stroke and other health problems led him to stop touring with the Four Tops in 2000.

Madonna and Guy Ritchie announce that their seven-year marriage is over because they have drifted apart. The press report that without a pre-nuptial agreement, Ritchie could receive up to £50m of Madonna's £300m fortune.

2009

Barbra Streisand goes to No. 1 on the US album chart with *Love Is the Answer,* also a UK No. 1.

October 18

Born on this day:

1926 Chuck Berry, guitar, singer, songwriter
1947 Laura Nyro, singer-songwriter
1949 Joe Egan, vocals (Stealers Wheel)
1977 Simon Rix, bass (Kaiser Chiefs)

1956
21-year-old Elvis Presley pulls into a Memphis gas station where he starts to attract a small crowd of autograph seekers. After station manager Ed Hopper repeatedly asks the singer to move on so he can resume normal business, he slaps Presley on the head and finds himself on the receiving end of a punch in the face from Elvis. Station employee Aubrey Brown tries to help his boss but is no match for Presley. After police are called, Hopper and Brown are charged with assault and are later fined $25 and $15 respectively.

1957
Paul McCartney makes his first appearance with The Quarry Men at The New Clubmoor Hall, Norris Green, Liverpool. The line-up is John Lennon, Paul McCartney, Eric Griffiths, Colin Hanton, and Len Garry.

1966
The newly formed Jimi Hendrix Experience appear at the Olympia, Paris, supporting French pop star Johnny Hallyday. The concert is recorded for French radio.

1967
'I Can See For Miles' by The Who enters the UK singles chart, peaking at No. 10.

The Bee Gees are at No. 1 on the UK singles chart with 'Massachusetts', the first of five UK chart-toppers for the group. Engelbert Humperdinck is at No. 2 with 'The Last Waltz' and Traffic are at 3 with 'Hole In My Shoe'.

1968
John and Yoko are taken to Paddington Green police station and charged with obstruction after cannabis is discovered at the flat in which they are staying. The following month Lennon pleads guilty to possession of cannabis (the obstruction charge was dropped) and he is fined £150.

1976
Buzzcocks make their first recordings at Revolution Studios, Cheadle, Manchester.

1979
Buggles (a studio band featuring producer Trevor Horn) are at No. 1 on the UK singles chart with 'Video Killed The Radio Star'. The song's video is the first ever to be shown on MTV in North America.

1986
Huey Lewis & The News are at No. 1 on the US album chart with *Fore!*

1987
On UK television *The South Bank Show* airs a documentary on The Smiths, filmed during the recording of the album *Strangeways, Here We Come*.

1996
Joni Mitchell is interviewed by Morrissey for a Reprise Records promotional CD 'Words and Music' used to promote her new release *Hits And Misses*.

2000
American singer and actress Julie London, who had a 1956 US No. 9 & UK No. 22 single with 'Cry Me A River', which was also featured in the 1956 film *The Girl Can't Help It*, dies aged 74 after suffering a stroke. She recorded 32 albums during her career and played the role of nurse Dixie McCall in the '70s television series *Emergency!*

2002
After a 15-year court battle, New York State's highest court rules that The Ronettes do not have the right to share the money earned by their producer Phil Spector through the use of the group's songs in movies, television and advertising. Citing a 1963 contract signed by the group, the court also substantially reduces

the amount they stand to gain from royalties on sales of records and compact discs.

2005
Live Aid co-founder Midge Ure collects his OBE from the Queen for his music and charity work. The 52-year-old ex-Ultravox singer wears a kilt for the occasion at Buckingham Palace, London.

2005
A foetal image of a naked John Lennon, taken on the last day of his life, is named the top US magazine cover of the past 40 years. The *Rolling Stone* front cover, by Annie Leibovitz, showing Lennon curled around Yoko Ono is picked by editors, artists and designers.

2009
The Editors go to No. 1 on the UK album chart with *In This Light And On This Evening*, the band's third studio album.

Born on this day:

1944 Peter Tosh, guitar, vocals (The Wailers, solo)

1957 Karl Wallinger, singer, songwriter (The Waterboys, World Party)

1960 Daniel 'Woody' Woodgate, drums (Madness, Voice Of The Beehive)

1972 Pras, rapper (The Fugees)

October 19

1967
The soundtrack to *The Sound Of Music* is at No. 1 on the UK album chart, its 132nd week on the chart. The Beatles are at No. 2 with *Sgt. Pepper's Lonely Hearts Club Band* and Scott Walker is at No. 3 with his first solo album, *Scott*.

1968
During their final North American tour Cream play the second of two nights at the Los Angeles Forum.

1974
Bachman Turner Overdrive are at No. 1 on the US album chart with *Not Fragile*.

1979
A 40-date 2-Tone Records UK tour starts in Brighton, featuring the ska bands The Selecter, The Specials and Madness.

1980
AC/DC commence a 20-date UK tour at Bristol's Colston Hall with new singer Brian Johnston. These are the band's first gigs since the death of their original vocalist Bon Scott.

1985
A-Ha are at No. 1 on the *Billboard* singles chart with 'Take On Me', making them the first Norwegian group to score a US No. 1.

1989
Alan Murphy, guitarist with Level 42 who also worked with Kate Bush, Go West and Mike & the Mechanics, dies of pneumonia related to AIDS.

1991
Oasis play The Boardwalk in their hometown of Manchester, the band's first gig with Noel Gallagher in the line-up.

1994
During a sold out Pink Floyd show at London's Earls Court a section of seating holding over 1,000 fans collapses, though there are no serious injuries.

1997
Glen Buxton, original guitarist with Alice Cooper and who co-wrote their hits 'School's Out' and 'Elected', dies aged 49 from pneumonia.

2000
A judge rules that Robbie Williams had substantially copied lyrics for his song 'Jesus Was A Camper Van' from the 1961 Woody Guthrie song 'I Am The Way' and also used parts of a parody by Loudon Wainwright III. EMI Records offers 25% royalties but Guthrie's publishers Ludlow Music demand 50%.

2005
A survey concludes that the average person spends around £21,000 on music during their life. That figure includes the amount spent on Hi-Fi equipment, concerts and CDs. Music enthusiasts are likely to spend more than double that, parting with just over £44,000, in a lifetime, according to the survey conducted by UK company Prudential.

2007
Johnny Marr is made a visiting professor of music at the University of Salford in Manchester. The former Smiths guitarist will deliver a series of workshops and masterclasses to students on the BA Popular Music and Recording degree.

2009
A clump of hair believed to have been trimmed from Elvis Presley when he joined the US Army in 1958 sells for $15,000 at an auction in Chicago. Other items sold belonging to Presley include a shirt for $52,000, a set of concert-used handkerchiefs for $732 and photos from the reception of Presley's 1967 wedding to Priscilla for nearly $6,000.

October 20

Born on this day:

1950 Tom Petty, guitar, vocals, songwriter
1958 Mark King, bass, vocals (Level 42)
1964 Jim Sonefild, drums, vocals (Hootie & The Blowfish)
1971 Snoop Doggy Dogg, singer, rapper

1962
Bobby 'Boris' Pickett & The Crypt Kickers start a two-week run at No. 1 on the US singles chart with 'Monster Mash', a No. 3 in the UK eleven years later in 1973. The song was deemed offensive by the BBC.

1969
The Who play the first of six nights at New York's Fillmore East, performing a two-hour show featuring the bulk of their latest album *Tommy*.

1976
Led Zeppelin's film *The Song Remains The Same* premieres in New York City. The charity night raises $25,000 for the Save The Children Fund.

1983
Country and western singer-songwriter Merle Travis, acknowledged as one of the most influential American guitarists of the twentieth century, who wrote 'Sixteen Tons', a 1955 US No. 1 for Ernie Ford and appeared in the 1953 movie *From Here To Eternity* singing 'Reenlistment Blues', dies aged 65 of a heart attack.

1984
Wham! start a three-week run at No. 1 on the UK singles chart with 'Freedom', the duo's second chart-topper. The song was used in a Japanese commercial for Maxell audio cassettes, with altered lyrics.

2003
A jury finds Girls Aloud's Cheryl Tweedy guilty of assaulting a nightclub worker. She is sentenced to complete 120 hours of unpaid community service and ordered to pay her victim £500 compensation, plus £3,000 in prosecution costs. The singer had denied attacking toilet attendant Sophie Amogbokpa, saying she only punched the woman in self-defence. The charges stemmed from an incident at the Drink nightclub in Guildford, Surrey, on 11 January.

2005
US rapper Sticky Fingaz is arrested after allegedly leaving an unlicensed gun in the Manhattan hotel Flatotel. Police say a handgun was found in a room where the rapper had been staying. Sticky Fingaz, real name Kirk Jones, was not licensed to carry a weapon.

Michael Jackson receives a jury summons at his Neverland ranch in California four months after he was acquitted on child molestation charges. A spokesperson said it was likely he would be excused from serving due to the fact that he had lived in Bahrain since his trial.

2006
George Michael is seen openly smoking a cannabis joint during an interview on a TV show. The singer is filmed backstage in Madrid, Spain where the drug is legal. "It's the only drug I've ever thought worth taking," Michael says. "This stuff keeps me sane and happy. But it's not very healthy."

2007
Paul Raven, bassist with post-punk band Killing Joke, dies aged 46 of a suspected heart attack in Geneva, Switzerland, where he was recording. He left the band in 1987 before forming Murder Inc and joining Ministry, Prong and Mob Research.

1977
Ronnie Van Zant, Steve Gaines and Cassie Gaines of Lynyrd Skynyrd are all killed along with the band's manager Dean Kilpatrick and two pilots when their rented plane runs out of fuel and crashes into a densely wooded thicket in the middle of a swamp near McComb, Missouri. The crash seriously injures the rest of the band and crew who were due to play at Louisiana University that evening.

1978
The Police make their US debut at CBGBs, New York. The trio had flown in from the UK on low cost tickets with Laker Airtrain, carrying their instruments as hand luggage.

1990
The Charlatans are at No. 1 on the UK album chart with their debut *Some Friendly*.

Born on this day:

1940 Manfred Mann, keyboards
1941 Steve Cropper, guitar, producer
(Booker T & The MGs)
1946 Lux Interior, singer (The Cramps)

1954 Eric Faulkner, guitar (The Bay City
Rollers)
1957 Julian Cope, bass, guitar, vocals (The
Teardrop Explodes, solo)

October
21

1967
Lulu starts a five-week run at No. 1 on the US singles chart with 'To Sir With Love', the theme from the film of the same name.

1972
Chuck Berry starts a two-week run on top of the *Billboard* singles chart with 'My Ding-A-Ling', his first and only US and UK No. 1, 17 years after his first chart hit.

1976
At the end of a North American tour, Keith Moon plays his last show with The Who in front of a paying audience at Maple Leaf Gardens, Toronto.

1989
Jive Bunny & The Mastermixes have their second UK No. 1 single with 'That's What I Like'. The *Hawaii Five-O* theme is the recurring hook in the record which also includes 'Lets Twist Again', 'Lets Dance', 'Great Balls Of Fire' and 'The Twist'.

1992
George Michael takes Sony Records to court in a fight over his contract with the company but loses the case in 1994. Michael works with Sony again less than 10 years later.

1997
Elton John's 'Candle In The Wind '97' is declared by *The Guinness Book Of Records* to be the biggest selling single record of all time, with 31.8 million sales in less than 40 days, raising more than £20 million for charity.

2001
Concerts at Madison Square Garden and RFK Stadium in Washington DC are expected to raise millions in funds for the victims of the 9/11 attacks. Stars who appear include Michael Jackson, Tom Petty, Aerosmith, *NSYNC, P Diddy, James Brown, Paul McCartney, David Bowie, Eric Clapton, The Who, Elton John, Mick Jagger and Keith Richards.

2006
It is revealed that British broadcaster John Peel left over £1.8m and over 25,000 vinyl records in his will. Peel died suddenly at the age of 65 from a heart attack in 2004.

2007
Kid Rock and five members of his entourage are arrested after an argument with a man escalated into a fight in a restaurant in Atlanta, Georgia. Kid Rock's tour bus is pulled over by police after it left the scene and Rock is released after posting $1,000 bail. Kid Rock has the No. 1 album in the US with *Rock 'N' Roll Jesus*, his eleventh album release and first to debut at the top of the *Billboard* chart.

2006
Evanescence top the US chart with their second album *The Open Door*, which becomes the 700th No. 1 album in *Billboard* since the chart became a weekly feature in 1956.

October 22

Born on this day:

1945 Leslie West, guitar (Mountain, West Bruce & Laing)
1946 Eddie Brigati, vocals (Young Rascals, Rascals)
1968 Shaggy, singer
1968 Shelby Lynne, US singer, songwriter
1985 Zachary Walker Hanson, drums, vocals (Hanson)

1964

The Who, then known as The High Numbers, receive a letter from EMI Records, asking them for original material after their recent audition for the company.

1966

The Beach Boys' 'Good Vibrations' makes its debut on the US singles chart. Written by Brian Wilson and Mike Love, the track was recorded over six weeks in four different Los Angeles studios, at a cost of over $16,000. The recording engineer is later quoted as saying that the last take sounded exactly like the first, six months earlier. The record reaches No. 1 on the US charts in December.

1969

American singer Tommy Edwards, who had a 1958 US & UK No. 1 with 'It's All In The Game', dies aged 47 after suffering a brain aneurysm in Henrico County, Virginia.

1971

Fleetwood Mac appear at The Felt Forum, New York City.

1978

On their first US tour, The Police appear at Grendel's Lair, Philadelphia, Pennsylvania.

1986

Jane Dornacker, a former member of The Tubes and Leila And The Snakes, is killed in a helicopter crash during a live traffic report for WNBC radio in New York.

1989

English folk singer, songwriter, poet, and record producer Ewan MacColl, who wrote 'Dirty Old Town' and 'The First Time Ever I Saw Your Face' and was the father of singer, songwriter Kirsty MacColl, dies aged 74. Acts including The Dubliners, Planxty, The Pogues, Roberta Flack, Rod Stewart, Elvis Presley and Johnny Cash recorded his songs.

1990

Pearl Jam play their first ever concert when appearing at The Off Ramp in Seattle.

1993

Nirvana appear at The Palmer Alumni Auditorium, Davenport, Iowa.

1996

A press release announces that: "The Beatles are now bigger than The Beatles". The statement is based on sales to date this year, taking in 6,000,000 albums from the group's back catalogue and a combined total of 13,000,000 copies of *The Beatles Anthology 1* and *Anthology 2*. With the release of *Anthology 3* a week away, it is anticipated that total Beatles album sales for 1996 will exceed 20 million. A poll shows 41 percent of sales are to teenagers who were not born when The Beatles officially disbanded in 1970.

2000

George Michael pays £1.45m for the Steinway piano on which John Lennon wrote 'Imagine'. "I know that when my fingers touch the keys of that Steinway, I will feel truly blessed," Michael says. "And parting with my money has never been much of a problem, just ask my accountant." The singer reportedly outbid Robbie Williams and the Gallagher brothers.

2005

'Waterloo' by Abba is voted the best song in the history of the Eurovision Song Contest. Viewers in 31 countries across Europe vote during a special show in Copenhagen to celebrate the annual event's 50th birthday.

2008

A homeless man claims a £2,000 reward by returning a waxwork head of ex-Beatle Sir Paul McCartney which had been left on a train. Anthony Silva found the item in a bin at Reading station after auctioneer Joby Carter left it under a seat at Maidenhead station. The homeless man thought it was a Halloween mask and had been using it as a pillow before realising what it was. The wax model sold the following week for £5,500 at auction.

1979

The Pretenders start a run of four consecutive Monday nights at London's Marquee Club.

October 23

1962
12-year-old Little Stevie Wonder records 'Thank You For Loving Me All The Way', his first single for Motown Records.

1963
Bob Dylan records 'The Times They Are A-Changin'' at Columbia Recording Studios, New York City.

1964
All three members of US band Buddy & The Kings are killed when their hired Cesna Skyhawk 172, piloted by the band's drummer Bill Daniels, taking them from a gig in Harris County crashes nose first killing all on board. Ironically, following the death of Buddy Holly, The Crickets used various lead singers on their records and Buddy & The Kings' singer Harold Box had sung lead on The Crickets' recording of 'Peggy Sue Got Married'.

1966
The Jimi Hendrix Experience record their first single 'Hey Joe' at De Lane Lea studios, London.

1976
Chicago start a two-week run on top of the US singles chart with 'If You

Leave Me Now'. It was the group's 18th Top 40 hit and first No. 1, also a chart-topper in the UK. It went on to win a Grammy Award for Best Pop Vocal Performance.

1982
Culture Club are at No. 1 on the UK singles chart with 'Do You Really Want To Hurt Me?', the group's first chart topper and the first of 12 UK Top 40 singles. The song becomes a major hit after the group's memorable debut performance on *Top Of The Pops*, when they stood in for Shakin' Stevens who was ill and unable to appear.

1989
Nirvana play their first ever European show at Newcastle's Riverside Club in north east England. It is the first night of a 36-date European tour for the group who are sharing the bill with fellow Sub Pop act, Tad.

1993
Meat Loaf has his first UK and US No. 1 with 'I'd Do Anything For Love (But I Won't Do That)', which stays in the top slot in Britain for seven weeks. It is also a No. 1 in 28 other countries.

1995
Def Leppard gain a place in *The Guinness Book Of World Records* by playing three gigs (Tangier, London and Vancouver) over three continents in 24 hours.

2002
Kanye West is involved in a car crash after he falls asleep at the wheel while driving home from a recording studio in West Hollywood. No other cars are involved in the incident which leaves West with his jaw fractured in three places.

A federal judge in St. Louis dismisses a lawsuit against Chuck Berry by Johnnie Johnson, a piano player and former collaborator, who wants royalties for more than 30 songs written between 1955 and 1966. The judge rules that too many years have passed to bring about a royalties suit.

2005
US rapper Cam'ron is taken to hospital in Washington DC after a man attempts to steal his sports car at traffic lights. A single shot passed through both of Cam'ron's arms.

Arctic Monkeys score their first UK No. 1 single with 'I Bet You Look Good On The Dancefloor', the Sheffield band's debut single.

October 24

Born on this day:

1936 Bill Wyman, bass, vocals (The Rolling Stones, solo)

1946 Jerry Edmonton, drums (Steppenwolf)

1947 Edgar Broughton, vocals, guitar (Edgar Broughton Band)

1948 Dale Griffin, drums (Mott The Hoople)

1948 Paul & Barry Ryan, singers

1979 Ben Gillies, drummer (Silverchair)

1962
James Brown records his *Live At The Apollo* album at the legendary soul and gospel venue in Harlem, New York City. The album is later ranked at 24 in *Rolling Stone* magazine's 2003 list of The 500 Greatest Albums Of All Time.

1969
Humble Pie appear at the Empire, Sunderland, supported by David Bowie.

1970
Santana score their first US No. 1 album with *Abraxas*.

1973
Rolling Stone Keith Richards is fined £205 after admitting having cannabis, Chinese heroin, mandrax tablets and a revolver at his Chelsea home.

1977
At a court in Toronto, Canada, Keith Richards pleads guilty to possessing heroin. He is later given a one year suspended sentence and ordered to perform a benefit concert for the blind.

1979
Paul McCartney receives a medallion cast in rhodium from the British arts minister after being declared the most successful composer of all time. According to the *Guinness Book Of Records*, from 1962 to 1978, McCartney had written or co-written 43 songs that sold over a million copies each.

1987
Michael Jackson starts a two-week run at No. 1 on the US singles chart with 'Bad'.

1998
Former Stone Roses lead singer Ian Brown is jailed for four months after being found guilty of disorderly behaviour during a flight from Paris to Manchester. Brown had threatened to chop the hands off an air stewardess during "a heated exchange".

2001
Kim Gardner, former bassist with British '60s groups The Birds and The Creation, and who, with Ashton Gardner & Dyke, had a 1971 UK No. 3 single with 'The Resurrection Shuffle', dies aged 55 of cancer in Los Angeles.

2002
American recording engineer and producer Tom Dowd, who worked on albums by many artists including The Drifters, The Rascals, Dusty Springfield, Cream, Eric Clapton, The Allman Brothers, Lynyrd Skynyrd, Rod Stewart, Aretha Franklin and Otis Redding, dies aged 67 of emphysema in Florida.

2005
Madonna gives a surprise lecture at New York City's Hunter College, discussing her career and her new documentary, *I'm Going To Tell You A Secret* as part of the MTV series *Stand In*. Students, who were only expecting a screening of the film, are also given the chance to question the singer.

2006
Foxy Brown is sentenced to three years probation for assaulting two New York nail salon workers during a dispute over payment for a pedicure and manicure in August 2004. The female rapper had been threatened with jail after failing to turn up to court.

2006
Forbes.com reveals that Kurt Cobain has overtaken Elvis Presley as the highest earning dead celebrity. Cobain's work earned $50m in the 12 months to October 2006, compared with Presley's $42m. Former Beatle John Lennon earned $35m.

October 25

1963
The Beatles start their first tour outside of Britain in Sweden. The local pop reviewer is not impressed, saying The Beatles should be grateful to their screaming fans for drowning out the group's terrible performance.

1964
The Rolling Stones appear for the first time on *The Ed Sullivan Show* from New York, performing 'Around And Around' and 'Time Is On My Side'. A riot breaks out in the studio, prompting Sullivan's infamous quote, "I promise you they'll never be back on our show again." The Rolling Stones went on to make a further five appearances on Sullivan's show between 1965 and '69.

1968
Led Zeppelin play a gig at Surrey University, England. Although there are unconfirmed reports of earlier shows, this appears to be the band's first gig with their new name after initially performing as The New Yardbirds. In 2003 a poster for the Surrey gig (billing the group as The New Yardbirds) sells at auction for £2,400.

The double album, *Electric Ladyland* by The Jimi Hendrix Experience is released in the UK. It was later made available as two separate albums with changed artwork in Britain after complaints about the naked women pictured on the British album sleeve. The female models, each being paid £5 for the shoot by photographer David Montgomery, were offered another fiver if they posed completely nude.

1969
'Sugar Sugar' by The Archies, a rock group based on comic book

characters, is at No. 1 on the UK singles chart, staying at the top for eight weeks. The song is also a chart-topper in the US, selling over six million copies worldwide.

1974
While taking a shower at his Memphis home Al Green receives second degree burns when his jealous ex-girlfriend Mary Woodson bursts into the house and pours boiling hot grits over him. She then shot herself dead.

1975
Art Garfunkel is at No. 1 on the UK singles chart with his version of 'I Only Have Eyes For You'. Written in 1934 for the film *Dames* the song was a No. 2 for Ben Selvin in 1934 and most notably a success for The Flamingos in 1959.

1980
Barbra Streisand starts a three-week run at No. 1 on the UK singles chart with 'Woman In Love', written by The Bee Gees.

1985
R.E.M., The Smiths and Tom Waits appear on *The Tube*, at Tyne-Tees Television Studios, Newcastle.

1986
Dire Straits guitarist and singer Mark Knopfler breaks his collarbone after crashing in a celebrity car race before the Australian Grand Prix.

1992
Roger Miller, who scored a 1965 UK No. 1 & US No. 4 single with 'King Of The Road' and won 11 Grammy Awards as a songwriter, dies aged 56 of lung and throat cancer in Los Angeles.

2001
Six years after his death it is announced that 13 law firms are still involved in claims to Grateful Dead guitarist Jerry Garcia's $10m estate,

with former wives and girlfriends continuing to fight about how to distribute his estate and annual royalties of $4.6m.

2003
Johnny Cash's step-daughter, Rosey Nix Adams and her fiddle player Jimmy Campbell are found dead on their tour bus in Clarksville, Tennessee from carbon monoxide poisoning. Heaters that had been left on were blamed for the accident.

2004
John Peel dies aged 65 in Cuzco, Peru of a heart attack. He was the BBC's longest-serving (and most influential) radio DJ, and the first to introduce T. Rex, Rod Stewart, Roxy Music, The Ramones, The Sex Pistols, The Smiths, The Fall, Blur and countless others to many loyal listeners. Peel, who was also renowned for his 'Peel Sessions', recording various bands in the Beeb's studios with producer John Walters for broadcast, was appointed an OBE in 1998.

Born on this day:

1946 Keith Hopwood, guitar (Herman's Hermits)

1951 Bootsy Collins, bass (James Brown, Parliament, Funkadelic, Bootsy's Rubber Band)

1952 David Was, multi-instrumentalist (Was Not Was)

1963 Natalie Merchant, singer (10,000 Maniacs)

1961
Thanks to the efforts of producer John Hammond, Bob Dylan signs with Columbia Records.

1962
The Rolling Stones (known as The Rollin' Stones), consisting of Mick Jagger, Brian Jones, Keith Richard, pianist Ian Stewart, bass player Dick Taylor, and drummer Tony Chapman, record their first demo tape at Curly Clayton Studios in Highbury, north London. It contains three songs: Jimmy Reed's 'Close Together', Bo Diddley's 'You Can't Judge A Book By The Cover' and Muddy Waters' 'Soon Forgotten'.

1965
Queen Elizabeth II invests The Beatles with their MBEs at Buckingham Palace, London. According to a later, by most reports, exaggerated account by John Lennon, the group smoked marijuana in one of the palace bathrooms to calm their nerves.

1974
Barry White scores his only US No. 1 album with *Can't Get Enough*.

1979
The scheduled date for an AC/DC gig at The Mayfair, Newcastle-upon-Tyne, supported by Def Leppard. The bands are booked to appear the night before but because of a fire at the venue in the afternoon, the show is cancelled.

1984
Having spent the day listening to Ozzy Osbourne records, 19-year-old John D. McCollum kills himself with a .22 caliber handgun. A year later, McCollum's parents take court action against Osbourne and CBS Records, alleging that the song 'Suicide Solution' from the album *Blizzard Of Ozz* contributed to their son's death. The case was eventually thrown out of court.

1985
Whitney Houston is at No. 1 on the *Billboard* singles chart with 'Saving All My Love For You', also a chart-topper in the UK.

1991
Legendary American promoter Bill Graham who opened his Fillmores West and East in San Francisco and New York in the '60s and did much to promote the Bay Area bands, is killed aged 60 when the helicopter in which he is travelling hits a 200ft. utility tower in Sonoma County, California. Graham's girlfriend and the pilot are also killed.

1993
Catholic churches in San Juan, Puerto Rico ask residents to tie black ribbons on trees in protest against Madonna's first live appearance in the country.

2004
Elvis Presley comes top of a Forbes.com list of the highest-earning deceased musicians over the past year with $40m. The others are John Lennon $21m, George Harrison $7m, Bob Marley $7m and George and Ira Gershwin $6m.

2006
Duran Duran guitarist Andy Taylor quits the band during the US leg of their world tour. A statement on behalf of the group describes the relationship with Andy Taylor as unworkable and one that cannot be resolved.

2007
Rapper TI is released on $3m bail in Atlanta after being charged with unlawfully possessing firearms, unregistered machine guns and silencers. Judge Alan Baverman says the singer must remain under house arrest in Henry County, Georgia, and be electronically tagged.

Pete Doherty is given a suspended prison term for drugs and motoring offences after admitting driving while uninsured, having no MoT and being in possession of crack cocaine, heroin, ketamine and cannabis. The Babyshambles singer was sentenced to four months in jail, suspended for two years.

Born on this day:

1949 Garry Tallent, bass (The E Street Band)
1958 Simon Le Bon, vocals (Duran Duran)
1967 Scott Weiland, vocals (Stone Temple Pilots)

1984 Kelly Osbourne, celebrity daughter of Ozzy Osbourne

October 27

1957

After a show at the Pan Pacific Auditorium in Los Angeles, local police prohibit Elvis Presley from wiggling his hips onstage and the local press run headlines saying the singer will have to clean up his act. The next night, the Los Angeles Vice Squad film Elvis' entire concert in order to study his performance.

1969

In Champagne, Illinois, Muddy Waters is seriously injured in a car accident that kills three people.

1979

During a US tour Elton John collapses on stage at Hollywood's Universal Amphitheatre suffering from exhaustion.

1980

Former T. Rex member Steve Took chokes to death on a cherry stone after some magic mushrooms he had eaten numb all sensation in his throat.

1984

During their current US tour, Grateful Dead allocate a specific recording area

1990

Michael Waite from one-hit-wonders Musical Youth ('Pass The Dutchie' in 1982) is jailed for four years for his part in a robbery.

2000

Lonnie Donegan receives an MBE for his services to pop music at Buckingham Palace. In the 1950s Donegan pioneered skiffle, a do-it-yourself form of fast folk music that inspired a generation of teenagers to start bands, including John Lennon with The Quarry Men.

2005

Paramount Pictures, the distributors of rapper 50 Cent's new film *Get Rich Or Die Tryin'* withdraw the advertising poster – showing the rapper holding a gun in his left hand and a microphone in the other – after complaints that it glorifies gun violence. Los Angeles County Supervisor Michael Antonovich writes to Paramount, urging them to take down the posters. The company says it had removed one from near a Los Angeles nursery school and planned to take down more.

1970

Black Sabbath play their first ever-live show in America at Glassboro State College, New Jersey – the first concert on a 16-date US tour.

1973

Mott The Hoople appear at The Orpheum Theatre, Boston, supported by local band Aerosmith.

1975

The relatively unknown singer-songwriter Bruce Springsteen receives the rare honour of simultaneous covers on both *Time* and *Newsweek*.

for fans to record each concert, tonight's home gig in Berkeley, California being no exception.

1989

U2 bassist Adam Clayton is convicted of a drink driving offence by a Dublin court after being found driving twice over the legal limit. He is fined £500 and banned from driving for a year.

2007

Former Moloko singer Roisin Murphy is reported as "recovering well" in hospital after damaging an eye socket during a show at Moscow's Ikra Club. The singer hit her head on a chair during the show and was rushed to hospital for surgery. A spokesman said Roisin had lost "a lot of blood" and had severe concussion, but her vision was unaffected.

October 28

Born on this day:

1941 Hank Marvin, guitar (The Shadows)
1945 Wayne Fontana, singer (Wayne Fontana & The Mindbenders, solo)
1948 Telma Hopkins, singer (Dawn)
1957 Stephen Morris, drums (Joy Division, New Order)

1958
Buddy Holly appears on Dick Clark's *American Bandstand*, where he lip-synchs 'It's So Easy' and 'Heartbeat'. It was to be Holly's last major TV appearance

1961
A local customer, Raymond Jones, walks into Liverpool's NEMS record store looking to buy a copy of 'My Bonnie' by The Beatles, which has been released in Germany. Shop manager Brian Epstein does not have the record in question but promises to investigate further.

1962
The Beatles play at the Empire in Liverpool, their first gig at Liverpool's top theatre. Eight acts are on the bill including Little Richard, Craig Douglas, Jet Harris and Kenny Lynch & Sounds Incorporated.

1964
The first of two nights billed as The T.A.M.I. (Teenage Music International) Show, being filmed for a cinematic release, takes place at the Civic Auditorium, Santa Monica, including Smokey Robinson & The Miracles, The Beach Boys, Chuck Berry, Marvin Gaye, The Supremes and The Rolling Stones.

1972
The United States Council for World Affairs announces it is adopting The Who song 'Join Together' as its official theme tune.

1974
David Bowie plays the first of seven sold-out nights on his 'Diamond Dogs' Tour at the Radio City Music Hall, New York City.

1978
Queen play the first night of their 79-date 'Jazz' Tour at the Dallas Convention Center, Dallas, Texas.

1982
The Jam announce they are splitting up at the end of their current UK tour.

1989
Janet Jackson starts a four-week run at No. 1 on the US album chart with *Janet Jackson's Rhythm Nation 1814*, only one of three albums to produce seven Top 10 US singles (the other two being *Thriller* by Michael Jackson and Bruce Springsteen's *Born In The USA*).

1995
Coolio featuring L.V. scores his first UK No. 1 single with 'Gangsta's Paradise', which samples the chorus of Stevie Wonder's 1976 song 'Pastime Paradise'. The song features in the 1995 movie *Dangerous Minds* (starring Michelle Pfeiffer).

1997
R.E.M. drummer Bill Berry announces that for health reasons he is leaving the group after 17 years to become a farmer.

2001
Afroman (Joseph Foreman) starts a two-week run at No. 1 on the UK singles chart with 'Because I Got High'. The song, about how cannabis use is degrading the singer's quality of life, rose from obscurity after it was circulated around the Internet.

2004
Courtney Love is ordered to stand trial on a charge of assault with a deadly weapon after complainant Kristin King tells a Los Angeles court that Love threw a bottle and a lit candle at her after turning up at the home of a former boyfriend in the early hours. King tells the court Love was "vicious" and "erratic" when she allegedly attacked her while she slept on a sofa on 25 April. King claims Love then sat on her, pulled her hair and pinched her left breast in the "worst pinch I ever had", before King managed to flee.

2005
Carl Morgan, a member of the rap collective So Solid Crew is jailed for at least 30 years for murdering a love rival in south London. The judge says the life sentence shows gun crime will not be tolerated. Morgan appears in the band's video for the track '21 Seconds'.

2007
The X Factor winner Leona Lewis is at No. 1 on the UK singles chart with the first track from her debut album *Bleeding Love*. Lewis has the biggest opening week sales to date in 2007, outselling the rest of the top five put together, with 218,000 copies.

Born on this day:

1944 Denny Laine, guitar, vocals (The Moody Blues, Wings)

1946 Peter Green, vocals, guitar (John Mayall's Bluesbreakers, Fleetwood Mac, solo)

1955 Kevin DuBrow, singer (Quiet Riot)

1955 Roger O'Donnell, keyboards (The Cure, The Psychedelic Furs, The Thompson Twins, Berlin)

October 29

1965

The Who release their third single, 'My Generation' in the UK, which peaks at No. 2 on the British charts.

1966

? & the Mysterians are at No. 1 on the US singles chart with '96 Tears' (only reaching 37 in the UK). The Stranglers' cover of the song reaches 17 in the UK in 1990.

1971
Duane Allman of The Allman Brothers Band is killed when he loses control of his motorcycle on a Macon, Georgia street while trying to swerve to avoid a tractor-trailer. He was three weeks shy of his 25th birthday.

1977

The Belgian travel service issues a summons against The Sex Pistols claiming the sleeve to the band's single 'Holidays In The Sun' infringes the copyright of one of its brochures.

1983

Pink Floyd's *The Dark Side Of The Moon* becomes the longest listed album in the history of the US chart with a total of 491 weeks on the chart.

1984

American drummer Wells Kelly from Orleans, who had two 1976 US hit singles with 'Still The One' and 'Dance With Me', dies aged 45 after choking to death on his vomit.

1987

David Bowie plays the first night of the Australian and New Zealand leg of his 'Glass Spider' Tour at the Boondall Entertainment Centre, Brisbane.

1991

Memphis City Council names Interstate 55 through Jackson, The B.B. King Freeway.

2001

In New York, U2 perform for the first time on *The Late Show With David Letterman*.

2003

Research in America finds that songs get stuck in our heads because they create a 'brain itch' that can only be scratched by repeating a tune over and over. Songs such as the Village People's 'YMCA' and the Baha Men's 'Who Let The Dogs Out' owe their success to their ability to create a 'cognitive itch', according to Professor James Kellaris, of the University of Cincinnati College of Business Administration.

2005

A set of waxwork heads of The Beatles from their *Sgt. Pepper* album cover sell for £81,500. The "pepperheads", used in 1967 by artist Peter Blake for the backdrop of the front sleeve, are auctioned after recently being discovered in a back room at London's Madame Tussauds.

2007

Walk The Line, a movie about the life of singer Johnny Cash, is voted the greatest music biopic in a poll. (The film, starring Joaquin Phoenix as Cash and Reese Witherspoon as his wife June Carter, won Witherspoon an Oscar in 2006.) It is followed by rapper Eminem's *8 Mile*, Mozart's' life story *Amadeus* is third and *Ray*, starring Jamie Foxx as musician Ray Charles, fourth. The most recent film in the Top 10 is Joy Division biopic *Control*.

Born on this day:

1939 Eddie Holland, Tamla-Motown producer, songwriter

1939 Grace Slick, vocals (The Great Society, Jefferson Airplane, Starship)

1947 Timothy B Schmit, bass, vocals (Poco, The Eagles)

1967 Gavin Rossdale, guitar, vocals (Bush)

1961

Two days after Raymond Jones asks Brian Epstein at NEMS record store in Liverpool for The Beatles' German single 'My Bonnie' (recorded with Tony Sheridan), two girls enquire about the same record. Epstein's difficulty in locating the record is due to him being unaware that the record is credited not to The Beatles, but to Tony Sheridan and 'The Beat Brothers' (Beatles too closely resembled 'peedles', a vulgar word for the male appendage in German so The Beatles' name was changed for this single).

1967

In a London court Rolling Stones' guitarist Brian Jones pleads guilty to cannabis possession and allowing his premises to be used for the smoking of the drug. His plea of 'not guilty' to the charge of possessing methedrine and cocaine is accepted. Jones is sentenced to nine months in Wormwood Scrubs prison but is released on bail the following day pending appeal.

Tyrannosaurus Rex record a session for the BBC Radio 1 *Top Gear* show, hosted by John Peel – the first group to do so without a recording contract.

1970

Jim Morrison of The Doors is fined and sentenced to six months in jail after being found guilty of exposing himself during a gig in Miami.

1971

John Lennon is top of the UK album chart with *Imagine*, which contains two thinly veiled attacks on former creative partner Paul McCartney in 'How Do You Sleep?' and 'Crippled Inside'.

1975

Bob Dylan plays the first night on his 31-date 'Rolling Thunder Revue' tour at the War Memorial Auditorium, Plymouth, Massachusetts.

1978

The animated cartoon, *Kiss Meets The Phantom Of The Park*, in which the rock band have to deal with a mad scientist who goes crazy in an amusement park, is shown on NBC-TV in America. All four members of Kiss have just released solo albums.

1988

Nirvana appear at The Evergreen State College dorm party, Olympia, Washington.

1990

Guns N' Roses singer Axl Rose is released on $10,000 bail, after being arrested for allegedly hitting a neighbour over the head with a bottle. The incident happened after a complaint to the police about loud music coming from the singer's house.

1998

The original Black Sabbath line-up momentarily reunites to play 'Paranoid' on US TV's David Letterman show.

2004

An arrest warrant is issued for Mötley Crüe singer Vince Neil after he allegedly knocked a soundman unconscious during a concert at Gilley's nightclub in Dallas. Neil is said to have punched Michael Talbert in the face after he asked for more volume on his guitar and attacked Talbert as he adjusted it, leaving him unconscious for 45 seconds.

2007

Linda Stein, former co-manager of punk band The Ramones and the ex-wife of Seymour Stein, former president of Sire Records, the launching pad for the Ramones, Talking Heads and Madonna, is found beaten to death at her Manhattan apartment. Stein had become one of New York's leading estate agents and her clients included Sting, Billy Joel and long-time friend Elton John who told the *New York Times* that he was "absolutely shocked and upset".

Born on this day:

1952 Bernard Edwards, producer (Chic)
1961 Larry Mullen, drums (U2)
1963 Johnny Marr, guitar, songwriter (The Smiths, Modest Mouse, Johnny Marr & The Healers, The Cribs)
1966 Ad-Rock, vocals (The Beastie Boys)
1981 Frank Anthony Iero, guitar (My Chemical Romance)

October 31

1952
Pianist Johnnie Johnson hires 26-year-old Chuck Berry as a guitarist in his band. While playing evening gigs in the St. Louis area, Berry keeps his day job as a hairdresser for the next three years.

1959
In Liverpool, when auditioning for the Carroll Levis *Discoveries* show, The Quarry Men, featuring John Lennon, Paul McCartney and George Harrison, decide to change their name to Johnny & The Moondogs.

1963
The Beatles return to London from Sweden and are greeted by hundreds of screaming fans and a mob of photographers and journalists. American television host Ed Sullivan is at Heathrow as The Beatles arrive, and is struck by the sight of Beatlemania in full swing. It prompts him to book the group to appear on his US television programme.

1964
Ray Charles is arrested by customs officials at Logan Airport, Boston and charged with heroin possession. This is Charles' third drug charge, following incidents in 1958 and 1961, but he avoids prison after kicking the habit in a Los Angeles clinic and spends a year on parole in 1966.

1967
Rolling Stone Brian Jones is released from Wormwood Scrubs prison on £750 bail pending appeal. Jones was found guilty of possession of cannabis. Several people, including Mick's brother, Chris, DJ Jeff Dexter and his girlfriend Caroline Coon are arrested and charged with obstructing the police after demonstrating on the King's Road.

1974
Led Zeppelin launch their new record label Swan Song with a Halloween party at Chislehurst Caves.

1986
The new series of Channel 4's *The Tube* starts with Jermaine Stewart, Troublefunk, Bob Geldof and Frankie Goes To Hollywood plus Spandau Ballet, who play live in the studio at Newcastle-upon-Tyne.

In the London High Court Roger Waters tries to stop Dave Gilmour and Nick Mason from using the name Pink Floyd for future touring and recording.

1987
Forbes magazine lists the Top 40 American entertainment earners from 1986-87; from music, eighth was Whitney Houston ($44m), seventh Madonna ($47m) and third Bruce Springsteen ($56m).

1990
During a gig in Seattle, Washington, Billy Idol dumps 600 dead fish in support act Faith No More's dressing room. They respond by walking on stage naked during Idol's set.

1995
James Brown is arrested in Aiken, South Carolina for assaulting his 47-year-old wife, Adrienne, who claims her husband hit her with a mirror. Adrienne dies in January 1996 and the assault charges against Brown are dropped.

1998
Cher starts a seven week run at No. 1 with her third UK chart-topping single 'Believe', taken from her 23rd studio album, making her (at 52) the first female artist to have a No. 1 single over the age of 50. The song was a No. 1 in 23 countries.

2004
R. Kelly is kicked off a tour with Jay-Z, a day after claiming he was attacked with pepper spray by a member of the rapper's entourage.

2005
At an auction in Las Vegas the white suit worn by John Lennon on the cover of The Beatles' *Abbey Road* album sells for $118,000. Also an Austin Princess hearse driven by Lennon in the documentary *Imagine* sells for $150,000. A portion of the proceeds from the sale of the items goes to Amnesty International.

November

Born on this day:

1949 David Foster, Canadian musician, producer, composer

1962 Anthony Kiedis, vocals (Red Hot Chili Peppers)

1962 Mags Furuholmen, guitar, keyboards (A-Ha)

1963 Rick Allen, drums (Def Leppard)

1981 LaTavia Roberson, singer (Destiny's Child)

November 1

1956

Elvis Presley buys a new Harley Davidson motorbike and spends the day riding round Memphis with actress Natalie Wood.

1966

The Doors play the first night of a month-long residency at the Ondine Discotheque, Manhattan, New York City.

1969

Elvis Presley is at No. 1 on the *Billboard* singles chart with 'Suspicious Minds', his 18th US No. 1 single.

1970

Matthews Southern Comfort are at No. 1 on the UK singles chart with their version of Joni Mitchell's 'Woodstock'.

1975

Wings kick off an 11-date Australian tour at The Entertainment Centre in Perth.

1987

LL Cool J, Eric B & Rankin and Public Enemy play the first of three shows at London's Hammersmith Odeon. Each night is marred by violence and crime.

1993

Flavor Flav from Public Enemy is arrested and charged with the attempted murder of his neighbour. Flav claims the man had sex with his girlfriend.

1996

U2 set up a video link to an Internet site from their Dublin recording studio so fans can watch them recording their new album.

1997

Scandinavian dance-pop act Aqua start a four-week run at No. 1 on the UK singles chart with 'Barbie Girl.' A massive world-wide hit the single has sold more than 8 million copies.

2000

All Saints come top of a poll to find the sexiest female act after being voted for by 12,000 UK television viewers. The Spice Girls finish second with Atomic Kitten third. The 1950s group The Beverley Sisters are voted into 11th place, beating TLC.

2001

In London two men are shot outside The Astoria, on Charing Cross Road, after a So Solid Crew concert.

2002

To celebrate his 33rd birthday in Morocco, P Diddy hires two private jets to fly 300 guests from New York to Marrakech.

2003

Organisers of the MTV Europe Awards 2003 recruit 500 'screamers' to attend this year's event. The music lovers are selected at an audition held in Edinburgh's Princes Street Gardens. About 1,500 pop-mad teenagers and adults scream themselves hoarse in a bid to get their hands on a ticket to the exclusive event.

2004

Terry Knight, the 61-year-old former DJ and manager of Grand Funk Railroad who began his music career by leading Michigan group Terry Knight & The Pack, is murdered at his home in Killeen, Texas. Knight was defending his daughter during a domestic disturbance, when he was stabbed by her boyfriend, 26 year old Donald Alan Fair.

A man who allegedly stalked Australian pop star Natalie Imbruglia is deemed too mentally ill to be interviewed by police. The 44-year-old fan was arrested after turning up on the doorstep of the singer's £2m home in Berkshire after flying to London from Australia.

2008

Jimmy Carl Black, the American Indian drummer with The Mothers Of Invention and who also worked with such artists as Captain Beefheart and Arthur Brown, dies aged 70 of lung cancer.

Shakir Stewart, a music promoter and vice-president of Def Jam Music Group, signing Rick Ross, Karina Pasian, Ciara and Young Jeezy and who worked with LL Cool J and Nas, shoots himself dead in the bathroom of his home in Atlanta.

Born on this day:

1941 Brian Poole, vocals (The Tremeloes)
1941 Bruce Welch, guitar (The Shadows)
1944 Keith Emerson, keyboards (The Nice, ELP)
1957 Carter Beauford, drums (Dave Matthews Band)
1961 kd Lang, singer, songwriter
1979 Nelly, rapper, singer

1956
Police use tear gas to break up a riot that broke out during a Fats Domino concert in Fayetteville, North Carolina. Fats and three of his sidemen suffer minor injuries.

1963
The Konrads (featuring 16-year-old David Bowie) appear at Shirley Parish Hall, Shirley, Croydon, England.

1964
The Rolling Stones record for the first time at RCA Studios, Hollywood where most of their records would be cut over the next two years.

1967
The Beatles complete recording on their next single, 'Hello Goodbye' at EMI Studios, London with a second Paul McCartney bass line. The McCartney song had been selected for the A-side with the flip being Lennon's 'I Am The Walrus'.

1968
The Doors play two shows at the Veterans Memorial Hall, Columbus, Ohio.

1969
'Sugar Sugar' by The Archies is at No. 1 in Britain, becoming the longest running one hit wonder in the UK with eight weeks at the top of the charts.

1974
In Vancouver, Canada, George Harrison plays the first show of a 30-night North America tour – the first Beatle to tour there solo.

1979
AC/DC play the second of three sold out nights at London's Hammersmith Odeon, with Def Leppard supporting.

1984
The Rev Marvin Gaye Sr. is sentenced to five years in prison for the manslaughter of his son, Marvin.

1985
The TV soundtrack from *Miami Vice* is top of the US album chart, spending a total of 11 weeks at No. 1.

1991
U2 score their second UK No. 1 with 'The Fly', taken from their album *Achtung Baby*.

1996
Counting Crows are at No. 1 on the US album chart with *Recovering From Satellites*.

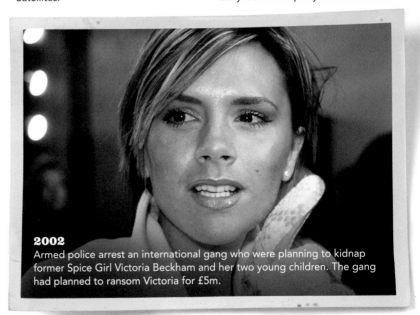

2002
Armed police arrest an international gang who were planning to kidnap former Spice Girl Victoria Beckham and her two young children. The gang had planned to ransom Victoria for £5m.

2004
Eric Clapton collects his CBE from Buckingham Palace, London for services to music.

2007
Led Zeppelin's eagerly-awaited reunion concert in London is postponed for two weeks after guitarist Jimmy Page breaks a finger.

The concert, in honour of late Atlantic Records' founder Ahmet Ertegun, scheduled for November 26 will now take place on December 10. More than a million fans applied for the 20,000 tickets available, which cost £125 each. Profits from the show will go towards scholarships in Ertegun's name in the UK, USA and Turkey, the country of his birth.

Ozzy Osbourne claims his reputation has been tarnished after he was used in a ruse organised by US police officers to round up missing criminal suspects. Over 500 people in North Dakota with outstanding arrest warrants were sent invitations to an Ozzy Osbourne party and more than 30 suspects turned up. Osbourne said it was "insulting" that his name had been used but police argued it was a "creative" way to fight crime. Ozzy had been selected because he was due to play a gig in a nearby arena, which helped to explain why he would supposedly have been attending the party.

Born on this day:

1943 Bert Jansch, UK folk singer
1948 Lulu, Scottish singer
1954 Adam Ant, singer, actor

1962 Ian McNabb, guitar, vocals (Icicle Works)

November 3

1957
Sun Records releases 'Great Balls Of Fire', by Jerry Lee Lewis, a No. 1 in the UK & No. 2 in the US, which goes on to sell over five million copies worldwide.

1990

Thanks to being featured in the film *Ghost*, The Righteous Brothers are at No. 1 on the UK singles chart with 'Unchained Melody', 25 years after their version was recorded. Written by Alex North and Hy Zaret, 'Unchained Melody' is one of the most recorded songs of the 20th century, with over 500 versions in many different languages.

'Ice Ice Baby' by Vanilla Ice becomes the first rap record to top the *Billboard* singles chart. The track was initially released as the B-side to the rapper's cover of 'Play That Funky Music', but becomes the A-side after US DJ's start playing the track.

1997

Metallica arrive at an out of court agreement with a fan who claims he lost his sense of smell after being dropped on his head at one of the band's shows four years earlier.

2002

Lonnie Donegan dies aged 71 midway through a UK tour and shortly before he was due to perform at a memorial concert for George Harrison. Donegan launched the '50s skiffle craze in the UK with his 1956 hit 'Rock Island Line' and went on to have over 30 UK Top 40 singles.

2003

P Diddy runs in the New York City marathon and raises $2,000,000 for the educational system for the children of New York. He finishes the marathon in four hours and 18 minutes.

2005

Winners at this year's MTV Europe Awards include Coldplay – Best UK Act and Best Song ('Speed Of Sound'), Green Day – Best Rock Act and Best Album, Alicia Keys – Best R&B Act, System Of A Down – Best Alternative Act, and The Black Eyed Peas – Best Pop Award.

1958

Elvis Presley goes on maneuvers for the first time with the US Army's 32nd Tank Regiment near the German-Czech border.

1964

During The Rolling Stones' North American tour a 17-year-old Stones fan falls from the balcony during a gig in Cleveland, Ohio. The Mayor of Ohio bans all future pop concerts, saying, "Such groups do not add to the community's culture or entertainment."

1967

The filming for The Beatles' *Magical Mystery Tour* is completed with sequences filmed at Ringo's house in Weybridge, Surrey.

1973

Neil Young, supported by The Eagles, appears at The Palace Theatre, Manchester.

1977

During a concert at the Empire Pool, Wembley, Elton John announces his retirement from live performances.

1979

One hit wonder M is at No. 1 on the US singles chart with 'Pop Muzik'.

1983

RCA Records signs Latin teen sensations Menudo for $30m. The line up of five young boys all have to sign a contract agreeing to leave the group when they reach the age of 16 (considered too old for the group). Ricky Martin was once a member.

1987

David Bowie plays the first of eight sold-out nights at The Entertainment Centre, Sydney, Australia. The shows were part of his 'Glass Spider' World Tour.

Born on this day:

1951 Dan Hartman, producer, multi-instrumentalist

1954 Chris Difford, guitar, vocals (Squeeze)

1957 James Honeyman-Scott, guitar (The Pretenders)

1970 P Diddy, rapper, US record producer

1963

The Beatles top the bill at The Royal Variety Show at The Prince Of Wales Theatre, London. With the Queen Mother and Princess Margaret in the audience, John Lennon introduces the group's last number 'Twist And Shout' with his famous remark: "Would the people in the cheaper seats, clap your hands. And the rest of you, if you just rattle your jewellery."

The night after coming off a 30-date UK package tour with The Everly Brothers and Bo Diddley, The Rolling Stones play a northern England ballroom date at the Top Rank, Preston.

1966

The Beach Boys' 'Good Vibrations' enters the British singles chart, going on to be a UK and US No. 1.

1971

The Who open up a new music venue, The Rainbow, in Finsbury Park, north London, appearing on the first of three nights.

1977

The Last Waltz, Martin Scorsese's movie of The Band's final concert, also featuring Joni Mitchell, Dr. John, Neil Young, Van Morrison, Neil Diamond, and Eric Clapton, premieres in New York.

1978

Crosby, Stills, Nash & Young are being sued for $1m by their former bass player Greg Reeves for royalties he claims he is owed from sales of the album *Deja Vu*.

1984

Prince plays the first of seven nights at the Joe Louis Arena in Detroit, Michigan at the start of his 87-date North American 'Purple Rain' Tour. The outing also marks the live debut of his new band The Revolution.

1989

Elton John scores his 50th UK chart hit when 'Sacrifice' enters the charts. Only Cliff Richard and Elvis Presley have also achieved this feat.

1993

Depeche Mode's Martin Gore is arrested at the Denver Westin Hotel after refusing to turn down the volume of music in his room.

1998

Mark E Smith appears at Manhattan Criminal Court on assault charges. The Fall singer is accused of kicking, punching and choking his girlfriend and band keyboard player Julia Nagle at a New York hotel.

Oasis singer Liam Gallagher is arrested after an alleged drunken brawl with photographer Mel Bouzac at a London pub. Bouzac had been tipped off that Gallagher was in the pub wearing a Russian hat and attempted to take photos.

2001

The Times newspaper publishes its 'Rich List' with Madonna as the highest earning woman in Britain, grossing £30m. All the Spice Girls had dropped out of the listings except for Victoria Beckham. Paul McCartney had earned £20.5m during the year.

2002

Elton John and his lyricist Bernie Taupin receive the Music Industry Trusts Award for one of the greatest songwriting partnerships of all time.

2007

The Eagles are at No. 1 on the UK album chart for the first time ever – 33 years after their debut album. *Long Road Out Of Eden* is the band's first full studio album since *The Long Run* in 1979.

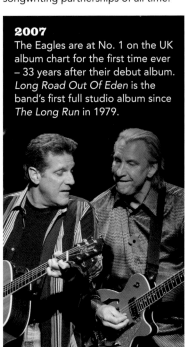

Born on this day:

1941 Art Garfunkel, singer, songwriter
1946 Gram Parsons, US singer, songwriter
(The Byrds, Flying Burrito Brothers)

1959 Bryan Adams, guitar, singer, songwriter
1971 Jonathan Greenwood, guitar,
keyboards (Radiohead)

November 5

1966
The Monkees are top of the *Billboard* singles chart with 'Last Train To Clarksville', the group's first No. 1. It was later revealed that due to filming commitments on their TV series, none of the group had played on this or most of the group's early recordings.

1967
Bee Gee Robin Gibb and his girlfriend are passengers on a train which crashes in Hither Green, south east London, killing 49 people and injuring 78. Robin was treated for shock after the accident.

1971
Elvis Presley kicks off a 15-date North American tour at the Metropolitan Sports Center, Minneapolis. At the end of the show, announcer Al Dvorin utters what would become a well known phrase: "Elvis has left the building." He was asked to make the announcement in an effort to quiet fans who continued to call for an encore.

1977
The manager of the Virgin record store in Nottingham, England is arrested for displaying a large poster advertising the new Sex Pistols album, *Never Mind The Bollocks, Here's The Sex Pistols*. High street stores ban the album after police warn they could be fined under the 1898 Indecent Advertising Act.

1982
The Tube debuts on Channel 4 in the UK. Presented by Paula Yates and Jools Holland from the Tynes-Tees studio in Newcastle-upon-Tyne, the show features The Jam (performing one of their last live sets) and an interview with Mick Jagger. First live act on the show is local band Toy Dolls.

1983
Billy Joel is at No. 1 on the UK singles chart with 'Uptown Girl', the song

written about his relationship with girlfriend later wife, supermodel Christie Brinkley, who appears in the accompanying video.

Topper Headon of The Clash is arrested for walking his dog while drunk on London's Fulham Road.

1986
Bobby Nunn of US vocal group The Coasters dies of heart failure in Los Angeles.

1988
The Beach Boys are at No. 1 on the US singles chart with 'Kokomo', which features in the film *Cocktail*. Co-written by producer Terry Melcher and John Phillips of The Mamas & The Papas, it peaks at No. 25 in the UK.

'The Locomotion' becomes the first song to reach the US Top 5 in three different versions, after Kylie Minogue's cover reaches No. 3 on the US chart. The song had also been a hit for Little Eva (in 1960) and Grand Funk Railroad (1974).

1998
Former Smiths' singer Morrissey loses an appeal ruling that all band profits should have been split equally and faces a backdated payout to former Smiths member Mike Joyce estimated at £1million.

2003
Bobby Hatfield of The Righteous Brothers is found dead aged 63 in a Michigan hotel room 30 minutes before he was due on stage. The autopsy report from the Kalamazoo County Medical Examiner says that Hatfield suffered a sudden, unexpected death due to acute cocaine toxicity.

2005
Link Wray, who was credited with inventing 'fuzz guitar' after punching a hole in a speaker giving him a distorted guitar sound, dies aged 76. Wray's best known recording, 'Rumble', which was banned on several radio stations on the grounds that it glorified juvenile delinquency, reached No. 16 in the US in 1958, a rare feat for a song with no lyrics.

1995
Producer Butch Vig's band Garbage make their US live debut when playing at The 7th Street Entry, Minneapolis.

November 6

Born on this day:

1941 Guy Clark, singer, songwriter
1947 George Young, guitar, vocals, songwriter, producer (The Easybeats)
1948 Glenn Frey, guitar, vocals (The Eagles)
1966 Paul Gilbert, guitarist (Mr. Big, solo)

1961
Jimmy Dean starts a five week run at No. 1 on the US singles chart with 'Big Bad John', a No. 2 on the UK chart. Jimmy goes on to present a prime time variety show on US TV.

1965
The Rolling Stones start a two-week run on top of the US singles chart with 'Get Off Of My Cloud', the group's second US No. 1.

1967
During a three hour session Bob Dylan records 'All Along The Watchtower' and 'John Wesley Harding' at Columbia Recording Studios in Nashville, Tennessee.

1968
The Monkees' three quarters of a million dollar feature film, *Head* opens in New York City. Instead of being aimed at their target audience of teenyboppers, the film contains a dark theme about the manipulation of the group with walk-on appearances by inappropriate guests and scenes of Vietnam War atrocities. Reviews are harsh and the picture is a box office disaster.

1970
Aerosmith perform their first ever gig at Nipmuc Regional High School, Mendon, Massachusetts.

1972
During a UK tour, Billy Murcia, drummer with The New York Dolls, dies in London after overdosing on Mandrax.

1973
Michael Martin and Phil Kaufman are charged and fined $300 each for the theft of a coffin containing Gram Parsons' body. The court hears that the two men are merely carrying out Parsons' wish to be cremated in the desert.

1975
The Sex Pistols make their live debut at St Martin's School Of Art in central London, supporting a band called Bazooka Joe, which includes Stuart Goddard (the future Adam Ant). The Pistols' performance lasts 10 minutes.

1977
Abba start a four-week run at No. 1 on the UK single chart with 'The Name Of The Game', the group's sixth chart-topper. The song was first called 'A Bit Of Myself'.

1982
Soft Cell's 'Tainted Love' achieves the longest unbroken run on the UK charts when it logs its 43rd week in the Top 100.

1984
U2 play the first of two nights at Glasgow's Barrowlands during their 'Unforgettable Fire' World Tour.

2000
Madonna plays her first show in eight years, a 20-minute set at New York's Roseland Ballroom. She wears a tight black vest bearing the sequinned name of 18-year-old Britney Spears.

2003
Winners at this year's MTV Awards include Christina Aguilera for Best Female Artist, Coldplay – Best Group and Justin Timberlake – Best Album for *Justified*.

2007
Meat Loaf cancels his European tour after being diagnosed with a cyst on his vocal cords. The singer had already scrapped two gigs on doctor's orders. Speculation had surrounded the tour after the 60-year-old cut short a gig in Newcastle, telling the audience it is "the last show I may ever do in my life".

1993
Pearl Jam are at No. 1 on the *Billboard* album chart with *Vs*, selling 950,378 copies – making it the highest selling US album in its first week.

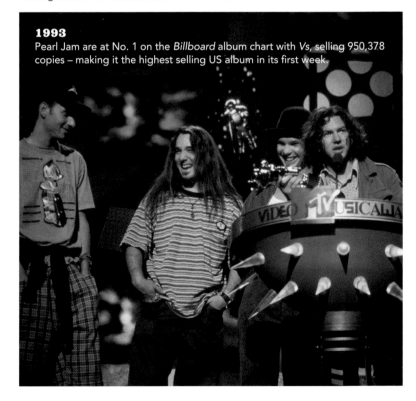

Born on this day:

1937 Mary Travers, singer (Peter, Paul & Mary)

1943 Joni Mitchell, singer, songwriter

1954 Robin Beck, singer

1960 Tommy Thayer, guitarist (Kiss)

1967 Sharleen Spiteri, vocals (Texas)

November 7

1958
Eddie Cochran makes his UK chart debut with 'Summertime Blues' which reaches No. 8 in the US and No. 18 in the UK.

1963
The Beatles fly to Ireland to play four shows (two each) at the Adelphi Cinema, Dublin and the Ritz Cinema, Belfast (on the 8th). Travelling with the group is screenwriter Alun Owen who has been appointed to write the screenplay for The Beatles' first (as yet untitled) motion picture. Owen spends three days with The Beatles observing their hectic lifestyle.

1967
Reg Dwight (Elton John) and his songwriting partner Bernie Taupin sign to DJM (Dick James Music) publishing. Their signatures have to be witnessed by their parents because both writers are under 21 years of age. Taupin had answered an advertisement for a lyric writer placed by Dwight in the *New Musical Express*.

1969
After a break of two and a half years The Rolling Stones return to the stage, opening a US tour at Fort Collins State University, Colorado. Also on the bill are Ike & Tina Turner, Chuck Berry and BB King.

1970
Led Zeppelin release their third album, which features a distinctive pinwheel revolving cover. It enters the UK chart at No. 1 and spends a total of 40 weeks in the Top 75.

1974
Ted Nugent wins a national squirrel-shooting contest after picking off a squirrel at 150 yards. The heavy rock guitarist also shoots dead 27 other mammals during the three-day event.

1975
A new world record is set for continuous guitar string plucking by Steve Anderson who plays for 114 hours, 17 minutes.

1986
Tracey Pew, former bassist with Australian art rock band The Birthday Party, dies aged 28 during an epileptic fit.

1987
Bruce Springsteen is at No. 1 on the US album chart with *Tunnel Of Love*.

Tiffany becomes the youngest act to score a US No. 1 since Michael Jackson ('Ben' in 1972) with a cover of Tommy James & The Shondells' 1967 hit, 'I Think We're Alone Now'.

2002
After a Guns N' Roses gig in Vancouver is cancelled, 12 fans are arrested during a riot. Promoters pull the gig after Axl Rose's flight from Los Angeles is delayed.

Whitney Houston's husband, Bobby Brown, is arrested and charged with possession of marijuana, speeding, driving without a licence and having no proof of insurance after he is stopped by police in Atlanta.

2004
Eminem is at No. 1 on the UK singles chart with 'Just Lose It', his fourth UK chart-topper. The UK top five this week consisted of all American acts: 2, Destinys Child – 'Lose My Breath', 3, Britney Spears – 'My Prerogative', 4, Christina Aguilera & Missy Elliott – 'Car Wash' and 5, Usher & Alicia Keys – 'My Boo'.

Elton John turns the airwaves blue, using the words; f****ing, w**k, and t**s, while appearing live on Chris Moyles' BBC Radio 1 breakfast show.

November 8

Born on this day:

1944 Bonnie Bramlett, singer (Delaney & Bonnie)

1944 Rodney Slater, sax (The Bonzo Dog Doo Dah Band)

1946 Roy Wood, guitar, vocals (The Move, Wizzard)

1947 Minnie Riperton, US singer

1949 Bonnie Raitt, singer, songwriter, guitarist

1976 Corey Taylor, singer (Slipknot)

1952
The first ever UK pop chart is published by *New Musical Express* after staff asked 53 record shops to divulge their sales returns. 'Here In My Heart' by Al Martino was the first No. 1. The song stayed at the top for nine weeks.

1958
The soundtrack to *South Pacific* is at the top of the UK album chart, becoming the longest running No. 1 album of all time spending a total of 115 weeks at the pole position.

1963
Dusty Springfield sets out on her first UK tour as a soloist, sharing the bill with The Searchers, Freddie & The Dreamers and Brian Poole & The Tremeloes.

1968
The Who, Joe Cocker & The Grease Band, The Mindbenders and The Crazy World of Arthur Brown start a UK package tour at The Granada, Walthamstow, London.

1969
'Something', the first Beatles A-side composed by George Harrison, enters the British singles chart, peaking at No. 4 in the UK and went on to be No. 1 on the US chart.

1975
David Bowie makes his US TV debut performing 'Fame' on Cher's CBS show.

Elton John is named godfather to John and Yoko Lennon's son Sean.

1980
Bruce Springsteen starts a four week run on top of the *Billboard* album chart with *The River*, his first US No. 1 album.

1986
Berlin start a four-week run at No. 1 on the UK singles chart with 'Take My Breath Away', taken from the film *Top Gun*.

1993
Take That kick off their 21-date, sold out 'Everything Changes' UK tour in Bournemouth.

1998
Robbie Williams scores his second UK No. 1 album with *I've Been Expecting You*.

2000
Spice Girl Mel C makes a foul-mouthed attack on Westlife, calling them "a useless bunch of talentless tossers" and "as hyped-up shit". The singer made the attack during The Spice Girls party to launch their new album *Forever*.

2001
Winners at the MTV Europe Awards include Robbie Williams – Best Male Artist and Best Song for 'Rock DJ', Craig David – Best R&B Act and Best UK & Ireland Act, Dido – Best New Act, Anastacia – Best Pop Act, Gorillaz – Best Song (for 'Clint Eastwood') and Best Dance Act and Eminem – Best Hip Hop Award.

2007
Four men are arrested on suspicion of perverting the course of justice after police raid a house in Camden in north London belonging to singer Amy Winehouse. The arrests are in connection to a court case involving Winehouse's husband Blake Fielder-Civil who faced charges of causing grievous bodily harm.

2009
Former Smiths frontman Morrissey stops a UK concert halfway through his second song after being hit in the eye by a plastic beer bottle. The 50-year-old singer says goodnight to the 8,000-strong crowd in Liverpool before walking off.

November 9

1955
The Everly Brothers make their first studio recordings, cutting four tracks in 22 minutes, at Nashville's Old Tulane Hotel studios.

1961
Brian Epstein sees The Beatles playing live for the first time during a lunchtime session at The Cavern Club, Liverpool. That night The Beatles appear at Litherland Town Hall on Merseyside.

1966
John Lennon meets Yoko Ono for the first time when he visits a preview of her art exhibition 'Unfinished Paintings and Objects' at the Indica Gallery, London.

1967
The first issue of *Rolling Stone* magazine is published in San Francisco, featuring a cover photo of John Lennon from his recent film, *How I Won The War* and a free roach clip to hold a marijuana joint. Editor Jann Wenner compiled the name of the magazine from three significant sources: the Muddy Waters song, the

first rock'n'roll record by Bob Dylan and The Rolling Stones.

1968
Led Zeppelin play their first high profile London show at The Roundhouse, Chalk Farm on the same bill as John Lee Hooker, Deviants, John James and Tyres. Zeppelin singer Robert Plant marries his girlfriend Maureen in London on this day and holds the reception at the gig.

1974
Bachman Turner Overdrive are at No. 1 on the US singles chart with 'You Ain't Seen Nothin' Yet'.

1978
During a North American tour Queen appear at the Cobo Arena in Detroit, Michigan.

1985
Jan Hammer is at No. 1 on the US singles chart with 'The Miami Vice Theme'.

1990
The Internal Revenue seize all of US country singer Willie Nelson's bank accounts and real estate holdings in connection with a $16million tax debt.

1991
American singer-songwriter Richard Marx plays in five cities in a day during a 'Rush-n Rush Out, Street Tour'. Marx appears in Baltimore, New York City, Cleveland, Chicago and Burbank Airport.

1993
The Dave Matthews Band release their first album, *Remember Two Things* on the Bama Rags label.

1996
Oasis singer Liam Gallagher is arrested after being stopped by police in London's Oxford Street and is charged with possession of a class A controlled substance.

Michael Jackson plays at the Ericsson Stadium in Auckland, New Zealand, the first of 11 dates in Australia and New Zealand on the 'HIStory' World Tour.

1997
Paul Weller is arrested and spends the night in a French jail after smashing up his hotel room in Paris. His record company pay £4,000 to cover the damage; Weller is released the following day.

1999
American producer, songwriter and co-founder of Atlantic Records, Herb Abramson, who wrote and produced Tommy Tucker's 1964 hit 'Hi-Heeled Sneakers', dies aged 82.

2002
Viewers of the UK music channel VH1 vote 'I Will Always Love You' by Whitney Houston as the number one most romantic song ever.

It is announced that Madonna's latest movie *Swept Away* would not be released in the UK because it had been such a box office flop in America. *The Washington Post* said the film was "as awful as you've heard and as bad as you've imagined."

2004
A Dutch man is jailed for nine months for harassing former Spice Girl Melanie Chisholm. The unnamed 39-year-old sent the singer parcels, letters and tapes during 2001. Dutch police searched the man's home after he tried to hand-deliver a parcel to Chisholm's London home.

November 10

Born on this day:

1948 Greg Lake, bass (King Crimson, ELP)
1957 Chris Joyce, drums (Simply Red)
1970 Warren G, US rapper

1975 Jim Adkins, singer, guitarist (Jimmy Eat World)

1955

Elvis Presley attends the fourth Country Music Disc Jockey Convention in Nashville, Tennessee. Back at his hotel Mae Boren Axton plays him a demo of a new song she had written with Tommy Durden called 'Heartbreak Hotel'.

1963

The Yardbirds (with Eric Clapton on guitar) appear at The Crawdaddy, Richmond Athletic Ground, Surrey, England.

1967

At the Saville Theatre in London, The Beatles film three promotional films, directed by Paul McCartney, for their new single 'Hello, Goodbye'.

1973

Elton John starts an eight-week run on top of the *Billboard* album chart with *Goodbye Yellow Brick Road*, the singer's third US chart-topping album.

1975

David Bowie is at No. 1 on the UK singles chart with 'Space Oddity', the track first released in 1969 to tie in with the Apollo 11 moon landing. Rick Wakeman (former keyboard player with Yes) provides keyboard backing. Bowie will later revisit his Major Tom character in the songs 'Ashes To Ashes' and 'Hallo Spaceboy'.

1979

The Eagles are at No. 1 on the US singles chart with 'Heartache Tonight', the group's fifth and final American chart-topper.

1984

Former Rufus singer Chaka Khan is at No. 1 on the UK singles chart with 'I Feel For You.' Written by Prince, the song features Stevie Wonder on harmonica and the rap is by

Grandmaster Melle Mel. The repetition of Khan's name by rapper Melle Mel at the beginning of the song was originally a mistake made by producer Arif Mardin, who then decides to keep it.

1984
After setting a new record for advanced orders (1,099,500 copies), Frankie Goes To Hollywood are at No. 1 on the UK album chart with their debut *Welcome To The Pleasure Dome*. Also on this day Frankie Goes To Hollywood make their debut TV appearance on *Saturday Night Live* performing 'Two Tribes' and 'Born To Run'.

1997

American session guitarist Tommy Tedesco dies aged 67 of lung cancer. Described by *Guitar Player* magazine as "the most recorded guitarist in history", Tedesco played on recordings by The Beach Boys, The Everly Brothers, The Supremes, The Monkees, The Association, Barbra Streisand, Elvis Presley, Ella Fitzgerald, Frank Zappa, Sam Cooke, Cher, and Nancy and Frank Sinatra. He also played on many TV themes including *Bonanza*, *The Twilight Zone*, *M*A*S*H* and *Batman*.

2004

Police question Sugababes singer Mutya Buena after she is involved in a fight at a beauty contest. A scuffle broke out in the audience as points were being awarded to girls in the Miss Teen Philippines contest in which Mutya's sister was competing.

2007

Kanye West's mother dies aged 58 after complications following surgery. She was taken to hospital in Los Angeles after she had stopped breathing at home and could not be resuscitated. Dr Donda West had managed her son's businesses and educational foundation and was the subject of his song 'Hey Mama'.

2008

Coldplay are declared the Biggest Selling Act of 2008 at the World Music Awards held in Monaco. The band picked up the prize – along with the Rock Act Of The Year award – after their current album *Viva La Vida Or Death And All His Friends* topped charts around the globe. Other winners at the awards included Leona Lewis for Best Pop Female and Best New Artist, Amy Winehouse was the recipient in the Female Pop/Rock award, while Alicia Keys was named best in the R&B category. Lil' Wayne bagged the Hip-Hop/Rap Artist Award, while Akon was declared the Biggest Internet Artist Of The Year.

Born on this day:
1938 Roger Lavern, keyboards (The Tornados)
1945 Vince Martell, guitar (Vanilla Fudge)
1946 Chris Dreja, guitar (The Yardbirds)

1953 Andy Partridge, singer, songwriter, guitarist (XTC)
1969 Gary Powell, drums (The Libertines)

November
11

1954
Bill Haley scores his first US Top 10 single with 'Shake, Rattle And Roll', originally made popular by Big Joe Turner. The song became the theme song for the Springfield Indians of the American Hockey League. Haley had dropped his cowboy image about a year and a half earlier, renaming his band The Saddlemen to Bill Haley & His Comets.

1957
Elvis Presley appears at Schofield Barracks, Hawaii, in what is his last concert of the 50s.

1965
The final recording session for The Beatles *Rubber Soul* album takes place at EMI Studios, London. The group need three new songs to finish off the album so an old song 'Wait' is pulled off the shelf and the group record two new songs, 'You Won't See Me' and 'Girl', both being completed in two takes.

1969
The FBI in Phoenix, Arizona arrest Jim Morrison for drunk and disorderly conduct aboard a plane. The Doors singer, who was on his way to a Rolling Stones concert with actor Tom Baker, had been drinking and annoying the stewardesses. The pair spend the night in jail and are released on $2,500 bail.

1972

Allman Brothers bass player Berry Oakley is killed when his motorcycle hits a bus, eerily at the same intersection as former band member Duane Allman who had died a year earlier. Oakley is 24 years old.

1977
During an Australian tour Fleetwood Mac appear at the RAS Sydney Showgrounds. Also on the bill are Santana, Little River Band and The Kevin Borich Express.

1978
The Cars release the first commercially available picture disc 7" single, 'My Best Friend's Girl' which made No. 3 in the UK charts.

1982
Prince kicks off his 87-date '1999' North American tour at the Soldiers and Sailors Memorial Auditorium in Chattanooga, Tennessee.

2004
The first UK Music Hall of Fame Awards are held at a ceremony in London. One act was chosen by TV viewers of a Channel 4 programme to be inducted, representing each decade since the 1950s. Robbie Williams represented the '90s, Michael Jackson the '80s, Queen the '70s, the Rolling Stones the '60s, and Cliff Richard the '50s.

2006
Grammy-nominated R&B star Gerald Levert, the son of O'Jays vocalist Eddie Levert, and who scored a UK top 10 single 'Casanova' with R&B trio LeVert in 1987, dies aged 40 of a heart attack.

1989
Chris Rea starts a three-week run at No. 1 on the UK album chart with *The Road To Hell*.

Born on this day:

1944 Booker T. Jones, organ (Booker T & The MGs)

1945 Neil Young, Canadian singer-songwriter

1948 Errol Brown, singer (Hot Chocolate)

1955 Les McKeown, vocals (The Bay City Rollers)

1956
Johnnie Ray is at No. 1 on the UK singles chart with 'Just Walking In The Rain'. Written in 1952 by Johnny Bragg and Robert Riley, two prisoners at Tennessee State Prison in Nashville, after a comment made by Bragg as the pair crossed the courtyard while it was raining.

1966
The Monkees' debut album starts a 13-week run at No. 1 on the US album chart, selling over three million copies in three months.

1968
British retail chain W.H. Smiths refuse to display the latest Jimi Hendrix Experience album *Electric Ladyland* due to the naked girls featured on the sleeve. The album is later made available as two albums with changed artwork after the complaints.

1977
The Sex Pistols are at No. 1 on the UK album chart with their debut LP *Never Mind The Bollocks, Here's The Sex Pistols*, the punk band's only chart-topping album.

1980
Bruce Springsteen scores his first No. 1 US album with *The River*.

1983
Lionel Richie starts a four week run at No. 1 on the US singles chart with 'All Night Long', becoming Motown's biggest seller to date.

1988
U2 start a six-week run at No. 1 on the US album chart with *Rattle And Hum*.

1990
Rolling Stone Ron Wood breaks both legs after being run over on the M4 motorway near Marlborough, Wiltshire. Wood was trying to wave traffic on past his car which had broken down when he was run over.

1998
Winners at this year's MTV Europe Awards include Madonna – Best Female Artist and Album (*Ray Of Light*), The Spice Girls – Best Group, All Saints – Breakthrough Artist, Robbie Williams – Best Male Artist and Natalie Imbruglia – Best Song ('Torn').

1999
Gary Glitter is sentenced to four months in a Bristol prison after being found guilty of downloading child pornography from the Internet.

2000
Destiny's Child start an 11-week run at No. 1 on the US singles chart with 'Independent Women Part 1'. The song first appeared on the soundtrack to the 2000 film *Charlie's Angels*.

2002
Beatles fans are enraged to find Paul McCartney has altered the songwriting credits on his latest live album *Back In The US 2002* from Lennon-McCartney to McCartney-Lennon.

2003
Session drummer Tony Thompson, who worked with Chic, David Bowie, Madonna and drummed with Led Zeppelin at Live Aid, dies aged 48 of renal cell cancer.

2007
Boy George is charged with the false imprisonment of a 28-year-old man. Police say the offence was alleged to have taken place at the 47-year-old's home in Hackney, London.

2008
Mitch Mitchell, former drummer with The Jimi Hendrix Experience, is found dead aged 61 in his Portland hotel room of natural causes. Mitchell had been drumming with Georgie Fame & The Blue Flames when in October 1966 he was invited to audition for a new band being formed to back American guitarist Jimi Hendrix.

1965
The Velvet Underground make their live debut when playing at Summit High School, New Jersey. The band are paid $75 for the gig.

Born on this day:

1949 Roger Steen, guitar (The Tubes)
1951 Bill Gibson, drums (Huey Lewis & The News

1953 Andrew Ranken, drums (The Pogues)
1979 Nikolai Fraiture, bass (The Strokes)

November
13

1968
Rolling Stone Brian Jones buys Cotchford Farm in Hartfield, East Sussex. The author AA Milne, who wrote the *Winnie The Pooh* books, had originally owned the cottage.

Hugo Montenegro is at No. 1 on the UK singles chart with 'The Good, The Bad And The Ugly', the soundtrack from a Clint Eastwood spaghetti western film, and the first instrumental to reach the top position since 1963.

1973
Jerry Lee Lewis Jr, who had been working as the drummer in his father's band, is killed in a car accident near Hernando, Mississippi.

1976
Rod Stewart starts an eight-week run on top of the *Billboard* singles chart with 'Tonight's The Night'. It is Stewart's second US No. 1; it makes No. 5 in the UK after being banned by many radio stations due to the song being about the seduction of a virgin.

1976
Melody Maker announce UK dates for the first major punk tour with The Sex Pistols and The Ramones co-headlining with Talking Heads, The Vibrators and Chris Spedding. The 14-date tour, due to start at Newcastle City Hall on November 29, never takes place.

1981
U2 kick off a 23-date North American 'October' tour at JB Scott's in Albany, New York.

1982
Men At Work start a 15-week run at No. 1 on the US album chart with their debut album *Business As Usual*, which went on to sell over five million copies in the US.

1990
Patricia Boughton, a Rod Stewart fan whose finger was hurt by a soccer ball the singer kicked into a Michigan audience during a gig at the Pine Knob Music Theatre in 1989, wins a settlement of $17,000. Boughton's ex-husband says the mishap made sex between the two "very difficult'" and contributed to the breakup of their 14-year marriage.

1992
Ronnie Bond, drummer with The Troggs, who scored a 1966 US No. 1 & UK No. 2 single 'Wild Thing' and 1966 UK No. 1 'With A Girl Like You', dies aged 52.

1999
A report shows that The Spice Girls are the highest earners in pop during the 90s with their debut album *Spice* selling over 20 million copies. Elton John is second with 1 million sales from *The Lion King*.

2000
The Beatles launch their official website www.thebeatles.com on the same day as the release of the retrospective compilation album *1* of the group's chart-toppers.

2004
Rap artist Ol' Dirty Bastard (real name Russell Jones) collapses and dies aged 35 at a Manhattan recording studio. A spokesman for his record company says the rapper, who had complained of chest pains, was dead by the time paramedics reached him. ODB was a founding member of the Wu-Tang Clan in the early '90s.

2005
Simon Cowell is named Show Business Personality of the Year by the Variety Club at the show business charity's annual awards show in London. Katie Melua wins Recording Artist of the Year at the event.

Born on this day:

1936 Freddie Garrity, vocals (Freddie & The Dreamers)

1951 Steven Bishop, US singer, songwriter

1956 Alec John Such, bass (Bon Jovi)

1966 Joseph 'Run' Simmons, rapper (Run-DMC)

1972 Douglas Payne, bass (Travis)

1960
Ray Charles goes to No. 1 on the US singles chart with 'Georgia On My Mind'. His cover of Hoagy Carmichael's 1930 standard became the first of three No. 1 hits for the singer, and in 1979 is adopted as the official state song by the Georgia legislature.

1962
The Beatles play the final show of a 14-night run at the Star-Club, Hamburg, West Germany.

1967
A 16-date UK package tour with Jimi Hendrix, Pink Floyd, The Move, Nice and Amen Corner kicks off at the Royal Albert Hall, London. All acts play two shows per night.

1975
Queen play the first of two nights at the Empire Theatre in Liverpool, the first nights on their 78-date A Night At The Opera World Tour.

1977
Kiss play the first date on their 51-date Alive II Tour at the Myriad Convention Center in Oklahoma City, Oklahoma.

1981
The Police have their fourth UK No. 1 single with 'Every Little Thing She Does Is Magic'.

1987
T'Pau open a five-week run at No. 1 on the UK singles chart with 'China In Your Hand'. According to singer Carol Decker, the song's title is the effect you get if you hold a china cup to a light and can see your hand through it.

1990
Record producer Frank Farin fires Milli Vanilli singers Rob Pilatus and Fabrice Morvan because they are insisting on singing on their new album.

1991
Over 1,000 New Kids On The Block fans are given medical treatment after a minor riot during a concert in Berlin, Germany.

1996
Michael Jackson marries Debbie Rowe in Sydney Australia. The couple met when he was diagnosed with vitiligo in the mid-1980s, and she was working as his dermatologist's assistant. The couple divorce on October 8, 1999, with Rowe giving full custody rights of their children to Jackson and receiving an $8-million settlement.

2000
Former Kajagoogoo singer Limahl narrowly misses death when a coach in which he is travelling crashes. Limahl (Chris Hamil) is on his way to perform at High Wycombe's Swan Theatre when the vehicle catches fire.

UK music chain HMV refuse to stock the new single by The Offspring, 'Official Prangster', after the band decide to give the track away as a free download on their official website. They had originally planned to release a whole album online.

2004
The Rolling Stones are refused permission to pursue a claim for unpaid royalties against their former record company Decca through the courts. A High Court judge in London says the dispute would go to arbitration and not be decided in court. The dispute is over their *Forty Licks* compilation CD, which was released in 2002 and was the first collection to span their entire career.

November
15

1965
The Rolling Stones make their US TV debut on *Hullabaloo*, performing 'Get Off Of My Cloud'.

1966
The Doors officially sign with Elektra Records in a deal for the band to produce seven albums. They also reluctantly agree to release 'Break On Through' as their first single. The lyric "She gets high/she gets high/she gets high" was changed to "She gets/she gets/she gets" in order to secure radio play.

1969
Janis Joplin is arrested during a gig in Tampa, Florida, after badmouthing a policeman and using vulgar and indecent language. Joplin becomes upset after police move into the hall, forcing fans to move back to their seats. As the singer leaves the stage she confronts a detective, calling him "a son of a bitch" and tells him she will kick his face in. She is released on $504 bail.

1976
The Sex Pistols appear at Notre Dame Hall, Leicester Place, London.

1980
Blondie have their fifth UK No. 1 single and third No. 1 of this year with 'The Tide Is High', a song written by reggae star John Holt, also a No. 1 in the US.

1984
R.E.M. play the first date on the band's second UK tour at Tiffany's Ballroom, Newcastle, England.

1986
Pop history was made when the Top 5 UK singles were all by female vocalists; Corinne Drewery from Swing Out Sister, Mel & Kim, Susannah Hoffs from The Bangles, Kim Wilde and Terri Nunn from Berlin, who were at No. 1 with 'Take My Breath Away'.

1987
Dire Straits become the first artist to sell over three million copies of an album in the UK. *Brothers In Arms* contains five top 40 singles: 'Money For Nothing', 'So Far Away', 'Walk of Life', 'Brothers In Arms' and 'Your Latest Trick'.

1991
French music producer and songwriter Jacques Morali dies of complications from AIDS. Morali formed The Village People and co-produced their film, *Can't Stop The Music*. Between 1974 and 1982 Morali produced over 65 albums.

1992
Ozzy Osbourne announces his retirement from live gigs after a gig in California, saying "Who wants to be touring at 46?"

2000
Michael Abram, the Liverpool man who stabbed George Harrison after breaking into his home, is awarded a not guilty verdict at Oxford's Crown Court. But the verdict was returned in view of Abram's mental history, and he is taken into care.

2007
Kenneth Donnell, from Glasgow, pays £83,000 for two tickets to see Led Zeppelin rehearse and perform at the O2 arena in London on December 10. Donnell bids for the tickets as part of an auction for the BBC's Children In Need.

Jay-Z goes to No. 1 on the US album chart with 'American Gangster', his tenth No. 1 album. This makes the rapper joint second with Elvis Presley for the most No. 1 albums on the chart. Only The Beatles have had more, with 19.

Mansion intruder attacks star
BEATLE GEORGE STABBED
Protection fails: George Harrison and his wife Olivia are both in hospital today after a knifeman beat the high security that surrounds their Friar Park estate

November 16

Born on this day:

1916 Herb Abramson, producer, co-founder of Atlantic records.

1962 Gary 'Mani' Mounfield, bass (The Stone Roses)

1964 Diana Krall, Canadian singer, songwriter

1965 David Kushner, guitarist (Velvet Revolver)

1968

The Jimi Hendrix Experience go to No. 1 on the US album chart with *Electric Ladyland*. The double album includes 'Crosstown Traffic', 'Voodoo Chile' and 'All Along The Watchtower' and features guest appearances by Dave Mason, Steve Winwood and Al Kooper.

Led Zeppelin play their first ever show in the north of England at Manchester College of Science & Technology.

1978

The Clash, supported by The Slits appear at the Odeon Theatre, Edinburgh, Scotland.

1985

Former Undertones singer Feargal Sharkey has his only UK No. 1 single with the Maria McKee song 'A Good Heart' written about her relationship with Tom Petty & The Heartbreakers keyboard player Benmont Tench. Sharkey follows up the single with the Tench written 'You Little Thief',

1991

Irish singer Enya scores her first UK No. 1 album with 'Shepherd Moons'.

1999

Grady Owen, guitarist with Gene Vincent & His Blue Caps, dies. They scored a 1956 US No. 7 & UK No. 16 single with 'Be Bop A Lula'.

2000

American rapper Joseph Calleja dies of chronic intestinal disorder. Calleja had celiac disease, an autoimmune disorder that causes stunted growth, and as a result he reached a maximum height of only three feet, nine inches by adulthood. He was a member of Kid Rock's band.

Elton John tells a London High Court that his former lover and manager John Reid betrayed him over touring costs. The singer says Reid had been "caught with his hands in the till." Elton is suing Andrew Haydon, former managing director of John Reid Enterprises, his management company, alleging Haydon was negligent in allowing JREL to charge him "several millions" in overseas tour expenses.

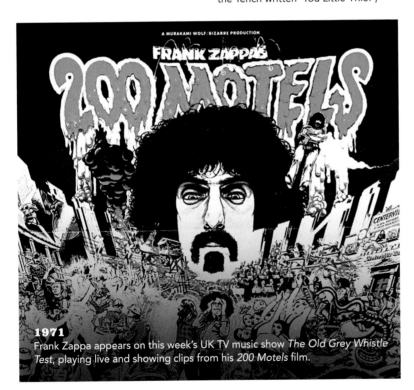

1971
Frank Zappa appears on this week's UK TV music show *The Old Grey Whistle Test*, playing live and showing clips from his *200 Motels* film.

1974

John Lennon is at No. 1 in the US singles chart with 'Whatever Gets You Through The Night'. Elton John played on the session and made a deal with Lennon that if the song reached No. 1, Lennon would have to appear on stage live with Elton. Lennon keeps his side of the deal and appears live with Elton on November 28.

this time about Tench's relationship with McKee.

1987

Former Clash drummer Topper Headon is jailed for 15 months at Maidstone Crown Court, England for supplying heroin to a man who later died.

2002

Texan multi-billionaire David Bonderman hires The Rolling Stones to play at his 60th birthday party held at the Hard Rock Hotel in Las Vegas. The band's fee is £4.4m.

Born on this day:

1938 Gordon Lightfoot, Canadian singer
1944 Gene Clark, singer, songwriter

1966 Jeff Buckley, US singer, songwriter
1981 Sarah Harding, singer (Girls Aloud)

November 17

1957
Harry Belafonte is at No. 1 on the UK singles chart with 'Mary's Boy Child', the first single to sell over one million copies in the UK.

1963
John Weightman, headmaster of a Surrey grammar school, bans all pupils from having Beatle haircuts, saying: "This ridiculous style brings out the worst in boys physically. It makes them look like morons."

1966
The Beach Boys are at No. 1 on the UK singles chart with 'Good Vibrations'.

1967
Pink Floyd release their third single 'Apples And Oranges', which fails to chart.

1973
The Who's double album *Quadrophenia* enters the UK album chart, peaking at No. 2. The 1979 film based on the album stars Phil Daniels, Leslie Ash, Toyah Willcox, Ray Winstone, Michael Elphick and Sting.

1979
Jethro Tull bass player John Glascock dies at the age of 28, as a result of a congenital heart defect. He had also been a member of Chicken Shack.

1985
Wham! are at No. 1 on the UK album chart with 'Make It Big' and No. 1 on the US singles chart with 'Wake Me Up Before You Go Go'.

1990
David Crosby is admitted to hospital after breaking a leg, shoulder and ankle after crashing his Harley Davidson motorbike.

1992
At the end of a long battle to claim royalties Jimmy Merchant and Herman Santiago, formerly of Frankie Lymon & The Teenagers, receive an estimated $4 million in back payments for their 1956 hit song 'Why Do Fools Fall In Love'.

1999
Mariah Carey is forced to abandon a performance on Rome's historic Spanish Steps after crowds of tourists swamp her. She takes shelter in a local shop before receiving a police escort to safety.

2003
American soul singer Arthur Conley dies of intestinal cancer in Ruurlo, The Netherlands, at the age of 57. He had a 1967 US No. 2 & UK No. 7 single 'Sweet Soul Music'. He first recorded in 1959 as the lead singer of Arthur & The Corvets.

21 year-old Britney Spears becomes the youngest singer to get a star on the Hollywood Walk of Fame. The only other performer with a Hollywood star at her age is *Little House On The Prairie* actress Melissa Gilbert.

George Michael signs a new contract with the record company he took to court in 1993. The singer re-signs to Sony in a deal that includes his extensive back catalogue. Michael had failed in his court wrangle with Sony after accusing it of "professional slavery". His contract is bought out by Virgin Records.

2003
American country music legend Don Gibson dies of natural causes aged 75. He scored the 1958 US No.7 single 'Oh Lonesome Me', (covered by Neil Young on his *After The Gold Rush* album) and the 1961 UK No. 14 single 'Sea Of Heartbreak'. His song 'I Can't Stop Loving You' has been recorded by over 700 artists, most notably by Ray Charles in 1962.

Born on this day:

1953 John McFee, guitar (The Doobie Brothers)

1954 John Parr, singer, songwriter

1960 Kim Wilde, singer

1962 Kirk Hammett, guitar (Metallica)

1956
Fats Domino appears on the US TV *Ed Sullivan Show* performing 'Blueberry Hill'.

1963
The Beatles receive silver LP discs for *Please Please Me* and *With The Beatles* at a ceremony held at EMI House in London. They also receive a silver EP for *Twist And Shout* and a silver single for 'She Loves You'.

1965
Manfred Mann, The Yardbirds and Paul & Barry Ryan all appear at the ABC Cinema, Stockton, Cleveland, north east England.

1971
Memphis blues singer Herman 'Junior' Parker dies aged 39 during surgery for a brain tumor. Parker was discovered in 1952 by Ike Turner, who signed him to Modern Records. In 1953 Parker signed to Sun Records where they produced three successful songs, including 'Feelin' Good', a No. 5 on the *Billboard* R&B charts.

1972
Danny Whitten dies of a drug overdose aged 29. He was a member of Neil Young's backing band, Crazy Horse, and the writer of 'I Don't Wanna Talk About It', covered by Rod Stewart, Rita Coolidge and Everything But The Girl. The Neil Young song 'The Needle And The Damage Done' was written about Whitten's heroin use before his death.

1975
Bruce Springsteen makes his live UK debut at London's Hammersmith Odeon.

1976
Richard Hell & The Voidoids make their debut at CBGBs in New York.

1983
R.E.M. make their first appearance outside the US when they appear on the Channel 4 UK TV show *The Tube*. The following night they make their live UK debut at Dingwalls, London.

1993
Nirvana record their MTV unplugged special at Sony Studios, New York.

1999
It is reported that Madonna has saved over £100,000 in the purchase of her new South Kensington home in London by doing a private sale and cutting out estate agents.

2003
More than 500 Britney Spears fans camp overnight outside the Virgin Records Megastore in New York's Times Square so as to obtain autographed copies of her new album *In The Zone*.

Following allegations of sexual abuse of a 12-year-old boy, police raid Michael Jackson's Neverland ranch. Jackson denies the allegations. The raid occurs on the same day that his latest greatest hits album, *Number Ones*, is released in the US.

American composer and orchestral arranger Michael Kamen dies of a heart attack in London aged 55. He worked with Pink Floyd, Queen, Eric Clapton, Roger Daltrey, Aerosmith, Tom Petty, David Bowie, Eurythmics, Queensryche, Rush, Metallica, Herbie Hancock, The Cranberries, Bryan Adams, Jim Croce, Sting, and Kate Bush. Kamen co-wrote Bryan Adams' ballad '(Everything I Do) I Do It for You'.

Britney Spears says that her first lover, Justin Timberlake, was a huge disappointment in the bedroom department. Talking during a MTV show, Spears says, "Forget trouser snake, it's more like trouser worm", when referring to her ex boyfriend.

2007
US celebrity publicist Paul Wasserman dies of respiratory failure aged 73. His clients included The Rolling Stones, The Who, Bob Dylan, Neil Diamond, Paul Simon, Tom Petty and James Taylor. His career ended in 2000 when he was jailed for six months for swindling some of his friends by selling shares in investment schemes that he falsely claimed were backed by stars like U2.

22-year-old *X Factor* winner Leona Lewis sets a British record for the fastest-selling debut album with *Spirit*. The singer sells more than 375,000 copies in seven days, 12,000 more than The Arctic Monkeys' 2006 release *Whatever People Say I Am, That's What I'm Not*. Oasis still have the overall record for the fastest selling British album, selling 813,000 copies of *Be Here Now* in 1997.

Born on this day:

1938	Hank Medress, vocals (The Tokens)
1943	Fred Lipsius, piano, sax (Blood Sweat & Tears)
1960	Matt Sorum, drummer (The Cult, Guns N' Roses, Velvet Revolver)
1971	Justin Chancellor, bass (Peach, Tool)

November
19

1955
Carl Perkins records 'Blue Suede Shoes' at Sun Studios in Memphis. The rock'n'roll classic becomes a US No. 2 and UK No. 10 hit for Perkins in 1956.

1964
The Supremes become the first all girl group to have a UK No. 1 single when 'Baby Love' goes to the top of the charts.

1965
The Who, Georgie Fame & The Blue Fames, The Hollies, Wilson Pickett and The Golden Apples Of The Sun all appear at the Glad Rag Ball, Empire Pool, London, with tickets costing 30 shillings (£1.50).

1976
UK music weekly *Sounds* makes The Sex Pistols' debut 45, 'Anarchy In The UK', its single of the week.

1979
Chuck Berry is released from prison after serving a four-month sentence for tax evasion.

1983
Tina Turner makes her first chart appearance in over ten years with her version of the Al Green hit 'Let's Stay Together'.

Tom Evans becomes the second member of Badfinger to commit suicide, hanging himself from a willow tree in his back garden. Family members say the singer and songwriter was never able to get over the suicide of his former bandmate Pete Ham. Evans and Ham co-wrote 'Without You', a massive hit for Harry Nilsson and Mariah Carey, but neither received a just reward in royalties.

1988
Robin Beck is at No. 1 on the UK singles chart with 'First Time'. The song is from a TV advertisement for Coca-Cola which session singer Beck

had recorded. It made the American a one hit wonder.

1990
Pia King, the wife of Level 42 main-man Mark King, is granted a 'quickie', divorce after her husband ran off with their children's nanny.

1994
David Crosby has a successful liver transplant operation at Dumont-UCLA in Los Angeles. Crosby's liver was deteriorated from extensive alcohol and drug abuse, as well as hepatitis-C.

1995
English singer-songwriter and founding member of folk rock band Lindisfarne Alan Hull dies of a heart attack aged 50. Lindisfarne scored the 1972 UK No. 3 single 'Lady Eleanor' and became local heroes in their home town of Newcastle where Hull was a city councillor.

2001
Scott Weiland, lead singer with The Stone Temple Pilots, is arrested after allegedly fighting with his wife at the Hard Rock Hotel in Las Vegas. Weiland was booked on one count of domestic battery and released 12 hours later. The band had performed at the club that night.

2002
Safety experts blast Michael Jackson after he dangles his baby from a third-floor hotel balcony. Jacko was in Berlin for an awards ceremony and was showing his nine-month old baby to his fans outside the hotel.

2003
American actor, dancer Gene Anthony Ray dies from a stroke aged 41. Best known for his portrayal of the street smart dancer Leroy in the 1980 film *Fame* and the television spin-off which aired from 1982 until 1987.

2004
Record producer Terry Melcher, who was behind hits by The Byrds, Ry Cooder and The Beach Boys, dies aged 62 after a long battle with skin cancer. The son of actress Doris Day, he co-wrote 'Kokomo' for The Beach Boys, produced 'Mr Tambourine Man' for The Byrds, as well as hits for The Mamas & The Papas.

2005
Former glam rock star Gary Glitter is arrested in Vietnam after being detained at Ho Chi Minh airport trying to board a plane to Bangkok. Police say Glitter was being held under suspicion of committing lewd acts with two girls under the age of 18.

2006
A guitar played by George Harrison is set to fetch more than £100,000 at a London auction. Harrison played the Maton MS500 guitar on The Beatles' first album.

Born on this day:

1947 Joe Walsh, guitar, vocals (James Gang, The Eagles)

1962 Gail Ann Dorsey, bass (David Bowie, Gwen Stefani)

1965 Mike Diamond, rapper (The Beastie Boys)

1986 Jared Followill, bassist (Kings Of Leon)

1955
Bo Diddley appears on the US TV *Ed Sullivan Show*. Sullivan had requested he sing his version of 'Sixteen Tons', but when he appears on the set he sings his own song, 'Bo Diddley', resulting in him being banned from further appearances on the show.

1961
Bob Dylan begins recording his debut album over two days at Columbia Recording Studios in New York City.

1967
Strawberry Alarm Clock are at No. 1 on the US singles chart with 'Incense And Peppermints'.

1971
Isaac Hayes starts a two-week run at No. 1 on the US singles chart with 'Theme From Shaft', which makes No. 4 in the UK. Hayes wins a Grammy award for Best Original Film Score with the track.

1974
Keith Moon, drummer with The Who, collapses twice during a concert in San Francisco after his drink is spiked with horse tranquiliser. After the second time, 19 year-old Scott Halpin, a fan who was in the audience, replaces him on drums for the remainder of the show.

1975
The Bay City Rollers' Les McKeown is found not guilty of causing the death of a 76-year-old woman he hit with his car the previous May. Witnesses say that Euphemia Clunie was walking across the road and had changed directions four times. McKeown is convicted of driving recklessly, fined £150 pounds and banned from driving for a year.

1976
Paul Simon hosts NBC's *Saturday Night Live* on which he performs duets with George Harrison on 'Here Comes The Sun' and 'Homeward Bound'.

1984
A large crowd of fans watch the unveiling of a Hollywood Walk of Fame Star for Michael Jackson in front of Mann's Chinese Theatre in Los Angeles. Jackson becomes star number 1,793 on the famed walk.

1991
The Rolling Stones announce they've signed a £20 million deal with Virgin Records to make three albums over six years.

2003
Michael Jackson flies to Santa Barbara to be arrested by police. He is seen in handcuffs being taken into the police station. The singer has his mug shot and fingerprints taken before being freed on $3m bail.

2004
Oasis singer Liam Gallagher is fined £40,000 after a fight in a German hotel. Gallagher is arrested along with drummer Alan White and three other members of the band's entourage after the brawl in Munich in December 2002. Gallagher loses two front teeth in the fight, which leads to the band abandoning their German tour.

2007
Velvet Revolver are forced to cancel a planned four-city Japanese tour after their request for visas is rejected. Officials are said to have refused the band entry to Japan due to previous drug convictions.

Radiohead frontman Thom Yorke admits he was among the thousands of people who paid nothing to download the band's latest album *In Rainbows*. Speaking to BBC 6 Music's Steve Lamacq, Yorke said: "There wasn't any point. I just move some money from one pocket to the other." According to one survey, three in five people paid nothing at all for it. Yorke adds that no one was allowed to have copies of the master recording in case it was leaked beforehand.

Born on this day:

1940 Dr John, US R&B pianist, singer
1965 Björk Gudmundsdottir, singer (The Sugarcubes, solo)

1968 Alex James, bass (Blur)
1970 Francis Macdonald, drummer (Teenage Fanclub)

November 21

1955
RCA Records purchase Elvis Presley's recording contract from Sam Phillips at Sun Records for an unprecedented sum of $35,000.

1960
Maurice Williams & The Zodiacs go to No. 1 on the US singles chart with 'Stay', the shortest ever US No. 1 single at one minute 37 seconds.

The Beatles play at the Kaiserkeller Club in Hamburg, Germany without George Harrison. Harrison had been deported earlier today for being underage (he was 17) and not legally allowed to remain in a nightclub after midnight.

1970
The Partridge Family start a three-week run at No. 1 on the US singles chart with 'I Think I Love You'. The song was featured in the first episode of the *Partridge Family* TV series, made by the same company that made *The Monkees* TV series.

1975
At the start of Elton John week in Los Angeles, the singer receives a Star on Hollywood's Walk Of Fame

1980
Don Henley is arrested after a naked 16-year old girl suffering from drug related seizures is found at his home in Los Angeles. He receives a $2,000 fine with two years probation.

1981
Queen and David Bowie are at No. 1 in the UK with 'Under Pressure'. They recorded the song together when both acts were working at Queen's studio in Montreux, Switzerland.

1987
Billy Idol knocks Tiffany from the No. 1 single position on the US singles chart with his version of Tommy James' 'Mony Mony'. Tiffany had been at

No. 1 with another Tommy James song 'I Think We're Alone Now'.

1990
Madonna is sued by her next door neighbour for having a hedge which blocks his view.

Mick Jagger marries Jerry Hall in Bali. The marriage was declared 'null and void' on August 13, 1999, after a judge ruled that the six-hour ceremony was never registered.

1995
Legendary Led Zeppelin manager Peter Grant dies from a heart attack aged 60. One of the shrewdest and most ruthless managers in rock history, Grant secured 90% of concert gate money for his clients and intimidated record store owners who dealt in bootlegs. A former wrestler, he also worked as a film extra and bodyguard. During the early 60s Grant was a tour manager for Bo Diddley, The Everly Brothers, Little Richard, Chuck Berry, Eddie Cochran, Gene Vincent and The Animals.

2003
An acoustic guitar on which the late Beatle George Harrison learned to play fetches £276,000 at a London auction. His father originally bought

the Egmond guitar for Harrison for £3.50. Another item auctioned is a signed invitation to the post-premiere celebrations for The Beatles' *A Hard Days Night* film, which goes for £17,250.

Record producer Phil Spector appears before a California court and is formally charged with murdering B-movie actress Lana Clarkson who was found at his mansion in February of this year with a fatal gunshot wound to

her face. Spector pleads not guilty to her murder during a brief hearing in Alhambra, near Los Angeles and is released on $1m bail.

November 22

Born on this day:

1949 Steve Van Zandt, guitar, vocals (Bruce Springsteen's E Street Band)

1950 Tina Weymouth, bass (Talking Heads)

1966 Francis Anthony 'Eg' White, songwriter, producer

1978 Karen O, singer (Yeah Yeah Yeahs)

1957
Paul Simon and Art Garfunkel appear as Tom and Jerry on ABC-TV's *American Bandstand*.

1965
Bob Dylan marries Sara Lowndes in New York. Sara will file for divorce on March 1, 1977.

1968
The Beatles double 'White Album' is released in the UK on Apple Records, the group's own label.

1969
Iron Butterfly, supported by Steel Mill, featuring Bruce Springsteen, appear at the Randolph-Macon College in Ashland, Virginia. The gig is held in the school's 3,500-seat Crenshaw Gymnasium.

1975
KC & The Sunshine Band start a two-week run at No. 1 on the US singles chart with 'That's The Way (I Like It)', the group's second US No. 1 of the year.

1986
The Human League go to No. 1 on the US singles chart with 'Human', making them the eighth UK act to score a US No. 1 single in 1986.

1987
Jesus and Mary Chain singer Jim Reid is arrested in Canada after being accused of assaulting members of the audience with his microphone stand. He is released on $2,000 bail.

1991
Alice Cooper comes to the rescue of two fans, Patrick and Dee Ann Kelly, whose California home is about to be re-possessed. Patrick had painted Cooper's face on the house to help sell the property. Alice signed autographs to help raise money for the couple

1997
INXS singer Michael Hutchence is found dead in his hotel suite in Sydney, aged 37. At 11.50am Hutchence's body is found naked behind the door to his room. He had apparently hanged himself with his own belt but the buckle broke away and he was found kneeling on the floor facing the door. It has been suggested that his death resulted from an act of auto eroticism, although no forensic or other evidence has been found to substantiate this suggestion.

2004
Ozzy Osbourne struggles with a burglar who escapes with jewellery worth about £2m from his Buckinghamshire mansion. Osbourne tells reporters that he had the masked raider in a headlock as he tried to stop him but the burglar broke free and jumped 30 foot from a first floor window. Two burglars were involved.

2005
Poems written by Bob Dylan in his college days sell for $78,000 at a New York City auction. The 16 pages of poems from his student days at the University of Minnesota during 1959-60 are believed to be the first time he used the name Dylan.

November 23

1956
Sheet metal worker Louis Balint is arrested after punching Elvis Presley at a Hotel in Toledo. Balint claims that his wife's love for Elvis has caused his marriage to break up. He is fined $19.60 but ends up being jailed because he is unable to pay the fine.

1962
The Beatles travel to St. James' Church Hall, London, for a ten-minute audition with BBC Television. The audition came about because Beatles fan David Smith of Preston, Lancashire, wrote to the BBC asking for The Beatles to be featured on BBC TV. Assuming that Smith was The Beatles' manager, the BBC wrote back to him, offering the group an audition. Smith brought his letter to NEMS Enterprises, and Clive Epstein (Brian's brother) arranged for the audition to take place. Four days later, Brian Epstein received a polite "thumbs-down" letter from the BBC.

1967
The Who appear at The New Barn, Lions Delaware County Fairgrounds, Muncie, Indiana.

1968
Pink Floyd appear at the The Large Hall, Regent Street Polytechnic, London, England.

1974
One hit wonder Billy Swan starts a two week run at No. 1 on the US singles chart with 'I Can Help', a No. 6 hit in the UK.

1975
Queen start a nine-week run at No. 1 on the UK singles chart with 'Bohemian Rhapsody'. The promotional video that accompanies the song cost only £5,000 to produce and is often cited as being the first pop video, although many other acts had already produced brief films to accompany their songs. When Queen

proposed releasing the single executives at their record label suggested to them that, at five minutes and 55 seconds, it was too long and would never be a hit.

1976
Ten hours after his last arrest, Jerry Lee Lewis is nicked again for brandishing a Derringer pistol outside Elvis Presley's Graceland's home in Memphis, and demanding a confrontation with the 'King'. When police arrive they find Lewis sat in his car with the loaded Derringer pistol resting on his knee.

1989
During a 104-date world tour, Paul McCartney plays the first of five nights at the Los Angeles Forum, California, his first appearances in North America in 13 years.

1992
American country music singer Roy Acuff dies aged 89. Known as the "King of Country Music", he was the first living artist elected to the Country Music Hall Of Fame. Acuff started his career in 1932 working for Dr. Hauer's Medicine Show, hired as one of its entertainers to draw a crowd to whom Hauer could sell medicines.

1994
Singer-songwriter Tommy Boyce commits suicide aged 55. With his professional partner Bobby Hart he had the 1968 US No. 8 single 'I Wonder What She's Doing Tonight'. They also wrote 'Last Train To Clarksville', 'I'm Not Your Stepping Stone' and 'Scooby-Doo Where Are You!', selling over 40 million records.

1995
American soul singer and saxophonist Junior Walker dies of cancer aged 64. He had the 1966 US & UK Top 20 single 'How Sweet It Is', and the 1969 US No. 4 single 'What Does It Take, To Win Your Love'. Walker also played sax on Foreigner's 1981 hit 'Urgent'.

2002
Otis Redding's widow and his former manager file a lawsuit against the author of a biography written in 2001 about the R&B legend, claiming the book is libelous. The lawsuit, filed in Atlanta's Fulton County, seeks $15 million in damages, claiming that information in the book about the singer's drug use, extramarital affairs and divorce causes "harm to the plaintiffs". It also cites rumours that Otis' manager plotted with the Mafia to kill Otis by causing the plane to crash in order to claim $1 million in life insurance.

2005
Dan McTeague, a Toronto MP, tries to have 50 Cent barred from entering Canada to perform a series of concerts later this year. McTeague had sent a letter to Immigration Minister Joe Volpe claiming that the controversial rapper shouldn't be permitted to cross the border because he promotes gun violence.

2007
Bono and The Edge from U2 make a surprise appearance at a charity gig, playing four songs before 250 people. The London gig at the Union Chapel is part of the Mencap's Little Noise Sessions.

November 24

Born on this day:

1944 Bev Bevan, drums (The Move, ELO)
1955 Clem Burke, drums (Blondie)
1962 John Squire, guitar (The Stone Roses)
1964 Tony Rombola, guitar (Godsmack)

1966
The Beatles get together for the first time since their return from the summer tour of the United States, ready to record a new album. The first song selected for recording is John Lennon's 'Strawberry Fields Forever'.

1968
Diana Ross & The Supremes are at No. 1 on the US singles chart with 'Love Child'.

1973
Ringo Starr goes to No. 1 on the US singles chart with 'Photograph', the first of his two US chart toppers as a solo artist.

1983
Irish group The Undertones split up. Lead singer Feargal Sharkey goes on to have a No. 1 UK single as a solo artist with 'A Good Heart' and later worked in A&R for various record labels. In October 2008, he became head of UK Music, which represents the collective interests of the UK's music industry in negotiations with the government and other commercial bodies.

1991
Kiss drummer Eric Carr (Paul Charles Caravello) dies aged 41, of complications from cancer in a New York hospital. Carr replaced Peter Criss in 1980 and remained a band member until he became ill in 1991. For his Kiss stage persona, Carr was known as "The Fox".

1992
Bill Wyman's divorce is finalised with the high court awarding his former wife Mandy Smith £580,000.

1993
American blues guitarist and singer Albert Collins dies of lung cancer aged 61. Known as "the master of the Telecaster", he shared a Grammy for the 1985 album *Showdown!*, which he recorded with Robert Cray and Johnny Copeland.

Janet Jackson plays the first night on her 'Janet' 120-date world tour at the Riverfront Coliseum in Cincinnati, Ohio.

1999
During a Bonhams of London rock auction, Buddy Holly's first driving licence sells for £3,795, and a copy of The Beatles 'White Album' numbered 00000001 sells for £9,775.

2003
'Agadoo' by Black Lace is named the worst song of all time by a panel of music writers. The song peaked at No. 2 on the UK charts in 1984.

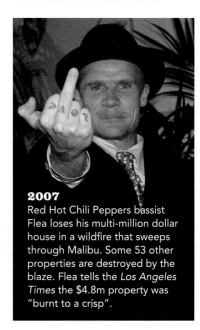

2007
Red Hot Chili Peppers bassist Flea loses his multi-million dollar house in a wildfire that sweeps through Malibu. Some 53 other properties are destroyed by the blaze. Flea tells the *Los Angeles Times* the $4.8m property was "burnt to a crisp".

2008
Snaresbrook Crown Court hears how Boy George chained a male escort to his bedroom wall and beat him with a metal chain after accusing him of hacking into his laptop. The singer had made contact with Audun Carlsen, 29, a gay male escort, on the social networking website Gaydar. Carlsen tells the court he was dragged along the floor towards the bed and a handcuff was put on his right hand. The manacle was attached to a hook drilled into the wall by the bed. The fire brigade had to be called to cut the cuffs off.

1991
Queen singer Freddie Mercury dies aged 45 of complications from AIDS at his home in London's Kensington, just one day after he publicly admitted he was HIV positive. Mercury was openly bisexual and enjoyed a colourful rock star lifestyle. During his career with Queen he scored over 40 Top 40 UK singles, including the worldwide No. 1 'Bohemian Rhapsody'.

November 25

Born on this day:

1940 Percy Sledge, soul singer
1950 Jocelyn Brown, singer

1959 Steve Rothery, guitar (Marillion)
1968 Tunde, singer (Lighthouse Family)

1961
The Everly Brothers start active service for the 8th Battalion Marine Corps Reserves, working as artillerymen.

1969
John Lennon returns his MBE to The Queen in protest against the UK's involvement in the Nigeria Biafra war, America in Vietnam, and his latest single 'Cold Turkey' slipping down the charts.

1974
UK singer, songwriter and guitarist Nick Drake dies in his sleep aged 26 of an overdose of tryptasol, an anti-depressant drug. Drake signed to Island Records when he was 20 years old, and recorded the classic 1972 album *Pink Moon*. In 2000, Volkswagen featured the title track

from *Pink Moon* in a TV advertisement, and within a month Drake had sold more records than he had in the previous thirty years.

1976
The Band make their final performance during 'The Last Waltz' at Winterland in San Francisco. The show also features Bob Dylan, Joni Mitchell, Dr John, Neil Young, Van Morrison, Neil Diamond, Eric Clapton and others. Martin Scorsese films the event.

1984
The cream of the British pop world gathers at SARM Studios in London to record the historic 'Do They Know It's Christmas?'. The single, written by Bob Geldof and Midge Ure, features Paul Young, Bono, Boy George, Paul Weller, Sting, George Michael and many others. It goes on to sell over three million copies in the UK, becomes the best selling record ever, and raises over £8 million worldwide.

1995
Radiohead singer Thom Yorke blacks out halfway through a show in Munich, Germany, suffering from exhaustion.

2000
A burglar breaks into Alice Cooper's home and makes off with over $6,000 worth of clothes, shoes and cameras belonging to the singer's daughter. The goods are all lifted from Cooper's house in Paradise Valley, Arizona, along with four of the star's gold discs.

2003
Michael Jackson launches a website to defend himself following allegations of sexual abuse of a 12-year old boy. The singer posts a message saying the charges were based on "a big lie" and he wanted to end "this horrible time" by proving they were false in court.

Glen Campbell is arrested in Phoenix, Arizona, with a blood alcohol level of .20 after his BMW strikes a Toyota Camry. He is charged with 'extreme' drunk driving, hit and run, and assaulting a police officer. A police officer reports that while in custody, Campbell hummed his hit 'Rhinestone Cowboy' repeatedly.

Meat Loaf undergoes heart surgery in a London hospital after being diagnosed with a condition that causes an irregular heartbeat. The 52-year-old singer had collapsed on November 17 as he performed at London's Wembley Arena.

2007
Kevin Dubrow, the frontman with metal band Quiet Riot, is found dead in his Las Vegas home aged 52. Their 1983 release *Metal Health* was the first metal album to top the US charts. The band's biggest hit was 'Cum On Feel The Noize', a cover of the Slade song which they are said to have grudgingly recorded in just one take.

2008
The legal dispute over a music contract between Michael Jackson and an Arab sheik ends with an "amicable settlement". Jackson had been due to fly in to the UK to give evidence at the High Court before an agreement in principle was reached. The King of Bahrain's son, Sheikh Abdulla Bin Hamad Bin Isa Al-Khalifa, was suing Jackson for £4.7m, claiming he reneged on a music contract.

Born on this day:

1939 Tina Turner, singer
1945 John McVie, bass (Fleetwood Mac)
1946 Burt Reiter, bass (Focus)
1981 Natasha Bedingfield, singer

November
26

1958
Johnny Cash makes his debut on the US country chart when 'Cry! Cry! Cry!' reaches No. 14. His next seven singles will all make the country top 10, with 'I Walk The Line' and 'There You Go' both hitting No. 1.

1968
Cream play their farewell concert at the Royal Albert Hall, London. Also on the bill are Yes and Taste.

1969
Pink Floyd and Mouseproof appear at The Civic Hall, Dunstable, England, with tickets at 14 shillings (70p).

1973
John Rostill, former bassist with The Shadows, dies after being electrocuted at his home recording studio. A local newspaper runs the headline: 'Pop musician dies, guitar apparent cause'. After the break up of The Shadows Rostill worked with Tom Jones and wrote songs that were recorded by Elvis Presley and Olivia Newton-John.

1976
The Sex Pistols release the single 'Anarchy In The UK'. It peaks at No. 38 on the UK charts.

1977
On their first visit to Australia, Blondie play the opening night of a 28-date tour at the Concert Hall, Perth, with support from The Ferrets.

1989
The Rolling Stones play a concert at Death Valley Stadium in Clenson, South Carolina to help raise money for the victims of Hurricane Hugo.

1991
US country singer Garth Brooks asks fans to bring 10 cans of food to a grocery store in exchange for a lottery envelope, some of which contain tickets to see Garth at a forthcoming show. Over 10,000 cans are donated to charity.

1994
Boyz II Men start their fourteenth and final week at No. 1 on the US singles chart with 'I'll Make Love To You', equalling the longest run in chart history with 'I Will Always Love You' by Whitney Houston.

2000
Fixtures and fittings from the Manchester club The Hacienda are auctioned off, raising £18,000 for charity. Madonna made her UK TV debut at the club when Channel 4 music show *The Tube* was broadcast live from the venue. Oasis, Happy Mondays, U2, New Order, Stone Roses, The Smiths and James all played at the club.

2006
Westlife go to No. 1 on the UK album chart with 'The Love Album', the Irish boy band's sixth UK No. 1 album.

2008
The parents of missing Manic Street Preachers guitarist and lyricist Richey Edwards are granted a court order for him to be declared presumed dead. He disappeared nearly 14 years ago, and despite alleged sightings all over the world many now believe Edwards, whose car was found near the Severn Bridge, took his own life at the age of 27.

1973
The New York Dolls make their live UK debut at Biba's Rainbow Room, London. During the afternoon two members of the group are caught switching price tags on clothing in the store.

November 27

Born on this day:

1942 Jimi Hendrix, guitar, singer, songwriter
1944 Dave Winthrop, sax (Supertramp)
1959 Charlie Burchill, guitar (Simple Minds)
1978 Mike Skinner, singer, songwriter (The Streets)

1964

Mick Jagger is fined £16 for driving offences by a court in Tettenhall, Staffordshire. His solicitor tells the court: "The Duke of Marlborough had longer hair than my client and he won some famous battles. His hair was powdered, I think because of fleas. My client has no fleas."

1966

The New Vaudeville Band are at No. 1 on the US singles chart with 'Winchester Cathedral'.

1970

George Harrison releases his first proper solo album *All Things Must Pass*. The triple album, which includes a number of Harrison's songs left over from the Beatles period, goes on to be certified six times platinum by the RIAA, making it the best selling album by a solo Beatle.

1973

Country artist Hank Snow's guitarist Jimmy Widener is shot dead and his body is dumped in an alley.

1974

Rod Stewart & The Faces appear at The Odeon, Lewisham, London. Paul and Linda McCartney join the band on stage for the encore.

1982

Lionel Richie is at No. 1 in the US with 'Truly'. For each year from 1978-85 as a writer, Richie achieved a chart-topper with 'Three Times A Lady', 'Still', 'Lady' (Kenny Rodgers), 'Endless Love' (Diana Ross), 'All Night Long', 'Hello', 'Say You, Say Me' and as co-writer of 'We Are The World'.

1986

Bon Jovi are at No. 1 on the US singles chart with 'You Give Love A Bad Name.'

1997

A disturbed fan brings the funeral of Michael Hutchence to a standstill when he tries to launch himself from a 20 ft high balcony with a cord around his neck. He is removed by police and taken away to a psychiatric unit.

2005

Multi-millionaire defence contractor David H. Brooks books New York's Rainbow Rooms and his daughter Elizabeth's favourite acts for her bar mitzvah coming-of-age celebration. The artists who appear include Aerosmith, Tom Petty, Don Henley, Joe Walsh and 50 Cent; the latter performed only four songs for a fee of $500,000. The party costs an estimated $10 million, including the price of corporate jets to ferry the mercenary performers to and from the venue.

2006

Cliff Richard loses a battle to extend the number of years that musicians can receive royalties for their records. Richard wants copyright to last 95 years, rather than the present 50 years, but an independent review recommends the terms would not change. Sir Cliff's earliest big hit 'Move It', recorded in 1958, would start to come out of copyright in 2008.

2005
Tony Meehan, former drummer with The Shadows who left the group in 1961 to work as a session drummer with Joe Meek, and also had a UK No. 1 hit, 'Diamonds' with Jet Harris, dies aged 62 from head injuries sustained in a fall at his London flat in Maida Vale.

Born on this day:

1929 Berry Gordy, founder of Motown Records

1943 Randy Newman, singer, songwriter

1948 Beeb Birtles, guitar, vocals (Little River Band)

1962 Matt Cameron, drums (Soundgarden, Pearl Jam)

November 28

1960
Elvis Presley starts a six-week run at No. 1 on the US singles chart with 'Are You Lonesome Tonight', his third US No. 1 of 1960. The single includes a spoken section based loosely on a passage from Shakespeare.

1964
The Shangri-Las go to No. 1 on the US singles chart with the teen death song, 'Leader Of The Pack'.

1968
On their first North American tour, Deep Purple play the first of four nights at the Fillmore West in San Francisco, California.

1970
Dave Edmunds is at No. 1 on the UK singles chart with his version of the 1955 Smiley Lewis hit 'I Hear You Knocking'.

1974
John Lennon makes his last ever concert appearance when he joins Elton John on stage at Madison Square Garden in New York City. Lennon performs three songs, 'Whatever Gets You Thru The Night', 'I Saw Her Standing There' and 'Lucy In The Sky With Diamonds'. Backstage after the concert, Lennon and Yoko Ono are reunited after their temporary split.

1975
The Sex Pistols appear at Queen Elizabeth College, Kensington, London.

1987
Taken from the film *Dirty Dancing*, the Jennifer Warnes' duet with Bill Medley '(I've Had) The Time Of My Life' goes to No. 1 on the US singles chart.

R.E.M. have their first entry in the Top 10 on the US singles chart with 'The One I Love'.

1991
Nirvana record a performance for BBC TV music show *Top Of The Pops* in London. Asked to lip-sync 'Smells Like Teen Spirit' to a pre-recorded tape Kurt Cobain protests by singing in a low-pitched funny voice with the rest of the band not even trying to mime in time to the track.

1992
Whitney Houston starts a record-breaking 14-week run at No. 1 on the US singles chart with 'I Will Always Love You', taken from *The Bodyguard* soundtrack. The song was written by Dolly Parton.

1993
Steppenwolf drummer Jerry Edmonton is killed in a car crash not far from his Santa Barbara, California home. He was 47. Steppenwolf had the 1969 US No. 2 & UK No. 30 single 'Born To Be Wild'.

2000
David Bowie is crowned the musician's musician. Bowie beats The Beatles and alternative rockers Radiohead in a survey by *NME* that asked hundreds of top rock and pop stars to name their biggest musical influence.

2002
Tony McCarroll the original drummer with Oasis fails in a bid to sue the group's lawyers after he was sacked because he took too long to file his claim. Judge Justice Gray, at the High Court in London, tells McCarroll his case could not proceed because he had brought his claim outside of the six-year time limit.

2004
Metallica play the last show on their 137-date 'Madly in Anger with the World' Tour at the HP Pavilion in San Jose, California. It becomes the fourth-highest grossing tour of 2004, reaping $60,500,000 in ticket sales.

2006
US actress Pamela Anderson files for divorce from rapper Kid Rock after four months of marriage. In a statement on her website the 39-year-old confirms she had split from Rock.

2007
Kanye West and stuntman Evel Knievel settle a copyright dispute over West's use of the name "Evel Kanyevel" in a music video. The 69-year-old daredevil had claimed his image was tarnished by the video's "vulgar, sexual nature". The clip for 'Touch The Sky' showed the rap star cavorting with Pamela Anderson and trying to jump a rocket-powered motorcycle over a canyon.

November 29

Born on this day:

1933 John Mayall, singer, songwriter
1947 Ronnie Montrose, guitar (Montrose, Edgar Winter Group)
1951 Barry Goudreau, guitar (Boston)
1974 Apl.De.Ap, vocals (Black Eyed Peas)

1960
Paul McCartney and Pete Best are deported from Hamburg in Germany after being arrested on suspicion of arson after premises where they were staying mysteriously caught fire. They are released and deported the next day.

1965
Colorado Governor John A. Love declares a Rolling Stones day throughout the state as the Stones appear at Denver Coliseum during a North American tour.

1975
During a UK tour Queen appear at the Hammersmith Odeon, London.

1976
Lancaster local council cancels the Sex Pistols' gig at Lancaster Polytechnic. The reason given in a statement by the council is: "We don't want that sort of filth (The Sex Pistols) in the town limits."

1980
Abba score their ninth and final UK No. 1 single with 'Super Trouper', the group's 25th Top 40 hit in the UK. The name "Super Trouper" refers to gigantic spotlights used in stadium concerts.

1985
Kiss play the first night on their 91-date North American 'Asylum' Tour at Barton Coliseum in Little Rock, Arkansas.

1996
American singer and ukulele player Tiny Tim (Herbert Khaury) dies from a heart attack on stage while playing his hit 'Tiptoe Through The Tulips' at a club in Minneapolis.

1997
Whitney Houston pulls out of a concert sponsored by the Unification Church, otherwise known as the Moonies, two hours before she is due on stage after finding out the event was a mass wedding for over 1,000 Moonie couples. The religious group say they had no intention of suing providing the singer returns the $1m fee she had received.

2000
U2's Larry Mullen comes to the rescue of a motorcyclist who has been involved in an accident. Larry is driving home when he sees the motorcyclist who had crashed and stops to call for help on his phone, then waits for the ambulance to arrive.

1993 to charges of attempted capital sexual battery by an adult on a victim younger than 12 and being principal to lewd and lascivious behavior on a child younger than 16. He is sentenced to eight years of probation.

2009
Susan Boyle's album becomes the best-selling debut in UK chart history when it goes to No. 1 on the UK chart. The 48 year-old runner-up in ITV's *Britain's Got Talent* sold 410,000 copies of *I Dreamed A Dream*. Boyle also tops the US charts, setting a first-week sales record for a female debut

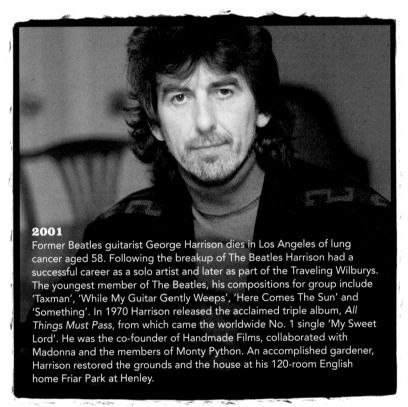

2001
Former Beatles guitarist George Harrison dies in Los Angeles of lung cancer aged 58. Following the breakup of The Beatles Harrison had a successful career as a solo artist and later as part of the Traveling Wilburys. The youngest member of The Beatles, his compositions for group include 'Taxman', 'While My Guitar Gently Weeps', 'Here Comes The Sun' and 'Something'. In 1970 Harrison released the acclaimed triple album, *All Things Must Pass*, from which came the worldwide No. 1 single 'My Sweet Lord'. He was the co-founder of Handmade Films, collaborated with Madonna and the members of Monty Python. An accomplished gardener, Harrison restored the grounds and the house at his 120-room English home Friar Park at Henley.

2007
Former Lynyrd Skynyrd drummer Artimus Pyle, a convicted sex offender, is arrested for failing to properly register a new permanent address. The 59-year-old had pleaded guilty in

album with 701,000 copies sold in its first week. Simon Cowell says he is proud of his protégé, adding: "She did it her way and made a dream come true."

Born on this day:

1945 Roger Glover, bass (Deep Purple)
1955 Billy Idol, vocals (Generation X, solo)
1968 Des'ree, UK singer, songwriter
1978 Clay Aiken, singer

November 30

1969

The Monkees make what will be their last live appearance for 15 years at The Oakland Coliseum, California.

The Rolling Stones play the final night on a 17-date North American tour at the International Raceway Festival, West Palm Beach, Florida. Also appearing are The Moody Blues, Ten Years After, King Crimson, Janis Joplin, The Band, Steppenwolf and Iron Butterfly.

1971

Sly & The Family Stone are at No. 1 on the US singles chart with 'Family Affair'.

1985

Wham! are at No. 1 on the UK singles chart with 'I'm Your Man', the duo's third UK No. 1; also a No. 3 hit in the US.

1991

Milli Vanilli singer Rob Pilatus attempts suicide while staying at The Mondrain Hotel, Los Angeles by taking an overdose of sleeping pills and slashing his wrists.

1996

Ice Cube obtains a restraining order to keep an obsessed fan away from him and his family. Cynthia Renee Collins is told to stop harassing the 26-year-old rapper, and stay at least 100 feet away from him.

1997

Chumbawamba's Danbert Nobacon is arrested by Italian police for wearing a skirt and is detained in police cells overnight.

1999

Don 'Sugarcane' Harris is found dead in his Los Angeles apartment at the age of 61. The American guitarist and violinist was part of 50s duo Don & Dewey. He also worked with Little Richard, John Mayall, Frank Zappa, John Lee Hooker and Johnny Otis.

Elton John is blasted by the Boy Scout Association after he appears on stage at London's Albert Hall performing 'It's A Sin' with six male dancers dressed as Boy Scouts. The dancers peeled off their uniforms during the performance.

2000

A block of East 2nd Street in New York City is officially renamed Joey Ramone Place. It is the block where Joey once lived with band mate Dee Dee Ramone, and is near the music club CBGBs, where the Ramones played their first gigs.

2002

High Court probate records show that George Harrison left his fortune of £99m in trust to his wife Oliva and his son Dhani, thus depriving the taxman of £40m. His mansion near Henley-on-Thames is said to be worth £15m.

2005

50 Cent is planning to create a vibrator of his manhood, so his female fans can pretend to have sex with him. The rapper is also planning to sell a line of condoms and waterproof sex toys designed to excite female fans. The rapper said: "I need to make a 50 Cent condom and motorised version of me, which will have to be waterproof so you can utilise it in the tub. Blue is my favourite colour so it will probably be blue."

Police are investigating claims that Michael Jackson is trafficking drugs to feed his 40 pills-a-day habit. The singer is suspected of flying antidepressants and painkillers from the US to his current home in Bahrain.

Babyshambles singer Pete Doherty is arrested on suspicion of possessing class A drugs after he is stopped by police while driving his car in Ealing, west London. Police stopped the vehicle because it was being driven "in an erratic manner" and recovered "substances" from the scene.

2006

Syd Barrett's final belongings are sold by Cheffins auctioneers in Cambridge, England. The sale of 77 items raises £119,890. Ten paintings alone raise over £55,000 and two bicycles over £10,000. The sale includes the armchair he used to sit in, his home-made bread bin, tools, notebooks and binders and books. The sale catalogue described Barrett – who quit Pink Floyd in 1968 – as a man with "total disinterest in materialism".

2008

Take That go to No. 1 on the UK singles chart with 'Greatest Day', their 11th UK No. 1. Taken from their 2008 album *The Circus*.

Born on this day:

1938 Sandy Nelson, US drummer
1944 Bette Midler, singer, actress

1944 John Densmore, drums (The Doors)
1977 Brad Delson, guitar (Linkin Park)

December 1

1957
Buddy Holly & The Crickets appear on *The Ed Sullivan Show*, performing 'That'll Be The Day' and 'Peggy Sue'. Sam Cooke is also a guest on the same show, performing 'You Send Me'.

1964
The Who play the first of 22 consecutive Tuesday night gigs at The Marquee Club in London. They are paid £50 for each gig.

1966
Tom Jones is at No. 1 on the UK singles chart with his version of 'Green Green Grass Of Home'. It stays at No. 1 for seven weeks, giving Decca records its first million selling single by a British artist. It is also a No. 11 hit in the US.

1976
The Sex Pistols appear on ITV's live early evening *Today* show (in place of Queen who pull out following a trip to the dentists by Freddie Mercury). Taunted by interviewer Bill Grundy, who asks the band to say something outrageous, guitarist Steve Jones says: "You dirty bastard... you dirty fucker... what a fucking rotter!"

1980
Talking Heads supported by U2 appear at the Hammersmith Palais in London.

1982
Michael Jackson's *Thriller* album is released. It spends 190 weeks on the UK album chart and becomes the biggest selling pop album of all time, with sales of over 50 million copies.

1987
A Kentucky teacher loses her appeal in the US Supreme Court after being sacked for showing Pink Floyd's film *The Wall* to her class. The court decides that the film's bad language and sexual content are unsuitable for minors.

1989
Sly Stone is sentenced to 55 days after pleading guilty to a charge of driving under the influence of cocaine. Two weeks later he also pleads guilty to possession of cocaine and is sentenced to spend 9-14 months in rehab.

1990
Vanilla Ice starts a four-week run at No. 1 in the UK with the single 'Ice Ice Baby'. The track samples the bass intro to the Queen and David Bowie No. 1 'Under Pressure'. 'Ice Ice Baby' is initially released as the B-side to the rapper's cover of 'Play That Funky Music', and becames the A-side after US DJs start playing it.

1997
Kenny G sets a new world record when he holds a note on his saxophone for 45 minutes and 47 seconds. (The record has since been broken by Geovanny Escalante, who held a note for 1 hour, 30 minutes and 45 seconds, using a technique that allows him to blow and breathe at the same time.)

2006
An Oasis fan enjoys "the best day of his life" when Noel Gallagher pops round to his house in Poynton, Cheshire, to play an intimate gig. Ben Hayes had won a BBC Radio 1 competition to have the star play in his front room as part of a week of gigs compered by DJ Jo Whiley. Some 15 people pack into his lounge for the tiny gig – with his mother on hand making cups of tea for the crew.

2008
Wham's 'Last Christmas' is the most played festive track of the last five years. The Performing Right Society puts the 1984 hit at the top of their

chart of seasonal songs, just ahead of Band Aid's 'Do They Know It's Christmas'. The Pogues come third with 'Fairytale Of New York', recorded with Kirsty MacColl and first released in 1987. Other featured artists include Slade, Mariah Carey and Bruce Springsteen.

December 2

Born on this day:

1941 Tom McGuinness, guitar, vocals (Manfred Mann)
1960 Rick Savage, bass (Def Leppard)
1968 Nate Mendel, bass (Foo Fighters)
1981 Britney Spears, US singer

1969
Cindy Birdsong of The Supremes is kidnapped at knifepoint by a maintenance man who works in the building where she lives. She later escapes unharmed by jumping out of his car on the San Diego freeway. The kidnapper is arrested in Las Vegas four days later.

1976
Elvis Presley plays the first of an 11-night run at the Hilton Hotel, Las Vegas.

1978
Rod Stewart is at No. 1 on the UK singles chart with 'Da Ya Think I'm Sexy', the singer's fifth UK chart topper. A plagiarism lawsuit by Brazilian musician Jorge Ben Jor confirms that the song is derived from his composition 'Taj Mahal'. Stewart agrees to donate all his royalties from the song to the United Nations Children's Fund.

1979
Neil Diamond and Barbra Streisand's 'You Don't Bring Me Flowers' is at No. 1 on the US singles chart. A radio station engineer had spliced together Neil's version with Barbra's version and received such a good response that the station added it to their play list. When Diamond is told about it, he decides to re-record the song with Streisand herself, and within weeks of its release the single goes to No. 1 in the US and No. 5 in the UK.

1982
US folk singer David Blue dies of a heart attack aged 41 while jogging in New York's Washington Square Park. A member of Bob Dylan's Rolling Thunder Revue during the mid-70s, he wrote 'Outlaw Man' which was covered by The Eagles on their 1973 *Desperado* album.

1983
MTV air the full 14-minute version of Michael Jackson's 'Thriller' video for the first time.

1999
It is reported that Stevie Wonder is to undergo an operation to regain his sight. The breakthrough by top eye specialists involves inserting a microchip in the retina.

2000
Thieves break into the London home Madonna shares with Guy Ritchie. The raiders force their way in through a basement door then take a set of car keys before loading up Guy Ritchie's car with some of the couple's possessions and driving off.

2002
Oasis singer Liam Gallagher is arrested and charged with assault after he kung-fu kicks a police officer at the Bayerischer hotel in Munich. The singer loses his two front teeth in the brawl and an Oasis minder is knocked out cold.

2006
David Mount, the drummer with Mud, dies in London. They had the 1974 UK No. 1 single 'Tiger Feet' (best-selling single of 1974), plus 14 other UK Top 40 singles.

2007
Sharon and Ozzy Osbourne make more than $800,000 for charity by selling off some of their possessions from their former US home.

Items sold include the family's custom pool table for $11,250 and a pair of Ozzy's trademark round glasses go for $5,250. The beaded wire model of the Eiffel Tower that adorned the kitchen fetches $10,000, while skull-adorned trainers worn by Ozzy sell for $2,625.

Born on this day:

1928 Andy Williams, US singer, TV host
1940 John Cale, singer, songwriter, multi-instrumentalist (Velvet Underground)
1948 Ozzy Osbourne, singer (Black Sabbath)
1979 Daniel Bedingfield, singer, songwriter

December 3

1965
The Beatles open what will be their last ever UK tour at Glasgow's Odeon Cinema. Also on the bill are The Moody Blues The Koobas and Beryl Marsden. The last show was at Cardiff's Capitol Cinema on December 12.

1966
Ray Charles is given a five-year suspended prison sentence and a $10,000 fine after being convicted of possessing heroin and marijuana.

1969
The Rolling Stones record 'Brown Sugar' at Muscle Shoals studios. The single goes on to be a UK & US No. 1.

1971
The Montreux Casino in Switzerland burns to the ground during a gig by Frank Zappa. The incident is immortalized by Deep Purple's 1973 hit, 'Smoke On The Water' – "Some stupid with a flare gun, burned the place to the ground..."

1975
Ronnie Wood's wife Chrissie is arrested for alleged possession of cannabis and cocaine after a raid on the couple's house in Richmond. Her friend Audrey Burgon is also arrested, and newspapers report that the two women were found "sleeping together".

1976
A giant 40ft inflatable pig can be seen floating above London after breaking free from its moorings. The pig was being photographed for Pink Floyd's *Animals* album cover. The Civil Aviation Authority issues a warning to all pilots that a flying pig is on the run.

An attempt is made on Bob Marley's life when seven gunmen burst into his Kingston home, injuring Marley, his wife Rita and manager Don Taylor. The attack is believed to be politically motivated.

1979
Some 11 Who fans are trampled to death after a stampede to claim unreserved seats before a concert by the group at The Riverfront Coliseum, Cincinnati.

1986
Judas Priest are sued by two families who allege that the band are responsible for their sons forming a suicide pact and shooting themselves after listening to Judas Priest records.

1999
U2 singer Bono is reunited with his missing laptop computer which he had lost. A man who bought it for £300 discovers he had the missing laptop, which contains tracks from the forthcoming U2 album, *All That You Can't Leave Behind*.

2000
American composer Hoyt Curtin dies of heart failure aged 78. He was the composer of many of the Hanna-Barbera cartoon theme songs, including *The Flintstones*, *Top Cat*, *Jonny Quest*, *Superfriends*, *The Jetsons*, *Josie & The Pussycats* and *The New Scooby-Doo Movies*.

2001
American session guitarist Grady Martin dies aged 72. A member of the legendary Nashville A-Team, he played guitar on hits ranging from Roy Orbison's 'Oh, Pretty Woman', Marty Robbins' 'El Paso' and Loretta Lynn's 'Coal Miner's Daughter'. During a 50-year career Martin played on records by such names as Elvis Presley, Buddy Holly, Woody Guthrie, Arlo Guthrie, Johnny Cash, Patsy Cline, Joan Baez and J. J. Cale.

2003
A Los Angeles court rules that the privacy of singer Barbra Streisand was not violated when a picture of her Malibu estate was posted on a website. Streisand had filed a $10m action against software entrepreneur Kenneth Adelman after he posted a photo of her home on his conservation site.

2007
Diana Ross and Brian Wilson both collect awards for contributions to US culture at a ceremony in Washington, attended by President Bush. Hootie & The Blowfish pay tribute to Wilson with a medley of some of The Beach Boys' best-known songs.

December 4

Born on this day:

1942 Chris Hillman, bass, mandolin, vocals (The Byrds, Flying Burrito Brothers)

1944 Dennis Wilson, drums, vocals (The Beach Boys)

1951 Gary Rossington, guitar (Lynyrd Skynyrd)

1969 Jay-Z, US singer, rapper

1956

The so-called 'Million Dollar Quartet' jam session takes place at Sun Studios in Memphis with Elvis Presley, Jerry Lee Lewis, Johnny Cash and Carl Perkins.

1965

The Byrds start a three week run at No. 1 on the US singles chart with 'Turn! Turn! Turn!' the group's second chart topper. It becomes a No. 26 hit in the UK. Unlike their first chart topper, 'Mr. Tambourine Man', the entire band plays on the recording, instead of studio musicians.

1971

Led Zeppelin start a two-week run at No. 1 on the UK chart with their untitled fourth album. Featuring the eight-minute track 'Stairway To Heaven', the album stays on the US chart for one week short of five years, selling over 11 million copies.

1976

Workers at EMI Records pressing plant in Hayes near London refuse to package The Sex Pistols single 'Anarchy In The UK' after the group's outburst on the *Today* TV programme.

1979

U2 appear at The Hope and Anchor, Islington, London. Misnamed 'The U2s', they play to only nine people and the show ends abruptly after The Edge breaks a guitar string.

1980

Prince plays the first night on his 31-date 'Dirty Mind' North American tour at Shea's in Buffalo, New York. After being told by his managers he can't wear spandex pants without any underwear, Prince appears in a long trench coat, black high heeled boots and leggings, and bikini brief trunks.

1988

Roy Orbison plays his last ever gig in Cleveland, Ohio. Orbison dies of a heart attack two days later.

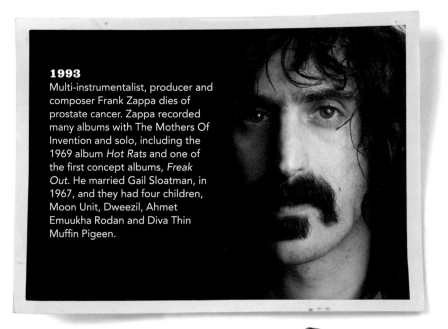

1993

Multi-instrumentalist, producer and composer Frank Zappa dies of prostate cancer. Zappa recorded many albums with The Mothers Of Invention and solo, including the 1969 album *Hot Rats* and one of the first concept albums, *Freak Out*. He married Gail Sloatman, in 1967, and they had four children, Moon Unit, Dweezil, Ahmet Emuukha Rodan and Diva Thin Muffin Pigeen.

1999

Rapper Jay-Z is released on $50,000 bail after being accused of attacking Lance Rivera when a fight broke out at a party for rapper Q-Tip at a Manhattan Club. Police decline to say what caused the dispute.

2002

Whitney Houston admits in a US TV interview that drink and drugs nearly killed her. She also admits to being addicted to sex. She says her business is sex, drugs and rock'n'roll, and got into the lifestyle after missing out on partying when her career kicked off aged 18.

2006

Yahoo reveals that 'Britney Spears' is the most searched for term of 2006 with more online searches for Spears than any other topic or person. Female celebrities dominate the top 10 overall search list, with Shakira at number three, Jessica Simpson at number four and Paris Hilton at number five.

Born on this day:

1899 Sonny Boy Williamson, harmonica player, singer

1932 Little Richard, singer, pianist

1938 JJ Cale, US guitarist, singer, songwriter

1952 Andy Kim, singer

1965 Johnny Rzeznik, singer, guitarist (Goo Goo Dolls)

1965

The Beatles play their last ever show in their hometown of Liverpool at The Liverpool Empire during the group's final UK tour. Only 5,100 tickets are available for the two shows, but there were 40,000 ticket applications. The group also have the UK No. 1 single with 'We Can Work It Out'/'Day Tripper'.

1968

The release of The Rolling Stones' new album, *Beggar's Banquet*, is celebrated at a party in London where a food fight with custard pies is the highlight of the event. Keith Richards, late as ever, misses the fun. The original cover for the LP featured a graffiti-strewn toilet but this was later changed to a plain white sleeve in the style of an invitation.

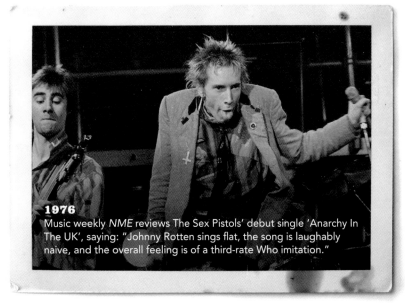

1976

Music weekly *NME* reviews The Sex Pistols' debut single 'Anarchy In The UK', saying: "Johnny Rotten sings flat, the song is laughably naive, and the overall feeling is of a third-rate Who imitation."

1970

'Amazing Grace' by Judy Collins enters the UK singles chart on the first of eight occasions. It spends a total of 67 weeks on the chart, never making the No. 1 position.

1987

Fat Larry James, drummer, singer and leader of Fat Larry's Band, dies of a heart attack aged 38. He scored the 1982 UK No. 2 single 'Zoom'. The opening drum break from 'Down On The Avenue', from the band's first album, *Feel It*, has been sampled by N.W.A. Ice-T, Jungle Brothers and Run-D.M.C.

The Jesus And Mary Chain are banned from appearing on a US music TV show after complaints of blasphemy when the group's name is flashed across the screen. The CBS TV network requests the band call themselves JAMC but they refuse.

1992

Whitney Houston starts a ten-week run at No. 1 on the UK singles chart with 'I Will Always Love You'. It is the longest ever run at No. 1 for a female artist. The Dolly Parton penned song was taken from *The Bodyguard* soundtrack.

1993

Co-founder of Gin Blossoms Doug Hopkins dies of self-inflicted gunshot wounds age 32. The guitarist and songwriter was in a detox unit of Phoenix's St. Luke's Hospital in Arizona when he snuck out and bought a .38 caliber pistol. The next day Hopkins committed suicide.

2006

Lyrics handwritten by Paul McCartney for an early version of 'Maxwell's Silver Hammer' sell for $192,000 at an auction in New York. A guitar owned by Jimi Hendrix fetches $168,000, a notebook containing lyrics written by Bob Marley sells for $72,000 and a poem penned by Doors frontman Jim Morrison makes $49,000 at a Christie's sale.

2007

Robbie Williams apologises to Nigel Martin-Smith, the former manager of Take That, and agrees to pay undisclosed damages over an allegation he made about him in a song. In the lyrics of 'The 90s' Williams had suggested that Nigel Martin-Smith had stolen funds from the band.

December 6

Born on this day:

1955 Rick Buckler, drums (The Jam)
1956 Peter Buck, guitar (R.E.M.)
1961 David Lovering, drums (Pixies)

1962 Ben Watt, singer, songwriter, guitar (Everything But The Girl)

1949
American blues artist Leadbelly dies. Among the many songs written by Huddie William Ledbetter were 'Goodnight Irene', 'Cotton Fields', 'The Rock Island Line', and 'The Midnight Special'. Leadbelly was jailed several times for fights and knife related incidents, once for shooting a man dead during an argument over a woman.

1961
John Lennon, Paul McCartney, George Harrison and Pete Best meet with Brian Epstein for further discussions about his proposal to manage them. Epstein wants 25% of their gross fees each week. He promises that their bookings will be better organised, more prestigious and will expand beyond the Liverpool area. He also promises that they will never again play for less than £15, except for Cavern lunchtime sessions, for which he will get their fee doubled to £10. Lennon, as leader of The Beatles, accepts on their behalf.

1962
Bob Dylan records 'A Hard Rain's A-Gonna Fall' during a session at Columbia Recording Studios in New York City.

1969
Led Zeppelin make their debut on the US singles chart with 'Whole Lotta Love', which reaches No. 4 on the chart, the first of six US Top 40 singles for the group. During their career, Zeppelin never released any singles in the UK.

The Rolling Stones play a free festival at Altamont in north California, along with Jefferson Airplane, Santana, The Flying Burrito Brothers and Crosby, Stills, Nash & Young. During their set, Rolling Stones fan Meredith Hunter (18) is stabbed to death by Hell's Angels who'd been hired to police the event. It's claimed Hunter was

waving a revolver. One other man drowns, two men are killed in a hit-and run accident and two babies are born.

1975
Rev Charles Boykin of Tallahassee, Florida organises the burning of Elton John and Rolling Stones' records, claiming they are sinful. Boykin was reacting to the results of a survey that indicated 984 of the 1,000 local unmarried mothers had sex when listening to rock music.

1978
Sex Pistol Sid Vicious smashes a glass in the face of Patti Smith's brother Todd Smith during a fight at New York City club Hurrah.

1980
The Police appear at the Fox Theater, Atlanta, Georgia, supported by R.E.M.

1986
Europe (below) are at No. 1 on the UK singles chart with 'The Final Countdown', its lyrics inspired by David Bowie's song 'Space Oddity'. They become only the second Swedish act to score a UK No. 1. The song reaches No. 1 in 25 countries.

1988
American singer songwriter Roy Orbison dies of a heart attack aged 52. He scored the 1964 UK & US No. 1 single 'Oh, Pretty Woman', plus over 20 US & 30 UK Top 40 singles, including 'Only The Lonely' and 'Crying'. Orbison formed his first band The Wink Westerners in 1949 and was a member of The Traveling Wilburys (known as Lefty Wilbury), alongside Bob Dylan, George Harrison, Tom Petty and Jeff Lynne.

1995
Michael Jackson collapses and is treated for dehydration while rehearsing for the HBO special *Michael Jackson: One Night Only* at The Beacon Theater in New York City.

2003
Elvis Costello marries jazz singer and pianist Diana Krall in a ceremony at Elton John's UK mansion. About 150 guests, including Paul McCartney, attend the wedding. It is Costello's third marriage.

December 7

1963
The Beatles' second album *With The Beatles* starts a 21-week run at No. 1 on the UK album chart, replacing their first album *Please Please Me* which had been at the top of the charts since its release 30 weeks previously.

1964
Beach Boy Brian Wilson marries Marilyn Rovell in LA. The couple will divorce in 1979.

1967
Otis Redding records '(Sittin' On) The Dock Of The Bay', which goes on to become his biggest hit, though Redding didn't see its release as he died three days later in a plane crash.

1969
The Byrds appear at the Senior High school gym, Baldwyn, Mississippi.

1974
Carl Douglas starts a two-week run at No. 1 on the US singles chart with 'Kung Fu Fighting'. Recorded in 10 minutes, the song started out as a B-side and went on to sell over 10 million.

1979
The Police have their second UK No. 1 single with 'Walking On The Moon', taken from their second album *Reggatta De Blanc*. The video for the song is filmed at Kennedy Space Center, interspersed with NASA footage.

1981
Duran Duran kick off a 14-date UK tour at Canterbury University.

1991
George Michael and Elton John are at No. 1 in the UK with a live version of 'Don't Let The Sun Go Down On Me', a hit for Elton in 1974. All proceeds from the hit go to AIDS charities.

1992
Mariah Carey's MTV *Unplugged* EP becomes the first Sony Minidisc to be released in the US.

1997
Shane MacGowan spends the night in police cells after being arrested in Liverpool. He is charged after throwing a mike stand into the crowd and injuring a fan.

2003
Britney Spears is at No. 1 on the US album chart with *In The Zone*, her fourth US No. 1 album. The singer breaks her own record from being the first female artist to have three albums enter the US chart at No. 1 to being the first female artist to have four albums enter at No. 1 consecutively.

2005
The MBE medal that John Lennon returned to the Queen is found in a royal vault at St James' Palace. Lennon returned his medal in November, 1969, with a letter accompanying saying, "Your Majesty, I am returning my MBE as a protest against Britain's involvement in the Nigeria-Biafra thing, against our support of America in Vietnam and against 'Cold Turkey' slipping down the charts. With Love, John Lennon." Historians call for the medal to be put on public display.

2007
Ray Charles Plaza is opened in Albany, Georgia, with a revolving, bronze sculpture of Charles seated at a piano.

2008
Leona Lewis goes to No. 1 on the UK singles chart with 'Run' which becomes the fastest-selling digital-only track.

Born on this day:

1942 Bobby Elliott, drums (The Hollies)
1943 Jim Morrison, vocals (The Doors)
1957 Phil Collen, guitar (Def Leppard)

1959 Paul Rutherford, vocals (Frankie Goes To Hollywood)

1963

Frank Sinatra Jr is kidnapped at gunpoint from a hotel in Lake Tahoe. He is released two days later after his father pays out the $240,000 ransom demanded by the kidnappers, who were later captured and sentenced to long prison terms. In order to communicate with the kidnappers via a payphone the senior Sinatra carries a roll of dimes with him throughout this ordeal. This became a lifetime habit, and he is even said to have been buried with a roll of dimes.

1965

The Rolling Stones record their ninth UK single '19th Nervous Breakdown' at RCA studios in Hollywood, California.

1968

Singer and guitarist Graham Nash leaves The Hollies to start work with David Crosby and Stephen Stills as Crosby, Stills & Nash.

1969

On trial in Canada on drug possession charges, Jimi Hendrix tells a Toronto court that he has only smoked pot four times in his life, snorted cocaine twice and taken LSD no more than five times. He tells the jury that he has now 'outgrown' drugs, and they find the guitarist not guilty.

1973

Roxy Music have their first UK No. 1 album when *Stranded* reaches the top for one week. The sleeve features *Playboy*'s Playmate of The Year, model Marilyn Cole.

1977

Four people are arrested after a riot breaks out when Blondie fail to arrive for a gig in Brisbane. Over 1,000 Australian fans had waited over an hour for the group to appear on stage, but the gig is cancelled due to singer Debbie Harry being unwell.

1980

John Lennon is shot five times by 25-year-old Mark Chapman outside the Dakota building in New York City where John and Yoko live. Chapman had been stalking Lennon for days outside the Dakota apartments and asked for an autograph as Lennon walked through the courtyard. As he signs a piece of paper Chapman fires. Lennon is pronounced dead from a massive loss of blood at 11.30pm.

1984

Frankie Goes To Hollywood are at No. 1 on the UK singles chart with 'The Power Of Love', the group's third No. 1 of the year and final UK No. 1. This makes them the first group since Gerry & The Pacemakers to have a UK No. 1 with their first three singles.

Vince Neil from Mötley Crüe is involved in a car accident in Redondo Beach, California, which kills Nick Dingley from Hanoi Rocks and injures two other passengers. Neil is jailed for 20 days and pays $2.6 million in compensation.

1999

1960s singer Heinz is given a formal caution by magistrates in Southampton for playing music too loud in his flat. The singer, who scored four Top 40 singles in the 60s, is now wheelchair bound.

2003

BPI figures show that UK sales of seven-inch singles have increased by 84% on the previous year. The report claims that bands such as The Darkness, The Strokes and The White Stripes have boosted sales by releasing special limited edition seven-inch records.

2004

Former Pantera guitarist Dimebag Darrell is one of five people killed after a man storms the stage during a Damageplan show at the Alrosa Villa Club in Columbus. Nathan Gale, aged 25, began firing at the band and crowd, and was then shot and killed by a police officer who arrives shortly after the first shots are fired.

Born on this day:

1940 Ginger Baker, drummer (Cream)
1940 Johnny Nash, singer
1945 Ian Gillan, vocals (Deep Purple)
1951 John Deacon, bass (Queen)

December 9

1961
The Beatles play at the Palais Ballroom in Aldershot to a crowd of just 18 people. The date had not been advertised, owing to the local newspaper's refusal to accept the promoter's cheque. After the show The Beatles become rowdy, and are ordered out of town by the local police.

1967
The Doors appear at the New Haven Arena, New Haven, Connecticut. Before the show a policeman finds singer Jim Morrison making out with an 18-year-old girl in a backstage shower and after an argument the policeman sprays mace in Morrison's face. Once on stage Morrison tells the audience about the backstage episode and starts taunting the police who drag him off the stage and arrest him. The crowd riots, leaving the venue in disarray and many are arrested. Later over 100 protestors gather at the police station to demonstrate and more arrests are made.

1968
Free appear at the Marquee Club in London, England. Other acts appearing at the club this month include Joe Cocker, The Who and Led Zeppelin.

1978
Chic start a seven week run at No. 1 on the US singles chart with 'Le Freak', a No. 7 hit in the UK.

1988
According to a poll released in the US, the music of Neil Diamond is favoured as the best background music for sex, Beethoven is the second choice and Luther Vandross is voted third.

1995
Michael Jackson scores his sixth solo UK No. 1 single when 'Earth Song' starts a six-week run at the top of the charts. It gives Jackson the UK Christmas No. 1 of 1995 and his best-selling UK single ever. The song keeps 'Free As A Bird', the first single released by The Beatles in 25 years, off the No. 1 position.

2000
Sharon Corr of The Corrs calls for the legalisation of cannabis, claiming that the drug has medicinal properties. Sharon says, "Certainly people with certain conditions can get a brief reprieve from their symptoms through cannabis."

2001
Channel 4 TV apologises to viewers after Madonna says 'motherfucker' during live UK TV coverage at The Tate Gallery, London. Madonna was presenting a prize to artist Martin Creed. A TV spokesman says that the bleeper system missed the offending word.

2003
Ozzy Osbourne is admitted to Wexham Park Hospital in Slough, Berkshire after being injured in a quad bike accident at his UK home. The 55 year-old singer breaks his collarbone, eight ribs and a vertebra in his neck. News of Osbourne's accident reaches the House of Commons, where the government sends a goodwill message.

2006
Mariah Carey threatens legal action against porn star Mary Carey in an attempt to stop her trademarking her similar-sounding stage name. The singer believes fans could get the two performers confused if the adult film actress Mary Carey's trademark application is successful.

December 10

Born on this day:

1947 Walter Orange, drums, vocals (The Commodores)

1965 Joseph Mascis, guitar, vocals (Dinosaur Jr)

1972 Brian Molko, guitar, vocals (Placebo)

1974 Meg White, drums (The White Stripes)

1967

American soul singer and songwriter Otis Redding is killed in a plane crash, aged 26. Redding and his band had appeared in Cleveland, Ohio, on the local *Upbeat* television show, the previous day. The plane carrying Otis Redding and his band crashed at 3.28pm into the icy waters of Lake Monoma near Madison. Also killed are members of the The Bar-Kays, Jimmy King, Ron Caldwell, Phalin Jones and Carl Cunningham. Trumpet player Ben Cauley is the only person to survive the crash.

1971

At the Rainbow Theatre, London, Frank Zappa is pushed off stage by jealous boyfriend Trevor Howell. He breaks a leg and fractures his skull.

1973

The club CBGBs opens on the Lower Eastside of Manhattan. It will become the home of many New York punk and new wave bands, including Blondie, Television and The Ramones.

1988

During their 222-date 'Damaged Justice' world tour, Metallica play the first of two nights at Cow Place in San Francisco, California.

1998

A recording of an August 1963 Beatles concert is sold at auction at Christies in London for £25,300. The tape of The Beatles' 10-song concert was recorded by the chief technician at the Gaumont Theatre in Bournemouth during one of six consecutive nights The Beatles played there, and includes their first ever live performance of 'She Loves You'.

1999

Rick Danko dies in his sleep at his home near Woodstock, New York, aged 56. In 1963 the Canadian bass guitarist and singer joined The Hawks, who went on to work as Bob Dylan's backing band (with Robbie Robertson, Richard Manuel, Garth Hudson and, later, Levon Helm). Renamed The Band, they released their debut album *Music From Big Pink* in 1968.

1999

A war of words breaks out between Cliff Richard and George Michael after George branded Cliff's hit 'Millennium Prayer' as 'vile'. Cliff hits back by saying that his single is a Christian celebration.

2003

Coldplay singer Chris Martin marries actress Gwyneth Paltrow in Santa Barbara, California. The couple also announce that Paltrow is pregnant and the baby is due next summer.

2004

One of three RCA microphones used by radio station KWKH for the historic Elvis Presley appearance at the Louisiana Hayride is sold for $37,500. The microphone is one of three used during 50 performances by Elvis Presley when he performed for the radio show in Shreveport from 1954 to 1956.

2007

Led Zeppelin play their first full-length concert for 19 years at London's 02 Arena as part of a tribute to Atlantic Records founder Ahmet Ertegun. Original band members Jimmy Page, Robert Plant and John Paul Jones are joined on stage by Jason Bonham, the son of their late drummer John Bonham. More than one million people had taken part in a ballot for the 10,000 pairs of tickets available for the show.

December 11

1961
Elvis Presley starts a 20-week run at No. 1 on the US album charts with *Blue Hawaii*, his seventh US No. 1 album. It's also a UK No. 1.

The Marvelettes go to No. 1 on the US singles chart with 'Please Mr Postman'. The session musicians on the track include 22-year-old Marvin Gaye on drums.

1964
Soul singer Sam Cooke is shot dead by his manager Bertha Franklin, who claims to have been assaulted by Cooke while staying at the Hacienda Hotel, Los Angeles.

circuited light. The guitarist is carried from the stage but returns 10 minutes later to finish the show.

1980
U2 appear at The Mudd Club in New York City, the first date of four US shows which also takes the band to Boston and Washington DC.

1982
Singer, TV actress and dancer Toni Basil goes to No. 1 on the US singles chart with 'Mickey', making her a US one hit wonder.

1989
The Recording Industry Association of America certifies four Led Zeppelin

2003
Bobby Brown is charged with battery after allegedly hitting wife Whitney Houston in the face. Brown turns himself in to the police three days after a reported domestic dispute at the couple's home in Atlanta, Georgia. Houston, who accompanied her husband to court, says they were trying to work out their problems "privately".

2008
Simon Cowell says he is "very embarrassed" after contracts signed by this year's X Factor contestants are leaked to the *Daily Mirror* newspaper. The 80-page document, which is enforceable "anywhere in the world

1968
Filming begins for *The Rolling Stones Rock & Roll Circus*. As well as clowns and acrobats, John & Yoko, The Who, Eric Clapton and Jethro Tull all take part. The film was eventually released in 1996.

1972
James Brown is arrested after a show in Tennessee for trying to incite a riot. Brown threatens to sue the city for $1m, and the charges are later dropped.

1973
Kiss guitarist Ace Frehley is nearly electrocuted during a concert in Florida when he touches a short-

albums as multi-platinum: *Presence* (two million), *Led Zeppelin* (four million), *Physical Graffiti* (four million) and *In Through The Out Door* (five million).

1998
During a gig in Tuscon, Arizona, a bottle thrown from the audience hits Black Crowes singer Chris Robinson. A security guard is then stabbed trying to eject a man from the crowd.

or the solar system", was signed by all 12 finalists before the live shows began. It includes a clause that prevents them from saying anything "unduly negative, critical or derogatory" about Cowell. Also the show claims the prize is a "£1m recording contract", but the contestants' contract says the prize money is £150,000.

Born on this day:

1915 Frank Sinatra, singer, actor
1940 Dionne Warwick, US singer
1944 Rob Tyner, singer (MC5)
1966 Sinead O'Connor, Irish singer, songwriter
1976 Dan Hawkins, guitar (The Darkness)

1957
Although still married to his first wife Jane Mitcham, Jerry Lee Lewis secretly marries his 13-year-old second cousin Myra Gale Brown.

1967
Rolling Stone Brian Jones is given three year's probation and a £1,000 fine for drug offences. Three psychiatrists agree that Jones is an extremely frightened young man with suicidal tendencies.

1970
The Doors play what turns out to be their last ever live show with Jim Morrison at the Warehouse in New Orleans.

1981
The Human League have their only UK No. 1 single with 'Don't You Want Me'. It is the Christmas hit of '81, the biggest seller of '81 and Virgin Records first No. 1 UK single. The group's singer Phil Oakey dislikes the song so much that it is relegated to the last track on their latest album *Dare*.

1985
Rolling Stones keyboard player Ian Stewart dies of a heart attack in his doctor's Harley Street waiting room in London. Co-founder of the Stones – he was the first to respond to Brian Jones's advertisement in *Jazz News* – Stewart was dismissed from the line-up by the band's manager, Andrew Loog Oldham, in 1963 but remained as road manager and piano player in the studio. He played on most of the Stones' albums between 1964 and 1983, and on Led Zeppelin's 'Rock And Roll' on their untitled fourth LP and 'Boogie With Stu' from *Physical Graffiti*.

1992
Whitney Houston starts a twenty-week run at No. 1 on the US album chart with *The Bodyguard*.

1998
A seven-inch single by The Quarry Men featuring John Lennon, Paul McCartney and George Harrison is named as the rarest record of all time, with only 50 copies that Paul had cut to give to close friends, each being valued at £10,000.

2001
Arthur Lee, guitarist and singer of Love, is released from prison after serving almost six years of an eleven-year sentence. Lee had been convicted of possession of a firearm and for allegedly shooting a gun in the air during a dispute with a neighbour.

2007
Ike Turner, the former husband of Tina Turner, dies aged 76 at his home near San Diego, California. Turner, a prolific session guitarist and piano player, played guitar on Jackie Brenston's 'Rocket 88' in 1951, which is credited by many music historians as the first rock'n'roll record. After marrying Tina Turner in 1959, the pair released a string of hits including the Phil Spector produced 'River Deep Mountain High'.

2008
It is announced that streets in a new estate in Dartford, Kent, the town where Mick Jagger and Keith Richards grew up, are to be named after Rolling Stones hits. The 13 streets will be given names such as Angie Mews, Babylon Close, Sympathy Street, Little Red Walk and Satisfaction Street. Leader of the council, Jeremy Kite, says he thinks Ruby Tuesday Drive sounds a "fantastic" place to live, but police are concerned the street signs will be stolen by fans.

Born on this day:

1948 Jeff 'Skunk' Baxter, guitar (Doobie Brothers, Steely Dan)

1948 Ted Nugent, guitar, vocals (The Amboy Dukes, solo)

1949 Tom Verlaine, guitar, vocals (Television)

1951 Tom Hamilton, bass (Aerosmith)

1952 Berton Averre, guitarist (The Knack)

1975 Tom Delonge, guitar, vocals (Blink 182)

1981 Amy Lynn Lee, vocals (Evanescence)

1961

The Beatles perform at the Cavern Club, Liverpool playing two shows at lunchtime and then again at night. Decca Records' Mike Smith attends the evening performance with a view to offering The Beatles a recording contract.

1966

Jimi Hendrix makes his TV debut on ITV's *Ready Steady Go!*. Marc Bolan is also on the show. The Experience also record 'Foxy Lady' on this day.

1969

Diana Ross takes the Latino Casino in Philadelphia to court for $27,500 after her two pet dogs die after eating cyanide tablets left in her dressing room by an exterminator.

1979

Simple Minds (below) play the first of two nights at The Marquee in London. Tickets are £1.25. Down the road at the Hope & Anchor, Islington, Tenpole Tudor play, with tickets costing 75p.

1986

Bruce Hornsby & The Range go to No. 1 on the US singles chart with 'The Way It Is', a No. 15 hit in the UK.

1999

Happy Mondays singer Shaun Ryder is ordered to pay £160,000 to his ex management team over a dispute in his contract. Ryder says he was so high after a 'joint' he didn't bother to read the small print. The court was told the contract had "done his nut in".

Winners in the *Smash Hits* readers poll include Backstreet Boys, who win best band, best album and best single; Britney Spears, who wins best female singer; Robbie Williams is best male singer; and S Club 7 best new band. The Spice Girls are voted worst group.

2002

UK music channel Music Choice analyses all the Christmas No. 1 singles from the past 30 years and identifies criteria for their success. These include the use of sleigh bells, children singing and church bells.

Cliff Richards' 1988 hit 'Mistletoe And Wine' was the perfect Christmas hit.

2003

Lauryn Hill launches a blistering attack on the Catholic Church, urging religious figures to "repent" whilst speaking on a stage regularly used by the Pope. The former Fugees singer is playing at a Christmas show in Vatican City and takes the opportunity to speak her mind about allegations of sexual abuse by priests in America, before an audience that includes top Vatican cardinals, bishops and the cream of Italian society.

2005

A cheque signed by John Lennon made out to the Inland Revenue sells for £2,000 at a UK auction. It was sold by former madam Lindi St Clair (formerly known as Miss Whiplash), after she decided she had no use for it. Clair, who now runs a duck farm in Herefordshire, had bought the cheque for £4,000 in 1988. It was signed by Lennon on January 23, 1968 on a District Bank Limited form and made out for £6,946.

December 14

Born on this day:

1946 Jane Birkin, actress, singer
1946 Joyce Vincent Wilson, singer (Dawn)

1949 Cliff Williams, bass (AC/DC)
1966 Tim Skold, bass (Marilyn Manson)

1962
Bill Wyman makes his live debut with The Rollin' Stones at the Ricky Tick Club, Star and Garter Hotel in Windsor, England. The group was known as The Rollin' Stones during this period.

1963
American blues and jazz singer Dinah Washington dies aged 39. Known as the 'Queen of the Blues', she scored the 1959 US No. 8 Grammy Award wining single 'What A Diff'rence A Day Makes' and the 1961 hit 'September In The Rain'.

1968
Marvin Gaye scores his first US No. 1 single when 'I Heard It Through The Grapevine' starts a five-week run at the top. It was Marvin's 15th solo hit and also his first UK No. 1 single in March 69.

1969
The Jackson 5 make their first network television appearance in the US when they appear on *The Ed Sullivan Show*.

1973
Bruce Springsteen appears at the Pinecrest Country Club, Shelton, Connecticut. Only 200 tickets are sold for the show.

1977
The film *Saturday Night Fever*, starring John Travolta, premieres in New York City.

1981
During their 'Ghost In The Machine' World Tour The Police play the first of three sold-out nights at Wembley Arena, London.

1985
Whitney Houston scores her first UK No. 1 single with 'Saving All My Love For You'. The song was a minor hit for Marilyn McCoo and Billy Davis Jr. in 1978 and was also a US No. 1 for Houston.

1999
Paul McCartney appears at The Cavern Club, Liverpool, with his 'rock'n'roll band' comprising David Gilmour and Mick Green on guitars, Pete Wingfield on keyboards and Ian Paice on drums. His last gig at the venue was in 1963. The show is filmed for TV and also goes out live on the Internet.

2003
Ozzy & Kelly Osbourne go to No. 1 on the UK singles chart with 'Changes', a remake of a track first sung by Ozzy on the Black Sabbath album *Volume IV* in 1972. It is the first father and daughter chart topper since Frank & Nancy Sinatra in 1967.

2004
The funeral takes place in Arlington, Texas, for Damageplan and Pantera guitarist Dimebag Darrell. Eddie Van Halen places Darrell's original black and yellow striped guitar into the Kiss Kasket in which he was buried. Several thousand fans and friends gather at the Arlington Convention Center to mourn the guitarist's death. Darrell was shot five times in the back of the head during a gig at the Alrosa Villa Club in Columbus on December 8, 2004, by a mentally ill former US Marine. Damageplan's drum technician, John Brooks, and tour manager, Chris Paluska, were both injured in the incident.

Born on this day:

1919 Max Yasgur, owner of the farm on which the Woodstock festival was held

1939 Cindy Birdsong, vocals (The Supremes)

1955 Paul Simonon, bass (The Clash)

1980 Sergio Pizzorno, guitar, vocals (Kasabian)

December 15

1969
John Lennon plays what will be his last ever gig in the UK at The Lyceum Ballroom, London, with The Plastic Ono Band in a UNICEF 'Peace For Christmas' benefit. George Harrison, Eric Clapton, Delaney & Bonnie, Billy Preston and Who drummer Keith Moon all take part.

1977
The Sex Pistols are refused entry into the USA two days before a scheduled NBC TV appearance; Johnny Rotten because of a drugs conviction, Paul Cook and Sid Vicious because of 'moral turpitude' and Steve Jones because of his criminal record.

1979
U2 appear at the Windsor Castle Pub, Harrow Road, London. Admission is free.

1984
'Do They Know It's Christmas' by Band Aid enters the UK chart at No. 1 and stays at the top for five weeks. It becomes the biggest selling UK single of all time with sales of over three and a half million. Band Aid is asterminded by former Boomtown Rats singer Bob Geldof, who was moved by a TV news story about famine in Ethiopia. Geldof decided to raise funds with a one-off charity single featuring the cream of the current pop world. Duran Duran, Spandau Ballet, Paul Young, Culture Club, George Michael, Sting, Bono, Phil Collins, Paul Weller, Francis Rossi and Rick Parfitt of Status Quo and Bananarama all appear on the recording.

1990
Rod Stewart marries New Zealand model Rachel Hunter in Beverly Hills. Stewart is quoted as saying: "I found the girl that I want. I won't be putting my banana in anybody's fruit bowl from now on." They split in 1999.

1997
Spice World – The Movie, featuring The Spice Girls, premieres at The Empire, Leicester Square, London. The following year it was nominated for the 'worst film' at the Golden Raspberry Awards.

1999
Boy George is knocked unconscious when a mirror ball falls on his head during a show in Dorset, England.

2001
American funk and soul singer Rufus Thomas dies of heart failure aged 84. He recorded on Sun Records in the 1950s and on Stax Records in the 1960s and '70s, scoring the 1963 US No. 10 single 'Walking The Dog' and the 1970 UK No. 18 & US No. 28 single 'Do The Funky Chicken'. A street is named in his honor, just off Beale Street in Memphis.

Eagles guitarist Joe Walsh is given an honorary Doctorate of Music from Kent State University in Ohio.

2003
Courtney Love is sentenced to 18 months in drug rehabilitation after she admits being under the influence of cocaine and opiates. She will undergo regular drug tests and is banned from taking non-prescription drugs, drinking alcohol or being in places that serve alcohol.

2006
The co-founder of Atlantic Records Ahmet Ertegun dies, aged 83. Ertegun, who founded Atlantic Records with Herb Abramson in 1947, helped make Ray Charles and Aretha Franklin stars and signed The Rolling Stones and Led Zeppelin in the early 70s. He suffered a head injury when he fell at a Rolling Stones concert at New York's Beacon Theatre in October, and dies after slipping into a coma.

2008
Madonna pays former husband Guy Ritchie around £50m as part of their divorce settlement. The singer's US spokeswoman Liz Rosenberg tells Associated Press the figure includes the value of the couple's Ashcombe home in England, and the financial part of the settlement had been worked out, but custody of the couple's children has yet to be finalised.

Born on this day:

1945 Tony Hicks, guitar (The Hollies)
1946 Benny Anderson, songwriter, keyboards, vocals (Abba)
1950 Bill Gibbons, guitar, vocals (ZZ Top)
1972 Michael McCary, vocals (Boyz II Men)

1966

The first Jimi Hendrix Experience single, 'Hey Joe', is released in the UK on Polydor records, having been rejected by the Decca label. It goes on to be a No. 6 hit in the UK but fails to chart in America.

1974

Guitarist Mick Taylor announces he is leaving The Rolling Stones, saying he feels that now is the time to move on and do something new.

1988

American soul and disco singer Sylvester James dies of complications from AIDS in San Francisco aged 41. He scored the 1978 US No. 36 & UK No. 8 single 'You Make Me Feel, Mighty Real', and sang back-up vocals for Aretha Franklin on her 1985 *Who's Zoomin' Who?* album.

1991

Chubby Checker files a lawsuit against McDonald's in Canada seeking $14 million for its alleged use of an imitation of his voice. The song 'The Twist' had been used on a French fries commercial.

1993

MTV airs Nirvana's *Unplugged* session for the first time.

With stories beginning to surface about Michael Jackson's alleged improprieties with young boys, St. Louis radio station KEZK announce it will be no longer playing the singer's records.

1997

American singer songwriter Nicolette Larson dies aged 45 of complications arising from cerebral edema. She worked with Neil Young (his *Comes A Time* and *Harvest Moon* albums), Emmylou Harris, Linda Ronstadt, Michael McDonald, Willie Nelson, Jimmy Buffett, The Beach Boys and The Doobie Brothers. She is best known for her 1978 cover of Neil Young's 'Lotta Love'.

2000

The estranged father and former manager of LeAnn Rimes makes embarrassing allegations during a legal battle involving millions of pounds. The court is told that LeAnn paid her mother £6,700 every time she styled her hair before a show.

2001

Stuart Adamson, lead singer of Big Country, is found dead in Hawaii a month after disappearing from his home in the US. The 43-year old Scottish musician had fought a long battle against alcoholism. His body is found in a hotel room.

2004

A Detroit studio where Eminem recorded 'My Name Is' is auctioned on the website eBay. Studio 8, in the Detroit suburb of Ferndale, was listed in eBay's commercial property section for 30 days, with a minimum bid of $215,000.

Gold and silver Black Sabbath discs are stolen from the Kent home of Ozzy Osbourne's former manager Patrick Meehan. Police recover the discs a week later after they are offered for sale on the internet auction site eBay.

2007

American singer songwriter Dan Fogelberg dies at his home in Maine at the age of 56. The US singer songwriter learned he had advanced prostate cancer in 2004. He had the 1981 album *The Innocent Age*, which featured the hits 'Leader Of The Band,' 'Hard To Say,' and 'Run For The Roses'.

Born on this day:

1926 Bill Black, bass player (Elvis Presley's first band, Bill Black Combo)
1949 Paul Rodgers, vocals (Free, Bad Company, Queen)
1958 Mike Mills, bass (R.E.M.)
1969 Micky Quinn, bass (Supergrass)

December 17

1962
Bob Dylan arrives in England for the first time, playing his first UK date the following night at the Troubadour Club in London.

1963
James Carroll at WWDC in Washington, DC, becomes the first disc jockey to broadcast a Beatles record on American radio. Carroll plays 'I Want To Hold Your Hand', which he had obtained from his air stewardess girlfriend, who brought the single back from the UK. Due to listener demand, the song is played daily, every hour. Since it hasn't yet been released in the States, Capitol Records initially considers court action, but instead releases the single earlier than planned.

1968
The Who play their Christmas party at the Marquee Club, London, their last ever appearance at the legendary Soho club. Also on the bill is a new group called Yes. Members pay 15 shillings (75p) or £1 on the night.

1975
Aerosmith and Blue Öyster Cult appear at the San Diego Sports Arena, San Diego, California.

1977
David Ackroyd purchases the one-millionth copy of 'Mull Of Kintyre' by Wings in the UK and becomes the first record buyer to receive a Gold Disc.

1982
Karen Carpenter makes her last live appearance with The Carpenters at Sherman, California.

1984
Frankie Goes To Hollywood, Big Country, Duran Duran, Ultravox, Paul Young and Wham! all appear on the UK TV show *Razzmatazz Solid Gold Christmas Special*.

1995
A statue of the late Frank Zappa is unveiled in Vilnius, the capital of the Republic Of Lithuania. It has been organised by Zappa fan club President Saulius Pauksty.

1997
David Bowie launches his BowieNet on the Internet.

1999
American jazz-funk, soul-jazz saxophonist Grover Washington Jr dies of a heart attack aged 56. He collapsed in the green room after taping four songs for *The Early Show*, at CBS Studios in New York City, He released over 20 solo albums and featured on the 1981 Bill Withers hit 'Just The Two Of Us'.

2004
Elvis Presley's daughter Lisa Marie Presley agrees to sell 85% of her father's estate to businessman Robert Sillerman in a deal worth $100m. Sillerman will run Presley's Memphis home Graceland and own Elvis' name and the rights to all revenue from his music and films. In the deal Lisa Marie will retain possession of Graceland and many of her father's personal effects.

2005
U2 has the top-grossing tour of 2005, according to an end-of-year chart compiled by US magazine *Billboard*. More than three million people watched the band's sell-out 90-date 'Vertigo' tour which grossed $260m. The Eagles took $117m from 77 shows and Neil Diamond grossed more than $71m. Kenny Chesney was fourth with $63m, Paul McCartney with $60m, Rod Stewart with $49m, Elton John with $45.5m, the Dave Matthews Band with $45m, Jimmy Buffett with $41m and Green Day with $36.5m.

1973
Slade are at No. 1 on the UK singles chart with 'Merry Xmas Everybody', their sixth chart topper. The song has re-entered the UK charts on eight other occasions.

Born on this day:

1938 Chas Chandler, bass (The Animals), manager of Jimi Hendrix and Slade

1943 Keith Richards, guitar, vocals (The Rolling Stones)

1953 Elliot Easton, guitar (The Cars)

1980 Christina Aguilera, US singer

1961

The Tokens start a three-week run at No. 1 on the US singles chart with 'The Lion Sleeps Tonight'. It reaches No. 11 in the UK.

1966

Socialite Tara Browne is killed when driving in his Lotus Elan after it collides at high speed with a parked lorry in South Kensington, London. A close friend of Rolling Stones Mick Jagger and Brian Jones, his death was immortalised in The Beatles' song 'A Day In The Life' ("He blew his mind out in a car") after John Lennon read a report on the coroner's verdict into Browne's death.

1971

Jerry Lee Lewis and his wife Myra, whom he married when she was 13, are divorced. Lewis now plans to marry 29-year-old Karen Elizabeth Gunn Pate.

1972

Bob Dylan starts filming his role for the film *Pat Garrett And Billy The Kid*.

1979

Joy Division play what will be their only gig in Paris at Les Bains Club.

1983

Keith Richards marries 27-year-old Patti Hansen on his 40th birthday.

American guitarist Jimmy Nolan dies of a heart attack in Atlanta, Georgia, aged 47. Known for his distinctive 'chicken scratch' lead guitar playing, he worked with James Brown from 1965 until his death.

1988

Mike Peters of The Alarm is rushed to hospital after having his eyes burnt by spotlights during a gig in Chester, causing the remaining dates on their UK tour to be cancelled.

1999

The Spice Girls unveil their waxwork look-alikes at Madame Tussaud's, London. Each model cost £35,000 to make.

2000

UK singer and songwriter Kirsty MacColl is killed off the coast of Mexico after being hit by a speedboat. MacColl was aged 41.

2000

*NSYNC fan Danielle McGuire files suit against group member Justin Timberlake, alleging that he harassed and verbally assaulted her. McGuire, 15, filed suit in St. Louis, Missouri, charging Timberlake with false imprisonment of a minor.

2001

English singer songwriter Clifford T. Ward dies aged 57 after suffering from multiple sclerosis since 1984. His first album, *Singer Songwriter*, was released in 1972 on Dandelion Records (a label formed by the disc jockey John Peel). He had the 1973 UK No. 8 single 'Gaye'. Working as an English teacher in the late '60s, one of his pupils was Trudie Styler, the future wife of Sting.

2004

A guitar played by George Harrison and John Lennon sells for £294,000 at auction in New York. The Gibson SG guitar was used by Harrison from 1966 to 1969, including the recording of *Revolver*, and by Lennon during the 'White Album' sessions. Other items sold in the Christie's auction include a letter from Kurt Cobain, which fetched £10,000, and a school book report by Britney Spears (£1,000).

2005

Babyshambles singer Pete Doherty is arrested on suspicion of driving under the influence of drink or drugs after being stopped by police in east London. Police say the 26-year-old had been driving erratically. Officers send suspicious substances found in the vehicle for analysis. Doherty is released on bail.

'Fairytale Of New York' is voted the favourite Christmas song ever in a VH1 poll. The song by The Pogues and Kirsty MacColl took the top spot, Mariah Carey's 'All I Want For Christmas Is You', was voted into second place and Wham's 'Last Christmas' came third. Other songs in the Top 10 were 'Mistletoe And Wine' by Cliff Richard at No. 4, 'Merry Xmas Everybody' by Slade at No. 5, 'I Wish It Could Be Christmas Everyday' by Wizzard at No. 6, 'Christmas Time' by The Darkness at No. 7, 'Saviour's Day' by Cliff Richard at No. 8, 'Do They Know It's Christmas' (1984) by Band Aid at No. 9 and 'Lonely This Christmas' by Mud at No. 10.

Born on this day:

1940 Phil Ochs, US folk singer, songwriter
1941 Maurice White, vocals (Earth Wind And Fire)
1944 Alvin Lee, guitar, vocals (Ten Years After)
1944 Zal Yanovsky, guitar, vocals (The Lovin' Spoonful)
1958 Limahl, vocals (Kajagoogoo)

December 19

1957

Elvis Presley is served with his draft notice by the US Army. He goes on to join the 32nd Tank Battalion third Armor Corps based in Germany.

1964

The Supremes score their third US No. 1 single of the year with 'Come See About Me'.

1967

Buffalo Springfield appear at the Community Concourse, San Diego, California.

1969

Mick Jagger is fined £200 plus 50 guineas (£52.50) costs at Marlborough Magistrates Court for possessing cannabis.

1970

Elton John's first US hit, 'Your Song', enters the *Billboard* Hot 100, where it goes on to reach number eight. The Hollies were offered the song and Three Dog Night had already recorded a version which was included on their *It Ain't Easy* album.

1976

During an interview with UK daily newspaper *The Daily Mail*, Sex Pistol Paul Cook's mother says he was no longer welcome at home and she is going to turn his bedroom into a dining room.

1979

Elvis Presley's personal physician, George Nichopoulos, is charged with 'illegally and indiscriminately' prescribing over 12,000 tablets of uppers, downers and painkillers for the star during the 20 months preceding his untimely death. Although he was acquitted this time, he was charged again in 1980 and again in 1992 and was stripped of his medical license in July 1995.

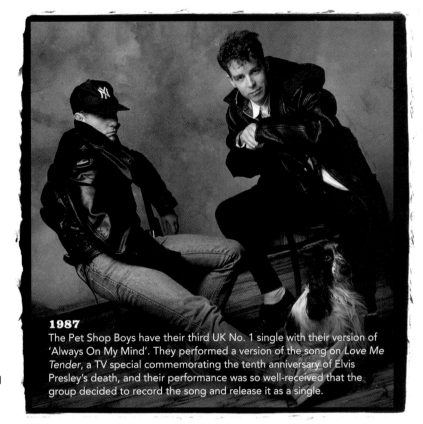

1987

The Pet Shop Boys have their third UK No. 1 single with their version of 'Always On My Mind'. They performed a version of the song on *Love Me Tender*, a TV special commemorating the tenth anniversary of Elvis Presley's death, and their performance was so well-received that the group decided to record the song and release it as a single.

1993

Michael Clarke, drummer with The Byrds, dies of liver failure aged 47. He also worked with the Flying Burrito Brothers and Jerry Jeff Walker. Before his death Clarke had expressed a desire to alert children to the dangers of alcoholism. Following his wishes, Clarke's girlfriend Susan Paul launches a foundation in Clarke's name called the Campaign for Alcohol-free Kids.

2000

10,000 Maniacs guitarist Robert Buck dies of liver failure aged 42. The group, fronted by singer Natalie Merchant, is best know for 'Hey Jack Kerouac', 'What's The Matter Here' and 'Candy Everybody Wants'.

Wu-Tang Clan rapper Ol Dirty Bastard is returned to New York from Philadelphia in police custody to face outstanding charges of possessing crack cocaine.

2001

Former Spice Girl Emma Bunton pays £3,000 for a custom built toilet. The singer ordered the hand painted porcelain loo complete with hand crafted toilet roll holder for her new £500,000 seaside apartment.

2006

Two giant eyeballs donated by Pink Floyd raise £16,500 for the homeless charity Crisis. The 6ft-high props, made to promote the *Pulse* DVD, were on the auction site eBay for a week and attracted 46 bids. Pink Floyd's David Gilmour, a vice-president of Crisis, said extra help was needed in the winter months.

December 20

Born on this day:

1947 Peter Criss, drums, vocals (Kiss)
1957 Billy Bragg, UK singer, songwriter
1957 Anita Ward, singer

1966 Chris Robinson, vocals (The Black Crowes)

1958
John Lennon, Paul McCartney and George Harrison appear as The Quarry Men at the wedding reception of George's older brother, Harry.

1962
The Osmonds appear for the first time on the NBC-TV *Andy Williams Show*. The brothers perform 'I'm A Ding Dong Daddy From Dumas'.

1967
Folk singer Joan Baez is sentenced to 45 days in prison after being arrested during an anti-war demonstration.

1968
Glen Campbell goes to No. 1 on the US album chart with 'Wichita Lineman'.

1969
Rolf Harris is at No. 1 on the UK singles chart with 'Two Little Boys', a song written in 1902. It is the Christmas No. 1 of 1969 and the last No. 1 of the 60s.

1973
American singer Bobby Darin dies aged 37. One of the first teen idols, he had the 1959 No. 1 with 'Dream Lover' plus 20 other US Top 40 hits during the 60s including 'Mack The Knife', which won the Grammy for Record of the Year in 1960.

1986
The Bangles start a four-week run at No. 1 on the US singles chart with 'Walk Like An Egyptian'.

1992
American blues singer and guitarist, Albert King dies from a heart attack in Memphis, Tennessee. He recorded dozens of influential songs, including 'Crosscut Saw' and 'As The Years Go Passing By', and the 1967 album, *Born Under A Bad Sign*.

1999
Readers of *UK Guitar* magazine vote Noel Gallagher the most overrated guitarist of the millennium. Jimi Hendrix is voted guitarist of the millennium with Nirvana's *Nevermind* winning best album.

Canadian Country singer Hank Snow dies. 'The Singing Ranger' released over 100 albums and scored more than seventy singles on the *Billboard* country charts from 1950 until 1980. A regular at the Grand Ole Opry, in 1954 Snow persuaded the directors to allow a new singer by the name of Elvis Presley to appear at the Grand Ole Opry.

2000
Figures from the RIA of America show that Teen Pop is alive and doing very well. Pop accounts for most of the record sales in America with Jive records, home to Britney Spears, The Backstreet Boys and *NSYNC, selling 31m records

2006
Eminem and his high school sweetheart divorce for a second time, less than a year after they remarried.

Matthew Fisher, a founding member of Procol Harum, wins a High Court battle over who wrote their song 'A Whiter Shade of Pale'. He played organ on the 1967 hit and argued he wrote the distinctive organ melody. Mr Justice

Blackburne rules he is entitled to 40% of the copyright. Fisher had wanted half but the court decided lead singer Gary Brooker's input was more substantial. Fisher's claim for back royalties – of up to £1m – was also rejected. For almost 40 years, the song has been credited to lead singer Gary Brooker and lyricist Keith Reid.

Rolling Stone magazine writer Ian Halperin claims that Michael Jackson is close to death. He says Jackson is suffering from a rare lung condition and needs a lung transplant. He also claims that the singer has lost 95% vision in one eye and is so ill he can barley speak.

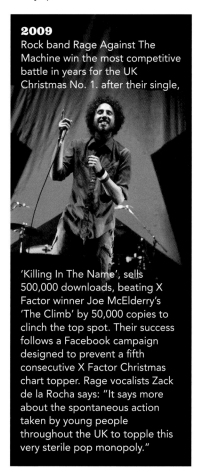

2009
Rock band Rage Against The Machine win the most competitive battle in years for the UK Christmas No. 1. after their single, 'Killing In The Name', sells 500,000 downloads, beating X Factor winner Joe McElderry's 'The Climb' by 50,000 copies to clinch the top spot. Their success follows a Facebook campaign designed to prevent a fifth consecutive X Factor Christmas chart topper. Rage vocalists Zack de la Rocha says: "It says more about the spontaneous action taken by young people throughout the UK to topple this very sterile pop monopoly."

Born on this day:

1940 Frank Zappa, multi-instrumentalist
1943 Albert Lee, UK country guitarist
1946 Carl Wilson, guitar, vocals (The Beach Boys)

1964 Patrick Murphy, drums (The Lemonheads, Dinosaur Jr)

1969

The Supremes make their last TV appearance with Diana Ross on *The Ed Sullivan Show*, singing their last No. 1 'Someday We'll Be Together'.

1970

A stretch limousine carrying Elvis Presley pulls up outside the White House in Washington, D.C. The driver hands over a letter from Elvis addressed to President Nixon requesting a meeting to discuss how the King of Rock and Roll could help Nixon fight drugs. The President agrees to give Presley a Narcotics Bureau badge – but only after learning that the Chief of the Narcotics Bureau had turned down the same request earlier that day and told Presley the only person who could overrule his decision was the President. At Elvis' request, the meeting remains secret for more than a year, until the *Washington Post* breaks the story on January 27, 1972.

1977

During a North American tour Queen appear at Long Beach Arena, California.

1984

Frankie Goes To Hollywood play the first of three sold out nights at Liverpool Royal Court. Tickets £5.30.

1985

Bruce Springsteen's album *Born In The USA* passes Michael Jackson's *Thriller* to become the second longest-lasting LP on the *Billboard* US Top 10. It stays there for 79 weeks. Only *The Sound of Music* with Julie Andrews lasted longer at 109 weeks.

1988

Former Cockney Rebel bass player Paul Jeffreys is one of the passengers killed by a terrorist bomb on Pan Am flight 103 which crashes over Lockerbie, Scotland. Former Sex Pistol John Lydon and his wife Nora were due to catch the same flight but missed it through being late, as were the Four Tops.

1991

'Bohemian Rhapsody'/'These Are The Days Of Our Lives' by Queen starts a five-week run at No. 1 in the UK. The 1975 word-wide hit was re-released following the death of Freddie Mercury.

1995

Former Oasis drummer Tony McCarrol issues a writ against the band seeking damages and royalties for his work on *(What's The Story) Morning Glory*.

2003

Eminem's ex-wife Kimberley Mathers pleads guilty to drug and driving offences. Mathers was pulled by traffic police in June and charged with possession of cocaine. Two other charges of driving with a suspended license and maintaining a drug house in which police discovered marijuana and Ecstasy are dropped.

Michael Andrews featuring Gary Jules goes to No. 1 on the UK singles chart with their version of the Tears For Fears song 'Mad World'. The song took just 90 minutes to record in 2001 and was featured in the film *Donnie Darko*.

2005

Sir Elton John and his partner David Furnish become the first gay celebrities to register their relationship as a civil partnership. The 20 minute ceremony takes place at The Guildhall, Windsor. Guests include Ringo Starr, Victoria Beckham, Joss Stone, Sting, Elvis Costello, Jamie Cullum, George Michael and The Osbournes – Ozzy, Sharon, Jack and Kelly.

Madonna is forced to cancel a romantic holiday at Skibo Castle in Scotland after her private jet breaks down with technical difficulties at London Airport.

December 22

Born on this day:

1949 Robin & Maurice Gibb, singers, songwriters (The Bee Gees)

1957 Ricky Ross, vocals, guitar, piano (Deacon Blue)

1968 Richard James Edwards, guitar (Manic Street Preachers)

1972 Vanessa Paradis, French singer, actress

1962

The Tornados start a three-week run at No. 1 on the US singles chart with 'Telstar'. Produced and written by Joe Meek, it is the first major hit from a UK act on the American chart. It is also a No. 1 in the UK.

1967

The Jimi Hendrix Experience, Pink Floyd, Keith West and Tomorrow, Eric Burdon & The Animals and Soft Machine all appear at The Olympia, London at an all night festival 'Christmas On Earth Continued'. The DJ is John Peel and the venue features a paddling pool, light shows and a movie theatre, with tickets costing £1.

1972

Little Jimmy Osmond is at No. 1 on the UK singles chart with 'Long Haired Lover From Liverpool'. Aged nine years and eight months he is the youngest person to have a No. 1 record, and it is also the biggest seller of 1972.

1973

Elton John starts a two-week run at No. 1 on the UK album chart with *Goodbye Yellow Brick Road*. It also has an eight-week run at No. 1 on the US chart.

1980

Stiff Records releases an album in the UK called *The Wit And Wisdom Of Ronald Reagan*. The disc contains 40 minutes of silence.

1981

At a rock & roll memorabilia auction in London, a stage suit worn by John Lennon sells for £2,300, a letter from Paul McCartney to a fan sells for £2,200 and a Perspex sculpture of John & Yoko is bought by singer Kate Bush for £4,200.

1987

Nikki Sixx from Mötley Crüe is pronounced 'dead on arrival' in an ambulance when his heart stops beating for two minutes. Sixx is given two shots of adrenaline in his chest to revive him. Fellow band members are prematurely informed of his death.

1988

The Smiths play their farewell gig at Wolverhampton Civic Hall, without guitarist Johnny Marr. To gain entrance to the gig fans have to wear a Smiths or Morrissey T-shirt.

1991

James Brown launches an unsuccessful lawsuit against the producers of the movie *The Commitments*, claiming one of the characters too closely resembles him.

single 'Rock The Casbah, 1991 UK No. 1 single 'Should I Stay Or Should I Go', first released 1982, plus 15 other UK Top 40 singles. The Clash's *London Calling* album was voted best album of the 1980s by *Rolling Stone* magazine. Strummer was also a member of the The Mescaleros.

2008

A cassette tape of a "drunk" John Lennon recording a cover version of a rock'n'roll song sells at auction in Los Angeles for $30,000. The six-minute recording, made in autumn 1973, is of Lennon performing Lloyd Price's 'Just Because'. "Debauched lyrics" improvised by Lennon include "just a

2000

Madonna marries film director Guy Ritchie at Skibo Castle, Scotland. Celebrities attending the wedding include Jon Bon Jovi, Bryan Adams, Sting and fashion designers Donatella Versace, Jean Paul Gaultier and Stellla McCartney. The couple divorce in Nov 2008.

2002

Former Clash singer and guitarist Joe Strummer (John Graham Mellor) dies of a suspected heart attack aged 50. The Clash scored the 1979 UK No. 11 single 'London Calling', 1982 US No. 8

little cocaine will set me right", and, "I wanna take all them new singers, Carol and the other one with the nipples, I wanna take 'em and hold 'em tight."

Born on this day:

1939 Johnny Kidd (Fred Heath), singer (Johnny Kidd & The Pirates)
1941 Tim Hardin, US singer, songwriter
1949 Ariel Bender (Luther Grosvenor), guitar (Spooky Tooth, Mott The Hoople, Widowmaker)

1958 Dave Murray, guitar (Iron Maiden)
1964 Eddie Vedder, vocals (Pearl Jam)

December 23

1959
Chuck Berry is arrested after taking 14-year-old Janice Norine, who unbeknown to Berry was working as a prostitute, across a state line. He is sentenced to five years jail, but after racist comments by the judge a mistrial is ruled. The case would drag on for three years.

1964
During a US tour Beach Boy Brian Wilson has a nervous breakdown during a flight from Los Angeles to Houston. Wilson leaves the band to concentrate on writing and producing. Glen Campbell replaces Wilson for the band's live shows.

1966
ITV broadcast Ready, Steady Go! for the last time. The special guests for the farewell show are Mick Jagger, The Who, Eric Burdon, The Spencer Davis Group, Donovan and Dave Dee, Dozy, Beaky, Mick & Tich.

1972
Former Grand Funk Railroad manager Terry Knight arrives during a concert

by the band with a court order to seize $1m in money or assets. Police inform the ex-manager that he can't take anything until after the show.

1985
Judas Priest fans Raymond Belknap and James Vance shoot themselves after listening to the Priest album Stained Class. The two had drunk beer, smoked marijuana and then listened to the album for several hours. Later they take a shotgun to a nearby school playground where Belknap shoots and kills himself. Vance then blows away his jaw, mouth and nose but lives for more than three years before dying of effects of the shooting.

1996
Mötley Crüe bassist Nikki Sixx marries TV's Baywatch star Donna Deruico.

1999
George Harrison's home in Maui is broken into by Cristin Keleher, who cooked a frozen pizza, drank beer from the fridge, started some laundry and phoned her mother in New Jersey. Keleher was arrested and charged with burglary and theft.

2000
Simply Red singer Mick Hucknall is given a police caution for possessing cocaine and cannabis. Police found the Class A and Class B drugs at his Surrey home after a woman falsely accused him of rape in November.

2005
Geezer Butler, the bass player with Black Sabbath, offers £5,000 for any information leading to the safe return of Toga, the three-month-old penguin that has been stolen from a zoo on the Isle of Wight a few days earlier.

2007
The Police are named as the highest earning touring group for the past year, bringing in nearly £66.5m. The band's 54 date North American tour had generated almost double the total of the second-placed act, country star Kenny Chesney.

Born on this day:

1945 Lemmy, bass, vocals (Hawkwind, Motörhead)
1946 Jan Akkerman, guitar (Focus)
1968 Doyle Bramhall II, guitarist, songwriter (Smokestack, Eric Clapton Band, Roger Waters)

1971 Ricky Martin, singer
1975 Joe Washbourne, vocals (Toploader)

1954
Johnny Ace shoots himself dead backstage at the City Auditorium in Houston, Texas. The R&B singer was playing with a revolver during a break between sets when someone in the room said, "Be careful with that thing…" He said, "It's OK the gun's not loaded… see?" and pointed it at himself with a smile on his face.

1963
The first night of The Beatles Christmas show at The Finsbury Park Astoria, London, with Billy J. Kramer, The Fourmost, Cilla Black and Rolf Harris.

1965
The Who appear at the Pier Ballroom, Hastings, England.

1975
AC/DC appear at The Hordern Pavillion, Sydney, Australia.

1977
The Sex Pistols play their last ever UK gig (until they reunite in 1996) before splitting, at Ivanhoes in Huddersfield. It is a charity performance before an audience of mainly children.

1983
The Police appear at The Brighton Centre, Brighton, England on their 'Synchronicity' Tour.

1988
Nirvana start recording their first album *Bleach* using a $600 loan from an old school friend.

2000
Four Seasons bassist Nick Massi dies of cancer. They scored the 1976 UK & US No. 1 single 'December 1963, Oh What A Night', as well as hits with 'Sherry' and 'Rag Doll'.

2003
Jack White of The White Stripes turns himself in to Detroit police to face aggravated assault charges stemming from a bar room altercation in which he allegedly attacked Jason Stollsteimer of The Von Bondies. White is fingerprinted and formally booked on the charges before being released on bail.

2005
Rapper Foxy Brown is handcuffed and threatened with jail after she sticks her tongue out at a New York judge who asked her to stop chewing gum. Judge Melissa Jackson tells the singer she has shown disrespect to the court. Brown was in court on charges of assaulting two nail salon workers during a row over payment.

2009
Tim Hart, a founding member of UK folk group Steeleye Span, dies aged 61 of lung cancer, in La Gomera on the Canary Islands.

1967
The Bee Gees perform their Christmas special live from Liverpool Cathedral, England which was broadcast on UK TV.

1971
Slade appear at London's Marquee Club, for a Christmas Eve party night.

1972
David Bowie appears at the Rainbow Theatre, London, England giving a special Christmas Eve concert.

1999
Zeke Carey of The Flamingos dies. They had the 1959 US No. 11 single 'I Only Have Eyes For You', which was also a 1975 UK No. 1 hit for Art Garfunkel.

Born on this day:

1937 O'Kelly Isley, vocals (The Isley Brothers)
1940 Phil Spector, producer
1944 Henry Vestine, guitar (Canned Heat)
1945 Noel Redding, bass (The Jimi Hendrix Experience)
1946 Jimmy Buffett, US singer, songwriter
1954 Annie Lennox, singer (The Tourists, Eurythmics)
1954 Robin Campbell, guitar, vocals (UB40)
1957 Shane MacGowan, guitar, vocals (The Pogues)
1971 Dido, singer, songwriter

December 25

1954
Bing Crosby's 'White Christmas' enters the *Billboard* Pop chart for the first time, seven years after it was recorded. Bing's rendition has sold over 100 million copies around the world, with at least 50 million sales as singles. It was the largest selling single in music history until it was surpassed by Elton John's 'Candle In The Wind 1997'.

1958
The first day of a 10-day residency in Alan Freed's Christmas Rock'n'Roll Spectacular in New York with Chuck Berry, Frankie Avalon, Dion, Jackie Wilson, Eddie Cochran, Bo Diddley and The Everly Brothers.

1964
The Supremes, Marvin Gaye, The Temptations, The Miracles, Stevie Wonder and The Marvelettes all appear at The Fox Theatre, Brooklyn, New York.

1965
The Beatles sixth album *Rubber Soul* starts a nine-week run at No. 1 on the UK chart. It spends a total of 42 week's on the UK chart and was also a No. 1 in the US.

1976
American MOR singer Johnny Mathis is at No. 1 on the UK singles chart with 'When A Child Is Born', the singer's only UK No. 1 and the Christmas hit of 1976.

1981
Michael Jackson phones Paul McCartney and suggests they write and record together, the first result being 'The Girl Is Mine'.

1995
American singer, actor and TV host Dean Martin dies. He had the 1956 UK & US No. 1 single 'Memories Are Made Of This' plus over 15 other UK Top 40 singles, including 'That's Amore', 'Everybody Loves Somebody' and 'Mambo Italiano'. In 1965, Martin launched his weekly NBC comedy-variety series, *The Dean Martin Show*.

1998
Bryan MacLean, guitarist with Love, dies of a heart attack aged 62 while having Christmas dinner with a young fan who is researching a book about the band. Love had the 1966 US No. 33 single '7 And 7 Is', and the 1968 album *Forever Changes*.

2003
Michael Jackson records his first interview since reports circulated of allegations of sexual abuse with a 12-year old boy. He tells the CBS TV network he would 'slit his wrists' before he would hurt a child. He also claims he suffered a dislocated shoulder after police 'manhandled' him and treated him 'very roughly' during his arrest.

2006
James Brown, the 'Godfather of Soul', dies at the age of 73 after being diagnosed with severe pneumonia. His hits included 'Papa's Got a Brand New Bag', 'I Got You (I Feel Good)' and 'Get Up (I Feel Like Being A) Sex Machine, Pt. 1'. Brown was married four times, and at the age of 16 was arrested for theft and served three years in prison. In 1988, Brown was arrested following a high-speed car chase along the Georgia-South Carolina state border. He was convicted of carrying an unlicensed pistol and assaulting a police officer and was sentenced to six years in prison.

December 26

Born on this day:

1935 Abdul 'Duke' Fakir, vocals, The Four Tops

1953 Henning Schmitz, Kraftwerk

1955 Lars Ulrich, drums (Metallica)

1979 Chris Daughtry, US guitarist, singer

1963
Little Stevie Wonder arrives in the UK for appearances on the TV shows *Ready Steady Go!* and *Thank Your Lucky Stars.*

1964
An advertisement attributed to The Rolling Stones appears in the music paper *New Musical Express* wishing starving hairdressers and their families a Happy Christmas.

1966
The Jimi Hendrix Experience play an afternoon show at The Uppercut Club, London. Hendrix writes the lyrics to 'Purple Haze' in the dressing room.

1967
BBC Television broadcast The Beatles' movie *Magical Mystery Tour* in black and white. The next day, the British press and the viewing public pronounce the film an utter disaster. The negative reaction is so strong that a US television deal for broadcasting the movie is cancelled.

1968
Led Zeppelin open their first North American tour, supporting Vanilla Fudge and Spirit, at Denver Auditorium, Colorado. Tickets for this Sunday night gig cost $5.

1970

George Harrison starts a four-week run at No. 1 on the US singles chart with 'My Sweet Lord', making him the first Beatle to score a No. 1 US hit. The song was originally intended for Billy Preston.

1976
The Sex Pistols record 'God Save The Queen' at Wessex Studios, London, England.

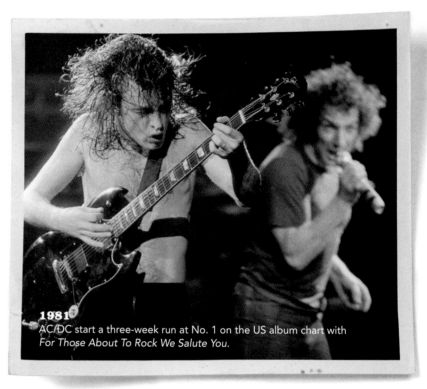

1981
AC/DC start a three-week run at No. 1 on the US album chart with *For Those About To Rock We Salute You.*

1988
Shane McGowan is arrested for smashing the glass of a shop window in a drunken rage. The Pogues singer is later fined £250.

The Spice Girls score their eighth UK No. 1 single with 'Goodbye' (the first single without Geri Halliwell). It gives the group the Christmas No. 1 for the third year in a row, equaling the record set by The Beatles from 1963, '64 and '65.

1999
American soul, R&B, and funk singer, songwriter Curtis Mayfield dies aged 57. He was a member of The Impressions (1965 US No. 7 single 'Lilies Of The Field') and solo (1971 UK No. 12 single 'Move On Up', 1972 US No. 4 single 'Freddie's Dead, Theme From Superfly').

2006
Michael Jackson files a lawsuit against his former accountants, claiming they withdrew $2.5 million a year from his bank accounts but did not properly pay his bills. Jackson hired the Los Angeles-based firm in 2003 for book-keeping, opening bank accounts and filing personal, corporate and real estate taxes.

2007
Amy Winehouse's second album *Back To Black* is named as the biggest-selling album of the year. Released at the end of 2006, the album has now sold more than 1.5m copies in the UK, achieving five platinum sales awards. Winehouse is also nominated for six Grammys, including song of the year. Leona Lewis's *Spirit* is the second best seller. Lewis sold 1.27m copies in just five weeks, becoming the fastest-selling debut in UK history and making the former X Factor winner the fastest female million-seller in the UK. Mika's *Life In Cartoon Motion* is the third best selling album of 2007.

Born on this day:

1931 Scotty Moore, guitarist in Elvis Presley's first band

1941 Mike Pinder, keyboards (The Moody Blues)

1944 Mike Jones, guitar (Foreigner)

1948 Larry Byrom, guitar (Steppenwolf)

1961 Youth (Martin Glover), bass, producer (Killing Joke)

December 27

1964
The Who appear at the Ealing Club, Ealing Broadway, London, England.

1967
The Doors appear on the CBS TV *Jonathon Winters Show* from Los Angeles, California.

1969
Led Zeppelin II is at No. 1 on the US album charts. It goes on to sell over six million copies in the US.

1975
The Faces split becomes official. Rod Stewart severs all connections with the group to work as a solo artist, Ron Wood is on permanent loan to The Rolling Stones, Ronnie Lane had already left to form Slim Chance and drummer Kenney Jones will join The Who following the death of Keith Moon.

A letter from future Smiths singer Steven Morrissey is published in this week's *NME*, complaining about the lack of media coverage for The New York Dolls.

1976
Blues guitarist Freddie King dies of heart trouble and ulcers aged 42. Eric Clapton covered his 'Have You Ever Loved A Woman' on his *Layla* album. He was a major influence on British and American blues-rock musicians such as Jimmy Vaughan, Ronnie Earl, Peter Green and Eric Clapton.

1981
American composer, pianist, singer, actor and bandleader Hoagy Carmichael dies aged 82. Among his many compositions were 'Georgia On My Mind' (covered by many acts including Ray Charles), 'Stardust' and 'Lazy River'.

1983
Walter Scott, lead singer of the St Louis, Missouri, band Bob Kuban & The In-Men, who scored a 1966 US hit with 'The Cheater', is seen alive for the last time. On April 10, 1987, his badly decomposed, bound body was found floating face down in a cistern. He'd been shot in the back. Scott's second wife, Jo Ann Calceterra, pleads guilty to hindering prosecution in his murder and receives a five-year sentence. Her boyfriend, James H. Williams Sr, whom she married in 1986, is found guilty of two counts of capital murder in the deaths of Walter Scott as well as his previous wife, Sharon Williams. He receives two life terms.

1983
The Police play the first of four sold-out nights at Wembley Arena in London, England, on their 'Synchronicity' world tour.

1986
Following its use in a commercial for Levi jeans, Jackie Wilson has the UK Christmas No. 1 single with 'Reet Petite' two years after his death. Written in 1957 by Berry Gordy and Tyran Carlo, the success of the song helped Gordy fund the launch of Motown Records.

1989
A former chef at the Chuck Berry owned restaurant Southern Air starts court proceedings against Berry, alleging that the singer had installed secret video cameras in the ladies toilets. A further 200 other women also take action, claiming that the recordings were for improper sexual use.

1992
Harry Connick Jr is arrested at Kennedy Airport, New York after police discover a 9mm pistol in his hand luggage.

2008
Thieves break into a house belonging to Allman Brothers band singer and keyboardist Gregg Allman in Georgia and steal a coin collection, knives and unreleased concert recordings. Two men are charged with the burglary two days later.

Singer, songwriter and guitarist Delaney Bramlett dies in Los Angeles from complications after gall bladder surgery. He was a member of Delaney, Bonnie & Friends and worked with George Harrison, The Everly Brothers, John Lennon, Janis Joplin, J.J. Cale, and Eric Clapton.

December 28

Born on this day:

1915 Roebuck Staples, vocals (The Staple Singer)

1943 Chas Hodges, keyboards (Heads Hands & Feet, Chas & Dave)

1946 Edgar Winter, singer, keyboards

1950 Alex Chilton, guitar, vocals, producer (The Box Tops, Big Star, solo)

1971 Anita Dels, vocals (2 Unlimited)

1978 John Legend, singer, songwriter

1979 Akon, US singer

1961

Danny Williams is at No. 1 on the UK singles chart with 'Moon River', the Oscar-winning song from the film *Breakfast At Tiffany's*. The Tokens are at No. 1 on the US singles chart with 'The Lion Sleeps Tonight'.

1966

Ike & Tina Turner appear at the El Cortez Hotel, San Diego, California.

1968

The three day Miami Pop festival takes place, the first major rock festival held on the East Coast of the US, with Chuck Berry, The McCoys, Joni Mitchell, Fleetwood Mac, Marvin Gaye, The Turtles, The Box Tops, Steppenwolf, Three Dog Night, Pacific Gas and Electric, Procol Harum, Canned Heat, Iron Butterfly and The Grateful Dead.

Vanilla Fudge appear at the Pacific Coliseum, Vancouver, Canada, supported by Led Zeppelin on their first US tour.

1972

David Bowie appears at The Hardrock, Stretford, Manchester, England on his Ziggy Stardust tour.

1974

Helen Reddy goes to No. 1 on the US singles chart with 'Angie Baby', the singer's third US No. 1. The song was turned down by Cher.

1978

Chris Bell, guitarist with Big Star, is killed aged 27 after his car crashes into a telephone pole.

1983

After a heavy day's drinking Beach Boy Dennis Wilson drowns while diving from a friend's boat moored in Marina Del Rey, California. He was attempting to retrieve jewellery thrown overboard from his own boat which used to be moored alongside. With permission from President Reagan he was given a burial at sea, a practice normally reserved for naval personnel. Dennis was the only genuine surfer in The Beach Boys.

1991

Red Hot Chili Peppers, Nirvana and Pearl Jam all appear at Del Mar O'brien Pavilion, San Diego, California.

1993

Canadian singer Shania Twain marries record producer Mutt Lange.

2003

50 Cent's debut album, *Get Rich Or Die Tryin'*, is named the biggest selling album in the US in 2003, going platinum six times over. Outkast come second with *Speakerboxxx/The Love Below* and Linkin Park's *Meteora* is the third biggest seller. The Top 10 albums of 2003 in the USA account for around 30 million sales.

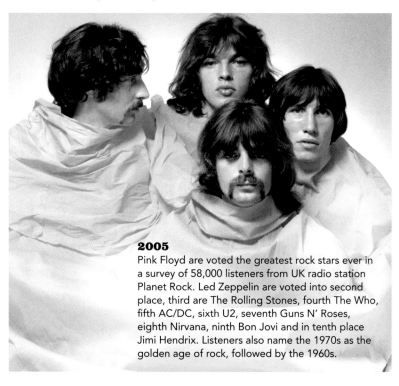

2005

Pink Floyd are voted the greatest rock stars ever in a survey of 58,000 listeners from UK radio station Planet Rock. Led Zeppelin are voted into second place, third are The Rolling Stones, fourth The Who, fifth AC/DC, sixth U2, seventh Guns N' Roses, eighth Nirvana, ninth Bon Jovi and in tenth place Jimi Hendrix. Listeners also name the 1970s as the golden age of rock, followed by the 1960s.

Born on this day:

1942 Ray Thomas, flute (The Moody Blues)
1946 Marianne Faithfull, UK singer
1947 Cozy Powell, drummer (Whitesnake, ELP, solo)
1951 Yvonne Elliman, singer
1961 Jim Reid, vocals (The Jesus & Mary Chain)
1966 Bryan Holland, vocals, guitar (The Offspring)

December
29

1956
Elvis Presley makes chart history by having 10 songs on *Billboard*'s Top 100.

1962
During his first visit to the UK Bob Dylan performs at The Troubadour in London.

1966
The Jimi Hendrix Experience make their debut on the UK TV show *Top Of The Pops* performing 'Hey Joe'.

At Abbey Road studios, London, The Beatles began work on a new Paul McCartney song, 'Penny Lane', recording six takes of keyboard tracks and various percussion effects.

1973
Jim Croce scores his second No. 1 US single of the year when 'Time In A Bottle' goes to the top of the charts. Croce was killed in a plane crash on September 20, 1973.

1980
American singer and songwriter Tim Hardin dies of a heroin overdose. Hardin wrote many songs, including 'If I Were A Carpenter' (covered by Bobby Darin, Johnny Cash and June Carter, The Four Tops, Leon Russell, Small Faces, Robert Plant and Bob Seger) and 'Reason To Believe', (covered by Rod Stewart). Hardin appeared at the 1969 Woodstock Festival.

1982
Commemorative stamps in memory of Bob Marley are issued in Jamaica.

1984
Band Aid are at No. 1 on the UK singles chart with 'Do They Know It's Christmas?' and Madonna is at No. 1 on the US singles chart with 'Like A Virgin'.

1999
Three ferrets named Beckham, Posh Spice and Baby Spice are used to lay power cables for a rock concert to be held in Greenwich, London. Workers are not allowed to dig the turf at the Royal Park.

UK music paper *Melody Maker* publishes its Music of the Millennium Poll of albums, placing The Smiths *The Queen Is Dead* at Number 1. This is the last issue of *Melody Maker*, which was first published in 1926.

2001
Aretha Franklin is suing a US newspaper which alleged that the star had alcohol problems. The singer's lawyers file a federal lawsuit against the Florida-based *Star* claiming she was defamed by an article in the paper in December 2000 and are seeking $50m in damages.

2002
Readers of *Sugar* magazine vote Pink as their No. 1 role model. Others in the top 10 are Britney Spears, Ms Dynamite, Kelly Osbourne, Kylie Minogue, Victoria Beckham, Avril Lavigne, Jennifer Lopez, Sarah Michelle Geller and Holly Valance.

2006
The wife of rock singer Marilyn Manson, burlesque dancer Dita Von Teese files for divorce after just a year of marriage. The couple married in December 2005 in a ceremony held at a castle in Ireland.

2009
James Blunt's *Back To Bedlam* is named Britain's best-selling album of the last ten years. The singer/songwriter's debut record topped a poll compiled by the Official Charts Company to find the US and UK's most popular artists. Dido's *No Angel* finished in second place, while Amy Winehouse's *Back To Black* came third. X Factor winner Leona Lewis' album *Spirit* and David Gray's *White Ladder* completed the top five. In the US, The Beatles' compilation *1* was named the best-selling album of the decade, making the Liverpudlian group the only British act to feature in the American Top 10. Boyband 'N Sync bagged second spot with their album *No Strings Attached*, Norah Jones took third place with *Come Away With Me*, and Eminem secured fourth and fifth place with *The Marshall Mathers LP* and *The Eminem Show* respectively.

Born on this day:

1928 Bo Diddley, guitarist, singer	**1945** Davy Jones, vocals (The Monkees)
1934 Del Shannon, singer	**1946** Patti Smith, singer, poet
1942 Mike Nesmith, vocals, guitar (The Monkees, First National Band)	**1947** Jeff Lynne, guitar, vocals, producer (The Move, ELO, Traveling Wilburys)
1942 Robert Quine, guitarist (Richard Hell & The Voidoids)	**1969** Jay Kay, singer (Jamiroquai)

1962

Singer Brenda Lee is hurt when she attempts to rescue her poodle, Cee Cee, from her burning house. Cee Cee later dies of smoke inhalation.

1967

The Beatles score their 15th US No. 1 with 'Hello Goodbye', Gladys Knight & The Pips are at No. 2 with 'I Heard It Through The Grapevine' and The Monkees at No. 3 with 'Daydream Believer'.

1969

Peter Tork quits The Monkees, buying himself out of his contract which leaves him broke.

1972

Brownsville Station, Sha-Na-Na and Bruce Springsteen (who was the opening act) all appear of the Ohio Theatre, Columbus, Ohio.

1978

XTC make their live debut in the US at a show in Philadelphia.

1989

Chris Novoselic, bass player with Nirvana, marries his long-time girlfriend Shelli Dilly in Washington.

1999

In the Queen's Millennium Honours List, former Slade singer Noddy Holder is awarded an MBE and guitarist Mark Knopfler is awarded an OBE.

2002

Diana Ross is arrested for drink driving by the Arizona highway patrol after a motorist calls to report a swerving vehicle in the western state of Arizona. Asked to walk in a straight line she falls over, and is unable to count to 30 or balance on one foot. Police say the singer was twice over the drink drive limit with a blood-alcohol of 0.20. The legal limit is 0.08.

The funeral of former Clash singer and guitarist Joe Strummer takes place in London. Strummer had died of a suspected heart attack on December 22, 2002 aged 50.

2003

Cris Kirkwood from The Meat Puppets is arrested and accused of hitting a federal post office security guard in the head with a baton that the musician took from the guard during a struggle. The guard then shot Kirkwood in the back. The incident began over a dispute about parking with another customer at a Phoenix post office.

2006

R&B singer Brandy is involved in a four-car crash that leaves one woman dead after the singer fails to slow down and hits the rear of another car. Brandy was alone in her car and no alcohol or drugs were involved.

2009

U2 had the most successful North American tour of 2009, according to music trade publication Pollstar. The Irish band's 360° stadium tour sold 1.3 million tickets in the US and Canada, worth $123m overall. Bruce Springsteen and The E Street Band come second, with tour takings amounting to $94.5m. U2's tour is the fifth most successful ever in North America. The Rolling Stones hold the record, for a 2005 tour that made $162m.

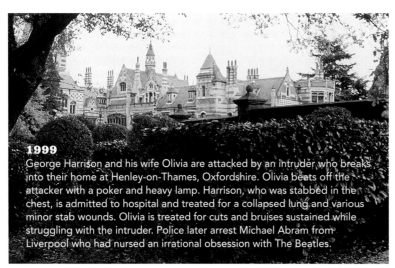

1999

George Harrison and his wife Olivia are attacked by an intruder who breaks into their home at Henley-on-Thames, Oxfordshire. Olivia beats off the attacker with a poker and heavy lamp. Harrison, who was stabbed in the chest, is admitted to hospital and treated for a collapsed lung and various minor stab wounds. Olivia is treated for cuts and bruises sustained while struggling with the intruder. Police later arrest Michael Abram from Liverpool who had nursed an irrational obsession with The Beatles.

Born on this day:

1942   Andy Summers, guitar (Zoot Money, The Animals, The Police)
1943   John Denver, singer, songwriter
1943   Peter Quaife, bass (The Kinks)
1948   Donna Summer, US singer

1960   Paul Westerberg, guitar, vocals (The Replacements)
1970   Danny McNamara, singer (Embrace)
1979   Bob Bryar, drummer (My Chemical Romance)

December 31

1961

The Beach Boys, previously known as Carl & The Passions, make their live debut using their new name at the Municipal Auditorium, Long Beach, California.

1963

The Kinks make their live debut at the Lotus House Restaurant, London.

1966

The Monkees start a seven-week run at No. 1 on the US singles charts with the Neil Diamond song 'I'm A Believer'. It was a No. 1 in the UK in 1967.

1967

American songwriter and producer Bert Berns dies of heart failure aged 38. He wrote many classic songs including 'Twist And Shout', 'Hang On Sloopy', 'Here Comes The Night', 'I Want Candy' and 'Brown Eyed Girl'.

1968

Joe Cocker, Amen Corner, John Mayall's Bluesbreakers, The Small Faces, Free and Bonzo Dog Doo Dah Band all appear at Alexandra Palace, London. Tickets cost 25 shillings (£1.25).

1970

Paul McCartney files a suit against the rest of The Beatles to dissolve their partnership.

1973

Australian band AC/DC make their live debut at Chequers Bar in Sydney.

1979

David Bowie performs an acoustic version of 'Space Oddity' on UK TV's *The Kenny Everett New Year's Show*.

1982

Max's Kansas City in New York City closes down. The venue had been a regular venue for such artists as The Velvet Underground and The New York Dolls, and in 1973 famously hosted a joint week of appearances by Bruce Springsteen supported by Bob Marley.

1984

Def Leppard drummer Rick Allen crashes his Corvette Stingray on the A57 outside Sheffield, losing his left arm in the accident. Allen was on his way to a New Year's Eve party at his family's home when a Jaguar passed him. The driver had been egging Allen on and would not allow him to overtake. In his attempts to pass this driver, he did not see a turn up ahead and lost control. He was thrown from the car, and his left arm was severed due to the seatbelt not being properly fastened.

1985

Ricky Nelson is killed along with six others when his charted light aircraft crashes in Texas. He scored the 1958 US No. 1 'Poor Little Fool', the 1961 UK No. 2 single 'Hello Mary Lou' plus over 30 US Top 40 hit singles.

1991

Pearl Jam, Nirvana and Red Hot Chili Peppers all appear on the same bill at the Cow Palace, San Francisco, California.

Ted Nugent donates 200 pounds of venison to a Salvation Army soup kitchen in Detroit with the message 'I kill it, you grill it'.

1996

Paul McCartney is awarded a knighthood in the Queen's New Year Honours List.

1999

The Manic Street Preachers perform to 57,000 fans at the Millennium Stadium, Cardiff. The *Guinness Book of Records* confirms that the concert sets a new record as the biggest indoor show ever staged in Europe.

2000

Black Crowes singer Chris Robinson marries actress Kate Hudson, the daughter of actress Goldie Hawn. The couple will separate in 2006.

2003

Kevin MacMichael, guitarist with Cutting Crew, dies of lung cancer aged 51. He also worked with Robert Plant and The Rankin Family.

Australian singer and actress Natalie Imbruglia marries Silverchair singer Daniel Johns.

2004

Pete Waterman is awarded an OBE for his services to music. Waterman had written and produced more than 200 hit singles in 25 years. The Who singer Roger Daltrey is awarded a CBE for services to music and charity.

2005

The John Lennon song 'Imagine' is voted the nation's favourite song a quarter of a century after his death. A UK radio station conducted the poll of 7,000 listeners. The Beatles are voted into second and third place with 'Hey Jude' and 'Let It Be'.

2006

George Michael is paid a reported £1.5m for an hour's concert at a Russian billionaire's New Year party.

2009

It is announced that Francis Rossi and Rick Parfitt, of Status Quo, have been awarded OBEs in New Year Honours List.

Access All Areas

Did you know?

The Rolling Stones
At the height of their success in 1966, all members of The Rolling Stones bought new cars. Keith Richards a Bentley, Bill Wyman an MGB sports car, Brian Jones a Rolls Royce and Mick Jagger bought an Aston Martin DB6, which came complete with its own record player.

Quincy Jones
The all-time most nominated Grammy artist is Quincy Jones with 77 nominations.

Elton John
Elton John once spent £293,000 over a 20 month period on flowers.

Eminem
The rapper's $5m mansion built on a six acre estate was once owned by Chuck Conaway, the chairman of supermarket giant Kmart.

Razorlight
Razorlight took their name form the make of the padlock worn by Sid Vicious.

Karen Carpenter
In 1975 a Playboy music poll ranked Karen Carpenter as the best drummer in the world. Led Zeppelin's John Bonham came second.

Bob Geldof
During the 1985 Live Aid concert, Bob Geldof took a call from the ruling family in Dubai who made the biggest single donation of £1m.

U2
The young boy featured on the front of the 1983 U2 album *War* is Peter Rowan, a brother of one of Bono's friends who was eight years old at the time of the photo shoot.

David Gilmour
In 2002 Pink Floyd guitarist David Gilmour sold his London house and gave the £4.2m he got for it to homeless charity Crisis.

Kurt Cobain
In 1988, Nikolas Hartshorne booked Nirvana to play at the Central Tavern in Seattle, the bands third ever gig. Six years later Hartshorne was the Medical Examiner at Kurt Cobain's death.

James Blunt
Working in the British army, James Blunt was one of the officers carrying the Queen Mother's coffin at her funeral on April 9, 2002.

Jim Morrison
Jim Morrison's grave at the Père Lachaise Cemetery in Paris is monitored by video cameras in an attempt to deter graffiti artists.

Led Zeppelin
The Led Zeppelin track 'Stairway To Heaven' is the biggest selling piece of sheet music in rock history, selling over 15,000 copies every year. The song has been broadcast on radio over three million times.

Lil' Kim
Hip Hop rapper Lil' Kim is just 4' 11" tall, making her an inch smaller than Dolly Parton who is 5'.

My first record

For a few of us, our first foray into the world of music can be an embarrassing one. Especially for those poor souls whose first record was 'Fan'dabi'dozi' by The Krankies or Black Lace's 'Agadoo'. Here, a few stars come clean about their first record.

Lily Allen
Crazy Sexy Cool (TLC)

Frank Black
Meet The Beatles (The Beatles)

James Blunt
Wish You Were Here (Pink Floyd)

Julian Casablancas (The Strokes)
Faith (George Michael)

Stewart Copeland
Help! (The Beatles)

David Crosby
All I Have To Do Is Dream (The Everly Brothers)

Sheryl Crow
Both Sides Now (Joni Mitchell)

The Edge
A Hard Day's Night (The Beatles)

Art Garfunkel
Rock Island Line (Lonnie Donegan)

Bobby Gillespie
Blockbuster (Sweet)

Natalie Imbruglia
Thriller (Michael Jackson)

Jewel
The Wall (Pink Floyd)

Elton John
Sgt Pepper's Lonely Hearts Club Band (The Beatles)

Norah Jones
The Humpty Dance (Digital Underground)

Lenny Kravitz
Philadelphia Freedom (Elton John)

Simon Le Bon
The Lamb Lies Down On Broadway (Genesis)

Gary Lightbody (Snow Patrol)
Thriller (Michael Jackson)

Johnny Marr
Jeepster (T Rex)

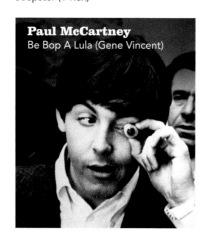

Paul McCartney
Be Bop A Lula (Gene Vincent)

Robert Palmer
Eight Miles High (The Byrds)

Lisa Marie Presley
Rocket Man (Elton John)

Nile Rodgers
Blue Suede Shoes (Elvis Presley)

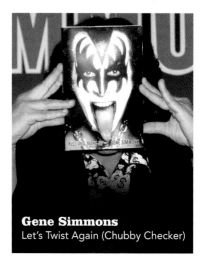

Gene Simmons
Let's Twist Again (Chubby Checker)

Meg White (The White Stripes)
Abracadabra (The Steve Miller Band)

Robbie Williams
Hello John, Gotta New Motor (Alexei Sayle)

Brian Wilson
Rock Around The Clock (Bill Haley & The Comets)

Bill Wyman
The World Is Waiting For The Sunrise (Les Paul)

Did you know ?

Sir Elton John

Some of the aliases Sir Elton John has used checking into hotels include Prince Fooboo, Sir Humphrey Handbag, Lillian Lollipop, Lord Choc Ice, Lord Elpus, Binky Poodleclip and Sir Henry Poodle.

David Rose

David Rose, who had a *Billboard* No. 1 hit in 1962 with an instrumental called 'The Stripper', also wrote the theme for the TV show *Little House On The Prairie*.

Jonny Trunk and Wisbey

At just 36 seconds in length 'The Ladies' Bras' by Jonny Trunk and Wisbey is the shortest song ever to make the Top 75 UK Singles Chart. At 1 minute 29 seconds The Buzzcocks 1978 single 'Love You More' is the second shortest UK single ever released. Maurice Williams & the Zodiacs 1960 hit 'Stay' is the shortest US No.1 hit at one minute 28 seconds. 'Some Kinda Earthquake', an instrumental single released in 1959 by Duane Eddy, clocked in at just 1 minute 17 seconds.

Beatlemania

Records released in the US during the early 60s to cash in on The Beatles craze included The Swans' 'The Boy With The Beatle Hair', Donna Lynn's 'My Boyfriend Got A Beatle Haircut', The Young World Singers' 'Ringo For

President', 'Ringo I Love You' by Bonnie Jo Maon' (sung by Cher), The Chipmunks Sing The Beatles and The Liverpools, who released an album called 'Beatlemania In The USA.'

Tinchy Stryder

At 5ft 1in Kwasi Danquah, better known by his stage name Tinchy Stryder, is the shortest ever male adult to reach the dizzy heights of the No. 1 spot in the UK charts. He hit the top spot with the aptly named song 'Number 1' (a collaboration with N-Dubz), which entered the UK chart at No. 1 on 26 April 2009.

Did you know ?

Keith Moon
During the 70s The Who drummer Keith Moon owned two Rolls-Royces (one of these may well have been the world's only lilac Rolls-Royce, which he painted with house paint), a Ferrari, an AC Cobra, a Mercedes, a Chrysler hot rod, a Hovercraft and a Milk Float. Moon couldn't drive and never had a driver's licence.

Jack Johnson
Singer songwriter Jack Johnson was a professional surfer until he had an accident - he broke his wrist, had his front teeth knocked out and received more than 150 stitches to his mouth and forehead.

Courtney Love
Courtney Love's father Hank Harrison was The Grateful Dead's tour manager.

Jimi Hendrix
The female models who posed for the 1967 Jimi Hendrix *Electric Ladyland* album sleeve were each paid £5 for the photo shoot and another £5 if they posed completely naked.

The Isle Of Wight festival
The Isle Of Wight festival started in 1968 because the local swimming pool association wanted to raise funds.

Pink Floyd
There are over 50 Pink Floyd tribute bands including: Think Floyd, Pink Voyd, Pink Noise, Macfloyd, Floydian Slip, Floydians, The Dark Side of the Wall, Bricks In The Wall and Which One's Pink.

Prince
Prince is a vegan and in 2006 he was voted the "world's sexiest vegetarian" in PETA's annual online poll.

Rush
The single 'Countdown' was inspired by the inaugural flight of the Space Shuttle *Columbia* on April 12, 1981. Rush were lucky enough to watch the launch from a VIP area called Red Sector A at Cape Kennedy. *Columbia* was destroyed on its 28th mission during re-entry on February 1, 2003.

Elton John
Elton John once auditioned for prog-rock bands King Crimson and Gentle Giant - he was rejected.

Walter Carlos
Walter Carlos, a collaborator with Richard Moog, inventor of the Moog Synthesiser, had a sex change operation in 1967. As Wendy Carlos, she went on to release the *Switched On Bach* album in 1969 and composed and performed on the soundtracks for *A Clockwork Orange*, *The Shining* and *Tron*.

The Darkness
A space probe that left Earth in 1982 contains a picture of Justin and Dan Hawkins from The Darkness aged 6 and 7 after an uncle entered a competition to have a photo on board the spacecraft.

Avril Lavigne
The Canadian won a singing contest on her local radio station in Ottawa when she was 14.